LAW AND POVERTY

PERSPECTIVES FROM SOUTH AFRICA AND BEYOND

LAW AND POVERTY

PERSPECTIVES FROM SOUTH AFRICA AND BEYOND

First published as
(2011) 22:3 *Stellenbosch Law Review*

Editors:
Sandra Liebenberg & Geo Quinot

JUTA

First edition 2012

ISBN 978 0 7021 9445 0

Typeset in 10 pt on 12pt Times

Cover by Comet Design
Typesetting by ANdtp Services, Cape Town
Print management

The artwork used on the front cover is a linocut entitled 'Making Democracy Work' by Sandile Goje. The artwork belongs to the South African Constitutional Court's art collection, and is used with the kind permission of the Constitutional Court Trust.

CONTENTS

CONTRIBUTORS

Catherine Albertyn (BA LLB MPhil PhD) is a Professor of Law in the School of Law, University of the Witwatersrand, where she teaches courses on constitutional law and human rights. Before joining the School, she was the Director of the Centre for Applied Legal Studies (2001 to 2007) and headed its Gender Research Programme for ten years (1992 to 2001). During that time she worked closely with the women's movement in seeking to influence the constitutional negotiations and, after 1994, on several policy and law reform processes. Her research interests include equality, gender studies, human rights and constitutional law. She has published extensively on equality, including the chapter on Equality in Woolman et al *Constitutional Law of South Africa* (with Beth Goldblatt), and is currently working on a book on Equality in South Africa. She has also written a number of articles on Gender and the Law, including 'Law, Gender and Equality in South Africa' (2011) *Oxford Development Studies* 139. She is also co-editor of *Gender, Law and Justice* (with Elsje Bonthuys). She is an editor of the *South African Journal on Human Rights*, and was a Commissioner at the South African Law Reform Commission from 2007 to 2011.

Henk Botha (BLC LLB LLM LLD) is a Professor of Law at the University of Stellenbosch, where he teaches constitutional law. Previously he taught at the University of South Africa, where he was Professor of Constitutional Law and head of the Verloren van Themaat Centre for Public Law Studies. He is a former editor of the journal *SA Publiekreg/Public Law*. He has also published widely in the fields of constitutional law, constitutional theory, legal philosophy and comparative constitutional law, and was awarded a fellowship by the Alexander von Humboldt Foundation in 2006.

Danie Brand (BLC LLB LLM LLD) is an Associate Professor in the Department of Public Law at the University of Pretoria, where he teaches constitutional and administrative law and land reform law. He works on the links between law, poverty and politics and he has published in this area, in particular on the adjudication of socio-economic rights claims in South Africa and the relationship between such adjudication and politics. He is the editorial manager of the Pretoria University Law Press (PULP) and an editor of *Southern African Public Law* and the *Constitutional Court Review*.

Lilian Chenwi (LLB LLM LLD) is as an Associate Professor at the School of Law, University of the Witwatersrand, South Africa. She has a record of publications in the area of socio-economic rights, housing rights and human rights and has been involved in advocacy and litigation initiatives in these areas. She has been involved in the discussions and drafting process of key international documents, such as the Optional Protocol to the International Covenant on Economic, Social and Cultural Rights (ICESCR), a milestone international treaty on the protection of human rights; and the recently adopted Maastricht Principles on Extraterritorial Obligations of States in the area of

Economic, Social and Cultural Rights. She is also a member of key international networks; a member of the Extraterritorial Obligations Consortium; one of the Convenors of the Social and Economic Rights in Africa working group of the African Network of Constitutional Lawyers; and a member of the Steering Committee of the NGO Coalition for an Optional Protocol to the ICESCR. Lilian has also been a consultant to the Office of the United Nations High Commissioner for Human Rights, amongst others; and has participated in a number of expert meetings of United Nations organs and mechanisms.

Emilios Christodoulidis (LLB LLM PhD) joined the Law School at Glasgow in 2006 as Professor of Legal Theory. From 1993 to 2006 he taught at the University of Edinburgh. He obtained his LLB degree from the University of Athens and his LLM and PhD from Edinburgh. As a doctoral student he won the IVR (International Association for Legal and Social Philosophy) "young scholar prize" in 1993. His book *Law and Reflexive Politics* won the European Award for Legal Theory in 1996 and the 1998 Prize for "Outstanding Legal Scholarship" by the UK Society of Legal scholars. He was Visiting Professor at the European Academy for Legal Theory in Brussels between 1996 and 1998, and at the Faculty of Law in Antwerp in 2008, and was a fellow at the Institute of Advanced Studies in Nantes in 2011. In June/July 2002 he gave the seventh series of the KOBE lectures in Japan. He is a member of the Executive Committee of the IVR.

Aninka Claassens (BA Hons) is a Senior Researcher in the Law, Race and Gender Unit at the University of Cape Town. She has been a land activist for many years and has worked with communities who resisted forced removals in the 1980s. Thereafter she worked at the Centre for Applied Legal Studies at the University of the Witwatersrand where she convened working groups that developed drafts for various land reform laws. She was also a technical advisor on land and property rights to the Constitutional Assembly. From 1996 to 2000 she worked for the Ministry of Land Affairs as a tenure specialist. More recently she worked for the Legal Resources Centre (LRC), co-ordinating research related to land rights and living customary law for the purposes of evidence in litigation. She is the co-editor, with Ben Cousins, of *Land, Power and Custom: Controversies generated by South Africa's Communal Land Rights Act.*

Dennis Davis (BComm LLB MPhil) is Judge of the High Court (Western Cape) and Judge President of the Competition Appeal Court. He is honorary Professor of Law at the University of Cape Town, where he teaches constitutional law, revenue law, competition law and legal theory. He has authored a number of scholarly books and articles in a range of fields, including transformative constitutionalism in South Africa, and the adjudication of socio-economic rights. He also regularly participates in public debates on issues of pressing concern to the deepening of constitutional democracy in South Africa.

Jackie Dugard (BA (Hons) MPhil PhD LLM LLB) is Executive Director at the Socio-Economic Rights Institute of South Africa (SERI) and a Visiting Senior Fellow at the School of Law, University of the Witwatersrand. With a background in social sciences and law, Jackie works to advance access to justice and basic services in poor South African communities, and has published widely on the role of law and courts in affecting socio-economic change, as well as on basic services-related rights. Her most recent publication, with Malcolm Langford, is "Art or Science? Synthesising Lessons from Public Interest Litigation and the Dangers of Legal Determinism" (2011) 27 *South African Journal on Human Rights* 39–64.

Ockert Dupper (BA LLB LLM SJD) is Professor of Labour Law and Social Security Law at the University of Stellenbosch, where he also serves as the Director of the Centre for International and Comparative Labour and Social Security Law (CICLASS). In 2002, he was a Faculty Fellow in Ethics at the Harvard University Center for Ethics and the Professions. Between 2004 and 2006, he was a visiting researcher at the Max Planck Institute for Social Law in Munich, Germany. He has published widely on a range of issues and, in particular, on affirmative action, non-discrimination and social security. He is the co-editor of *Equality in the Workplace: Reflections from South Africa and Beyond* (Juta 2009), and the forthcoming *Affirmative Action: A View from the Global South* (Sun Media 2012). He regularly consults to the ILO, and as a consultant to the Institute for Social Law and Policy (ISLP) and the International Institute for Social Law and Policy (IISLP), he has been involved in a range of social security-related projects for various South African government departments and agencies.

Nancy Fraser (BA MA PhD) is the Henry A and Louise Loeb Professor of Philosophy and Politics at the New School for Social Research in New York. Her books include *Scales of Justice: Reimagining Political Space for a Globalizing World* (2008); *Adding Insult to Injury: Nancy Fraser Debates her Critics* ed Kevin Olson (2008); *Redistribution or Recognition? A Political-Philosophical Exchange* (2003) with Axel Honneth; *Justice Interruptus: Critical Reflections on the "Postsocialist" Condition* (1997); and *Unruly Practices: Power, Discourse, and Gender in Contemporary Social Theory* (1989). She received the American Philosophical Association's Alfred Schutz Prize in 2010, and is currently Einstein Visiting Fellow at the Free University of Berlin and holder of a Chair at the College of Global Studies in Paris.

Sandra Fredman (BA MA BCL FBA) is the Rhodes Professor of the Laws of the British Commonwealth and the USA at Oxford University, a Fellow of the British Academy, and an Honorary Professor at the University of Cape Town. She has published widely in the fields of equality, labour law, and human rights. Her published books include *Human Rights Transformed* (OUP 2008); *Discrimination Law* (OUP 2002; 2 ed 2011); *Women and the Law* (OUP 1997); *The State as Employer* (Mansell 1988) with Gillian Morris, and *Labour Law and Industrial Relations in Great Britain* 2 ed (Kluwer 1992) with Bob Hepple. She has also edited two books: *Age as an Equality Issue* (Hart 2003) with Sarah Spencer, as well as *Discrimination and Human Rights: the Case of Racism* (OUP 2001). She was a scientific director of the EU Network of Legal Experts in the Non-Discrimination field; and she has been an expert adviser to the proposed Single Equality Bill in Northern Ireland, the Equalities Review in the UK, the Canadian Review of Federal Labour Law, the UN Human Rights Commission working group on national action plans against racism, the UN Working Group on Women's Rights, the World Development Report 2013, and Indian gender discrimination legislation. She is a barrister, holding an academic tenancy at Old Square Chambers, and became a QC (honoris causa) in 2012.

Avinash Govindjee (BA LLB LLM LLD) is a Professor in the Department of Public Law and Deputy Head of the Labour and Social Security Law Unit in the Faculty of Law, Nelson Mandela Metropolitan University, where he has taught since 2003. Avinash is an attorney of the High Court of South Africa, practising as a consultant to the firm Burmeister de Lange Soni Incorporated in Port Elizabeth. He serves the Commission for Conciliation, Mediation and Arbitration on a part-time basis as a senior commissioner, and arbitrates disputes for various bargaining councils. He holds a standing Visiting Professorship from the National Law School of India University, Bangalore. As a consultant to the Institute for Social Law and Policy (ISLP) and the International Institute for Social Law and Policy (IISLP), he has been involved in a range of social security-related projects for various South African government departments and agencies.

Anna Kamkuemah (LLB) attended Deutsche Höhere Privatshule in Windhoek. She completed her Bachelor of Laws at the University of Stellenbosch (2006 to 2009). In 2009, she was selected and worked as a research assistant for the South African Research Chair in Property Law hosted by the University of Stellenbosch. Anna is currently a second year LLM student and research assistant at the Strategic Research and Outreach Initiative on Combating Poverty, Homelessness and Socio-Economic Disadvantage under the Constitution at the Stellenbosch University's Faculty of Law. Her area of research is land reform, and the title of her thesis is "A Comparative Study of Women's Tenure Security in South Africa and Namibia".

Karl Klare (BA MA JD) is George J and Kathleen Waters Matthews Distinguished University Professor at Northeastern University School of Law, Boston, USA, where he has taught since 1977. He has been a Visiting Professor at the Universities of British Columbia, Cape Town, Michigan and Toronto, and he held a Fulbright Chair at the European University Institute in Florence. He was active in the Critical Legal Studies movement and was a founder of the International Network on Transformative Employment and Labour Law. Much of his career has been devoted to labour and employment law. In recent years he has focused on social and economic rights and particularly on questions of law and social transformation in South Africa.

Pius N Langa (Bluris LLB) obtained his degrees while working at the Department of Justice in various capacities as interpreter, messenger and magistrate. After being admitted as an advocate in 1977, he attained the rank of Senior Counsel in 1994, with his practice reflecting the struggle against apartheid. He has served on the boards of various law-related institutions, such as the National Association of Democratic Lawyers, for which he was President from 1988 to 1994. He has also served as the Commissioner of Human Rights and has been awarded honorary doctoral degrees in law by numerous universities. In 1994, Langa was appointed as one of the first Judges of the Constitutional Court. He became the Court's Deputy President in 1997, and in 2001, he became the Deputy Chief Justice of South Africa. In 2005 he was appointed as the country's Chief Justice and head of the Constitutional Court. In 2008 he received the Presidential Order of the Boabab (in gold), one of the various awards he has received for his work in the advancement of human rights. Justice Langa was discharged from active service in 2009 and is currently an acting Judge of Appeal in the Namibian Supreme Court.

Sandra Liebenberg (BA LLB LLM LLD) currently holds the HF Oppenheimer Chair in Human Rights Law in the Law Faculty of the University of Stellenbosch. She was academic director of the Faculty's post-graduate research project on Combating Poverty, Homelessness and Socio-Economic Vulnerability under the Constitution, and is now Co-Director of the Faculty's Socio-Economic Rights and Administrative Justice Research Project (SERAJ). She previously served as a member of the Technical Committee advising the Constitutional Assembly on the Bill of Rights in the 1996 Constitution of South Africa. In 1997, she founded and directed the Socio-Economic Rights Project based at the Community Law Centre (University of the Western Cape), where she was involved in research, advocacy and supporting litigation in the area of socio-economic rights. She serves on the editorial board of the *South African Journal on Human Rights*, the *African Human Rights Law Journal*, and the *Human Rights Law Journal*. She is also Chairperson of the Board of SERI (Socio-Economic Rights Institute of South Africa). She has been involved in research, litigation and advocacy in the area of socio-economic rights for a number of years, and is the author of *Socio-Economic Rights: Adjudication under a Transformative Constitution* (Juta 2010).

Sue-Mari Maass (BComm LLB LLD) joined the Department of Public, Constitutional and International Law at Unisa as a Senior Lecturer in 2012. She is involved in the teaching of administrative law, constitutional law and local government law. Her research interests are property law, constitutional property law, housing law and land reform. In 2011 she was employed as a Postdoctoral Research Fellow at the South African Research Chair in Property Law. In 2010 she finished her LLD dissertation on "Tenure Security in Urban Rental Housing" which she completed under the supervision of André van der Walt.

Frank I Michelman (BA LLB) is Robert Walmsley University Professor, Harvard University, where he has taught since 1963. He is the author of *Brennan and Democracy* (1999), and has published widely in the fields of constitutional law and theory, comparative constitutionalism, property law and theory, local government law, and general legal theory. He is a fellow of the American Academy of Arts and Sciences and a past President (1994 to 1995) of the American Society for Political and Legal Philosophy. He has served on the

Committee of Directors for the annual Prague Conference on Philosophy and the Social Sciences, the Board of Directors of the United States Association of Constitutional Law, and the National Advisory Board of the American Constitution Society. In 2005, he was awarded the American Philosophical Society's Phillips Prize in Jurisprudence and, in 2004, the Brigham-Kanner Property Rights Prize. In January 1995, and again in January 1996, he served as a co-organiser and co-leader of Judges' Conferences sponsored by the Centre for Applied Legal Studies of the University of the Witwatersrand, devoted to matters of constitutional law in South Africa.

Sindiso Mnisi Weeks (BA LLB MSt DPhil) is a Senior Researcher in the Law, Race and Gender Research Unit at the University of Cape Town (UCT), where she has worked on the Rural Women's Action-Research project – which combines research and policy work on women, land and customary law – since 2009. She is also a Senior Lecturer in UCT's Department of Private Law where she co-teaches African Customary Law. She has published on customary law, women's rights to land, traditional institutions and the Constitution. She holds a doctorate from the University of Oxford where, as a Rhodes Scholar, she conducted empirically-based research on the interface between living customary law(s) and South African state law, specifically focusing on the law of succession. Prior to studying at Oxford, she clerked for Dikgang Moseneke, the Deputy Chief Justice of the Constitutional Court. Her current research focuses on traditional courts and vernacular dispute resolution forums in South Africa.

Khulekani Moyo (LLB (Hons) LLM) obtained his LLB (Hons) from the University of Zimbabwe and his LLM in public international law from the University of Oslo, Norway. He also holds two diplomas in the international protection of human rights and justiciability of economic, social and cultural rights from Abo Akademi University in Finland. He was admitted to practise law in Zimbabwe in 2003 as legal practitioner, conveyancer and notary public. He has practised law in Zimbabwe, worked in Namibia as a legal advisor to an insurance company and has worked for the Norwegian Centre for Human Rights at the University of Oslo. He is currently a doctoral researcher at Stellenbosch University focusing on privatisation and the human right to water, and is a member of the Socio-Economic Rights and Administrative Justice Research Project (SERAJ). His other areas of interest include international criminal law and regional integration law.

Gustav Muller (LLB LLD) is a Lecturer at the Faculty of Law, Rhodes University where he teaches the law of contract and company law to commerce students, legal interpretation, legal skills and jurisprudence. Stellenbosch University conferred the degree of Doctor of Laws on him in December 2011 for his dissertation on "The Impact of Section 26 of the Constitution on the Eviction of Squatters in South African Law" which he completed under the supervision of Sandra Liebenberg and André van der Walt. His dissertation investigates whether unlawful occupiers can be afforded greater protection through a substantive interpretation of section 26 of the Constitution as influenced by a contextual understanding of evictions and international law. He is interested in constitutional law (especially socio-economic rights), administrative law, the use of international law as an interpretive tool, legal theory and the inter-disciplinary study of law.

Juanita M Pienaar (Bluris LLB LLM LLD) is a Professor in Private Law at the University of Stellenbosch. She lectures customary law, property law and statutory property law. Her research focus is property law in general and land reform and related matters in particular. She has co-authored some of the standard property law publications, including *Silberberg and Schoeman's Law of Property* (with PJ Badenhorst and H Mostert) and *Principles of the Law of Property* (H Mostert and A Pope (eds)). She is also responsible for the land reform section of the "Land" title in *LAWSA* (2010, with H Mostert and J van Wyk) and the chapter on "Land" in *Constitutional Law of South Africa* (with J Brickhill). She is a member of the Advisory Committee of the Law Commission (Land Legislation: 2008 to 2010) and was an acting judge in the Land Claims Court (2006 to 2007).

Geo Quinot (BA LLB LLM LLD) is a Professor in the Department of Public Law at Stellenbosch University, Co-Director of the Socio-Economic Rights and Administrative Justice Research Project (SERAJ) and Director of the African Public Procurement Regulation Research Unit (APPRRU). He mainly teaches administrative law and constitutional law. His research focuses primarily on administrative law and he has a particular interest in the intersection between administrative law and other areas of law and the impact of such intersection on efforts of the administration to pursue social justice under South Africa's transformative Constitution. He is the author of *State Commercial Activity: A Legal Framework* (Juta 2009) and *Administrative Law: Cases and Materials* (Juta 2008), and is currently the editor of the *Stellenbosch Law Review*.

Solange Rosa (BA LLB LLM) is a doctoral candidate at the University of Stellenbosch and a Senior Policy Analyst in the Premier's Department in the Western Cape Provincial Government, responsible for social policy and planning. She worked as a senior researcher at the Children's Institute, University of Cape Town, from 2002 to 2006, focusing on children in poverty and the right to social security. She was also Advocacy Coordinator for the Alliance for Children's Entitlement to Social Security and Chairperson of the Basic Income Grant Coalition, based in Cape Town. She has worked internationally for Oxfam International and the United Nations Development Program. She has also researched, written and published broadly on human rights, social justice and development, and in particular on freedom of expression, access to information, prisoner's rights, criminal justice, gender, children's rights, social security rights, participatory rights, socio-economic rights and poverty.

Sanele Sibanda (BA LLB LLM) is a Senior Lecturer at the Wits School of Law, Johannesburg, South Africa. Since joining the School in 2002, he has taught a wide range of subjects at undergraduate level, including customary law, introduction to constitutional law, insurance law, persons and family law and administrative law. His current research interests are in the areas of constitutional law and customary law reform, and he has also published on these areas. He is also an editor of the *South African Journal on Human Rights*.

Lucy A Williams (BA JD) has been a Professor of Law at Northeastern University School of Law, Boston since 1991, and was named its Public Interest Distinguished Professor in 1994/1995. She has written and lectured widely in the area of social assistance/security law, poverty, low-wage labour law, and the justiciability of social and economic rights, focusing on race, class and gender in a global context. She was appointed by President Clinton to the Advisory Council on Unemployment Compensation, evaluating all aspects of the US unemployment compensation program and making policy recommendations to the President and Congress. She is Co-Director of the Project on Human Rights in the Global Economy at Northeastern University School of Law and coordinates the International Social and Economic Rights (SER) Project, an international network of lawyers, judges, academics and other human rights advocates, which seeks to encourage and develop critical and transformative thinking about SER and SER-based legal strategies.

Stuart Wilson (MA LLB) is a practising advocate and a member of the Johannesburg Bar. He is currently the Director of Litigation at the Socio-Economic Rights Institute of South Africa. He specialises in constitutional and administrative law and has appeared in a number of leading socio-economic rights cases in the Constitutional Court. He also practises in the areas of criminal defence, defamation and consumer protection. He runs the property law course at the University of the Witwatersrand where he holds an appointment as a Visiting Senior Fellow. He studied at Oxford University (where he took an MA in Philosophy, Politics and Economics) and the University of the Witwatersrand, Johannesburg, where he received a Bachelor of Laws degree (with distinction).

TABLE OF CASES

United States of America

INTRODUCTION: LAW AND POVERTY COLLOQUIUM

According to the *Development Indicators 2010*, 49% of persons in South Africa live below a poverty line of R524 per month (approximately 75 US dollars per month).[1] The official unemployment rate in South Africa was in the vicinity of 25% (excluding discouraged work-seekers) in 2010.[2] Most concerning is the unemployment rate of 51% for youth in the age group of 15–24 years.[3] About two-thirds of all unemployed are below the age of 35 with significantly higher unemployment rates for black youth.[4] To add to this mix, South Africa's levels of income inequality are amongst the highest in the world. According to the National Planning Commission's recently published *Diagnostic Overview*, the "poorest 20% of the population earns about 2.3 percent of national income, while the richest 20 percent earns about 70 percent of the income".[5]

And yet we have a Constitution[6] which proclaims in its preamble that it was adopted so as "to heal the divisions of the past, and to establish a society based on democratic values, social justice and fundamental human rights". In addition, the Constitution aims to "improve the quality of life of all citizens and free the potential of each person".[7] How must a legal system which gains its force and validity from this Constitution respond to the dire reality which the few statistics above crudely sketch?

It is this fundamental question which the Strategic Postgraduate Research and Outreach Project of the Law Faculty at Stellenbosch University, entitled *Combating Poverty, Homelessness and Socio-Economic Vulnerability Under the Constitution*[8] has sought to grapple with since its inception in 2009. The Project forms part of the "Hope Project" initiative of Stellenbosch University[9] which seeks to stimulate socially relevant research aimed at addressing the crucial political and developmental problems of South Africa's young democracy within a broader African context. It is rooted in the University's three core functions of teaching and learning, research, and community interaction.

---

[1] The Presidency of the Republic of South Africa *Development Indicators 2010* (2010) 23 <http://www.presidency.gov.za/MediaLib/Downloads/Home/Publications/NationalPlanningCommission4/Development%20Indicators2010.pdf> (accessed 27-11-2011).

[2] 20-21.

[3] National Planning Commission *Diagnostic Overview* (2011) 11 <http://www.npconline.co.za/MediaLib/Downloads/Home/Tabs/Diagnostic/Diagnostic%20Overview.pdf> (accessed 28-11-2011).

[4] 11.

[5] 9.

[6] Constitution of the Republic of South Africa, 1996 ("the Constitution").

[7] Preamble.

[8] The Law Faculty's Project's website is at <http://www.sun.ac.za/lawandpoverty> (accessed 28-11-2011).

[9] On the broader University Hope Project, see <http://thehopeproject.co.za> (accessed 28-11-2011).

The Law Faculty's contribution to the Hope Project aims to explore how the rights and institutions created by the Constitution can contribute to redressing poverty and inequality. Postgraduate research and training constitute a major focus of the Project. Apart from in-depth supervision and involvement in the various seminars, workshops, and other activities conducted under the auspices of this Project, students are provided with intensive training and advisory support to enable them to succeed in their academic programmes. Students accepted into the project benefit from good library and infrastructure facilities, exposure to critical scholarship and debate, as well as participation in test case litigation and community outreach activities. In this way the Project seeks to directly challenge the *status quo* by equipping a new generation of lawyers with postgraduate qualifications in topics related to overcoming socio-economic disadvantage through law.

The main research and postgraduate training focus areas (with the leading researcher in each particular area) are:

* socio-economic rights (Sandra Liebenberg);
* transformative property law and theory (AJ van der Walt);
* land reform and security of tenure in housing and land (Juanita Pienaar);
* administrative justice (Geo Quinot);
* consolidating and deepening democracy (Henk Botha);
* equality, redress and poverty relief (Ockert Dupper); and
* legal and constitutional interpretation (Lourens du Plessis).

The community outreach and litigation component of the Project's work has been primarily conducted through the Faculty's Legal Aid Clinic.

The Law and Poverty Colloquium held at the Stellenbosch Institute for Advanced Studies (STIAS) from 29 to 31 May 2011 was intended to highlight the research done under the auspices of the Project by both academic staff and some of the postgraduate students working within the Project. In addition, we also invited a range of national and international experts working on a diverse array of theoretical and applied research topics closely related to the themes of our colloquium. The bulk of the papers presented at the colloquium were published in a special edition of the *Stellenbosch Law Review* (volume 22:3, 2011), and now also in this volume. We are grateful to all our national and international guest presenters for participating in the colloquium and for contributing papers to this volume.

The colloquium was attended by 126 delegates, representing a cross-section of academics, postgraduate students, and representatives of the legal profession, government, Chapter 9 Institutions and civil society organisations. We were also honoured by the attendance of former Constitutional Court Justices Pius Langa, Albie Sachs and Kate O'Regan. We are particularly grateful to former Chief Justice Pius Langa, who delivered the keynote address at the official colloquium dinner and whose address is also published in this special volume of the *Stellenbosch Law Review*.

The range of papers presented at the colloquium and the ensuing debates highlighted the contested nature and complexity of poverty, as well as the possibilities and limits of the law in responding to it. We are grateful to

Professor Karl Klare for capturing, with grace and insight, the key themes and richness of the debates which took place at the colloquium in his closing address, which is also published in this volume. Given his excellent account of the papers and the debates it will be redundant to provide a similar overview of the papers contained in this volume here. Two of our international guests, Professor Nancy Fraser and Professor Frank Michelman, were STIAS fellows over the period of the colloquium and we are grateful to STIAS and its director, Professor Hendrik Geyer, for making their participation in the colloquium possible.

A special word of thanks is due to Gustav Muller, the Project Manager of the Law Faculty's Law and Poverty Project who co-organised the colloquium together with Professor Sandy Liebenberg, the Project's Academic Director.

This book and the special edition of the *Stellenbosch Law Review* that preceded it were made possible by the expert editorial assistance of the two technical editors of the *Stellenbosch Law Review*, Shanelle van der Berg and Michael Clark. They were ably assisted in this task by the following team of postgraduate students working within the Project: Gustav Muller, Khulekani Moyo, Margot Strauss, Tarryn Bannister, Sibusiso Radebe, Hugo Murray and Christine Botha. We are indebted to them for their expert assistance and hard work in getting this volume ready in a record period of time.

It is our hope that this collection of the colloquium proceedings will contribute to deepening critical reflection and debate on law's contribution to social justice and building a better life for all in South Africa.

Sandra Liebenberg & Geo Quinot
Editors

CHAPTER 1

THE ROLE OF THE CONSTITUTION IN THE STRUGGLE AGAINST POVERTY

Pius N Langa

1 Introduction

It is a great honour to be asked to speak at this colloquium on *Law and Poverty*. I understand the Constitution of the Republic of South Africa, 1996 ("the Constitution") as urging us to eradicate poverty, and for me and others here, the instrument we have available to us is the law. The theme has particular resonance to me, and to those of us who have battled poverty in various ways and on a number of terrains. I thank you, the organisers of this colloquium, for the opportunity to address this subject at this forum.

2 South Africa's constitutional democracy: The challenge of poverty

What I have said in the past (and others have said today in the papers delivered at this colloquium) is that how we respond to poverty is critical to democracy, development and the stability of our constitutional state. In South Africa, in particular, it is of the utmost relevance to reconciliation. I agree with those who say that not enough attention has been paid to the subject of poverty, and even less to its eradication. Many just throw up their hands in despair, while others simply accept it as a fact of life that South Africa and the continent will never be able to rid themselves of this problem. I need hardly mention that the concession to failure is an extremely dangerous one as it affects the sense of urgency with which we attack the problem. It is dangerous further because it contradicts the Constitution which speaks of the commitment to "social justice and fundamental human rights"; improving "the quality of life of all citizens" and freeing "the potential of each person".[1]

It is dangerous on another score as well. Poverty, and our attitudes to it in a country like South Africa, may bring with it complex and interrelated challenges that threaten to interfere with our society's commitment to the rule of law, which is a foundational concept and element of our constitutional existence. Of course there are those living in this beautiful and well-endowed country who are simply indifferent to the fact that it still has perhaps the widest poverty gap on the planet.

In many conferences, speaker after speaker focus on various direct challenges to the rule of law. These include the inadequacy of economic

---

[1] Preamble, Constitution of the Republic of South Africa, 1996.

development, the abuse of human rights and the law, and corruption. In more recent years, we have recognised the existence of less direct – but no less powerful – challenges to the rule of law that exist throughout our societies from other sources, some posed by poverty itself. We have just been through countrywide elections and are witnessing, as a result, much breast-beating, back-patting and finger-pointing. The elections were preceded by unprecedented levels of service delivery protests, as the people flexed their muscles and voiced their dissatisfaction rather volubly against their political leaders. More often than not, the trigger for these protests and upheavals is poverty. The question then is: do we at least have a plan to solve this problem?

3   Placing poverty at the forefront of the human rights agenda

In large part, addressing issues of human rights requires grappling with issues of the economic conditions under which the majority of our people live. Sometimes this aspiration is referred to as economic development for all our people. That is where the battlefront is. That is what our people fought for. That is in fact what the Constitution urges us to aspire to achieve.

I have walked among the shacks and I have seen little children without food. I have asked myself what the real meaning of the Constitution is in the context of the founding constitutional values of human dignity, equality and freedom.

Legal guarantees of political rights are indivisible from constitutional protection for social and economic rights. Without economic security and independence, individuals will be unable to realise individual freedom and express themselves freely in the social and political sphere. They will be unable to educate themselves, a prerequisite for robust political participation. Without economic security and independence, culture and civil society cannot flourish. Individuals without the means to support themselves will find themselves turning to crime and violence and disrespecting the legal system. Keba M'Baye spoke out powerfully in favour of a right to development when he remarked

> "[w]hat does freedom in effect mean for him that will die of hunger? The rights of man and of the citizen have no meaning for the men who stagnate in famine, sickness, and ignorance."[2]

It is no secret that women and children often bear the brunt of poverty. Studies in South Africa have indicated that there is even a relationship between poverty and violence against women. Internationally, poverty has been recognised as a serious problem and halving it by 2015 is included as one of the Millennium Development Goals. However, we are told elsewhere that about 50% of the population in sub-Saharan Africa survives on less than $1.00 per day. Poverty is therefore an issue that must be placed firmly at the forefront of the human rights agenda. The continued prevalence of poverty is related to lack of education and is tied to lack of economic growth and

---

[2]   K Mickelson "Rhetoric and Rage: Third World Voices in International Legal Discourse" (1998) 16 *Wis Int'l LJ* 353 383 n 154 citing K M'Baye "Le Droit au Développement Comme un Droit de l'Homme" (1972) 5 *Revue des Droits de l'Homme* 505 524.

opportunities. This has resulted largely from wars, fiscal mismanagement and corruption. We know that in recent years, there have been attempts to turn this around with a renewed focus on good governance as well as initiatives such as NEPAD, the African Peer Review Mechanism, and the African Union Convention on Preventing and Combating Corruption. These initiatives can only succeed if civil society gets involved in holding governments and relevant institutions accountable and exposing them when they fail to uphold the requirements of these Conventions and values. The fact is, true leadership means putting people first.

4 Human rights, the rule of law and poverty eradication

I thought I might say a word or two about the interrelationship between human rights, the rule of law, and the impact of poverty in our journey to being the type of society our Constitution envisages. Human rights and the rule of law are foundational values of most democratic states. However, they remain shallow platitudes without a solid foundation of basic health care, saleable skills, education, and security of the person, in combination with a total dedication from government to the equitable application and interpretation of human rights.

In our time, we have witnessed a sea change in attitudes, what has been referred to as a "wave of democratisation" that has swept the African continent. Yet it is trite to observe that this is but a first step in establishing respect for the rule of law and human rights. Though democratic elections are a critical foundation of the rule of law, they do not begin to guarantee it. Even in states that have established constitutions based on powerful notions of freedom, these notions may, in fact, do little to practically affect the daily lives of individuals – many of whom frequently face violations of their human rights.

Addressing issues of human rights goes hand in hand with efforts to support the rule of law. Without proper respect for the rule of law, legal guarantees of human rights cannot be effectively implemented and remain relatively meaningless. Respect for the rule of law is also of central relevance to economic development, since it protects property rights and provides the certainty necessary for business transactions and development. Thus, human rights, which embrace the concept of economic development for all, and the rule of law cannot be neatly compartmentalised or assessed in a vacuum, but must be viewed as interdependent.

5 Socio-economic justice and reconciliation

The fight against poverty also has major implications for national reconciliation in South Africa. I say I have walked among the shacks. The poorest of the poor also walk the streets of the more affluent, and look at what we throw away in our dirt bins. Poverty speaks to our history, to where we come from. National reconciliation therefore has to have resonance with that past. Thus, we fight poverty because we aim to correct a past that went horribly wrong. This is an aspect we should pay attention to, if only out of our own national self-interest. I am convinced that unless we redress this very wide gap between the poorest of the poor and the most affluent in our country, the reconciliation that will facilitate our development as a nation will remain a pipe dream.

There is hope in projects and gatherings like this one: hope that they will help bring about the desired understanding of the challenges that poverty poses for our constitutional democracy and the possibilities of addressing these – at least partially – through the legal system. They also provide encouragement to the national effort to eradicate poverty from our midst.

I would place the emphasis on the national level, rather than the international assistance agencies. In contrast to external assistance, national programmes offer our country, civil society, and the public at large the opportunity to realise the potential we have in our midst to develop locally appropriate solutions. Addressing the problems of the most disadvantaged members of society through the promotion of social and economic rights requires efforts that are sensitive to the specific context and circumstances of our nation.

6 Protecting, promoting and fulfilling socio-economic rights

In this country, we have made a promising start in addressing these problems. We have established a constitution based on the principles and values of human dignity, equality and freedom, and we have recently started uncovering the constitutional significance of the African indigenous value of *ubuntu*. Our foundational document recognises the unjust past of this nation and documents the suffering and hardship, and the persistence and dedication of those who made this democratic nation a possibility. The preamble of the Constitution states that its aim is to "[i]mprove the quality of life of all citizens and free the potential of each person". In so doing, it recognises that the proper response to injustice and division is not further division, but rather equal protection, common citizenship, and human dignity for all people. In protecting these principles, the Constitution seeks to create a better life for all citizens, not just those with access to political power or military force.

As part of the Constitution's commitment to uplifting the quality of life of all people, it specifically protects a broad array of social rights, including specific provisions protecting the rights to health care, food, water, social security, education, housing, land and the environment. This is fortified by the *Grootboom* judgment, in which the Court reasoned:

"All the rights in our Bill of Rights are inter-related and mutually supporting. There can be no doubt that human dignity, freedom and equality, the foundational values of our society, are denied to those who have no food, clothing or shelter. Affording socio-economic rights to all people therefore enables them to enjoy the other rights enshrined in Chapter 2. The realisation of these rights is also key to the advancement of race and gender equality and the evolution of a society in which men and women are equally able to achieve their full potential. Socio-economic rights must all be read together in the setting of the Constitution as a whole. The state is obliged to take positive action to meet the needs of those living in extreme conditions of poverty, homelessness or intolerable housing. Their interconnectedness needs to be taken into account in interpreting the socio-economic rights, and, in particular, in determining whether the state has met its obligations in terms of them."[3]

---

[3] *Government of the Republic of South Africa v Grootboom* 2001 1 SA 46 (CC) paras 23-24.

And yet, for all our progress, we cannot rest because we still have a long way to go to achieve our goals. Our jurisprudence thus far establishes that the Constitution protects individuals from negative infringements of their socio-economic rights. For example, in assessing the constitutionality of the socio-economic rights provisions of the Constitution, we held that "[a]t the very minimum, socio-economic rights can be negatively protected from improper invasion".[4] The right to be protected from interference with the enjoyment of socio-economic rights stems directly from the obligation of the state to protect the rights in the Bill of Rights.

However, in order to make progress towards the full realisation of the rights and their implementation by the state, there is room to go beyond a mere enforcement of negative duties. The Constitution's ideal could be said to impose a duty not only to protect rights, but also to promote and fulfil them as well. After all, the Court has also reasoned that

> "where a breach of any right has taken place, including a socio-economic right, a Court is under a duty to ensure that effective relief is granted. The nature of the right infringed and the nature of the infringement will provide guidance as to the appropriate relief in a particular case. Where necessary this may include both the issuing of a mandamus and the exercise of supervisory jurisdiction."[5]

Socio-economic rights in their positive dimension have been interpreted as being subject to progressive realisation and the requirement that the government must take reasonable steps within the constraints of its available financial resources. To that end, the Court in *Soobramoney* reasoned that

> "[w]hat is apparent from these provisions is that the obligation imposed on the state by sections 26 and 27 in regards to access to health care, education, food, water and social security are dependent on the resources available for such purposes, and that the corresponding rights are limited by the lack of resources. Given the lack of resources and the significant demands on them that have already been referred to, an unqualified obligation to meet these needs would not presently be capable of being fulfilled."[6]

While cognisant of the various constraints facing the legislature, we should recognise that the Constitution aspires to create a fair, equal, and developed society. We must therefore remain mindful of the possibilities available within our legal system to help bridge the chasm between the constitutional ideals and the dire realities of life for many in the society that we inhabit. The following observation in *Soobramoney* is no less true today:

> "We live in a society in which there are great disparities in wealth. Millions of people are living in deplorable conditions and in great poverty. There is a high level of unemployment, inadequate social security, and many do not have access to clean water or to adequate health services. These conditions already existed when the Constitution was adopted and a commitment to address them, and to transform our society into one in which there will be human dignity, freedom and equality, lies at the heart of our new constitutional order. For as long as these conditions continue to exist that aspiration will have a hollow ring."[7]

---

[4]   *Ex Parte Chairperson of the Constitutional Assembly: In re Certification of the Constitution of the Republic of South Africa, 1996* 1996 4 SA 744 (CC) para 78.

[5]   *Minister of Health v Treatment Action Campaign (No 2)* 2002 5 SA 721 (CC) para 106.

[6]   *Soobramoney v Minister of Health, KwaZulu-Natal* 1998 1 SA 765 (CC) para 11.

[7]   Para 8. This was confirmed in *Government of the Republic of South Africa v Grootboom* 2001 1 SA 46 (CC) para 25.

7   Conclusion

These issues are complex and do not have easy answers. Yet, a commitment to social programmes and specific support for basic health care, saleable skills, education, security of person, combined with government's total dedication to an equitable application of the Constitution, may offer a way forward. Human rights, social and economic development for all, and the rule of law are foundational principles of our constitutional order. Maintaining our commitment to the Constitution and the rule of law is a promising first step, but we must continue to enforce rights robustly, including socio-economic rights. This represents a positive contribution to realising the transformative potential inherent in the ideals and values of our Constitution.

CHAPTER 2

SOCIAL EXCLUSION, GLOBAL POVERTY, AND SCALES OF (IN)JUSTICE: RETHINKING LAW AND POVERTY IN A GLOBALISING WORLD

Nancy Fraser

1 Introduction

Most discussions of law and poverty are pitched at the national level. Tacitly presuming what I call "the Westphalian frame", they envision the arena for addressing poverty as a modern territorial state. As a result, they imagine the victims of poverty as citizens of a bounded political community. Likewise, they picture the law that might help to rectify poverty as national law. Finally, they see the agency that might effect redress as a modern national state with sovereignty over a delimited territory.[1]

These assumptions are intuitively plausible. In the modern era, anti-poverty activists have in fact chiefly sought redress within bounded political communities that have been understood in Westphalian terms. And legal advocates for the poor have mainly focused on whatever resources they could find in the constitutions of such communities, especially resources for realising the social rights of member citizens. To the extent that legal efforts to mitigate poverty have achieved results, moreover, they have done so by mobilising national law to compel action from national states on behalf of national citizens. Thus, the Westphalian frame has a measure of real-world traction. No wonder, then, that it is commonly used to frame discussions of poverty and law.

Nevertheless, the Westphalian framing of poverty and law is problematic in a globalising world. Its constitutive assumptions are belied by the increasingly salient fact of "global poverty". That expression names modes of impoverishment whose causes and manifestations cannot be located within a single territorial state. Generated by transborder processes, the harms suffered by "the global poor" largely escape the parameters of national law and the control of national states. To locate them within the Westphalian frame is in fact to *misframe* them. With the picture cropped to exclude transnational vectors of domination, that framing obscures the offshore sources of the poverty that currently afflicts many in the "global South". Channelling the claims of the global poor into the domestic legal arenas of states that lack the capacity to redress them, it deprives them of the ability to challenge some

---

[1] For a fuller account of "the Westphalian frame" see N Fraser "Reframing Justice in a Globalising World" (2005) 36 *New Left Review* 69 69-88, reprinted in N Fraser *Scales of Justice: Reimagining Political Space in a Globalising World* (2008).

of the major architects of their dispossession. Effectively insulating offshore powers from critique and control, the Westphalian frame obfuscates the need for legal instruments and agencies of redress that operate on a broader scale than that of the modern territorial state. Obscuring the question of *scale*, it adds the insult of (national) misframing to the injury of (transnational) poverty.

That, at any rate, is the intuition that underlies the present essay. In what follows, I shall maintain that sensitivity to the problem of *scale* is a *sine qua non* for understanding, let alone overcoming, some of the most characteristic forms of poverty in the 21st century. Far from simply assuming the Westphalian frame, I shall treat the question of scale as a problem requiring interrogation. I shall assume, accordingly, that injustices operate at a variety of different scales in a globalising world – hence, that their analysis requires a variety of different frames. Some injustices, such as the US government's abdication of its responsibilities to the (largely non-white) victims of hurricane Katrina, are situated squarely on the national scale and can be adequately understood *via* the Westphalian frame. Others, such as that same government's practice of extra-legal "rendition", whereby suspected terrorists are kidnapped and flown secretly to "black sites" in foreign locations for "enhanced interrogation", are more plausibly located on a broader, transnational scale and so require a broader, transnational frame. Still others, such as the rise throughout the global South of mega-slums utterly cut off from formal work, are credibly imagined even more broadly, on a global scale, and require yet a larger frame. The trick is to know when to use which frame.

In general, then, I shall assume that discussions of law and poverty need to reckon with the existence of a plurality of *scales of (in)justice*. I shall assume, also, that they need to contemplate the possibility that some forms of poverty cannot be overcome by appealing exclusively to national law. In such cases, it may also be necessary to deploy law at other scales – and where such law is absent, to create it.

But that is not all. I shall also suggest that some important injustices are best located not on any one single scale but rather at the intersection of several scales. This, I will argue here, is the case for one of the core characteristic injustices of the present era: namely, "the social exclusion of the global poor". To understand this injustice requires an analytical approach that admits a multiplicity of intersecting scales. To overcome this injustice requires a political struggle that operates simultaneously at several scales. The same holds for the legal front of such a struggle. Legal advocates for the global poor must devise a coordinated strategy that integrates several levels of law and scales of justice.

I shall make this argument in several steps. After some preliminary reflections on terminology, I shall present a general conceptual account of *social exclusion*. In this first step, I shall draw on a three-dimensional view of (in)justice, encompassing (mal)distribution, (mis)recognition, and (mis)representation, in order to distinguish multiple forms of social exclusion and to identify those experienced by the global poor. In a second step, I shall complicate this account by introducing the problem of scale. After defining the injustice of *misframing* as a mismatch of scale, I shall theorise the situation of the global poor in terms of exclusions that are rooted *transnationally*, at the intersection of processes that operate at different scales. In a third step, I shall consider how such injustices might best be combated. Analysing the multi-scalar strategy of the Zapatistas, I shall try to clarify the moral stakes and political grammar of contemporary struggles over globalisation. In a brief *coda*, I shall return to the problem of terminology, arguing for reflection on the political implications of analytical categories, especially the terms "global poverty" and "the global poor".

2 "Social exclusion": A preliminary terminological note

I begin by noting that the phrase "social exclusion" has fast become a keyword of our age. Widely used throughout the world, this expression now headlines a large social-science literature and a surprising number of major policy initiatives. Under Tony Blair, the British government established a "Unit on Social Exclusion" in the Deputy Prime Minister's Office. Several years ago, the European Union adopted a policy aimed at eradicating "poverty and social exclusion by 2010",[2] although I don't recall reading any announcement of success. Within the last decade, moreover, the Inter-American Development Bank published a "mission statement" on social exclusion;[3] the United Nations Educational, Scientific and Cultural Organization ("UNESCO") held a major conference on the theme "From Social Exclusion to Social Cohesion";[4] and the London School of Economics established a Centre for the Analysis of Social Exclusion ("CASE").[5] Finally, a May 2011 Google search of "social exclusion South Africa" yielded a remarkable 5 360 000 results.

Nevertheless, the literature sheds little light on what "social exclusion" actually means. In some accounts, it is assigned to the same general field as such concepts as poverty and inequality. In others, it belongs rather with denial of recognition and disrespect. In still others, social exclusion is part of a discourse about social disintegration and the rupturing of social bonds. As yet, there exists no authoritative survey of the relative merits of those perspectives. As a result, there are major conceptual deficits in our understanding of an expression that is playing an increasingly important role in political life.

At the risk of muddying the waters still further, I want to introduce yet another way of thinking about social exclusion. In the view I will elaborate here, social exclusion is a species of injustice, but it is reducible neither to economic deprivation, on the one hand, nor to cultural disrespect, on the other. In the case of global poverty, rather, social exclusion arises from the intersection of three distinct genres of social injustice, which operate at

---

[2] European Parliament & Council of the European Union *European Year for Combating Poverty and Social Exclusion (2010)* Decision No 1098/2008/EC (2008).

[3] See Inter-American Development Bank *Action Plan for Combating Social Exclusion due to Race or Ethnic Background* (2002) <http://idbdocs.iadb.org/wsdocs/getdocument.aspx?docnum=1481940> (accessed 19-10-2011).

[4] UNESCO Conference *From Social Exclusion to Social Cohesion: Towards a Policy Agenda* International Symposium held at Roskilde University, 02-03-1995 – 04-03-1995.

[5] For more information visit *The Centre for the Analysis of Social Exclusion* <http://sticerd.lse.ac.uk/case/> (accessed 19-10-2011).

several scales. To understand this phenomenon requires attention to multiple cross-cutting scales and dimensions of justice.

3   Social exclusion: A three-dimensional account

I have already said that social exclusion belongs to the family of social injustices. But what sort of injustice is it? Is social exclusion an especially severe case of distributive injustice? Or is it a case of culturally constructed disrespect? Or is it something else altogether?

How one answers these questions depends, of course, on how one understands justice. In what follows, I shall rely on the view of justice, which I have elaborated elsewhere, as *parity of participation*.[6] According to this norm, justice requires social arrangements that permit all members of society to interact with one another as peers. For participatory parity to be possible, however, at least three conditions must be met. First, the distribution of material resources must be such as to ensure participants' equal capacity for social interaction. This condition precludes economic structures that institutionalise deprivation, exploitation, and gross disparities in wealth, income, labour and leisure time, which prevent some people from participating on a par with others in social life. Second, the status order must express equal respect for all participants and ensure equal opportunity for achieving social esteem. This condition precludes institutionalised patterns of cultural value that systematically depreciate some categories of people and the qualities associated with them, thus denying them the status of full partners in social interaction. Finally, the political constitution of society must be such as to accord roughly equal political voice to all social actors. This condition rules out electoral decision rules and media structures that systematically deprive some people of their fair chance to influence decisions that affect them. All three conditions are necessary for participatory parity. None alone is sufficient. The first brings into focus concerns traditionally associated with the theory of distributive justice. The second stresses concerns recently highlighted in the philosophy of recognition. The third emphasises concerns that have long been central to the theory of democratic representation.

This view of justice is "three-dimensional". Encompassing economic, cultural and political considerations, it treats redistribution, recognition, and representation as three analytically distinct facets of justice, none of which can be reduced to the others, although they are practically intertwined.

Given the view of justice as participatory parity, how should we understand social exclusion?[7] Consider, first, that this view of justice is very demanding. It holds that social arrangements that institutionalise obstacles to parity of participation are unjust. But anyone who is structurally excluded from participation in social interaction is *eo ipso* denied the possibility of

---

[6]   For a fuller account of this conception, see N Fraser "Social Justice in the Age of Identity Politics" in N Fraser & A Honneth (trans J Golb, J Ingram & C Wilke) *Redistribution or Recognition? A Political-Philosophical Exchange* (2003) 7.

[7]   The following account draws on N Fraser "Identity, Exclusion, and Critique: A Response to Four Critics" (2007) 6 *European J of Political Theory* 305 305-338.

participating as a peer. On this account, therefore, social exclusion is an injustice because it represents a denial of participatory parity. As denials of parity go, moreover, it is very severe. Being excluded, after all, is considerably worse than being included but marginalised or being included in a subordinate way. Those who are marginalised or subordinated can still participate with others in social interaction, although they cannot do so as peers. Those who are excluded, by contrast, are not even in the game.

On the view of justice as participatory parity, therefore, social exclusion is a grave moral wrong. But what exactly are the excluded excluded from? As I understand it, the norm of parity of participation applies broadly, across all major arenas of social interaction, including family and personal life, employment and market relations, formal and informal politics, and voluntary associations in civil society.[8] In principle, one can be excluded from some of these arenas and not from others. Thus, social exclusion can take a plurality of different forms, depending on which arenas are affected. Historically, many (white, heterosexual) women have lacked the standing and resources to participate in official politics, while enjoying the cultural and material prerequisites for participating meaningfully (if not fully equally) in family life. Homosexuals, in contrast, have until very recently lacked the standing to participate openly in sexual relations and family life, even in contexts where some of them have had access to decently remunerated work. In such cases, exclusion remains contained within a given sphere or set of spheres and does not spill over into others. In other cases, however, exclusion is highly convertible, spreading freely from sphere to sphere. We need only recall the Nazi treatment of Jews to appreciate the possibility of total and radical exclusion. In such cases, a class of persons is systematically stripped of participatory rights in sphere after sphere until they are denied the right to have any rights at all, including the right to exist. Such cases attest to the possibility of extreme and wholesale exclusion, a possibility that contrasts sharply with more "ordinary" sphere-specific exclusions, whose convertibility is far more limited.[9]

If exclusion can take a variety of forms, it can also be effected by a variety of means. I can envision at least five possibilities. In one scenario, exclusion is grounded in political economy, as when economic structures deny some categories of social actors even the minimal economic resources that are needed for marginalised or subordinated interaction. This, I take it, is what Hegel had in mind when he wrote in the *Philosophy of Right* of "the rabble".[10] In a second scenario, exclusion is rooted in the status order, as when the institutionalisation of a hierarchical pattern of cultural value denies some the chance even for second-class participation in some arenas. This is how Max

---

[8]   Because access to these arenas is so fundamental for people's well being, I construe all of them as "spheres of justice" in which the requirement of participatory parity applies. Here I break with the common view that focuses exclusively on political participation, often understood very narrowly in terms of voting. For me, in contrast, the requirement of participatory parity applies broadly, in all the major arenas of social life.

[9]   Whether exclusion from one sphere converts into exclusion from others is in the end an empirical question, which depends on the character of the society in question.

[10] GWF Hegel *Philosophy of Right* (1821) para 244A.

Weber understood the situation of ethnically constituted pariah groups.[11] In a third scenario, exclusion is grounded in the political constitution of society, as when the architecture of political space denies some people the chance to have even a marginal say in disputes about justice. This is the situation of undocumented immigrants in many countries. In a fourth scenario, exclusion arises from the combined operation of culture and political economy, as when class differentials map onto status hierarchies to prevent some actors from participating at all in mainstream arenas of social interaction. This, I suppose, is the situation of some indigenous peoples in settler societies, as well as of Romany people in East/Central Europe. In a fifth scenario, exclusion is rooted jointly in all three dimensions of social ordering, as when economic, cultural, and political structures work together to obstruct participation. This, I shall argue next, is the situation of those who are often referred to today as "the global poor".

4   Scales of exclusion: An intersectional approach

My claim is that the three-dimensional framework of redistribution, recognition, and representation affords an illuminating account of the situation of the global poor. But it can only do so after it has been modified to take account of the question of scale. Let me explain.

So far, I have discussed social exclusion without explicit attention to the problem of scale. As a result, I have glossed over a crucial question: parity of participation *among whom*? *Who* exactly is entitled to participate on a par *with whom* in *which* social interactions? By not raising this question explicitly, I have conveyed the impression that we already know and agree upon the answer. The effect, however unwitting, is to ratify an answer that goes by default: the appropriate frame for thinking about justice is the modern territorial state. The scale of justice is "Westphalian".

As I noted at the outset, however, this answer is problematic. It forecloses consideration of the situation of the global poor as a matter of injustice. If the subjects of justice are by definition fellow citizens, then the very idea of transborder injustice is inconceivable. The most disadvantaged citizens of a poor country may well have valid justice claims against their own government and their own better-off fellow citizens. But by definition they can have no such claims against offshore exploiters or beneficiaries. In this view, rather, social exclusion is exclusively a domestic problem, internal to a Westphalian state. There can be no such thing as transnational social exclusion. Strictly speaking, the very expression "the global poor" is an oxymoron.

This result itself is patently unjust. The foreclosure by definition of the very possibility of transborder social exclusion is itself a form of social exclusion: namely, the exclusion of the "global poor" from the universe of those who can press justice claims against those outside their borders who exploit them

---

[11]   M Weber "Class, Status, Party" in HH Gerth & C Wright Mills (eds) *From Max Weber: Essays in Sociology* (1958) 180 188-190; M Weber "India: The Brahman and the Castes" in HH Gerth & C Wright Mills (eds) *From Max Weber: Essays in Sociology* (1958) 396 399.

or benefit from their dispossession. The point can also be put like this: by presupposing that the Westphalian frame is the only legitimate framing of questions of justice, we commit a special kind of meta-injustice, in which we "misframe" first-order injustices, wrongly excluding some who deserve inclusion.[12] Assuming an inappropriate Westphalian frame, we airbrush away all actors, processes, and mechanisms that operate at the global or transnational scale.

How can we avoid this sort of meta-injustice? The strategy I propose draws on a distinctive conception of the political dimension of justice. So far, I have considered this dimension in the usual way, as concerned exclusively with injustices of "ordinary-political misrepresentation". These are political injustices that arise within a political community whose boundaries and membership are widely assumed to be settled – when, for example, the polity's decision rules deny some who are counted in principle as members the chance to participate fully, as peers. Important as such matters are, they represent only half the story. In addition to ordinary-political injustice, which arises *within* the frame of a bounded polity, we can also conceptualise a second level, of "meta-political injustice", which arises as a result of the division of political space *into* bounded polities. This second level comprehends injustices of *misframing*. Such injustices occur when a polity's boundaries are drawn in such a way as to wrongly deny some people the chance to participate *at all* in its authorised contests over justice. In such cases, those who are constituted as non-members are wrongly excluded from the universe of those entitled to consideration within the polity in matters of distribution, recognition, and ordinary-political representation. The injustice remains, moreover, even when those excluded from one polity are included as subjects of justice in another – as long as the effect of the political division is to put some relevant aspects of justice beyond their reach. An example is the way in which the international system of supposedly equal sovereign states gerrymanders political space at the expense of the global poor, channelling their claims into the domestic political arenas of weak or failed states, and shielding more powerful predator states and transnational private powers from the reach of justice.

The introduction of this second level of meta-political injustice can be used to clarify the social exclusion of the global poor. Oriented to the possibility that first-order framings of justice may themselves be unjust, this level grasps the question of the frame *as* a question of justice. As a result, it provides the sort of sensitivity to questions of scale that we need to understand social exclusions that arise transnationally, when processes that operate at different scales intersect – as, for example, when global economic forces converge with local status hierarchies, on the one hand, and with national political structures, on the other. With its sensitivity to frames and to questions of scale, this framework illuminates such exclusions.[13]

One example is the sexual enslavement of girls sold by impoverished parents to middlemen who proceed to sell them to Thai brothels, a case in

---

[12] For a fuller account of "misframing", see Fraser (2005) *New Left Review* 69-88.
[13] The following account, too, draws on Fraser (2007) *European J of Political Theory* 305-338.

which gender status hierarchies intersect with the collapse of rural farming economies in the wake of a regional banking crisis sparked by a global speculative currency run, as well as with a shift in transnational sex tourism toward child prostitution in the wake of the global HIV-AIDS epidemic.[14] Another example, documented in the film, *Darwin's Nightmare*, is the devastation of Tanzanian shore communities as a result of the introduction of large-scale, transnational-corporate perch fishing in Lake Victoria, a case in which post-Cold War structural adjustment policies, forcing developmental states to open their economies to foreign direct investment on terms dictated by transnational capital, intersect with ethno-racial stigmatisation and political voicelessness.[15] The result, in both cases, is a vicious circle of transnationally rooted exclusions, which spread unhindered from one arena of social interaction to another.

Other cases, in contrast, belie the model of free-spreading social exclusion. In such cases, the existence of multiple scales affords some protection against total all-enveloping exclusion. Thus, those who suffer from globally caused poverty may retain capacities for (subordinated) participation in some nationally defined arenas of social interaction. An example is the situation of former copper miners in Zambia who, despite having been disconnected involuntarily from the official production circuits of the global economy, as a result of the collapse of world copper prices, still manage to exercise their political voice at the national level.[16]

What none of the transnationally excluded can do, however, is make efficacious claims against the offshore architects of their dispossession. That option is foreclosed by the Westphalian gerrymandering of political space, which misframes disputes about justice as national matters and insulates transnational malefactors from critique and control. Among those shielded from the reach of justice are foreign investors and creditors, international currency speculators, and transnational corporations. Also protected are the governance structures of the global economy, which set exploitative terms of interaction and then exempt them from democratic control. Finally, the Westphalian frame is self-insulating, as the architecture of the interstate system excludes democratic decision-making on framing questions.

5   Contesting social exclusion in multiple scales

But the absence of formal-institutional channels of democratic transnational politics does not mean the absence of all contestation. Rather, some segments of the global poor have organised resistance to transnationally rooted exclusions.

---

[14] KC Bond, DD Celentano, S Phonsophakul & C Vaddhanaphuti "Mobility and Migration: Female Commercial Sex Work and the HIV Epidemic in Northern Thailand" in G Herdt (ed) *Sexual Cultures and Migration in the Era of AIDS: Anthropological and Demographic Perspectives* (1997) 185 185-215.

[15] H Sauper (director) *Darwin's Nightmare* (2004) Film: Celluloid Dreams/International Film Circuit.

[16] J Ferguson "Global Disconnect: Abjection and the Aftermath of Modernism" in J Ferguson *Expectations of Modernity: Myths and Meanings of Urban Life on the Zambian Copperbelt* (1999) 234 234-254.

Consider the case of the Zapatistas. Mobilising impoverished peasants and indigenous people, their movement linked claims against despotic local elites and a corrupt, authoritarian federal government to claims against transnational corporate predation, the US-dominated North American Free Trade Area pact ("NAFTA"), and the non-democratic governance structures of global capitalism. The result was a powerful strategy for contesting multiple sources and scales of exclusion. Thus, the Zapatistas combined a redistributive struggle against dispossession from communal lands, a recognition struggle against a neocolonial ethno-racial hierarchy, and a representation struggle against exclusion from political decision-making at several different scales. At the local scale, they sought to replace quasi-feudal subjection with communal self-government. At the national scale, they contested the effective exclusion of indigenous peasant communities from Mexican citizenship. At the regional scale, they protested popular exclusion from the design and control of NAFTA. At the global scale, they contested meta-injustices of misframing and convened a transnational public conversation about how to reframe questions of justice in a globalising world – a discussion that has since been continued in the meetings of the World Social Forum.[17] With its several dimensions and multiple scales, the Zapatista movement offers a textbook illustration of the sorts of injustices, and struggles against them, that I have been considering here under the rubric of "the social exclusion of the global poor". It also demonstrates the merits of a three-dimensional theory of justice that is sensitive to scale for understanding these injustices and struggles.

I have been arguing that this theory affords a good account of the various dimensions and scales of exclusion that afflict the global poor. Encompassing first-order exclusions from domestic arenas of social interaction, it also conceptualises meta-exclusions that result from the misframing of first-order harms. Clarifying, as well, exclusions that are rooted transnationally, at the intersection of multi-scaled processes, it illuminates the moral stakes and political strategies of contemporary struggles over globalisation.

6 "The global poor": A concluding terminological note

Having begun with a terminological reflection on the expression "social exclusion", I want to end with some thoughts on the phrase "the global poor". Although I have used this phrase repeatedly here, I nevertheless consider it problematic. To speak of "the poor" (global or otherwise) is to cast the people in question as passive victims defined by what they lack, instead of as agents who manage, despite all, to provide for themselves and their families, and who either are or could become political actors. But this language does more than erase the agency of "the poor". To name their plight "poverty" is to also suggest that they somehow inexplicably *lack* the means of subsistence, without inquiring as to whether they have been *deprived* of those means. Thus, "poverty" talk also erases the agency of the forces of dispossession

---

[17]   D la Botz *Democracy in Mexico: Peasant Rebellion and Political Reform* (1995); J Nash *Mayan Visions: The Quest for Autonomy in an Age of Globalization* (2001).

and exclusion. Presenting "the poor" and their "lack" in a free-standing, decontextualised way, this language obscures the mechanisms that produce poverty. For all these reasons, the expression "the poor" fails to convey that the issue in question is one of *injustice*. Efforts to overcome the injustice would be better served by an expression that forthrightly names it as such, focusing attention on the forces that generate it, on the one hand, and on the agency of those who experience it, on the other. Phrases like "the exploited" and "the excluded" strike me as better than "the poor", although they are still not entirely satisfactory. Better still, I believe is "the precariat". This expression suggests multiple degrees and forms of inclusion/exclusion. Able to encompass people engaged in various combinations of formal work, informal work, and household unpaid work, it stresses their shared vulnerability and the ease with which those in the relatively favoured categories can slip back into the disfavoured ones.

But the term "poverty" is not the only source of linguistic difficulty. In addition, the modifier "global" is problematic. It suggests that the only scale of justice implicated here is that of the globe as a whole. In fact, however, as I have shown, many of today's characteristic forms of dispossession and exclusion arise from the convergence of multi-scaled processes, as when global economic structures intersect with local status hierarchies and national political structures. To speak of those who experience such injustices as if they existed on one plane alone is to reduce them to a global abstraction, stripped of the particularities in and through which sociality is lived. Once again, they would be better served by an expression that signals the full complexity of their situation, by situating them in the context of such multiple intersecting scales of justice. Although it may not itself be fully satisfactory, the modifier "transnational" strikes me as better than the adjective "global" at signalling such complexity. My suggestion, therefore, is to replace the expression "the global poor" with "the transnational precariat".

Yet terminological change is of little use unless it helps us envision social change. As I see it, law is one important front of the struggle to effect such change. The legal front of the struggle to end poverty could be strengthened, I think, if its practitioners ceased thinking of their subjects as "the national poor" and began thinking of them instead as (a fraction of) "the transnational precariat". That shift might incline them to think outside the Westphalian box of national law. Appreciating the transnational, multi-scalar roots of much contemporary dispossession and exclusion, they might be inspired to invent new, coordinated legal strategies that integrate multiple levels of law and scales of justice – strategies that befit a globalising world.

SUMMARY

Most discussions of law and poverty are pitched at the national level and tacitly presume what this chapter terms "the Westphalian frame", which envisions the arena for addressing poverty as a modern territorial state. As a result, they imagine the victims of poverty as citizens of a bounded political community and picture the law that might help to rectify poverty as national law. Finally, they see the agency that might effect redress as a modern national state with sovereignty over a delimited territory.

In this chapter I argue that the Westphalian framing of poverty and law is problematic in a globalising world. Its constitutive assumptions are belied by the increasingly salient fact of "global poverty". Generated by transborder processes, the harms suffered by "the global poor" largely escape the parameters of national law and the control of national states. To locate them within the Westphalian frame is in fact to *misframe* them. I maintain that sensitivity to the problem of *scale* is a *sine qua non* for understanding some of the most characteristic forms of poverty in the 21st century. The question of scale is treated as a problem requiring interrogation.

Discussions of law and poverty need to reckon with the existence of a plurality of *scales of (in) justice* and need to contemplate the possibility that some forms of poverty cannot be overcome by appealing exclusively to national law. I suggest that some injustices are best located at the intersection of several scales.

This argument is made in several steps. After some preliminary reflections on terminology, I present a general conceptual account of *social exclusion*. In this first step, a three-dimensional view of (in)justice, encompassing (mal)distribution, (mis)recognition, and (mis)representation is proposed. In a second step, the problem of scale is introduced. In a third step, I consider how such injustices might best be combated. In a brief *coda* on terminology, I argue for reflection on the political implications of analytical categories, especially the terms "global poverty" and "the global poor".

THE LEGAL CONSTRUCTION OF POVERTY: GENDER, "WORK", AND THE "SOCIAL CONTRACT"

Lucy A Williams

1 Introduction

A late-20th century version of social contract theory has enormously influenced public policy initiatives regarding poverty taken by both conservative (Reagan/Thatcher) and so-called "third way" administrations (Clinton/Blair). This approach has been marketed globally, particularly in "developing nations"[1] such as South Africa. Central to this policy vision is a certain understanding of waged work and labour markets. As I will argue, a key characteristic of this understanding of waged work is that it ignores the fragmentation of labour markets and is oblivious to the gender implications of dual or fragmented labour markets. This distorted view of waged work is incorporated in one of the fundamental tenets of the new social contract, namely that single mothers must contribute to society by supporting their families as breadwinners in formal-sector waged work.[2] In return, these mothers theoretically acquire a sense of "dignity" and pride in the fact that they are "self-sufficient" and "independent". This chapter's central claim is that, as decision-makers translated the supposedly universal values of "dignity", "self-sufficiency" and "independence" into policies, institutions, and legal rules, they consistently filled them with gendered content that ultimately reinforces the social and economic subordination of women. Specifically, policymakers did not incorporate the concept of dual labour markets into their

---

[1] I recognise the problematic nature of current terminology used to describe economic levels. I use "developed" and "developing" countries quite tentatively, understanding the ways in which that formulation incorporates a Western perception of development.

[2] I distinguish several forms of work in this chapter under two overarching headings of "subsistence work" and "caregiving work". Of course, much has been written about the distinction between waged work and caregiving. See generally J Conaghan & K Rittich (eds) *Labour Law, Work and Family: Critical and Comparative Perspectives* (2005) and citations therein. However, as I have explored elsewhere, I have attempted to develop what I hope are more nuanced definitions of the various forms of work that women largely provide. As I use it here, the term "subsistence work" encompasses all forms of effort to produce and provide the means to maintain the subsistence needs of family members, that is, work that produces what society recognises as value. "Subsistence work" includes both "formal-sector waged work", that is, employer-employee relationships within the formal sector (which often fragment into primary and secondary labour markets), and paid work in the informal sector, such as street vendoring, home laundering, *et cetera*. It also includes "non-waged work" that involves in-home production for consumption by the family, such as farming. "Caregiving work" includes effort expended to sustain and nurture family members, but which does not produce what society recognises as "value" or "potentially commodifiable value". I discuss these definitions more fully in L Williams "Poor Women's Work Experiences: Gaps in the 'Work-Family' Discussion" in J Conaghan & K Rittich (eds) *Labour Law, Work and Family* (2005) 195 195-214.

analyses, thereby ignoring the way in which marginalised populations interact with formal-sector waged work.

This chapter has a limited scope and ambition. It is not an original research contribution. Rather, drawing on the rich, emerging literature in the field of law and poverty, as well as my own prior work, I attempted here to identify some framing themes and questions in the context of the Law and Poverty Colloquium to which this collection is dedicated. I hoped no more than to ignite discussion among the scholars, lawyers, and activists attending, who brought a wide range of perspectives and experiences to the conference. In what follows, I have reluctantly set aside several major considerations due to the constraints of time and space on a piece of this kind. For example, although I allude to distinctions between white women and women of colour, I focus on gender as the lens through which I present my themes, fully realising that I am not covering major racial considerations. In other work, I have discussed how – both in South Africa and the US – race, ethnicity, and class have also been defining factors in the social construction of poverty and, in particular, in the evolution of contemporary "social contract" approaches to social assistance policy.[3] In addition, due to the brevity of the piece, I emphasise the US experience and short-change the South African, about which I have also written elsewhere.[4] I believe the themes identified will resonate with the South African reader, and I hope the chapter raises both useful and controversial thematic questions.

I begin with a brief description of the history of US welfare policy, later incorporating the experiences of poor women in "developing countries". I then raise questions about several threads of that history and discuss how blindness toward gender consequences of social policy and legal rules:

(i)   Obscures the roots of poverty that are in part constructed by common-law background legal rules of property, contract, tort, and family law. Of particular significance for this chapter are the background rules of inheritance which create asset- or opportunity-inequality that undermines equal opportunity in waged work.

(ii)   Induces decision-makers to ignore the conditions of and sex segregation in low-wage labour markets and the lack of upward mobility for poor women, thus appearing to legitimate the central, but flawed, assumption of neo-liberal poverty reduction policy (namely, that formal-sector waged work can and will provide adequate family support).

---

[3]   I have previously written about the significant racial discrimination encoded in US social assistance or social insurance policy. See, for example, LA Williams "The Ideology of Division: Behavior Modification Welfare Reform Proposals" (1992) 102 *Yale LJ* 719 (providing a racial critique of state welfare initiatives prior to 1996); LA Williams "Race, Rat Bites and Unfit Mothers: How Media Discourse Informs Welfare Legislation Debate" (1995) 22 *Fordham Urb LJ* 1159 (exposing the racial underpinning of US social assistance policy initiatives); LA Williams *Decades of Distortion: The Right's 30-Year Assault on Welfare* Political Research Associates (1997). More recently, I have drawn connections between the racial dimensions of social assistance policy in the US and South Africa in LA Williams "Issues and Challenges in Addressing Poverty and Legal Rights: A Comparative United States/South African Analysis" (2005) 21 *SAJHR* 436.

[4]   See Williams (2005) *SAJHR* 436-472; LA Williams, "The Role of Courts in the Quantitative-Implementation of Social and Economic Rights: A Comparative Study" (2010) 3 *CCR* 141 141-199.

(iii) Renders invisible what I call the non-formal sector subsistence work and caregiving work, and in particular ignores the contribution of this work to economic productivity and efficiency as conventionally understood.

(iv) Fails to appreciate that the legal definitions characterising many poor women workers as "non-workers" reinforce an artificial dichotomy between waged work and social assistance receipt (a distinction often framed as independence *versus* dependence) and eliminates, by magical thinking, the alienation and subordination experienced by low-wage workers, particularly women, from poverty discourse.

How US public policy historically has treated poor people, especially low-income single mothers and their children, reflects a particular understanding of the causes of poverty that is deeply embedded in US political culture. The US tradition of social welfare finds its genesis in the Elizabethan Poor Laws – concepts of local control, family responsibility, residency, and definitions of who is worthy or unworthy as determined by the non-poor were central to the framing of US social welfare policy. In brief, US social welfare policy historically has been based on the theory that poverty is caused by individual human failure and a deficit of "traditional" family values. Political leaders early in the 20th century often claimed that providing outdoor relief (assistance outside the context of a poorhouse or work house) would undermine poor people's initiative and dignity. Some elements of the reformists' movements tried to control the behaviour of – or "Americanise" – immigrant poor mothers who were felt to have inadequate moral values.[5] Importantly, public provision for poor women and children has historically reflected a tension between the conflicting imperatives of family care and waged work.

Although this was often not reflected in the stated goals of social assistance programmes, such programmes and their recipients have always been significantly connected to low-wage labour markets. Consider, for example, the predecessors to the first federally sanctioned programme for single-parent families enacted in 1935 (Aid to Dependent Children and later Aid to Families with Dependent Children), the "Mother's Pensions" or "Widow's Pensions" Acts enacted in numerous states in the early 20th century. One goal of these programmes was to provide cash assistance to enable single mothers to fulfil the "woman's role" of homemaker, rather than placing their children in institutions. To avoid the stigma of immorality attached to unmarried mothers or deserted wives, the proponents of these programmes highlighted an image of the worthy white widow. Programmes were highly discretionary, allowing localities to exclude "immoral" women and women of colour.[6]

---

[5] L Gordon *Pitied, But Not Entitled* (1994) 28, 45-46. Even widows were often scrutinised for their housekeeping, cleanliness, and moral habits. W Bell *Aid to Dependent Children* (1965) 29.

[6] Gordon *Pitied, But Not Entitled* 27. The National Congress of Mothers, in lobbying for mother's aid, initially framed the programme as providing support for mothers of "the race" (62-63). See also Bell *Aid to Dependent Children* 29-31, 34-35. Gordon *Pitied, But Not Entitled* 48 n 41 notes that in 1931 only 3% of recipients of mother's pensions were African American.

But even for a "deserving" woman eligible for such assistance, the benefit amount was so low that she (and often her children), in order to survive, either had to do paid labour or to attach themselves to a male breadwinner, or both. It was always a feature of US social assistance programmes that poor women needed to seek additional income by, for example, laundering, sewing, or taking in boarders. However, whenever a single mother *did* do waged work, usually in the informal economy, she was stigmatised and moved into the category of a "bad" mother.

Thus, poor women were faced with irreconcilable pressures: they were expected not to earn, yet they were required to earn; they were expected to be chaste, yet needed to find a man; they were expected to care for their children, yet they were forced to leave their children to perform paid labour.

These ideas and value judgments remain central to the contemporary version of social contract theory fashioned and deployed to support neo-liberal "welfare reform" in the US and the UK (now being touted throughout the globe). Espousing the values of dignity, self-sufficiency and independence as components of the social contract,[7] advocates of this social assistance model now assume that participation in formal-sector waged work can be and is the solution to poverty, the path to independence and the cornerstone for individual dignity and full social citizenship.[8] This framing of the problem presupposes an institutional structure within which a breadwinner's paid labour in the formal-sector provides for family subsistence, without incorporating the contribution of unpaid work to the production of wealth. More importantly, this approach is oblivious to distinctions between formal sector waged work, informal-sector paid work and unpaid family work (which I have characterised and will later discuss as "subsistence work" and "caregiving work").[9] In so doing, it fails to recognise the complexity of women's, particularly poor women's, work.

For example, in 1996 the US Congress passed the Personal Responsibility and Work Opportunity Reconciliation Act ("PRWORA"),[10] replacing the Aid to Families with Dependent Children programme (the major US cash assistance programme for single parents, largely female-headed families) with the Temporary Assistance to Needy Families ("TANF") programme. The PRWORA contained two major provisions relating to mandatory work programmes and the role of formal-sector waged work in US poverty-reduction policy for single

---

[7]   See generally E Gillespie & B Schellhas (eds) *Contract with America: The Bold Plan by Rep. Newt Gingrich, Rep. Dick Armey and the House Republicans to Change the Nation* (1994), who state:
      "*Contract with America* is an agreement and a covenant between our now elected representatives and the American people with whom we sought a common bond." (6).
      "[W]e require that welfare beneficiaries *work* so they can develop the *pride* and *self-sufficiency* that comes from holding a *productive* job." (65) (emphasis added).
      "[O]nce welfare recipients become *dependent* on public assistance, they are caught in the now-familiar welfare trap." (67) (emphasis added).
[8]   One could analyse the gendered nature of the social contract underlying the neo-liberal welfare policy from a number of perspectives, for example, concepts of what constitutes female respectability *versus* immorality or views of women's sexual and reproductive independence. However, these are beyond the scope of this chapter.
[9]   See n 2 and part 4 below.
[10] Pub L No 104-193, 110 Stat 2105, 42 USC § 601 *et seq.*

mothers and their families. First, states must require significant percentages of primarily single mothers who receive TANF to participate in designated work activities for 30 hours a week.[11] Virtually all forms of job and skill training, ie activities that would contribute to the upward mobility of single mothers, are excluded from the definition of "core work activity" for purposes of fulfilling the states' mandate for work participation.[12] Specifically, the US Department of Health and Human Services' final rule implementing the TANF reauthorisation does not include jobs skills training directly related to employment, education directly related to employment, or secondary school attendance for those who have not completed secondary school as "core work activities".[13] In addition, activities that would address barriers to employment, such as mental health treatment or rehabilitation services, can only count toward work participation under the category of "job readiness assistance", which many states limit to six weeks in any given year.[14]

Second, the PRWORA prohibits most claimants from receiving welfare for more than five years in one's lifetime, and many states have an even shorter period of lifetime eligibility.[15] This restriction on the period of time a single mother and her family can receive governmental cash assistance rests on the assumption that formal sector waged work can and will provide adequate family support at all other times. In this sense, the PRWORA is the modern reincarnation of the idea that poverty is caused by human failure, in that a person is assumed to be able to overcome poverty by one's own individual action of participating in waged work.

The PRWORA specifically incorporates a "social contract", authorising states to require recipients to contract with the state through written "individual responsibility plans" ("IRPs"), which, among other things, set forth obligations of the individual recipient and services that the state is obligated to provide the recipient.[16] As of 1999, 33 states require recipients to sign "employability plans" (which focus exclusively on employment-related issues), 35 states require "responsibility contracts" (which cover a variety of employment and non-employment obligations), and 17 states require recipients to sign both.[17]

The rhetoric underlying this formulation of "welfare reform" was seemingly oblivious to gender (and racial) considerations. Instead, the debate relied on

---

[11]   42 USC § 607(c)(1); 45 CFR § 261.31(a)(1).

[12]   42 USC § 607(c) and (d).

[13]   45 CFR § 261.31(b) and (c).

[14]   Center on Budget and Policy Priorities, Center on Law and Social Policy *Implementing the TANF Changes in the Deficit Reduction Act* (2007) 17.

[15]   42 USC § 608 (a)(7) (2003); 45 CFR § 264.1 (a)(1).

[16]   42 USC § 608 (b).

[17]   For more information visit *State Policy Documentation Project* <http://s242739747.onlinehome.us/spdp/ tanf/tanfapps.htm> (accessed 19-05-2011). More recent data can be found by querying the *Welfare Rules Database* <http://anfdata.urban.org/wrd/WRDWelcome.cfm> (accessed 19-05-2011). A query of whether or not that state has a formal, written agreement listing the recipient's responsibilities for the year 2009 was run by selecting "Query the Database" and the category "Contracts and Agreements" and the data element "ca_exist". Based on this query, as of 2009, 35 states require some form of contract. For a fuller discussion of IRPs, see CM Miller "The New Contract: Welfare Reform, Devolution, and Due Process" (2002) 61 *Md L Rev* 246.

facially neutral (and therefore inevitably patriarchal) concepts of dignity, self-sufficiency and dependency,[18] without recognising that identical social assistance programmes can have quite different consequences for various populations as I will show below.

2 Background legal rules construct poverty

The above described reductions in social welfare benefits and reliance on low-waged work as the source of family support assumes that entry into the generic "labour market" is the silver bullet that allows single mothers to have "equal opportunity" to succeed. That assumption is false and is based on an understanding of our legal system that ignores how historically and culturally contingent legal rules have skewed distributive effects, in particular, negative consequences for women, minorities, and other subordinated groups.

The dominant political discourse in Western nations, reinforced by our legal cultures, teaches that poverty arises naturally and that the legal system bears no responsibility for causing it. Private law concepts of family, tort, property, and freedom of contract are made to appear as the necessary and neutral framework of social and economic power relations, arising independently of law. The dominant political culture denies that these background rules privilege any group or have anything to do with allocating wealth or income. The role of law in distributing property, valuing waged labour, and consequently devaluing other forms of "subsistence work" and "caregiving work",[19] is almost always invisible.

In fact, the stubborn persistence of poverty, in both developed and developing countries, results in significant part from political and legal decisions and institutions that generate and sustain a sharply unequal distribution of wealth and resources. The substantive content and distributive effects of a wide range of legal entitlements are not matters of accident; rather they are chosen, and reflect and enact distinct political values. Legal entitlements are created by human actors who make moral or philosophical decisions, explicitly or implicitly, about who is deserving or undeserving, and who is worthy of reward within a chosen economic structure. The politics of race, gender, and class are filtered through these choices. Far from being natural or neutral, legal rules, norms, and practices play a central role in maintaining poverty by

---

[18] House of Representatives *Welfare and Medicaid Reform Act of 1996: Report of the Committee on the Budget House of Representatives to accompany HR 36734* (1996) HR Rep 104-651, reprinted in 1996 USCCAN 2183:

"It [the current welfare system] traps recipients in a cycle of *dependency*. It undermines the values of *work* and family that form the foundation of America's communities." (HR Rep 104-651 3; 1996 USCCAN 2184 (emphasis added)).

"The welfare system contradicts fundamental American values that ought to be encouraged and rewarded: *work*, family, personal responsibility, and *self-sufficiency*. Instead, the system subsidizes dysfunctional behavior." (HR Rep 104-651 4; 1996 USCCAN 2185 (emphasis added)).

"As welfare discourages *work*, it encourages long-term *dependency*." (HR Rep 104-651 4; 1996 USCCAN 2185 (emphasis added)).

[19] See part 4 below.

perpetuating and by according cultural legitimacy to severe wealth inequality, privileging certain interests and disadvantaging others.[20]

Legal rules also shape social roles by assigning power and responsibility in social relationships, whether in the workplace, landlord/tenant structure or within the family,[21] always eroding the independence of some in favour of empowering others. For example, those with greater property rights generally have greater bargaining power in the market; they are more capable of living without or replacing elsewhere the goods that the other participant in the bargain has to trade or offer.

Contrary to the dominant political imagery, which effaces the power of the state in structuring social life, the state has always intervened in social life through the design and enforcement of non-neutral, value-laden entitlements established by market-structuring background rules. The question is not when or whether government should step in; the question is rather whose interests, and what distribution of power, are protected by these entitlements.

One specific illustration that is important to the understanding of waged work as a focus of poverty reduction is reflected in the inheritance law in many countries. Building on prior legal definitions of "private property" (notably, in the US, developed at a time when only moneyed white males could own property or had the right to vote), inheritance law provides protections for wealthy individuals' economic interests. Through the rules on ownership and succession, the law privileges those with wealth by allowing them to maintain and pass on their assets to their chosen heirs. Thus the heirs of those originally able to own or purchase property are, likewise, economically privileged.

The ramifications of these common-law principles are evident in gender (as well as racial) income disparity. For example, the vast majority of women and people of colour in many Western developed nations do not have resources. Put differently, most resources, in the form of assets, are controlled primarily by white men. Thus, those with the major amount of assets can invest and continue to generate income for themselves and their families, income that is not based on their own formal-sector waged work. The continuation of privileges, benefits and inheritance are classic examples of legal entitlements guaranteed by the state. The wealthy and their children have choices that those without resources simply do not have.

The mainstream legal concept of "equal opportunity", particularly within the formal-sector waged work force, ignores the imbalance and the privilege derived from "asset advantage" and the resulting disadvantage for those previously discriminated against because of gender, disability, sexual

---

[20] An overview of the strand of critical legal realism that focuses on background rules is provided in DM Davis & K Klare "Transformative Constitutionalism and the Common and Customary Law" (2010) 26 *SAJHR* 403 435-449. See also D Kennedy "The Stakes of Law, or Hale and Foucault!" in D Kennedy *Sexy Dressing Etc.: Essays on the Power and Politics of Cultural Identity* (1993) 83 83-125; KE Klare "Legal Theory and Democratic Reconstruction: Reflections on 1989" (1991) 25 *University of British Columbia LR* 69 69-103.

[21] FE Olsen "The Myth of State Intervention in the Family" (1985) 18 *University of Michigan JL Reform* 835 835-864.

orientation or race.[22] Those without assets are treated as if they were on an equal footing within the formal-sector waged work setting. Once any person has been given an "equal" opportunity to compete for a job, the appearance of imbalance is obscured. Thus popular culture often ignores the role of legal institutions in reproducing hierarchy and thereby preventing the emergence of a gender/racial/class-neutral world of "equal opportunity". But any conception of equal right to employment opportunities and pay that ignores the legal rules which determine what assets various social groups are able to bring to the labour market is theoretically deficient. To correct this error requires a re-examination of the traditional common law of property that perpetuates the asset, or "opportunity" inequality, something that is simply not factored into the debate about poverty reduction.

A similar analysis applies in many of the so-called "developing countries" where legal systems establish that men hold much, if not all, of the land and other asset wealth.[23] The continuing power of the background rules of inheritance is dramatically illustrated by the landmark case of *Bhe v Magistrate, Khayelitsha*[24] in which the South African Constitutional Court exposed the colonialist imposition of racial hierarchy or white supremacy by maintaining separate black/white systems of inheritance. Specifically, the Court exposed the power of inheritance apartheid[25] and customary law as applied to blacks (or at least the reified version of customary law imposed by the colonist oligarchy) and its central importance in fostering and sustaining male supremacy and the total economic marginalisation of women.[26]

3   Segmented labour markets

One result of this unequal opportunity structure partially created by the legal background rules is that poor women, and particularly poor women of colour, do not have the resources to develop sufficient human capital to obtain living-wage employment. They are relegated to the lowest wage level and highly unstable jobs and have difficulty obtaining training and education that would facilitate upward mobility.

In the US, as noted above, social welfare programmes never provided sufficient income to sustain poor families. Therefore, many single mothers either combined some form of formal- or informal-sector paid work with

---

[22] See generally ML Oliver & TM Shapiro *Black Wealth, White Wealth: A New Perspective on Racial Inequality* (1995).

[23] For a discussion of this issue in Latin America, see generally CD Deere & M Léon *Empowering Women: Land and Property Rights in Latin America* (2001).

[24] *Bhe v Magistrate, Khayelitsha; Shibi v Sithole; South African Human Rights Commission v President of the Republic of South Africa* 2005 1 BCLR 1 (CC).

[25] See the discussion of the centrality of the rights to human dignity and equality (paras 48-51, 71-73).

[26] The consolidated cases were brought by African women who were next of kin under the Intestate Succession Act 81 of 1987 applicable to whites, but were barred from inheriting by the primogeniture principle of customary law. In holding that the rule of primogeniture was unconstitutional, the Court stated:

"The exclusion of women from heirship and consequently from being able to inherit property was in keeping with a system dominated by a deeply embedded patriarchy which reserved for women a position of subservience and subordination and in which they were regarded as perpetual minors under the tutelage of the fathers, husbands, or the head of the extended family." (Para 78).

receipt of social benefits or cycled between formal-sector, low-wage work and social assistance programmes. Studies performed immediately preceding the 1996 passage of PRWORA documented that receipt of welfare and waged work were inextricably intertwined, giving the lie to the widely held assumption that welfare recipients are a separate and distinct category from formal-sector paid workers. A majority of women receiving governmental social assistance benefits move in and out of low-wage work regularly.[27] However, they never escape welfare for the jobs and programmes available to higher and more regular earners.

Far from recipients of governmental social assistance being unwilling to work, these studies suggest that most recipients, even before the stringent work requirements mandated by PRWORA, preferred and endeavoured to earn wages despite the most trying personal circumstances. Their efforts are frequently frustrated by barriers for which legal rules and public policies are responsible. The problem, by and large, is not lack of work-effort, but the legal and social structure of low-wage labour markets. Often, poor people cannot find employment for which they are qualified. Even in times of low unemployment, low-wage work conditions are so precarious as to guarantee that many low-wage earners will periodically cycle through periods of unemployment. Low-wage jobs in the US and many other developed nations pay below-subsistence wages (thereby ensuring that workers cannot provide for their families) and provide little or no training or advancement opportunities. They have the least family-necessary benefits, such as health insurance, sick days and vacation time. They typically have inflexible work schedules, allowing no adjustment for the caregiving needs of low-income families who do not have nannies or others available to care for their children and elders (resulting in frequent job loss). In addition, low-wage employers often induce employee turnover to depress wages and prevent vesting of benefits. Far from providing a site for self-actualisation, independence, autonomy, and empowerment, these jobs generate alienation, depression, poverty within wage-work, and disempowerment.

---

[27] One study found that of the 64% of women on Aid to Families with Dependent Children for the first time who left the rolls within two years, almost half left for waged work. But of those who left, three-quarters eventually returned; 45% returned within a year. See LD Pavetti *The Dynamics of Welfare and Work: Exploring the Process by Which Young Women Work Their Way Off Welfare* (1993) PhD thesis JFK School of Government, Harvard University. Another study found that 70% of Aid to Families with Dependent Children recipients participated in some way in the waged labour force over a two-year period: 20% combined paid work and welfare, 23% worked intermittently, receiving welfare between jobs, 7% worked limited hours and looked for more paid work, and 23% searched for, but could not obtain, paid work. The women in this study held an average of 1.7 paid jobs over the two-year period and spent an average of sixteen weeks looking for paid work. R Spalter-Roth *Making Work Pay: The Real Employment Opportunities of Single Mothers Participating in the AFDC Program* (1994).

If one used "point in time" data, ie counting the percentage of those *on a given day both* receiving welfare *and* participating in wage work, there appears to be very little overlap, figures showing only about 7% of welfare recipients are also in paid labour. Staff of the House Committee on Ways and Means *Background Material and Data on Programs Within the Jurisdiction of the Committee on Ways and Means* 104th Cong 2nd Sess (1996) 474. But this type of data collection does not take into account the "cyclical welfare/work population".

For example, according to the US 2000[28] census, millions of full-time, year-round workers in waged work in the formal economy live below the officially designated poverty wage. Women predominate in the lowest wage-work positions. Of the 25 occupations with the lowest median earnings, nineteen are predominantly filled by women, in both the full-time and part-time categories. The percentage of workers in these occupations who are women is often in the 80-95% range. For the average-sized family receiving TANF benefits (a single mother with two children), the *median* earnings of women working full-time, year-round in eighteen of these occupations is below the designated, and quite conservative, federal poverty level. Reflecting poor women's history, these occupations fall into categories such as maids and housecleaning attendants (1.12 million), childcare workers (1.19 million), waitresses (1.04 million), cashiers (1.7 million), and a variety of food preparation and serving jobs (including fast food, cafeteria, and counter attendant jobs).[29]

A 2003 study that focused specifically on US low-income, single-parent household-heads found that 78.2% of those in waged work were concentrated in four typically low-income occupations: service, administrative support and clerical, sales, and operators, fabricators and labourers. That figure rose to 81% for single mothers. When broken down by industry classifications, 71% of low-income single mothers worked in services or retail trade compared to 53.1% of low-income single fathers. The percentage of all single parents participating in low-wage work rose from 60.4% to 69.0% after the social protection reductions (PRWORA) in 1996. However, the number of low-income, single-mother household-heads increased even more dramatically, from 58.5% to 68.1%. Only 7.3% of all single-parent household-heads were affiliated with unions, with an even smaller figure for women.[30]

The legal rules and patterns of gender discrimination and job segregation that make low-wage labour markets so hostile to women workers are virtually

---

[28]   As of the publication date of this chapter, commensurate data from the 2010 census has not been made available. However, based on the C DeNavaz-Walt, BD Proctor & JC Smith (US Census Bureau) *Income, Poverty, and Health Insurance Coverage in the United States, 2008: Current Population Reports* (September 2009) P60-236(RV), and Detailed Tables – Table HIMC-01, 4.495 million households in which at least one member of the household worked at a full-time job more than 50 weeks per year had median income less than $25 000. Of that 1.031 million had income less than $15 000. US Census Bureau *The 2011 Statistical Abstract, The National Data Book, Income, Expenditures, Poverty, and Wealth: Table 691 – Money Income of Households – Distribution by Income Level and Selected Characteristics, 2008* (2011) <http://www.census.gov/compendia/statab/2011/tables/11s0691.pdf> (accessed 15-05-2011).

[29]   Data compiled from: D Weinberg *Evidence From Census 2000 About Earnings by Detailed Occupation for Men and Women* Census 2000 Special Reports CENSR-15 (2004) 9; US Census Bureau "TABLE 1: Earnings Distribution of All US Year-Round Full-Time Workers by Occupation: 1999" (02-06-2004) *US Census Bureau* <http://www.census.gov/population/cen2000/phc-t33/tab01.pdf.> (accessed 05-08-2011); US Census Bureau "TABLE 3: Earning Distribution of the Female US Year-Round Full-Time Workers by Occupation: 1999" (02-06-2004) *US Census Bureau* <http://www.census.gov/population/cen2000/phc-t33/tab03.pdf.> (accessed 05-08-2011); US Census Bureau "Income: TABLE 2: Earnings by Detailed Occupation: 1999: United States, Both Sexes" (03-06-2010) *US Census Bureau* <http://www.census.gov/hhes/www/income/data/earnings/call2usfemale.html> (accessed 15-05-2011).

[30]   A Jones-DeWeever, J Peterson & X Song *Before & After Welfare Reform: The Work and Well-Being of Low-Income Single Parent Families* (2003) 11 (Table 2.1), 15 (Table 2.3), 16 (Table 2.4), 19 (Table 2.5). I am here referring to the data from August 1999 to February 2000. National union density at the time was 13.5%.

invisible in the discourse of neo-liberal welfare reform.[31] When advocated in South Africa, the problematic nature of the argument that formal-sector waged work is the solution to poverty is even more stark. South Africa is faced not just with segmented labour markets, but with the lack of *any* formal sector jobs for a substantial percentage of its population.[32]

However, ignoring these factors enables neo-liberal policymakers and ideologues to advance with a straight face the plainly false thesis, a product of wishful thinking, that income from formal-sector waged work is sufficient to provide adequate family support to all who are willing to work. Both the legal effacement of "work" outside of the formal-sector waged work structure and the factually unsupportable and intellectually dishonest "welfare-dependency thesis" provide cover for this myth.

4 Value is created outside the wage-work sector

As noted earlier, the version of the social contract theory invoked to support neo-liberal welfare reform privileges formal-sector waged work as the site for creating value and producing dignity, self-sufficiency and independence. This framing of a primary answer to poverty ignores the vast amounts of work performed by women, particularly poor women, outside of the formal-sector. Yet women's work in all of its complexity creates wealth and contributes to society. Formal-sector production could not occur without women's unwaged work. That such work often fails to promote the definitions of dignity, self-sufficiency and independence contained in neo-liberal social assistance policy results not from any intrinsic lack of worth, but from legal structures and social practices that devalue it and deny its importance.

In my effort to de-centre formal-sector waged work in the neo-liberal social contract discussion, I have used two terms, not mutually exclusive, to describe effort expended to sustain, nurture and develop human beings – "subsistence work" and "caregiving work".[33] Recall that "subsistence work" includes formal- and informal-sector paid work and in-home production for consumption by the family, while "caregiving work" includes effort expended to sustain and nurture family members.[34]

Unpaid labour, particularly the unpaid labour of women in the home, is an indispensable factor in the production of social wealth. Specifically,

---

[31] Note the earlier discussion of the restrictions in the US Department of Health and Human Services' final rule implementing the TANF reauthorisation that severely restricts states' ability to provide education and training that might assist a mother in low-waged work to develop upward mobility, as such programmes are not considered "core work activities".

[32] In South Africa, depending on the definition of unemployment, between 23.6% and 32.5% of the working age population are unemployed – not as a result of lack of initiative, but rather the lack of job-availability (a legacy of colonialism and apartheid). The Presidency of Republic of South Africa *Development Indicators* (2009) 21, 26.

[33] See n 2 above.

[34] Some activities cross these categorical lines, for example, grooming children for school might be seen as both caregiving (nurturing, imparting pride and self-respect) and as subsistence work (socialisation as investment in the family's human capital). In addition, the distinction between women's work "in the home" and women's work "outside the home", while significant for some analytical purposes, cross-cuts these categories. For example, in-home craft production for barter or sale would be subsistence work, whereas transporting children to the doctor would be caregiving.

unpaid subsistence and caregiving work subsidises the production of value
in the formal economy. Mainstream economic theory and social policy
has historically ignored this and, consequently, is oblivious to the gender
consequences of a system that relies on unpaid labour in the home to support
formal-sector waged work.[35] Firms cannot function to produce value without
socialised, clothed, and fed workers appearing at the factory gate. If the formal
wage were truly a "family wage", employers would be paying for a share of
the unpaid labour upon which they rely. However, for well-known reasons that
I cannot explore here, it is highly doubtful that waged work fully compensates
the unpaid labour in the home on which it depends. Legal rules and policies
tacitly based on the assumption that unpaid labour in the home will subsidise
the formal economy devalue women, particularly poor women, and exclude
them from genuine participation in the social contract.

Whether in the informal economy, subsistence farming, in-kind bartering
or caregiving, the vast majority of "work" performed in the world, particularly
by poor women, is performed outside of the formal-sector. However, the role
that poor women play both as subsistence workers outside of the formal-sector
and as caregivers historically has been, and continues to be, largely denigrated
by the mainstream in most societies and by contemporary legal systems.

As noted, many poor women in the affluent Western nations frequently
move in and out of low-wage work in the formal economy – holding jobs that
routinely create barriers to women fulfilling their caregiving work. A wealth
of scholarship[36] criticises the tensions between these competing work demands
and points out that the version of the social contract that supports neo-liberal
welfare policy renders invisible the caregiving needs of poor single-parent
families in Western nations.[37]

The absence of any attention to or appreciation of women's experiences of
work in the marketing of neo-liberal social contract theory to developing and
postcolonial countries is equally unpardonable. Poor mothers in the rest of
the world still largely work in subsistence agricultural and, to a lesser extent,

---

[35]   There are some promising new conceptual and research developments in this area. See, for example, JE
Stiglitz, A Sen & J-P Fitoussi *Report by the Commission on the Measurement of Economic Performance
and Social Progress* (2009), specifically 40, where the authors state:
> "Many services that households produce for themselves are not recognized in official income and
> production measures, yet they constitute an important aspect of economic activity. While their
> exclusion from official measures reflects uncertainty about data more than it does conceptual dissent,
> more and more systematic work in this area should be undertaken."

[36]   See, for example, Conaghan & Rittich (eds) *Labour Law, Work, and Family*; ND Zatz "Supporting
Workers by Accounting for Care" (2011) 5 *Harv L & Pol'y Rev* 5 (also available as ND Zatz *Supporting
Workers by Accounting for Care* UCLA School of Law Research Paper No 11-17 (2011) <http://ssrn.
com/abstract=1852707> (accessed 06-14-2011)); PB Edelman "Changing the Subject: From Welfare to
Poverty to a Living Income" (2009) 4 *NW J L & Soc Pol'y* 14; DE Roberts "Welfare Reform and Economic
Freedom: Low-Income Mothers' Decisions About Work at Home and in the Market" (2004) 44 *Santa
Clara L Rev* 1029.

[37]   Even within the PRWORA, the concept of "work" is highly contextual and contested. For example,
providing child care services (whether paid or unpaid) to another TANF recipient so that she can participate
in a community service programme is a "work activity", whereas providing care to your own children is
not. More generally, lack of pay does not disqualify an activity from being defined as "work", as unpaid
community service constitutes a "core work activity". See generally ND Zatz "Welfare to What?" (2006)
57 *Hastings LJ* 1131. The "worker" *versus* "non-worker" distinction is highly ideological, drawing upon
and developing the messages of the legal culture generally.

domestic work. Of the 6.39 billion people in the world, only 0.9 billion live in the 50 developed countries, less than one-sixth of the world's population. Five billion live in developing countries. As of 2005, 1.4 billion people lived on less than $1.25 a day, the international poverty level. About 75% of the world's poor people live in rural areas and depend on agriculture for their livelihood.[38]

Women comprise, on average, 43% of the agricultural labour force in developing countries, ranging from 20% in Latin America to 50% in Eastern Asia and sub-Saharan Africa.[39] They do so primarily through small-scale cultivation for household consumption. After harvest, poor women provide much of the labour for storage, handling, stocking and processing. The number of poor female-headed households has significantly increased, largely because of the HIV/AIDS epidemic in some developing countries,[40] resulting in what certain international organisations have termed a "feminization of agriculture".[41] Yet, because much of women's work in crop production consists of unpaid labour for family consumption rather than for market sale, it is unrecorded in labour statistics.

While waged work in the formal-sector does provide a source of income for many poor families within developing countries, the vast majority of poor people, and especially poor women, provide for their families through small-scale production for sale (for example, fruits and vegetables, sewn goods), domestic work, subsistence agriculture and other forms of subsistence work, and support from family and community networks, all of which falls outside of the formal economy. These strategies for family subsistence are not limited to rural areas; urban dwellers also engage in backyard farming and animal husbandry.

This work is, of course, on top of caregiving work that is quite different from that experienced in developed countries; for example, collecting firewood and water for many hours each day, primarily women's tasks. In developing countries, women can spend up to two hours each day on these tasks, and several times longer in deforested areas. In addition, households are

---

[38] Bread for the World Institute "Hunger and Poverty Facts" (undated) *Bread for the World* <http://www. bread.org/hunger/global/facts.html> (accessed 15-05-2011); A Rahman "Rural Development is Key to Tackling Global Poverty" (2004) *Choike.org* <http://www.choike.org/nuevo_eng/informes/2459.html> (accessed 15-05-2011); United Nations Development Programme ("UNDP") *Human Development Report 2003 – Millennium Development Goals: A Compact Among Nations to End Human Poverty* (2003) 91 <http://hdr.undp.org/en/media/hdr03_complete.pdf> (accessed 15-05-2011).

[39] United Nations Food and Agriculture Organization ("FAO") *The State of Food and Agriculture, 2010-2011: Women in Agriculture, Closing the Gender Gap for Development* (2011) 5-8 <http://www.fao.org/docrep/013/i2050e/i2050e.pdf> (accessed 15-05-2011). In sub-Saharan Africa, women contribute 60 to 80% of the labour in food production both for household consumption and for sale. FAO Economic and Social Department *Rural Women and Food Security: Current Situation and Perspectives* (1998) 2.1 <http://www.fao.org/DOCREP/003/W8376E/w8376e02.htm> (accessed 15-05-2011).

[40] A joint FAO and UNAIDS study found that since 1985, AIDS has killed approximately 7 million agricultural workers, often a family's main provider, and will probably kill another 16 million by 2020. D Taponzis (FAO & UNAIDS) *Addressing the Impact of HIV/AIDS on Ministries of Agriculture: Focus on Eastern and Southern Africa* (2003) 1 <http://www.fao.org/hivaids/publications/moa.pdf> (accessed 15-05-2011).

[41] UNDP and FAO "Gender and Biodiversity Management: India" in *Sharing Innovative Experiments 5: Examples of Successful Initiatives in Agriculture and Rural Development in the South* (2011) 296 294-312 <http://ssc.undp.org/uploads/media/foreword_Content.pdf> (accessed 24-11-2011).

responding to poverty caused by the loss of formal-sector jobs by increasing home-based production of goods previously purchased in the market. This burden predominantly falls on women.[42]

Unfortunately, Western governments are not alone in devaluing poor mothers' caregiving and non-formal-sector subsistence work and assuming that installing a "work ethic" in poor people will provide the means for them to support their families in the formal-sector. I have previously written about South Africa's Expanded Public Works Programme ("EPWP"), which provides very short-term employment and for which one of the major target populations are women.[43] Interestingly, the government's reasons given for embracing the public works model are reminiscent of previously quoted neo-liberal social contract rhetoric assuming formal-sector wage work as the source of independence, dignity and self-reliance and ignoring caregiving and other subsistence work. [44]

Public works programmes, properly implemented, can be an important tool in reducing poverty. But the unproblematised incorporation of Western neo-liberal constructions of "dignity", "self-sufficiency", and "dependency" once again denigrates the multiple forms of work that poor women perform and ignores the dependent and subordinated status of low-wage formal-sector work in this picture.[45]

5   Legal construction of identities: Defining independence

While assuming that single mothers should participate in formal-sector subsistence work and that low-wage labour will provide a site of dignity, US social welfare programmes for "worthy" claimants, ie Social Security and particularly the Unemployment Insurance programme, legally define poor subsistence workers and even many formal-sector low-wage workers as "non-workers". Rather than giving dignity to poor women, legal constructions undermine dignity, reposition poor women as dependent and lazy, and erase the dependency inherent in wage work.

Social welfare policies and statutes are typically based on the fiction that the people who are the subjects of these laws and policies have fixed identities independent of law (for example, a person who is, in medical terms, permanently disabled from waged work). But drafting and administering welfare laws are political practices with discursive as well as instrumental consequences. Legal discourses and practices create meanings and identities.

---

[42]   For example, in Bulgaria, the share of home-based production for own consumption in household income doubled from 14.1% in 1990 to 27.5% in 1995. M González de la Rocha *Private Adjustments: Household Responses to the Erosion of Work* UNDP/SEPED Conference Paper Series (2000) 25.

[43]   Williams (2005) *SAJHR* 460-462.

[44]   P Stober "Getting Down to Business" *Mail & Guardian Online* (16-04-2004) <http://mg.co.za/ article/2004-04-16-getting-down-to-business> (accessed 30-11-2011); F Haffajee "Ideals of an African Utopia Hamper the BIG, Big Time" *Mail & Guardian Online* (15-05-2003) <http://mg.co.za/article/2003-05-30-ideals-of-an-african-utopia-hamper-the-big-time> (accessed 30-11-2011). See also President T Mbeki "Address to the National Council of Provinces, 11 November 2003" (03-09-2004) *Department of International Relations and Cooperations of the RSA* <http://www.dirco.gov.za/docs/speeches/2003/ mbek1111.htm> (accessed 15-05-2011).

[45]   See part 5 below.

Social welfare-related legal practices partially construct the identities of deserving and undeserving claimants.

As in most Western nations, the US legal discourse defines "worker", for purposes of determining eligibility for benefits under programmes such as Unemployment Insurance ("UI") based on an artificial dichotomy between formal-sector waged workers and welfare recipients. For example, through minimum earnings requirements and disqualifying reasons for termination, UI rules exclude many low-waged workers, including significant numbers of single mothers, from the definition of "employee", and such workers are rendered ineligible for unemployment insurance.[46] Many of the single mothers who move from welfare to unstable wage labour in secondary labour markets and then lose their jobs, find that they are *ineligible* for UI benefits and have no choice but to reapply for social assistance benefits. Indeed, in 41 of the 50 US states, men are more likely to receive UI than women.[47] In one study of women-maintained families, in which the mother was employed for at least three months, almost three times as many families turned to welfare as turned to UI. In another study of 1 200 single mothers who received welfare for at least two months in a 24-month period, 43% also worked, averaging just about half-time. However, only 11% of those who worked later qualified for UI. They returned to welfare as their "unemployment insurance".

The 1996 imposition of a five-year lifetime limitation on receipt of TANF has substantially reduced single mothers' ability to utilise TANF as their "unemployment insurance" when they become unemployed. However, in spite of that, a recent study shows that the percentage of low-educated single mothers entering a spell of unemployment who reported receipt of unemployment insurance *fell* from 28.7% in the years 1990-1994 to 21.4% in the years 2001-2005.[48] Among other factors, this decrease is based on the fact that the jobs that low-educated single mothers largely hold tend not to "lay off" workers in the traditional sense, but use informal shifts in hours and other means associated with secondary labour markets to encourage workers to quit "voluntarily" (see part 3 above), thereby disqualifying the individual from eligibility for unemployment insurance. As a result, the only social assistance that many of these unemployed single mothers were receiving was food stamps under the Supplemental Nutrition Assistance Program.[49]

---

[46] For example, two-fifths of high-wage unemployed receive UI, as compared to less than one-fifth of low-wage unemployed (note that 60% of low-wage workers are women). V Lovell & C Hill *Today's Women Workers: Shut Out of Yesterday's Unemployment Insurance System* (2001) 1. Women are four times more likely to be working part-time during their prime earning years than men, and 25 US states deny UI benefits to part-time workers. National Employment Law Project *Why Unemployment Insurance Matters to Working Women and Families: An Important Tool in the Work-Family Balance* (2004) 1 <http://nelp.3cdn.net/160e9cc27e3f2a6d6e_bwm6b5dz6.pdf> (accessed 19-05-2011). Because only fifteen states allow individuals who must leave their employment because of compelling family circumstances to receive UI benefits, women who leave are 32% less likely than men to receive benefits (National Employment Law Project *Why Unemployment Insurance Matters* 1).

[47] National Employment Law Project *Why Unemployment Insurance Matters* 1.

[48] HL Shaefer & L Wu *Unemployment Insurance and Low-Educated Single Working Mothers Before and After Welfare Reform* Upjohn Institute Working Paper No 11-173 (2011) 9.

[49] 5-7.

By denying many low-wage earning mothers transitional support when they become unemployed, UI law *constructs* them as persons who are "not attached to the labour force", that is, as social deviants who cause their own poverty by refusing to work and who therefore are unworthy of assistance from society. They then are viewed as "dependent" on the state and the economic dependency on employers that is a structural feature of low-wage labour markets is rendered invisible. In other words, the power of legal discourse creates a disconnect between people's *self-understanding as workers* and society's *recognition of them as non-workers*. Like the background rules that divide the family and the market into independent "private" spheres, separated from "state-imposed" social programmes, social welfare laws create and reinforce identities and images that deeply influence welfare policy debates.[50]

The conceptual bifurcation of wage work and welfare receipt performs the discursive magic of severing the concept of dependency from any connection to the sale of labour power in the market, erasing the alienation and subordination that characterise low-wage work. The legal system defines who is a worker, ie who is independent, and then legal discourse stigmatises those who fail to meet the legal definition of "worker" as trapped in dependency. Dependency becomes a concept excised from market structure. Likewise there is no concept of independence outside the formal-sector market structure (unless one has sufficient wealth of one's own or through a male breadwinner so that wage work is not required).[51]

My contention is that the low-wage experiences of many women reinforce increased dependency both in the work setting and in domestic situations. However, by defining "dependency" as "reliance on welfare" and excluding capital–labour relations from the concept of dependency, current discourse on welfare policy has largely ignored the structure of low-wage work.

For example, Lourdes Benería and Martha Roldán,[52] in discussing the increase in female employment in Mexican industries, note that firms prefer women workers for certain tasks because they assume stereotypical female

---

[50] That is not to say that imaginative re-envisioning of legal rules cannot make a difference to thousands and perhaps hundreds of thousands of people. It is worth noting that, at the point of his highest popularity (immediately after taking office), President Obama included very progressive, often quite technical, changes to the UI system in his stimulus package – changes that are barely known to the general public. He provided $7 billion to states for three years if they modernised their UI systems in several ways. One-third of this amount was made available to states if they changed their system to count wages in the quarter immediately prior to the quarter in which the unemployed person files for benefits. This method of computing wages has a major impact on low-wage workers who move in and out of unstable secondary labour market jobs on a regular basis. The remaining two-thirds was made available to states if they revised their system in two of four possible ways, each of which benefits women and/or low-wage workers: provide that a person shall not be disqualified because she is seeking part-time work in certain circumstances; provide that a person shall not be disqualified if she left her job for "compelling family reasons" which includes domestic violence, the illness or disability of an immediate family member, or to accompany a spouse changing employment; provide that benefits shall be available to a person taking an approved training programme; and provide allowances for dependents. American Recovery & Reinvestment Act of 2009, PL 111-5 [HR1], February 17, 2009, 123 Stat 115.

[51] N Fraser & L Gordon "A Genealogy of Dependency: Tracing a Keyword of the Welfare State" (1994) 19 *Signs: Journal of Women in Culture and Society* 309 314-319.

[52] L Benería & M Roldán *The Crossroads of Class and Gender: Industrial Homework, Subcontracting, and Household Dynamics in Mexico City* (1987) 40-74.

characteristics: that women workers will be reliable and stable, able to follow orders, and less troublesome; will do careful manual work; and will have discipline and patience. Some employers stated that single mothers were "among their 'best workers' because their responsibility as heads of households implies that they cannot rely on anybody else for family subsistence".[53]

In discussing Mexican industrial homework, the authors noted that the structure of homework is based on and reinforces pre-existing social relations and gendered division of labour within the domestic unit. Likewise they discuss how homework, which is unstable and offers little security, develops relationships of dependency by workers both on jobbers (those who distribute the homework) and on other sites of production outside of the homeworker's "control". The authors conclude that "society's and women's own perception of themselves as secondary income earners prepares them for involvement in unstable and low-pay jobs".[54]

Karen Hossfeld,[55] studying the model of labour control in Silicon Valley for female electrical production workers who are primarily immigrants, notes that supervisors affirm the workers' sense of their factory jobs as non-feminine. The supervisors then use flirting and dating as "refeminisation" strategies, subtly undermining the desire to file conditions complaints or join unions. Likewise, she notes the workers' internalisation or acceptance of capital's relegation of immigrants to secondary status in labour markets.

Chandra Mohanty[56] describes how Indian lacemakers have internalised ideologies that define them as "non-workers" whose work is "leisure time activity". They view themselves as selling products rather than labour, and are invisible as workers in census figures. Mohanty contrasts these homeworkers to Hossfield's immigrant women in Silicon Valley and migrant women in Britain who work in family firms as an extension of their family role, and concludes that "[i]n all these cases, ideas of *flexibility, temporality, invisibility* and *domesticity* in the naturalization of categories of work are crucial in the construction of Third-World women as an appropriate and cheap labor force".[57]

Several themes emerge from these studies that are instructive in providing a critique of low-wage labour markets as part of an anti-poverty agenda. First, the structure of low-wage paid labour often legitimates and reinforces existing patterns of gender subordination and dependency within the family and supports existing racial hierarchies. Second, the structure of low-wage labour contributes to and constructs increased "dependency" of women in the workplace, and a devaluing of all of women's work, both paid and unpaid. This dependency creates a constant fragility of the work experience, in the actual job site and in the self-construction and expectations of women workers.

---

[53] 48.

[54] 71.

[55] K Hossfeld "'Their Logic against Them': Contradictions in Sex, Race and Class in Silicon Valley" in K B Ward (ed) *Women Workers and Global Restructuring* (1990) 149 149-178.

[56] CT Mohanty "Women Workers and Capitalist Scripts: Ideologies of Domination, Common Interests and the Politics of Solidarity" in MJ Alexander & CT Mohanty (eds) *Feminist Genealogies, Colonial Legacies, Democratic Futures* (1997) 3 3-29.

[57] 20 (original emphasis).

However, a critical understanding of this construction of dependency has been largely absent from the debate about "welfare reform". In that discourse, dependence is synonymous with receipt of social assistance benefits, and independence is constructed as being in waged work. Yet as Nancy Fraser and Linda Gordon[58] have set out, prior to the rise of industrial capitalism, the definition of dependence was that of being subordinate to someone else or gaining one's livelihood by working for someone else. Virtually everyone was considered dependent; there was no deviancy associated with the concept. Only those owning sufficient property to live without working were deemed independent.

With the rise of industrial capitalism, as white male workers demanded electoral rights, they expanded and reconstructed the concept of economic independence to include wage labour. Economic inequality or relationships of subordination among white men no longer created dependency, capital–labour relations were exempted from dependency relations. In abolishing capitalist economic dependency by definition, and in "legally abolishing" political-exclusion dependency, many believed that structural bases of dependency had been eliminated in the US.

In contrast, the concept of dependency became tied to exclusion from wage work and receipt of social welfare programmes. Rather than dependence being viewed as normal and pervasive, it was viewed as deviant, and resulting from individual fault. Both conservatives and liberals increasingly did not question that independence was good, and tied to wage work, failing to incorporate or recognise how the structure of low-wage labour contributes to creating increased "dependency" of women.

The jurisprudence of the South African Constitutional Court is instructive in illustrating how the abstract concepts of "independence" and "dignity" can be filled with meanings that result in quite different redistributive effects than that of the neo-liberal social contract. *Khosa v Minister of Social Development*[59] was the first Constitutional Court case directly to address the constitutional provisions relating to the socio-economic right to social security. In finding that the statutory exclusion of permanent residents from specific social programmes violated the South African Constitution, the Constitutional Court recognised that reliance on other family members for support may have serious negative consequences for poor families. Rather than viewing receipt of a state social grant as creating dependency, the Court in *Khosa* saw social grants as a way to ensure the dignity of a recipient who would otherwise be dependent on the family:

"The exclusion of permanent residents in need of social-security programmes forces them into relationships of *dependency* upon families, friends and the community in which they live, none of whom may have agreed to sponsor the immigration of such persons to South Africa. These families or dependants, who may be in need of social assistance themselves, are asked to shoulder burdens not asked of other citizens. The denial of the welfare benefits therefore impacts not only on permanent residents without other means of support, but also on the families, friends and communities with whom they have contact. Apart from the undue burden that this places on those who take on this

[58]   Fraser & Gordon (1994) *Signs* 312-327.
[59]   2004 6 SA 505 (CC).

responsibility, it is likely to have a serious impact on the *dignity* of the permanent residents concerned who are cast in the role of supplicants."[60]

6   Conclusion

Drawing on the contributions of many colleagues, I have attempted in this chapter to articulate three central themes or assumptions that can usefully inform our discussions going forward. First, legal rules and discourses play a significant role in constructing society's understanding of poverty. Second, the rules historically in place in our societies work to keep people in poverty rather than to ameliorate their situation. And, third, contemporary neo-liberal social contract discourse – based in part on these embedded legal understandings – is an ideological initiative that legitimises and sustains gender subordination (among other forms of illegitimate hierarchy and domination). It is difficult to imagine a hopeful future either in law or social policy unless we can counteract the grip of this initiative on policymaking.

SUMMARY

In this chapter I attempt to provide a broad thematic framework for discussing critical and sometimes controversial issues in the field of law and poverty. Using gender as the lens through which to view a late 20th-century version of social contract theory, I discuss how blindness toward gender consequences of social policy and legal rules: (i) obscures the roots of poverty that are in part constructed by common-law background legal rules of property, contract, tort, and family law; (ii) induces decision-makers to ignore the conditions of and sex segregation in low-wage labour markets and the lack of upward mobility for poor women, thus appearing to legitimate the central, but flawed, assumption of neo-liberal poverty reduction policy (namely, that formal-sector waged work can and will provide adequate family support); (iii) renders invisible non-formal-sector "subsistence work" and "caregiving work," as defined herein, and in particular ignores the contribution of this work to economic productivity and efficiency as conventionally understood; and (iv) fails to appreciate that the legal definitions characterising many poor women workers as "non-workers" reinforce an artificial dichotomy between waged work and social assistance receipt (a distinction often framed as independence *versus* dependence) and eliminates by magical thinking the alienation and subordination experienced by low-wage workers, particularly women, from poverty discourse.

I articulate three central themes or assumptions that can usefully inform our discussions going forward. First, legal rules and discourses play a significant role in constructing society's understanding of poverty. Second, the rules historically in place in our societies work to keep people in poverty rather than to ameliorate their situation. And, third, contemporary neo-liberal social contract discourse – based in part on these embedded legal understandings – is an ideological initiative that legitimises and sustains gender subordination (among other forms of illegitimate hierarchy and domination).

---

[60]   Para 76 (emphasis added).

CHAPTER 4

NOT PURPOSE-MADE! TRANSFORMATIVE CONSTITUTIONALISM, POST-INDEPENDENCE CONSTITUTIONALISM, AND THE STRUGGLE TO ERADICATE POVERTY

Sanele Sibanda[*]

1 Introduction

It is a generally accepted assertion that constitutionalism – namely "the idea that government should derive its powers from a written constitution and that its powers should be limited to those set out in the constitution"[1] – is viewed as one of the most important tenets upon which the South African post-apartheid state has been established. Further, the proposition that one of the most pressing social and economic problems facing our post-apartheid state is a deeply entrenched structural poverty that continues to track closely the racist policies and spatial logic of previous colonial and apartheid governments could hardly be described as controversial.[2] However, in my engagement with South African constitutional discourse, I have noted that there is little scholarship that seeks to interrogate the relationship between constitutionalism and poverty eradication. In the scholarship the eradication of poverty is not regarded as a benchmark or a measure to determine the ultimate success or failure of South Africa's constitutional project of transforming society. By this I am making a claim that within our constitutional discourse engagement with poverty seems to be mainly confined to, and mediated through, rights discourses rather than seeing the eradication of poverty as forming an integral part of the *raison d'être* of the conception of South Africa's post-apartheid (or post-independence)[3]

---

[*] I would like to thank the following people for their insightful and helpful comments: Cathi Albertyn, Tshepo Madlingozi, Marius Pieterse, Silindiwe Sibanda and Chaka Uzondu. I would also like to thank Frank Michelman for his generous engagement with my chapter. More generally I would like to thank the organisers and participants of the Law and Poverty Colloquium for their valuable questions and comments; in this regard special thanks goes to Sandra Liebenberg for her patience and encouragement. Usual disclaimers apply.

[1] I Currie & J De Waal *The Bill of Rights Handbook* 5 ed (2005) 8.

[2] See generally S Terreblanche *A History of Inequality in South Africa, 1652–2002* (2002). See also N Nattrass & J Seekings *Class, Race and Inequality in South Africa* (2005).

[3] Although not a term often used within the South African political or constitutional lexicon I shall be using it here in reference to South Africa as an alternative to post-apartheid. In the chapter the terms are used interchangeably. My reason for this is simply that both historically and structurally South Africa resembles many a post-independence African state with their shared colonial history of discrimination, dispossession and disenfranchisement of the black majority; a negotiated independence settlement that produced a liberal constitutional document; and rich endowments of natural resources including land and minerals but a majority poverty-stricken population under the government of a liberation movement that has become the dominant political party.

constitutionalism.[4] What should be clear in my broad characterisation of what, in my view, is a disconnect between constitutionalism and poverty is at once an explicit and, indeed, an implicit recognition of the fact that there are numerous other instances in our constitutional scholarship wherein poverty is engaged with relative to specific areas such as the relationship between poverty and socio-economic rights;[5] poverty and access to justice;[6] and so forth. So in other words, my interest here is not with questions of how access to courts, the right to equality or socio-economic rights impact upon or are impacted upon by poverty it is rather the question of what the relationship of constitutionalism to the eradication of poverty is – or at least, what it should or could be. In this chapter I explore this relationship and in the process raise pertinent questions and make some tentative observations. For example, should constitutionalism be connected to poverty eradication in the sense of it being, at least, one of the primary end goals of South Africa's constitutional project? Is it in fact necessary or even desirable to formulate issues around poverty within the rubric of constitutionalism? Is South Africa's constitutional project, as currently conceived, formulated in such a way that it will withstand the pressures of seemingly deepening cycles of racialised, intergenerational poverty and social decay?[7] Or does its constitutional structure, its value system, its institutions and its norms and rules – in other words its model of constitutionalism have the wherewithal to insulate it from the stereotypical constitutional demise of many a post-colonial or post-independence African state?

However, before proceeding any further, and as a way to set the tone of the chapter, I want to start by providing, firstly, a brief description of how I understand and use the concept of constitutionalism in this chapter; and, secondly, a brief outline of two crudely constructed approaches to constitutionalism through which one could view the nature of transformation in post-apartheid South Africa. It must be conceded at the outset that these two approaches are not necessarily mutually exclusive; indeed I shall demonstrate they have some level of overlap. Their construction and presentation here are mainly for purposes of contrast, emphasis, and eventually as a means to expose their inherent limits in addressing a project of poverty eradication.

---

[4] Naturally some will refute the validity of the claims made in this chapter with assertions such as "we will never eradicate poverty; the poor will always be among us". Rather than this type of knee-jerk response I invite readers to engage their imaginations and contemplate, *not* the detail of a world free of poverty, but rather the implications of committing to, and to actually working towards, poverty eradication. In this imaginative space poverty is not a naturalised and accepted facet of our existence to be "alleviated", "reduced" or curbed, but an unacceptable aspect of our society to be eradicated. Interestingly the National Planning Commission states that its "key strategic objectives are the elimination of poverty and the reduction of inequality". See National Planning Commission *Diagnostic Overview* (2011) 8.

[5] For example, D Bilchitz *Poverty and Fundamental Rights: The Justification and Enforcement of Socio-Economic Rights* (2007); S Liebenberg "South Africa's Evolving Jurisprudence on Socio-Economic Rights: An Effective Tool in Fighting Poverty?" (2002) 6 *LDD* 159.

[6] For example, J Dugard & T Roux "The Record of the South African Constitutional Court in Providing an Institutional Voice for the Poor: 1995-2004" in R Gargarella, P Domingo & T Roux (eds) *Courts and Social Transformation in New Democracies* (2006) 107. See also J Dugard "Courts and the Poor in South Africa: A Critique of Systemic Judicial Failures to Advance Transformative Justice" (2008) 24 *SAJHR* 214.

[7] See generally National Planning Commission *Diagnostic Overview*.

It is probably apposite at this juncture to briefly set out my understanding of constitutionalism and its particular usage within this chapter. It is acknowledged that constitutionalism does not lend itself to easy definition.[8] Therefore, in this chapter, I shall use constitutionalism to refer to the notion of a system of governance established under a constitutional document whose primary functions are to structure, delineate, distribute and limit state power within a defined political community. Implicit in this understanding of constitutionalism is the idea that constitutional norms, values and principles are not predetermined, but they are rather the product of the political, economic, social and cultural history (both local and global) prevailing at the time of a constitution's adoption.[9] Thus, while modern constitutionalism has come to be associated with particular norms, values and principles, these are no less the product of an evolutionary process that is closely associated with particular histories.[10] Therefore, strongly influencing my understanding is the idea that, as a notion, constitutionalism is *not so much* about delivering a preordained form of state than it is an expression of choices made by those collectively responsible for establishing a particular system of constitutionalism.[11] With this in mind, I now turn to the two approaches alluded to above.

The first of these approaches I shall refer to as the orthodox or liberal democratic approach to constitutionalism. Those subscribing to this orthodox approach to constitutionalism would tend to view South Africa since the adoption of the post-apartheid constitutions[12] as steadily transforming over the past seventeen years from autocratic rule to a stable liberal democracy. In giving credence to this view, its proponents would point to a peaceful and by most accounts a successful transition; a stable democratic government; an arguably free media; the holding of regular free and fair elections; a multi-party system of representative democracy; an independent judiciary enjoying powers of substantive judicial review and a general respect for the rule of law. In brief, emphasis by proponents of an orthodox constitutionalism would be placed on the gains of political transformation and the limits placed on state power in the post-1994 period.[13]

---

[8]   C Fombad "Challenges to Constitutionalism and Constitutional Rights in Africa and the Enabling Role of Political Parties: Lessons and Perspectives from Southern Africa" (2007) 55 *Am J Comp L* 1 6-10.

[9]   G Devenish *A Commentary on the South African Constitution* (1998) 4.

[10] I Currie & J de Waal *The New Constitutional and Administrative Law I: Constitutional Law* (2001) 10-24. See also H Klug *Constituting Democracy: Law, Globalism and South Africa's Reconstruction* (2000) 1-4, 48.

[11] See Currie & De Waal *Constitutional Law* 12-21, in particular the descriptions of British constitutionalism as contrasted with US constitutionalism.

[12] The Constitution of the Republic of South Africa Act 200 of 1993 ("the Interim Constitution") and the Constitution of the Republic of South Africa, 1996 ("the Final Constitution" or "the Constitution").

[13] See generally Currie & De Waal *Constitutional Law* 10-11. While briefly outlining the history of constitutionalism and some of its different conceptions focusing on the limitation of state power, the authors also point out that modern constitutionalism has developed into a "prescriptive and normative" doctrine. Understood thus, modern constitutionalism is said to be characterised by, amongst other things, the following: a shared concern with democratic theory for human worth and dignity that demands the participation of citizens in governance; a prescribed structure of government in accordance with the doctrine of separation of powers; and the incorporation of judicial review as a "fundamental institutional mechanism for enforcing the specific arrangements and guarantees of the constitution".

The second approach is one that I shall refer to as a transformative approach to constitutionalism. Proponents of this approach, while recognising the importance of political transformation that has ushered in a democratic era, will point out that despite the Constitution's preambular commitment to "improve the lives of all citizens" and the inclusion of socio-economic rights in the Bill of Rights,[14] living conditions in South Africa from a social and economic perspective remain fundamentally unchanged for many black citizens for whom apartheid's multiple legacies continue to be a living and lived reality.[15] Of major concern to those subscribing to this approach is the fact that despite the political transformation described above, South Africa continues to suffer from increasing income inequality;[16] deeply entrenched structural poverty;[17] sharp increases in rural–urban migration;[18] and a growing educational crisis.[19] In brief, those subscribing to this approach would view transformation as entailing *both* political and socio-economic change. This second approach to constitutionalism is arguably the prevalent understanding in contemporary South African constitutional scholarship under the Final Constitution.

Although outlined in the briefest of terms, what is sought to be shown is that the two approaches are easily portrayed as differing significantly in terms of how they conceive of the legitimate goods or concerns of constitutionalism. Or put differently, they outwardly differ in terms of what it is that they conceive constitutionalism to be about and for. The question is just *how* different are they? What is the source of these differences? Do these differences matter in terms of outcomes, in other words how the use of state power and resources are experienced in a practical sense? Do these differences reflect a deviation of thought on constitutionalism and its goods? Or do these differences merely reflect a slightly divergent extension in thought? And therefore, do these differences reflect a truly radical departure from a liberal democratic constitutionalist paradigm or are they more reflective of a progressive gradualism within that paradigm?

A major premise of this chapter is that while a transformative conception of constitutionalism (or, as it is usually referred to, "transformative constitutionalism"[20]) is within our current constitutional discourse the

---

[14] See ch 2 of the Constitution.

[15] See National Planning Commission *Diagnostic Overview* 7, where it is tellingly conceded that "[f]or those South Africans who are excluded from the formal economy, live in informal settlements, depend on social services which are either absent or of poor quality; the political transition is yet to translate into a better life". See also S Liebenberg *Socio-Economic Rights: Adjudication under a Transformative Constitution* (2010) 25-27.

[16] H Bhorat, C van der Westhuizen & T Jacobs *Income and Non-Income Inequality in Post-Apartheid South Africa: What are the Drivers and Possible Policy Interventions?* Development Policy Research Unit (DPRU) Working Paper 09/138 (2009) 1, 5-15. See also A Sparks "At Home and Abroad: Losing the Battle of the Wealth Gap" (13-10-2009) *Business Day* <http://www.businessday.co.za/articles/Content. aspx?id=83913> (accessed 16-10-2011).

[17] Terreblanche *History of Inequality* 26.

[18] Bhorat et al *Income and Non-Income Inequality* 13.

[19] For a concise, comprehensive and well presented overview of the current state of South Africa's education system see: G Bloch *The Toxic Mix – What's Wrong with South Africa's Schools and How to Fix It* (2009).

[20] K Klare "Legal Culture and Transformative Constitutionalism" (1998) 14 *SAJHR* 146.

preferred approach to reading and understanding our Constitution, it has major pitfalls that make it ill-suited to delivering a project of poverty eradication. In particular, as I shall argue in this chapter, one major pitfall relates to the understanding of constitutionalism (including transformative constitutionalism) that prevails within our constitutional discourse that is deeply imbedded in liberalism. Or to put it slightly differently, the question that I shall grapple with in this chapter is, does transformative constitutionalism – that is clearly imbedded within a liberal democratic constitutional paradigm – have within it the potential to bring about the necessary structural change that will enable the poor to become true political agents rather than the recipients of welfare style handouts that will keep them and future generations "in their place"? In essence I shall be arguing here that (i) transformative constitutionalism finds a clear textual basis in the Constitution; (ii) academic commentators have gone to great lengths to articulate its vision and goals; and (iii) the courts have sought to enforce its principles and aspirations in adjudication, however the prevalence of a liberal democratic constitutional paradigm in South African constitutional discourse – despite the best intentions of transformative constitutionalism – has had the effect of defining the goods of constitutionalism in narrower terms than is in fact necessary or desirable for purposes of pursuing a truly transformative project of poverty eradication. In short, I will argue that it is transformative constitutionalism's ostensible weddedness to liberal democratic constitutionalism that makes it ill-suited for achieving the social, economic and political vision it proclaims.

Therefore, the overarching aim of this chapter is to offer a critique that engages the nature and role of constitutionalism in the post-apartheid era, particularly that of transformative constitutionalism. At the heart of this critique is a desire to interrogate whether constitutionalism, as conceptualised, is alive to the possibility of delivering a substantively more egalitarian society committed to true social and economic emancipation in which poverty is not only alleviated so as to assuage the collective conscience of the haves, but totally eradicated to address the needs, and indeed the demands, of the have-nots.

Very briefly, my argument will develop as follows: In part 2, I shall proffer transformative constitutionalism as representing an important political project that seeks to capture in many ways the vision and ideals of a society that many of us would have wanted to see South Africa become post-1994. In part 3, I will present some of the limits of transformative constitutionalism that have been put forward as presenting a challenge to the overall project of transformative constitutionalism. In part 4, drawing upon a Fanonian critique,[21] I shall argue that transformative constitutionalism presents certain pitfalls that impede the attainment of a truly egalitarian and emancipated society. In part 5, I shall discuss the crisis of constitutionalism in post-independence Africa, particularly the failure of liberal constitutionalism to take hold and the contestation around the Constitution. In part 6, I shall make some tentative propositions as to the importance and possibility of making more direct

---

[21]   F Fanon *The Wretched of the Earth* (1967 reprint 1990).

connections between constitutionalism and poverty eradication. In this part and the concluding one, my aim will be to begin to explore the imaginary of constitutionalism and what it could mean for the eradication of poverty.

2   Transformative constitutionalism as a discourse of hope

The amount of literature, both academic and non-academic, that the post-apartheid era of South African constitutionalism has spawned is nothing short of phenomenal. However, it is not the purpose of this chapter to engage in the many debates that have arisen as a result of this immense body of literature. The main thrust of this part is to briefly and in a generalised sense present transformative constitutionalism as an important project that has sought to account for contemporary developments in South Africa. Because this chapter seeks to draw a link between constitutionalism and poverty, I start by focusing on the concept of "transformative constitutionalism" because this project seeks to consciously argue for redress of the multiple legacies of apartheid. From early on in South Africa's constitutional project the pre-eminence of the notion of transformation as being at the heart of the project has been evident in the literature.[22] The depths to which the idea of transformation runs within the South African constitutional context is powerfully captured by Albertyn and Goldblatt when they state as follows (with respect to right to equality):

> "[W]e understand transformation to require a complete reconstruction of the state and society, including redistribution of power and resources along egalitarian lines. The challenge of achieving equality within this transformation project involves the eradication of systematic forms of domination and material disadvantages based on race, gender, class and other grounds of inequality. It also entails the development of opportunities which allow people to realise their full human potential within positive social relations."[23]

However, it was the seminal article by Klare that placed the concept or idea of "transformative constitutionalism" firmly within the lexicon of South African constitutional discourse.[24] The term has arguably become the most frequently and approvingly used term in South African constitutional discourse to describe South Africa's project of constitutionalism.[25] Both as a conception of constitutionalism and as a term seeking to define South Africa's constitutional project, transformative constitutionalism has, arguably, assumed a near hallowed status as a descriptor of the current South African project of constitutionalism. It is, admittedly, not without good reason that this is the case, as Klare's articulation of transformative constitutionalism has resonated

---

[22]   On the meaning and varied use of transformation in South African constitutional discourse since 1994 and a useful discussion of the literature, see M Pieterse "What Do We Mean When We Talk about Transformative Constitutionalism?" (2005) 20 *SAPL* 155.

[23]   C Albertyn & B Goldblatt "Facing the Challenge of Transformation: Difficulties in the Development of an Indigenous Jurisprudence of Equality" (1998) 14 *SAJHR* 248 249.

[24]   Klare (1998) *SAJHR* 146.

[25]   T Roux "Transformative Constitutionalism and the Best Interpretation of the South African Constitution: Distinction without a Difference?" (2009) 20 *Stell LR* 258 259 makes a similar point. However, a few more examples well illustrate the point: D Moseneke "The Fourth Bram Fischer Memorial Lecture – Transformative Adjudication" (2002) 18 *SAJHR* 309; Pieterse (2005) *SAPL* 155; P Langa "Transformative Constitutionalism" (2006) 17 *Stell LR* 351; S Liebenberg "Needs, Rights and Transformation: Adjudicating Social Rights" (2006) 17 *Stell LR* 5, K van Marle "Transformative Constitutionalism as/and Critique" (2009) 20 *Stell LR* 286; S Liebenberg *Socio-Economic Rights* ch 2.

with many within the judiciary, the academic and the legal professions alike. In his own, oft-quoted words, Klare puts forward the concept of transformative constitutionalism as entailing

> "a long term project of constitutional enactment, interpretation, and enforcement committed ... to transforming a country's political and social institutions and power relationships in a democratic, participatory, and egalitarian direction. Transformative constitutionalism connotes an enterprise of inducing large-scale social change through non-violent political processes grounded in law."[26]

Commenting on the notion of transformation as a constitutional imperative within the context of adjudication, Deputy Chief Justice Moseneke, writing extra-curially, boldly asserts that "the judiciary is commanded to observe with unfailing fidelity the transformative mission of the Constitution".[27] In a similar vein, Pieterse – in addressing the meaning of transformative constitutionalism – has located its imperatives in the text of the Constitution *via* a collective reading of some provisions of the Constitution that "indicate a marked departure from 'traditional' liberal conceptions of constitutionalism".[28] In particular, Pieterse points us[29] to the following provisions, namely: (i) the founding values;[30] (ii) the duty placed on the state to "respect, promote, protect and fulfil the rights in the Bill of Rights";[31] (iii) the extension of applicability of the Bill of Rights to private relations;[32] (iv) the substantive conception of the right to equality, including the prohibition of private discrimination;[33] (v) the inclusion of social and economic rights;[34] and (vi) the limitation clause.[35]

Of course, transformative constitutionalism, or even transformation as an idea, is not uncontested as to its scope or meaning; quite the contrary – such contestation is readily acknowledged by those engaging in constitutional discourse. This contestation as to the meaning of transformative constitutionalism is, arguably, one of its primary limitations. I turn to consider some of these limits below.

3   The limits of transformative constitutionalism

Klare is mindful to point out the "disconnect or chasm between the Constitution's substantively transformative aspirations and the traditionalism of South African legal culture".[36] According to Klare, if there is a threat to the success of the transformational constitutional project it is the imbedded traditionalism and conservatism that is characteristic of South African legal culture. The danger, Klare asserts, lies in the political nature of the project, meaning that transformative constitutionalism's reliance on politically progressive interpretation will always leave it at risk of being undermined

---

[26]   Klare (1998) *SAJHR* 150.
[27]   Moseneke (2002) *SAJHR* 319.
[28]   Pieterse (2005) *SAPL* 161.
[29]   161-163.
[30]   S 1 of the Constitution.
[31]   S 7(2).
[32]   S 8(2) and (3).
[33]   S 9(2), (3) and (4).
[34]   Ss 26, 27 and 28.
[35]   S 36.
[36]   Klare (1998) *SAJHR* 170.

by those who believe that political goals should not be pursued through adjudication.[37] Also wise to this threat is Pieterse, who contends as follows:

"[I]t is in this third contribution [namely, the need for the provisions of the Constitution to be interpreted to accord with the transformative vision] to transformation that the Constitution poses the most significant challenge to the South African judiciary and legal community. Constitutional provisions come alive mainly through interpretation and by being applied in particular concrete contexts. *This becomes controversial when the provisions that are to be interpreted and applied require that those tasked with interpretation and application aspire to achieve political goals embodied by the provisions.*"[38]

Pieterse adds further:

"South African legal culture with its pronounced preference for 'political neutrality' in adjudication (which requires lawyers and judges to remain 'neutral' in their interpretation and application of legal texts by abstaining from interpretations or orders that have 'political' (or social and economic) significance or consequences) has ... rightly been accused of masking a strong preference for the political structures and rights discourses associated with classic liberalism ... and accordingly of condoning the inequalities occasioned, reinforced and sustained by the unfettered operation of classical liberal economic and social structures."[39]

Therefore, the main challenge facing transformative constitutionalism identified by Klare, Pieterse and others[40] is that adjudicators may, owing to the prevailing legal culture and/or their politics, interpret and enforce the Constitution in ways that subvert the progressive and egalitarian social and political vision of transformation.[41] This challenge is, further, well illustrated by AJ van der Walt who has lucidly captured this conservative trend. In his discussion of those within the legal community who have sought to preserve the common-law tradition in its pristine condition by the exclusion of politics in legal interpretation, Van der Walt comments as follows:

"[T]he idea is that law is (or should be) neutral and free of political influence; the issue (as far as transformation is concerned) is to eradicate the political legacy of apartheid and not change the politics of law. Accordingly, law without politics – that is law that has been cleansed of the pernicious influence of apartheid politics but that is also free from reform politics – will necessarily serve the process of transformation better than a politically influenced process."[42]

Van der Walt's observation best demonstrates this conservatism, that while accepting that transformation may be important, there is the additional demand that it be achieved while maintaining a clear law and politics divide. The irony, of course, is that it was on the basis of this law and politics dichotomy that the apartheid courts were able to perform the dubious role of being unquestioning enforcers of patently racially discriminatory apartheid laws while purportedly staying out of politics.[43]

More recently, Davis, in a critique of the progression of South Africa's project of transformation, has sought to demonstrate the impact of South

---

[37] 171-172.
[38] Pieterse (2005) *SAPL* 164 (emphasis added).
[39] 164 (references omitted).
[40] See also Dugard (2008) *SAJHR* 214.
[41] See also Moseneke (2002) *SAJHR* 315-316.
[42] AJ van der Walt "Legal History, Legal Culture and Transformation in a Constitutional Democracy" (2006) 12 *Fundamina* 1 7.
[43] See H Klug *The South African Constitution: A Contextual Analysis* (2010) 225-229.

Africa's "untransformed" or traditionalist legal culture.[44] In this critique, Davis argues that despite an ambitious and enabling constitutional text embodying the possibility of a far-reaching transformation of South African society, its economy and indeed its legal principles, what has happened instead is a narrowing of this vision to a very formalised and legalistic conception of transformation.[45] Further, Davis argues that instead of the courts seizing upon the possibilities created by the Constitution to take South Africa forward in pursuit of a "social democratic" vision, the courts have retrogressed[46] and allowed for the "traditional laissez faire norms of a minimalist state"[47] and "traditional legal techniques"[48] to prevail in their adjudication. Davis, in his critique, airs his disappointment with this failure to fully exploit the constitutional text in line with the demands of the transformation as follows:

> "The [constitutional] text may have been seen as a bridge between apartheid and a democratic society but given the prevailing political discourse, the democratic society promised by the Constitution which, in part at least, would have required a radical transformation of the legal concepts which underpinned the entire society was replaced by a narrow vision: the eradication of what admittedly was a significant cancer in the body of the legal system prior to 1994."[49]

Davis' lament is well made and I would tend to concur with the general tenor of his views; and more generally in his critique that details the disappointing, untransformative jurisprudence emanating from the courts. That said, in this present chapter it is my purpose to take matters a little further and suggest that beyond what may be termed as retrogressive interpretation,[50] the root of the problem may well be the liberal democratic paradigm in which the project of transformative constitutionalism is embedded and operates. This fact, as will be argued below, is a serious pitfall of transformative constitutionalism that has a grave potential to undermine its aspirations of reimagining South Africa.

4   The pitfalls of transformative constitutionalism

While acknowledging that transformative constitutionalism has much to commend itself, it is subject to certain limitations, such as South Africa's conservative legal culture and its over-reliance on interpretation, that have been outlined above. Further, it also presents certain pitfalls that leave it susceptible to the charge that it promises more than it can actually deliver. I will elaborate upon this point shortly. However, before doing that I shall briefly discuss an important chapter entitled "The Pitfalls of National Consciousness",

---

[44]   D Davis "Transformation: The Constitutional Promise and Reality" (2010) 26 *SAJHR* 85.

[45]   99-101.

[46]   Please note that this is my term to characterise what I deem to be the essence of Davis' critique rather than a term used by Davis.

[47]   Davis (2010) *SAJHR* 93. Here Davis is referring to the courts' interpretive practices with respect to the law of contract.

[48]   97. Here Davis is referring to the courts' interpretive practice of conducting a reasonableness review of socio-economic rights that is grounded in the old administrative review which in turn encourages the courts to take a deferential stance *vis à vis* the executive.

[49]   101.

[50]   Again, please note that this is my term to characterise what I deem to be the essence of Davis' critique rather than a term he uses.

from which the title of this part borrows, in Frantz Fanon's *magnum opus*, *The Wretched of the Earth*.[51]

Those familiar with Fanon's work will no doubt be aware that he was not a constitutional theorist (at least in a conventional constitutional-law sense). However, Fanon is an an interlocutor whose work, in my view, constitutes and remains one of the most probing and prescient critiques of the condition of the post-independence African state.[52] Fanon's ideas remain important, especially in the context of this chapter, for the powerful and precise elaboration of the types of deep, structural challenges that would plague post-independence African states. More pointedly, I refer to Fanon here as I make the claim that he also speaks to us in South Africa as a post-independence state.

Fanon recognised that the struggles to end colonialism and the subsequent establishment of independent nation states were accompanied by the development of nationalist sentiment as all "nationals" struggled together to bring down the colonial power.[53] Of course, it is trite to suggest that the nation states that emerged from colonialism were almost exclusively as a result of European intervention rather than through the agency of population groups that saw themselves as nations.[54] The national consciousness that arose as a result of independence statehood was, thus, in many instances a new notion touted by the ruling political elites as being an important moral and political foundation upon which the new nation would be built. While Fanon acknowledged the importance of establishing consciousness – both social and political – as part of the broader emancipatory project of decolonisation,[55] he was not only sceptical of an elite-driven project of establishing national consciousness, but was in fact deeply critical of it and warned of the pitfalls it presented. Carefully noting the fragility of the constructed idea of the nation in the post-independence state and the fact that rather than a genuine national consciousness, what evolved was a conjured up "national" identity forged together often *via* disparate "native" struggles to overcome the various forms of colonial subjugation,[56] Fanon decries this kind of national consciousness when he states:

> "[N]ational consciousness, instead of being the all-embracing crystallization of the innermost hopes of the whole people, instead of being the immediate and most obvious result of the mobilization of the people, will be in any case only an empty shell, a crude and fragile travesty of what it might have been."[57]

---

[51] Fanon *The Wretched* 119.
[52] See also N Gibson "The Pitfalls of South Africa's 'Liberation'" (2001) 23 *New Political Science* 371 374-375.
[53] Fanon *The Wretched* 119.
[54] The formation of Africa's colonial borders is generally accepted as being the result of the Berlin Conference of 1884-1885. See, in general, B Davidson *The Black Man's Burden: Africa and the Curse of the Nation-State* (1992).
[55] See Fanon *The Wretched* 164-165.
[56] 119.
[57] 119.

Fanon proceeds further and asserts that:

"[T]his traditional weakness, which is almost congenital to the national consciousness of under-developed countries, is not solely the result of the mutilation of the colonized people by the colonial regime. It is also the result of the intellectual laziness of the national middle class, of its spiritual penury, and of the profoundly cosmopolitan mould that its mind is set in."[58]

Integral to Fanon's critique is an understanding of *how* the project of nation-building was a reaction to colonialism rather than as a project arising out of a truly shared sense of nationhood among the disparate groups within the colony. In other words, within colonial struggles, the quests for independence demanded that ethnic, class, rural–urban and other differences be put aside in the name of nation-building in order to establish a "national" force to overcome the colonial power. Therefore, the post-independence domination by the political elites and the middle class in the affairs of the state – both political and the economic – and their deployment of an elite-driven national consciousness to achieve this domination, caused Fanon to denounce it as being inimical to the interests of the masses or ordinary people. Fanon, according to Gibson, recognised that "[u]nless developed into a new humanism, into a social and political program that addresses the elemental needs of the mass of the people and includes them in the very discussion of the 'nation', national consciousness becomes an empty shell, a slogan cynically repeated at rallies and anniversaries and for the advance of the new huckstering elite".[59]

Based on these inherent tensions and imbalances of the new post-independence society, Fanon's view was accordingly that while the project of forming a truly inclusive and emancipatory (transformational) national consciousness was necessary, it was, owing to the dominance of the elites, always going to be fraught with pitfalls.[60]

I return to transformative constitutionalism. Using Fanon to draw a rough parallel, I would like to suggest that for a moment we imagine transformative constitutionalism to be a form of social and political consciousness that informs how we perceive the South African constitutional project. In so doing I am suggesting that in a political and legal community where there is a shared sense of this consciousness, the value-laden, forward-looking, and purposive interpretive approach established by transformative constitutionalism would be regarded as its strength and boon. Within such an approach, informed by a transformative consciousness, so to speak, the possibilities of establishing a truly transformed society would be, within the bounds of reason and the constitutional text, virtually limitless.[61]

However, in a political and legal community in which the vision of transformation is contested, as demonstrated above, the overriding dependence of transformative constitutionalism on the "right" kind of interpretation also

---

[58]   119.

[59]   Gibson (2001) *New Political Science* 383.

[60]   Fanon *The Wretched* 123. See also N Gibson "The Limits of Black Political Empowerment: Fanon, Marx, 'the Poors' and the 'New Reality of the Nation' in South Africa" (2005) 52 *Theoria* 89 96-97.

[61]   "Limitless" in this particular instance is used to convey the idea that the number of different contexts or situations to which transformative constitutionalism as an idea, ideal and interpretive approach can be applied are immense.

becomes a pitfall or fatal weakness. In other words, if the entrenchment of transformative constitutionalism, beyond disparate constitutional provisions that demand a collective reading as suggested by Pieterse above,[62] is primarily through interpretation by lawyers and judges of different political persuasions and inclinations, then the goals of transformation will always be at risk of being undermined or reduced to being merely of rhetorical value. Without the translation of the goals of transformation into explicitly entrenched constitutional provisions that demand reconstruction, redistribution and more deeply democratic popular participation that go beyond the Bill of Rights, it is arguable that transformative constitutionalism was always going to struggle to entrench itself, particularly in light of the overall constitutional scheme which is a liberal democratic one. This assertion is based on the fact that methodologically, in a constitution that structurally and institutionally accords with the basic tenets of liberal democratic constitutionalism (a few innovations notwithstanding),[63] transformative constitutionalism would, in a practical sense, only appear to be achievable through sustained and purposeful legal and judicial interpretation demanding a shared consciousness. Therefore, it is my contention that within the context of South Africa's prevailing conservative legal culture, the *extent* to which the success of transformative constitutionalism as an enterprise depends on legal and judicial interpretation leaves the project in danger of remaining an incomplete project at best. At worst, it runs the risk of failing to deliver true transformation by promising that which many charged with delivering it are not committed to, owing to its potential to undo already entrenched elite or middle-class interests. Closely related to this, and potentially the most significant pitfall limiting the possibilities of transformation is, in my view, the prevailing understanding of constitutionalism (including transformative constitutionalism) within constitutional discourse that is deeply embedded in liberalism and the seemingly unquestioning acceptance and commitment of many within the discourse of this fact.

While understandings of constitutionalism have developed over time, the liberal roots of the concept have continued to inform how it is understood.[64] As suggested at the outset of this chapter, I am of the view that few within our constitutional discourse would dispute the understanding of constitutionalism

---

[62] Pieterse (2005) *SAPL* 161-163.

[63] By this I mean that structurally the South African Constitution retains many of the same structures and institutions that one might find in a classic liberal democratic constitution. It contains, among other things, a bill of rights (admittedly one that goes beyond classic civil and political rights); makes provision for the three branches of government; separation of powers; provides for a further federative division of power; and establishes a democratic state with periodic elections. This fact read in conjunction with the clearly expressed goals of transformation in the Constitution led Klare (1998) *SAJHR* 153 to describe the South African constitution as "post-liberal".

[64] R Kay "American Constitutionalism" in L Alexander (ed) *Constitutionalism: Philosophical Foundations* (1998) 16 17. According to Kay, modern constitutionalism, from a historical standpoint, is widely regarded as having been influenced by the works of John Locke (who is widely viewed as one of the founding fathers of liberalism). In terms of the Lockean view, constitutionalism as a concept arose out of the realisation that government as the repository of ever increasing state power needed to have limitations imposed upon it to avoid it encroaching unjustifiably or tyrannically into the private sphere that was the preserve of private citizens.

as essentially a limiting doctrine. This means that it is primarily understood as being designed to ensure that the exercise of governmental power is subject to structural, procedural and substantive limits. Therefore, it is my contention that there would appear to be a general acceptance, at least on a normative level, that constitutionalism within the South African context is grounded on liberal tenets.[65] Further, so implicit is this understanding that the philosophical roots of South African constitutionalism are a sound basis for the transformation of South Africa that the question rarely, if ever, arises. In fact, I would venture to suggest further that liberal democratic constitutionalism is accepted implicitly, if not posited, as a good in itself of unquestionable or unimpeachable virtue. Rather than questioning whether liberal democratic constitutionalism is actually up to the demands of transformation that entail the "reconstructing" of South Africa so as to achieve the "redistribution of power and resources along egalitarian lines", to borrow from Albertyn and Goldblatt,[66] much more attention is being paid to questions around perceived threats to constitutionalism posed by an increasingly populist African National Congress government often portrayed as being blinded by the arrogance of incumbency.[67]

The point I seek to make here is that *if* transformative constitutionalism is at its heart an interpretive enterprise that can be undermined by a conservative legal culture, then what is one left with when such erosion of the Constitution's transformative vision occurs? My answer to this question would be as follows. What one is left with then is a prevailing system of liberal democratic constitutionalism with its emphasis on procedural democracy in the form of free and fair elections and the balancing of institutional power dynamics between the branches of government. Put differently, shorn of its transformative potentialities through retrogressive interpretation, transformative constitutionalism offers precious little in the form of an armoury with which to continue the fight to fundamentally reconstruct South Africa and contribute to the eradication of poverty. In fact, viewed from this perspective, transformative constitutionalism may end up being perceived as not being "post-liberal",[68] but merely an extension of liberal democratic constitutionalism. In this respect, transformative constitutionalism's greatest pitfall may well turn out to be the fact that rather than giving rise to a truly post-liberal discourse, it is a variant or derivative of liberal democratic constitutionalism. But, one could ask, is this necessarily a problem? My answer would have to be, while not necessarily an immediate problem, it may eventually become one, considering that liberal constitutionalism in post-independence Africa has, for the most part, been in something of a perpetual crisis. Before considering the implications of this argument for the fight against poverty, I shall briefly sketch some broad themes in the history of constitutionalism in post-colonial Africa.

---

[65]   See Currie & De Waal *Constitutional Law* 23-24.

[66]   Albertyn & Goldblatt (1998) *SAJHR* 249.

[67]   See D Dyzenhaus "The Pasts and Future of the Rule of Law in South Africa" (2007) 124 *SALJ* 734; T Roux (2009) *Stell LR* 258 in particular n 5; F Venter "Liberal Democracy: The Unintended Consequence. South African Constitution-Writing Propelled by the Wind of Globalisation" (2010) 26 *SAJHR* 45.

[68]   See Klare (1998) *SAJHR* 151-156.

5   The crisis of constitutionalism in Africa's post-independence era

It is not my intention here to engage at any great length with the details of the constitutions that were introduced in African states as a result of decolonisation – the so-called independence constitutions. Where I do refer to them my comments will be made in general terms with respect to some of the themes concerning such constitutions. That there has been a general failure of a progressive development-oriented, in other words a transformative, constitutional culture taking root in Africa in the post-independence era is a point few would dispute. What is controversial, however, is why this failure occurred, especially in light of the fact that the principal driving forces of the struggles for independence were political, social and economic liberation; ie the same goals that animate a transformational constitutional project. Rather than liberation, what followed for the most part was the conversion of a colonial state to an independent state that in many ways mirrored the former colonial state in terms of the structures and forms of governance. Power upon independence was generally transferred to a mass-based liberation movement that over time morphed into an elite-dominated ruling party.

According to Shivji, the post-independence constitutional order, although broadly premised on a liberal conception of constitutionalism, did not manage to usher in a new era of equal citizenship and liberation. Instead, as Shivji points out, the new independence order established under the new constitutions was little more than an "excrescence" of the despotic colonial political and legal order.[69] The implications this had for constitutionalism is that the independence constitutions for all their classic liberal features were after a period amended, modified or simply overthrown in order to accord with the aspirations of the new independence leadership.[70] In short, liberal constitutionalism with its emphasis on processes and institutions as we have come to know it in the modern era never really took firm root in most post-independence African states. Even in those instances where it did appear to do so, under the weight of expectation and social upheaval, things seemed to unravel after a while.[71]

The state of affairs described briefly above led to what Okoth-Ogendo has described as Africa's constitutional paradox.[72] Okoth-Ogendo asserts that this paradox lies in the fact that the attainment of independence brought with it "a clear commitment to the idea of the constitution and an equally emphatic rejection of the classical notion of constitutionalism".[73] In explaining the nature of the paradox, Okoth-Ogendo tells us that it is necessary to initially recognise the overwhelming acceptance by the political elites that negotiated

---

[69] IG Shivji "State and Constitutionalism: A New Democratic Perspective" in IG Shivji (ed) *State and Constitutionalism: An African Debate on Democracy* (1991) 27 27-29.

[70] Shivji "State and Constitutionalism" in *State and Constitutionalism* 39. For a more recent account of the failure of constitutionalism in Africa see Fombad (2007) *Am J Comp L* 2-5.

[71] Fombad (2007) *Am J Comp L* 2-5.

[72] HWO Okoth-Ogendo "Constitutions without Constitutionalism: Reflections on an African Political Paradox" in IG Shivji (ed) *State and Constitutionalism: An African Debate on Democracy* (1991) 3.

[73] 5.

independence of the fact that a constitution was a *sine qua non* for the establishment of the newly independent state.[74] He identified two important senses in which this was true. Firstly, it was true in the sense that the constitution was seen as constitutive, in a foundational sense, of the new state. In other words, the constitution was seen as the bedrock of the sovereignty upon which all other acts in the name of the state would be done.[75] Secondly, the constitution was seen as forming the *basic law* of the newly established state. In this sense, *basic law* must be understood as denoting a legal regime that established minimum rules to be observed,[76] and not necessarily denoting a sacrosanct set of laws that demands observance in all matters relating to state power and the law.

In further describing the development or actual manifestation of the paradox which entails the actual subversion of the constitutional order, Okoth-Ogendo identifies two particular forms of subversion by state elites that cement the paradox. These two forms, according to Okoth-Ogendo, worked hand in hand as the elites "*politicise* the constitution; *initially* by declaring it a liability, and subsequently by converting it into an instrument of warfare."[77] In terms of the first form of subversion of the constitutional order, the constitution is viewed as an obstacle to rapid economic development. The constitution is, in the words of Okoth-Ogendo, seen as "a liability", and as such it must be changed or simply done away with.[78] The subsequent subversion of the constitutional order then posits the constitution as a political instrument that has the power to rectify its own shortcomings by allowing those in power to amend it so as to place more power in the hands of the executive.[79] In his own words Okoth-Ogendo sets out the essence of his argument as follows:

> "As these and other devices found their places within the 'constitutional' framework, so did the view that the constitutional arena, if properly controlled by the state elite offered a more efficient and effective environment for the resolution of *political* conflicts than even the party and certainly the electorate at large. Indeed by translating a political option or decision into a *constitutional* device or norm, state elites gained the added advantage of passing on the problem of enforcement or supervision ultimately to the judicial arm of government. A *run to amend the constitution* whenever a political crisis emerged or was apprehended, therefore, became increasingly attractive as a method of re-establishing equilibrium within the body politic."[80]

---

[74] 6.

[75] 6.

[76] 6-7. Okoth-Ogendo points out that it was actually this particular sense or understanding of the basic law that was instrumental in permitting or promoting some of the most drastic amendments that proved destructive to Africa's nascent constitutionalism. See in particular the examples cited here. Another way to look at this particular understanding of what the *basic law* stood for is that to those who interpreted it this way the Constitution represented ground zero on which to build rather than revered or holy ground. This view can be starkly contrasted with the understanding of the term "basic law" in South Africa, which is premised on the idea that the Constitution as the basic law is the source of all law and any law that is found to be in conflict with or contravenes it is unconstitutional.

[77] 11 (original emphasis).

[78] 11.

[79] Under the rubric of constitution as a political instrument, Okoth-Ogendo identifies some of the devices that were deployed to concentrate power in the hands of the executive: (i) granting power to the chief executive to appoint and dismiss all public service appointees, (ii) "subjecting the process political party recruitment at all levels to strict party sponsorship", and (iii) amending the constitution so that it accords with the rest of the legal order, particularly repressive legislation (12).

[80] 13 (original emphasis).

Although the crisis of constitutionalism discussed above speaks mainly to post-independence Africa before the so-called "winds of democratic change" swept through Africa in the mid 1990s,[81] the place, function and entrenchment of a culture of constitutionalism in many African countries continues to be in question.[82] While readily conceding that Okoth-Ogendo's paradox does not apply to South Africa, a recent calling into question of the Constitution by a deputy minister of the incumbent government has brought to the fore issues of contestation of the very meaning of the Constitution to the transformation of South Africa. Ramatlodi, the deputy minister in question, argues that in the pre-democratic constitutional negotiations the African National Congress made "fatal concessions" that have resulted in "a Constitution that reflects the great compromise, a compromise tilted heavily in favour of forces against change".[83] While not expressing an official government position, the position of power Ramatlodi holds and the ensuing silence from official circles makes his utterances worthy of attention.

6   Constitutionalism and the fight against poverty

There is no obvious constitutional crisis in South Africa at present. In fact, the constitutional centre seems to be holding in spite of the palpable contradictions that are South Africa's socio-economic reality, particularly the visible opulent and grandiose living of the haves as opposed to the equally visible gut-wrenching poverty of the have-nots. This fact, however, does not mean that things cannot change or that we should not ask difficult questions as to whether or not transformative constitutionalism, embedded as it is in a liberal democratic constitutional scheme, is up to meeting the challenges that South Africa faces. In my view, it is necessary for us to ask some probing questions about whether the direction being chartered within the confines of the prevailing constitutional discourse holds within it the potential in terms of language, ideas and an imaginary to make positive steps towards a truly more egalitarian society in which we strive not to alleviate poverty, but to eradicate it. Or to put it a bit differently, does the discourse of transformative constitutionalism that is clearly conceived within a liberal democratic paradigm have within it the potential to bring about the necessary structural changes that will enable the impoverished to become true political agents rather than the recipients of welfare-style handouts that will keep them and future generations "in their place"? I, for one, certainly doubt it.

---

[81]   HK Prempeh "Africa's 'Constitutional Revival': False Start or New Dawn" (2007) 5 *I Con* 1 6.

[82]   See, generally, Fombad (2007) *Am J Comp L* wherein he focuses on constitutional developments in twelve Southern African countries.

[83]   N Ramotlodi "ANC's Fatal Concessions" (01-09-2011) *The Times Live* <http://www.timeslive. co.za/opinion/commentary/2011/09/01/the-big-read-anc-s-fatal-concessions> (accessed 16-10-2011). See also related articles: P de Vos "Why Ramatlhodi Promotes an Autokratic Kleptocracy" (01-09-2011) *Constitutionally Speaking* <http://constitutionallyspeaking.co.za/why-ramatlhodi-promotes-an-autokratic-kleptocracy/> (accessed 16-10-2011); J Duncan "The Problem with South Africa's Constitution" (05-09-2011) *The South African Civil Society Information Service* <http://www. sacsis.org.za/site/article/741.1> (accessed 16-10-2011); D McKinley "The Majority and the 'Meaning' of the Constitution" (04-10-2011) *The South African Civil Society Information Service* <http://www. sacsis.org.za/site/article/760.1> (accessed 28-10-2011).

While not claiming to possess the answers, what I can say is that for South African constitutionalism to be truly transformative, or more appropriately emancipatory, greater commitment needs to be made towards ensuring that our conception of constitutionalism encompasses significant advances in: (i) mass bottom-up truly participatory democracy in that it allows people to take an active part in the decision-making processes that concern them;[84] (ii) a greater commitment to structural interventions targeted at delivering a more equitable and sustainable distribution of wealth and resources; and (iii) more generally striving towards a more just and fair society that rejects the deepening of the legacies of colonialism and apartheid. I turn now to reflect upon and raise concerns about the current failure of South Africa's constitutional discourse to better locate South Africa's development within the post-independence paradigm and the implications of this for any project of long-term poverty eradication.

Firstly, as mentioned above, I contend that by seeking to entrench transformative constitutionalism *via* interpretive devices within a liberal democratic constitutional paradigm the goods of constitutionalism have come to be defined in narrower terms than is in fact necessary or desirable for purposes of pursuing a truly transformative project of poverty eradication. As has been discussed, the goals of transformative constitutionalism can, through narrow constitutional interpretation, be negated, leaving us with a conception of transformation that is narrowly focused on limiting state power. If we are to draw a lesson from post-independence constitutionalism in Africa, it is that when constitutionalism becomes subsumed in the regulation of power relations within government, then it is power politics that dominates the constitutional terrain rather than the demands of society more broadly speaking; let alone the imperative of eradicating poverty. Put differently, in the South African context the failure to more directly and concretely connect the goals of the Constitution's transformative vision with ideals of delivering truly egalitarianism outcomes and poverty eradication creates room for a charge to be levelled that asserts that currently conceived constitutionalism is viewed as an end in itself, rather than as a means to an end. In the context of South Africa as a post-independence society that end was and must, surely, continue to be political, social and economic liberation – especially for those whose current destitution is as a direct consequence of violent and racist policies of former governments.

Secondly, following on from above, within the confines of the prevailing discourse there appears to be little or no room for the consideration of ideas that the renowned African historian Basil Davidson would describe as "radical innovations".[85] The current trajectory of our constitutional discourse is such that even arguably necessary reforms, such as land reform, will be evaluated in terms of their ability to comport with liberal democratic models,

---

[84] For example, Brazil's participatory budgeting system involves citizens in the budgetary decision-making processes at local government. See generally J van Speier "Citizen Participation Influencing Public Decision Making: Brazil and the United States" (2009) 69 *Public Admin Rev* 156.

[85] Davidson *Black Man's Burden* 193.

values, norms and principles.[86] As a result, the tendency is then to replicate or mimic models from more established Western liberal democracies with whom we do not have an obviously similar or shared history. My point here is that the appropriateness of replicated structures and institutions must always be questioned, especially in light of the fact that the material conditions and stages of development between South Africa and the countries where these models have been developed are vastly different. Instead of a constitutional discourse that acknowledges that there may be cause for radical innovation or experimentation, especially in terms of thinking, our discourse bases itself on a model of replication that promotes "prudent continuity"[87] or more precisely, at least in the context of constitutional law, legal continuity.[88]

7 Conclusion

In this chapter I have intentionally sought to raise more questions than provide answers. In particular, I have also sought to question the potential, and indeed the ability, of transformative constitutionalism to deliver on the large-scale promise it makes while it remains, consciously or unconsciously, embedded in a liberal democratic constitutional paradigm. In my view, this is an important question that demands some honest and open reflection, particularly if one is also willing to look beyond South African exceptionalism and locate South Africa within a wider continental history and context. Yes, South Africa is a different country and our Constitution is quite different to that of many other countries on the continent, particularly those that attained independence in the 1960s. But that said, once one pries beneath the surface one sees that South Africa's history and positioning within a global context is actually not that far removed from that of other African countries. In other words, just because we have a much lauded constitutional document does not in itself provide some form of immunity or indemnity from the social decay that ensued after a point in other post-independence states where the governments of the day failed to deliver social and economic emancipation. Of course, the point is not to portray such an end as inevitable; it need not be.

In the main, this chapter serves as an invitation to others to have a conversation about what are clearly some exploratory ideas about constitutionalism and how it is made to react in a tangible and real way to poverty and its resultant social, economic and political marginalisation. More generally, the ideas, questions and critiques discussed here seek to spark some critical engagement with questions of how we try to forge firm links between constitutionalism and poverty eradication in a way that is informed by South Africa's history and current context, and above all recognises that to be truly committed to dignity, equality and freedom demands that we unlock our collective imaginary and reject the *status quo*. By this I mean that if we can imagine a world without

---

[86] See generally L Ntsebeza "Land Redistribution in South Africa: The Property Clause Revisited" in L Ntsebeza & R Hall (eds) *The Land Question in South Africa: The Challenge of Transformation and Redistribution* (2007) 107.

[87] Davidson *Black Man's Burden* 192.

[88] See Klug *The SA Constitution* 13-17.

poverty and are indeed serious about attaining it, then we must continue to engage with questions that force us to re-imagine how constitutionalism can contribute to this fight unapologetically, even if it means robustly critiquing and laying bare that which we identify with almost as a matter of course – like transformative constitutionalism.

SUMMARY

In this chapter I interrogate the relationship between constitutionalism and poverty eradication. Motivating this inquiry is the fact that in South African constitutional scholarship poverty eradication is not articulated as a benchmark or even a measure to determine the ultimate success or failure of social transformation. By this the chapter makes the claim that within constitutional discourse engagement with poverty seems to be mainly confined to, and mediated through, rights discourses rather than being seen as forming an integral part of the *raison d'être* of post-apartheid constitutionalism.

The main argument of this chapter is that whilst transformative constitutionalism is rightly regarded as the preferred approach to reading and understanding the Constitution, it suffers from certain pitfalls that render it ill-suited to delivering a project of poverty eradication. In particular, I argue here that one major pitfall is that transformative constitutionalism, whilst claiming to be post-liberal, is deeply embedded in and comfortably co-exists with liberal discourses. In essence I argue here that (i) transformative constitutionalism finds a clear textual basis in the Constitution; (ii) academic commentators have gone to great lengths to articulate its vision and goals; and (iii) the courts have sought to enforce its principles and aspirations in adjudication, however the prevalence of a liberal democratic constitutional paradigm, has had the effect of defining the goods of constitutionalism in narrower terms than is in fact necessary or desirable.

In making this argument I critically engage with transformative constitutionalism, in particular its limits and pitfalls. In so doing, I draw upon a Fanonian critique to illustrate the pitfalls of elite dominated transformations. In addition to this I engage the crisis of constitutionalism in post-independence Africa. It is against this background that I make calls for a constitutional conversation that more directly connects between constitutionalism and poverty eradication.

CHAPTER 5

DE-POLITICISING POVERTY: ARENDT IN SOUTH AFRICA

Emilios Christodoulidis[*]

1 South Africa: the "social" and the "political"

Post-apartheid South Africa stands at the crossroads of the "political" and the "social" in a way that calls us to put to question conventional conceptions of the two, and of their *separateness*. I take Hannah Arendt's to be the most robust and influential of the theorisations of this separateness. If Dana Villa is right – and he is certainly not alone in this kind of acclamation – to say that "the *Human Condition* (1958) and the essays collected in *Between Past and Future* (1961) … mark Arendt's emergence as a political thinker of truly staggering range and depth; [and] that these books, together with *On Revolution* (1963) constitute her most enduring legacy in political theory",[1] then it becomes all the more urgent to challenge her "enduring legacy" of theorising the political *as a denial of the social*. For "one of the most unapologetic champions of the political life in the history of Western thought"[2] this theorisation is, startlingly, a move aiming to *de*-politicise and, in effect, to undercut our ability to understand and redress poverty as a political issue.

A decade and a half after what so many of us, as fascinated observers, saw in South Africa as an extraordinary opportunity for a different *political imaginary*, "*the social question*" – or what "we may better and more simply call the existence of poverty"[3] – remains alarmingly alive. Anticipating the analysis of key terms that follows, the *political* moment in South Africa testifies to much of what Arendt identifies as worthy (even constitutive) of the "political". Take her concept of *natality* for example. The seismic change in the country was not marked by bloodshed, but instead by an astonishing effort at reconciliation; something genuinely *new* was born which was *unanticipated* both as to its magnitude and as to its momentum. With it we had the emergence of a new collective identity-in-plurality, an *acting-in-concert*, as Arendt would put it, across racial groups and political divides, the government itself an alliance of the ANC, the communists and the trade unions. At the same time, the emergence of the politically new is neither anti-institutional nor anomic:

---

[*] Many thanks to the participants of the Law and Poverty Colloquium at Stellenbosch, to the editors, and to Ruth Dukes for helpful comments. I owe a debt also to Andrew Schaap who familiarised me with the work of Arendt when he was my doctoral student in Edinburgh and in conversation with whom many of the ideas developed, though Andy remains a great deal more sympathetic than me to her thought and certainty more erudite about it. We have co-written an earlier paper on "Arendt's Constitutional Question" forthcoming in M Goldoni & C McCorkindale (eds) *Hannah Arendt and the Law* (2012).
[1] DR Villa "Introduction" in D Villa (ed) *The Cambridge Companion to Hannah Arendt* (2000) 1 8.
[2] 8.
[3] H Arendt *On Revolution* (1963) 60.

it is born out of *institutions* in the way Arendt understood their function as supporting or undergirding political processes. We could borrow from Andrew Arato the language of "constitutional learning"[4] to describe how the new is harboured in the institutions and born of them. Or we could turn our gaze to the extraordinary experiment that was the setting up of the Truth and Reconciliation Commission ("TRC") and the institutional imagination it took both to institutionalise a forum that served as tribunal and public confessional, and to defend it with such judicial creativity in *Azanian Peoples Organisation (AZAPO) v President of the Republic of South Africa*.[5] As to the *intensity* of political *mobilisation* and commitment to the public sphere, that Arendt treasures, one would be able to pick amongst a vast number of instances here: from the political momentum in the townships to the extraordinary numbers of those who queued all day to vote in the first elections. Or perhaps one might single out as exemplary the event that Jeremy Cronin describes, when over 100 000 attended the Communist Party's launch party in Johannesburg after the fall of apartheid and completely overwhelmed the Party's preparedness to meet the demands for membership.[6] How eventfully indeed the "new" broke into being in South Africa, with Arendt's lexicon of the political spelt out in the entirety of its impressive range.

And yet, at the same time, how stark the opposition with the "social"! The poverty that ravaged the country under apartheid ravages it still. The looting of the country's wealth continues unabated, with new, reconfigured, minorities taking over the process from the old ones, or simply joining them. We witness today an unprecedented level of wealth polarisation, the debacle of the "reparations" promise, the political dominance of demagogues, privatisers and tax-cutters, the crony capitalism of "Black Economic Empowerment", unemployment rocketing, and the provision of basic services limping along.

All this is well known and documented and I will not dwell on it much longer. I would recommend Patrick Bond's excellent response to Richard Johnson's more familiar tale that South Africa's woes lie in the fact that, despite its efforts, the government never provided the kind of stability that would realise the levels of capital investment foreseen and necessary.[7] Bond analyses how state provision of housing, water, sanitation, electricity, healthcare and education are currently widely considered inferior or more expensive than during apartheid as a result of macro-economic strategies put in place during the Kempton Park negotiations, intended to bind the post-apartheid regime to a neo-liberal structural adjustment programme that it never showed the will or the power to resist. My own concern in this chapter is with the severed link between the first set of conditions fulfilled (the political) and the denial of the second set (the social). What, might one ask, does this elevation of the *political* moment mean above the realities of *social* devastation wrought

---

[4]   See, for example, A Arato "Constitutional Learning" (2005) 52 *Theoria* 1-36.

[5]   *AZAPO v President of the Republic of South Africa* 1996 4 SA 671 (CC).

[6]   P Bond "In Power in Pretoria?" (2009) 58 *New Left Review* 77. See also P Bond *Against Global Apartheid* (2003).

[7]   Bond (2009) *New Left Review* 77; RW Johnson "False Start in South Africa" (2009) 58 *New Left Review* 61-76.

by a post-apartheid neo-liberal structural adjustment programme, to which the ANC government committed the continent's most developed state from the very start? How does it come about that in two decades, during which huge mass political and syndicalist forces have been assembled, there has never arisen the kind of self-confident mass-power which could control its leaders and avoid the transmutation of the Alliance's proclaimed overall socialist goals into investment-driven narratives of growth? And how does it transpire that the main role that the Alliance of political forces in government – the anti-apartheid movement, the communists, and the trade unions – sets for itself is that of appeasement and conflict avoidance, channelled into an endless series of "consultations and discussions" during "Alliance summits", and the appointment of leaders of the Left in relatively marginal governmental positions?[8] In this disturbing conjunction the political, having been so successfully separated off from the social, is made to yield to market imperatives, and the whole cohort of "natality", "wordliness", "acting-in-concert" and the rest, become hollowed out to the point where "democratic experimentalism" means nothing but market adjustment, and delivers nothing but the reproduction of privilege.

Perhaps the question that we face most directly and urgently as constitutional lawyers is how we might think with, or trouble, such distributions, these "guiding distinctions" of the political imagination? My contribution to this discussion centres on that question, and that contra-distinction between the "political" and the "social". I will attempt to trace the genealogy of the entrenchment of this separation, initially through a discussion of Arendt who has emerged in the last decade, partly also due to Habermas's debt to her, as the theorist *par excellence* of the political. I look at how the distinctions her work is based on have informed – sometimes unwittingly, but for the most part consciously – theories of differentiation. In part 2, I will thus visit what Arendt says about the question of poverty in her unflinching attack on Marxism, and the devastating analysis she offers of the French Revolution as the most explicit attempt in European history to "emancipate the suffering masses".[9] I will then look more specifically at how she famously expounds the concept of "the political" (in part 3), and following that I will return to draw out more fully the political–social contradistinction, and how it undercuts the way we might otherwise have made sense of the political redress of poverty (part 4). In the final part (part 5), I will return to South Africa today, to trace some limits and put some concerns on the table about what, in the face of this prevalent understanding of the public sphere, we may achieve in terms of a "transformative" social rights constitutionalism.

---

[8]   See Bond (2009) *New Left Review* 85 on this and on how massive protests were diverted into a fight around personalities.

[9]   Arendt *On Revolution* 111; "explicit" in the sense that the professed emancipation of the "suffering masses" does not involve them as "prospective citizens but as *malheureux*".

2   Arendt rescues the political (from Marx and Robespierre)

In the customary periodisations of Arendt's work, the early *Origins of Totalitarianism*[10] is seen as a work that, while rich in ideas that inform the later oeuvre, nonetheless stands apart from that, more explicit, theory of the political. This periodisation misses an important link of the early and late work that centres on the critique of Marx, a link Arendt traces between the theory of totalitarianism and her identification of the "totalitarian elements in Marxism". While it is true that Arendt felt that her early work had focused too heavily on Nazism rather than Soviet totalitarianism, the approximation of the two is more than a remedy of a skewed emphasis, and, I would argue, revealing, especially as it is developed with exceeding urgency in her later work.

Key in this approximation is, firstly, how her defence of "plurality" is pitted against mass society (totalitarianism) and collective subjecthood (Marxism). Secondly, as she develops it at length in the last chapter of *Origins of Totalitarianism*, totalitarianism, in both its national-socialist and soviet varieties, attempts to "still" action through terror in order to pursue the Law of History, whose laws of movement replace the spontaneous action of free men. With it "terror", the "essence of totalitarian domination", is deployed to "stabilize men", "to liberate the forces of nature or history"[11] in the name of the "fabrication of mankind", "eliminating individuals for the sake of the species, sacrificing the 'parts' for the sake of the 'whole'".[12] Thirdly, and most crucially for our discussion, in both cases the "political" becomes subsumed to the "social". The political hubris of totalitarianism, which Arendt defines as a "climactic pathology" of modern European history, stands at the counterpoint of what it means to preserve and share a "world". A "world" for Arendt involves the institutions and structures that mediate man's relation to nature, mark civilised life, and constitute man's medium of freedom.[13] Totalitarianism collapses that space and subsumes the political to the state's direct administration. And with this comes another approximation, or a second "subsumption", not just to the state, but also to economics. Arendt develops the argument about the subsumption of politics to economics predominantly in *The Human Condition*. What is interesting is that there is a likening of the two pathologies in Arendt's thought, in that both constitute instances of decisive absolution of civic responsibility: in the case of totalitarianism the absolution is to powerful government, in the case of economics to policymakers and the administrative apparatus of the state.

For Arendt, that the political sphere came to be identified with the "national household" involved a category mistake that collapsed the two spheres that in their contradistinction upheld the autonomy of the political and the social respectively.[14] The significance of this separation and the conceptual work

---

[10]   H Arendt *The Origins of Totalitarianism* (1973).
[11]   465.
[12]   465.
[13]   For this analysis see H Arendt *The Human Condition* (1958) 193-198.
[14]   28-37.

that these stark contradistinctions do for Arendt cannot be exaggerated. The intrinsic dignity itself of the political depends on the specific modality of drawing the public/private distinction and at stake is the ability of people to create and share a world as equals. Further distinctions correlate: political/ social, public/private, equality/hierarchy, freedom/necessity. We will explore much of what Arendt builds on and makes dependent on these stark binarisms that, I will argue, operate in her theory as blindspots.

But how does this relate to her critique of Marx? Already in 1951, convinced as Dana Villa puts it that "Marx's thought could not be easily isolated from its Stalinist deformation", Arendt begins her more systematic engagement with Marxism in the context of a work she undertook but never saw through on the "totalitarian elements in Marxism".[15] These include "his preference for collective subjects – like the proletariat or mankind – which act in accordance with supposed class or species interests".[16] It is important to note that the deployment of collective subjects by Marx undercuts the very thing that Arendt identifies as quintessential to politics: diversity amongst equals, and with it the constitutive plurality of the political.[17]

What begins in 1951 as a tentative attempt to trace the totalitarian elements in Marxism reaches its apogee twelve years later in *On Revolution*, her treatise on the American and French Revolutions. Her attack on Robespierre allows her a debunking of Marx too, in whom, Arendt tells us, "the transformation of the Rights of Man into the Rights of the Sans-Culottes" will find its most "brilliant theorist" half a century later.[18] The second chapter of the book is dedicated to the "social question" or what "we may better and more simply call the existence of poverty".[19] When Robespierre declared that everything which is necessary to maintain life must be common good and only the surplus can be recognised as private property, for Arendt he was subjecting the welfare of the people, "to the most irrefragable of all titles, necessity".[20] For her it was necessity, the urgent needs of the people, that unleashed the terror and sent the Revolution to its doom. She cites Jefferson approvingly, when he declared that a people "so loaded with misery would [not] be able to achieve what had been achieved in America".[21] And about John Adams' "conviction" that a free republican government "was as unnatural ... as it would be over elephants, lions, wolves [*et cetera*] in the royal menagerie at Versailles" she proclaims, rather disturbingly, that "years later, events to an extent proved him right".[22]

---

[15] Villa "Introduction" in *Cambridge Companion to Hannah Arendt* 7.

[16] 7.

[17] Compare M Dietz "'The Slow Boring of Hard Boards': Methodical Thinking and the Work of Politics" (1994) 88 *Am Pol Sci Rev* 873 882:
  "Arendt's condition of plurality itself provides the *ethical* dimension that a truly emancipatory politics requires." (Original emphasis).

[18] Arendt *On Revolution* 61.

[19] 60.

[20] 60.

[21] 67.

[22] 68.

Why do the cries of the dispossessed masses not resonate politically; what is it about their movement that "sent the revolution to its doom"?[23] The "transformation of the Rights of Man into the Rights of the Sans-Culottes" Arendt argues, abandons the foundation of freedom to the "powerful conspiracy of necessity and poverty", Robespierre's relentless insistence on the latter forcing him to miss the "historical moment" to "found freedom".[24] Arendt's unreserved admiration for the American Revolution is nowhere thrown into starker contrast with her misgivings about the French Revolution than in these pages on the "social question", and this in the context of the acutest of analyses of Robespierre's claim to speak on behalf of the dispossessed. The guiding distinction that operates here to set up freedom against necessity as involving contrasting logics, is the distinction between *the social as sphere of necessity*, and *the political as sphere of freedom*.

Arendt will make recourse to Marx to explain what it was about the French revolution that imported the element of totalitarianism while claiming to realise freedom. Let me repeat the earlier quote:

> "It took more than half a century before the transformation of the Rights of Man into the Rights of the Sans-Culottes, the abdication of freedom before the dictate of necessity, had found its theorist in Marx."[25]

What a strange formulation this is, couched in a vocabulary of abdication, and thus of a certain refusal of a different route. What, one might pause to ask, does "abdication of freedom" mean for the sans-culottes? What possibility of freedom did the Parisian mob really forego in bringing the "needs of the body"[26] into the streets? Let us leave that question open for the moment and return to Arendt. Marx's genius and ultimately his theoretical error, she says, is that he *read the social question in political terms*. That means that he read the question of *poverty* as a question of the suppression of *freedom*, and the way he achieved this was through the theory of *exploitation*. This allows the connection between the two spheres to be "mediated".

> "Marx's transformation of the social question into a political force is contained in the term 'exploitation', that is in the notion that poverty is the result of exploitation through a 'ruling class' which is in the possession of the means of violence."[27]

> "His most explosive and indeed most original contribution … was that he interpreted the compelling needs of mass poverty in political terms as an uprising, not for the sake of bread or wealth, but for the sake of freedom as well."[28]

His achievement was to conjure up a "spirit of rebelliousness that can spring only from being violated, not from being under the sway of necessity"; and to "persuade them that poverty itself is a political not a natural phenomenon, the result of violence and violation rather than scarcity".[29]

---

[23] 60.

[24] 61.

[25] 61.

[26] As Robespierre formulates them: "dress, food, and the reproduction of the species" in Arendt *On Revolution* 60.

[27] 62.

[28] 62.

[29] 62.

Arendt sets out to prove Marx wrong to have interpreted the "predicament of poverty in categories of oppression and exploitation",[30] by returning to the embeddedness of her own founding distinction, the foundational character of the disconnect. The recovery of the ability to act cannot spring from necessity because the logic of "emancipation" is too rooted in the release of a natural propensity, a problematic for Arendt *becoming-political* in the absence of the preconditions of such action in freedom. It is this absence that drives Marx to attach himself to the Hegelian dialectic in which "freedom would directly rise out of necessity", a dialectic and a coincidence that Arendt has earlier characterised as "perhaps the most terrible and, humanly speaking, least bearable paradox in the body of modern thought".[31] It is unclear why the denunciation is so vehement here but let us retain from it Arendt's unflinching insistence that the two spheres are not and cannot be tied dialectically.

Having repeated her premises, Arendt's rebuttal of Marx becomes fairly cursory. Her first criticism is that he abandons "the revolutionary élan of his youth" to redefine the revolutionary moment in economic terms, which means also the "iron laws of historical necessity", "necessity" again serving to fold the revolutionary moment back into the binarism from which it seemingly can never depart.

Her second criticism is that he "strengthened more that anybody else the politically most pernicious doctrine of the modern age, namely that life is the highest good and that the life process of society is the very centre of human endeavour".[32] With this new emphasis

"the role of revolution is no longer to liberate men from the oppression of their fellow men, let alone to found freedom, but to liberate the life process of society itself from the fetters of scarcity so that it would swell into a stream of abundance. Not freedom but abundance became the new aim of revolution".[33]

This circumvents "oppression" too quickly and unreflectively, given the lengths Arendt went to earlier to argue that Marx deployed "exploitation" to short-circuit precisely these terms (freedom and scarcity), but the message is nonetheless clear, against a displacement of the very aspiration of the political, a falling short that turns out to be a radical undercutting of the logic of political action. To aspire to establish the free association of producers in a classless society and to harness political action to that aspiration, makes the final goal of politics something beyond politics and cancels out plurality, world-making, and the rest, in the process.

We will return to this in part 4. For now, let us retain from her analysis that the French Revolution throws up the social question in its most stark form: as addressing the quest for liberation from the burden of poverty, as a violent demand on the national "household" (*oikos*), and is as such pre-political. It does not express, as Hauke Brunkhorst puts it, "the admirable 'will to freedom'

---

[30] 63.
[31] 57.
[32] 64.
[33] 64.

and political participation that we find in those who are already free of such burdens (such as men of the American Revolution)".[34]

Incidentally only, if this appears a rather odd rendering of Marx, or at least a rather facile turning of the later Marx against his earlier better self, it is because it is that, both odd and facile, based on an impatient misreading that identifies in Marx the "ambition to raise his science to the rank of a natural science".[35] "Incidentally" because the point here is not to defend Marx against Arendt.[36] Rather it is this, which goes to the heart of our discussion and what is staked on the concept of the political.

Arendt famously returns to the flowering of democracy in the Athenian polis to retrieve above all the purity of the public/private dichotomy in order to support and defend the unencumbered public sphere.[37] It is a distinction "the sheer clarity" of which, Villa clarifies, "the Athenian citizen experienced every time he left the household in order to take part in the assembly or the agora".[38] The household (*oikos*), as concerned with "material reproduction", represented the

"part of human life where necessity held sway and where coercion was both unavoidable and legitimate. The public realm on the other hand, was the realm of freedom."[39]

For Marx of course the only "sheer clarity" that the citizen would "experience every time he left the household" would be that of the "robbing of his real life" and its substitution with an "unreal universality", as he famously put it in *On the Jewish Question*.[40] It is remarkable that Arendt is silent about the young Marx's seminal piece, since it addresses precisely her founding distinction. Marx's argument in that piece is that the "political" emancipation of the Rights of Man falls short of "human" emancipation by deploying the distinction between private man and public citizen, subjecting to the realm of the private property relations all the elements of social labour, and thus constitutively undercutting any form of emancipation that engaged him as

---

[34] H Brunkhorst "Equality and Elitism in Arendt" in D Villa (ed) *The Cambridge Companion to Hannah Arendt* (2000) 178 192.

[35] Arendt *On Revolution* 65.

[36] Arendt *On Revolution* 64 states: "The trouble is of a theoretical nature." Marx's economic explanations simply merge violence and necessity together back into the sphere that, properly understood, is on the other side of the political.

[37] Arendt looks to the experience of the Greek polis because "a freedom experienced in the process of acting and nothing else – though, of course, mankind never lost this experience altogether – has never again been articulated with the same classical clarity" (H Arendt *Between Past and Future* (1961) 165). As she puts it in the *Human Condition*:
      "The 'good life', as Aristotle called the life of the citizen ... was 'good' to the extent that having mastered the necessities of sheer life, by being freed from labour and work, and by overcoming the innate urge of all living creatures for their own survival, it was no longer bound to the biological life process. At the root of Greek political consciousness we find an unequalled clarity and articulateness in drawing this distinction. No activity that served only the purpose of making a living, of sustaining only the life process, was permitted to enter the political realm..." (Arendt *The Human Condition* 36-37).

[38] Villa "Introduction" in *Cambridge Companion to Hannah Arendt* 9.

[39] 9.

[40] K Marx *On the Jewish Question* (1843) in D McLellan (ed) *Karl Marx: Selected Writings* (1977) 39 46:
      "Man in the reality that is nearest to him, civil society, is a profane being. Here where he counts for himself and others as a real individual, he is an illusory phenomenon. In the state, on the other hand, ..., he is an imaginary participant in an imaginary sovereignty, he is robbed of his real life and filled with an unreal universality."

a social being in the materiality of his real life. On the one side we have the rights of property, or as Marx puts it in his seminal text, the rights of "egoistic man, separated off from other men and the community",[41] and on the other the "illusory rights of an illusory sovereignty". Arendt's social and political fall neatly on either side of Marx's divide, and his argument about the ideological effects of this displaced manifestation of the political become lost to Arendt; because, if the private/public distinction becomes Arendt's starting point for her phenomenological exercise, it is also the distinction behind which she cannot step without cancelling out that exercise, and with it, as far as Arendt is concerned, the very possibility of the political.

"The more she thought about Marx", summarises Villa, "the more Arendt came to the conclusion that he was no friend of human freedom at all, and that his fundamental ideas and categories had effaced the phenomenal basis of the most basic political experiences, such as debate amongst diverse equals".[42] Note that what is staked on the term *phenomenal* here is the very possibility of appearance, and "effaced" is an interesting term for what might have otherwise appeared. It is Marx's categories that are argued to be doing the "effacing", those "fundamental categories" that constitute the basis of the analysis, including as we saw, collective subjectivity and *species-being*, freedom as emancipation, exploitation as deprivation, and most fundamentally that of social labour as the basis of human association. We will return to this discussion in part 4. For now, let us look, with Arendt, at the "space of appearance" that she draws insightfully from the European philosophical tradition of phenomenology.

3   The phenomenology of the political

"The concern with appearance", as Johan van der Walt puts it in an important recent paper, "the fundamental concern of the tradition of European philosophical inquiry that came to be called *phenomenology*, runs like a constant thread through Hannah Arendt's work".[43] And famously the phenomenology of the political is what breaks into the world as irreducibly plural. In one of the most quoted passages in political theory she says:

"Action, the only activity that goes on directly between men without the intermediary of things or matter, corresponds to the human condition of plurality, to the fact that men, not Man, live on the earth and inhabit the world. While all aspects of the human condition are somehow related to politics, this plurality is specifically *the* condition – not only the *conditio sine qua non*, but the *conditio per quam* – of all political life."[44]

"While all aspects of the human condition are somehow related to politics" is an interesting formulation, though perhaps the "somehow" holds a key and introduces a qualification. Let us leave that question suspended for now to focus instead on the phenomenological thread in Arendt's thought that she clearly adopts from Heidegger. Like him, Arendt avoids the metaphysical

[41]   46.
[42]   Villa "Introduction" in *Cambridge Companion to Hannah Arendt* 7.
[43]   J van der Walt "Law and the Space of Appearance in Arendt's Thought" forthcoming in M Goldoni & C McCorkindale (eds) *Hannah Arendt and the Law* (2012).
[44]   Arendt *The Human Condition* 7.

distinctions between essence and existence, being and becoming, to conceive of freedom not as something that somehow resides in the will, but that which is performed in the world.[45] Key to this freedom-in-action is that it enjoins plurality (or "action-in-concert"), and the political is thus constitutively linked with the initiation of the new, or as Arendt beautifully puts it, the performance of the "infinitely improbable": "the fact that man is capable of action means that that the unexpected can be expected from him".[46] In this, the new breaks into being in moments that exhibit something of the purely constituent.

There are other aspects of Heidegger's influence that can be traced in Arendt's phenomenology of the political, and in that respect one can note: (i) the *disclosive* function of the political working against what is forgotten – a Heideggerian thread in her thought, which is coupled, in Arendt's idiom with natality, spontaneity and the unexpectedness of beginnings; (ii) the situatedness of political action, the fact that we are always in *media res* and that our action seeks its coordinates in situations already in the world. There are no clean slates. We act from the position in which we find ourselves with all the attendant contingencies. There are obvious resonances of Heidegger's "throwness" here. But crucially for Arendt the fact that action is situated in the world does not cancel out its radical potential for newness.

Significantly it is Arendt's point about plurality that is her most valuable and original phenomenological insight. She returns to this argument throughout her oeuvre, that not man but the interaction of men in irreducible diversity, in their plurality, marks the entry point of the political. "To the extent that man in the singular", as Andrew Schaap puts it well, "corresponds to any experience it would be to mere life, a life deprived of public appearance".[47] Man, in the singular, does not cross the threshold of the political.

This is insightful stuff and the power of its imagination goes some way to explaining Arendt's sweeping influence in political theory today. Praxis, natality, world-disclosive activity, acting-out the infinitely improbable, are terms that carry a radical potential for rethinking political thought. But it is a renewal of praxis philosophy in the direction of a distinctly bourgeois philosophy of the public sphere. As this may strike many scholars who have been influenced by Arendt as unfair or sweeping, let me clarify right away what I mean, by means of showing that if it is indeed sweeping, it is because Arendt herself has so raised the stakes. The crucial question she invites us to ask, repeatedly, is this: what are the conditions of thinking the political? If thinking politically depends on what appears, with the help of which distinctions does the "new" break into the world? And the answer that Arendt gives is unwaveringly the same: thinking politically involves its constitutive disconnect from, and unburdening of, the social dimension.

Amongst Arendt scholars there is no disagreement that, as Villa puts it,

---

[45] The analysis in this part owes much to two excellent pieces: Van der Walt's "Law and the Space of Appearance in Arendt's Thought" forthcoming in *Hannah Arendt and the Law*; and Brunkhorst's "Equality and Elitism in Arendt" in *Cambridge Companion to Hannah Arendt* 178.

[46] Arendt *The Human Condition* 158.

[47] A Schaap "Enacting the Right to have Rights: Jacques Ranciére's Critique of Hannah Arendt" (2011) 10 *European J of Political Theory* 22 22.

"Arendt's primary energy is devoted to distinguishing the fundamental experiences and preconditions of the political or public realm from other spheres of life. In *The Human Condition* particularly, Arendt seems obsessed with demarcating the specificity of the political realm in contrast to all others."[48]

"All others" include mainly the social and the personal, and where any possibility of encroachment arises Arendt will excise it with the restatement of the purity of the criteria.

Even amongst her ardent fans, Arendt's relentless exercise in conceptual purity has sometimes drawn some objections, and in the example of her final, controversial essay *Reflections on Little Rock* even some signs of fatigue and despair. In a recent book,[49] Vikki Bell attempts a sympathetic reading of that text which contains Arendt's disturbing critique of the US Supreme Court's 1954 celebrated decision in *Brown* to integrate schools.[50] Bell rightly observes that if Arendt takes the side of the advocates of discrimination, it is because, in her mapping of the political/social/personal, discrimination makes the "social" possible. She comments that freedom to associate and to form groups with whomever one wishes means that discrimination becomes for Arendt a right.

And Bell quotes her:

"Discrimination is as indispensable a social right as equality is a political right."[51]

What is the reason for this? It is because groups form and crystallise around differences, they congeal around preferences, and that proliferation of groups that segregate against others in their pursuit of their preferences in turn undergirds plurality, and therefore politics proper.

Rather than viewing Arendt's trajectory therefore as a progressive endorsement of a conservative US constitutionalism, one might understand *On Revolution* and *Little Rock* as Arendt's fixating on the separateness of spheres (political, social, personal) and the principles proper to them: equality for the political, discrimination for the social, uniqueness for the personal. These principles of differentiation operate as conditions of appearance, and therefore as fundamental and constitutive.

4   Revisiting the "social question"

Our concern, in these discussions, is with poverty and its relationship to politics. It is this fundamental aspect of the "human condition", the imperative to satisfy basic needs, and thus the correlative obligation placed upon our political institutions to deliver a certain threshold of subsistence, that forms a key (and for us here the main) focus of attention. The question that has arisen for us is this: could it be that this, for Arendt, is the wrong *kind* of imperative? Could it be that it falls foul of a *categorical* mistake?

---

[48]   Villa "Introduction" in *Cambridge Companion to Hannah Arendt* 8.

[49]   V Bell *Feminist Imagination: Genealogies in Feminist Theory* (1999).

[50]   The enforced desegregation of schools in the South, Arendt argued, meant depriving parents "of rights which clearly belong to them in all free societies: the private right over their children and the social right to free association". (H Arendt *Reflections on Little Rock* (1959) 55).

[51]   Arendt *Reflections on Little Rock* 53.

The subsumption of politics to economics, as we discussed in part 2 above, is characteristic for Arendt of the inability to preserve the autonomy of politics. Her critique of the welfare state pivots on that distinction. As Villa summarises it:

> "The tendency to interpret political phenomena in accordance with hierarchical models derived from ... the realm of production conspired ... to undercut whatever limited autonomy politics might have had in modern life. Indeed as economic concerns came to dominate the political sphere during the nineteenth and early twentieth centuries, it became increasingly difficult to maintain even the *idea* of a relatively autonomous public realm, one characterized by the debate and deliberation of public-spirited citizens. Arendt confronts the difficulty by ... challenging at every turn our received ideas of what politics is and should be."[52]

The form that the challenge takes, Villa says, is "to excavate and reveal what has been doubly hidden by contemporary experience and inherited categories".[53]

In her critique of the welfare state, Arendt joins a long list of critics from both the Right and the Left, though her angle is perhaps novel. As is well known, while the Right has tirelessly argued that the welfare state is unaffordable, and that it undercuts the labour market by providing labour with exit opportunities in the form of benefits, the radical Left in the 60s and 70s argued that it created a culture of dependency that weakened resistance and undercut working-class militancy. Arendt attacks the welfare state on a more conceptual, if unremarkable level, which Habermas too is quick to take up in his post-*Legitimation Crisis* work, which calls for resistance to the welfare state in the name of the *purity of the political as deliberative*. Undertaken in the guise of a critique of ideology – "to reveal" as Villa writes approvingly above "what has been doubly hidden" – the emancipatory call for an autonomous politics will remain, in Arendt, unsullied by claims to redistribution or support for the weak. Against the penetration of "national household" concerns into the realm of the properly political, what Arendt's clearing exercise aspires to is a call for a genuine politics of plurality and equality, each of these terms in turn cleansed of their contamination by the social to emerge as properly political categories. The phenomenological exercise marks precisely this space of appearance of the political phenomenon *as such*. What is shed in the process are the kind of collective identities that people may have assumed in the workplace, family, neighborhoods, movements, *et cetera*, or – perhaps this is, more charitably, what Arendt means – shed as *constitutive* of political participation, one might say as "points of entry" into the public sphere. Syndicalism for example can only be a pseudo-political form given that it involves, for her, corporate identities which are pre-political in that they are not hammered out in political exchange amongst equals, and undercut genuine plurality in engaging collective actors. Instead, Arendt will proclaim that the hallmarks of the political: *isonomia*, political equality, political life as the *vita activa* of sharing words and deeds establish in an *initiatory*, performative way what it means to share; it does not and cannot rely on inherited, already shared, and thus pre-political forms.

---

[52]   Villa "Introduction" in *Cambridge Companion to Hannah Arendt* 9.
[53]   9.

In parts 2 and 3, we saw how Arendt draws the distinction that increasingly in her theorising became stark, pivotal, resistant, insubordinate to mediation, synthesis and sublation. It is the distinction between the social and the political. It came to lie at the basis of the constitutional question and as foundational to inform not just the remit of the constitutional *but its very possibility*. Because, as foundational, the distinction does not allow us to step behind it, and to put *it* to question *politically*.

Of course the "social question" in Arendt has been the object of criticism, sometimes severe, but it is treated typically as a moment of aberration in the otherwise near-hagiographic treatment that the Academy has reserved for her. Even Hauke Brunkhorst, to my mind one of the most acute of her readers and critics, warns that we "should be somewhat sceptical about certain elements of [her] critique (Arendt's entirely negative view of politics as the quest for social justice, for example) even as we utilize her profounder insights about the nature of politics and freedom".[54]

My argument is that there is a constitutive connection between the two, such that if we are "somewhat sceptical" about her view of social justice, we cannot but remain equally sceptical as to her "profounder insights". Because the clearing exercise that Arendt performs in regard of social justice founds her view of politics and freedom. Arendt's work is above all an ingenious and stubborn exercise at drawing conceptual distinctions which aim to release the new and bring the possibilities of initiatory action into view. What is initiatory depends on what is left behind, and one cannot but remain "somewhat sceptical" if the price for political engagement proper is social justice.

Against the qualifications and the excuses, the bracketing and the apologia, let us dignify Arendt's work by treating the later outputs *as* continuous with the earlier work, or at least let us read her account of the social question in *On Revolution* against her powerful phenomenological theory of the political in the *Human Condition*. If the latter celebrates what breaks into the world as political, what is disclosed and what initiated, one must ask "with the help of what distinctions?" is that effected. Speaking from the phenomenological point of view, disclosure has to be based on a reduction that can be operationalised *because* it cannot be queried. Let us be clear about what are the stakes of the unquestionability of Arendt's guiding social/political distinction.

To return briefly to her attack on the Jacobins: "Since the revolution had opened the gates of the political realm to the poor", she says,

> "this realm had indeed become 'social'. It was overwhelmed by the cares and worries which actually belonged in the sphere of the household and which, even if they were permitted to enter the public realm, could not be solved by political means, since they were matters of administration, to be put into the hands of experts, rather than issues which could be settled by the twofold process of decision and persuasion."[55]

And further:

---

[54] Brunkhorst "Equality and Elitism in Arendt" in *Cambridge Companion to Hannah Arendt* 178-198.
[55] Arendt *On Revolution* 90-91.

"Their [the revolutionaries'] need was violent, and as it were, pre-political; it seemed that only violence could be strong and swift enough to help them."[56]

This dire section of the chapter on the "social question" finds its disturbing culmination in the concluding paragraph where she asserts:

"Nothing we might say today, could be more obsolete than to attempt to liberate mankind from poverty by political means; nothing could be more futile and more dangerous."[57]

Note how the extraordinary analysis of the phenomenology of the constituent event and of the novelty of the concept of beginning of the *Human Condition* winds up as a kind of bourgeois alarmism in *On Revolution* at the prospect of anything like a political claim for redistribution. Significantly Arendt appends the denial of social justice on a meta-political argument. The constitutive severing of the political from the social props it up as autonomous from the vagaries of social encumberment. Phenomenologically speaking, it is the reduction[58] that allows phenomena to appear on a political register. The continuity between the two books, that I claim matters, has to do with how the process where the drawing of distinctions has selectively opened up and simultaneously foreclosed a space for the appearance of the political. What is at stake is the withdrawal of that space of appearance, as in the case where the social demands of recognition and distribution are denied a political register. The denial is then effaced, doubly forgotten, when the very purity of the constitutional question demands that its statement in political terms proper – as condition of freedom – is *its unburdening from the social question*.

We have seen how the political is first enabled in the mapping out through the specific binarisms and the opportunities they sustain. As in ideology's most pervasive move, the enabling move displaces alternatives that are simultaneously occluded and forgotten: forgotten in that their occlusion is what enables the appearance, furnishes the modality of appearance. If freedom cannot be dialectically tied to necessity it is because to retrieve necessity is to deny freedom; it is to fold or collapse the space for the appearance of freedom. There is no political space in which the social question can find political expression because political expression – the realm of the in between, of freedom and the rest – is what necessity *is not*. The effacement is at the level of context, at the level of what opens up meaningfully to perception.

When, in part 2, we looked at Arendt's critique of Marx, we saw how she set out to prove Marx wrong to have interpreted the "predicament of poverty in categories of oppression and exploitation",[59] by returning to the embeddedness of her founding distinction, the foundational character of the disconnect between political and social. Marx's attachment to the Hegelian dialectic in which "freedom would directly rise out of necessity" was for Arendt, as we

---

[56] 91.

[57] 114.

[58] On Edmund Husserl's theory of the "phenomenological reduction" see in particular his *General Introduction to a Pure Phenomenology* (1982).

[59] Arendt *On Revolution* 63.

already saw, "perhaps the most terrible and, humanly speaking, least bearable paradox in the body of modern thought".[60]

But at this juncture, couldn't the tables be turned to suggest that the "least bearable paradox" is perhaps Arendt's, since it involves the disconnection of all that presents itself as *necessary* to men from that which is *at stake* regarding political freedom, and *challengeable* politically? It is a severing that founds the bourgeois public sphere as cleansed of the social, a sphere that makes nonsense of claims to recognition other than the attribution of the status of equal citizen (politically impossible *as a demand* because already granted), that collapses the concept of the political economy, and expels democratic categories from the sphere of production. Out of this disarticulation and severing is the public sphere hoisted, eloquently, radically, gloriously vacuous.[61]

5   Social rights and the social question

I began this chapter with a quandary about the radical separation of the social from the political in South Africa that hollows out equality and makes disempowerment politically un-addressable. But it is perhaps worth noting that the same logic has taken hold across the African continent in the extraordinary mobilisations of the peoples of North Africa and Arab States in Asia. Political exaltation in Egypt has today been replaced by sober disillusionment at the stalling of social reform. What sparked the rebellions was undoubtedly political resistance to the odious dictatorships of the region. Yet it would be deliberately blind to ignore the social pressures that brought the thousands into the squares of Tunis and Cairo: rising food prices, homelessness, massive unemployment across social strata, excessive income polarisation and social dislocation. The exercise of political freedom cannot be disconnected from the social question without making a mockery of revolting peoples' aspirations. Of course, as Perry Anderson puts it, after "decades of police repression and the stamping out of collective organization of any kind amongst the dispossessed", "the vocabulary of revolt could not but concentrate on dictatorship".[62] He adds, however, that "the strategic priority" must be to "fight for the forms of *political* freedom that will allow *social* pressures to find optimal collective expression".[63]

As constitutional lawyers and theorists involved in a discussion of "social rights jurisprudence" we are confronted with the separation between the "social" of *social* rights and the "political" dimension of a *transformative* constitutionalism; the latter committed, like very few other constitutional regimes today, to defending and guaranteeing a level of satisfaction of demands

---

[60]   54.

[61]   On a lighter note, and as Seyla Benhabib relates the story, an exasperated Mary McCarthy put it thus to her friend during a frank exchange at the University of Toronto:

"'[S]peeches can't be just speeches. They have to be speeches about something.' ... At one point or another Arendt had excluded poverty, welfare and housing provisions, procreation, nourishment, family life and even education from the realm of the public, as social or pre-political by nature." (S Benhabib *The Reluctant Modernism of Hannah Arendt* (1996) 155).

[62]   P Anderson "On the Concatenation in the Arab World" (2011) 68 *New Left Review* 1 11.

[63]   11 (own emphasis).

that are elementary conditions of human flourishing or what it means to secure its citizens a life of dignity. As Henk Botha put it recently, "[d]eprivation of basic material needs constitutes an impairment of a person's human dignity as the Constitutional Court was at pains to point out in *Grootboom* and other cases".[64] In his contribution to the proceedings Karl Klare goes even further:

> "A tacit premise of the colloquium that merits explicit statement is that poverty-eradication is not only a desirable policy-direction for South Africa, it is a *constitutional imperative*."[65]

What a remarkable development in legal history; he adds that while "[t]his observation may be trite in South Africa ... it is decidedly novel almost elsewhere in the world".[66] What is the specifically constitutional contribution in this context? It is that the Constitution offers a precise language to conceptualise the imperative and to give expression and sanction to the public sphere in the form of social rights.[67]

I do not want to either deny or belittle this suggested contribution, and I think also that on strategic grounds it makes sense to commit constitutionalism to such a promise and to suggest to judges that they should do their best to live up to it.[68] And so they have, in a number of rightly celebrated decisions. But I also want to suggest that there are limits, sometimes severe, to how far social rights jurisprudence will take us in the direction of securing for South Africa's citizens what is owed to them materially; and to suggest that we need to be sober about those limits if we are to remain aware of what political choices confront us. The severity of those limits has to do with the entrenchment of the social/political divide, in the way that we have seen it developed with Arendt, at the very heart of South Africa's constitutional settlement. With it social equality becomes something separate from political equality. And if we take the latter to find complete expression in the equal distribution of political rights amongst citizens to participate in the political transactions available to them constitutionally, then its fulfilment as constitutive *political* condition pits it against the aspiration of *social* equality. The distinction as harnessed to the logic of the bourgeois public sphere[69] celebrates political empowerment on the back of an indifference to social conditions of engagement, and collapses any notion of equality as adequate to the promotion of dignity. Equality, split down the middle, ceases to do the gathering, rationalising work that would make it the genuine aspiration of the political.

---

[64] H Botha "Equality, Plurality, and Structural Power" (2009) 25 *SAJHR* 17.

[65] K Klare "Concluding Reflections: Legal Activism after Poverty has been Declared Unconstitutional" in S Liebenberg & G Quinot (eds) *Law and Poverty* (2012) 423.

[66] 865-866.

[67] As Klare "Concluding Reflections" in *Law and Poverty* 427 summarises Danie Brand's paper (D Brand "Judicial Deference and Democracy in Socio-Economic Rights Cases in South Africa" in S Liebenberg & G Quinot (eds) *Law and Poverty* (2012) 172):
     "Danie Brand argued that the constitutional vision of democracy embraces the idea that poverty-eradication is not a technical problem for solution by experts and elites but fundamentally a political problem. The implication is that the poor must be actively engaged in the design and implementation of measures to eliminate poverty."

[68] See S Liebenberg *Socio-Economic Rights: Adjudication under a Transformative Constitution* (2010).

[69] What Lenin famously called "the ideal political shell for capitalism" in the first chapter of *The State and Revolution* (1917).

So let us draw from our discussion so far some caution about the potential of a social rights constitutionalism to deliver South Africa from its current predicament and effects of twenty years of neoliberalism. Given the government's political choices and priorities, what redress can a robust social-rights constitutionalism offer and what opportunities of engagement?

I will tentatively sketch three ways in which the transformative potential of social-rights constitutionalism yields to the market. The aim of this exercise is to warn against the ways in which good intentions and energies may fall short of the aspirations of social justice; and to urge that we deploy legal devices *strategically* rather than entrust the delivery of poverty eradication to the aspirations of an inflated paradigm.

The first form of such yielding links to the proliferation of constitutions and, crucially, the distinction between the "economic constitution" and the "political" and "social" constitution(s). It is often in the name of constitutional pluralism that these conceptual lines are drawn, but in any case they replicate Arendt's organising dichotomy between the reproduction of social life in the realms of necessity and need (social), that of the regulation of production and the economy (economic), and the action-in-concert of the purely political. Take the example of the protection of people at work and, crucially, also the protection of their employment as such. If one begins with the *labour market* and allows it to do all the work of allocating value to work and deciding between possible uses of labour, according to market-protective and maximising rules of the *economic* constitution, then the redress of those effects in terms of the *social* constitution comes too late, and the *political* constitution has remained irrelevant throughout. Obviously in order to attain demand and supply equilibria, a labour market must maintain an element of unemployment as structural; no constitutional right to work will ever remedy that. The measure of the "healthy" labour market will dictate what constitutes the threshold of "normality" with, at best, only indirect regard to issues of job satisfaction and fulfilment, the maintenance of some threshold of protection of workers' dignity against new management techniques, job security and career development. The social constitution entrusted with the redress of the effects of profit maximisation can only be mobilised at the extreme end of managerial abuse and remains toothless with regard to the majority of those effects. Alain Supiot refers in this context to what he calls the "Matthew effect",[70] where the very commitment of national economies to political redress of the social costs of globalisation becomes self-defeating because it weakens the state's ability to deliver it. Accordingly those most in need of protection are those most bereft of it, due to the global labour market's flexibility at circumventing the costs of social protection by relocating to cheaper sites. The separation of the economic from the social and the political constitution creates the conditions of a staggering asymmetry between the damage that labour markets wield and the remedies available in terms of social rights jurisprudence. For the Left to seek answers exclusively in the latter is then to once again be wrong-footed by

---

[70] A Supiot *L'esprit de Philadelphie: La justice sociale face au marché total* (2010) 56-57.

theorists of the market who have long argued for entrenching and protecting the sphere of the economic from the regulatory efforts to contain it.

A second argument elevates the same point to a higher level of abstraction to warn against what is so often taken as the inviolable premise of functional differentiation. On the Right such a defence of differentiation draws on the integrity of systems and their distinct logics, on arguments about spontaneous order and the inevitable failures of regulatory states or "command" economies to intervene when they inevitably lack requisite information, the inevitable reduction in complexity and therefore freedom that such intervention would entail, *et cetera*. On the part of those who do not necessarily associate themselves with the Right, the argument has usually been advanced in terms of "spheres of justice", the distinctiveness of which apparently preventing injustices that appear in one sphere from spilling over into another. I have no space to argue my objection fully except to say that that which keeps spheres apart to prevent the spillover of injustice also prevents the kinds of links and overlaps between spheres that make public life and social justice meaningful, in allowing the *political* pursuit of *economic* objectives possible in the name of *social* goals.[71] I have said too much about the constitutive disconnect that Arendt builds her theory on, to repeat it again here. But do we really need reminding that this disconnect is what collapses as meaningless the concepts of the democratic control of the workplace and of production, which dignified political economies in the past and made social-democratic societies humanly functional?

Thirdly, at a more obvious level perhaps, theorists of regulation have developed highly sophisticated accounts of the problematic and multi-faceted articulations of the social, the political and the legal under conditions of heightened complexity. The relevant point here is that under market conditions a constitutional intervention to "alleviate poverty" or even, more modestly, direct the provision of services is highly likely to misfire.

Take for example an early, much quoted, contested and debated article, in which Gunther Teubner introduced the terminology of "reflexive law" in the context of regulatory pathologies of the welfare state.[72] This was still the era of a weakly globalised society, and the problem that occupied sociologists of law working against the neoliberal assumptions that were about to sweep the theoretical as well as the political agenda was how to integrate some of the important insights regarding the separateness and integrity of functional systems in order to salvage something of the steering function of law and its ability to redress distributional injustices and social need. At least that is how I interpret the normative priorities that underlie Teubner's earlier work. The reflexivity of "reflexive law" had a meaning in terms of the "constellation politics/law/regulated field" in which the reflexivity of the law was harnessed to its "performance" as navigating the triad of risks (the "regulatory trilemma"[73]

---

[71] This includes perhaps also Nancy Fraser's three-axis conception of justice, comprising distributive justice, equal recognition, and representation. See N Fraser "Social Exclusion, Global Poverty, and Scales of (In) Justice: Rethinking Law and Poverty in a Globalising World" in S Liebenberg & G Quinot (eds) *Law and Poverty* (2012) 10.

[72] G Teubner "Substantive and Reflexive Elements in Modern Law" (1978) 17 *Law & Society Review* 239.

[73] G Teubner "Juridification" in G Teubner (ed) *Juridification of Social Spheres* (1987) 3 19.

Teubner called it) which faced the legal scientist in her efforts to regulate society: those of "mutual indifference", juridification and regulatory capture. Reflexive law was a suggestion for reciprocal adaptation rather than direct intervention and reflected the anxiety of sociologists of law about the limitations of attempts to deal with social problems through direct enactment of laws.

What at the time appeared perhaps a slightly over-cautious and overly complex theorisation may appear today, under conditions of globalisation, optimistic. I spoke earlier of the regulation of the labour market and the negative effects (the "Matthew effect") that it produces under "total market" conditions.[74] Another example is one much discussed during the colloquium, the recent case of *Mazibuko v City of Johannesburg*,[75] which concerned the sufficiency of the City of Johannesburg's policy relating to the quantum of a free basic water supply.[76] Under the authorship of the World Bank and the tutelage of neoliberal think-tanks water had been priced at "full-cost recovery" by Kader Asmal, in a ruling which, according to Patrick Bond, generated "massive numbers of disconnections, a cholera epidemic, protest riots and illegal reconnections".[77] The problem of water provision was revisited in this important case. And the Court was widely criticised[78] for its narrowing the remit of the "reasonableness review" standard for assessing the positive duties imposed by socio-economic rights that it had set itself in the celebrated line of cases going back to *Grootboom*.[79]

Critics may well be right in criticising the Court for its deferential stance in this case, or for its reluctance to move beyond vague recommendations to the government to "take reasonable steps" to meet its constitutional obligations. I am not in a position to intervene in that debate except to point out the following: that under conditions of privatised or semi-privatised provision, direct intervention is likely to prove counterproductive by imposing increased costs and thus a flight of capital to more productive areas, the result of all of which is likely to be a rise in the cost of the commodity. This pattern is too depressingly familiar, forever repeated across the spectrum dictated by capital's incessant drive to maximise its rate of return. We may of course protest that water is not a commodity,[80] or that the Court should face up honestly to its constitutional mandate. None of this is likely to take us very far, however loud our protestations to the judges that their stance is not robust

---

[74] I have developed this in E Christodoulidis "A Default Constitutionalism? A Disquieting Note on the Many Constitutions of Europe" in K Tuori & S Sankari (eds) *The Many Constitutions of Europe* (2010) 31 31-47.

[75] 2010 4 SA 1 (CC). For an illuminating discussion of the criteria of the "reasonableness review" see G Quinot & S Liebenberg "Narrowing the Band: Reasonableness Review in Administrative Justice and Socio-Economic Rights Jurisprudence in South Africa" in S Liebenberg & G Quinot (eds) *Law and Poverty* (2012) 197.

[76] The Court was requested to consider whether the decision by the City to limit its supply of free basic water to six kilolitres of free water per month to every accountholder in the city was in conflict with the right of access to "sufficient" water in s 27(1)(b) of the Constitution, read with subs (2), or with s 11 of the Water Services Act 108 of 1997.

[77] Bond (2009) *New Left Review* 79.

[78] See a number of contributions to this collection. See also P O'Connell "The Death of Socio-Economic Rights" (2011) 74 *Modern Law Review* 532 550-551.

[79] *Republic of South Africa v Grootboom* 2001 1 SA 46 (CC).

[80] See for example P de Vos "Water is Life (But Life is Cheap)" quoted by O'Connell (2011) *Modern Law Review* 551.

enough. Yielding to the dictates of the market will remain the "solution" to the social question unless a *political* decision is taken either to nationalise the industry[81] or to embark on a programme of radical redistribution.

If there is one argument that I hope to have adequately set out in this chapter it is this: that the "social question" is the political question *par excellence* – political because it has to do with people's *participation* in production, which involves (on any register that might do justice to the dignity of those participating) both the use of democratic categories in the economy, and the shielding of that participation from subsumption to other imperatives. It involves, in other words, the political determination to render key aspects of our participation in social life and social labour irreducible to the logic of price. Analytical exercises that separate the social from the political, the "sphere" of social equality from the "sphere" of political participation, are suspect attempts to sever significant connections and reciprocities. As *metapolitical* moves to draw "proper" boundaries of the social and the political, these exercises are from the point of view of the plight of social justice nothing short of catastrophic for those who find their life-chances increasingly sacrificed to the false necessities of markets.

SUMMARY

In this chapter I argue against the significant structuring effect of the distinction between the political and the social as it informs theories of constitutionalism, and with specific reference to South Africa. The distinction underlies the constitutional separation of political from socio-economic constitutionalism and concerns directly the "social question", or, in other words, the question of poverty. I trace the distinction back to the theory of Hannah Arendt that has been so extraordinarily influential to the conceptualisation of "the political" today. I argue that the distinction political/social is not incidental but instead constitutive of the way in which Arendt offers a phenomenology of the political, on the back, as it were, of the exclusion of the social. I argue that the leverage that this separation offers to the political imaginary comes at a crucial cost, because it diminishes the power of social and economic rights to offer political redress to the continuing devastating effects of poverty in South Africa, and across the countries of the South.

---

[81] I note here the Congress of South African Trade Unions (COSATU) economist Chris Malekane's statement to the South African Chamber of Commerce and Industry, in Johannesburg in August 2011 as quoted in N Bauer "Nationalisation: It's about When, not If, Says Cosatu" *Mail & Guardian Online* (04-08-2011) <http://mg.co.za/article/2011-08-04> (accessed 26-11-2011):

"If business needs certainty on this issue, they should be certain that the ANC is not researching the feasibility of nationalisation – it is researching models of implementation."

While the focus of the discussion was on the mining industry, the model of nationalisation, Malekane is quoted as saying, would not be restricted to the mining sector.

CHAPTER 6

REPRESENTING THE POOR: LAW, POVERTY, AND DEMOCRACY

Henk Botha[*]

1 Introduction

The title of the chapter refers to the representation of the poor. "Representation" is used here to refer to different contexts and institutional settings. First, it denotes the ways in which the interests and viewpoints of the poor are voiced, championed, overlooked and effaced in and through representative legislative bodies.[1] Secondly, it refers to the ways in which courts, through constitutional interpretation and enforcement, affirm and reinforce the rights of the poor to democratic participation and citizenship, or fail to challenge their exclusion from effective democratic representation. The representation of the poor in and through representative institutions and through constitutional litigation and adjudication also touches upon a third meaning, which refers to the portrayal of "the poor" and the construction of their interests in legal and political discourse. This dimension is closely connected to the first two. The scope and meaning assigned to the rights of the poor to democratic representation and participation are, after all, inseparably linked to whether they are portrayed as active citizens or largely passive subjects of state authority.

I consider different judicial constructions of democracy, and ask whether and to what extent these understandings can help reinforce the effective representation of the poor and affirm their rights to democratic citizenship and participation. Conversely, to what extent do these interpretations insulate relations of inequality and subordination from democratic debate and contestation and contribute to the silencing of the poor? The emphasis on judicial understandings of democracy draws attention to the adjudicative setting, and raises questions about the capacity of courts to serve as open democratic spaces in which the meaning of constitutional norms and

---

[*] Thanks to Thabani Matshakaile for research assistance and to the participants in the Law and Poverty Colloquium for valuable suggestions. The chapter also benefited from the incisive comments of an anonymous referee.

[1] Representation, in this sense, is intimately bound up with the claim of democratic states to rest on the consent of the governed or to institute the right of the people to self-government. At the same time, however, it raises questions about distortions in the democratic process, through which the right of the poor to participate in and influence the outcomes of political decisions is substantially diminished.

commitments can be contested.[2] At the same time, however, the topic points beyond the judiciary to legislatures as the primary institutions representing the people and to the people themselves. How is "the people" conceived in constitutional discourse? How is the relationship between the people and their representatives construed? And what are the conditions under which legislative bodies can be said to have made authoritative pronouncements in the name of the people they claim to represent?

Two conflicting conceptions of democracy are juxtaposed in this chapter, which are both derived from the Constitutional Court's jurisprudence. The first can be labelled a dialogic, participatory and pluralistic model of democracy. This model underscores the agency and voice of those traditionally excluded from full citizenship; posits a dialogue between the people and their representatives; and requires the state to take positive steps to secure conditions under which citizens can exercise rights of democratic participation. It also embraces a vision of political equality which is suspicious of laws and practices which may have the effect of insulating social and political power from mechanisms designed to promote democratic accountability, or allowing the wealthy and powerful to pass off their particular interests as the common good. This understanding sets the bar quite high for legislative enactments to qualify as authoritative pronouncements made in the name of the people. It is suspicious of the idea of an identity of the people and their representatives, and assumes an active role for the courts in policing legislative and bureaucratic decisions to ensure that they emanate from inclusive participatory processes and do not impinge on basic norms of democratic accountability and responsiveness. The second conception, by contrast, conceives of democracy in more formal terms as the capacity of duly elected legislatures to enact law within their constitutional area of competence. Between elections, there is little that the people can do to hold their representatives accountable. Moreover, except in the case of a breach of clear, unambiguous constitutional provisions, courts should defer to the democratic legitimacy and institutional competence of the political branches.

The interplay between these two understandings calls for a far more extensive study of the Constitutional Court's jurisprudence than can be undertaken here, as judicial understandings of democracy influence decisions on issues as diverse as access to court, the application of the Bill of Rights to private relations, limitation analysis, remedies, and the substantive meaning of a broad range of constitutional norms such as equality, freedom of

---

[2]   These include questions about the extent to which the courts' actual jurisprudence has secured a space in which the poor can challenge official interpretations of constitutional norms which entrench their continued social, economic and political marginalisation. See, generally, J Dugard & T Roux "The Record of the South African Constitutional Court in Providing an Institutional Voice for the Poor: 1995-2004" in R Gargarella, P Domingo & T Roux (eds) *Courts and Social Transformation in New Democracies: An Institutional Voice for the Poor?* (2006) 107. More theoretical questions relate to the spatial and aesthetic dimensions of adjudication (see W le Roux "From Acropolis to Metropolis: The New Constitutional Court Building and South African Street Democracy" (2001) 16 *SAPL* 139) and to whether the diverse needs and voices of the poor can be adequately represented in the language of the law. Much of the latter debate has centred on the tension between the Constitution's transformative aspirations and the conservatism of South African legal culture. See K Klare "Legal Culture and Transformative Constitutionalism" (1998) 14 *SAJHR* 146.

expression and socio-economic rights. I focus here instead on two areas of the Constitutional Court's jurisprudence. The first deals with public participation in the legislative process, while the second relates to constitutional challenges to the hegemony of political elites who are in a position to use their power and influence to privilege their own particular interests over the public interest. Throughout, the emphasis will be on the ways in which the two conceptions of democracy under consideration relate to the rights, needs and voices of the poor.[3]

2   Public participation in the legislative process

2 1   *Doctors for Life* and *Matatiele II's* promise

In *Doctors for Life International v Speaker of the National Assembly*[4] the Constitutional Court held that the Constitution of the Republic of South Africa, 1996 ("the Constitution") imposes an enforceable obligation on legislatures to facilitate public participation in the legislative process, and that non-compliance with this requirement must result in the constitutional invalidity of the legislation in question. Ngcobo J, writing for the majority, interpreted section 72(1)(a) of the Constitution[5] in view of the right to political participation in international and foreign law and the importance of democratic participation in the struggle against apartheid and under the Constitution.[6] On this construction, it is not enough simply to allow public participation. Parliament is under a positive obligation to ensure that citizens have an effective opportunity to participate in the legislative process. This is to be done through public education, the provision of information, and various other initiatives to bring democracy closer to the people.[7] Although Parliament and the provincial legislatures must be allowed a broad discretion in deciding how best to fulfil this duty in a given case, the Constitutional Court has the power to test whether they afforded the public a reasonable opportunity to participate in the legislative process. What is reasonable will depend on a range of factors, including the nature and importance of the legislation, its impact on the public, its urgency, and Parliament's

---

[3] These are of course not the only areas relating to the political participation of the poor. Other contexts of interest include the participation of the poor in administrative decision-making, their exercise of democratic rights and freedoms (for example freedom of expression, association and assembly) and, indeed, contexts in which political participation occurs outside of the formal opportunities offered by state institutions (for example where alliances, communities or groups seize the political initiative through mass action, protests or petitions). My decision in this chapter to focus on channels of participation relating directly to the logic and mechanisms of representative government does not signal the privileging of "formal" or "state-centred" conceptions of democracy over "informal" or "decentred" understandings of democratic participation. In fact, the chapter's resistance to the reduction of "the people" to a particular institutionalisation (for example "the people" as represented in Parliament) is perfectly consistent with an account of democracy which emphasises the capacity of the people to challenge decisions of their representatives, whether through formal or informal mechanisms.

[4] 2006 6 SA 416 (CC); 2006 12 BCLR 1399 (CC) (*"Doctors for Life"*).

[5] S 72(1)(a) of the Constitution states that
      "[t]he National Council of Provinces must facilitate public involvement in the legislative and other processes of the Council and its committees".

[6] *Doctors for Life International v Speaker of the National Assembly* 2006 6 SA 416 (CC); 2006 12 BCLR 1399 (CC) paras 90-117.

[7] Paras 130-134.

own views on what would be appropriate.[8] Ngcobo J held that the failure of the National Council of Provinces (NCOP) to hold public hearings was unreasonable in relation to two of the four Acts that were being challenged. These two Acts – one of which dealt with the termination of pregnancies and the other with traditional health practitioners – related to controversial matters and were the subject of great public interest. He also emphasised the special role assigned to the NCOP in the legislative process. Since the NCOP is charged with the representation of the provinces in the national sphere of government, the facilitation of public involvement by the National Assembly is no substitute for public participation at the level of the NCOP and/or of the provincial legislatures.[9]

It is instructive to compare this judgment with the dissenting judgment of Yacoob J. Yacoob J's disagreement with the majority turns in part on his use of grammatical and structural modes of interpretation. In his view, the majority judgment conflates "public involvement" with the stronger notion of "public participation",[10] overlooks the fact that section 72(1)(a) requires the NCOP merely to "facilitate" public involvement (which, he insists, is a less exacting requirement than to "promote" involvement),[11] and misses the significance of the fact that section 72(1)(a) does not form part of the constitutional provisions relating to the legislative process.[12] His insistence that it is the Court's task to determine what the Constitution requires, and not to engage in theoretical speculation about the meaning of "democracy" or the ideal balance between its representative and participatory dimensions, is consistent with the textualist leaning of his judgment.[13] However, the disagreement between the majority and minority judgments ultimately turns on more than differences in interpretive methodology. Yacoob J's interpretation of the constitutional text is informed by a particular understanding of democracy, in which the decisions of elected representatives are seen as identical with the will of the people. In the absence of a clear and unambiguous constitutional requirement of public participation in the legislative process, judicial enforcement of a "right" to political participation would "undermine the political will of the people" and "negate their choice at free and fair elections".[14] Such "failure to accord due weight to the actions and decisions of the representatives of the people of South Africa would demean the very struggle for democracy"[15] and impact fundamentally on "the value of the right to vote acquired through bitter struggle".[16]

In this vision, there is a perfect identity of the people and their representatives, which is secured through the expression of the will of the people during free and fair elections. This unity or identity is bolstered through

---

[8]   Paras 118-129, 145-146.
[9]   Paras 79-88.
[10] Paras 308-312.
[11] Paras 303-307.
[12] Paras 315-318.
[13] Para 269.
[14] Para 292.
[15] Para 294.
[16] Para 319.

a variety of mechanisms designed to give effect to the constitutional values of accountability, responsiveness and openness. However, such mechanisms must either be rooted directly and unambiguously in the Constitution or in the decisions of the people's representatives, and must not be judicially imposed on legislative majorities. Judicial imposition of a requirement of public participation would disturb the direct and "uninterrupted chain of legitimacy" running from the people to their representatives,[17] and would thus demean the value of the right to vote.

Where Yacoob J sees unity and identity, Ngcobo J in his majority judgment perceives a certain distance between the people and their representatives. The people, in his view, did not confer absolute authority on their representatives, but "reserved for themselves part of the sovereign legislative authority that they otherwise delegated to the representative bodies they created".[18] This residue of the people's originary power precludes representative bodies from making totalising claims in the name of the people. Far from having an absolute claim to represent the people, based on the latter's participation in elections every five years, representative institutions need to strengthen their legitimacy through an ongoing dialogue with the people who elected them. On this view, the right to vote is an important, but by no means the only institutionalisation of the right to political participation.[19] Other forms of democratic participation help provide vitality to representative institutions and enhance the civic dignity of participants. They also counter the disproportionate effects of private wealth and power in the legislative process. Ngcobo J states that public participation

"because of its open and public character acts as a counterweight to secret lobbying and influence peddling. Participatory democracy is of special importance to those who are relatively disempowered in a country like ours where great disparities of wealth and influence exist."[20]

For these reasons, participatory democracy has an important role to play in promoting political equality and integrating the marginalised and poor into the democratic community.[21]

---

[17] The phrase is borrowed from E-W Böckenförde "Demokratische Willensbildung und Repräsentation" in J Isensee & P Kirchhof (eds) *Handbuch des Staatsrechts der Bundesrepublik Deutschland Bd III* 3 ed (2004) 31 38.

[18] *Doctors for Life International v Speaker of the National Assembly* 2006 6 SA 416 (CC); 2006 12 BCLR 1399 (CC) para 110.

[19] Para 98.

[20] Para 115.

[21] See paras 171, 174 on the importance of adequate consultation with traditional healers, particularly in view of their previously marginalised status. See also the concurring judgment of Sachs J para 234:
   "Public involvement will also be of particular significance for members of groups that have been the victims of processes of historical silencing. It is constitutive of their dignity as citizens today that they not only have a chance to speak, but also enjoy the assurance they will be listened to. This would be of special relevance for those who may feel politically disadvantaged at present because they lack higher education, access to resources and strong political connections."

In *Matatiele Municipality v President of the Republic of South Africa (2)*[22] the constitutionality of the Constitution Twelfth Amendment Act of 2005 and the Cross-Boundary Municipalities Laws Repeal and Related Matters Act 23 of 2005 was at issue. The effect of this legislative package was, *inter alia*, that the Matatiele Municipality was removed from the province of KwaZulu-Natal and incorporated into the Eastern Cape. This triggered section 74(8) of the Constitution, which requires a constitutional amendment which alters the provincial boundaries of a particular province or provinces to be approved by the legislature[s] of the province[s] concerned. While the Eastern Cape Legislature did hold public hearings, the KwaZulu-Natal Legislature approved the constitutional amendment without facilitating public involvement. Ngcobo J in his majority judgment rejected the contention that it was not necessary to facilitate public consultation as the legislature was speaking on behalf of the people of the province. The Constitution, in his view, does not unquestioningly assume the identity of the people and their representatives, but envisages "a dialogue between the elected representatives of the people and the people themselves".[23]

The majority advanced a number of reasons for holding that the provincial legislature's conduct fell short of section 118(1)(a) of the Constitution, which requires a provincial legislature to facilitate public involvement in its legislative and other processes. Chief among these was the impact of the legislation on the community of Matatiele. Their emotional attachment to KwaZulu-Natal, their right to live in the province of their choice and the practical significance of the move for service delivery militated against the idea that their relocation to the Eastern Cape could be effected without proper consultation. The conclusion that they should have been afforded an opportunity to make submissions was also supported by other considerations. These include: the fact that they were "a discrete and identifiable section of the population";[24] the unique nature of the provincial power to veto constitutional amendments and its centrality to the constitutional scheme;[25] and the fact that both the NCOP and the KwaZulu-Natal Legislature considered public hearings to be desirable.[26]

The reasoning in *Doctors for Life* and *Matatiele II* seems particularly promising when viewed from the perspective of the representation of the poor and other vulnerable groups. This is so for at least four reasons. First, these judgments emphasise the agency and voice of those traditionally excluded from democratic citizenship. Far from being viewed as helpless victims, the poor are regarded as bearers of fundamental human dignity who are entitled

---

[22] 2007 1 BCLR 47 (CC) ("*Matatiele II*"). The legislative package was originally challenged on the basis that Parliament had usurped the powers of the Municipal Demarcation Board to re-determine municipal boundaries. In *Matatiele Municipality v President of the Republic of South Africa (1)* 2006 5 SA 47 (CC); 2006 5 BCLR 622 (CC) ("*Matatiele I*") this challenge was rejected. However, although the point was not relied on by the applicants, the Court directed the parties to make submissions on whether the KwaZulu-Natal Provincial Legislature was obliged to facilitate participation, and if so, whether it had complied with this obligation.

[23] *Matatiele Municipality v President of the Republic of South Africa (2)* 2007 1 BCLR 47 (CC) para 58.

[24] Para 79.

[25] Paras 46-48.

[26] Paras 76-78.

to participate in processes of collective decision-making. Secondly, this jurisprudence does not content itself with a merely abstract understanding of the opportunity to participate in democratic processes, but requires the state to take positive steps to secure conditions under which citizens – including the poor and marginalised – can exercise rights of democratic participation. Thirdly, because the judgments in question resist assumptions about the unity of the citizenry or the identity of the electorate and their representatives, they are less prone to subsuming the needs and interests of the poor under vague notions of the "common interest". One-size-fits-all solutions imposed from above do not sit well with the Court's emphasis on the particularity of needs and the distinctness of the voices of those affected. Finally, these judgments rest upon a conception of political equality which is inconsistent with the capacity of the wealthy and powerful to pass off their private interests as the public interest or to insulate their power and influence from mechanisms designed to promote democratic accountability. The right to public participation vests in every person affected by a decision, regardless of her income or social status. It can therefore be expected to play an important role in countering private power and influence, and ensuring that a broader range of interests and viewpoints – including those of the marginalised and poor – are heard.

Subsequent to these two judgments, the theme of public participation has also made its influence felt in other contexts. The state has been required to engage meaningfully with individuals and communities affected by intrusive forms of government action such as evictions.[27] In these cases, too, the Court has emphasised the agency and voice of the poor and has treated them as equal participants in a constitutional dialogue involving the state, land owners and poverty-stricken communities.[28] The Court has also held that the President's failure to afford victims an opportunity to participate in proceedings concerning the possible pardoning of individuals claiming to have been convicted of offences committed with a political motive was irrational and hence unconstitutional.[29]

---

[27] See *Occupiers of 51 Olivia Road, Berea Township v City of Johannesburg* 2008 5 BCLR 475 (CC) and *Residents of Joe Slovo Community, Western Cape v Thubelisha Homes* 2009 9 BCLR 847 (CC) on the requirement of meaningful engagement in eviction cases. See also *Beja v Premier of the Western Cape* 2011 3 All SA 401 (WCC), where the City of Cape Town failed to adhere to the National Housing Code's community participation requirements and the "agreement" between the City and the residents for the installation of unenclosed toilets was found to be neither valid nor enforceable.

[28] In an earlier case concerning an application for the eviction of occupiers from privately owned land, Sachs J declared that
"those seeking evictions should be encouraged not to rely on concepts of faceless and anonymous squatters automatically to be expelled as obnoxious social nuisances. Such a stereotypical approach has no place in the society envisaged by the Constitution; justice and equity require that everyone is to be treated as an individual bearer of rights entitled to respect for his or her dignity. At the same time those who find themselves compelled by poverty and landlessness to live in shacks on the land of others, should be discouraged from regarding themselves as helpless victims, lacking the possibilities of personal moral agency. The tenacity and ingenuity they show in making homes out of discarded material, in finding work and sending their children to school, are a tribute to their capacity for survival and adaptation. Justice and equity oblige them to rely on the same resourcefulness in seeking a solution to their plight and to explore all reasonable possibilities of securing suitable alternative accommodation or land." (*Port Elizabeth Municipality v Various Occupiers* 2005 1 SA 217 (CC); 2004 12 BCLR 1268 (CC) para 41).

[29] *Albutt v Centre for the Study of Violence and Reconciliation* 2010 3 SA 293 (CC); 2010 5 BCLR 391 (CC).

2 2 *Merafong* and *Poverty Alleviation Network*'s rider

The duty of provincial legislatures to facilitate public involvement in relation to constitutional amendments which affect the boundaries of a specific province or provinces also came up in *Merafong Demarcation Forum v President of the Republic of South Africa*.[30] The legislation in question abolished cross-boundary municipalities and transferred the part of Merafong which had formerly formed part of Gauteng to North West. From the outset, the proposed amendment gave rise to vehement opposition. Against the background of mass protests and calls for a public hearing, the Gauteng Provincial Legislature held a joint public hearing with the North West Legislature. After the conclusion of the hearing, the relevant portfolio committee of the Gauteng Legislature adopted a written negotiating mandate which detailed the reasons for the community's opposition. The mandate mirrored the community's demands. It supported the phasing out of cross-border municipalities, and recommended the inclusion of the municipal area of Merafong in Gauteng. When this mandate was presented to the Select Committee of the NCOP, the latter's legal advisors pointed out that it was not competent for the Gauteng Provincial Legislature to propose amendments to the Bill in question. Three days later, the portfolio committee reversed its original decision and authorised its delegation to the NCOP to vote in favour of the Bill. The Bill was passed, and Merafong was incorporated into North West.

The majority of the Court rejected the applicants' contention that the Gauteng Provincial Legislature had failed to facilitate public involvement. Van der Westhuizen J pointed out that, while the legislature was constitutionally obliged to be open to the views expressed by the public, they were not bound by them.[31] In his view, the fact that the provincial legislature changed its line after consulting with the NCOP does not suggest that the public meeting was a mere charade, or that the incorporation of Merafong into North West was always a done deal. The legislature was open to persuasion by the views of the community, as reflected in its negotiating mandate, and there is no evidence that the reversal of that position in the final voting mandate points to a lack of good faith. Moreover, the legislature's failure to inform the community that it was no longer possible to adhere to the position taken in the negotiating mandate was "possibly disrespectful",[32] but not unreasonable. Another round of public consultation would have served little or no purpose, as it was unlikely that either the legislature or the community would be swayed by the other's arguments. The judge also rejected the argument that the legislature's decision was irrational, and found that it was not based on a mistaken understanding

---

[30] 2008 5 SA 171 (CC); 2008 10 BCLR 968 (CC) (*"Merafong"*).

[31] "Government certainly can be expected to be responsive to the needs and wishes of minorities or interest groups, but our constitutional system of government would not be able to function if the Legislature were bound by these views. The public participation in the legislative process, which the Constitution envisages, is supposed to supplement and enhance the democratic nature of general elections and majority rule, not to conflict with or even overrule or veto them." (Para 50).

[32] Para 55.

of its powers or responsibilities under the Constitution or of the consequences of a legislative veto.[33]

Only one of the judges held that the provincial legislature had acted in breach of its constitutional obligation to facilitate public consultation. Sachs J found that its failure to go back to the community and explain its about-turn was unreasonable in view of the nature of the legislation, its potentially drastic impact on the community and the expectations created by the recommendations of the Municipal Demarcation Board and the adoption of the negotiating mandate. It slighted the civic dignity of the people of Merafong and created the perception that the consultation process was a sham.[34] The Court was more evenly split on the question whether the legislature had acted irrationally. Moseneke DCJ, in a dissent concurred in by three other judges, held that the legislature had laboured under a fundamental misconception of its powers under section 74(8). It appeared to believe that its exercise of the veto power would result in the withdrawal of the entire amendment Bill and a consequent return to a system of cross-boundary municipalities. This, stated Moseneke DCJ, was clearly incorrect, as the province only had a veto over changes to its specific boundaries. Its exercise of the veto would therefore not prevent the abolition of cross-border municipalities, and would be perfectly consistent with its stated objectives of phasing out cross-border municipalities and preventing the incorporation of Merafong into North West. The legislature's about-turn was accordingly not in pursuance of a legitimate objective and was therefore irrational.[35]

A fourth case arose from the legislative response to the *Matatiele II* judgment. Legislation (including a constitutional amendment) providing for the incorporation of Matatiele in the Eastern Cape was adopted anew, this time after a fairly extensive process of public consultation at the national and provincial levels. In *Poverty Alleviation Network v President of the Republic of South Africa*,[36] the Constitutional Court held unanimously that the relevant legislative bodies had complied with their constitutional obligation to facilitate public consultation. The Court rejected the contention that the consultation facilitated by Parliament and the KwaZulu-Natal Legislature was a sham, and pointed out that the applicants' submissions had been discussed during the deliberations of the portfolio committees and that a report on issues relating to service delivery had been compiled. A challenge based on the alleged irrationality of the decision was also dismissed.

2 3   Reassessment

The judgments in *Merafong* and *Poverty Alleviation Network* raise several questions. Do these judgments stand for the proposition that legislative majorities are free to push through their party-political agendas, provided that they first go through the motions of public consultation? Do they signal a return

---

[33] Paras 62-115.
[34] Paras 292-298.
[35] See paras 166-192.
[36] 2010 6 BCLR 520 (CC) (*"Poverty Alleviation Network"*).

to the more deferential approach that characterised the Court's political rights jurisprudence prior to *Doctors for Life* and *Matatiele II*?[37] Do they renege on the promise of those two cases, and revert back to a thinner conception of democracy that has relatively little to say to the struggles of the poor and destitute to overcome their economic, social and political marginalisation?

These questions may appear rather too harsh. After all, there is nothing in *Doctors for Life* or *Matatiele II* that suggests that legislatures are bound by the views expressed during rounds of public consultation. The reasoning in *Merafong* and *Poverty Alleviation Network* seems consistent with the insistence in those two cases that legislatures must be allowed a broad margin of discretion in deciding how best to facilitate public consultation. It also seems consistent with the idea, reiterated in numerous cases, that judges inquiring into the rationality of exercises of public power are not to substitute their own views on policy issues for those of the relevant authorities. Once meaningful public consultation has taken place, a court must respect the legislature's power to make a final, binding decision, as long as that decision is rational.

Indeed, one should not be too quick to conclude, simply on the basis of the outcomes of these cases, that the Court has reverted to a shallow conception of democracy and an overly deferential posture which has little to offer the poor. The value of public participation cannot and should not be reduced to the question whether participants were able to convince the legislature of their views. Even when measured in purely instrumental terms, public participation may be of value in cases in which the participants' views ultimately did not carry the day. Neither in *Merafong* nor in *Poverty Alleviation Network* can it be said that the communities' concerns over service delivery fell on deaf ears. In *Merafong* the portfolio committee proposed, in their report to the Gauteng Provincial Legislature, a service delivery audit on the basis of which recommendations would be made to North West Province. And in *Poverty Alleviation Network*, a report on service delivery issues was compiled on the basis of the community's inputs. Therefore, even in cases where the legislature is not swayed by the inputs of communities and groups, the latter's participation in public processes of engagement may help raise public and legislative awareness of their needs and concerns, and may provide occasion for further democratic engagement and mobilisation.

And yet, it is hard to shake the feeling that, in these cases, the vision of democracy articulated in *Doctors for Life* and *Matatiele II* has either been diluted or has stumbled upon its own limits. In the first place, the majority judgment of Van der Westhuizen J (who was one of the dissenters in the two earlier cases) in *Merafong* rests on assumptions that are hard to square

---

[37] See the discussion of *United Democratic Movement v President of the RSA* 2002 11 BCLR 1179 (CC) in part 3 below. It must, however, be pointed out that not all the earlier decisions were informed by a shallow conception of democracy. Important precursors to the deeper understanding of democracy articulated in *Doctors for Life International v Speaker of the National Assembly* 2006 6 SA 416 (CC); 2006 12 BCLR 1399 (CC) and *Matatiele Municipality v President of the Republic of South Africa (2)* 2007 1 BCLR 47 (CC) include the minority judgments of O'Regan J and Sachs J in *Democratic Alliance v Masondo* 2003 2 SA 413 (CC); 2003 2 BCLR 128 (CC); and *Minister of Health v New Clicks SA (Pty) Ltd* 2006 2 SA 311 (CC); 2006 1 BCLR 1 (CC) (see particularly paras 111-113 and the judgment of Sachs J).

with the depth of the vision of democracy embraced in *Doctors for Life* and *Matatiele II*. Consider, for instance, his argument that a further round of public consultation would serve little purpose – beside showing courtesy to the inhabitants of Merafong – as it was unlikely that the parties would be able to reach a common understanding. This argument is surprising in view of his conclusion that it could not be proved that the provincial legislature's reversal of its original decision was "directly or indirectly influenced by previously formulated policies of the ruling party".[38] Seeing that the legislature offered no cogent explanation for its sudden about-turn and since the judge rejected the contention that the change was dictated by political superiors, it is not clear how he could be so certain that the legislature would not be open to ideas that might result from a new round of consultation. One possible explanation is proffered: the effect of an exercise of the legislative veto would be that the municipality of Merafong would be split into two, one falling in Gauteng and the other in North West. This was apparently not what either the community or the legislature had envisaged. In view of this reality, the judge seems to suggest, there was not much to discuss – the legislature simply had to choose between two options, one of which would result in the bigger part of Merafong remaining in Gauteng, while the other would bring about the relocation of the entire municipality to North West.

The judgment assumes that participation primarily has instrumental value as a means to the coordination of conflicting interests or as a mechanism to bolster the legitimacy of laws in the eyes of the people. Where participation in the legislative process cannot reasonably be expected to forge consensus among legislative majorities and members of the public, the legislature is not obliged to report back to the community or to initiate a further round of public consultation in cases in which it has reversed its original decision. Where, as here, the positions of the legislature and general public appear irreconcilable, a further round of consultation would serve little or no purpose. This reasoning makes sense if we accept the judgment's assumption that democratic deliberation consists in arm's-length transactions between rational actors each seeking to maximise their own interests. There are, however, good reasons to be wary of this understanding of democracy. For one, this vision of democracy is far from uncontested. There is a tradition in democratic theory that is critical of the reduction of the political process to the coordination of conflicting interests and insists that democratic participation has an expressive and constitutive value that cannot be captured in purely instrumental terms.[39] In this view, it is through political participation that citizens become aware of their mutual dependence, learn to respect each other's viewpoints and, through their deliberations about the common good, engage on a path of moral self-discovery which may give rise to a reconsideration of their private beliefs and perceptions of their own interests. For another, this second vision

---

[38] *Merafong Demarcation Forum v President of the Republic of South Africa* 2008 5 SA 171 (CC); 2008 10 BCLR 968 (CC) para 50.

[39] See J Habermas *Between Facts and Norms* (1996) 18-19 on the distinction between communicative and strategic action; and D Held *Models of Democracy* 3 ed (2006) on the distinction between theories viewing democracy as an end in itself and those seeing it as a means to the end of securing private freedom.

of democratic deliberation resonates with the deliberative and participatory stands in the South African Constitution[40] and with the reasoning in *Doctors for Life* and *Matatiele II*, which posits a dialogue between citizens and their representatives. That this dialogue does not simply have instrumental value and is not premised solely on the idea of arm's-length negotiations between self-interested actors is clear from the judgment of Ngcobo J in *Doctors for Life*, which emphasises that public participation enhances the civic dignity of participants and "promotes a spirit of democratic and pluralistic accommodation".[41]

The majority judgment of Van der Westhuizen J in *Merafong* vividly illustrates the limits of an instrumental vision of democracy. His judgment apparently views public consultation as a one-off event and is unconcerned with building more lasting forms of civic engagement and trust.[42] It is blind to the possibility that democratic deliberation could persuade political actors to reconsider their perceptions of their own interests or open up novel ways of seeing and thinking about the problem.[43] It is fixated on established institutions, and finds it hard to conceive of the possibility that political contestation and struggles outside these institutions could have a significant bearing on the democratic character of the law. Ultimately, this construction of the legislature's duty to facilitate participation does little to challenge or interrupt a merely formal conception of democracy as the capacity of duly elected legislatures to enact law within their constitutional area of competence. In fact, it is perfectly congruent with it.

Secondly, the facts in *Merafong* and *Poverty Alleviation Network* draw attention to the power of the ruling party to instruct its members how to vote. In both these cases, the Court dismissed claims that ANC legislators were under instructions from the party and were therefore not open to be persuaded by the public's views. In *Merafong*, it was held that it was "not possible to determine whether and to what extent the final voting mandate and the debate in the NCOP Select Committee were directly or indirectly influenced by previously

---

[40] A number of authors have argued that the South African Constitution envisages a heterogeneous public sphere in which democratic participation is an end in itself and the public interest cannot and should not be reduced to the sum of private interests. See, for example, AJ van der Walt "Un-Doing Things with Words: The Colonisation of the Public Sphere by Private-Property Discourse" in G Bradfield & D van der Merwe (eds) *"Meaning" in Legal Interpretation* (1998) 235; H Botha "Civic Republicanism and Legal Education" (2000) 41 *Codicillus* 23; Le Roux (2001) *SAPL* 139; K van Marle "Lives of Action, Thinking and Revolt – A Feminist Call for Politics and Becoming in Post-Apartheid South Africa" (2004) 19 *SAPL* 605; J van der Walt *Law and Sacrifice: Towards a Post-Apartheid Theory of Law* (2005).

[41] *Doctors for Life International v Speaker of the National Assembly* 2006 6 SA 416 (CC); 2006 12 BCLR 1399 (CC) para 115.

[42] Sachs J implicitly levels this critique against the majority when he states, in relation to the legislature's failure to explain its decision to the community:

"Arms-length democracy is not participatory democracy, and the consequent and predictable rupture in the relationship between the community and the Legislature tore at the heart of what participatory democracy aims to achieve." (*Merafong Demarcation Forum v President of the Republic of South Africa* 2008 5 SA 171 (CC); 2008 10 BCLR 968 (CC) para 300).

[43] One would have expected a new round of consultation not only to create a better understanding on the part of residents of the reasons for the legislature's change of mind, but also to provide some insight into the community's views on the possible division of Merafong into two municipalities falling in two separate provinces. It is even conceivable that a clearer understanding of the options available to the legislature under the Constitution might crystallise in the course of such consultation, or that new political alliances might be forged or alternative strategies be devised.

formulated policies of the ruling party".[44] And in *Poverty Alleviation Network*, the rationality challenge was brushed off with reference to the distinction between the purpose of the legislation and Parliament's motives in enacting it. It was held that while the court can test for rationality, it is not in a position to inquire into the motives of legislators.[45] These judgments raise questions about the capacity of the Court's jurisprudence to respond to situations in which an open-minded consideration of inputs is precluded by the hegemony of particular interests masquerading as the ruling party's understanding of the public interest. It is to these issues that I now turn.

3 Keeping private interests at bay

Allegations that a political party or parties have used their numerical majority to introduce legislation to cement their own position or to shield politicians or officials from oversight by the legislature or independent institutions, have featured in a number of cases. In *United Democratic Movement v President of the RSA*,[46] the Constitutional Court considered the constitutionality of legislation (including a constitutional amendment) which allowed members of legislatures at the national, provincial and local government levels to cross the floor to another party without losing their seats. The Court rejected the contention that the legislation, which was triggered by a split in the Democratic Alliance, undermined the basic structure of the Constitution, was inconsistent with the idea of multiparty democracy as entrenched in section 1 of the Constitution, or violated the constitutional right to vote. The Court's restrictive understanding of democracy and failure to give content to "multiparty democracy" have been widely criticised. Its rejection of the argument that a system of proportional representation requires an anti-defection clause[47] and its finding that the 10% threshold, which made it considerably easier to defect from smaller parties than from larger ones did not result in the unconstitutionality of the legislation,[48] appear to rest on the premise that the courts will generally defer to the electoral scheme devised by Parliament, and will intervene only in cases where it is in clear and direct conflict with the Constitution. This, together with its insistence that between elections, "voters have no control over the conduct of their representatives",[49] raises questions over the depth of the Court's understanding of democracy and over the capacity of its jurisprudence to help secure conditions in which representatives can be held accountable by the electorate.

Subsequent judgments have shown a somewhat richer and more nuanced understanding of "multiparty democracy". The concurring judgment of Sachs J in *Democratic Alliance v Masondo*[50] – a case concerning the

---

[44] *Merafong Demarcation Forum v President of the Republic of South Africa* 2008 5 SA 171 (CC); 2008 10 BCLR 968 (CC) para 50.
[45] *Poverty Alleviation Network v President of the Republic of South Africa* 2010 6 BCLR 520 (CC) para 73.
[46] 2002 11 BCLR 1179 (CC) ("*UDM*").
[47] Paras 28-35.
[48] Paras 46-47.
[49] Para 49.
[50] 2003 2 SA 413 (CC); 2003 2 BCLR 128 (CC).

question whether opposition parties are entitled to representation on mayoral committees – evinces a strong commitment to a pluralistic and deliberative democracy, and shows sensitivity to the intersections and tensions between deliberation and majority rule and between inclusivity and effective service delivery. And in *African Christian Democratic Party v The Electoral Commission*,[51] the Court preferred an interpretation of a legislative provision which promoted multiparty democracy and citizens' political rights over a more restrictive interpretation. Whether the Court's sensitivity in these cases to democratic participation, inclusivity and citizenship signals a greater willingness to subject measures to rigorous scrutiny which are purportedly aimed at upholding the hegemony of a particular party or parties, or insulating party bosses from accountability is, however, uncertain.[52]

If that is indeed the case, the message was apparently lost on the Cape High Court in *IDASA v African National Congress*.[53] In that case it was held that political parties are private bodies in relation to their fundraising activities. Applications for access to their fundraising records in terms of the Promotion of Access to Information Act 2 of 2000 can, as a result, only succeed if the applicants can show that they reasonably require the information in order to exercise their rights. In the view of the Court, section 19 of the Constitution does not confer a right to the disclosure of political parties' sources of funding. The applicants were accordingly not entitled to access these records. The judge noted, however, that the applicants had made out a "compelling case" in favour of the need for specific legislation to regulate the disclosure of private donations to political parties.[54] Although he is right that the legislature would be better equipped than the courts to deal with the complexity of these issues, one cannot help but feel that an important opportunity was lost for establishing the principle that political parties, which occupy such a central role and wield so much public power in a list system of proportional representation, are constitutionally required to conduct themselves in an open, responsive and transparent manner. The finding that parties do not act as public bodies when receiving private funding is particularly ironic. It is precisely the "fluidity" and "permeability" of the distinction between their "public" and "private" functions[55] which make it imperative to require political parties to disclose their sources of funding, as corruption, nepotism and secret lobbying thrive in that grey area between public power and private influence. To hold that they act in a private capacity when

---

[51] 2006 5 BCLR 579 (CC). The Court held that the ACDP had complied with a requirement in the Local Government: Municipal Electoral Act 27 of 2000 that a party contesting an election must submit a deposit to the IEC's local representative in circumstances where the party, not having submitted a deposit to the local office in Cape Town, requested the IEC to allocate a surplus payment made by it as a deposit for the Cape Town Metro. But see also *Electoral Commission v Inkatha Freedom Party* 2011 9 BCLR 943 (CC). The Court distinguished the facts from those in *ACDP*, and held that the requirement that election documentation be submitted at the local office of the IEC served a central and significant legislative purpose and helped maintain the integrity of the electoral process.

[52] See G Quinot "Snapshot or Participatory Democracy? Political Engagement as Fundamental Human Right" (2009) 25 *SAJHR* 392 for a critique of the courts' fixation on the act of voting and neglect of the democratic processes leading up to and underpinning elections.

[53] 2005 10 BCLR 995 (C).

[54] Para 58.

[55] Para 29.

receiving funding is to submit rather meekly to the power of private interests to determine, twist and distort the public interest.

A recent judgment of the Constitutional Court has been hailed by some as an important victory for the rights of the poor. In *Glenister v President of the Republic of South Africa*,[56] the Court held that the independence of the Directorate for Priority Crime Investigation (DPCI) was not adequately safeguarded. To that extent, the impugned legislation was in violation of the state's constitutional obligation to establish and maintain an independent anti-corruption entity. In their majority judgment Moseneke DCJ and Cameron J relied on section 7(2) of the Constitution, which obliges the state to "respect, protect, promote and fulfil" the rights in the Bill of Rights, to construe a positive state duty to create an effective and integrated anti-corruption strategy. Viewing this duty through the prism of section 39(1)(b), which states that a court interpreting the Bill of Rights "must consider international law", they concluded on the basis of a range of international conventions and agreements acceded to by South Africa that it includes the obligation to establish an anti-corruption unit that is sufficiently independent. The legislation in question fell short of this requirement in several respects. Members of the DPCI enjoyed no special security of tenure, and a ministerial committee was given the power to issue policy guidelines and to oversee the DPCI's functioning. In the judges' view, these features created a real risk of political influence on investigations, which compromised the capacity of the DPCI to act fearlessly and independently, particularly in high profile cases involving senior politicians and government officials.

The judgment has drawn sharp criticism. Ziyad Motala has lashed out at the majority: in his view, their judgment takes leave of the constitutional text and accepted canons of interpretation, makes questionable use of international law, and usurps Parliament's policymaking function. In the absence of clear constitutional guidelines on the institutional home of and lines of command within the anti-corruption unit, the Court ought to have respected the legislature's decision to locate it within the Department of Police.[57] These sentiments are echoed in statements by President Zuma[58] and Gwede Mantashe. Mantashe warned that judgments like *Glenister* "cast aspersions on the work of Parliament", involve the Court in the "political weighting of views", and

---

[56] 2011 3 SA 347 (CC); 2011 7 BCLR 651 (CC) ("*Glenister*"). There was a narrow five/four split between the majority and minority. In his dissenting judgment, Ngcobo J held *inter alia* that international law cannot be used to create constitutional obligations (paras 88-103), that the state's obligation to protect the rights in the Bill of Rights can be fulfilled in a number of ways (paras 105-113), that the legislature enjoys considerable leeway in deciding how best to ensure the DPCI's independence (paras 107, 111, 114) and that the Act contains adequate safeguards to ensure the DPCI's independence (paras 132-156).

[57] Z Motala "Divination through a Strange Lens" *Sunday Times* (27-03-2011).

[58] Zuma's recent admonition to judges not to usurp the executive's policymaking function has been understood as a reference to the *Glenister* ruling. Zuma's address, which was delivered at the Third Access to Justice Conference in Pretoria, is available at *PoliticsWeb* <http://www.politicsweb.co.za/politicsweb/view/politicsweb/en/page71656?oid=244907&sn=Detail&pid=71616> (accessed 29-08-2011).

represent a "slippery road" which may lead to the judiciary "seeking to arrest the functioning of Parliament".[59]

The decision to locate a crime investigating unit within a particular government department and the setting up of mechanisms to provide lines of accountability and oversight are issues over which Parliament typically enjoys a wide margin of discretion. The conventional wisdom that a court, in deciding the constitutionality of laws, should not concern itself with the wisdom of particular policy choices would, ordinarily, preclude courts from interfering with decisions that are intimately bound up with the policy choices informing the design of law-enforcement agencies. In the absence of a clear constitutional preference for one model over another, a decision which overturns the legislative scheme designed by Parliament risks being seen as an unauthorised judicial transgression on the powers and functions of legislative bodies. Because they believe that the constitutional rights and values and the international legal materials relied upon by the majority are inconclusive as to the specific institutional framework within which an anti-corruption entity must operate, the critics aver that the majority judgment ultimately rests on ideological rather than legal premises and usurps legislative power.

I find some of these criticisms problematic. A constitution does not always wear its meaning on its sleeve and interpretations arrived at through rigorous and sometimes arduous engagement with the constitutional text, structure and values and the social and historical context are not for that reason less compelling than interpretations that immediately strike us as right or even inevitable. I am also uncomfortable with the binary opposition between "legal" and "ideological" decision-making. The right question to ask is not whether this is a legal or political judgment, but whether it is based on a plausible interpretation of the Constitution – a legal document that structures public power through an intricate network of institutions, procedures, rights and values that is political at its core. If the judgment places too much strain on the constitutional text or fails to integrate the various reasons advanced for it into a coherent and defensible reading of the Constitution, that is cause for criticising the Court's reasoning, not for concluding that it has forsaken its judicial mandate in favour of an overtly political role.

Despite the progressive tone of the majority judgment, there is nevertheless something odd about the way it jumps from the state's obligation to respect, protect, promote and fulfil the rights in the Bill of Rights to an analysis of the extent to which the DPCI's independence is secured. For a start there is no rights analysis. It is simply stated, without arguing, that the rights infringed by the state's failure to establish a sufficiently independent anti-corruption unit include "the rights to equality, human dignity, freedom, security of the

---

[59]   See Anonymous "Mantashe's ConCourt Remarks Scandalous: DA" (18-08-2011) *News 24* <http://www. news24.com/SouthAfrica/Politics/Mantashes-ConCourt-remarks-scandalous-DA-20110818> (accessed 29-08-2011).

person, administrative justice and socio-economic rights, including the rights to education, housing, and health care".[60]

The foray into international law, which is expressly undertaken in terms of section 39(1)(b) (the Constitution's injunction to consider international law in the interpretation of the Bill of Rights), does not shed any light on the content of these rights either. The inquiry centres on institutional issues of independence, and no attempt is made to explain how a failure to adhere to international standards impacts on the rights in question.[61] Given the paucity of rights analysis, it does not come as a surprise that there is no limitation analysis either. Noting that the respondents offered no justification of the limitation, the Court concludes the limitation inquiry simply by stating that a justification would in any event be "hard to advance".[62]

The only clue to the link between the rights in the Bill of Rights and institutional issues of independence comes in the form of statements, references and quotations which refer, in the most general terms, to the effects of corruption on democracy, the rule of law, societal safety and security, and the socio-economic upliftment of the poor. For instance, we are told that corruption

> "blatantly undermines the democratic ethos, the institutions of democracy, the rule of law and the foundational values of our nascent constitutional project. It fuels maladministration and public fraudulence and imperils the capacity of the state to fulfil its obligations to respect, protect, promote and fulfil all the rights enshrined in the Bill of Rights. When corruption and organised crime flourish, sustainable development and economic growth are stunted. And in turn, the stability and security of society is put at risk."[63]

The judges also quote from a statement by Kofi Annan, which emphasises corruption's detrimental effects on the rights of the poor:

> "[I]t is in the developing world that [the effects of corruption] are most destructive. Corruption hurts the poor disproportionately by diverting funds intended for development, undermining a government's basic ability to provide basic services, feeding inequality and injustice, and discouraging foreign investment and aid. Corruption is a key element in economic under-performance, and a major obstacle to poverty alleviation and development."[64]

The first statement notes the negative impact of corruption on the "democratic ethos" and the "institutions of democracy", but does not explain how this negative impact occurs. The second statement does not

---

[60] *Glenister v President of the Republic of South Africa* 2011 3 SA 347 (CC); 2011 7 BCLR 651 (CC) para 198. No attempt is made to relate these findings to the Court's earlier jurisprudence or to explain how they fit in with the standards (for example, the reasonableness standard in relation to socio-economic rights) enunciated in earlier cases. The specific subsections that are infringed are not even mentioned.

[61] See paras 179-202.

[62] Para 203. Perhaps it does not really matter that the judges' recourse to a two-stage inquiry is more apparent than real. As an anonymous referee helpfully points out, the judgment does not hinge on a finding of a direct infringement of the Bill of Rights, but relies instead on the state's more general failure to respect, protect, promote and fulfil the rights in the Bill of Rights. Given corruption's threat to a number of rights it may have been sufficient for the majority to find, as it did with reference to international law, that the failure to establish an independent anti-corruption unit was at odds with the state's obligations in terms of s 7(2) of the Constitution. This may be so, but it would nevertheless have contributed significantly to the judgment's persuasive value if the Court engaged in a more rigorous analysis of corruption's impact on constitutional rights and values.

[63] Para 166.

[64] Para 167.

refer to democracy, but can be read to imply that one of the ways in which corruption impacts on basic service delivery and perpetuates inequality is by undermining a government's democratic legitimacy and by obstructing the mechanisms of democratic accountability. Democracy, it seems, is viewed mainly in instrumental terms. Norms of democratic accountability are valued to the extent that they boost the state's capacity to alleviate poverty, redress inequality and ensure a dignified life for all. The possibility that democracy may be constitutive of – at least some of – the rights in question[65] or that the rights of citizens to political participation may be at stake here is apparently not considered.

These lines of inquiry might have provided a sounder basis for the Court's attempt to establish a link between the Bill of Rights and institutional issues of independence. Representatives and officials whose primary allegiance is to those who fund their lavish lifestyles or whose donations oil the party's machinery make a mockery of the ideals of democratic accountability, openness and responsiveness. In the first place, their willingness to place private interests above the public interest dilutes the importance of the right to vote and diminishes the impact of democratic participation. Corruption and political patronage thus strike at the heart of democratic citizenship and rights of political participation. They deny basic political equality and re-introduce gradations and hierarchies based on wealth and influence into the very notion of citizenship.[66] Secondly, as Choudry points out, corruption and patronage flourish in dominant party democracies in which there has been a shift of power from the ruling party's parliamentary to its non-parliamentary wing. In such societies the separation between state and party gets increasingly blurred, legislators and officials come to depend on the goodwill of party leaders whose mandate derives not from the electorate but from the party, and public resources (for example state contracts and government positions) become an indispensable tool in struggles for political power and influence. Democratic accountability becomes a sham, and attempts to curb the independence of institutions that are able to expose corruption become common.[67] Thirdly, the political manipulation of public resources enables ruling parties to stifle political competition and prevent the formation of a strong and credible opposition. Corruption and political patronage are therefore fundamentally

---

[65] See H Botha "Equality, Plurality and Structural Power" (2009) 25 *SAJHR* 1 on the links between democracy and equality. See also S Liebenberg *Socio-Economic Rights: Adjudication under a Transformative Constitution* (2010) 28-34, 36-42 and 63-66 on the relation between democracy and socio-economic rights.

[66] Classical-republican thinkers already theorised the relationship between corruption and inequality in the 16th and 17th centuries. For them, civic virtue signified the capacity of citizens to place the common good above their own particular interests. Corruption, by contrast, referred to the propensity of rulers and citizens to elevate their private interests above the public interest. For thinkers like Machiavelli and Harrington, inequality was the root cause of corruption, as material dependence gave rise to "a state of affairs in which some individuals look to others ... when they should be looking to the public good and public authority" (JGA Pocock *The Machiavellian Moment: Florentine Political Thought and the Atlantic Republican Tradition* (1975) 209). In the absence of a material basis for independence, individuals lack the positive freedom to pursue the common good in concert with others. Inequality is thus irreconcilable with citizenship and threatens the very life of the republic.

[67] S Choudry "'He Had a Mandate': The South African Constitutional Court and the African National Congress in a Dominant Party Democracy" (2009) 2 *CCR* 1 22-32.

at odds with the idea of a multiparty democracy and with the right of every citizen to make political choices which, according to section 19(1) of the Constitution, includes the right to form a political party and to participate in its activities and recruit members.

Seen thus, the independence of anti-corruption agencies does not simply have a remote bearing on a range of constitutional rights, but goes to the heart of our constitutional system of representative democracy and fundamentally affects rights of democratic citizenship. The order made in *Glenister* is, accordingly, not a misguided attempt by an unelected court to substitute its views on policy issues and its preference for a particular institutional design for those of Parliament, but an important victory for a constitutional vision of democracy which precludes laws and conduct which effectively insulate political elites from democratic supervision and contestation.

4 Concluding remarks

The Constitutional Court's jurisprudence wavers uneasily between two rival conceptions of democracy and its relationship to the poor. On the first view, regular elections secure a direct link between the government and electorate. It is this chain of democratic accountability and legitimacy which ultimately provides the strongest guarantee that the voices of the poor will be heard and that their needs will be attended to. The power of judicial review should, accordingly, be used sparingly. In the absence of clear and unambiguous constitutional authorisation, judicial review of decisions of the political branches amounts to unwarranted interference with the chain of legitimacy running from the people to their representatives. Besides resting on shaky hermeneutical foundations, this understanding of democracy is based on dubious assumptions about the relationship between the people and their representatives in government. Effectively reducing the role of "the people" to participation in elections every five years, it grounds the state's legitimacy in the people's supreme democratic power and, in the very same move, removes power from the people by insisting that they relinquished it to elected representatives. Moreover, this view overlooks the link between economic and political power and fails to resist the capacity of private power and influence to shape political outcomes. In addition, it accepts the uninterrupted chain of democratic legitimacy as a given rather than as a critical ideal, and legitimates the political marginalisation of the poor and other vulnerable groups in the name of a formal conception of democracy and of political equality.

The second view resists a too glib identification of the people with their representatives and posits a dialogical, participatory and pluralistic understanding of democracy. Rejecting the first view's fixation on a single act through which voters delegate power to their elected representatives, it starts from the idea of an ongoing dialogue between the people and representative institutions. Here the supposed unity and identity of "the people" keeps getting interrupted by a plurality of needs and viewpoints, as individuals and communities participate in decision-making processes affecting them. This vision seems better able to uphold the civic dignity of the poor; to ensure open, accountable and responsive government; and to resist the capture of public decision-making processes by particular interests.

Despite the progressive tenor of the judgments in *Doctors for Life* and *Matatiele II*, the first, more restrictive view of democracy continues to reassert itself in Constitutional Court judgments. A number of reasons have been mooted for its persistence. According to Roux, judgments like *UDM* in which the Court relies on a formal, rather shallow conception of democracy should not be seen as a renunciation of the deep principle of democracy articulated elsewhere. They rely, rather, on a countervailing principle in terms of which "the judiciary should defer to the legislature in politically sensitive cases concerning the design of the electoral system",[68] or amount to a pragmatic concession to the Court's vulnerable institutional position.[69] Choudry takes a somewhat different view. For him, judgments like *UDM* and *Merafong* result from the Court's lack of a conceptual framework for understanding the dynamics of a dominant party democracy.[70] To these a third explanation can be added, which relates to the Court's reliance on human dignity in cases concerning political rights. The Court has invalidated measures which, by denying the vote to prisoners[71] or nationals residing abroad,[72] could be construed as a denial of the equal dignity of those categories of citizens. However, the Court has struck a far more deferential pose in cases in which laws dilute the importance of the right to vote through structural changes to the electoral system,[73] or effectively prevent some citizens from casting their vote as a result of the interplay between electoral rules and material and other forms of disadvantage.[74] This raises fundamental questions over the relationship between dignity and democracy, and over the political marginalisation and silencing of the poor.[75]

It is hard to square the current socio-political reality with the Constitutional Court's vision of an inclusive, egalitarian and participatory democracy in which the poor are treated as active citizens rather than faceless subjects or passive beneficiaries of government largess. Recent protests over poor service delivery, police brutality in the face of these protests, and countless allegations of corruption, nepotism and political patronage have once again

---

[68]   T Roux "Democracy" in S Woolman, T Roux & M Bishop (eds) *Constitutional Law of South Africa (CLoSA)* 2 ed (OS 7 2006) 10-64.

[69]   10-57.

[70]   Choudry (2009) *CCR* 5, 34.

[71]   *August v Electoral Commission* 1999 3 SA 1 (CC); 1999 4 BCLR 363 (CC); *Minister of Home Affairs v NICRO* 2004 5 BCLR 445 (CC).

[72]   *Richter v Minister of Home Affairs* 2009 3 SA 615 (CC); 2009 5 BCLR 448 (CC).

[73]   *United Democratic Movement v President of the RSA* 2002 11 BCLR 1179 (CC).

[74]   *New National Party of South Africa v Government of the RSA* 1999 5 BCLR 489 (CC).

[75]   Danie Brand has argued that some of the Constitutional Court's "meaningful engagement" orders in socio-economic rights cases overemphasise the specific, individual interests at stake in a particular dispute, at the expense of the underlying structural causes of poverty and deprivation. JFD Brand *Courts, Socio-Economic Rights and Transformative Politics* LLD thesis University of Stellenbosch (2009) 162-176. The Court's emphasis in political rights cases on the dignity of individual voters has arguably had a similar effect, in that it has shifted the attention away from the underlying structural causes of political inequality, the silencing of marginalised and poor communities and a lack of democratic accountability and responsiveness.

drawn attention to the staggering gap between rich and poor and the ways in which political elites appear to have extricated themselves from the logic of democratic accountability. The critical challenge is to articulate the Court's deeper vision of democracy, in which dialogue, participation and voice take centre stage, with an understanding of the ways in which electoral rules and the party system combine with inequality, corruption and patronage to entrench the exclusion and silencing of the poor. Only thus can we hope to resist the strange logic in terms of which the poor are effaced in the very act of their representation.

SUMMARY

I juxtapose two judicial understandings of democracy in relation to their implications for the poor. Some constitutional judgments conceive of democracy in formal terms as the capacity of duly elected legislatures to enact law within their constitutional area of competence. These judgments are loath to impose requirements that would guarantee the participatory nature of the lawmaking process, and reluctant to raise questions about the ruling party's use of their numerical majority to stifle political opposition or shield officials from legislative oversight. Other judgments conceive of democracy in dialogic, participatory and pluralistic terms. I argue that this second judicial conception of democracy is better placed to challenge laws and practices which effectively insulate social and political power from mechanisms designed to promote democratic accountability, or allow the wealthy and powerful to pass off their particular interests as the common good. This vision of democracy needs to be supplemented with a better understanding of the ways in which electoral rules and the party system tend to intersect with inequality, corruption and patronage to entrench the exclusion and silencing of the poor.

CHAPTER 7

TRANSFORMATIVE CONSTITUTIONALISM IN A DEMOCRATIC DEVELOPMENTAL STATE

Solange Rosa*

1 Introduction

Mass poverty in South Africa continues to present a considerable challenge in various forms. Notwithstanding ongoing debates about how best to describe and measure poverty, while poverty remains very widespread, the available data point to a reduction in extreme destitution in recent years. This is to a large extent due to the redistributive targeting and successful impact of a number of laws, policies and programmes aimed at addressing poverty and inequality implemented in the country since the demise of apartheid. The transformation from a racially based, resource-biased society to an egalitarian one where all enjoy the aims, values and rights upheld in the Constitution of the Republic of South Africa, 1996 ("the Constitution" or "the South African Constitution"), requires a concerted effort by all institutional players to redress the material as well as the psycho-socio-political deficiencies that continue to inhibit the full enjoyment of our new democracy for approximately half the population.

This chapter commences with a discussion of the origin and evolution of the concept of transformative constitutionalism in South Africa and what it means for addressing poverty and inequality. The Constitution, and in particular the Bill of Rights, has a critical role to play in advancing poverty reduction through the courts, the legislature and the executive. The rights to life, equality, dignity, administrative justice and socio-economic rights are all instruments that can be sharpened further to tackle poverty and inequality and thereby transform our society.

In the next part I discuss Amartya Sen's analysis of the links between public reasoning, democracy and justice. Sen argues that the attainment of social justice, without public reasoning based on participatory and deliberative democratic models, is not possible. I then examine the participatory and deliberative dimensions of democracy in the South African Constitution that support the transformation project.

In the final part I outline the political-economy underpinnings of the South African government's historical and current policy responses to poverty reduction and inequality. The South African government's discourse has shifted in the last five years from a welfare state approach to a democratic developmental state approach. Both welfare and developmental states aim at a more equitable redistribution of resources in society, but developmental states differ from welfare states mostly in the free market alliances between government and business, soft authoritarianism and

* I would like to thank Professors Sandra Liebenberg and Geo Quinot for their valuable comments.

a strong public sector bureaucracy. I argue that a shift to a *democratic developmental state* – as a transitional state – is necessary in order to achieve equitable socio-economic transformation in South Africa. The democratic developmental state emphasises the collaborative role of all players in society and the empowerment of the poor in the development project. Participation and empowerment are central means and ends in our transformative Constitution. There is a limit to what lawyers can say about models of the developmental state; however, lawyers can contribute to an understanding of the type of state that we need in order to realise the rights in the Constitution. Participatory democracy is the most powerful guarantee for the poor that their interests will not be disregarded.

2 Transformative constitutionalism and poverty

It is widely acknowledged that the South African Constitution is a progressive and transformative legal instrument.[1] As the supreme law, its purpose is to regulate public power and to frame "an objective, normative value system"[2] in a post-apartheid society. All law and conduct must conform to its provisions, failing which it is invalid.[3] This system of normative values seeks to fulfil a constitutional imperative to remedy South Africa's past and "transform our society into one in which there will be human dignity, freedom and equality".[4] This is vividly expressed in the Preamble to the Constitution, and then in section 7(1),[5] in the Bill of Rights (Chapter 2), and throughout the Constitution. The Bill of Rights binds the legislature, the executive, the judiciary, all organs of state, and, where applicable, a natural or juristic person.[6]

---

[1] KE Klare "Legal Culture and Transformative Constitutionalism" (1998) 14 *SAJHR* 146, where the term "transformative constitutionalism" was first coined. See discussion of the "transformative" vision of the Constitution in C Albertyn & B Goldblatt "Facing the Challenges of Transformation: Difficulties in the Development of an Indigenous Jurisprudence of Equality" (1998) 14 *SAJHR* 248; AJ van der Walt "Tentative Urgency: Sensitivity for the Paradoxes of Stability and Change in the Social Transformation Decisions of the Constitutional Court" (2001) 16 *SAPL* 1 1-27; D Moseneke "The Fourth Bram Fischer Memorial Lecture: Transforming Adjudication" (2002) 18 *SAJHR* 309; H Botha, AJ van der Walt & J van der Walt (eds) *Rights and Democracy in a Transformative Constitution* (2003); H Botha "Metaphoric Reasoning and Transformative Constitutionalism (Part 2)" (2003) *TSAR* 20 20-36; M Pieterse "What Do We Mean When We Talk about Transformative Constitutionalism?" (2005) 20 *SAPL* 155 155-166; AJ van der Walt "Legal History, Legal Culture and Transformation in a Constitutional Democracy" (2006) 12 *Fundamina* 1 1-47; S Liebenberg "Needs, Rights and Transformation: Adjudicating Social Rights" (2006) 17 *Stell LR* 5 5-36; P Langa "Transformative Constitutionalism" (2006) 17 *Stell LR* 351 351-360; S Liebenberg *Socio-Economic Rights: Adjudication under a Transformative Constitution* (2010) 23-78.

[2] *Carmichele v Minister of Safety and Security* 2001 4 SA 938 (CC) para 54.

[3] S 2 of the Constitution.

[4] *Soobramoney v Minister of Health (Kwazulu-Natal)* 1998 1 SA 765 (CC) para 8. See also Liebenberg *Socio-Economic Rights* 25-28.

[5] S 7(1) of the Constitution states:
"This Bill of Rights is a cornerstone of democracy in South Africa. It enshrines the rights of all people in our country and affirms the democratic values of human dignity, equality and freedom."

[6] S 8 of the Constitution.

The South African Constitution embraces notions of participatory democracy, social, and economic equality, protection of culture, openness, and transparency. As Karl Klare points out in his seminal article:

"[T]he South African Constitution, in sharp contrast to the classical liberal documents, is social, redistributive, caring, positive, at least partly horizontal, participatory, multicultural, and self-conscious about its historical setting and transformative role and mission."[7]

His was the first explicit characterisation of the South African Constitution as transformative, from a political, economic and social perspective. This view of the Constitution took hold firmly and has been quoted many times in academic literature[8] and court judgments.[9] The transformative nature of the Constitution provides a legal normative framework, which will guide "the redress of the injustices of the past as well as to facilitate the creation of a more just society in the future".[10]

Klare described the South African Constitution as a "transformative" project in the following terms:

"[A] long-term project of constitutional enactment, interpretation and enforcement committed (not in isolation, of course, but in a historical context of conducive political developments) to transforming a country's political and social institutions and power relationships in a democratic, participatory, and egalitarian direction. Transformative constitutionalism connotes an enterprise of inducing large-scale social change through nonviolent political processes grounded in law."[11]

Marius Pieterse describes the South African Constitution as an essentially social-democratic model, quite distinct from the traditional, liberal model of constitutionalism, and links this understanding to at least three critical aspects, which make the Constitution transformative.[12]

Firstly, the South African Constitution mandates the achievement of substantive equality and social justice through the provisions of sections 9, 26, 27, 28 and 29. Section 9 of the Constitution incorporates the concept of substantive equality, which involves a contextual, group-based approach to discrimination and domination and requires remedial measures designed to rectify the destructive effects of entrenched structures of past oppression. The achievement of substantive equality also necessitates that the material consequences of social and economic subjugation be addressed.[13] These ends are further supported by the inclusion of justiciable civil, political *and* socio-

---

[7]   Klare (1998) *SAJHR* 153 (footnotes omitted).
[8]   See Liebenberg *Socio-Economic Rights* 23-78.
[9]   See *S v Makwanyane* 1995 3 SA 391 (CC) para 262; *Du Plessis v De Klerk* 1996 3 SA 850 (CC) para 157; *Bato Star Fishing (Pty) Ltd v Minister of Environmental Affairs and Tourism* 2004 4 SA 490 (CC) paras 73-74; *Minister of Finance v Van Heerden* 2004 6 SA 121 (CC) para 142; *City of Johannesburg v Rand Properties (Pty) Ltd* 2007 1 SA 78 (W) paras 51-52; *Rates Action Group v City of Cape Town* 2004 5 SA 545 (C) para 100; *Residents of Joe Slovo Community, Western Cape v Thubelisha Homes* 2010 3 SA 454 (CC) paras 343-344, 360; and *Head of Department: Mpumalanga Department of Education v Hoërskool Ermelo* 2010 2 SA 415 (CC) para 77.
[10] Liebenberg *Socio-Economic Rights* 25.
[11] Klare (1998) *SAJHR* 150.
[12] For a summary of the literature on the meaning of "transformative constitutionalism" see Pieterse (2005) *SAPL* 156.
[13] Pieterse (2005) *SAPL* 160; Albertyn & Goldblatt (1998) *SAJHR* 250-251, 253; Moseneke (2002) *SAJHR* 318-319; S Liebenberg & M O'Sullivan "South Africa's New Equality Legislation: A Tool for Advancing Women's Socio-Economic Equality?" (2001) *Acta Juridica* 73 81.

economic rights in the Bill of Rights.[14] This embodies recognition that full transformation from an apartheid society requires both a reconfiguration of the legal-political structures that upheld it, as well as the transformation of the devastating social and economic consequences of its policies and laws. The overwhelming levels of poverty still felt to a disproportionate extent by those discriminated against during apartheid, will undermine the transformation project if not addressed.

Socio-economic rights have been increasingly used as a tool in litigation and in monitoring and advocacy related to the government's obligations to secure for all members of society a set of social goods – education, social security, health care, food, water, shelter, access to land and housing. Justiciable socio-economic rights assist in monitoring the state's progressive realisation of its constitutional obligations to the poor, and ultimately holding the state accountable to these obligations.

Secondly, the achievement of political and socio-economic transformation requires a "collaborative enterprise". The legislature, the executive, the judiciary and all organs of state are all bound by the Bill of Rights and are obliged to "respect, protect, promote and fulfil" its mandates.[15] This collaborative enterprise is not only an obligation upon the state, but also upon non-state actors.[16]

Finally, linked to this is the fostering of a "culture of justification"[17] for every exercise of public power, where public power is kept in check for compliance with human rights standards as essential for the transformative project.[18] Pieterse argues that this is starkly provided for in section 36 of the Constitution,[19] which determines that rights may only be limited by laws that are reasonable and justifiable in "an open and democratic society based on human dignity, equality and freedom". It can also be derived from reasonableness review in sections 26(2) and 27(2), which requires an "exercise in proportionality informed by a proper analysis of the normative commitments of the relevant rights and the impact of the deprivation of the particular resource or service at issue on the claimant group".[20] The rights of access to information (section 32) and just administrative action (section 33) similarly play a critical role in societal transformation in that they seek to keep a check on public power by providing citizens with the information and procedural and substantive protection required for empowerment and autonomy of the poor and vulnerable in our society. The right to just administrative action is an increasingly constructive and transformative tool, for the assessment and enforcement of efforts to address poverty and

---

[14] Ss 26-29 of the Constitution protect the rights to housing, health care, food, water, social security and education, as well as the rights of children to "basic nutrition, shelter, basic health care services and social services" (s 28(1)(c)).

[15] Ss 7(2) and 8(1) of the Constitution.

[16] S 8(3) and (4). S 39(2).

[17] See E Mureinik "A Bridge to Where? Introducing the Interim Bill of Rights" (1994) 10 *SAJHR* 31 32.

[18] Pieterse (2005) *SAPL* 161, 163.

[19] 163.

[20] Liebenberg *Socio-Economic Rights* 198.

inequality. It focuses on the implementation of legislation[21] based on the broad, overarching requirements of lawfulness, procedural fairness and reasonableness – elements which require a "culture of justification" when rights are at risk.[22] The reasonableness component of administrative justice, in particular, insists on *substantive justification* for all public action.[23]

Finally, Danie Brand[24] draws a distinction between two understandings of transformative constitutionalism among legal commentators: the first explains transformation as the "achievement of certain tangible results or outcomes",[25] such as the reduction of poverty, through adjudication; the second "refers to the radical change of the institutions and systems that produce results themselves".[26]

In this chapter, I embrace both of the above understandings of transformative constitutionalism. I assert that the courts should aspire to contribute to a reduction in poverty in material terms, while at the same time using its adjudicatory powers and powers of judicial review to examine and influence "the systems and institutions themselves" in terms of "their processes" and "modes of reasoning". The participatory and empowerment elements of achieving social justice require a more modest and less quantifiable – but no less important – account of the role of institutions in facilitating socio-economic transformation.

3 Participatory democracy and social justice

Sen asserts that the attainment of social justice, without public reasoning based on participatory and deliberative democratic models, is not possible.[27] Democracy in the South African Constitution can be characterised as representative, participatory and direct.[28] The *participatory* provisions that support the transformation project are: public participation in legislative

---

[21] Administrative justice deals with implementation of legislation rather than policy directly – ie only implementation of the legislature's translation of policy into law. See the exclusion of s 85(2)(b) of the Constitution from the definition of administrative action in s 1 of the Promotion of Administrative Justice Act 3 of 2000 ("PAJA").

[22] Note that s 33(2) of the Constitution includes the right to be given reasons for administrative action, in circumstances where rights have been adversely affected.

[23] See *Bato Star Fishing (Pty) Ltd v Minister of Environmental Affairs and Tourism* 2004 4 SA 490 (CC) paras 44-45; *Minister of Health and Another NO v New Clicks South Africa (Pty) Ltd* 2006 2 SA 311 (CC) paras 187-188.

[24] D Brand *Courts, Socio-Economic Rights and Transformative Politics* LLD thesis Stellenbosch (2009) 2-3.

[25] 4.

[26] 4 and n 12-15. See Nancy Fraser's distinction between "affirmative" and "transformative" redistribution in N Fraser "Social Justice in the Age of Identity Politics: Redistribution, Recognition, and Participation" in N Fraser & A Honneth *Redistribution or Recognition? A Political-Philosophical Exchange* (2003) 7 45-46.

[27] See generally A Sen *The Idea of Justice* (2009).

[28] For a discussion of the conceptions of democracy in the South African Constitution, see I Currie & J de Waal *The Bill of Rights Handbook* 5 ed (2005) 13; T Roux "Democracy" in S Woolman, T Roux & M Bishop (eds) *CLoSA* 2 ed (OS 2008) 10-1-10-77. See also G Quinot "Snapshot or Participatory Democracy? Political Engagement as Fundamental Human Right" (2009) 25 *SAJHR* 392, 397-399 on participatory democracy; and Liebenberg *Socio-Economic Rights* 28-34 on deliberative democracy.

processes,[29] in the public administration,[30] just administrative action,[31] and socio-economic rights.[32] I argue here, that the vision of participatory democracy laid down in our Constitution is necessary to facilitate the transformation of South African society into one "based on democratic values, social justice and fundamental human rights",[33] and thus to holistically ameliorate the lives of the poor and marginalised members of our society. This model requires vigorous discussion, debate and activism in the process of transformation and responsiveness "to the inequalities and material deprivation that prevent certain groups from participating as equals in the creation of a new society".[34] I argue that this theory explains the work that rights in a transformative constitution are able to do for the poor and marginalised, alongside the conception of the role of the state and its citizens in a *democratic* developmental state.

3 1 Theoretical dimensions of participatory democracy

In Sen's *The Idea of Justice*, he states that the institutional structure of the contemporary practice of democracy hails largely from the experience of Europe and America over the last few centuries.[35] He remarks that these institutional forms have been ultimately effective. However, he is at pains to point out that while democracy in its current institutionally elaborate form may be quite new and Western-centred, *participatory governance* in practice has a much wider and longer history in the world.[36] He states that in fact the practice of elections has a long history in non-Western societies, as does "the broader view of democracy in terms of *public reasoning* that makes it abundantly clear that the cultural critique of democracy as a purely regional phenomenon fails altogether".[37]

He goes on to give the example of Nelson Mandela's autobiography, *Long Walk to Freedom*, where Mandela describes how impressed and influenced he was, as a young boy, by seeing the democratic nature of the proceedings of the local meetings that were held in the regent's house in Mqhekezweni:

> "Everyone who wanted to speak did so. It was democracy in its purest form. There may have been a hierarchy of importance among the speakers, but everyone was heard, chief and subject, warrior and

---

[29] Ss 57, 59, 70, 72, 74, 116, 118, 160 of the Constitution.

[30] S 195(1)(e).

[31] S 33.

[32] Ss 25-29. The Constitutional Court has interpreted particular socio-economic rights to include participatory elements, most notably in eviction cases where "meaningful engagement" with affected parties has been read into s 26. See *Port Elizabeth Municipality v Various Occupiers* 2005 1 SA 217 (CC) paras 39, 42; *Occupiers of 51 Olivia Road, Berea Township, and 197 Main Street, Johannesburg v City of Johannesburg* 2008 3 SA 208 (CC) paras 9-18; *Residents of Joe Slovo Community, Western Cape v Thubelisha Homes* 2010 3 SA 454 (CC) paras 167, 237-244; *Abahlali baseMjondolo Movement SA v Premier, KwaZulu-Natal* 2010 2 BCLR 99 (CC) paras 113-114.

[33] Preamble to the Constitution.

[34] Liebenberg *Socio-Economic Rights* 34.

[35] Sen *Idea of Justice* 322-354. On the institutional history of democracy, see also generally J Dunn *Democracy: A History* (2005).

[36] Sen *Idea of Justice* 323.

[37] 330-331 (emphasis added).

medicine man, shopkeeper and farmer, landowner and labourer .... The foundation of self-government was that all men were free to voice their opinions and equal in their value as citizens."[38]

As Sen highlights, Mandela's understanding of democracy was not rooted in the political practice that he saw around him during the reign of apartheid based on a European system, but on his general ideas about political and social equality, which had global roots, and from his observations of the practice of participatory public discussion that he found in his local town.[39]

This recognition, argues Sen, points to a connection between the idea of justice and the practice of democracy. In contemporary political philosophy the view that democracy is best seen as "government by discussion" has gained widespread support.[40] This contemporary view of democracy has broadened considerably, so that democracy is no longer seen just in terms of public balloting, but in terms of what John Rawls calls the "exercise of public reason".[41]

While there are differences among contemporary democracy theorists about the role of public reasoning in politics, these distinctions are not critical to the argument here. What is important to note, is that these contributions have elevated the central issues in a broader understanding of democracy as being political participation, dialogue and public interaction. Sen argues that the vital role of public reasoning in the practice of democracy makes the entire subject of democracy relate closely with notions of justice. He thus reasons that since the "demands of justice" must be assessed with the help of public reasoning, and public reasoning is constitutively related to the idea of democracy, there is a direct connection between justice and democracy.[42] The value of this broadened form of democracy, he explains, is firstly the ability to make people take an interest, through public discussion, in each other's predicaments, and to have a better understanding of the lives of others. The second concerns the informational role of democracy which goes beyond its incentive functions, to improved policymaking.

His argument, based on global evidence, is that democracy and political and civil rights tend to enhance freedoms of other kinds (such as human security) through giving a voice to the marginalised and vulnerable on important policy

---

[38]   330-331; N Mandela *Long Walk to Freedom* (1994) 21. See the concept of "participatory parity" in Fraser "Social Justice in the Age of Identity Politics" in *Redistribution or Recognition?* 730-731. She posits that a prerequisite for justice are social conditions that enable people to engage with one another as peers. For "participatory parity" to exist, "it is necessary but not sufficient to establish standard forms of formal legal equality" (31). She highlights two additional conditions that must be satisfied: the first requires that material resources be distributed across society in such a way as "to ensure participants" independence and "voice"; the second requires that "institutionalised cultural patterns of interpretation and evaluation express equal respect for all participants and ensure equal opportunity for achieving social esteem" (26).

[39]   Sen *Idea of Justice* 332.

[40]   324.

[41]   324. See J Rawls *A Theory of Justice* (1971); J Rawls *Political Liberalism* (1993); J Rawls *Collected Papers* (1999) 579-580. See also proponents of deliberative democracy referred to in Sen *Idea of Justice* 324-326, in particular J Habermas "Three Normative Models of Democracy" in S Benhabib (ed) *Democracy and Difference: Contesting the Boundaries of the Political* (1996) 21 21-30. See further the discussion in Liebenberg *Socio-Economic Rights* 28-34 on deliberative democracy.

[42]   Sen *Idea of Justice* 324.

issues, and thereby influencing greatly their developmental outcomes.[43] He provides examples of areas where social change has been brought about as a result of a "determined use of political and social voice",[44] such as the feminist revolution and achievement of gender equality in certain instances. This mounting action in organised movements is based broadly on demands for human rights, such as the right to education, food, basic healthcare, environmental preservation and employment. Sen says that these movements raise awareness of particular societal failures, in addition to public debates in the media, by providing "a politically harder edge to socially important demands".[45]

Democratic freedom can thus be used to improve social justice and a better and fairer politics. However, the process is not ingrained and requires engagement and activism both by those affected by injustice, poverty and marginalisation, as well as those who contribute intellectually to the transformation of society, such as the legal fraternity, academics and the media.[46]

This leads us to the distinction between participatory democracy[47] and deliberative democracy.[48] As explained by the chief theoretical exponent of participatory democracy, Carole Pateman:

> "The existence of representative institutions at national level is not sufficient for democracy; for maximum participation by all the people at the level socialisation, or 'social training', for democracy must take place in other spheres in order that the necessary individual attitudes and psychological qualities can be developed. This development takes place through the process of participation itself. The major function of participation in the theory of participatory democracy is therefore an educative

---

43 348.

44 348.

45 348.

46 351. For example, the current sweep of protest action against financial greed and corruption under the banner of "Occupy Wall Street" ("OWS") that began in New York City and has spread around the world. See *Occupy Wall Street* <http://www.occuywallstreet.org> (accessed 14-10-2011). Their website states that the OWS demonstrations are emulating the tactics of the revolutionary "Arab Spring", which is an example of participatory democracy overturning authoritarianism in African states.

47 See Roux "Democracy" in *CLoSA* 10-14–10-15; Quinot (2009) *SAJHR* 397-399. For a more detailed examination of participatory democracy, see C Pateman *Participation and Democratic Theory* (1970) 22-44; D Held *Models of Democracy* 3 ed (2006) 209-216; F Cunningham *Theories of Democracy: A Critical Introduction* (2002) 123-141.

48 Roux "Democracy" in *CLoSA* 10-15–10-18 elaborates further on the contemporary accounts of democracy found in the Constitution and distinguishes between deliberative democracy and participatory democracy, although they are both closely aligned to the model of direct democracy. He explains that "deliberative democracy and participatory democracy are superficially similar since both can be seen as a reaction against the tendency of modern representative democracies to produce passive citizens, whose power to control their elected representatives is reduced to their right to participate in periodic elections" (10-17).

He goes on to explain that the difference between these two forms of democracy, however, is that for theorists of deliberative democracy "a particular form of participation – deliberation – may legitimate collective decisions even in the presence of fundamental moral disagreement" (10-17) while participatory democracy in contrast, assumes "that sufficient, or the right kind of, participation, will eventually produce agreement between citizens on a single right decision most conformable with the public interest" (10-17).

one, educative in the very widest sense, including both the psychological aspect and the gaining of practice in democratic skills and procedures."[49]

David Held describes participatory democracy as part of the same model as direct democracy, since they both stress the value of citizen participation in the making of collective decisions.[50] In contemporary terms, Theunis Roux explains participatory democracy as "an attempt to re-inject elements of direct democracy into modern systems of representative democracy".[51] Participatory democracy is thus, in this sense, "essentially about the question whether, and if so, how, citizens should be given the right to participate in the making of decisions that affect them, notwithstanding the fact that the basic form of political organisation in the modern nation-state is, and is likely to remain, representative democracy".[52] As Held also notes, proponents of these models "often emphasise ... as vital for the transformation of politics [that] ... the state must be democratised by making parliament, state bureaucracies and political parties more open and accountable".[53]

3 2   Participatory democracy in the South African Constitution

The South African Constitution is said to recognise three forms of democracy: representative democracy, participatory democracy and direct democracy. There are minimal manifestations of direct democracy in the Constitution: the right to freedom of assembly (section 17), the provision for the holding of referenda and a greater degree of citizen participation in local government (section 152(1)(e)). All formal legislative and policymaking bodies are representative. I argue here that at the heart of South Africa's transformative Constitution lies a *participatory* democratic culture that is integral to the achievement of social justice and development for all. This is evident both in the legal text of the Constitution and the judgments of the

---

[49] Pateman *Participation and Democratic Theory* 42. According to CB Macpherson, the "circular" problem with the approach of participatory democracy is that the two "virtues" of participation, that of promoting a more active citizenry and reducing poverty and inequality, "are also its prerequisites". See CB Macpherson *The Life and Times of Liberal Democracy* (1977) 99-100, quoted in Roux "Democracy" in *CLoSA* 10-15. In relation to the well-known "circularity problem" of justice as democratic participation also see Liebenberg *Socio-Economic Rights* 32 (and sources cited by her in n 40-42). Fraser "Social Justice in the Age of Identity Politics" in *Redistribution or Recognition?* 44, argues that this circularity is not vicious but reflects the nature of justice from a democratic perspective, and that the solution to the problem is rather to focus on "changing social reality".

[50] Held *Models of Democracy* 210; Pateman *Participation and Democratic Theory* 42; Quinot (2009) *SAJHR* 397. Roux "Democracy" in *CLoSA* 10-9 defines direct democracy as:
"a system of government in which major decisions are taken by the members of the political community themselves, without mediation by elected representatives ... [S]uch a system has only ever existed in its pure form in the ancient city-state of Athens and certain other isolated and relatively short-lived polities ... It is also possible for direct democracy to be implemented in subsidiary institutions within an over-arching system of representative democracy."

[51] Roux "Democracy" in *CLoSA* 10-14.

[52] 10-14.

[53] Held *Models of Democracy* 211, quoted in Quinot (2009) *SAJHR* 397.

Constitutional Court over the past fifteen years,[54] as well as in the culture of social, economic and political activism and debate that has emerged out of democracy in South Africa.

The realm of public debate and activism around issues of poverty, inequality and development in South Africa spans the work of research organisations, trade unions, civil society organisations, the media, and academia; and is vividly expressed in the service delivery protests of poor communities and demonstrations of mass movements. All of this exchange has contributed to an ongoing policy debate in the country concerning government's macro-economic and distributional policies.[55] As Sandra Liebenberg writes:

> "Active debate and contestation concerning the nature of social change, and the political and legal reforms necessary for achieving it, should not be viewed as antithetical to transformation, but rather as integral to its achievement."[56]

This is the notion of participatory democracy of which deliberative democracy is a significant component, discussed by Sen above, that will aid in the transformation of the current *status quo* and achievement of a more just society. Deliberative democracy can contribute to making participatory democracy more meaningful, where all actors/participants are open to changing their views and there are no fixed or preconceived policy positions.

Besides the value of general discussion and debate in the public arena, public participation in the processes of government is also an integral part of our Constitutional democracy. One of the founding constitutional values is a multiparty system of democratic government based on accountability, responsiveness and openness.[57] The Constitution expressly provides for public access to and participation in legislative processes,[58] as well as the executive processes by providing that among the "basic values and principles governing public administration"[59] is that "people's needs must be responded to, and the public must be encouraged to participate in policy-making".[60] The Constitutional Court has in several cases underscored the centrality of participatory democracy to the achievement of constitutional goals and

---

[54] Cases dealing with participatory democracy that have come before the courts include: *Affordable Medicines Trust v Minister of Health* 2006 3 SA 247 (CC); *Doctors for Life International v The Speaker of the National Assembly* 2006 6 SA 416 (CC); *Minister of Health and Another NO v New Clicks South Africa (Pty) Ltd* 2006 2 SA 311 (CC); *Poverty Alleviation Network v President of the Republic of South Africa* 2010 6 BCLR 520 (CC).

[55] See part 4 below on the conception of the South African democratic developmental state.

[56] Liebenberg *Socio-Economic Rights* 29.

[57] S 1(d) of the Constitution.

[58] Ss 57, 59, 70, 72, 74, 116, 118, 160.

[59] S 195.

[60] S 195(1)(e). Ss 50 and 51 of the Municipal Systems Act No 32 of 2000 affirm the application of the constitutional principles governing public administration to the provision of municipal services.

values,[61] the necessity of this participation for purposes of informed decision-making[62] and affirmed the duty of the state to take positive measures to ensure that the public has the effective capacity and opportunity to participate in decision-making processes.[63] In particular, it has highlighted the need to listen to the voices of the poor and marginalised in society.[64]

The Constitutional Court has affirmed that the participation of the poor in the determination of their access to benefits and services serves the values of dignity and freedom as well as gives substance to the deliberative and participatory democracy envisaged in the Constitution.[65] As Liebenberg states:

> "A major factor contributing to a sense of powerlessness and lack of autonomy is the absence of the opportunity to voice our concerns in relation to decisions which have a major impact on our lives. Meaningful participation in decisions that affect our lives affirms the close relationship between freedom and human dignity ... It not only gives people a sense of control over their lives, but it affirms their equal worth as members of a political society ... Participation in public and private processes of decision-making is not only an affirmation of individual dignity and freedom, but gives substance to a participatory and deliberative concept of democracy. This is the best reading of the value of accountable, responsive and open democracy in the Constitution."[66]

Most recently, a number of cases have gone before the courts in relation to administrative justice[67] and access to material benefits, which have asserted the importance of the participation of those affected by the decisions. These cases have affirmed the importance of administrative justice rights of affected persons in relation to the rights of access to housing,[68] water,[69] education,[70]

---

[61] In *Masetlha v President of the Republic of South Africa* 2008 1 SA 566 (CC) para 181, the Constitutional Court elaborated upon the goals and values of the Constitution in relation to democracy and participation:
>   "[I]t is apparent from the Constitution that the democratic government that is contemplated is a participatory democracy which is accountable, transparent and requires participation in decision-making."
See also *Doctors for Life International v The Speaker of the National Assembly* 2006 6 SA 416 (CC) para 121; *Poverty Alleviation Network v President of the Republic of South Africa* 2010 6 BCLR 520 (CC) para 40.

[62] *Poverty Alleviation Network v President of the Republic of South Africa* 2010 6 BCLR 520 (CC) para 33.

[63] See *Doctors for Life International v The Speaker of the National Assembly* 2006 6 SA 416 (CC) paras 108, 112-117.

[64] Para 115.

[65] See paras 115, 234; *Minister of Health and Another NO v New Clicks South Africa (Pty) Ltd* 2006 2 SA 311 (CC) para 627.

[66] Liebenberg *Socio-Economic Rights* 167-168.

[67] In cases where a determination of what constitutes "administrative action" has had to be made, and where executive public power falls outside the strict definition of "administrative action", the courts have still insisted that the executive must abide by the values of accountability, responsiveness and openness in a participatory constitutional democracy. See *Albutt v Centre for the Study of Violence and Reconciliation* 2010 3 SA 293 (CC).

[68] See *Joseph v City of Johannesburg* 2010 4 SA 55 (CC) (right to procedural fairness when electricity supply disconnected by municipality); and *Nokotyana v Ekurhuleni Metropolitan Municipality* 2010 4 BCLR 312 (CC) (right to sanitation).

[69] See *Mazibuko v City of Johannesburg (Centre on Housing Rights and Evictions as amicus curiae)* 2010 4 SA 1 (CC) (right to sufficient water and legality of prepaid water meters).

[70] See *Head of Department: Mpumalanga Department of Education v Hoërskool Ermelo* 2010 2 SA 415 (CC) (exclusive language policy set by school governing body thwarts right to education).

and social security.[71] For instance, in *Joseph v City of Johannesburg,* the Constitutional Court stressed the importance of participation within the executive branch of government, at the level of local government.[72] The Court asserted the right to procedural fairness of tenants whose electricity was disconnected by the municipality due to non-payment by the landlord as crucial "not only for the protection of citizens' rights, but also to facilitate trust in the public administration and in our participatory democracy".[73]

The courts have also begun to develop a body of jurisprudence on "meaningful engagement" with communities potentially affected by evictions, based on an interpretation of section 26(3). "Meaningful engagement" refers to the requirement on the part of municipalities to hold consultations with communities potentially affected by evictions. The Court's reading of this requirement from section 26(3) also has the potential to be extended to policy-making in relation to other socio-economic rights.

The Constitutional Court has thus repeatedly affirmed that deliberative and participatory democracy seeks to enhance and deepen representative democracy and the values of freedom and dignity, by expanding the opportunities for people's active participation in decision-making processes, including in cases dealing with their access to public goods (socio-economic rights). It is about more than merely "participating in periodic elections and in the formal mechanisms created for allowing citizens input in the institutions of representative democracy",[74] but also going beyond to creating numerous forums for dialogue and mechanisms for participation. The aim is to promote greater participation in the public and private institutions, which affect diverse aspects of people's lives.[75] Those particularly disadvantaged groups who are not easily able to participate in deliberative processes as peers or political equals, must be given real and *meaningful* opportunities for participation.[76]

In this part I have argued that the combination of opportunities for participatory democracy to thrive in policy- and law-making, administrative decision-making and adjudication of rights, will enhance the responsiveness of the state to conditions of poverty and inequality in South Africa and move us closer to the constitutional ideal of social justice.

I will now locate this discussion in the growing discourse in South Africa on the role of a *developmental state* in achieving higher rates of growth and development to address the challenges of eradication of poverty,

---

[71] See a number of successful court challenges that were brought under administrative law by indigent individuals affected by the withdrawal of social security benefits amidst the ongoing systemic problems in the administration of social grants in the Eastern Cape: *Bushula v Permanent Secretary, Department of Welfare, Eastern Cape* 2000 2 SA 849 (E); *Mahambehlala v Member of the Executive Council for Welfare, Eastern Cape Provincial Government* 2001 9 BCLR 899 (SE); *Mbanga v Member of the Executive Council for Welfare* 2002 1 SA 359 (SA); *Nomala v Permanent Secretary, Department of Welfare* 2001 8 BCLR 844 (E); *Permanent Secretary, Department of Welfare, Eastern Cape Provincial Government v Ngxusa; Rangani v Superintendent-General, Department of Health and Welfare, Northern Province* 1999 4 SA 385 (T).

[72] *Joseph v City of Johannesburg* 2010 4 SA 55 (CC) para 46.

[73] Para 46.

[74] Liebenberg *Socio-Economic Rights* 30.

[75] 30.

[76] 32.

underdevelopment and inequality. Though located in a constitutional framework of justiciable socio-economic rights, the conceptualisation of anti-poverty policies, laws and programmes and the way in which the state sees its role in delivering services to people in order to address poverty and inequality, is still highly influenced, in design, by the model of the state and its guiding ideology for socio-economic transformation.

4　The emerging South African democratic developmental state: Implications for socio-economic transformation

Since 2002, there has been a shift by the South African government, away from a market-oriented economic-policy approach towards a more "developmental state" approach.[77] This is primarily driven by a focus on the need for public-sector action to remove binding constraints to growth through a range of strategic public-sector interventions.[78] The concept of the "developmental state" emerged out of East Asia and is generally used to mean a state that drives development, in a centralised manner in contrast to a more *laissez faire*, decentralised free-market approach.[79] It embodies particular economic and political connotations for policies and institutional make-up of states, and is transitional by its very nature.[80] It applies to lesser developed or transitional states that are striving to achieve greater economic and social success.

The concept of a developmental state has evolved from the traditional notion into the 21st century so-called *democratic* developmental state. This implies that the latter types of developmental states also require "effective and efficient bureaucracies, resilient leadership, sustainable organisational structure, strong state and national building initiatives, democracy, rule of law, sustainable economic growth and redistribution, social capital and social equity".[81]

---

[77]　See F Cloete & C Auriacombe *Measuring Empowerment in Democratic Developmental States* (2011) unpublished conference paper presented at the Centre for International Policy Exchanges Conference on *Improving the Quality of Public Services* in Moscow, Russia, 27-06-2011 – 29-06-2011 (on file with author).

[78]　See national macro-economic policy documents: National Treasury *Growth, Employment and Redistribution ("GEAR")* (1996) <http://www.treasury.gov.za/publications/other/gear/default.aspx> (accessed 27-11-2011) and Presidency *Accelerated and Shared Growth Initiative for South Africa ("ASGI-SA")* (2006) <http://www.info.gov.za/asgisa> (accessed 27-11-2011).

[79]　See discussions on the evolution of the concept of a "developmental state" from East Asia in C Johnson *MITI and the Japanese Miracle: The Growth of Industrial Policy 1925-1975* (1982); A Amsden *Asia's Next Giant: South Korea and Late Industrialisation* (1989); R Wade *Governing the Market: Economic Theory and the Role of Government in East Asian Industrialisation* (1990); Z Onis "The Logic of the Developmental State" (1991) 24 *Comparative Politics* 109 109-126; M Woo-Cumings (ed) *The Developmental State* (1999), and in particular C Johnson "The Development State: Odyssey of a Concept" in M Woo-Cumings (ed) *The Developmental State* (1999) 32; P Evans *Embedded Autonomy: States and Industrial Transformation* (1995); PB Evans *What Will the 21st Century Developmental State Look Like?* (2006) unpublished paper presented at conference on *The Role of Government in Hong Kong* organised by the Central Policy Unit of HKSAR Government, Public Policy Research Centre of The Chinese University of Hong Kong and the Hong Kong Sociological Association in Hong Kong (SAR, China), 03-11-2006 (on file with the author); and United Nations Conference on Trade and Development ("UNCTAD") *Economic Development in Africa: Domestic Resource Mobilization and Developmental States* (2007) <http://www.unctad.org/en/docs/aldcafrica2007_en.pdf> (accessed 27-11-2011).

[80]　Cloete & Auriacombe *Measuring Empowerment in Democratic Developmental States* 2.

[81]　2.

Scholars have recently begun to describe the South African state as a "democratic developmental state".[82] Broadly speaking, the discourse in South Africa is captured by a state that is determined to influence the direction and pace of economic development by directly intervening in the development process with the co-option of selected business and social elites, rather than relying on the uncoordinated influence of market forces to allocate resources. This is achieved through collaboratively establishing substantive social and economic goals to guide the long-term process of development and placing responsibility on all actors to collectively strive towards those goals.[83]

The main proposition of this part is that South Africa can at least be said to be an emerging democratic developmental state due to its developmentalist approach, the increasingly interventionist role of the state in the economy, the emergent institutional support for the state's capacity to realise its developmental objectives, and the acknowledgement that participatory democracy lies at the heart of the transformation project. However, the undemocratic impulses of the state are severely limiting its achievements thus far, as witnessed for example in the limitations on freedom of information, the corruption and culture of impunity that is rife and the impact that will have on the poor.

4 1   The origins and characteristics of the "developmental state"

The concept of a "developmental state" arose from an endeavour by Chalmers Johnson to generalise about the model pursued by many of the East Asian nations post the Second World War, in order to rapidly modernise their economies. In his well-known study of Japan's modernisation, Johnson characterised the basic framework of the East Asian developmental state as one where the state sets specific development goals and then mobilises society to achieve industrial modernisation.[84] The idea of "a centralised state interacting with the private sector from a position of pre-eminence so as to secure development objectives"[85] is generally called the "developmental

---

[82]   See W Gumede *Delivering the Democratic Developmental State in South Africa* DBSA Development Planning Division Working Paper Series No 9 (2009); and various chapters in O Edigheji (ed) *Constructing a Democratic Developmental State in South Africa* (2010).

[83]   For discussions on South Africa's evolution from a welfare state to a "developmental state" see: M Pieterse "Beyond the Welfare State: Globalisation of Neo-Liberal Culture and the Constitutional Protection of Social and Economic Rights in South Africa" (2003) 14 *Stell LR* 1 1-28; G Rapholo "Towards Becoming a Developmental State: A Focus on Poverty Alleviation" (2003) 2 *Service Delivery Review* 24 24-27; R Levin "Building Service Effectiveness" (2004) 3 *Service Delivery Review* 25 25-28; O Edigheji *A Democratic Developmental State in Africa?* Research Report 105, Centre for Policy Studies (2005) <http://www.cps.org.za/cps%20pdf/RR105.pdf> (accessed 31-03-2010); R Southall "Introduction: Can South Africa be a Developmental State?" in S Buhlungu, J Daniel, R Southall & J Lutchman (eds) *State of the Nation: South Africa 2005-2006* (2006) xvii xvii–xxiv; Congress of the South African Trade Unions (COSATU) *A Developmental State for South Africa?* (2005) unpublished (on file with author); S Gelb *A South African Developmental State: What is Possible?* (2006) unpublished paper presented at the Harold Wolpe Memorial Trusts' Tenth Anniversary Colloquium *Engaging Silences and Unresolved Issues in the Political Economy of South Africa* in Cape Town, South Africa, 21-09-2006 – 23-09-2006 (on file with author); and B Fine *The Curious Incidence of the Developmental State in the Night-Time* (2007) paper presented at the *SANPAD Poverty Conference* held in Durban, South Africa, 26-06-2007 – 30-06-2007 <http://eprints.soas.ac.uk/5611/> (accessed 27-11-2011).

[84]   See generally Johnson *MITI and the Japanese Miracle*.

[85]   Gumede *Delivering the Democratic Developmental State in SA* 4.

state" theory. Analysing these processes, Johnson pointed out four critical elements in the Japanese developmental state: firstly the bureaucracy was assigned the tasks of planning, constructing and supervising industry; secondly a political system was established to support the bureaucracy; thirdly when the government wanted to intervene in the market, it left plenty of scope for activities of private enterprises; and lastly, political direction was given by the Ministry of International Trade and Industry.[86] Co-opted elites, soft authoritarianism and a submissive population are all constitutive elements of the original developmental state.

Since Johnson, the developmental state has been defined differently by scholars and development agencies alike. Some scholars tend to emphasise the role of the state. In this category are scholars like Manuel Castells, who defines a developmental state "as one which establishes – as its principle of legitimacy – its ability to promote and sustain development, understood as the combination of steady high rates of economic growth and structural change in the productive system, both domestically and in its relationship with the international economy".[87]

Other scholars have stressed the organisational features of the developmental state. They identify that a developmental state must also have the capacity to *formulate* and *implement* its developmental agenda. Key structural characteristics are "autonomy" of state institutions, which enables it to define and promote its strategic developmental goals, and its "embeddedness" – that is, "a concrete set of social ties that binds the state to society and provides institutionalised channels for the continual negotiation and renegotiation of goals and policies".[88] In this perspective, autonomy implies the presence or high degrees of coherent state agencies that are able to formulate and implement coherent developmental goals. A significant feature of the autonomous state is greater coordination of industrial change and economic adjustment.

Though not widely acknowledged in the literature, developmental states at the same time also implemented social policies, focusing on non-state entities such as families and firms, with the state implementing social welfare programmes.[89] They made substantial efforts to ensure more equitable development through land reform, relevant education and training, support for small enterprise and provision of housing and infrastructure.[90] Improvements in social protection focused on measures that would reduce the cost of employment and raise productivity. Increasing employment was supported by restrictions on retrenchment and elevated spending on skills development.[91]

---

[86]   See generally Johnson *MITI and the Japanese Miracle*.

[87]   M Castells "Four Asian Tigers with a Dragon Head: A Comparative Analysis of the State, Economy and Society in the Asian Pacific Rim" in R Appelbaum & J Henderson (eds) *States and Development in the Asia Pacific Rim* (1992) 33 56. See also Gumede *Delivering the Democratic Developmental State in SA* 4-6, who provides a useful summary of the common characteristics of East Asian developmental states.

[88]   Evans *Embedded Autonomy* 12.

[89]   O Edigheji "Constructing a Democratic Developmental State in South Africa: Potentials and Challenges" in Edigheji (ed) *Constructing a Democratic Developmental State in South Africa* (2010) 1 9-10.

[90]   Gumede *Delivering the Democratic Developmental State in SA* 6.

[91]   6.

In summary, the concept of a developmental state has a particular intellectual history, grounded primarily in the experience of industrialisation in East Asian states. It emphasises the ability of the state to drive development by guiding capital towards new activities – achieved under largely authoritarian and centralised governance. East Asian developmental states reached their developmental goals under authoritarian conditions and dominant party democratic systems.

4 2　The evolution of the democratic developmental state

Peter Evans provides the theoretical grounding for the *democratic* developmental state – what he terms the 21st-century developmental state.[92] The 21st-century democratic developmental state that Evans depicts is grounded in three strands of development theory: the "new growth theory"; "institutional approaches"; and the "capability approach".[93] These theories converge into Evan's main proposition that "enhancing human capabilities" is the central goal of the 21st-century developmental state. He states thus:

> "Enhancement of human capabilities is not, however, just a welfare goal but is also an important foundation for sustained economic growth: investment in human capital has the potential to lead to social inclusion and economic growth. From this premise, human capability is both a means and an end."[94]

Furthermore, this latter approach places great importance on equity concerns. Similar to the Asian developmental states, equity is a focal goal and institutional architectures must be designed and policies promoted to attain that goal.[95] The state capacities required for the enhancement of human capabilities and the attainment of equity, Evans argues, are the efficient provision of collective goods. This in turn depends on both administrative capacity and political foundations that are anchored on "active democratic structures".[96] The latter is also a foundation for effective economic management. Effective provision of public goods, including health, education, social welfare and the like, is a manifestation of social citizenship, enhancing the well-being of ordinary citizens; and public goods are themselves major economic infrastructure required by market agents.[97]

With development theory, in particular Sen's work, as his basis, Evans notes that, because development is about human well-being, "development strategies and policy cannot be formulated by technocrats, but must be

---

[92] P Evans "Constructing the 21st Century Developmental State: Potentialities and Pitfalls" in O Edigheji (ed) *Constructing a Democratic Developmental State in South Africa* (2010) 37 37-58.

[93] 37-58. His three strands of development theory are largely based on A Sen *Development as Freedom* (1999), the initiator of the "capability approach" in development theory.

[94] Edigheji "Constructing a Democratic Developmental State" in *Constructing a Democratic Developmental State in SA* 13.

[95] 13. Eidgheji defines "equitable growth" as:
    "[A] high rate of economic growth combined with equitable distribution of income and wealth, with egalitarianism meaning that all segments of society are able to share in the benefits of growth."

[96] Evans "Constructing the 21st Century Developmental State" in *Constructing a Democratic Developmental State in SA* 38.

[97] 38.

derived from democratically organised public deliberation".[98] Deliberative and participatory democratic institutions are thus essential to 21st-century development.[99] In light of this theoretical foundation, Evans presents the 21st-century model as fundamentally different to the Asian developmental state and rather more similar to the Nordic democratic developmental state where "human welfare and public policy were driven by deliberative mechanisms that are more broad-based than those made up of government and capital".[100]

This understanding leads me to the discussion of the evolution of a democratic developmental South African state, and how this notion can be adapted to suit our constitutional democracy in support of broad-based socio-economic transformation.

4 3   An emerging South African democratic developmental state

There is no definitive conception of the developmental state in South Africa in the academic literature and policy documents of government, the ruling African National Congress ("ANC") party and its alliance partners, the South African Communist Party ("SACP") and the Congress of South African Trade Unions ("COSATU"). The literature and policy documents are filled with rhetoric and ideology with reference to the developmental state. Nevertheless, it is argued that the concept is useful as an evolving and transitional political framework to guide South Africa's socio-economic transformation.

South Africa's transition to democracy took place under changing global conditions. These were characterised by the collapse of the communist bloc and the ascendancy of neo-liberal market ideology. A key element of this ideology argued for the primacy of the market over the state. This was in stark contrast to the newly elected ANC government's Reconstruction and Development Programme ("RDP"),[101] which called for a strong interventionist and redistributive state. The RDP focused on meeting basic needs, developing the country's human resources, building the economy and democratising the state and society. The RDP document defines development in terms of a growing economy in which redistribution is a critical element. It includes the preservation and development of human resources in the form of skills-training, job-creation and the provision of education, health services, services, infrastructure and an adequate social security system. It also strongly embeds the notions of representative and participatory democracy.[102]

During the first decade of freedom, some progress was achieved in addressing RDP priorities, but global pressure saw government adopt the Growth, Employment and Redistribution ("GEAR") policy framework. Left-orientated social movements, trade unions and commentators saw this framework as a shift towards identifying the market as the supreme agent for

---

[98] 43.

[99] Edigheji "Constructing a Democratic Developmental State" in *Constructing a Democratic Developmental State in SA* 14.

[100] 14.

[101] Office of the Presidency *White Paper on Reconstruction and Development* (15-11-1994) <http://www.info.gov.za/view/DownloadFileAction?id=70427> (accessed 28-11-2011).

[102] 9.

resource allocation and an acknowledgement that the inherited formal economy would be the determinant of growth and development. One consequence of the adoption of GEAR was that development priorities, including the provision of social services and economic infrastructure, were subject to fiscal discipline, cost recovery and financial sustainability.[103] GEAR is widely acknowledged to have succeeded in bringing about macro-economic stability, but critiqued for its limited ability to equitably distribute the economic benefits of stability and substantially reduce poverty and inequality in the country.[104]

In a context of resource scarcity, growing inequality and ongoing wide-spread poverty, the making of strategic choices on where and how to invest scarce resources to maximise social and economic return became imperative in South Africa. Since GEAR, market failure in addressing the abovementioned developmental challenges provided a strong rationale for government intervention. This position was reinforced by a resurgent belief in the role of the state as a driver of economic development, where government leads growth creation and identifies the major beneficiaries of growth through active interventions, such as infrastructure investment, job creation, State-Owned Enterprise ("SOE") initiatives, sector and small enterprise support, industrial policy, targeted procurement and spatial development.[105] In fulfilling its developmental role, government recognised its position as a key facilitating, partnering and collaborative economic agent through planning, fixed investment and developmental spending. Public investment has therefore become a key mechanism for the achievement of higher GDP growth, as this guides private investment decisions and facilitates social and economic spin-offs.[106] The Accelerated and Shared Growth Initiative for South Africa ("ASGI-SA") economic policy framework announced by the government in late 2005 confirmed the return into policy discourse of the role of the state, as compared with the mid-1990s.

Increasingly, over the past five years, the state has thus asserted the objective to build and consolidate a strong developmental state in South Africa – a developmental state that excels in the basics of public administration and intervenes strategically in the economy to promote socio-economic transformation.[107]

Fine divides the discourse on the developmental state in South Africa into two schools, the economic and the political.[108] The economic school focuses on the economic policies that the state needs to adopt in order to bring about development, namely through the array of interventions associated with

---

[103] Edigheji "Constructing a Democratic Developmental State" in *Constructing a Democratic Developmental State in SA* 12-13.

[104] 12-13.

[105] 12-13.

[106] 12-13.

[107] T Manuel *Budgeting Challenges in the Developmental State* (2004) speech by the Minister of Finance at the *Senior Management Service Conference* held in Cape Town, South Africa, 20-09-2004 <http://www. treasury.gov.za/comm_media/speeches/2004/2004092001.pdf> (accessed 31-03-2010); T Mbeki *Address of the President of the Republic of South Africa* on the occasion of the *Budget Vote of the Presidency: National Assembly* held in Cape Town (07-06-2006) <http://www.dfa.gov.za/docs/speeches/2006/ mbek0607.htm> (accessed 28-11-2011).

[108] Fine *The Curious Incidence of the Developmental State in the Night-Time* 2.

the East Asian model, especially protection, export promotion, targeted investment and finance, and so on. The political school, on the other hand, is more or less entirely concerned with addressing the issue of whether the state has the capacity and motivation to adopt and implement developmental policies. In particular, the focus is upon whether the state has the autonomy, in some sense, both to adopt policy independent of special interests and to deploy that independence for broader developmental aims.[109]

The reason for the lack of clarity on the definition of a developmental state in the literature appears to be that the developmental state has sprung into South African discourse from the political arena and has, until recently, largely been rhetorical and unexamined. The concept first began appearing in policy documents of the ANC, COSATU and the SACP.[110]

In 2005 the previous Minister of Finance, Trevor Manuel introduced the concept and trajectory:

"A developmental state is one that is determined to influence the direction and pace of economic development by directly intervening in the development process, rather than relying on the uncoordinated influence of market forces to allocate resources."[111]

Manuel, in quoting Sen's book *Development as Freedom*, stated:

"The task of a developmental state is to fight poverty and expand economic opportunities for the poor."[112]

Manuel's text is then heavily quoted in President Mbeki's *Budget Speech* for 2006.[113] The developmental state has since appeared in the speeches of a range of Ministers over the last five years, both during the Mbeki era and under President Jacob Zuma.[114]

The State President has over the past couple of years elaborated on the commitment to build a developmental state, which among other things entails the improvement of public services and strengthening of democratic institutions.[115] Two Ministries in the Presidency have been established to enhance strategic planning and performance monitoring and evaluation. The inclusion of State-Owned Enterprises and Development Finance Institutions in government planning processes and enhanced administration of service delivery, are some of the ways in which the government is attempting to create

---

[109] 3.

[110] See eg: ANC *The State, Property Relations and Social Transformation* (1998) <http://amadlandawonye. wikispaces.com/1998,+ANC,+State,+Property+Relations,+Social+Transformation> (accessed 28-11-2011); ANC *National Policy Conference Report* (2007); South African Communist Party *African Communist* (1998) <http://www.sacp.org.za/list.php?type=African%20Communist&year=1998> (accessed 28-11-2011); COSATU *A Developmental State for South Africa?*.

[111] Manuel *Budgeting Challenges in the Developmental State*.

[112] Manuel *Budgeting Challenges in the Developmental State*.

[113] President Mbeki *Budget Speech* (2006).

[114] Presidency *State of the Nation* addresses available at <http://www.info.gov.za/speeches/son/index.html> (accessed 28-11-2011).

[115] President JG Zuma *State of the Nation Address 2009* (2009) delivered at the *Joint Sitting of Parliament* held in Cape Town, South Africa (03-06-2009) <http://www.thepresidency.gov.za/pebble.asp?relid=310> (accessed 01-11-2011).

a developmental state.[116] In his *State of the Nation Address 2010*,[117] President Jacob Zuma also committed to five priorities: education, health, rural development and land reform, creating decent work, and fighting crime, with education and skills development at the centre of the government's policies.

It is clear that the indigenous South African model of the developmental state, as distinct from the Asian or any other model, at least in theory and rhetoric, means that intervention in the economy to generate higher rates of "shared" growth and employment is a means to an end to poverty, and participatory democracy where the poor can "act as their own liberators"[118] is central to that enterprise.

Gumede and others identify a number of essential conditions for a successful ongoing project of establishing a South African democratic developmental state.[119]

First, it requires the political will and a long-term developmental vision based on broad national consensus among political parties, civil society, business and organised labour, to industrialise and modernise.[120] This requires mature, quality leadership and determination on the part of the country's political elite. All stakeholders must then collaboratively implement an integrated long-term development plan based on a holistic vision. Successful long-term development plans integrate action for the short-term, medium term and long term. A long-term development plan is crucial for the identification of the core priorities of a nation. But these development plans must have public and stakeholder legitimacy.[121]

Second, a fundamental feature of the South African democratic developmental state is that it must allow for participation and be capable of addressing the socio-economic needs of its entire population, especially the poor, marginalised and historically disadvantaged. The conception of the South African democratic developmental state is the kind of state that fosters the empowerment of people. It is vital that ordinary people are involved in the process of development and as they get more involved, they must also own the process. Whenever policies are developed, which are aimed at addressing existing socio-economic imbalances, ordinary people should be involved.

---

[116] Zuma *State of the Nation Address 2009*.

[117] President JG Zuma *State of the Nation Address 2010* (2010) delivered at the *Joint Sitting of Parliament* held in Cape Town, South Africa (11-02-2010). <http//www.info.gov.za/speeches/2010/10021119051001. htm> (accessed 01-11-2011).

[118] Commonly used phrase in various speeches and documents of the ANC.

[119] See Gumede *Delivering the Democratic Developmental State in SA* 2-4; and generally Edigheji (ed) *Constructing a Democratic Developmental State in SA*; Cloete & Auriacombe *Measuring Empowerment in Democratic Developmental States*.

[120] See Anonymous "Mont Fleur Scenarios" (July 1992) <http://www.generonconsulting.com/publications/papers/pdfs/Mont%20Fleur.pdf> (accessed 28-11-2011); Presidency "SA Scenarios 2025: The Future We Chose?" (September 2008) <http://www.info.gov.za/view/DownloadFileAction?id=89109> (accessed 28-11-2011); and Anonymous "Dinokeng Scenarios" (2009) <http://www.dinokengscenarios.co.za/> (accessed 28-11-2011). These scenario exercises were developed at different points in South Africa's recent history, with the participation of a wide spectrum of society for purposes of identifying a long-term vision for the country, which would then be translated into a plan.

[121] Gumede *Delivering the Democratic Developmental State in SA* 11 explains that although most of the East Asian developmental states were autocratic, their development plans had wider legitimacy among the key stakeholders in society. In Malaysia for example, the New Economic Policy – its long-term development plan – became the official "ideology".

The most critical aspect of this kind of developmental state is participatory democracy.[122]

Third, at the core of the developmental effort is an efficient, well-coordinated state, staffed with skilled employees. The state must have the administrative, technical and political capacity and competency to facilitate the setting of national goals, develop the right policies to deliver on those goals, and implement these policies. This also means that widespread corruption and the policy of cadre deployment must be systematically abolished. Furthermore, the most successful developmental states had a central coordinating centre driving socio-economic transformation.[123] This centre not only determinedly pushes the economy's vulnerabilities, and makes it competitive, by diversifying and identifying new niche manufacturing, but directly coordinates industrial investment, actively directs macro-economic policy towards developmental goals and protects and promotes the national interest.[124] It facilitates the setting of national goals, makes use of the market, and monitors whether policies are implemented and are having the desired effect. This is not compatible with more advanced economies that necessitate less state intervention and more transparency and accountability. A successful democratic developmental state therefore leads to its own demise as a developmental state, and is forced to accept the empowerment of its people and democratise increasingly. A developmental state is therefore a transitional state form and is not sustainable in the long term if its developmental goals are increasingly achieved.

I will now briefly assess the current state of South Africa's development in practice, as opposed to in theory and rhetoric, applying Gumede's pre-conditions for a democratic developmental state.

Firstly, the National Planning Commission ("NPC") was established in 2009, to support Cabinet in long-term planning and coordination. The NPC is chaired by the Minister in the Presidency: National Planning Commission Trevor Manuel, with ANC heavyweight and business leader Cyril Ramaphosa as his deputy. Also on the team are ANC national executive committee member Joel Netshitenzhe and Business Unity South Africa chief executive officer Jerry Vilakazi. The 24 people on the commission come from a cross-sector of society and have expertise in areas including finance, industry, telecommunications, biotechnology, energy, education, food security and climate change. The NPC is responsible for developing a draft long-term vision and strategic plan for South Africa. They have thus far delivered a diagnostic report of all the critical issues facing the country and engaged in a process of discussion with people across the country. This led to the first draft of South Africa's long-term plan, which was released on 11 November

---

[122] 4.

[123] In 2001, the Policy, Coordination and Advisory Services Unit ("PCAS") was established to coordinate policy formulation and monitoring and evaluation of policy implementation.

[124] See R Davies (Minister of Trade and Industry) *2010/11 – 2012/13 Industrial Policy Action Plan (IPAP2)* (18-02-2010) <http://www.dti.gov.za/parliament/022310_Min_briefing_revised_ipap.pdf> (accessed 23-11-2011).

2011.[125] This is evidence, in part, of the political will to develop a long-term developmental vision for South Africa, based on broad national consensus and to allow for participation in addressing the socio-economic needs of the poor. Other examples of participation include the Constitutional Court cases requiring the state to "meaningfully engage" with citizens on their needs and solutions to socio-economic problems, before they implement housing programmes.[126]

However, the recent attempts by the Executive and the Legislature to introduce and pass the Protection of State Information Bill B6 of 2010,[127] which allows state information to be categorised as secret and does not allow for a public interest defence for whistleblowers and journalists who expose state wrongdoing, is contrary to the spirit of participatory democracy. The introduction of the Bill met with strong opposition from civil society and opposition parties. It is seen as a return to the apartheid-era repression, and as a severe curtailment of the right of access to information and the principles of transparency and accountability.[128]

Secondly, in relation to an efficient, well-coordinated state, staffed with skilled employees, the state still has a long way to go. The efficiency of the state leaves a lot to be desired, and is constantly mired by widespread corruption among officials and politicians alike. This situation will be made worse with the adoption of the Information Bill.

Thirdly, the Industrial Policy Action Plan ("IPAP2")[129] builds on the National Industrial Policy Framework ("NIPF")[130] and the 2007/08 IPAP,[131] and represents a scaling up of the government's efforts to promote long-term industrialisation and industrial diversification beyond the reliance on traditional commodities and non-tradable services. Its purpose is to expand production in value-added sectors with high employment and growth multipliers that compete in export markets as well as compete in the domestic market against imports. In so doing, the action plan also places emphasis on more labour-absorbing production and services sectors, the increased participation of historically disadvantaged people and regions in the economy and seeks to facilitate, in the medium term, South Africa's contribution to

---

[125] National Planning Commission "National Developoment Plan" (11-11-2011) <http://www.npconline. co.za/medialib/downloads/home/NPC%20National%20Development%20Plan%20Vision%202030%20 -lo-res.pdf> (accessed 28-11-2011). See also SAPA "Ramaphosa, Godsell on National Planning Commission" (30-04-2010) *Mail & Guardian* <http://mg.co.za/article/2010-04-30-ramaphosa-godsell-on-national-planning-commission> (accessed 24-11-2011).

[126] *Port Elizabeth Municipality v Various Occupiers* 2005 1 SA 217 (CC) (*"PE Municipality"*); *Occupiers of 51 Olivia Road, Berea Township and 197 Main Street, Johannesburg v City of Johannesburg* 2008 3 SA 208 (CC) (*"Olivia Road"*); *Residents of Joe Slovo Community, Western Cape v Thubelisha Homes* 2010 3 SA 454 (CC) (*"Joe Slovo"*).

[127] The Bill was passed by the National Assembly on 22-11-2011.

[128] See SAPA "Info Bill Will Hide Corruption" (12-10-2011) *News24* <http://www.news24.com/SouthAfrica/ Politics/Info-bill-will-hide-corruption-20111012> (accessed 24-11-2011).

[129] Department of Trade and Industry *Industrial Policy Action Plan II.*

[130] Department of Trade and Industry *National Industrial Policy Framework* (2010) <http://www.info.gov. za/view/DownloadFileAction?id=108831> (accessed 28-11-2011).

[131] Department of Trade and Industry *Industrial Policy Action Plan* (2007) <http://www.tips.org.za/ node/1402> (accessed 28-11-2011).

industrial development in the African region. The government's New Growth Path[132] reiterates these elements.

In conclusion, whereas developmental states in East Asia were authoritarian; in the South African context, the developmental state has to be democratic. While this is different to Johnson's conceptualisation of the developmental state as a soft authoritarian state, it is closer to Evans' broader definition of "state embeddedness". As Gumede suggests:

> "South Africa is a constitutional democracy, and the constitution provides for both a representative and a participatory democracy. This means that ordinary citizens will not only have to be consulted but also to be involved and participate in the decisions, whether economic, political or social, that affect them. This makes the challenge of building a developmental state very different in South Africa from elsewhere: the state must deliver development in both the economic and democratic spheres."[133]

South Africa's prospects of overcoming its historic legacy of poverty and inequality and offering a way ahead for a transformed society rests on a vision of a *democratic developmental state*. But this vision remains somewhat undefined, its implications have only just begun to be thought out and the undemocratic tendencies of the state have to be overcome.

5   Conclusion

The South African Constitution is a legal framework underpinning the socio-economic transformation of South African society from its unequal and unjust past. It lays the foundation for participatory and deliberative processes and forums to imagine and conceive what is required to transform this society. These processes and forums must be sufficiently inclusive of a diversity of voices, and enable all groups, including those affected by poverty and marginalisation, to participate meaningfully as equals. This requires positive measures to remedy various manifestations of widespread socio-economic deprivation and disempowerment in South Africa.

The analysis has pointed to a number of conclusions. The first is that the developmentalist reorientation of the South African state has been tempered by the globalisation imperatives, which give primacy to the needs of the market, as well as by the non-participatory tendencies of the state. While the government continues to stress the relevance of the people in its policy, in actual practice citizens and people are frequently passive clients, users and customers. With respect to the structural features of the state, South Africa is gradually establishing institutional features of a transitional democratic developmental state, notably collaborative centralised leadership with a collective vision and plan, to promote a process of accumulation whose fruits would be shared by all. The key challenges remain the inclusion of the non-elites – the ordinary people – in the preparation and implementation of a democratic developmental state, and the elimination of corruption. Once these goals are eventually achieved, the state also has to change its character

---

[132] Department of Economic Development "New Growth Path" (2011) <http://www.info.gov.za/view/DownloadFileAction?id=135748> (accessed 24-11-2011).

[133] Gumede *Delivering the Democratic Developmental State in SA* 11-12.

to a more traditional democracy in order to acknowledge the successful empowerment of its citizens.

However, as Chief Justice Langa elaborates, the view of transformation envisaged by the Constitution is a process of constant dialogue and contestation in the pursuit of a more just society:

"[T]ransformation is not a temporary phenomenon that ends when we all have equal access to resources and basic services and when lawyers and judges embrace a culture of justification. Transformation is a permanent ideal, a way of looking at the world that creates a space in which dialogue and contestation are truly possible, in which new ways of being are constantly explored and created, accepted and rejected and in which change is unpredictable but the idea of change is constant. This is perhaps the ultimate vision of a transformative, rather than a transitional Constitution. This is the perspective that sees the Constitution as not transformative because of its peculiar historical position or its particular socio-economic goals but because it envisions a society that will always be open to change and contestation, a society that will always be defined by transformation."[134]

SUMMARY

In order for socio-economic transformation to have a real impact on the lives of the poor and marginalised, meaningful participation in the development of law and policy as well as administrative decision-making, is required. Opportunities for informed participation can lead to transparent, accountable dialogue and debate on key policy choices to address the impact of poverty and inequality. This resonates with a participatory constitutional democracy, which requires decisions to be considered in the light of certain fundamental norms and values. The policy discourse in South Africa around solutions to poverty eradication has evolved over the past five years from a "welfare state" approach to a "developmental state" approach which must have the strategic capacity to mobilise society around the developmental agenda and bring technical and organisational capacity to bear in order to create fundamental change. The developmental state theory in South Africa is being grounded in principles of representative democracy, participatory democracy and accountability of the state.

---

[134] Langa (2006) *Stell LR* 354.

CHAPTER 8

THE POTENTIAL AND LIMITS OF AN EQUAL RIGHTS PARADIGM IN ADDRESSING POVERTY

Sandra Fredman[*]

1 Introduction

Poverty is increasingly recognised as a human rights issue. As Paul Hunt, previous Special Rapporteur for Health, tellingly put it, "[h]uman rights are not just about prisoners of conscience, they are also about prisoners of poverty".[1] But how do we address poverty through human rights? The focus of most of the chapters in this book is on socio-economic rights. The aim of this chapter is to consider what role the right to equality can and should play in relation to poverty. The right to equality is important for reasons which are both pragmatic and principled. While socio-economic rights are still fighting for full recognition within the human rights arena, the right to equality has an old and well established position. Indeed, in jurisdictions without express socio-economic rights within their constitutional bills of rights, the right to equality, together with rights to life and security, are potentially the primary vehicles for establishing a human rights approach to poverty. Thus Brodsky and Day have forcefully argued that women's right to equality brings with it a justiciable right to income security.[2] This makes it important on a pragmatic level to explore the role of the right to equality in addressing poverty.

This in turn requires a deeper understanding of the relationship between poverty and the traditional constituency of equality rights, namely inequality on the grounds of race, gender or other status. With the growing recognition of the concentration of poverty within status groups has come an increasing overlap between the areas of concerns of anti-poverty policy and equality law. Researchers and policymakers continue to wrestle with the extent to which inequality should be part of the definition and measurement of poverty. Equally contested is the question of whether equality should be the desired outcome of anti-poverty measures, and if so, what this would entail. At the same time, deepening understandings of substantive equality have illuminated the continuities between "status" inequalities (or inequalities on the grounds

---

[*] I am grateful to the anonymous reviewers for their helpful comments and to Laura Hilly and Chris McConnachie for their research and assistance in the final draft of this chapter.

[1] P Hunt "Statement to the Panel on Maternal Mortality and the Human Rights of Women" (2008) *UN Human Rights Council* 1 <http://www.essex.ac.uk/human_rights_centre/ research/rth/pressreleases. aspx> (accessed 11-11-2011).

[2] G Brodsky & S Day "Beyond the Social and Economic Rights Debate: Substantive Equality Speaks to Poverty" (2002) 14 *Canadian J of Women & L* 185 189.

of race, gender, disability, *et cetera*) and poverty. Groups which suffer from discrimination on status grounds are disproportionately represented among people living in poverty. Conversely, people living in poverty experience many of the elements of discrimination experienced by status groups, including lack of recognition, social exclusion and reduced political participation.

I begin by considering the relationships between poverty and inequality, firstly from the perspective of distributive inequalities, and then from the perspective of status inequality or discrimination. In the third part, I briefly sketch an analytic framework within which both poverty and status inequality might be located. In the fourth part, I consider how a right to equality might function in order to contribute towards addressing poverty, drawing on the experience in four English-speaking jurisdictions: Britain, the US, Canada and South Africa. Always bearing in mind the need to be sensitive to legal and social differences between countries, I focus on three approaches which have been attempted in these jurisdictions. The first is to include poverty as a protected characteristic or a ground of discrimination. Secondly, the right to equality can be used to challenge those anti-poverty measures which are under-inclusive in that they exclude status groups (such as same-sex partners, Gypsies and Travellers, or asylum-seekers) or entrench status inequalities (for example by constructing women as dependants). The third arises in relation to "fourth generation" or proactive understandings of equality, which recognise that human rights are not merely about refraining from discrimination, but also include a positive duty to address inequality. The strong correlation between status inequality and poverty means that positive duties to address status inequality bring with them a duty to address the distributive disadvantage attached to status.

The chapter concludes that viewing poverty through the lens of substantive equality allows us to illuminate the ways in which poverty, like status discrimination, generates stigma, social exclusion and loss of autonomy. It also demonstrates that a genuine commitment to addressing status inequality necessarily entails addressing the poverty and economic disadvantage that have resulted from structural discrimination against women, black people, people with disabilities and other status groups. This in turn suggests that the right to equality can have important traction in the field of poverty and distributive inequality. However, in the jurisdictions examined here, there remains a deep reluctance to regard the right to equality as generating social rights in its own right. The result is that, while the right to equality potentially makes a valuable contribution to aspects of poverty based on mis-recognition and social and political exclusion, it has not yet been sufficiently developed to address distributive inequalities in its own right. The alliance with socio-economic rights, as is the case in South Africa, is more likely to yield progress on both redistributive and recognition fronts.

2   Poverty and inequality

The relationship between poverty and inequality is complex and contested. There are several dimensions to this debate. The first concerns the conceptualisation of poverty.[3] To what extent should poverty be defined in relative terms, focusing on inequalities between people, rather than in absolute terms, focusing on the ability to meet one's basic physical needs? This debate tends to focus on distributive inequalities, particularly income inequality. The second dimension brings inequalities of status into the frame, and examines the intersection between poverty on the one hand, and gender, race, disability and age discrimination on the other. The aim of this section is to air these debates rather than resolve them. Ultimately, the focus of concern in this chapter is the role that the right to equality can play in addressing poverty. Since the conceptualisation of poverty is closely related to the kind of policy prescriptions which might follow, it is important to ask how an equality perspective on poverty might enhance such policy responses.

2 1   Poverty and distributive inequality

One view is that poverty should be defined by the

"actual needs of the poor and not by reference to the expenditure of those who are not poor. A family is poor if it cannot afford to eat."[4]

According to this approach, poverty can be determined regardless of levels of inequality in society, and regardless of the social or physical context within which it is found. In Britain, the seminal work on defining and measuring poverty was done by Seebohm Rowntree, beginning in 1901. According to his definition, families living in poverty were those "whose total earnings are insufficient to obtain the minimum necessaries for the maintenance of merely physical efficiency".[5] This required an estimate of the nature and cost of "minimum necessities". Rowntree developed such a list, under the headings of food, clothing, fuel and household sundries, and worked out how much it would cost to buy them.[6] The "basic needs", or "existential minimum", approach has remained influential in a number of contexts. Thus Alexy argues that the German Constitution recognises a constitutional right to an existential minimum.[7] In a more modern manifestation, the Millenium Development Goals seek to halve the number of people living on less than $1 dollar a day, regarding this as the threshold of extreme poverty.[8] Even in relation to the more sophisticated theories, such as the capabilities approach, equality is seen as distinct from the issues surrounding poverty. Thus Nussbaum argues for a minimum threshold of capabilities, which should be separated from issues of equality. She states:

---

[3]   R Lister *Poverty* (2004) ch 1.
[4]   KJ Joseph & J Sumption *Equality* (1979) 27; see also Lister *Poverty* 21.
[5]   BS Rowntree *Poverty: A Study of Town Life* (1901) 86.
[6]   P Townsend "The Meaning of Poverty" (1962) 13 *The British Journal of Sociology* 210 215.
[7]   R Alexy *A Theory of Constitutional Rights* (2004) 290.
[8]   UN General Assembly *Millennium Declaration* (2000) UN Doc A/55/L.2 para 19.

"On the whole the [capabilities approach] holds that the question we need to ask is what is *adequate* – what basic minimum justice requires. Thus it employs the notion of a threshold, and does not comment on what justice requires us to do about inequalities over the threshold."[9]

This absolutist view presents itself as scientific definition, based on the notion of the minimum needed to sustain life.[10] Poverty can be measured and dealt with entirely separately from inequality: as long as people can obtain what they need to live, the problem of poverty is removed, regardless of the extent of inequalities in society.[11] This is not to say that inequalities are not important on this approach; just that inequality is a separate and distinct problem compared to poverty.

However, it is immediately clear that it is impossible to keep inequality wholly outside of the definition of poverty. In his path-breaking work, Townsend argued that a central mistake is to assume that "physical efficiency of individuals can be divorced from their psychological well-being and the organization and structure of society".[12] In particular, it is wrong to assume that there can be a "list of absolute necessities of life to maintain even physical efficiency or health which applies at any time and in any society, without reference to the structure, organization, physical environment and available resources of that society".[13] Instead, he advocates a relative definition of poverty, one which regards people as poverty stricken if "their income, even if adequate for survival, falls markedly behind that of the community".[14] Similarly, in the German context, Alexy argues that "what belongs to the constitutionally guaranteed existential minimum can hardly be determined without comparisons".[15]

There are several dimensions of inequality implicit in the claim that poverty is relative. The first denies the possibility of an absolute measure of basic subsistence. The amount of food required clearly depends on how much energy must be expended in one's daily life, as well as on physical constraints such as the availability of particular foodstuffs and access to cooking facilities. Similarly, the amount of shelter required for basic subsistence depends on climate, materials, *et cetera*. In this sense, poverty is relative to the location, rather than to the ways in which others live. A second dimension of relative poverty, however, relates to the social expectations and customs of particular societies, which vary not only with location but also over time. Even basic needs, such as food, are defined by social and customary expectations.

But the thoroughgoing nature of relative poverty extends even further, to the ways in which people are perceived by others in society. Even the earliest economists, such as Adam Smith, recognised that poverty entailed more than subsistence: lack of dignity can itself be an aspect of poverty. He therefore

---

[9]   M Nussbaum "Constitutions and Capabilities: 'Perception' Against Lofty Formalism" (2007) 121 *Harv L Rev* 4 12 (original emphasis).
[10] P Alcock *Understanding Poverty* 3 ed (2006) 64.
[11] 64.
[12] Townsend (1962) *The British Journal of Sociology* 218-219.
[13] 219.
[14] 221 citing JK Galbraith *The Affluent Society* (1958) 252.
[15] Alexy *Constitutional Rights* 284.

included in his notion of necessaries, "not only the commodities which are indispensably necessary for the support of life, but whatever the custom of the country renders it indecent for creditable people, even of the lowest order, to be without".[16] For him, then, a linen shirt was indispensable. The role of basic needs in defining a person as a full and respected member of society has been further elaborated in more recent research. For example, Dowler and Leather argue that food is "an expression of who a person is".[17] There are many ways in which food represents a social as well as physiological need. People in poverty lack more than the basic nutrients calculated strictly according to necessary calories. They also lack the ability to maintain conventional eating patterns, of experimenting with new diets or of enjoying eating as a social activity.[18]

The absolutist definition of poverty does more than ignore the central relationship between poverty and inequality. It can also entrench inequality in important ways. Firstly, it assumes inferiority on the part of people in poverty by defining their needs on their behalf. Rowntree, for example, used the work of nutritionists to calculate the number of calories and amount of protein thought to be required by the average man. On the basis of this, he determined the cost of purchasing a standard diet. This assumes that people should not have personal tastes; and ignores the role of social expectations and advertising. It may also set the standard of poverty much too low. As Townsend points out, individuals may not have the available expertise or the access to the appropriate shopping or cooking facilities, to translate their own budgets into precisely the standard diet Rowntree had assumed for them.[19] Secondly, the absolutist definition makes assumptions about people's needs on the basis of stereotypical roles assigned for them. Most seriously, Rowntree and other poverty analysts assumed that women need less than men, thus setting the poverty standard for women at a particularly low level. The absolutist approach also ignores the fact that time is itself a resource. As Lister points out, time is needed to convert resources into living standards, and this is frequently women's time.[20] Thus women's unpaid work is, as in many other contexts, denuded of value. Thirdly, by setting the standard at a level unrelated to a general rise in living standards, the absolutist approach makes it appear that people are no longer in poverty if they have benefited from a general rise in living standards. When translated into anti-poverty policies, this means that success in decreasing poverty can legitimate continuing extreme inequalities.[21]

---

[16]   A Smith *An Inquiry into the Nature and Causes of the Wealth of the Nations* (1892) Book V, ch 2, part I.
[17]   E Dowler & S Leather "Spare Some Change for a Bite to Eat? From Primary Poverty to Social Exclusion: The Role of Nutrition and Food" in J Bradshaw & R Sainsbury (eds) *Experiencing Poverty* (2000) 200.
[18]   200.
[19]   Townsend (1962) *The British Journal of Sociology* 217.
[20]   Lister *Poverty* 41.
[21]   There are also important critiques of a minimalist approach from within the field of socio-economic rights which are beyond the scope of this chapter. See B Porter "The Crisis in ESC Rights and Strategies for Addressing It" in J Squires, M Langford & B Thiele (eds) *The Road to a Remedy: Current Issues in the Litigation of Economic, Social and Cultural Rights* (2005) 9-10; D Bilchitz *Poverty and Fundamental Rights: The Justification and Enforcement of Socio-Economic Rights* (2007) 197-207.

The relative definition of poverty has several advantages. Perhaps the most important is its ability to capture the ways in which social expectations can themselves structure poverty. Thus, as Sen shows, African Americans may well be many times richer in terms of incomes than poorer people in the rest of the world, even when taking account of price differences. However, they are decidedly poorer than American whites.[22] As a start, even when one's income is high in terms of absolute standards, more income is needed to buy enough commodities to achieve the same social functioning:

"The need to take part in the life of a community may induce demands for modern equipment (televisions, videocassette recorders, automobiles and so on) in a country where such facilities are more or less universal (unlike what would be needed in less affluent countries), and this imposes a strain on a relatively poor person in a rich country even when that person is at a much higher level of income compared with people in less opulent countries."[23]

The logical conclusion of the critique of the absolute standard might seem to entail rejecting an inevitably artificial line below which individuals are considered poor, and instead focusing on the gaps between the best off and the worst off in society. However, the relative definition of poverty has its own difficulties. Most importantly, does a relative definition of poverty simply collapse the distinction between inequality and poverty in unhelpful ways? Given that there will always be some sections of society that are badly off in relative terms, it would, on this approach, be impossible to eliminate poverty: a society might improve its general living standards without ever reducing the number of those in poverty. More problematically, if the vast majority have insufficient for an adequate life, there might seem to be little or no poverty; and if there is a rapid decline due to a recession or natural disaster, poverty would not seem to increase.[24] It is also difficult to determine whether anti-poverty programmes have been successful. Sen concludes that

"[i]t is clear that somewhere in the process of refining the concept of poverty from what is viewed as the crudities of Charles Booth's or Seebohm Rowntree's old-fashioned criteria, we have been made to abandon here an essential characteristic of poverty, replacing it with some imperfect representation of *inequality* as such."[25]

Sen therefore argues for an "irreducible absolutist core in the idea of poverty".[26] One particularly obvious element of the absolutist core is starvation and hunger:

"If there is starvation and hunger, then – no matter what the relative picture looks like – there clearly is poverty."[27]

Conversely,

"[i]t would be absurd to call someone poor just because he had the means to buy only one Cadillac a day when others in that community could buy two of these cars each day. The absolute considerations cannot be inconsequential for conceptualising poverty."[28]

---

[22] A Sen *Development as Freedom* (1999) 96.
[23] 89.
[24] A Sen "Poor, Relatively Speaking" (1983) 35 *Oxford Economic Papers* 153 156-157; Lister *Poverty* 27.
[25] Sen (1983) *Oxford Economic Papers* 156 (original emphasis).
[26] 159.
[27] 159.
[28] 159.

This has resonances with the minimum core debate within the socio-economic rights dispute. The question of minimum core is not, however, dealt with here.[29]

One widespread way of distinguishing poverty from inequality between those with acceptable living standards while maintaining a relativist view is to establish a poverty line. Thus the European Union counts people as poor if their income falls below 60% of the median of the income distribution.[30] While this is a good start, it still runs into difficulties if it ignores inequalities between those beneath the poverty line. Therefore as Alcock shows, anti-poverty measures may appear successful because they lower the numbers of people below the poverty line. However, it is easier to move those just below the line to just above it than to achieve the same result with those well below the line.[31] It is therefore important to pay attention to the distribution of income among the poor themselves. This can be expressed in the form of an "income gap", which measures the additional income that would be needed to bring all of the poor up to the level of the poverty line.[32]

The above assumed that income should be the main measure of relative poverty. However, it is now well recognised that income is not the only type of poverty. Townsend argues that inequitable distribution of housing, medical, educational and other resources should also be taken into account.[33] This approach is now reflected in the European Commission's definition, adopted in 1984, which defines the poor as "persons, families and groups of persons whose resources (material, cultural and social) are so limited as to exclude them from the minimum acceptable way of life in the Member State in which they live".[34]

More far-reaching still has been Sen's recognition that the same level of income might yield very different levels of quality of life depending on the individual's personal and social capacity. Therefore it is not so much income but an individual's ability to be and do what they choose to be and do which measures whether a person is in poverty. This is the basis of Sen's ground-breaking "capabilities approach". This judges individuals in terms of the "capabilities a person has, that is, the substantive freedoms he or she enjoys to lead the kind of life he or she has reason to value".[35] It may not be feasible for a person to achieve the goals she values due to social, economic, or physical constraints, as well as due to political interference. Sen states:

"What people can positively achieve is influenced by economic opportunities, political liberties, social powers, and the enabling conditions of good health, basic education, and the encouragement and cultivation of initiatives."[36]

---

[29] For further discussion of the minimum core approach see S Fredman *Human Rights Transformed: Positive Rights and Positive Duties* (2008) 84-87.

[30] Alcock *Understanding Poverty* 16-17; Lister *Poverty* 42.

[31] Alcock *Understanding Poverty* 85.

[32] A Sen *Inequality Reexamined* (1995) 103.

[33] Townsend (1962) *The British Journal of Sociology* 223-224.

[34] Council of the European Communities "Council Decision on Specific Community Action to Combat Poverty" (1984) 85/8/EEC art 1(2).

[35] Sen *Development as Freedom* 86; see also M Nussbaum *Women and Human Development* (2000).

[36] Sen *Development as Freedom* 5.

Broadening the perspective beyond that of income inequalities illuminates the fact that the relationship between low income and low capabilities varies between different communities, different families and different individuals.[37] This renders visible types of inequality which might otherwise be obscured. Reverting to the example of African Americans, Sen points out that although African American men may well be richer in terms of incomes; in terms of life expectancy, they fall well behind the immensely poorer men in China, Kerala, Sri Lanka, and Costa Rica.[38] Thus the primary concern of poverty analysis should be inadequacy of income to achieve minimally acceptable capabilities, rather than lowness of income as such.[39]

It is through his capabilities theory that Sen achieves a synthesis between the absolute core and the relative characteristics of poverty. Deprivation of capabilities is absolute, whereas the resources needed to fulfil those capabilities are relative to the society. In particular, he recognises the shame accompanying poverty as a deprivation in itself. Therefore although some commodities are not necessary for survival, they may be necessary for the avoidance of the shame that accompanies poverty. Avoidance of shame is absolute: an individual's desire is to avoid shame, not to be less ashamed. However, the commodities needed to avoid that shame are relative to a particular society. In Adam Smith's society, a linen shirt was what was needed; in modern society, it may be a pair of shoes or a fixed address.[40] The same is true of the ability to participate in society, or the ability to be educated. Sen therefore sees poverty as "the failure of basic capabilities to reach certain minimally acceptable levels".[41] The relevant functionings range from "such elementary physical ones as being well-nourished, being adequately clothed and sheltered, avoiding preventable morbidity, [et cetera], to more complex social achievements such as taking part in the life of the community, being able to appear in public without shame, and so on".[42] The specific form of these general functionings varies from society to society.

Whether the capabilities approach has satisfactorily married the concept of absolute deprivation of needs with a definition of poverty which takes relativities into account remains contested. Stein, for example, argues that Nussbaum's attempt to draw a clear distinction between minimum threshold capabilities and inequality fails to take account of important equality issues below the threshold.[43] The definition of poverty clearly needs to take account of such thoroughgoing distributional issues. Moreover, it remains problematic to regard inequalities above the minimum as unrelated to the fulfilment of threshold capabilities. Recent research demonstrates that unequal societies have higher levels of social problems than more equal societies.[44] This affects

---

[37]   88.
[38]   96.
[39]   Sen *Inequality Reexamined* 111.
[40]   Sen (1983) *Oxford Economic Papers* 161.
[41]   Sen *Inequality Reexamined* 109.
[42]   110.
[43]   M Stein "Nussbaum: A Utilitarian Critique" (2009) 50 *Boston College LR* 489 494-497, 508-509.
[44]   R Wilkinson & K Pickett *The Spirit Level: Why More Equal Societies Almost Always Do Better* (2009) 15-24.

not just the most deprived, but also the better off. Thus an individual from the lowest-earning 20% of society in a more equal society is more likely to live longer than her counterpart from a less equal society. By the same token, perhaps surprisingly, someone from the highest-earning 20% in a more equal society has a longer life expectancy than an equivalently well off person in a less equal society.[45] Similarly, more equal societies tend to have lower infant mortality,[46] and lower levels of crime[47] than more unequal societies, even where the latter have higher average rates of income.

Conversely, distributive equality should not be determined independently of minima. Otherwise, distributive equality could simply be achieved by removing resources from the better off (levelling down), without redistributing such resources to the worst off. To avoid such a response, it is necessary to have regard both to absolute basic requirements for survival and those which are relative to what others have.[48] Of particular interest in this respect is the Child Poverty Act 2010, which gives government the task of eliminating child poverty in Britain by 2020. This includes four specific measures of poverty: relatively low income; combined low income and material deprivation; absolute low income; and persistent poverty.[49]

2 2   Poverty, socio-economic disadvantage and anti-discrimination law

The above analysis focused on the relationship of poverty to distributive inequality. In this section, I examine the close interaction between poverty and status inequalities, particularly of gender, race, age and disability. These interactions are complex and multi-directional. On the one hand, it is well established that women, ethnic minorities, black people, people with disabilities, older people and children are disproportionately represented among people in poverty. On the other hand, people in poverty suffer from many of the elements of discrimination and substantive inequality experienced by these status groups.

Particularly striking is the relationship between gender and poverty. In countries as diverse as the UK and South Africa, women are generally poorer than men, have fewer opportunities for employment and earn less than men.[50] Moreover, women's risk of poverty is specifically gendered.[51] Whereas for men, this risk is predominantly connected to exclusion from

---

[45] Ch 6.

[46] 82-83.

[47] Ch 10-11.

[48] R Goodin "Relative Needs" in A Ware & R Goodin (eds) *Needs and Welfare* (1990) 15 15-20.

[49] Ss 1-5 of the Child Poverty Act.

[50] G Rosenblatt & K Rake "Gender and Poverty" (2003) *Fawcett Society* <http://www.fawcettsociety.org.uk/ documents/pov_000.pdf> (accessed 12-10-2011); B Goldblatt "The Right to Social Security – Addressing Women's Poverty and Disadvantage" in B Goldblatt & K McLean (eds) *Women's Social and Economic Rights: Developments in South Africa* (2011) 35. See generally World Bank *World Development Report 2011: Gender Equality and Development* (2011) 201 <http://econ.worldbank.org/WBSITE/EXTERNAL/ EXTDEC/EXTRESEARCH/EXTWDRS/0,,contentMDK:20227703~pagePK:478093~piPK:477627~the SitePK:477624,00.html> (accessed 20-11-2011).

[51] This section is taken from S Fredman "Engendering Socio-Economic Rights" (2009) 25 *SAJHR* 1.

the labour market, whether due to low skills, previous unemployment or lack of regional job opportunities, for women, there are other, gender-based factors leading them into poverty. In particular, women's poverty is closely linked to their role in the family, particularly their caring roles. Therefore, as Goldblatt shows, South African women are "overwhelmingly responsible for childcare, housework and care of the sick and aged".[52] Unpaid caring roles can significantly limit women's access to decent paid work, leaving many women with no choice but to accept precarious and low-paid work.[53] Part-time work is particularly at risk of low pay;[54] yet part-time workers are predominantly women.[55] Women also predominate in the informal-sector, especially in the lowest-paid segment – as homeworkers or industrial outworkers.[56] Caring roles have an impact on women's lifetime earnings, which in turn significantly affect pension entitlements. Furthermore, divorce, widowhood, separation and teenage motherhood are major triggers of women's poverty in a way they are not for men.[57] This is aggravated by lack of power. For example, as Chant notes, household income may bear no relation to women's poverty because women may not be able to access it.[58] Brodsky and Day powerfully argue that "poverty is a sex equality issue because women's poverty is a manifestation of persistent discrimination against women".[59] Similar interactions have been well documented between poverty and age, race, disability and other status.[60]

Thus measures directly addressing poverty might tackle some of the main causes of status disadvantage. For example, minimum-wage legislation, which directly addresses socio-economic disadvantage, has made a significant contribution to narrowing the gender pay gap in the UK.[61] Minimum-wage jobs are more likely to be held by women, young workers, those of retirement age, ethnic minorities, those with a disability, and those with no qualifications.[62] Directly addressing socio-economic disadvantage would have an impact on all these status groups.

However, the interaction does not travel in only one direction. This is because poverty is not just about distributive inequality: it also carries with it the stigmatic effects often thought to be confined to status inequalities such

---

[52] Goldblatt "The Right to Social Security" in *Women's Social and Economic Rights* 35.
[53] Rosenblatt & Rake "Gender and Poverty" *Fawcett Society* 1.
[54] J Hills, M Brewer, S Jenkins, R Lister, R Lupton, S Machin, C Mills, T Modood, T Rees & S Riddell *An Anatomy of Inequality in the UK* (2010) 11-13.
[55] Low Pay Commission *National Minimum Wage Report* (2009) 98; Report from the Commission to the Council, the European Parliament, the European Economic and Social Committee, the Committee of the Regions *Equality Between Women And Men – 2009* (Com (2009) 77 Final) 4.
[56] International Labour Office *Global Employment Trends for Women: 2009* (2009) 10-12; World Bank *World Development Report 2011* 79-80.
[57] Rosenblatt & Rake "Gender and Poverty" *Fawcett Society* 3.
[58] S Chant "Rethinking the 'Feminisation of Poverty' in Relation to Aggregate Gender Indices" (2006) 7 *J Hum Dev* 201 208.
[59] Brodsky & Day (2002) *Canadian J of Women & L* 189.
[60] Hills et al *Anatomy of Inequality* 26.
[61] Low Pay Commission *National Minimum Wage Report* 15.
[62] Low Pay Commission *National Minimum Wage Report* xii. For earlier reports containing equivalent findings see *Low Pay Commission* <http://www.lowpay.gov.uk/lowpay/rep_a_p_index.shtml> (accessed 12-10-2011).

as racism, sexism or homophobia. Thus Porter points to a "disturbing pattern of scapegoating the poor" in Canada in the 1990s, where welfare recipients were seen in "unremittingly negative terms by the economically secure".[63] As he concludes:

> "It is difficult to appreciate just how profound is the social exclusion that results from this kind of government-endorsed promotion of discrimination and scapegoating. It transforms social assistance from an entitlement of citizenship linked with the right to security and dignity, into a source of shame, guilt, and insecurity."[64]

Moreover, when poverty becomes a source of stigma, this can in turn reinforce poverty. For example, in the UK, free school meals have played a central role in the nutrition of children from poorer families; yet research shows that 20% of children who are entitled to free school meals do not use their entitlement. A third of pupils surveyed and over two-fifths of parents identified embarrassment or fear of being teased as factors which put them off taking their free meal.[65]

From the other direction, measures addressing distributive disadvantage should also take into account their effect on status. Ignoring the interaction might risk aggravating status based inequalities. For example, social security benefits which are based on a "breadwinner" model aggravate gender discrimination by treating women as dependants.[66] Similarly, basing assessments of eligibility for benefits on "household income" assumes that the income is evenly shared between the partners within the household. Also specifically affected by gender is access to social protection or pensions, where the latter are linked to continuous, full-time employment in the formal-sector.[67] In the European Union, for example, pension schemes in many member states still leave many women with only derived rights based on their husband's employment record.[68]

3   Substantive equality and poverty: An analytic framework

As seen above, it is increasingly recognised that poverty is a multi-dimensional phenomenon. It is not simply about insufficient income, although income is an important means to combat poverty. It is also about relative deprivation, absence of agency, stigma and exclusion. Each of these has resonances in the rapidly developing theoretical and practical understanding

---

[63]   B Porter "Claiming Adjudicative Space: Social Rights, Equality and Citizenship" in S Boyd, G Brodsky, S Day & M Young (eds) *Poverty: Rights, Social Citizenship and Legal Activism* (2007) 77 82.

[64]   85.

[65]   P Storey & R Chamberlin (Thomas Coram Research Unit, Institute of Education) *Improving the Take Up of Free School Meals* (Research Report No 270) Department of Education and Employment (2001) <http://www.cpag.org.uk/campaigns/school_meals.htm#stigma> (accessed 20-06-2011).

[66]   See, for example, S Fredman *Women and the Law* (1997) 83-85.

[67]   World Bank *World Development Report 2012: Gender Equality and Development* (2012) 154–156; F Lund "A Framework for Analyzing Social Protection for Workers in the Informal Economy" in C Piras (ed) *Women at Work: Challenges for Latin America* (2004) 229.

[68]   Report from the Commission to the Council, the European Parliament, the European Economic and Social Committee & the Committee of the Regions *Equality Between Women And Men – 2009* 5, 8; European Parliament *Non-Discrimination Based on Gender and Intergenerational Solidarity* Non-Legislative Resolution INI/2008/2118 <http://www.europarl.europa.eu/oeil/FindByProcnum.do?lang=en&procnum =INI/2008/2118> (accessed 12-10-2011).

of substantive equality. Putting the insights of the poverty analysis together with theories of substantive equality potentially yields a powerful analytic tool both to assess and to develop policy responses to poverty.

Substantive equality goes beyond formal equality in that it is not simply about equal treatment, or a comparison between two groups.[69] Some regard substantive equality as requiring a focus on equality of results; others stress equality of opportunity. In both cases, unequal treatment may be necessary to achieve the ultimate goal. However, both equality of results and equality of opportunity are vague and difficult to measure. A further potential "substantive core" to the concept of equality is the concept of dignity. On this approach the ultimate aim of equality is to achieve equal dignity.[70] However, as the Canadian jurisprudence has shown, dignity on its own may have the perverse effect of erecting barriers to claimants, who have to show not just that they have suffered disadvantage, but that this reflects a breach of their dignity.[71] Drawing together these perspectives yields a multi-dimensional concept of substantive equality pursuing four overlapping aims.[72] First, it aims to break the cycle of disadvantage associated with status or out-groups. This reflects the redistributive dimension of equality. Secondly, it aims to promote respect for dignity and worth, thereby redressing stigma, stereotyping, humiliation, and violence because of membership of an identity group. This reflects a recognition dimension.[73] Thirdly, it should not exact conformity as a price of equality. Instead, it should accommodate difference and aim to achieve structural change. This captures the transformative dimension. Finally, substantive equality should facilitate full participation in society, both socially and politically. This is the participative dimension.

It can immediately be seen that this conception of equality is relevant to people in poverty in a number of important ways. The distributive dimension brings together status inequalities and poverty by recognising that disadvantage is often disproportionately associated with status. The first aim of substantive equality is therefore to correct the cycle of disadvantage experienced because of status or other protected characteristic. However, focusing on disadvantage also carries with it some important challenges. The most important is to specify the nature of disadvantage. Disadvantage is most easily understood in the context of redistribution of resources and benefits, and therefore is of most relevance to poverty. However, as Iris Marion Young argues,[74] the distributive paradigm ignores social structures such as decision-making power, the division of labour and culture, or the symbolic meanings attached to people, actions, and things.[75] Thus disadvantage should encompass

---

[69]   For valuable analyses of substantive equality, see C Albertyn "Substantive Equality and Transformation in South Africa" (2007) 23 *SAJHR* 253; C McCrudden "Equality and Non-Discrimination" in D Feldman (ed) *English Public Law* 2 ed (2009) 499; Brodsky & Day (2002) *Canadian J of Women & L* 185.

[70]   *Law v Canada* [1999] 1 SCR 497 (Canadian Supreme Court) para 51.

[71]   *Law v Canada* [1999] 1 SCR 497 (Canadian Supreme Court); *Gosselin v Quebec* [2002] SCC 84 (Canadian Supreme Court); *R v Kapp* [2008] SCC 41 (Canadian Supreme Court).

[72]   S Fredman *Discrimination Law* 2 ed (2011) ch 1.

[73]   N Fraser & A Honneth *Redistribution or Recognition? A Political-Philosophical Exchange* (2003) 1.

[74]   IM Young *Justice and the Politics of Difference* (1990) 16.

[75]   16.

more than maldistribution of resources. It needs also to take on board the constraints which power structures impose on individuals because of their status. For example, women who are trapped in the private sphere will suffer disadvantage in this sense even if they live in affluent households.

Disadvantage can also be understood as a deprivation of genuine opportunities to pursue one's own valued choices. This again draws on the insights of Sen[76] and Nussbaum's[77] "capabilities" theories, which stress the importance of considering the extent to which people are actually able to exercise their choices, rather than simply having the formal right to do so. It is not enough to treat everyone equally, since the same treatment of individuals with very different constraints can replicate disadvantage. Similarly, Griffin stresses that human rights are grounded in the value attached to "normative agency", or "our autonomously choosing and freely pursuing our conception of a worthwhile life".[78] Like Sen, he argues that "[t]he value [of normative agency] resides not simply in one's having the undeveloped, unused capacities for autonomy and liberty but also in exercising them – not just in being able to be autonomous but also in actually being so".[79]

One of the aims of the redistributive dimension of equality therefore is to redress disadvantage by removing obstacles to genuine choice. At the same time, it needs to be recognised that choice itself can be problematic, since people often adapt their choices to their circumstances. For example, women might prefer part-time work even if it is insecure and low paid because it permits them to combine paid work and childcare. But this choice is made within a context in which women are assumed to be the primary childcarers. The fact that women make these choices should not imply that there is no further need for legal intervention. Substantive equality should also aim to remove the disadvantages attached to part-time work; and indeed to achieve more wide-ranging structural change, which includes an equitable division of childcaring obligations between mothers, fathers and the broader community. Moreover, there are circumstances in which the concern is not solely to increase the range of feasible options but to address the disadvantage attached to the circumstances a person actually finds herself in. This is particularly true in the context of some kinds of disability; as well as of caring obligations.

Even in its most expansive sense, disadvantage does not cover all the wrongs associated with inequality. Stigma, stereotyping, humiliation, and violence on grounds of gender, race, disability, sexual orientation, or other status can be experienced regardless of relative disadvantage. Thus the second main aim of substantive equality should be to promote respect for the equal dignity and worth of all. This is the dimension of equality which speaks to our basic humanity. Equality attaches to all individuals, not because of their merit, or their rationality, or their citizenship or membership of any particular

---

[76] Sen *Development as Freedom.*
[77] Nussbaum *Women and Human Development.*
[78] J Griffin *On Human Rights* (2009) 179.
[79] 183.

group, but because of their humanity. Individuals should not be humiliated or degraded through racism, sexism, violence, or other status-based prejudice.

The particular value of the dignity or recognition dimension of equality is to highlight the fact that the stigma often associated with poverty is itself a harm which needs to be addressed. This was captured, as we have seen, in Adam Smith's recognition that a linen shirt might be a basic need because it signified the very minimum of respectability. Indeed, as we have seen, stigma can itself perpetuate poverty. Lister also points to the ways in which black people have been stereotyped and stigmatised through associating them with poverty and welfare dependency.[80] More generally, she argues, the ways in which the non-poor construct the poor as "Other" can have a profound impact on how poverty is experienced.[81] The line between "us" and "them" is "imbued with negative value judgements that construct 'the poor' variously as a source of moral contamination, a threat, an 'undeserving' economic burden, an object of pity or even as an exotic species".[82] This also legitimates the privilege of the wealthy, defining and affirming their identity by diminishing others.

Locating dignity as one of several dimensions of equality also enables us to see that dignity is not a separate and additional element to socio-economic disadvantage in an equality claim. Socio-economic disadvantage is itself an assault on an individual's basic humanity. This was highlighted in the South African case of *Khosa v Minister of Social Development; Mahlaule v Minister of Social Development*,[83] which concerned a legislative measure which confined the right to child benefit and old-age pensions to South African citizens, to the exclusion of permanent residents. In striking down this measure as a breach of equality, Mokgoro J emphasised that the consequences of exclusion were not only socio-economic. In addition, the exclusion of permanent residents had a strong stigmatising effect, creating the impression that they were inferior to citizens and less worthy of social assistance.[84]

The third dimension of equality, the transformative dimension, entails recognising and accommodating difference. It also entails changing underlying structures, rather than expecting individuals to conform. This dimension of equality taps into a complex debate in relation to poverty: the relationship between agency and structure. The agency approach to poverty is based on the central assumption that, on the whole, people can be regarded as responsible for their own poverty. Only those who are genuinely incapacitated should be entitled to assistance from the state. This approach has directly influenced policy, from the punitive Poor Laws of 19th century Britain to modern day welfare-to-work programmes in the US and elsewhere. It puts people living in poverty in a double bind from which it is difficult to escape. Those who are regarded as capable of work are attributed more power and agency than they truly have. On the other hand, those who are regarded as incapacitated are

---

[80] Lister *Poverty* 64.
[81] 100.
[82] 101.
[83] 2004 6 SA 505 (CC).
[84] *Khosa v Minister of Social Development; Mahlaule v Minister of Social Development* 2004 6 SA 505 (CC) para 77.

deprived of all agency. In 19th century Britain, this manifested as a distinction between the "deserving" and the "undeserving" poor. The undeserving poor were treated punitively, whereas the deserving poor were characterised as objects of charity rather than as individual agents. These epithets endure into modern day debates.

At the other extreme, the structural approach recognises that poverty is based on forces beyond the control of any one individual. However, there is a risk that such an approach leads to policy prescriptions which denude individuals of any agency. Instead, the object of policy should be to facilitate agency by removing some of the central constraints and obstacles. The transformative dimension thus frees individuals from constraints without expecting that they use their agency in predetermined ways.

The fourth dimension of substantive equality relates to participation. Given that past discrimination or other social mechanisms have blocked the avenues for political participation by particular minorities, equality laws are needed both to compensate for this absence of political voice and to open up the channels for greater participation in the future. Participation also refers to the importance of community in the life of individuals. Rather than the universal, abstract individual of formal equality, substantive equality recognises that individuals are essentially social. To be fully human includes the ability to participate on equal terms in community and society more generally. Thus Young argues that the focus of theories of justice should be on structures which exclude people from participating in determining their actions.[85] Fraser puts particular emphasis on participation, regarding parity of participation as the normative core of her conception of justice, encompassing both redistribution and recognition without reducing either one to the other.[86] Collins, in searching for a justification for departure from the equal treatment principle, develops the concept of social inclusion as central to his notion of substantive equality.[87]

Both the political and the social aspects of participation are similarly central to the characterisation of poverty and therefore to the determination of appropriate policy. Indeed, the concept of social exclusion has to some extent eclipsed that of poverty in the European debate.[88] Social exclusion refers to those who are systematically excluded from participation in society, where participation refers to the capacity to purchase goods and services; participation in economically or socially valuable activities, political engagement and social interaction.[89] The concept of social exclusion highlights the interaction between status and distributive equalities: it is closely correlated with living in a deprived area, suffering partnership breakdown, or being a member of an ethnic minority, the elderly or disabled. It is particularly valuable in that

---

[85]   Young *Justice and the Politics of Difference* 31-32.
[86]   N Fraser "Social Justice in the Age of Identity Politics" in *Redistribution or Recognition?* 36 36-77.
[87]   H Collins "Discrimination, Equality and Social Inclusion" (2003) 66 *Modern LR* 16 24.
[88]   Lister *Poverty* 74.
[89]   T Burchardt, J Le Grand & D Piachaud "Degrees of Exclusion: Developing a Dynamic, Multidimensional Measure" in J Hills, J Le Grand & D Piachaud (eds) *Understanding Social Exclusion* (2002) 30 30-32.

its focus is on the relationship between the included and the excluded, and in particular on the role of the former in causing or perpetuating exclusion.[90]

4   Equality as a potential paradigm for addressing poverty: Some current approaches

It has been demonstrated above that poverty and inequality intersect in complex and often contested ways. This raises the central question to be considered in this chapter, namely, what possible role can be played by a constitutional right to equality or statutory anti-discrimination laws in addressing poverty? This section draws on the experience of four English-speaking jurisdictions – Britain, the US, Canada and South Africa – to examine three possible points of entry. The first is to address the stigmatic, exclusionary and structural aspects of poverty directly through a right to equality. This would entail explicitly or implicitly incorporating poverty as a protected characteristic or a ground of discrimination. A second is to address the intersection between status based and distributive poverty by subjecting anti-poverty measures to equality analysis. In particular, poverty measures which entrench gender, race, age or disability disadvantage, or which exclude status groups from their reach, should be regarded as violating the right to equality. In affluent societies, this may be particularly important in addressing "pockets of poverty", such as the poverty experienced by the Roma in Europe. A third point of entry is to benefit from the advances in the right to equality beyond simple individual entitlements. Such advances include proactive duties to promote equality and policies which "mainstream" equality by insisting that equality considerations are included in all policy measures. Each of these is considered in turn.

4 1   Poverty as a ground of discrimination

The first point of entry recognises the parallels between poverty and status inequality when considered through the lens of substantive equality. As we have seen, poverty shares many of the elements captured by the four-dimensional understanding of equality. As well as the obvious distributive dimension, substantive equality is well placed to address the stigmatic, exclusionary and structural aspects of poverty. One way to make this link is to give individuals a right not to be discriminated against on grounds of poverty. This would entail including poverty in the list of grounds protected by equality guarantees. This approach is now recognised at international level by the United Nations Committee on Economic, Social and Cultural Rights. Thus in General Comment 20, it is stated that discrimination on grounds of "economic and social situation" should be prohibited by contracting states.[91] Notably, both the stigmatic and redistributive dimensions are highlighted. According to the General Comment:

---

[90]   Lister *Poverty* 98.
[91]   UN Committee on Economic, Social and Cultural Rights *General Comment No 20: Non-Discrimination in Economic, Social and Cultural Rights* (2009) UN Doc E/C 12/GC/20 para 35.

"A person's social and economic situation when living in poverty or being homeless may result in pervasive discrimination, stigmatization and negative stereotyping which can lead to the refusal of, or unequal access to, the same quality of education and health care as others, as well as the denial of or unequal access to public places."[92]

However, as yet this has not been achieved in the four jurisdictions examined here. In some jurisdictions, such as UK domestic anti-discrimination legislation, the equality guarantee includes an exhaustive list of grounds.[93] Including poverty entails convincing the legislature to amend the statute. Although a new Equality Act was adopted in 2010, with an expanded list of grounds, poverty was not included. As will be seen below, a short-lived provision included socio-economic disadvantage among the proactive equality duties introduced by the statute. But it was made clear that this should not include an individual right to claim on the grounds of socio-economic disadvantage.

Other equality guarantees are open-ended[94] or non-exhaustive.[95] Including poverty would entail convincing courts that it should be regarded as an analogous ground. Most resistant to this possibility is the US Supreme Court, which has been particularly adamant in its insistence that policies which discriminate against poor people cannot attract heightened judicial scrutiny. Unlike racial classifications, which are suspect because they concern a "discrete and insular minority",[96] poor people should not be regarded as discrete or insular.[97] Therefore a system which funded schools on the basis of local taxes, leading to under-resourced schools in poor areas, was not subject to the heightened scrutiny which would have been appropriate had the system provided inferior schools to African Americans.

More progress has been made in Canada, where, at provincial level, three Canadian jurisdictions have adopted "social condition" as a prohibited ground of discrimination,[98] and the remaining jurisdictions recognise narrower grounds such as social origin, source of income and receipt of public assistance.[99] At federal level, the Canadian Human Rights Act Review Panel, which reported in 2000, found "ample evidence of widespread discrimination based on characteristics related to social conditions, such as poverty, low education, homelessness and illiteracy".[100] It strongly recommended the inclusion of "social condition" as a ground of discrimination under the federal Canadian

---

[92] Para 35.

[93] Ss 4-12 of the Equality Act.

[94] Amendment XIV of the US Constitution (1868).

[95] See for example s 9 of the Constitution of the Republic of South Africa, 1996 and s 1 (definition of "prohibited grounds") of the Promotion of Equality and Prevention of Unfair Discrimination Act 4 of 2000; art 14 of the European Convention on Human Rights 1950 ETS 5; 213 UNTS 221; s 15 of the Canadian Charter of Rights and Freedoms (Part I of the Constitution Act, 1982).

[96] *United States v Carolene Products Co* 304 US 144, 152 n 4 (US Supreme Court).

[97] *San Antonio Independent School District v. Rodriguez* 411 US 959 (1973) (US Supreme Court).

[98] See s 10 of the Quebec Charter of Human Rights and Freedoms, RSQ C-12 Quebec, New Brunswick and the Northwest Territories. See W MacKay & N Kim *Adding Social Condition to the Canadian Human Rights Act* Canadian Human Rights Commission (2009) 2.

[99] See the summary in Canadian Human Rights Act Review Panel *Report of the Canadian Human Rights Act Review Panel, Ottawa: Department of Justice and Attorney General "Promoting Equality: A New Vision"* (2000) 107.

[100] 114.

Human Rights Act.[101] Indeed, social condition should be added to the list of permitted grounds for affirmative action and equity programmes. However, a decade has passed without further action, although a Bill to this end was proposed in 2010.[102] So far as the constitutional guarantee is concerned, recognising poverty as a ground would entail convincing the Court that people living in poverty fulfil its criteria for an unenumerated ground, namely, irrelevance, a history of prejudice, political exclusion and immutability. As we have seen, people living in poverty readily fit these criteria. Even the characteristics of "immutability" can be applied to those living in poverty in that poverty is frequently structural and beyond the individual choice of the individual. However, attempts to persuade the Court to regard poverty or social condition as an unenumerated ground have met with little success. Like its US counterpart, the Canadian Court is unwilling to engage in distributive issues, which it regards as the province of the legislature.[103]

Other jurisdictions have similarly flirted with the possibility of including an express ground, variously formulated, which includes poverty, but they too have drawn back from carrying this to fruition. Thus in South Africa, the Promotion of Equality and Prevention of Unfair Discrimination Act 4 of 2000 does not include socio-economic status within its long and inclusive list of protected grounds, but instead refers to it as a "directive principle" to which the Minister should give special consideration for inclusion.[104] However, no legislative amendments have been forthcoming. This leaves open the possibility of judicial extension. As in the Canadian Charter, the list of enumerated grounds is non-exhaustive and the statute expressly permits courts to include any other ground which "(i) causes or perpetuates systemic disadvantage; (ii) undermines human dignity; or (iii) adversely affects the equal enjoyment of a person's rights and freedoms in a serious manner that is comparable to discrimination [as defined in the Act]".[105] Whether an argument to this effect would find favour with a South African court or confront a similar deference to the legislature in relation to economic issues, remains to be seen.

So far as definition is concerned, there is a general reluctance to include poverty *per se*, with a preference for such terms as "social condition", "socio-economic status" or "social and economic condition". However, such definitions are symmetric, running the risk of permitting claims by better-off people challenging pro-poor policies. More appropriate would be a definition which is expressly asymmetric, such as "socio-economic disadvantage" as used in the British Equality Act 2010. The 2010 Canadian Bill defined "social condition" as "experiencing social or economic disadvantage on the basis of their source of income, occupation, level of education, poverty, lack of adequate housing, homelessness or any other similar circumstance".[106] Jurisprudence from

---

[101] 117.
[102] Bill C-559 Third Sess, 40th Parliament, 59 Elizabeth II, 2010 <http://www.parl.gc.ca/HousePublications/Publication.aspx?DocId=4640207&File=24&Language=E&Mode=1> (accessed 12-10-2011).
[103] MacKay & Kim *Adding Social Condition to the Canadian Human Rights Act* 64.
[104] S 34 of the Promotion of Equality and Prevention of Unfair Discrimination Act.
[105] S 1(xxii).
[106] S 1 of Bill C-559 Third Sess, 40th Parliament, 59 Elizabeth II, 2010.

Quebec, which has included social condition since its Charter was adopted in 1975, is of particular interest, in that it includes both an objective element, referring to factors such as income, occupation or level of education, and a subjective component, which reflects the recognition dimension of poverty, namely social perceptions or stereotypes associated with low levels of income, education or occupation.[107] The South African statute uses the term "socio-economic status", but goes on to define it as including "the social or economic condition or perceived condition of a person who is disadvantaged by poverty, low employment status, or lack of or low-level educational qualifications".[108]

What would be the added value of such a ground? As the Canadian Human Rights Panel put it, "at the very least, the addition of this ground would ensure there is a means to challenge stereotypes about the poor in the policies of private and public institutions".[109] In Quebec, the inclusion of "social condition" has meant that stereotypical assumptions, such as those of landlords refusing to let premises to social assistance recipients or precarious workers, can be challenged.[110] Equally, there are a range of indirectly discriminatory practices which could be challenged. The Canadian Panel found evidence of barriers to employment (for example, unnecessarily high educational requirements, costs of paying for aptitude tests, tools or uniforms, or transport to interviews) and services, particularly in banking, telephone services (for example, through the need to provide a deposit), and housing. It is of course possible that the same effect could be achieved without an express ground, if the experience of discrimination can be fitted into that of a "status" group such as gender or race. But this would not include disadvantaged or socially excluded individuals such as poor white men who are not members of historically stigmatised status groups. The same is true for indirect discrimination. The correlation between poverty and status would need to be proved statistically, and may exclude areas where all people in poverty, not just women, blacks, ethnic minorities or people with disabilities, are affected.[111] Nevertheless, this is not a complete solution, particularly if housed within an individualistic complaints system. While recognition claims may succeed, distributive inequalities are unlikely to be addressed. Indeed, even if a claim succeeds in principle, redistributive issues may re-emerge as a potential defence.

4 2   Challenging the inclusiveness of anti-poverty strategies

A second point of entry for equality laws is to challenge anti-poverty measures which themselves reinforce status discrimination. For example, women might be constructed as dependants for the purposes of social security benefits; or household income might be used as a measure of poverty.

---

[107] MacKay & Kim *Adding Social Condition to the Canadian Human Rights Act* 22-23.
[108] S 1(xxvi) of the Promotion of Equality and Prevention of Unfair Discrimination Act. It should be noted that socio-economic status is only a directive principle, not a ground as such. See s 34(1).
[109] Canadian Human Rights Act Review Panel *Promoting Equality* 110.
[110] MacKay & Kim *Adding Social Condition to the Canadian Human Rights Act* 24.
[111] 108.

Alternatively, particular groups, such as asylum seekers or migrants, might be excluded.

Courts in various jurisdictions have been reasonably open to this analysis. Reluctant to impose obligations on legislatures to provide social security in the first place, courts may nevertheless be willing to scrutinise such schemes for under-inclusiveness. This has been a familiar approach in Canada. Thus McLachlan J stated in *Auton v British Columbia (Attorney General):*[112]

> "This Court has repeatedly held that the legislature is under no obligation to create a particular benefit. It is free to target the social programs it wishes to fund as a matter of public policy, provided the benefit itself is not conferred in a discriminatory manner."[113]

Although this has been criticised as not going far enough,[114] it can in practice function as a valuable way of extending existing benefits to excluded groups, or challenging the rules of eligibility on the grounds that they reinforce stereotypes or exclude marginalised groups. In a surprisingly similar approach, the European Court of Human Rights ("ECtHR") has held that a member state is not obliged to provide welfare to its citizens. But if it does, its scheme is subject to the equality guarantee.[115] Similarly, the state has no duty to provide housing[116] or education,[117] but if it does, it must provide them without discrimination.[118] This approach has been replicated in the UK courts, applying the European Convention on Human Rights ("ECHR") *via* the Human Rights Act 1998.[119]

The South African Constitution has the advantage of containing express socio-economic rights. However, these rights are qualified: they do not give rise to immediate entitlements, but instead require the state to take reasonable measures within available resources to progressively realise the right.[120] The equality guarantee in section 9, by contrast, gives an immediate right to equality. By interpreting the Constitution so that rights reinforce one another,[121] the equality guarantee can considerably strengthen socio-economic rights. This use of the equality guarantee to extend benefits to an excluded class is most clearly seen in *Khosa*, where permanent residents were denied the right to child benefit and old age pensioners provided to citizens.

---

[112] *Auton v British Columbia (Attorney General)* [2004] 3 SCR 657 (Canadian Supreme Court).

[113] Para 42.

[114] B Porter "Expectations of Equality" (2006) 33 *Supreme Court LR* 23.

[115] *Stec v United Kingdom* (2006) 43 EHRR 47 (ECtHR) para 53.

[116] *Chapman v United Kingdom* (2001) 33 EHRR 18 (ECtHR) para 99.

[117] *Belgian Linguistic Case (No 2)* (1968) 1 EHRR 252 (European Court of Human Rights) para 3.

[118] *Ghaidan v Godin-Mendoza* [2004] UKHL 30, [2004] 2 AC 557 (HL); *DH v Czech Republic* Application No 57325/00 (2008) 47 EHRR 3 (ECHR (Grand Chamber)).

[119] *Ghaidan v Godin-Mendoza* [2004] UKHL 30, [2004] 2 AC 557 (HL).

[120] See for example ss 26(2), 27(2).

[121] This follows from s 39(1)(a) of the Constitution which provides that when interpreting the Bill of Rights courts "must promote the values that underlie an open and democratic society based on human dignity, equality and freedom". As a result, the Constitutional Court has affirmed that "constitutional rights are mutually interrelated and interdependent and form a single constitutional value system". See *De Reuck v Director of Public Prosecutions, Witwatersrand Local Division* 2004 1 SA 406 (CC) para 55. See further S Liebenberg & B Goldblatt "The Interrelationship Between Equality and Socio-Economic Rights under South Africa's Transformative Constitution" (2007) 23 *SAJHR* 335.

The Court held that this was a breach of the equality guarantee and the right to social security.[122]

The question then becomes whether a court is prepared to recognise that the boundaries drawn by a particular classification are in fact stereotypical. In *Auton*, the Canadian court concentrated on finding an appropriate comparator group. In a highly restrictive decision, the claim was ultimately rejected because no "mirror" group could be found which was treated less favourably.[123] However, in the more recent case of *Withler v Canada (Attorney General)*,[124] the Court rejected the emphasis on a mirror group, recognising that by looking for sameness, the Court might find it impossible to identify substantive inequalities. Instead, the key test was whether the law perpetuates disadvantage or negative stereotypes. Nevertheless, the Court rejected the claim that a law reducing pensions in the armed forces as a person got older was based on age-based stereotypes that people needed less as they got older. As a broad-based scheme meant to cover the competing interests of various age groups, distinctions on general criteria, including age, had to be made. Since these were effective in achieving the goal of the provisions, the scheme as a whole did not breach the equality guarantee.

In ECHR jurisprudence, the most successful claims for inclusion into socio-economic benefits have been on behalf of same-sex couples,[125] a pattern which is mirrored in Canada and South Africa. This is possibly because sexual orientation is ground which resonates most strongly with the recognition dimension of substantive equality, rather than the distributive dimensions. This approach has also been effective in relation to groups, such as the Roma, where there is an almost complete overlap between status and poverty. Roma in Europe are not only the largest single minority, but are the most disadvantaged on all measures, whether in terms of income, housing, health or education. Using the equality principle to challenge such policies is potentially more effective than requiring minimum standards on their own, since it measures deprivation relative to local standards. This means that such measures can address "pockets of poverty", relative deprivation and social exclusion. A series of challenges have been mounted in the European Court of Human Rights against exclusion and segregation of Roma children in schools in several countries in Eastern Europe.[126] In these cases, the state has argued that placing Roma children in "special" schools and classes was aimed at addressing their specific needs. In reality, however, such special schools and classes provided inferior education and reinforced the marginalisation of Roma children. Initially, the Court took a formal view of equality, holding that the fact that these policies were not expressly directed against Roma meant that there was no breach of prohibition on race discrimination. However, in an important breakthrough, the Court recognised the indirectly discriminatory

---

[122] *Khosa v Minister of Social Development* 2004 6 SA 505 (CC) paras 68-85.

[123] *Auton v British Columbia (Attorney General)* [2004] 3 SCR 657 (Canadian Supreme Court).

[124] *Withler v Canada (Attorney General)* [2011] 1 SCR 396 (Canadian Supreme Court).

[125] *Ghaidan v Godin-Mendoza* [2004] UKHL 30, [2004] 2 AC 557 (HL).

[126] *DH v Czech Republic* (2008) 47 EHRR 3 (ECtHR); *Sampanis & Others v Greece* Application no. 32526/05, unreported judgment of 5 June 2008 (ECtHR); *Oršuš & Others v Croatia* (2011) 52 EHRR 7 (ECtHR).

effects of these policies. Particularly important was its rejection of the state's argument that parents had agreed to these measures, and its corresponding acceptance of the real constraints on choice.[127]

However, as the excluded class more closely resembles a group defined by its poverty, the standard of scrutiny tends to be diluted. In both the UK and Canada, equality guarantees have been used to challenge welfare to work programmes which prescribe a lower welfare rate for claimants under a given age or make the full benefit conditional on participation in training or work programmes. In both these cases, the Court did not regard socio-economic disadvantage as itself infringing on an individual's dignity. Thus the UK case of *R (on the application of Reynolds) v Secretary of State for Work and Pensions*[128] concerned regulations pursuant to which applicants under 25 years of age were entitled to less by way of jobseeker's allowance and income support than those of 25 years and over. It was argued that this breached Article 14 of the ECHR by discriminating against the applicant on grounds of her age. In the House of Lords, Lord Rodgers stated:

"There is no doubt that the relevant Regulations, endorsed by Parliament, deliberately gave less to those under 25. But this was not because the policymakers were treating people under 25 years of age as less valuable members of society."[129]

This is remarkably similar to the Canadian case of *Gosselin v Quebec*,[130] where the claimant challenged a scheme according to which full benefit was only available to welfare recipients over 30 years of age. The majority of the Supreme Court of Canada held that "[t]he provision of different initial amounts of monetary support to each of the two groups does not indicate that one group's dignity was prized above the other's".[131]

A similar pattern can be seen in relation to cases concerning the exclusion of a subset of a status group, where the distinguishing feature of the subset is its poverty. Thus in a British case, a challenge was mounted against a measure which excluded homeless disabled people from a benefit available to all other disabled people.[132] Although the UK Supreme Court held that homelessness was a characteristic protected under Article 14 of the ECHR, and therefore the policy *prima facie* discriminated against homeless people, there was no breach of that article in this case. This was because the court should be slow to substitute its opinion for that of the state in a policy area such as this.[133]

---

[127] *DH v Czech Republic* Application No 57325/00 (2006) 43 EHRR 41 (ECtHR) para 142.

[128] *Carson, R (on the application of) v Secretary for State for Work and Pensions* [2005] 2 WLR 1369; [2005] UKHL 37 (UKHL).

[129] *R (on the application of Reynolds) v Secretary of State for Work and Pensions, R (on the application of Carson) v Secretary of State for Work and Pensions* [2005] 2 WLR 1369; [2005] UKHL 37 (UKHL) para 45.

[130] *Gosselin v Quebec* [2002] SCC 84 (Canadian Supreme Court).

[131] *Gosselin v Quebec* [2002] SCC 84 (Canadian Supreme Court) para 61 (per McLachlin J). See *R v Kapp* [2008] SCC 41 (Canadian Supreme Court).

[132] *Regina (RJM) v Secretary of State for Work and Pensions* [2008] UKHL 63 (HL).

[133] Para 56.

4 3   Positive duties in anti-discrimination law

A third point of entry arises within the context of "fourth generation" equality laws, which recognise that the duty on a state is more than to refrain from discrimination, but includes taking positive steps to ameliorate inequality. The intricate interaction between status and distributive inequalities should entail that such duties incorporate both dimensions. This was indeed the expectation of the Canadian equality guarantee, section 15 of the Canadian Charter. Thus Porter demonstrates that section 15, with its new guarantee of the right to the "equal benefit of the law", was originally conceived by equality seekers as a positive notion of equality, which went "beyond prohibition of government action that violates the equality guarantees to require positive government measures to eradicate inequality, including social and economic inequality".[134] However, in 2005, he concluded that

> "the unique vision of equality behind section 5 is in serious jeopardy ... In 20 years of equality claims, the Supreme Court has on no occasion considered evidence of persistent or worsening socio-economic disadvantage of an enumerated group, and found on the basis of that evidence that positive action must be taken to ameliorate it."[135]

In Britain, over the past two decades, positive duties in relation to equality have been imposed by statute on public bodies. The duty is a light-touch one: instead of requiring public bodies to take steps to achieve equality, on the model of socio-economic rights, it requires such bodies to "have due regard to" the need to eliminate discrimination, advance equality of opportunity and foster good relations.[136] This "public sector equality duty" has been concerned with status inequality, rather than distributive inequality or poverty, although the Equality Act[137] briefly signalled a recognition of the role of equality in relation to poverty by including a specific duty in relation to socio-economic disadvantage. However, a change of heart came with the change of government in 2010, and the relevant Minister announced that the socio-economic duty would not be brought into effect.[138]

In the event, the status-based equality duty will continue to bear the burden of litigation on behalf of people in poverty in Britain. Indeed, there has been a spate of litigation challenging cuts in welfare on the basis that the public authority failed to pay due regard to the impact on women, people with disabilities, or ethnic minorities. In the absence of the express socio-economic disadvantage duty, these claims must be framed in terms of status inequality. At times the intersection is close enough for all people living in poverty to benefit from the gains made by a particular status group.[139] However, the duty has proved to

---

[134]   Porter (2006) *Supreme Court LR* 27.

[135]   40-41.

[136]   See s 76A of the Sex Discrimination Act 1975; s 71 of the Race Relations Act 1976 and s 3 of the Disability Discrimination Act 2005 (all repealed by the Equality Act).

[137]   S 1 of the Equality Act.

[138]   The Honourable Theresa May, Minister for Women and Equality *Equality Strategy Speech* (2010) speech delivered at the Colin Street Community Centre, London, 17-11-2010 <http://www.homeoffice.gov.uk/media-centre/speeches/equality-vision> (accessed 21-06-2011).

[139]   *The Queen (on the Application of Meany, Glynn, Sanders) v Harlow District Council* [2009] EWHC 559 (Admin) (HC).

be a fragile platform for launching challenges on behalf of people in poverty. As a start, the duty is only to pay due regard. Cuts are unassailable if the court finds that the authority has indeed paid due regard to the statutory criteria.[140] Secondly, in some cases, the challenge has simply created competition for scarce resources between status groups and other individuals in poverty.[141] The third difficulty is to do with the potential weakness of equality itself, if applied in a purely comparative or formal sense. Where a policy has a deleterious effect on all users, there is no cause for complaint.[142]

More optimistically, the most recent formulation of the status-based duty draws the linkages between status and distributive equality for the first time, providing that public bodies must have due regard to the need to address disadvantages suffered by persons sharing a protected characteristic, to meet different needs, and to encourage under-represented groups to participate in public life.[143] As we have seen, all three of these elements are related to socio-economic disadvantage and social exclusion, and potentially open up a channel for factoring socio-economic disadvantage into decisions in regard to status.

5 Conclusion

Analysing poverty through the lens of substantive equality reveals that many of the stigmatic and exclusionary aspects of status discrimination are also a feature of poverty. Moreover, measures aimed at addressing poverty can themselves reinforce status discrimination. It is in these cases that the right to equality has most traction. Indeed, lifting some of the stigmatic and exclusionary barriers associated with poverty can have important redistributive consequences in themselves. However, courts and legislatures remain reluctant to regard the right to equality, interpreted and enforced by judges, as the appropriate arena for addressing what are viewed as the essentially distributive and polycentric issues that arise in relation to poverty. It is possibly in the area of "fourth generation" equality rights, entailing positive duties in relation to both socio-economic disadvantage and status inequality, that attention should be focused.

SUMMARY

My aim here is to consider what role the right to equality can and should play in relation to poverty. Unlike socio-economic rights, which are still fighting for full recognition within the human rights arena, the right to equality is well established and could therefore be a primary vehicle for establishing

---

[140] *R (Brown) v Secretary of State for Work and Pensions* [2008] EWHC 3158 (Admin) (HC).

[141] *R (on the application of Kaur & Another) v London Borough of Ealing* [2008] EWHC 2062 (HC) (review of decision to close loss-making branches of the postal service, impacting on access to postal services by the disabled, elderly and "vulnerable" persons); *The Queen (on the application of Harris) v London Borough of Haringey* [2010] EWCA Civ 703 (CA) (planning permission for a substantial development set aside for failing to show due regard to the need "to promote equality of opportunity and good relations between persons of different racial groups" under s 71(1)(b) of the Race Relations Act); *The Queen (on the Application of Hajrula) v London Councils* [2011] EWHC 448 (Admin) (HC) (review of decision to cut funding to a Roma Support Group as part of a scheme to prioritise social spending).

[142] *R (Domb) v London Borough of Hammersmith* [2009] EWCA Civ 941 (CA) para 67.

[143] S 149(3) of the Equality Act.

a human rights approach to poverty. This in turn requires a deeper understanding of the relationship between poverty and the traditional constituency of equality rights, namely inequality on the grounds of race, gender or other status. In the first part of the chapter I examine the relationships between poverty and inequality first from the perspective of distributive inequality and then from that of status inequality. While the relationship between poverty and distributive inequality remains contested, deepening understandings of substantive equality have illuminated the continuities between status inequalities and poverty. I then develop an analytic framework within which both poverty and status inequality might be located. In the last section, drawing on the experience in Britain, the US, Canada, and South Africa, consider three possible ways in which a right to equality could function in relation to poverty: including poverty as a ground of discrimination; using equality to challenge under-inclusive or discriminatory anti-poverty measures; and "fourth generation" models of equality, which include positive duties. I conclude that viewing poverty through the lens of substantive equality allows us to illuminate the ways in which poverty, like status discrimination, generates stigma, social exclusion and loss of autonomy. Conversely, status inequality will only be fully addressed by addressing distributive inequalities. It is in these cases that the right to equality has most traction. However, in the jurisdictions examined here, there remains a deep reluctance to regard the right to equality on its own as generating social rights if the latter are not explicit in the constitution. The result is that while the right to equality potentially makes a valuable contribution to aspects of poverty based on mis-recognition and social and political exclusion, it has not yet been sufficiently developed to address distributive inequalities in its own right.

CHAPTER 9

GENDERED TRANSFORMATION IN SOUTH AFRICAN JURISPRUDENCE: POOR WOMEN AND THE CONSTITUTIONAL COURT

Catherine Albertyn

1   Introduction

Most people in South Africa are poor, and most of the poor are women.[1] It is no surprise that the achievement of equality, human dignity and freedom under South Africa's Constitution[2] is closely tied to the eradication of poverty and inequality.[3] These goals are an essential part of South Africa's transformative constitutional project, part of the wider constitutional commitment to "improve the quality of life and free the potential of all persons".[4]

Central to this transformative project, although often not recognised as such, is the need to address the distinctive forms of poverty and inequality experienced by women. This chapter explores the extent to which, and how, poor women have been included within the constitutional project, firstly, by an acknowledgment of the complexity of poor women's lives and then through a brief analysis of cases and jurisprudence on equality and socio-economic rights. Underlying these two facets of the chapter are two key questions: What does the experience of poor women tell us about the meaning of transformation and a transformative Constitution? And how can we seek a more transformative (and gendered) understanding of equality and socio-economic rights jurisprudence? In respect of the latter, the chapter explores whether we can move beyond a progressive liberal egalitarianism in achieving transformative outcomes that address gendered poverty and inequality.

---

[1]   In the most recent official unemployment statistics the formal unemployment rate for men was 22.2% and for women 28.2%. Statistics South Africa "Quarterly Labour Force Survey, Quarter 1, 2011" (2011) *Stats Online*<http://www.statssa.gov.za/PublicationsHTML/P02111stQuarter2011/html/P02111stQuarter2011. html> (accessed 05-08-2011). In addition, women are more likely than men to live in poor households and have lower earnings, and female-headed households are much more vulnerable to poverty than male-headed households. D Posel & M Rogan "Women, Income and Poverty: Gendered Access to Resources in Post-Apartheid South Africa" (2009) 23 *Agenda* 25.

[2]   Preamble and s 1 of the Constitution of the Republic of South Africa, 1996 ("the Constitution").

[3]   See the much cited *Soobramoney v Minister of Health (Kwazulu-Natal)* 1998 1 SA 765 (CC) para 8:
   "We live in a society in which there are great disparities in wealth. Millions of people are living in deplorable conditions and in great poverty. There is a high level of unemployment, inadequate social security, and many do not have access to clean water or to adequate health services. These conditions already existed when the Constitution was adopted and a commitment to address them, and to transform our society into one in which there will be human dignity, freedom and equality, lies at the heart of our new constitutional order. For as long as these conditions continue to exist that aspiration will have a hollow ring."

[4]   Preamble of the Constitution. See also P Langa "Transformative Constitutionalism" (2006) 3 *Stell LR* 351.

2   Poor women, gender inequality and transformation

2 1   Poverty and gendered inequalities

Transformative jurisprudence must be grounded in a court's understanding of the actual conditions in which people are living.[5] These often give rise to a complexity that law struggles to tame. Although it is well known that the burdens of poverty fall disproportionately on women, the multiple, intersectional inequalities that shape women's vulnerability to, and experience of, poverty produce a complex and diverse picture. This part provides an overview of some of the main issues that shape poor women's lives.

If poverty is measured solely in terms of income and formal employment, then black women fare the worst. Where women cannot *earn* a living, they *make* a living in any way that is possible.[6] This includes social grants (if they have children up to age seventeen, are disabled, or are over sixty years of age) that help lift households out of extreme poverty,[7] as well as a variety of kinds of informal and subsistence work, and, sometimes, prostitution.[8]

Women's economic inequality is significantly influenced by their reproductive roles and primary care-giving responsibilities, which mean that they bear additional (and often sole) responsibilities for children and other dependants.[9] This care-giving role is significantly under-recognised and means that women devote a disproportionate amount of time and resources in unpaid, domestic labour.[10] As Justice O'Regan has noted:

"It is unlikely that we will achieve a more egalitarian society until responsibilities for child-rearing are more equally shared."[11]

The practical and normative consequences of this "sexual division of labour" affect women's ability to find work and their place in the labour

---

[5]   D Moseneke "Transformative Adjudication" (2002) 18 *SAJHR* 309 318-319.

[6]   Karl von Holdt and Eddie Webster distinguish between earning a living (in regular paid employment) and making a living (in any form of income generating or subsistence income): K von Holdt & E Webster "Work Restructuring and the Crisis of Reproduction: A Southern Perspective" in K von Holdt & E Webster (eds) *Beyond the Apartheid Workplace: Studies in Transition* (2005) 3 4.

[7]   M Leibbrandt, I Woolard, A Finn & J Argent *Trends in South African Income Distribution and Poverty since the Fall of Apartheid* OECD Social, Employment and Migration Working Papers No 101 (2010) 66.

[8]   See, for example, S Benjamin "The Feminization of Poverty in Post-Apartheid South Africa: A Story Told by the Women of Bayview, Chatsworth" (undated) *Centre for Civil Society, UKZN* <http://ccs.ukzn. ac.za/files/The%20Feminization%20of%20Poverty%20in%20Post-Apartheid%20South%20Africa%20. pdf> (accessed 30-08-2011).

[9]   B Clark & B Goldblatt "Gender and Family Law" in E Bonthuys & C Albertyn (eds) *Gender, Law and Justice* (2007) 195 201.

[10]   Statistics South Africa *A Survey of Time Use: How South African Women and Men Spend Their Time* (2010).

[11]   The full quote recognises the social and economic disadvantage experienced by women because of the sexual division of labour:
       "For many South African women, the difficulties of being responsible for the social and economic burdens of child-rearing, in circumstances where they have few skills and scant financial resources, are immense. The failure by fathers to shoulder their share of the financial and social burden of child-rearing is a primary cause of this hardship. The result of being responsible for children makes it more difficult for women to compete in the labour market and is one of the causes of the deep inequalities experienced by women in employment. [This] ... is one of the root causes of women's inequality in our society ... It is unlikely that we will achieve a more egalitarian society until responsibilities for child-rearing are more equally shared." (O'Regan J minority concurring judgment *Hugo v President RSA* 1997 4 SA 1 (CC) para 38).

market that is already marked by high levels of unemployment. As a result, women are most likely to be found in low-paid formal work, domestic work, casual and informal work. Women in these sectors are particularly vulnerable to exploitation, violence and coercion.[12]

Hunter argues that rising unemployment and increased female mobility (largely in pursuit of work) have contributed to a significant decline in marriage amongst poor women. While some women live in informal, long-term relationships,[13] many seek to survive within a network of relationships that also serve an economic function of providing for women's basic needs, including care of children.[14] Many poor women live in women-headed households that are statistically poorer than male-headed households, poignantly illustrated by the fact that members of women-headed households are more likely to be hungry.[15]

Not surprisingly, poor African women are more likely to live in informal housing, in poorer rural areas and are least likely to enjoy access to formal housing and basic services.[16] In addition, women living in rural areas are most likely to be subject to traditional forms of power, which may contribute further to their poverty and vulnerability.[17]

Poverty and inequality affect women's ability to exercise autonomy over their bodies and lives. Poor women are more vulnerable to HIV infection, as a complex mix of poverty and gendered inequalities drive the epidemic.[18] Poor women are also more vulnerable to all forms of sexual violence and coercion.[19]

---

[12] These include the exchange of sex for protection as women working in least protected informal spheres might exchange sex to secure protection for their goods and belongings. B Karumbidza *Criminalising the Livelihoods of the Poor: The Impact of Formalising Informal Trading on Female and Migrant Traders in Durban* SERI Research Report (February 2011) <http://www.seri-sa.org/index.php?option=com_cont ent&view=article&id=17&Itemid=29> (accessed 15-08-2011). Women who earn an income through sex work often have to protect themselves from arrest and abuse by having sex with police officers, security guards and other "gatekeepers".

[13] About 7% of South Africans report living together (more than three million people), a number that is gradually increasing. D Budlender "Marriage Patterns in South Africa: Methodological and Substantive Issues" (2004) 9 *Southern African Journal of Demography* 1 1.

[14] M Hunter "The Changing Political Economy of Sex in South Africa: The Significance of Unemployment and Inequalities to the Scale of the HIV/AIDS Pandemic" (2007) 64 *SocSci Med* 689 692-693; A Harrison *A Context of 'Non-Marriage': Non-Marital Unions in the Transition to Adulthood in South Africa* (2007) a paper prepared for the symposium *Rethinking Relationships* hosted by the Population Studies and Training Center, Brown University, 19-04-2007 <http://www.pstc.brown.edu/nmu/Harrison%20-%20 Non%20Marital%20Unions%204-12-2007.pdf> (accessed 25-08-2011). As Hunter points out, these relationships fulfil a range of social, personal, emotional and economic needs.

[15] According to the 2007 Household Survey, persons living in a female-headed household were 67% more likely to go hungry than those in a male-headed household. Statistics South Africa *General Household Survey 2007* (2008) 46. Female-headed households are much more vulnerable to poverty than male-headed households. See also generally Posel & Rogan (2009) *Agenda* on greater poverty of women-headed households .

[16] J Kehler "Women and Poverty: The South African Experience" (2001) 3 *Journal of International Women's Studies* <http://www.bridgew.edu/soas/jiws/fall01/kehler.pdf> (accessed 22-11-2011).

[17] See, generally, S Mnisi Weeks & A Claassens "Tensions Between Vernacular Values that Prioritise Basic Needs and State Versions of Customary Law that Contradict Them: 'We Love These Fields that Feed Us, But Not at the Expense of a Person'" in S Liebenberg & G Quinot (eds) *Law and Poverty* (2012) 381.

[18] See M Hunter *Love in the Time of AIDS: Inequality, Gender and Rights in South Africa* (2010) 24-28.

[19] See, generally, Michigan Domestic Violence Prevention and Treatment Board *The Intersection of Poverty and Sexual Violence* (February 2008).

Poor women bear the burden of blame in our society, as they become the scapegoat for a range of social ills from HIV/AIDS to teenage pregnancies to abortion.[20] Underlying this attribution of blame is a range of gendered stereotypes of women held by women and men, which deepen and reinforce women's unequal position in our society.[21]

It is impossible, in this short space, to capture the diversity and complexity of poor women's lives. However, it is clear that their lived experiences are found in the intersection of race, gender, class, sexuality, space and place, *et cetera*, in which a range of social and economic inequalities are inextricably bound up with each other. Yet women are not passive in the face of enormous obstacles to leading a decent and secure life. Rather, poor women are constantly negotiating "multiple, complex and simultaneous subject positions, identities, inequalities, marginalities and resistances to differing and similar oppressions" in order to secure their lives and livelihoods.[22] Thus, while poverty and inequality undoubtedly deepen women's experience of powerlessness and subordination, this does not mean that women are rendered eternally powerless and dependent. Despite their circumstances, women are resourceful, exercising agency and rational choices within particular contexts of vulnerability and inequality.[23]

2 2   Transformative constitutionalism and transformative strategies

How do we think about transformation and transformative constitutionalism in this context? Clearly the lives of poor women suggest a complexity that cannot be simply reduced to either "poverty" or gendered inequality and subordination.

2 2 1   Substantive, gendered and contested transformation

The lived realities of poor women suggest a vision of the Constitution, and an interpretation of its values of equality, dignity, freedom and democracy, that speak of a society in which individuals are afforded equivalent, substantive conditions for exercising the choices that matter to them, about how to live their lives, maintain their relationships, raise their children and pursue their aspirations. This requires a substantial equality of resources (including remedial measures and redistribution) to satisfy basic needs and

---

[20] See, for example, S Leclerc-Madlala "Virginity Testing: Managing Sexuality in a Maturing HIV/AIDS Epidemic" (2001) 15 *Medical Anthropology Quarterly* 533; S Panday, M Makiwane, C Ranchod & T Letsoala *Teenage Pregnancy in South Africa: With a Specific Focus on School-Going Learners* (2009) 26-28 <http://www.hsrc.ac.za/Research_Publication-21277.phtml> (accessed 25-08-2011).

[21] D Everatt "The Undeserving Poor: Poverty and the Politics of Service Delivery in the Poorest Nodes of South Africa" (2008) 35 *Politikon* 293 315-316.

[22] M O'Neill & R Campbell "Desistence from Sex Work: Feminist Cultural Criminology and Intersectionality: The Complexities of Moving In and Out of Sex Work" in Y Taylor, S Hines & S Casey (eds) *Theorizing Intersectionality and Sexuality* (2010) 163 165.

[23] There are many examples of this in research. See Claassen's work on women's resourcefulness in negotiating access to land: A Claassens & S Ngubane "Women, Land and Power: The Impact of the Communal Land Rights Act" in A Claassens & B Cousins (eds) *Land, Power and Custom: Controversies Generated by South Africa's Communal Land Rights Act* (2008) 154. See also Hunter on poor women's agency in negotiating condom use: M Hunter *Love in a Time of AIDS* (2010) ch 9.

enable equivalent levels of well-being, meaningful recognition of diversity and community, unfettered participation in local and national politics and a state that is responsive and accountable.[24]

There is no doubt that addressing economic inequalities, joblessness and redistribution is critical to alleviating the plight of the poor, including and especially poor women. Poor women focus particular attention on how these economic inequalities are gendered. The lives of poor women also demonstrate the interaction of social and economic inequalities, and thus the need *also* to shift those gendered norms, values and social rules that place women in an unequal position in society, affect patterns of (re)distribution, impede their agency, and render them vulnerable to exploitation and violence. In addition, the effective participation of poor women in their community, and in local and national politics requires a particularly inclusive and interactive form of participatory democracy that extends to the public and private spheres. Therefore the lived realities of poor women remind us that the kind of transformation – and transformative strategies – that are necessary to generate meaningful change require attention to structure and agency, to redistribution and recognition, to individual and community, to public and private (especially care-giving roles in family), to inequality and poverty.

There is a significant degree of consensus over the general meaning of constitutional transformation amongst progressive lawyers in South Africa.[25] However, it is a "transformation consensus" that operates at a fairly high level of abstraction, and the differences that exist at the more detailed level of theory, concepts and strategies are not always apparent. Nor is there much engagement with whether and how the experiences of poor women, and of gendered poverty and inequality, might shape this idea of transformation.

Roux has pointed to the commonalities that progressive and egalitarian liberals may share with a more critical and radical mode of thinking, at least at a general level of constitutional interpretation.[26] However, it is in the detail of the ideas that Klare identified as typifying a "post-liberal" view (such as egalitarianism and equality, multi-culturalism and diversity, gender identity, participatory democracy and the public/private divide)[27] that the dividing line between progressive, liberal egalitarian (on the one hand) and more critical and radical interpretations and outcomes (on the other) exists. While liberalism may not have "clear conceptual boundaries",[28] and its reach has certainly extended beyond its more classic liberal forms, it nevertheless has conceptual

---

[24] This is developed in the South African context of poverty and inequality from ideas expressed by authors such as Martha Nussbaum, Anne Phillips, Iris Marion Young and Nancy Fraser. This is developed in more detail in relation to constitutional values in a South African context in C Albertyn *Equality Law* (forthcoming).

[25] See S Sibanda "Not Purpose-Made! Transformative Constitutionalism, Post-Independence Constitutionalism and the Struggle to Eradicate Poverty" in S Liebenberg & G Quinot (eds) *Law and Poverty* (2012) 40.

[26] T Roux "Transformative Constitutionalism and the Best Interpretation of the South African Constitution: Distinction without a Difference" (2009) 20 *Stell LR* 258 261-262. However, Roux does not address the very real differences that exist in the actual interpretation and content of these "shared" ideas and concepts, and the degree of contestation within and between them.

[27] See, generally, K Klare "Legal Culture and Transformative Constitutionalism" (1998) 14 *SAJHR* 146.

[28] Roux (2009) *Stell LR* 262.

limits. It is clear that the interaction between liberal and radical or critical intellectuals produces an overlapping middle ground in some instances,[29] but there are also significant differences as will be discussed in relation to equality below. Although beyond the scope of this chapter, identifying these commonalities and differences is an important component of developing a more radical, indigenous jurisprudence that meets the needs of South Africa: one that is characterised by "local" ideas of, *inter alia*, redistribution, stronger positive duties and remedial action by a more interventionist state; recognition of a strong and positive cultural diversity; robust ideas of choice; and an understanding of separation of powers that appreciates the judiciary's positive role in a "pro-poor" constitutional democracy.[30]

A key question for critical scholars is whether the Constitution's liberal focus and interpretation, and the necessary engagement with legal liberalism that this entails, limits the interpretation and application of the Constitution to a struggle between the reach permitted by the tenets of classic liberalism,[31] and to a more egalitarian and progressive, but nevertheless, liberal approach (thus excluding critical approaches). What space is there for a more critical understanding? Does a more critical or radical approach offer something different from progressive and strongly egalitarian forms of liberalism?

2 2 2   *Transformative strategies in law*

Although there is a fairly vigorous scholarship on transformation, and a strong critique in areas of law where courts are seen to fall short of transformative outcomes,[32] there is less concrete legal debate on what transformation might mean in any particular context, for a particular group, as well as how we might get there, and the role of law within this.

Most of us agree that opportunities for transformation in and through law are limited, contingent upon a range of legal and other factors that include the state of jurisprudence and legal doctrine, the culture of judicial decision-making and values, the facts of a particular case, the values and choices of lawyers, and the wider political, social and economic context. However, social change literature alerts us to the importance, also, of understanding the direct

---

[29] Here the work of Michael Walzer on multi-culturalism in *Politics and Passion: Towards a More Egalitarian Liberalism* (2004) or Martha Nussbaum *Women and Human Development: The Capabilities Approach* (2000) on capabilities, choice and family are excellent examples of "liberals" articulating more critical views, and thus of the impact of the radical critique on liberalism.

[30] See Klare (1998) *SAJHR* 151-156; J Baker, K Lynch, S Cantillon & J Walsh *Equality: From Theory to Action* 2 ed (2009) 33-41; Albertyn *Equality Law* (forthcoming).

[31] See, for example, M Pieterse "What Do We Mean When We Talk About Transformative Constitutionalism?" (2005) 20 *SAPL* 155.

[32] Especially in relation to equality, socio-economic rights and private law. See, generally, C Albertyn "Substantive Equality and Transformation in South Africa" (2007) 23 *SAJHR* 253; P de Vos "Same-Sex Sexual Desire and the Re-imagining of the South African Family" (2004) 20 *SAJHR* 187; D Bilchitz *Poverty and Fundamental Rights* (2007); S Liebenberg *Socio-Economic Rights: Adjudication under a Transformative Constitution* (2010); D Davis & K Klare "Transformative Constitutionalism and the Common and Customary Law" (2010) 26 *SAJHR* 403.

and indirect benefits of litigation, and of conceiving of court action as part of wider political struggles for change.[33]

The opportunities for transformative legal action present in many different ways and have multiple possible outcomes. These might be purely practical legal rights and remedies that positively affect the lives of the poor and marginalised. They might be more normative advances, restating the values and norms that shape social and economic inequalities. Or they might be steps in wider political struggles with a range of outcomes. Transformative legal action might be particularly powerful, with a potential "multiplier effect" if it also affects the norms, values and background rules that underlie different areas of the law.[34] For example, Wilson argues that *Government of the Republic of South Africa v Grootboom*[35] generated developments in property law (over a series of cases) that dislodged the normality assumption that an owner is entitled to exclusive possession of his property, at least insofar as evictions that might lead to homelessness were concerned.[36] Some of this did not occur by accident, but was the result of conscious litigation strategies. Wilson argues that this is an incomplete and uncertain trajectory where the principles have "yet to be stated as a coherent whole".[37] This argument is based on the suggestion that building a transformative jurisprudence takes place over time, requiring strategic lawyers to take advantage of destabilising moments to bring about small actual or potential, intended or unintended, shifts in the background rules. These moments need to be exploited to push the law in a progressive direction, build jurisprudence and achieve conceptual and practical results.

Positive outcomes to cases are often difficult enough. Transformative outcomes, which not only address poverty and/or inequality, but also do so in a way that opens up the possibility of substantial shifts in social and economic relations and alters the underlying norms and rules, are rare and difficult. But opportunities for such transformative outcomes might present more often than we think. The challenge is to recognise and understand these opportunities for change. Even though the construction of critical alternatives is inevitably circumscribed by the need to work with existing jurisprudence, there are spaces and opportunities presented by law that are potentially transformative.[38]

---

[33] M McCann *Rights at Work: Pay Equity Reform and the Politics of Legal Mobilization* (1994). See also new work in South Africa, especially issue 2 of (2011) 27 *SAJHR* (a special issue on public interest litigation).

[34] See Davis & Klare (2010) *SAJHR* 435-449 on the manner in which background rules shape social and economic relations, and can also potentially "undo" them.

[35] 2001 1 SA 46 (CC).

[36] See, generally, S Wilson "Breaking the Tie: Evictions from Private Land, Homelessness and a New Normality" (2009) 126 *SALJ* 270.

[37] 290.

[38] See, for example, Liebenberg *Socio-Economic Rights*, which takes the court's socio-economic rights reasonable review jurisprudence and seeks to push the boundaries in more transformative directions. See also Davis & Klare (2010) *SAJHR* 403-509 (identifying a range of transformative judgments); Albertyn (2007) *SAJHR* 253-276 on transformative possibilities in equality.

2 2 3   *Women and transformation*[39]

For women, transformation in general means that each woman is afforded the ability and the resources to pursue her well-being, so that the vision of the Constitution, set out in broad terms above, is fulfilled.[40] Poor women require the resources necessary not only to meet their basic needs, but also to enhance their control over their lives and ability to make real choices for themselves and their dependants. As stated above, this includes attention to recognition and redistribution, to poverty and inequality, to structure and agency, and to inclusion and transformation. Poor women present the challenge of overcoming such dualisms, and of finding legal ways of doing so.

What that means practically in any given case or context is open for debate. However, it usually entails choices about legal arguments, in terms of content and approach, characterisation of the case, rights arguments, and remedies. Certainly, there is often a choice of inclusive or transformative strategies, those that affirm the *status quo* and those that seek to dislodge its rules, norms and institutions.[41] However, what is actually transformative, and in what manner, in any particular case – and whether it is capable of legal argument and resolution – remains contested.

For example, it is transformative to extend equal rights within marriage and inheritance, as well as to land, resources and leadership, to women living under customary law. As occurs under civil law, the shifting of a normative framework of inequality (that defers to men as heads of households and providers, and women as subordinates serving the sexual and reproductive needs of men within patriarchal families) to one of equality (which recognises the entitlements of women to power, status and resources within the family), fundamentally affects underlying legal and social norms. It is true that this does not immediately translate into actual equality, nor does it necessarily challenge embedded gender roles (such as women's social position as mother and sole care-giver). However, it enables a revaluing of women's status and constitutes a real shift in recognition. It also enhances the possibilities of redistribution of resources within the family and even beyond.[42] It opens up the opportunity to advance a more sex- and gender-equal society in which women are not the sole custodians of child and male welfare. Perhaps the most important cases concerning poor women in the Constitutional Court were therefore the equality cases of *Bhe v Magistrate, Khayelitsha*[43] (that found the rule of patriliny to be unfair gender discrimination and extended inheritance rights to women); *Gumede v President of the Republic of South Africa*[44] (which removed the discriminatory proprietary consequences of

---

[39]   For more detail on these arguments, see C Albertyn "Law, Gender and Inequality in South Africa" (2011) 39 *Development Studies* 139.

[40]   Part 2 2 1 above. See also C Albertyn & B Goldblatt "Facing the Challenge of Transformation: Difficulties in the Development of an Indigenous Jurisprudence of Equality" (1998) 14 *SAJHR* 248.

[41]   For a discussion on this in relation to gender, see Albertyn (2007) *SAJHR* 253-276.

[42]   Women's access to family property for example, extends their ability to secure credit for income generating purposes.

[43]   2005 1 SA 580 (CC).

[44]   2009 3 SA 152 (CC).

customary marriages concluded prior to the enactment of the Recognition of Customary Marriages Act 110 of 1998); and *Shilubana v Nwamwita*[45] (which accepted that women could be traditional leaders). Equally important are cases extending rights to women in Muslim marriages.[46]

It is also transformative to amend the law to recognise and protect partners in a broad range of relationships outside of marriage, so that parties to these relationships are afforded status, rights and opportunities, and their relationships recognised as valuable social institutions. For poor women, who are least likely to be able to rely on the income of a spouse within marriage, but who tend to live in more informal relationships of various kinds, the failure of cases such as *Volks NO v Robinson*[47] to recognise their plight in any meaningful way is a missed opportunity for both protection and transformation. (In *Robinson* the Court denied that the exclusion of cohabiting partners from claiming maintenance from the estate of a deceased partner – a right extended to spouses in a marriage – was unfair discrimination based on gender and marital status). Although a case concerning spousal maintenance from a deceased estate does not reflect the reality of the limited resources available in the relationships of poor women, *Robinson* nevertheless presented the Court with a chance to address the underlying norms and rules of cohabiting relationships in a transformative manner. At the very least, the Court might have established a normative framework that was inclusive of the needs and relationships of poor women (for whom marriage is not the norm).[48]

At the same time, judgments that produce positive outcomes for poor women are not necessarily transformative. It is hugely significant to grant women access to life-saving treatment to prevent HIV transmission to their babies, but it is only transformative to do so on terms that recognise the agency of poor young women in doing so. If women are granted access to such treatment solely out of a need to "save" their children, they tend to be viewed as mere vessels of reproduction rather than as rights-bearing citizens. Arguably, this was the outcome of *Minister of Health v Treatment Action Campaign (No 2)*,[49] as discussed in more detail below.[50] Indeed, I would suggest that the practical extension of socio-economic rights to women (whether housing, water, social assistance or health care) is always significant in terms of alleviating the burden of poverty, but is rarely transformative if it does not address – and undermine – the gendered barriers to access and full enjoyment of these rights.

Given the invisibility of women in all socio-economic rights cases so far (except for *Minister of Health v TAC*), the mere inclusion of women, as women rather than (gender neutral) applicants, would be significant. It would begin to recognise women as citizens and rights-bearers to whom the state

---

[45] 2009 2 SA 66 (CC).

[46] *Daniels v Campbell* 2004 5 SA 331 (CC); *Hassam v Jacobs* 2009 5 SA 572 (CC).

[47] 2005 5 BCLR 446 (CC) (denying partners in cohabitating couples the same rights as married couples to maintenance from the estate of a deceased spouse).

[48] This was more evident in the two minority, dissenting judgments of O' Regan and Mokgoro JJ and Sachs J in *Volks NO v Robinson* 2005 5 BCLR 446 (CC).

[49] 2002 5 SA 721 (CC).

[50] See part 3 2 below.

is accountable. Developing a gendered understanding of women's particular position and needs in relation to socio-economic rights, and shaping arguments and remedies around this, is potentially transformative.

Seeking transformative outcomes for women thus entails attention to social and economic inequalities, to recognition and redistribution, and to the connections between them. Put another way: poverty is always, also, a matter of gendered inequalities. For example, improving access to jobs or resources will not assist women in the long term unless this takes into account the particular social and economic ways in which women are excluded from work. Broadening access to basic services will reproduce gendered social and economic hierarchies unless the extra burdens caused by women's gender roles and economic marginalisation are addressed. Extending social grants to women to address the additional social and economic burden of care might alleviate economic hardship, but reinforce unequal recognition.[51] It is always important to address gendered inequalities in a manner that subverts, rather than reinforces, the gender roles and stereotypes that place women in unequal positions. Improving the lives of poor women must comprehend the multiple barriers that poor women face in accessing rights, including the resistance of overlapping systems of law, power and authority: the state and state law, community, custom and tradition, and family.

What does this mean for transformation through law? It seems that there are at least three areas that could be fruitfully addressed. They are listed briefly here, and discussed further below.

Firstly, the context of an alleged rights violation should be understood to include these intersecting social and economic inequalities – the particular complexity of women's lives. When (poor) women bring their claims to court, lawyers and judges need to understand this context: how gender inequality and poverty intersect; how gendered material conditions relate to gendered norms and social attitudes. This information needs to be introduced in court as part of the contextual analysis that is required in determining whether a right has been violated. The importance of context is discussed further in parts 3 and 4 below.

Secondly, attention needs to be paid to overcoming the divides between gender and poverty manifest in, for example, equality and socio-economic rights cases. Poor women fall between the different conceptual approaches that address gender *or* poverty. Thus poor women may find that a court's reluctance to entertain arguments of poverty and class (or redistribution) in equality cases results in a narrow focus on recognition issues that does not meet their specific needs.[52] Alternatively, a court might acknowledge the complexity of their plight but defer it to social policy to address (often as a matter of redistribution). In socio-economic rights cases, lawyers and

---

[51] N Fraser "Social Justice in the Age of Identity Politics: Redistribution, Recognition and Participation" in N Fraser & A Honneth *Redistribution or Recognition? A Political-Philosophical Exchange* (2003) 1 64.

[52] See, for example, the manner in which the majority in *Volks NO v Robinson* 2005 5 BCLR 446 (CC) acknowledges the plight of poor cohabiting women, and then leaves this issue for Parliament or the Executive to address through policy and legislative measures (especially paras 63-66). See further part 3 1 below.

judges tend to address the problem of poverty without reference to gender.[53] Transformative cases need to address poverty and gender, recognition and redistribution.

Thirdly, remedies need to be shaped to meet the particular needs of women. Here the practical and normative effects of judgments and remedies must be considered. Courts need to worry about practical relief at the same time as they consider the message about women that is present in a particular judgment and remedy. Although space prevents a detailed discussion of this, it is important to pursue remedies that shift the traditional understandings of gender.[54]

What all of this means practically in any given case or context is always open for debate, involving choices about legal arguments, in terms of content and approach, *amicus curiae* briefs, and remedies. Certainly, there is often a choice of inclusive or transformative strategies, those that affirm the *status quo* and those that seek to dislodge its underlying rules, norms and structures. However, what is actually transformative, and in what manner, in any particular case remains contested. Sometimes, transformative outcomes might not be practically or strategically possible. For example, the case of *Minister of Health v TAC* discussed in part 3 2 below was – subjectively – determined by lawyers to be strategically problematic, even dangerous. The cases of *Volks NO v Robinson* and *S v Jordan*[55] suggest that judicial attitudes might prevent transformative outcomes.

3   Determining poor women's claims – legal choices and constraints

Lawyers play a crucial role in selecting and characterising the cases that end up in the Constitutional Court. A particular experience of poverty or inequality is given meaning, evidence is chosen, applicants identified, legal arguments are developed. These decisions and choices set important limits to the kinds of gendered outcomes that are possible, so a few points on these choices are relevant.

3 1   Poverty and/or inequality?

Both equality and socio-economic rights jurisprudence place some emphasis on notions of disadvantage and vulnerability. How important is it to select applicants and cases on the basis of extreme disadvantage or vulnerability? Marius Pieterse has argued that the "certain unique circumstances or characteristics of individual plaintiffs, [including the degree of privilege] may

---

[53] See part 4 below. Whether socio-economic rights cases, in fact, address issues of poverty is beyond the scope of this chapter. See, for example, S Wilson & J Dugard "Taking Poverty Seriously: The South African Constitutional Court and Socio-Economic Rights" in S Liebenberg & G Quinot (eds) *Law and Poverty* (2012) 222 for further reading on this subject.

[54] See Albertyn (2007) *SAJHR* 262.

[55] 2002 6 SA 642 (CC).

influence ... outcome[s]" in equality cases.[56] Choosing the "right" poor or disadvantaged claimant is arguably significant in equality cases. The framing of claims around the needs of relatively privileged claimants in both *S v Jordan* (criminalisation of prostitution not considered to be a violation of equality rights) and *Volks NO v Robinson*[57] (providing benefits to married couples, but not unmarried, heterosexual co-habiting partners not unfair discrimination) was certainly important in the court's rejection of those claims. Yet it was not determinative.[58] In both instances, the majority judgments are better explained by the Court's resistance to recognising cohabiting couples on the same basis as married couples, and accepting prostitution as a legitimate activity chosen under difficult circumstances. Poor applicants might have elicited more sympathy, but not necessarily different results. The real problem in these cases was not the absence of poor women as applicants, but judicial attitudes that valorised marriage over other relationships, misunderstood the nature of women's choices in an unequal world, and were uncomfortable with women who fell outside the traditional norms of wife and mother.[59] It is questionable whether more emphasis on the plight of poor women would have shifted such attitudes towards gender, sexuality, choice and relationships.

Indeed, had the Court wanted to address the plight of poor women, there was arguably sufficient contextual evidence in *amici curiae* briefs to enable a much more sensitive gendered analysis of the plight of women in unprotected relationships and in sex work. In addition, although neither Ellen Jordan nor Mrs Robinson could be classified as "poor", their lives certainly reflected a combination of gendered inequalities that place women in positions of dependence upon men and in precarious work, and that demonstrate continuities with the plight of poor women. As both minority judgments show, a more sensitive analysis of the impact of the law on "poor" prostitutes or women in cohabiting relationships was clearly possible.

Although the Constitutional Court has previously recognised the persistence of "deep patterns of disadvantage" in our society, which are "particularly acute in the case of black women",[60] the Court's approach to unfair discrimination in terms of section 9(3) has largely sidestepped the intersection of poverty and complex, group-based inequality. Instead, the Court has tended to focus on the implications of status-based discrimination arising from singular grounds.[61]

---

[56] M Pieterse "'Finding for the Applicant': Individual Equality Plaintiffs and Group-Based Disadvantage" (2008) 24 *SAJHR* 397 423.

[57] 2005 5 BCLR 446 (CC).

[58] In *Volks NO v Robinson* 2005 5 BCLR 446 (CC), the Court suggests that it would be sympathetic to claims of poor women for protection within their relationships (paras 66-68). However, it seems clear from its readiness to accept a legitimate distinction between the regulation of married and unmarried couples, that this could not be achieved through the broadening of legislated rights of married couples to unmarried couples. Similarly, in *S v Jordan* 2002 6 SA 642 (CC), the Court's finding that sex work is not gender-based discrimination was not dependent upon who the sex worker was.

[59] Albertyn (2007) *SAJHR* 253-276; E Bonthuys "Institutional Openness Resistance to Feminist Arguments: The Example of the South African Constitutional Court" (2008) 20 *Can J Women & L* 1 23-26; Pieterse (2008) *SAJHR* 405-413.

[60] *Brink v Kitshoff* 1996 4 SA 197 (CC) para 44.

[61] See S Liebenberg & B Goldblatt "The Interrelationship between Equality and Socio-Economic Rights under South Africa's Transformative Constitution" (2007) 23 *SAJHR* 335 349.

As discussed in more detail in part 5 below, women are largely invisible in socio-economic rights jurisprudence. These cases have focused on poverty at the expense of equality. This is at least partly due to legal choices by lawyers. Therefore, in both equality and socio-economic rights cases, legal choices might exclude, subvert or limit the particular experiences, needs and concerns of poor women (and thus limit the possible outcomes). The development of a jurisprudence that is truly reflective of the needs and interests of poor women at the very least requires that public interest lawyers understand and present the complex context of poor women's lives, but also that they are alert to the kind of jurisprudential developments that are needed for more transformative legal outcomes. This is discussed further in parts 4 and 5 below.

3 2   Poor women and non-transformative outcomes[62]

Sometimes poor women are the primary claimants because they are central to the case. The question that then arises is whether such cases are "transformative". *Minister of Health v TAC*[63] is a particularly fascinating case-study of how the context of a case, and the choices made by lawyers about that case, can shape the possibilities of transformative outcomes in courts.

Minister of Health v TAC is a rightly praised case, securing the rights of poor, HIV-positive pregnant women to obtain antiretroviral therapy in public sector hospitals to reduce the risk of transmitting HIV to their babies. Although this was a triumphant outcome to a case fought within a hostile political climate, as part of a highly successful public campaign for access to affordable treatment for HIV-positive poor people,[64] it also represented a missed opportunity for a more transformative jurisprudence on reproductive choice and the rights of access to reproductive healthcare.

The *TAC* case is the only socio-economic rights case that has directly addressed gender issues, in this case women's role as mothers. Initially conceived as a violation of multiple rights, the case eventually turned on section 27 of the Constitution, the right of access to health-care services, including reproductive health care. Central to a transformative idea of reproductive health care is the idea of women as able to make real choices about their sexuality, reproduction and fertility. Rather than cast as "vessels" of reproduction – mothers whose primary role it is to bear and raise children – the centrality of reproductive and sexual choice sees women as independent and equal agents and rights-bearing citizens, able to act to secure their bodily and moral autonomy. This idea of gender and choice is also critical to an ideological and policy context concerning HIV/AIDS that affirms the right of

---

[62] This part is based on C Albertyn & S Meer "Citizens or Mothers? The Marginalization of Women's Reproductive Rights in the Struggle for Access to Health Care for HIV-Positive Pregnant Women in South Africa" in M Mukhopadhyay & S Meer (eds) *Gender, Rights and Development: A Global Sourcebook* (2008) 27 <http://www.kitpublishers.nl/net/KIT_Publicaties_output/ShowFile2.aspx?e=1456> (accessed 31-05-2011).

[63] 2002 5 SA 721 (CC).

[64] For an excellent study of the context of this case, see M Heywood "Preventing Mother-to-Child HIV Transmission in South Africa: Background, Strategies and Outcomes of the Treatment Action Campaign Case against the Minister of Health" (2003) 19 *SAJHR* 278.

women to choose when and whether to have sex, to act to protect themselves from HIV, to choose whether to have children, and to be entitled to treatment in their own right.

The dominant characterisation of the *TAC* case, as a campaign to "save babies", while undoubtedly laudable, ends up by casting poor women as victims and dependants, their decisions subordinated to the overriding goal of treatment, and the lives of their children. This approach reinforces, rather than undermines, "the ethical and legal inequalities inherent in a societal structure that places more value on a women's reproductive capacity than her ... individual well being".[65]

Mindful of these problems, feminist groups had sought to intervene as an *amicus curiae* in the *TAC* case to raise the choice arguments, to assert the conditions necessary for women to exercise their own choices, and to illustrate the consequences of an approach that treated women solely as mothers. These arguments were withdrawn after lawyers in the case indicated a concern with court time available, given the multiplicity of parties to the case. There was also evidence of a concern that feminist arguments about choice would undermine the case, suggesting that women might choose not to take the potentially life-saving nevirapine.[66]

Although the withdrawal of these arguments was the immediate result of the approaches of the TAC lawyers and their legal choices about the best strategic approach to the case; it also reflected a political context that was characterised by state–civil society conflict over HIV/AIDS and a weaker women's movement.[67] The hostile political context of HIV policy was certainly influential in how the case was fought and won. Nevertheless, it illustrates that the strategic choices that lawyers make in framing cases means that they are important gatekeepers to transformative outcomes.[68] The case also suggests that strongly gendered arguments are difficult to make in courts, and that these difficulties are both political and legal. Lawyers make legal choices within a particular political and legal context.

It is important to note that ten years after the judgment, "choice" arguments remain contested in HIV policy, which is consistently criticised for its focus on women as "vessels of reproduction":

> "Women of reproductive age bear the brunt of the epidemic. For prevention to work, we need to be affirming women and providing them with better choices. There is a need to move away from a maternal paradigm that conceptualises treatment for women only as mothers. With the highest rate of infection, women of reproductive age need a continuum of care that takes into account their sexual, reproductive and fertility intentions."[69]

---

[65] C Eyakuze, D Jones, A Starrs & N Sorkin "From PMTCT to a more Comprehensive AIDS Response for Women: A Much-Needed Shift" (2008) 8 *Developing World Bioethics* 33 36 (writing about the intersection of HIV and pregnancy generally).

[66] See Albertyn & Meer "Citizens or Mothers?" in *Gender, Rights and Development* 41.

[67] 47-49.

[68] A second, and different, example in which strategic legal choices possibly trumped arguments of poverty and inequality is the constitutional challenge to CLARA in *Tongoane v Minister for Land and Agricultural Affairs* 2010 6 SA 214 (CC).

[69] M Stevens "Sacrificing the Woman for the Child" (2008) 28 *RJR* 60 60-61.

The courtroom offers an important space to challenge these ideas and comparable assumptions in other policy areas (especially in the absence of widespread political support). Judgments play an important symbolic and standard-setting role. But this requires public-interest lawyers, as gatekeepers of litigation, to be responsive to these claims, and incorporate them into the manner in which a case is conceptualised, characterised and presented through evidence and argument.

4   Equality jurisprudence and poor women

To what extent does equality jurisprudence (in theory and practice) address issues of poverty and gender inequality?

The shift from "formal" to "substantive" equality adopted by the South African Constitutional Court enabled a jurisprudence that moves away from an abstract analysis of discrimination to one that is more focused on the actual context in which rights violations occur. In theory, the Court's emphasis on context and impact, as well as its concern with disadvantage, should allow a proper examination of the actual impact of law and policies on the poor, including poor women.[70] In addition, the adoption of a value-based approach should facilitate a nuanced engagement with the extent to which a law or policy falls short of the kind of society that is envisaged in the Constitution. In practice, two fault-lines appear in the jurisprudence: one between formal and substantive equality, and a second between a liberal egalitarian model of substantive equality and a more critical or radical idea of substantive equality.[71]

The distinction between formal and substantive equality has been widely discussed by legal scholars. Important to understanding the ambit of this debate is the distinction between formal and substantive equality as philosophical goals and as legal means. In addressing equality jurisprudence, I am more concerned with the latter. Here formal equality, as the abstract, mechanical, "value-free" and acontextual comparison of two groups, is found in cases such as *Jordan* and *Robinson*. Underlying the majority judgments in these cases are more dominant, libertarian views of freedom and individual choice, an acceptance of certain norms as inherently dominant (over egalitarian difference), as well as a more limited role for the courts, even in deciding issues of status and recognition.[72]

Legal ideas of substantive equality are characterised by an understanding that difference is an aspect of equality, and that the problem is with disadvantageous impact. An understanding of context is necessary to decide when differentiation is indeed discrimination, and when (re)distribution is permitted. Values and mediating principles are important to the determination of inequality.

---

[70]   See Albertyn (2007) *SAJHR* 258-261.

[71]   These models and fault-lines are examined in more detail in Albertyn *Equality Law* (forthcoming).

[72]   See, generally, Albertyn (2007) *SAJHR* 253, Bonthuys (2008) *Can J Women & L* 1; Pieterse (2008) *SAJHR* 397; H Botha "Equality, Plurality and Structural Power" (2009) 25 *SAJHR* 1.

However, there is also a difference between a liberal egalitarian model of substantive equality and one that might be constructed within a more critical approach. This difference has not always been clearly drawn, but is significant in understanding the limits and possibilities of South African equality jurisprudence, especially in addressing the role of equality jurisprudence in addressing poverty and inequality, and the connections between them.

A liberal egalitarian model is characterised by a concern with equality and distribution, accepting that individual freedom must, on occasion, defer to equality concerns. The balance is sought through the application of values and mediating principles, including the remedying of (group-based) disadvantage and the importance of dignity, as well as legitimate, equality-related, state purposes. The idea of fairness achieves this balance. The context of discrimination is important in the sense that the history and impact of the impugned law on an outsider or disadvantaged group must be interrogated.

Underlying this model is the idea of fair equality of opportunity: the idea that a degree of redistribution is necessary to enable the fair pursuit of individual freedom. However, the separation of social and economic inequalities that this entails tends to mean that anti-discrimination law (and courts) addresses status-based discrimination (although more widely defined to include forms of group-based disadvantage) and affirmative action, especially in employment and education. Although courts play a far greater role in adjudicating discrimination and affirmative action than under a more classic liberal model, for the most part, economic redistribution remains within the purview of government, and is protected (by courts) from constitutional attack where the purposes are legitimate and remedial.[73] The model permits important, and even transformative, advances for outsider groups. Ultimately, however, this model does not fundamentally challenge the structures and institutions of society (broadening the ambit of inclusion rather than transforming them) and tolerates significant socio-economic inequalities.

A more critical perspective on substantive equality is characterised by a more robust approach to redistribution (requiring a greater equality of resources and substantive conditions to enable individuals to pursue their well-being) and recognition of the need to transform structures and institutions to achieve actual "substantive" equality. Grounded in actual socio-economic inequalities, this approach also entails a more nuanced idea of individual choice and the conditions in which it can be more freely exercised. In legal terms, it differs from a more egalitarian liberalism in (at least) the following respects: a deeper understanding of structural disadvantage and the manner in which social and economic inequalities are bound up together; a broader approach to the context (and impact) that are relevant to a legal dispute; a more complex understanding of intersectional discrimination; greater attention to difference and diversity; a concrete reliance on values as constituting an articulated standard for adjudication and thus for forward movement by our society; a

---

[73] Under s 9(2) of the Constitution. See *Minister of Finance v Van Heerden* 2004 6 SA 121 (CC).

more robust role for courts; and a willingness to engage redistribution and to formulate innovative remedies to manage separation of powers issues.

Ultimately, it is the South African courts' tendency towards the former model of egalitarian liberalism that limits the reach of equality jurisprudence, especially where poor women are concerned. This is not to deny the huge importance of judgments in terms of this model: the cases concerning sexual orientation and the minority judgments in *Jordan* and *Robinson* all testify to its power (and the extent to which it has moved equality jurisprudence from a formal model). However, its reach is limited.[74]

A detailed exposition of this approach is beyond the scope of this chapter,[75] but a useful way of illustrating the differential approach, reach and impact of liberal and critical models of equality is to consider the different phrasing of the "equality question" under each. For example, in *Jordan* the minority considered how to address, and reduce the harm of, the gendered patterns of stigma and stereotype that characterised the criminalisation of female, but not male, sex workers. A more critical approach might phrase the question in terms of the structural social *and* economic inequalities that shape the choices faced by women (and men) in particular contexts and mean that they end up in sex work. In such circumstances, is it discriminatory to criminalise this conduct? The latter question is much wider in terms of understanding context and impact (and thus scope of evidence), as well as inequality itself (social and economic, not just a matter of stigma and stereotype), thus allowing a more detailed consideration of poor women within sex work. It also speaks to a different interpretation of the values of dignity and freedom (choice).[76]

Perhaps the most interesting recent example of the liberal/critical split in substantive equality is the case of *Mazibuko v City of Johannesburg*,[77] a matter directly concerned with poverty and redistribution in relation to the right of access to sufficient water by the poor.

Mazibuko concerned two major constitutional questions, does the right of access to sufficient water include a right to a basic minimum supply? Was the installation of prepaid water meters constitutionally permissible? An equality argument was raised in relation to the second question. The applicants argued that the instalment of prepaid water meters in poor areas of Soweto, but not in more affluent, largely white, suburbs constituted unfair racial discrimination. In support of this, the applicants argued the prepaid water meters resulted in water cut-offs without notice, and thus in poor people not having access to water once cut off.[78]

---

[74] Albertyn (2007) *SAJHR* 265-273.

[75] This is part of a larger project. See Albertyn *Equality Law* (forthcoming).

[76] See J Barrett "Dignatio and the Human Body" (2005) 21 *SAJHR* 529 for a discussion of how dignity could have been more transformatively conceived in *S v Jordan* 2002 6 SA 642 (CC). A more radical notion of choice would have elicited more compassion for the rational nature of choices made by poor women in difficult circumstances.

[77] 2010 4 SA 1 (CC).

[78] The High Court found this to be unfair discrimination: *Mazibuko v City of Johannesburg* 2008 4 All SA 471 (W) paras 94 and 155. However the matter was not addressed in the SCA: *City of Johannesburg v Mazibuko* 2009 3 SA 592 (SCA).

However, the Constitutional Court differed. It accepted the presence of discrimination, but in weighing up the nature of the disadvantage, the purpose of the policy and the harm inflicted, it found that this discrimination was not unfair. In brief, the Court accepted that Soweto residents constituted a historically disadvantaged group, although less so than poor, black residents of informal settlements such as Orange Farm or Ivory Park.[79] However, the Court concluded that the differential treatment did not necessarily deepen this disadvantage, especially as its purpose was both necessary and desirable (the eradication of severe water losses in Soweto).[80] Overall, the Court found the policy not to be harmful or disadvantageous to consumers, especially when compared to the flat rate policy and credit meter customers. In particular, prepaid customers paid less for their water than credit meter customers, and avoided negative consequences of non-payment in the form of interest and blacklisting as creditors.[81] In sum:

> "The group affected by the installation of pre-paid water meters is a vulnerable group, the purpose for which the meters are installed is a laudable, indeed necessary government objective, clearly tailored to its purpose. Moreover the difference between the pre-paid water meter system and a credit system is not disadvantageous to the residents of Phiri ... [I]t cannot be said that the introduction of a pre-paid water meter system in Phiri was unfairly discriminatory."[82]

The equality analysis is brief. The comparative nature of equality, context and impact are all present, but narrowly defined. The equality question is defined as a comparison of the impact of policy provisions that address payment rates and consequences. The nature of disadvantage is not poverty, but race (poverty is not a permitted, prohibited ground). Gender was not argued, and is absent. The long-term remedial aspects of the policy in relation to overcoming apartheid inequalities are broadly stated,[83] thus justifying differential policies as a form of substantive equality.[84] The context is thus the nature and purpose of the policy in relation to scarce water, rather than the actual conditions of poor people's (and women's) lives in a situation of insufficient water. Most surprisingly, there is no mention of the standard of dignity in determining fairness.

In line with some of the components of substantive equality, the Court is concerned with context, disadvantage and difference (although not with values), but in a limited manner. Thus *Mazibuko* finds the limits of substantive equality in the liberal egalitarian model, largely, I suggest, because of a consequent discomfort with matters of poverty and redistribution (unless defending state action), rather than status and recognition, and of the courts' role in such matters.

How might the matter be better addressed under a more critical approach to substantive equality? Here, the delineation of context, the assessment of impact and the role of values would play out differently, as would the willingness to find creative remedies.

---

[79] *Mazibuko v City of Johannesburg* 2010 4 SA 1 (CC) paras 149-150.
[80] Para 151.
[81] Paras 152-153.
[82] Para 154.
[83] Para 148.
[84] Paras 151 and 156.

Instead of limiting the equality question to narrow policy provisions, the problem could be phrased as follows (starting with the nature of inequality): Should impoverished communities in Soweto's poorer neighbourhoods, whose position is a result of deep structural social and economic inequalities of apartheid, be given prepaid water meters (without a sufficient basic supply) that allow water to be cut off without notice and without the financial means to reconnect to ensure basic needs for water are met? The "comparator group" would be found amongst those who live in areas that benefited from apartheid and where higher income levels mean that they have the means to pay for sufficient water. Here the context would require evidence and/or judicial notice of the inherited and current socio-economic inequalities that structure the inability of the poor to pay for water, as well as how the prepaid water meters and a limited basic supply affected this. To insert a necessary gendered analysis, one would demonstrate how a lack of water always impacts disproportionately on women, making poor women especially vulnerable in this context. One would expect the Court to take account of the detailed and diverse picture of poor households and their struggle to live a dignified life with adequate water.

A conscious articulation of the values underlying equality[85] might see the court envisaging a society in which women and men were afforded the substantive conditions necessary to exercise meaningful choices: the provision of adequate and affordable water being one of these. Fairness would require the state to enable these conditions.

Such an approach would begin to set standards for non-discriminatory conduct in relation to the right to water and is a significant component of a legal approach to reducing poverty and inequality. The Court's extensive remedial powers would allow it to enhance accountability and accommodate any separation of powers concerns that it might have in requiring a different mode of water provision that does not amount to unfair discrimination, including structural interdicts that allow government to address the problem.[86]

Although sketchy in the confines of this chapter, I suggest that the development of such a critical approach would enable courts to grapple with more substantive redistribution within an equality framework, mediated through remedial powers.

In the end, the Court's egalitarian liberal approach, although capable of significant judgments and important equality gains, sets boundaries to equality jurisprudence that tend to marginalise the experiences and concerns of poor women. Poor women thus fall outside the protections of legal liberalism. While a critical engagement with legal liberalism might sometimes secure important rights (such as in status-based gains in customary law), in most instances issues of poverty and gender inequality are not adequately addressed. In the end, therefore, equality jurisprudence needs to rest on different philosophical and conceptual foundations to those based on a liberal egalitarian model. Those

---

[85]   See C Albertyn "'The Stubborn Persistence of Patriarchy?' Gender Equality and Cultural Diversity in South Africa" (2009) 2 *CCR* 165 for a development of these in relation to gender and cultural diversity issues.

[86]   See L Williams "The Role of Courts in the Quantitative-Implementation of Social and Economic Rights: A Comparative Study" (2010) 3 *CCR* 1 on this. See also Liebenberg *Socio-Economic Rights* ch 8.

foundations require not merely an equality of equal concern and respect, but of substantive conditions for a decent life. More conceptual work is required to advance a more critical and indigenous model of substantive equality.

5   Socio-economic rights and poor women

5 1   Why women?

As alluded to earlier, women are largely invisible in socio-economic rights cases. For example, the *Grootboom* community represented a "textbook" example of gendered poverty: an informal settlement in which the majority of residents were women and children,[87] and arguments would clearly have been available about the particular plight of poor woman-headed households. While the absence of gendered arguments might not have affected the eventual outcome, it can be seen as a missed opportunity in the development of socio-economic rights jurisprudence. Introducing a gendered analysis could have set important standards for the evaluation of reasonableness, as discussed below. Similarly, in *Mazibuko*, a case concerning the right of access to adequate water by poor households living within a formal township, three out of five applicants were women living in woman-headed households. Household water shortages have a disproportionate impact on women who bear the burden of domestic reproduction, meaning that it is women who usually have to seek out available water for the needs of the entire household: drinking, cooking, cleaning and care work. It is also women who usually defer their own needs to those of the family. However, nothing was made of this in the application or judgment.

The emphasis on poverty at the expense of other forms of inequality and exclusion, or on singular rather than intersectional forms of discrimination, is commonplace in political and legal discourse. Single issues simplify the complexities of life, making them easier to describe and adjudicate. However, if addressing *gendered* poverty and inequality is central to our constitutional project – rather than an afterthought, an add-on, or a rhetorical device – then gender is a nettle that must be grasped.

Firstly, Everatt has written about the failure of government anti-poverty programmes to target the specific needs of different groups of the poor. He suggests that a general concern with disadvantage and the "poorest of the poor" tends to translate into large (and unmanageable) groups and undirected programmes.[88] Similarly judgments might be ineffective or reinforce inequalities. Courts can assist with more nuanced judgments, but this would only be possible if the cases are argued in a more gender-conscious manner.

Secondly, a more careful consideration of the gendered context of claims can affirm women as citizens, build a more "gendered" accountability through courts (a primary function of socio-economic rights jurisprudence), and help publicise the issue for political action. Legal action is almost always a moment

---

[87] *Government of the RSA v Grootboom* 2001 1 SA 46 (CC) n 2, which states that 510 children and 390 adults lived in desperate circumstances. Although no gender breakdown is provided, it is statistically probable that the majority of adults were women.

[88] Everatt (2008) *Politikon* 305-311.

in a longer political battle – positive judgments can be significant weapons in those bigger battles for gender equality.

Finally, properly conceived and argued, such cases will assist in more transformative outcomes at a practical or symbolic level. Judgments are important indicators of how we can or should see the world.

5 2   Engendering "reasonableness"

Despite the preponderance of women amongst the poor, and substantial qualitative and statistical evidence of gendered access to socio-economic rights, gender issues are almost completely absent in socio-economic rights jurisprudence. A small, but important, body of academic literature has begun to engage this gap. Beth Goldblatt and Sandra Liebenberg have called for the interpretive interdependence of socio-economic rights and equality,[89] while Sandra Fredman has extended this approach to argue for a more engendered conception of socio-economic rights.[90] In the same edition of the *South African Journal of Human Rights*, various authors have begun to document the ways in which women's enjoyment of socio-economic rights is gendered, meaning that we need to rethink some of our conceptual approaches to socio-economic rights as well as our understanding of women's (lack of) enjoyment of these rights.[91]

The current jurisprudence of reasonableness is ultimately limited by the same kind of constraints as equality jurisprudence. There is no doubt that a more critical and gendered approach to socio-economic rights is required, and that this needs to be located in a substantive understanding of our democratic values of freedom, equality and dignity, and a nuanced consideration of differing material conditions of poor people's lives.

A more pressing concern is the absence of poor women from the current jurisprudence. Within the confines of this chapter I want to suggest (albeit very briefly) that there is substantial room to engage in a more gendered analysis within this jurisprudence: firstly, in the depiction of context; secondly in the procedural and "governance" criteria of reasonableness; thirdly, in a more nuanced understanding of "the needs of the most desperate"; fourthly, in a more gendered idea of the accountability that underpins the jurisprudence; and fifthly, within the meaning of "meaningful engagement" as a form of remedy.

As with equality, the Constitutional Court has emphasised that socio-economic rights must be judged within their social, economic and historical context of inequality and deprivation,[92] even if it has not always addressed this context sufficiently. There is ample scope for the development of a gendered analysis in respect of the context of socio-economic rights claims generally, and not merely those that refer to women claimants alone. Building gender

---

[89] Liebenberg & Goldblatt (2007) *SAJHR* 335-361.
[90] See, generally, S Fredman "Engendering Socio-Economic Rights" (2009) 25 *SAJHR* 410.
[91] See, generally, the articles in issue 3 of (2009) 25 *SAJHR*.
[92] *Government of the RSA v Grootboom* 2001 1 SA 46 (CC) para 43.

inequality within this contributes to the idea that a gendered analysis should be the norm.

The courts' test for reasonableness tends to focus on process and accountability rather than substance. It looks at whether government action to give effect to socio-economic rights is appropriate or fair, but omits an engagement with the objective norms promoted, or the specific goods and services guaranteed, by the rights themselves. Thus, as is well known, the Court has identified a number of criteria to assess reasonableness including availability of resources; flexibility; the comprehensive, coherent and effective nature of the policy; its balance in terms of short- medium- and long-term needs; and the allocation of governmental responsibilities.[93] It appears that a carefully crafted engagement with these elements of reasonableness could be used to hold government to account for ensuring that its policies are appropriately "engendered", and that the needs of women and men are built into the conceptualisation, resource allocation, budgeting et cetera of government policies.[94]

The most "substantive" criterion of reasonableness is that a policy needs to pay special attention to the needs of the poorest and most vulnerable, the most desperate.[95] This remains an undeveloped category within the Court's jurisprudence and it is not always clear who the most desperate are. What is clear, however, is that more specificity is required and, again, a gendered analysis of the "most desperate" will always be important to addressing the needs of poor women.

In Mazibuko, the Constitutional Court highlighted the accountability aspect of justiciable socio-economic rights.[96] This provides important space to develop an idea of state accountability, that the delivery of goods and services must be structured in a manner that meets the needs of women and men. It also develops notions of equal participation within the structures of civil society. Socio-economic rights cases could be used to set standards for a more gendered form of accountability. Similarly, any imposition of "meaningful engagement"[97] over the implementation of socio-economic rights needs to take account of gender, especially of how women participate equally within this engagement.

The development of a more critical and transformative jurisprudence of socio-economic rights remains important. However as described above, even within the confines of reasonableness currently utilised by the Constitutional Court, there are opportunities to begin to address the intersections of gender inequality and poverty.

---

[93] Paras 40-46.

[94] For example, the manner in which the Court assesses reasonableness in *Mazibuko v City of Johannesburg* 2010 4 SA 1 (CC) shows a lack of consideration of context of poverty and impact of policy on living poor and women (paras 82-88 provide just one example of the absence of any reference to the lived reality of the applicants).

[95] *Government of the RSA v Grootboom* 2001 1 SA 46 (CC) paras 42 and 44.

[96] Paras 61 and 70.

[97] *Occupiers of 51 Olivia Road v City of Johannesburg* 2008 3 SA 208 (CC).

6 Conclusion

If the constitutional project is to effect change and transformation in the lives of women and men, then all of us who engage in that project have limited its potential: in how we select cases, prepare our arguments, write our judgments, and engage in the jurisprudence. Gender inequalities, like poverty, raise particularly difficult issues about the connections between reform and transformation, recognition and redistribution, law and politics, and between a "strategic engagement with legal liberalism" and something more than that.

While it remains important to engage critically with legal liberalism and the jurisprudence that we have, in order to pursue those transformative claims and judgments that are possible within the bounds of liberal egalitarianism; an important academic and legal pursuit continues to be to construct more critical and "indigenous" conceptions of equality and socio-economic rights. Importantly, these should be shaped within the particular context ("political economy" and cultural or social values) of South Africa as a constitutional democracy and a developing state. While the ideas generated by welfare liberalism and social democracy of Western welfare states are important footholds in equality and socio-economic rights jurisprudence, they require significant development to meet the challenges of South Africa's constitutional project.

SUMMARY

Central to the transformative project of the South African Constitution, although not always recognised as such, is the need to address the distinctive forms of poverty and inequality experienced by women. In this chapter I explore the extent to which, and how, poor women have been included within the constitutional project, firstly, by describing the complexity of poor women's lives and then through a brief analysis of cases and jurisprudence on equality and socio-economic rights. Underlying these two facets of the chapter are two key questions: What does the experience of poor women tell us about the meaning of transformation and a transformative Constitution? How can we seek a more transformative (and gendered) understanding of equality and socio-economic rights jurisprudence? I argue that the lived realities of poor women remind us that the kind of transformation – and transformative legal strategies – that are necessary to generate meaningful change require attention to structure and agency, to redistribution and recognition, to individual and community, to public and private (especially caregiving roles in family), to inequality and poverty. To achieve this through equality and socio-economic rights jurisprudence entails greater care in the choices made by lawyers in selecting and arguing cases, and in advancing critical arguments that push the boundaries of progressive and strongly egalitarian forms of liberalism. It also requires a more gendered jurisprudence in courts where attention to women's socio-economic context is combined with a conscious attempt to give meaningful content to the values informing constitutional rights, the gendered interests at stake and the manner in which application of legal principles, such as reasonableness and fairness, can be shaped to include women. In the end transformation requires the construction of a society in which women and men are afforded equivalent, substantive conditions for exercising the choices that matter to them, about how to live their lives, maintain their relationships, raise their children and pursue their aspirations.

CHAPTER 10

JUDICIAL DEFERENCE AND DEMOCRACY IN SOCIO-ECONOMIC RIGHTS CASES IN SOUTH AFRICA

Danie Brand[*]

1 Introduction

In this chapter I evaluate the manner in which South African courts have chosen to deal with the range of institutional problems (problems with institutional capacity, legitimacy, integrity and security, as well as pure separation of powers problems) they face in the adjudication of constitutional socio-economic rights claims. I investigate, that is, judicial deference in socio-economic rights cases – the strategy of courts, when faced with difficult technical or contested social questions in such cases to leave decision of those issues, in different ways and to varying degrees, to the other branches of government.[1]

I attempt an evaluation, or, more directly, a particular critique of the strategy of judicial deference in socio-economic rights cases. I ask how comfortably or uncomfortably judicial deference fits with what I see as the constitutional imperative that courts should, through their work in socio-economic rights cases, seek to advance, or at least to avoid limiting, the kind of democracy (a thick, or empowered conception of democracy) envisaged in the South African Constitution.[2]

Of course, neither judicial deference nor the institutional problems it is intended to address are unique to socio-economic rights adjudication. Deference operates also more generally in constitutional and in administrative

---

[*] My thanks to colleagues at the Department of Public Law at the University of Pretoria for comments of an earlier version of this chapter presented at a departmental research seminar; to Sandra Liebenberg and Geo Quinot for inviting me to participate in the Law and Poverty colloquium in Stellenbosch, where I presented yet another version of this chapter; to the participants in the colloquium for questions and subsequent discussions; to the two anonymous referees who reviewed the chapter for searching and challenging observations; and to Karl Klare, Koos Malan, Karin Van Marle and Lucy Williams for reading and commenting on the chapter in various stages of its development.

[1] See K McLean *Constitutional Deference, Courts and Socio-Economic Rights in South Africa* (2009) 3-4 and 25-26 for a similar description of deference. See also, more recently, K McLean "Towards a Framework for Understanding Constitutional Deference" (2010) 25 *SAPL* 445.

[2] Constitution of the Republic of South Africa, 1996 ("the Constitution" or "the South African Constitution"). More about this conception of democracy later, but see in general terms for a description D Brand "Writing the Law Democratically: A Reply to Theunis Roux" in S Woolman & M Bishop (eds) *Constitutional Conversations* (2008) 97; T Roux "Democracy" in S Woolman, T Roux & M Bishop (eds) *CLoSA* 2 ed (OS 2006); B Cousins & A Claassens "Communal Land Rights and Democracy in Post-Apartheid South Africa" in P Jones & K Stokke (eds) *Democratising Development: The Politics of Socio-Economic Rights in South Africa* (2005) 245 246-247; S Liebenberg *Socio-Economic Rights: Adjudication under a Transformative Constitution* (2010) 63-65.

law review in South Africa and elsewhere.[3] I focus on deference specifically in socio-economic rights adjudication for no deep conceptual reason, nor because I claim that deference operates differently in this context than elsewhere. I do so, simply put, because my interest is in the first place in the effective enforcement of socio-economic rights specifically and in deference only to the extent that it relates to that enforcement. From the point of view of claimants, deference has so far in our courts' socio-economic rights jurisprudence operated as an obstacle to effective enforcement, leading in those cases where claims are successful to attenuated forms of relief[4] and explicitly forming the basis for rejection of claims in the few cases so far where claimants have been unsuccessful.[5] My focus on deference is intended to address this problem – I seek to debunk deference *as an obstacle to the effective enforcement of socio-economic rights.*[6]

To do so, the chapter consists of a description, an evaluation and a modest proposal. I first, in part 2 below, describe the manner in and extent to which judicial deference and the democratic justification for it operates in South African socio-economic rights adjudication. I then, in part 3 below, present a critique of such deference along two distinct but related lines: that judicial deference both reflects a conception of democracy at odds with the constitutional vision of democracy and, more importantly, actively counteracts the construction of that constitutional vision of democracy – that

---

[3] For engagements with deference in constitutional review generally in South Africa see H Klug "Introducing the Devil: An Institutional Analysis of the Power of Constitutional Review" (1997) 13 *SAJHR* 185; P Lenta "Democracy, Rights Disagreements and Judicial Review" (2004) 20 *SAJHR* 1; T Roux "Legitimating Transformation: Political Resource Allocation in the South African Constitutional Court" (2003) 10 *Democratization* 92; T Roux "Principle and Pragmatism on the Constitutional Court of South Africa" (2009) 7 *I Con* 106. For the most prominent engagements with deference in administrative-law review in South Africa, see H Corder "Without Deference, with Respect: A Response to Justice O'Regan" (2004) 121 *SALJ* 438; DM Davis "To Defer and When? Administrative Law and Constitutional Democracy" (2006) *Acta Juridica* 23; C Hoexter "The Future of Judicial Review in South African Administrative Law" (2000) 117 *SALJ* 484; C Hoexter *Administrative Law in South Africa* (2007) 138-147; K O'Regan "Breaking Ground: Some Thoughts on the Seismic Shift in Our Administrative Law" (2004) 121 *SALJ* 424. For a sample of engagements with deference in administrative-law review outside South Africa, see TRS Allan "Common Law Reason and the Limits of Judicial Deference" in D Dyzenhaus (ed) *The Unity of Public Law* (2004) 289; J Jowell "Of Vires and Vacuums: The Constitutional Context of Judicial Review" (1999) *Public Law* 428; DJ Mullan "Deference: Is it Useful Outside Canada?" (2006) *Acta Juridica* 24; D Dyzenhaus "The Politics of Judicial Deference: Judicial Review and Democracy" in M Taggart (ed) *The Province of Administrative Law* (1997) 279.

[4] See, for example, *Government of the Republic of South Africa v Grootboom* 2001 1 SA 46 (CC) para 41.

[5] See, for example, *Mazibuko v City of Johannesburg* 2010 4 SA 1 (CC) paras 63 and 159. For a fuller description of this point, see Liebenberg *Socio-Economic Rights* 67-68.

[6] The most prominent engagements with deference in the context of socio-economic rights in the South African context (M Pieterse "Coming to Terms with Judicial Enforcement of Socio-Economic Rights" (2004) 20 *SAJHR* 383; DM Davis "Adjudicating the Socio-Economic Rights in the South African Constitution: Towards 'Deference Lite'?" (2006) 22 *SAJHR* 301; DM Davis "Socio-Economic Rights in South Africa: The Record of the Constitutional Court after Ten Years" (2004) 5 *ESR Review* 3; McLean *Constitutional Deference*; and Liebenberg *Socio-Economic Rights* 66-76) all share my assumptions that deference is a prominent feature of the approach of South African courts to the adjudication of socio-economic rights cases and additionally that it either can or in fact does operate as an important obstacle to the robust enforcement of these rights (see, for example, Liebenberg *Socio-Economic Rights* 67 and in particular Davis (2006) *SAJHR* 301-327). For an additional insightful engagement with deference in the context of socio-economic rights from outside South Africa that operates on the same assumptions (although drawing on the experience of South African courts) see R Dixon "Creating Dialogue over Socio-Economic Rights: Strong-Form Versus Weak Form Judicial Review Revisited" (2007) 5 *I Con* 391.

it is both a limited and an inappropriate response to the problem of democratic illegitimacy of review in socio-economic rights cases. I end up, in part 4 below, arguing that deference should be abandoned in favour of an alternative approach – one which I begin to describe in conclusion.

2 Description

I assume that I do not have to defend the claim that a set of institutional concerns – concerns about the institutional capacity, legitimacy, integrity and security of courts and about classical separation of powers requirements (otherwise referred to as "comity"[7] or "constitutional competence"[8]) – have centrally influenced the development of our courts' approach to deciding socio-economic rights cases.[9] Explicitly our courts have in these cases expressed concern for their capacity – both with respect to the ability to process the volumes of information at issue in such cases and with respect to technical expertise to engage with choices under scrutiny – to analyse, evaluate and decide the complex questions of social and economic theory and planning that arise in these cases.[10] Courts have also voiced concern for the threat to their institutional integrity that might arise from them reaching decisions and issuing orders that, for reasons out of their control, prove to be impossible to implement.[11] In addition, our courts have shown themselves to be concerned for their institutional illegitimacy, in democratic terms, in evaluating decisions of the supposedly democratically accountable branches of government;[12] and for maintaining their proper place in the scheme of separation of powers.[13] Implicitly our courts have certainly also been aware of

---

[7]   McLean *Constitutional Deference* 25.

[8]   Hoexter *Administrative Law* 139; Jowell (1999) *Public Law* 451.

[9]   For an excellent early review of the role these concerns have played in shaping judicial thinking about socio-economic rights, see Pieterse (2004) *SAJHR* 383-417. See also McLean *Constitutional Deference* 89-115; and, most recently, Liebenberg *Socio-Economic Rights* 71-75. With respect to the role of these concerns more generally in constitutional review in South Africa, where they obviously also play a role, see Lenta (2004) *SAJHR* 1-31; Roux (2003) *Democratization* 92-111; Roux (2009) *I Con* 106-138.

[10] See, for example, Sachs J in *Soobramoney v Minister of Health, KwaZulu-Natal* 1998 1 SA 765 (CC) para 58:
     "Courts are not the proper place to resolve the ... medical problems that underlie these choices. Important though our review functions are, there are areas where institutional incapacity ... require[s] us to be especially cautious."
     See also *Minister of Health v Treatment Action Campaign* 2002 5 SA 721 (CC) para 128; *Mazibuko v City of Johannesburg* 2010 4 SA 1 (CC) paras 61-62. See Liebenberg *Socio-Economic Rights* 71-75 for a fuller discussion of the manner in which this concern has featured in socio-economic rights cases. For an overview of the operation of this concern in administrative-law review, see Hoexter *Administrative Law* 139-142.

[11] For example, *Soobramoney v Minister of Health, KwaZulu-Natal* 1998 1 SA 765 (CC) para 11; *Mazibuko v City of Johannesburg* 2010 4 SA 1 (CC) para 57.

[12] For example, *Mazibuko v City of Johannesburg* 2010 4 SA 1 (CC) paras 61-62. See also Liebenberg *Socio-Economic Rights* 63-66.

[13] For example, *Soobramoney v Minister of Health, KwaZulu-Natal* 1998 1 SA 765 (CC) para 58. See also Liebenberg *Socio-Economic Rights* 66-71; McLean *Constitutional Deference* 86. In the context of administrative law, see Hoexter *Administrative Law* 139.

the threat to their institutional security that their deciding controversial and contested social and political questions might bring about.[14]

It is certainly not surprising, nor would I claim that it is inappropriate, that these institutional concerns should play a role and indeed a central role in shaping courts' approach to deciding socio-economic rights cases. Such institutional concerns, after all, were important considerations at play in the debate about whether or not to include socio-economic rights in the South African Constitution[15] and indeed have shaped approaches to constitutional review and related forms of review such as administrative law review in probably all jurisdictions with systems of constitutional judicial review.[16] I regard all of these institutional concerns as reflecting real problems with constitutional review in general and constitutional review in the context of socio-economic rights in particular, and problems that are difficult – perhaps even intractable. Consequently, I believe that, for courts to develop in any way a useful and sustainable approach to deciding socio-economic rights cases they cannot avoid – they have in some way to take account of – all of these institutional problems.[17]

However, for me the interesting question is not so much the institutional problems themselves, which I accept as a given – rather, it is the response of courts to them. South African courts have in the main so far accounted for the institutional problems they face in socio-economic rights cases by depicting these problems in binary[18] institutional relations terms. That is, our courts habitually describe these institutional problems as problems that courts face relative to the other branches of government. Courts do not simply describe themselves as institutionally incapable or illegitimate to decide certain

---

[14] See in general in this respect Roux (2009) *I Con* 106-138; and with respect to socio-economic rights in particular S Gloppen "Social Rights Litigation as Transformation: South African Perspectives" in P Jones & K Stokke (eds) *Democratising Development: The Politics of Socio-Economic Rights in South Africa* (2005) 153 173-174.

[15] For an overview of this history and in particular the debate about the wisdom of rendering socio-economic rights justiciable (which centred on the institutional concerns dealt with here) see S Liebenberg "South Africa's Evolving Jurisprudence on Socio-Economic Rights: An Effective Tool in Challenging Poverty?" (2003) 6 *LDD* 159 161-162; Liebenberg *Socio-Economic Rights* 7-21; D Brand "Introduction to Socio-Economic Rights in the South African Constitution" in D Brand & CH Heyns (eds) *Socio-Economic Rights in South Africa* (2005) 1 21-22.

[16] For an overview of the pervasive influence of these institutional concerns in administrative-law review, see in particular Hoexter *Administrative Law* 139-142; Hoexter (2000) *SALJ* 490 and 501; O'Regan (2004) *SALJ* 435-436. See also the sources listed in this respect in n 1 above.

[17] Which is not to say that courts are ever able to overcome these problems definitively, whatever approach to doing so they follow. In this sense I align myself with Emilios Christodoulidis when, in his "Paradoxes of Sovereignty and Representation" (2002) *TSAR* 108 108, he makes the point that the problem of democratic institutional illegitimacy of constitutional review, despite stock attempts either to deny it or explain it away, remains "real, fascinating and persistent". In another sense, Hoexter's development of what she calls a "theory of deference" – a set of principles to guide the employment of deference in specific cases – is also premised on the realisation that institutional problems with review are not either there or not there, but are always to some degree present and have to be accounted for (Hoexter *Administrative Law* 142-143; Hoexter (2000) *SALJ* 501-502; see also Liebenberg *Socio-Economic Rights* 67 and L Williams "The Role of Courts in the Quantitative-Implementation of Socio-Economic Rights: A Comparative Study" (2010) 3 *CCR* 141, both arguing for an engagement with institutional problems rather than simply a "ritualistic", either-or invocation of them to avoid decision).

[18] I use "binary" here in its ordinary, literal sense: "dual, of or involving pairs"; or as it is used in astronomy: "two stars revolving round common centre or each other" (HW Fowler & FG Fowler (eds) *The Concise Oxford Dictionary of Current English* 4 ed (1959) 116).

issues – they describe themselves as such in relation or in comparison to the other branches of government. In short, in Michelman's terms, these problems are depicted as "com[ing] down mainly, if not solely, to a matter of separation of powers".[19] Against this background, courts have then sought to deal with the institutional problems also in binary institutional relations terms – through the judicial strategy of deference, of deferring *to the other branches of government* those questions that they feel incapable of deciding, or with respect to which they feel democratically illegitimate, or which they feel threaten their institutional integrity or security, or require them to violate principles of separation of powers. So, for example, when Sachs J raises the problems of institutional capacity and constitutional comity in *Soobramoney v Minister of Health, KwaZulu-Natal*[20] to justify his choice not to interfere with a decision about provision of medical treatment, he does not simply choose not to interfere with the decision, but explicitly defers to "those better equipped" than the Court to make the allocational choices at issue, ie the provincial legislature and health care executive.[21] When Yacoob J in *Government of the Republic of South Africa v Grootboom*[22] declines to prescribe a particular solution to the problem of emergency shelter provision to the state on institutional capacity grounds, he does not simply decline such prescription, but defers explicitly to the legislature and executive the determination of the "precise contours and content of the measures to be adopted".[23] When O'Regan J declines the invitation to attribute a particular substantive content to the right to have access to sufficient water on institutional capacity and democratic legitimacy grounds in *Mazibuko v City of Johannesburg*,[24] again she does not simply hold that she is incapable of making such a determination and leave it at that – she explicitly defers this question to the "two other arms of government".[25] In sum, the solution is always not simply to leave difficult question alone or engage with them only to a certain degree or in a different way, but rather to defer those issues for decision *to the other branches of government*.

This strategy of deference in such binary institutional relations form is pervasive in all aspects of our courts' socio-economic rights jurisprudence. Deference operates in the first place in its most extreme form[26] in the choice by courts of which questions to engage with at all and which to leave alone. We saw this in *Minister of Health v Treatment Action Campaign*[27] in the Constitutional Court's decision not to decide the question whether a breast milk substitute should be provided to HIV-positive women who had given

---

[19]   FI Michelman "The Constitution, Social Rights, and Liberal Political Justification" (2003) 1 *I Con* 13 15.

[20]   1998 1 SA 765 (CC).

[21]   Para 58.

[22]   2001 1 SA 46 (CC).

[23]   Para 41.

[24]   2010 4 SA 1 (CC).

[25]   Para 65.

[26]   See McLean *Constitutional Deference* 25-26, where she describes the "overlap" between the concept of justiciability and deference, and describes a decision by a court that a matter is non-justiciable as reflecting "a position of extreme deference".

[27]   2002 5 SA 721 (CC).

birth at public health facilities and had not transferred the HI virus to their children at birth, to avoid transmission later on. The decision not to decide this question was explicitly motivated by the complexity of the issue and the perceived technical incapacity of the Court, *as opposed to the legislature and executive* properly to analyse and decide the issue.[28] More recently we have seen this expression of deference in *Mazibuko*, with the court there again declining at all to determine the content of the right to have access to sufficient water – that is, declining to engage with that issue at all – on the argument that this is an exercise best and properly left to the legislature and executive.[29]

Deference has also determined central aspects of the Court's doctrine in deciding socio-economic rights cases where the court in fact elects to engage with the issues. In *Grootboom* already the Court indicated, for example, that its reasonableness test was to be understood as what in administrative-law terms is referred to as a dialectical reasonableness test – that is, that the purpose of the test is simply to determine whether or not a measure under evaluation falls within the bounds of reasonableness and not to determine what would be the best or most appropriate measure to address the social problem at issue.[30] This choice, so the approach related in the abstract at least goes, is always to be left to the relevant other branch of government – deference in operation.[31] More recently, again in *Mazibuko*, we see deference operating in the formulation of the reasonableness test in absolute procedural or structural, rather than substantive terms that O'Regan J provides in that case. Again the motivation is explicitly that the content of social provisioning measures should be left to the other branches of government due to problems of institutional incapacity and illegitimacy, with the role of the court limited to evaluating form and process only.[32]

Finally, we see deference operating as a strategy to avoid or account for institutional problems also in the penchant our courts have shown in socio-economic rights cases for broad-ranging forms of declaratory rather than directory relief, and their insistent avoidance of structural relief of any kind.[33] One example will suffice: the choice of the Court in *Grootboom* to issue a declaratory order only without any more specific prescription to the government and, perhaps more importantly, without in any way retaining jurisdiction over compliance with its order.[34]

This tendency to see the institutional problems in binary terms – as problems of institutional relations between the courts on the one hand and the other branches of government on the other – and to attempt to account for them through the binary strategy of deference (deferring *to the other*

---

[28] Para 128.

[29] *Mazibuko v City of Johannesburg* 2010 4 SA 1 (CC) paras 63-65.

[30] L Baxter *Administrative Law* (1984) 485. See also Hoexter *Administrative Law* 302.

[31] *Government of the Republic of South Africa v Grootboom* 2001 1 SA 46 (CC) para 41.

[32] *Mazibuko v City of Johannesburg* 2010 4 SA 1 (CC) paras 65-67.

[33] For an early review and critique of the Constitutional Court's approach to remedies in socio-economic rights cases, see M Swart "Left Out in the Cold? Crafting Constitutional Remedies for the Poorest of the Poor" (2005) 21 *SAJHR* 215. See also, for a more recent account, Liebenberg *Socio-Economic Rights* 75-76 and 377-460.

[34] *Government of the Republic of South Africa v Grootboom* 2001 1 SA 46 (CC) paras 96-97.

branches of government) is not limited to the courts. Academic commentary on the operation of institutional concerns in socio-economic rights cases and more broadly the operation of these concerns in judicial review has equally been limited to a binary institutional relations perspective. This is true of those who respond to the accusation of the democratic illegitimacy of judicial review in socio-economic rights cases through problematising perceptions of the democratic accountability of the legislature and executive relative to the courts[35] or positing such review as instigating a "democratic dialogue" between the courts and other branches of government.[36] It is also true of those who engage the problem of institutional capacity by pointing out that, in particular in a developing state such as South Africa it is not self-evident that the legislature or executive has capacity for resolving issues of social policy superior to the courts.[37] Rich and nuanced as it undoubtedly is, such commentary in the main does not move outside of an institutional relations paradigm, that is, a paradigm in terms of which these institutional problems are seen as operating between the courts and the other two branches of government alone.[38]

The point need not be belaboured: in sum, institutional concerns have, as can be expected, been prevalent in socio-economic rights adjudication. Further, the manner in which our courts have almost exclusively sought to deal with those concerns has been to employ in various ways and contexts and to differing degrees the strategy of deference, in a binary institutional relations mode – that is, by deferring decision to the other branches of government.

---

[35] Pieterse (2004) *SAJHR* 388 and 391.

[36] McLean *Constitutional Deference* 77-78; Liebenberg *Socio-Economic Rights* 69-71; Dixon (2007) *I Con* 391 393.

[37] McLean *Judicial Deference* 77; Pieterse (2004) *SAJHR* 395; Liebenberg *Socio-Economic Rights* 74-75.

[38] Also Davis, who criticises the Constitutional Court for what he sees as its overly deferential approach in socio-economic rights cases, remains within the binary institutional relations depiction of the problems of judicial review (Davis (2006) *SAJHR* 315-316 and 319-320), depicting in particular the problem of institutional capacity as a problem operating between the courts on the one hand and the other branches of government on the other. The same is clearly true of engagements with institutional problems of review in the context of administrative law. Hoexter, for example, in her influential and nuanced development of what she has variously referred to as a "theory", a "doctrine" and a "view" of deference – a set of principles, that is, to "guide legal intervention and non-intervention" (A Cockrell "'Can You Paradigm?' – Another Perspective on the Public Law/Private Law Divide" in TW Bennett, A Cockrell, R Jooste, R Keightly & CM Murray (eds) with H Corder (editorial consultant) *Administrative Law Reform* 227 247) – describes deference as judicial response to institutional problems with review as "ineluctably bound up with the separation of powers and the area of competence associated with each of the three branches of government" (Hoexter *Administrative Law* 139) and as "a judicial willingness to appreciate the legitimate and constitutionally-ordained province of administrative agencies; to admit the expertise of those agencies in policy-laden or polycentric issues; to accord their interpretations of fact and law due respect; and to be sensitive in general to the interests legitimately pursued by administrative bodies and the practical and financial constraint under which they operate" (Hoexter (2000) *SALJ* 501; see also Hoexter *Administrative Law* 142-143, slightly misquoting herself in this respect). Rich as her account is, it does not conceive of the problem and the strategy of deference outside the institutional relations mould. See also Dyzenhaus "The Politics of Deference" in *Province of Administrative Law* 279. It is important to state that my observation here that these engagements with deference still operate in a binary institutional paradigm does not amount to criticism of those engagements. The literature in South Africa on deference, both in administrative law and in the context of constitutional adjudication, is rich and varied and the various proposals that have emanated from this literature for approaches to deference that take account of institutional problems without jeopardising constitutional principles and constitutional rights are equally rich and nuanced. But all of these engagements and critiques amount to internal critiques of deference – that is, they engage with deference on its own terms.

One final descriptive point: as noted in the introduction, judicial deference from the point of view of claimants in socio-economic rights cases is of course not a neutral feature of review. The employment by courts of the strategy of deference results in courts refusing to decide issues claimants place before them, which sometimes results in their claim being rejected. This was most clearly the case in *Mazibuko*, where the Court's decision not to determine the substantive content of the right to sufficient water resulted in the rejection of the applicant's challenge to the city's free basic water policy.[39] There, where deference does not result in a court refusing to entertain issues, it causes courts to deal with issues in what to claimants must seem to be a superficial manner only. Here again the *Mazibuko* Court's proceduralist description of the reasonableness test, leading to the failure of the applicants' case, provides an example.[40] Finally, even there where claimants succeed in persuading the court to their view, the employment of deference results in the court handing down indirect, generalised, attenuated forms of relief – here *Grootboom*'s unsupervised declaratory order is the best example.[41] It might seem obvious, but when courts employ deference in socio-economic rights cases to deal with problems of institutional capacity, legitimacy, integrity, security or constitutional comity, they favour the point of view with respect to the issues in dispute of one of the parties to that dispute (the state) over another (the claimants).[42] In short, for claimants in socio-economic rights cases deference operates as an important obstacle to having their plight properly addressed.

3 Evaluation

3 1 Democracy in the Constitution

To develop my critique of deference in socio-economic rights adjudication I must digress somewhat.

---

[39] *Mazibuko v City of Johannesburg* 2010 4 SA 1 (CC) paras 63 and 159.

[40] Paras 67 and 159.

[41] *Government of the Republic of South Africa v Grootboom* 2001 1 SA 46 (CC) paras 96-97.

[42] Lucy Williams has recently meticulously described the manner in which the Constitutional Court in *Mazibuko v City of Johannesburg* 2010 4 SA 1 (CC), through the employment of a rather extreme degree of deference, in effect accepted without interrogating the state's depiction of technical issues in contention at the expense of the version put forward by the claimants in that case (Williams (2010) *CCR* 178-181). See also, for a similar description of the administrative-law aspects of that case G Quinot "Substantive Reasoning in Administrative Law Adjudication" (2010) 3 *CCR* 111 128-136. See in general with respect to this kind of exclusionary reasoning in socio-economic rights adjudication D Brand *Courts, Socio-Economic Rights and Transformative Politics* LLD thesis Stellenbosch (2009) 217-256. It is interesting to compare the favouring of the point of view of one party to a case at play here, with the Constitutional Court's response to an argument that in a case involving a dispute between a school and one of its pupils (*MEC for Education: Kwazulu-Natal v Pillay* 2008 1 SA 474 (CC)), the supposedly superior experience and expertise of one of those parties must be acknowledged through employment of deference. In that case, which dealt with the question whether prohibition by a school of a form of outward expression of religious belief and culture (the wearing of a nose ring) amounted to unfair discrimination, the school argued that a degree of deference should be accorded the school governing body's (SGB's) experience and expertise in managing diversity at schools. The court rejected this contention, holding that it amounted to an argument that the SGB's judgment of what is fair in this context should be accorded deference; that the SGB was bound to show that its conduct was fair; and that "[a] court cannot defer to the view of a party concerning a contention that that same party is bound to prove" (para 81).

I subscribe to the notion first put forward by Karl Klare[43] and later developed by many others[44] that the South African Constitution is a transformative document in that it has a certain political character; in short that it embodies a certain vision of society[45] and requires positive action on the side of all agencies of the state toward the attainment of that vision.[46] This transformative duty – the duty to work toward the achievement of the constitutional vision of society – is one that rests also on courts. Courts must also, in both the outcomes they generate in their judgments and the manner in which they reach their judgments (their reasoning and judicial "method"), to the extent that it "innovate[s] and model[s] intellectual and institutional practices"[47] for the rest of society, work toward the achievement of the society envisaged in the Constitution.[48]

One important aspect of the society envisaged in the Constitution is the establishment and maintenance of a particular kind of democracy – a "thick" conception of democracy, or what Klare has described as an "'empowered' model of democracy".[49] Glossing over a complex and contested topic I will for the moment only say that this constitutional conception of democracy shows to my mind two important characteristics. First, and most basically, the Constitution envisages a representative/participatory democracy – a democracy that operates most obviously through formal representative institutions, but allows for and indeed requires participation in decision-making outside of the formal representative institutions of the state, ie outside of regular general

---

[43] K Klare "Legal Culture and Transformative Constitutionalism" (1998) 14 *SAJHR* 146.

[44] See, for a sample of a by now very extensive literature, H Botha "Metaphoric Reasoning and Transformative Constitutionalism (Part 1)" (2002) *TSAR* 612; H Botha "Metaphoric Reasoning and Transformative Constitutionalism (Part 2)" (2003) *TSAR* 20; H Botha "Freedom and Constraint in Constitutional Adjudication" (2004) 20 *SAJHR* 249; H Botha "Democracy and Rights. Constitutional Interpretation in a Postrealist World" (2000) 63 *THRHR* 561; T Roux "Transformative Constitutionalism and the Best Interpretation of the South African Constitution: Distinction without a Difference?" (2009) 20 *Stell LR* 258; AJ van der Walt "Resisting Orthodoxy – Again: Thoughts on the Development of Post-Apartheid South African Law" (2002) 17 *SAPL* 258, AJ van der Walt "Dancing with Codes – Protecting, Developing and Deconstructing Property Rights in a Constitutional State" (2001) 118 *SALJ* 258; AJ van der Walt "Tentative Urgency: Sensitivity for the Paradoxes of Stability and Change in Social Transformation Decisions of the Constitutional Court" (2001) 16 *SAPL* 1; K van Marle "Transformative Constitutionalism as/and Critique" (2009) 20 *Stell LR* 286; and, in particular in relation to socio-economic rights, Liebenberg *Socio-Economic Rights* (in general) and Brand *Transformative Politics* 13-73.

[45] Klare speaks of a "highly egalitarian, caring, multicultural community, governed through participatory, democratic processes in both the polity and large portions of what we now call the 'private sphere'" (Klare (1998) *SAJHR* 150). He also describes the societal ethos embodied in the Constitution as "post-liberal", in that it "embraces a vision of *collective self-determination* parallel to (not in place of) its strong vision of individual self-determination" (original emphasis) (153).

[46] 149-150.

[47] 147.

[48] In subscribing to this notion, I assume that it is no longer necessary to justify it: the basic idea that the Constitution is generally transformative in nature and that this means that courts also should through their work – both through the outcomes they generate and in their interpretive method and the reasoning through which they reach those outcomes – participate in that transformative project is accepted by South African legal scholars of virtually all theoretical persuasions (even though there might be difference in opinion about what this basic fact implies in more concrete terms) (see, for example, Roux (2009) *Stell LR* in particular 283-285 for an argument supporting the basic transformative premise not from Klare's own Critical Legal Studies/Critical Realist-inspired theoretical position but from a theoretically rather more centralist Dworkinian position).

[49] Klare (1998) *SAJHR* 153.

elections and the representative institutions that result from them.[50] In short, in the words of O'Regan J in *Mazibuko*, the Constitution requires "a form of ... democracy that holds government accountable and requires it to account between elections over specific aspects of government policy".[51]

Second, and perhaps a little more tenuously, I would claim that the Constitution also envisages a substantive rather than only a procedural conception of participatory democracy. That is, the Constitution requires not only that processes and institutions for participation – opportunities for participation – should be available for people to make use of if they so wish. It also requires that state agencies should act in such a way that actual participation is enabled. This means that state agencies should work to enhance the capacity of people to participate in political life, to ensure that they are able in fact to make use of opportunities for participation.[52] My argument in this respect is the following:[53] The Constitution clearly posits the ideal of a democratic society – that is, a society in which democracy in fact operates.[54] In order for that ideal society to be constructed, it explicitly requires that the basic institutional arrangements for a representative/participatory democracy be put in place and maintained – regular elections, democratically elected legislatures at national, provincial and local level, and structures, institutions and processes to enable participation in decision-making outside those institutions and in between elections.[55]

But that cannot be all the Constitution requires. A collection of democratic institutions and processes (elections, representative decision-making bodies, processes for direct participation in decision-making) is not democracy itself. Such institutions and processes constitute only the structure within which

---

[50] See Klare (1998) *SAJHR* 155:

"The Constitution envisages inclusive, accountable, participatory, decentralized and transparent institutions of governance."

See also T Roux "The Principle of Democracy in South African Constitutional Law" in S Woolman & M Bishop (eds) *Constitutional Conversations* (2008) 79 where he describes the "principle of democracy" emanating from the text of the Constitution in part as follows:

"Government in South Africa must be so arranged that the people, through the medium of political parties and regular elections, in which all adult citizens are entitled to participate, exert sufficient control over their elected representatives to ensure that: (a) representatives are held to account for their actions, (b) government listens and responds to the needs of the people, in appropriate cases directly, (c) collective decisions are taken by majority vote after due consideration of the views of minority parties; and (d) the reasons for all collective decisions are publicly explained ..."

See also Liebenberg *Socio-Economic Rights* 63-64.

[51] *Mazibuko v City of Johannesburg* 2010 4 SA 1 (CC) para 160.

[52] See D Beetham *Democracy and Human Rights* (1999) 92 (arguing that institutions are not democratic only by providing space for democratic action but must operate in such a way as to promote and realise the basic democratic principles of popular control of decision-making and political equality between citizens). See also Cousins & Claassens "Communal Land Rights and Democracy" in *Democratising Development* 246-247, where they distinguish "democratic institutions" (the procedural aspect of participatory democracy I refer to) and "democratic politics" (the substantive aspect of democracy I refer to). With the latter term they refer to the struggle for power over decision-making or for access to power and goods (246). They then proceed to point out that for democratic politics to function and for a substantive democracy to operate, the key is to enhance "citizen capacity [for participation]" (247).

[53] For my own more complete elaboration of this point, see Brand "Writing the Law" in *Constitutional Conversations* 99-101.

[54] See, for example, the Preamble to the Constitution, referring to a "society based on democratic values", a "democratic society" and a "democratic South Africa".

[55] S 19 coupled with s 7(2) of the Constitution.

democracy operates, the mechanisms, if you will, through which democracy operates. Rather than that it consists of this collection of institutions, processes and structures, democracy is what must happen within these institutions, processes and structures. Democracy is in this sense a value system,[56] a discursive practice,[57] a societal grammar,[58] a mode of political action (a "politics")[59] or a culture – in short, a way of doing things. In this light, a simply institutional or procedural understanding of democracy (or, more contentiously, a solely representative understanding of democracy) is an empty shell – it is the structure for democracy without the necessary content of democratic culture/practice. And further: a society in which all of the structures, processes and institutions of democracy exist and function smoothly is not yet the "democratic society" or "society based on democratic values" that the Constitution envisages. It is instead simply a society that has complied with a range of the essential preconditions for a democratic society to develop. If coupled with the affirmative, transformative democracy-related ethos of the Constitution (for example, a society based on democratic values must be "established"; a democratic South Africa must be "built"),[60] the democratic society envisaged in the Constitution requires not only the creation of democratic institutions and processes, but also the fostering and maintenance of democratic substance, of the practice of democracy.

The duty to work toward the achievement of this conception of substantive participatory democracy as a transformative goal rests on all state agencies, but of course also on the courts. Also courts should, both in the outcomes they generate in their judgments and in the manner in which those judgments are arrived at, be sensitive to the impact that their work might have on the achievement of this substantive constitutional conception of democracy.[61]

3 2   Deference and democracy

If this description of the constitutional conception of democracy is accepted, my critique of judicial deference becomes possible. In short it entails that the strategy of deference amounts to a failure in the democracy-related aspect of the transformative duty on courts, in two ways. First, the strategy of judicial deference embodies a conception of democracy simply at odds with the constitutional conception of democracy. Judicial deference in socio-economic rights cases – as is the case more generally – is often justified with reference to democracy. Along hackneyed "counter-majoritarian dilemma" lines, the argument goes that courts should defer to the legislature or executive on a particular point, because it is democratically inappropriate for a court, an

---

[56]   Roux "Democracy" in *CLoSA* 23.
[57]   N Fraser "Talking about Needs: Interpretive Contests as Political Conflicts in Welfare-State Societies" (1989) 99 *Ethics* 291 297.
[58]   B de Sousa Santos & L Avritzer "Introduction: Opening up the Canon of Democracy" in B de Sousa Santos (ed) *Democratizing Democracy: Beyond the Liberal Democratic Canon* (2007) xxxiv xliii-xlv.
[59]   Cousins & Claassens "Communal Land Rights and Democracy" in *Democratising Development* 246.
[60]   See the Preamble to the Constitution:
        "We ... adopt this Constitution to ... establish a society based on democratic values [and to] ... build ... a democratic South Africa."
[61]   Klare (1998) *SAJHR* 149.

essentially non-accountable institution, to question the choices made or determine choices that should be made by the democratically accountable branches of government. In the words of O'Regan J in *Mazibuko*:

> "[O]rdinarily it is institutionally inappropriate for a court to determine precisely what the achievement of any particular social and economic right entails and what steps government should take to ensure the progressive realisation of the right. This is a matter, in the first place, for the legislature and executive ... Indeed, it is desirable as a matter of democratic accountability that they should do so for it is their programmes and promises that are subjected to democratic popular choice." [62]

Although this justification for deference is clearly motivated by a concern for democracy, it is a concern for exactly the kind of democracy that the Constitution does not require, or require alone: an institutional, procedural or structural conception of democracy, in terms of which democracy is equated with the formal representative institutions that result from it (the legislature and, more indirectly, the executive and the regular elections that give rise to them). In short, the deference accorded the legislature and the executive by equating democracy with the institutions and mechanisms for its operation, privileges and confirms a limited procedural/institutional conception of democracy that falls substantially short of the broader constitutional vision.

This, so I would argue, is problematic not only because it simply does not accord with the Constitution's transformative vision. It is also problematic because the limited conception of democracy underlying an approach of judicial deference leads to a limited understanding of what the tension between judicial review and democracy in fact entails. Stated differently, judicial deference becomes in this light a limited and insufficient response to the very problem it is intended to account for, being the counter-democratic effect of judicial review.

At the time that the entrenchment of justiciable socio-economic rights in the eventual 1996 Constitution was being debated, the democratic objection to making these rights subject to judicial review was prominent. Interestingly, however, it did not in the main take the usual counter-majoritarian dilemma line that also motivates judicial deference – that to give courts the power to pronounce on the validity of social and economic policy choices would allow them to limit the democratic will as expressed through the formal institutions of democracy, while lacking the democratic credentials to do so. Instead the concern most often expressed in this respect was with the extent to which adjudication of claims based on socio-economic rights would lead to the "judicialisation of politics" – would impact adversely precisely on the broader, substantive constitutional vision of democracy outlined above by allowing judges and courts authoritatively to decide issues which should properly be the subject of broad political contestation ("democratic politics"). Along Critical Legal Studies lines, for example, the concern was expressed that the entrenchment of these rights would lead to political energy and organisation being channelled into the courts instead of being directed at community organisation, advocacy and other forms of political action, with limited

---

[62] *Mazibuko v City of Johannesburg* 2010 4 SA 1 (CC) para 61.

prospects of real social transformation resulting from that.[63] The concern then seemed to be, in other words, about the impact that justiciable socio-economic rights could have on the practice or culture of democracy, rather than only on its possible impact on the structures or mechanisms of democracy. With the subsequent judicial focus on deference as a way in which to mitigate the tension between socio-economic rights adjudication and democracy, this, to my mind much more important aspect of the tension – the tension between socio-economic rights adjudication and democracy more broadly conceived – was lost sight of. Consequently courts have in the subsequent fifteen years or so failed to come up with coherent judicial strategies to deal with this broader aspect of the problem.[64] This leads to my second democracy-related critique of judicial deference in socio-economic rights cases.

For this second critique I must digress again, this time into the realm of political theory. Lucy Williams refers in her chapter in this volume to the tendency in political and other discourses to depict impoverishment and deprivation as somehow natural – caused by things outside of our control – or at least so prevalent and pervasive that nothing can be done about it.[65] We are, for example, used to hearing that impoverishment is caused by character deficiencies of impoverished people themselves (their perceived "laziness" or lack of entrepreneurial spirit); or by what are presented as "inexorable" movements of global markets; or uncontrolled population growth.[66] The intention with and effect of these depictions is to deny societal responsibility for and the political causes of impoverishment and so to depoliticise issues of impoverishment and deprivation – to remove them from the arena of political contestation. After all, if we cannot do anything about impoverishment because it is caused by forces outside of our control, we cannot be blamed for

---

[63] The strongest proponent of this view in the South African debate at the time was Dennis Davis, in his "The Case Against the Inclusion of Socio-Economic Demands in a Bill of Rights Except as Directive Principles" (1992) 8 *SAJHR* 475. For a more recent rehearsal of such arguments, see M Pieterse "Eating Socio-Economic Rights: The Usefulness of Rights Talk in Alleviating Social Hardship Revisited" (2007) 29 *Hum Rts Q* 796.

[64] See Pieterse (2007) *Hum Rts Q* 796-822 for a detailed account of the manner in which this tension, more broadly conceived, appears in the socio-economic rights jurisprudence of South African courts, focusing on Critical Legal Studies "false consciousness" arguments. See also P Bond & J Dugard "Water, Human Rights and Social Conflict: South African Experiences" (2008) 1 *Law, Social Justice and Global Development* <http://www.go.warwick.ac.uk/elj/lgd/2008_1/bond_dugard> (accessed 09-11-2011); J Dugard "Civic Action and Legal Mobilisation: The Phiri Water Meters Case" in J Handmaker & R Berkhout (eds) *Mobilising Social Justice in South Africa: Perspectives from Researchers and Practitioners* (2010) 71.

[65] L Williams "The Legal Construction of Poverty: Gender, 'Work' and the 'Social Contract'" in S Liebenberg & G Quinot (eds) *Law and Poverty* (2012) 21, 23, 26-28. See also L Williams "Welfare and Legal Entitlements: The Social Roots of Poverty" in D Kairys (ed) *The Politics of Law. A Progressive Critique* 3 ed (1998) 569; T Ross "The Rhetoric of Poverty: Their Immorality, Our Helplessness" (1991) 79 *Georgetown LJ* 1499.

[66] Of course none of these forces to which poverty is attributed, despite the fact that they are assumed and presented by those who employ them in this context as somehow natural and apolitical, are in fact themselves apolitical. Quite the contrary: what are perceived as negative character traits are determined by relative positions of power and the understanding of social dynamics; the movements of markets, despite being fondly described by those involved in them in apolitical terms, are at the same time acutely politically determined and driven, the subject of acute political contestation, and have diverse consequences depending on one's position of power (one's political position in society). The point, as becomes clearer below, is that these descriptions of the determinants of poverty are used for political purposes to deny the political nature of poverty – their description as apolitical is itself a political move.

it, so the argument seems to go, and it certainly does not help talking about it in the political world.[67]

In the broader political debate, this has an obvious effect on the capacity of impoverished people to engage in political action to address their plight – to participate, that is, in political life or democracy. Before they can contest politically the causes of and possible solutions to their situation of deprivation and need, they must first struggle to have these problems recognised as the subject of political contestation.[68] This significantly limits the democratic space available to them.

These forms of "naturalisation" and "personalisation" of poverty are but one set of examples of strategies that operate in political discourses about impoverishment intended to remove questions of need, deprivation and poverty from political contestation – to depoliticise them. One other such way was highlighted by Nancy Fraser in an article she wrote in the late 1980s. There she describes the pervasive tendency in discourses about need and poverty to depict these issues as technically complex in nature and as such suitable for discussion only in technically proficient forums – the state bureaucracy, expert think tanks and other technocratic institutions.[69] The effect of this depiction of poverty and deprivation is equally depoliticising. Their description as technically complex is intended to convey exactly the message that they are unsuited to political contestation and cannot be engaged with in a useful fashion by those that are not technically proficient.[70]

This technicisation of issues of impoverishment is of course also a move central to proceduralist or institutional models of democracy – the limited conception of democracy that motivates judicial deference. De Sousa Santos and Avritzer distinguish such proceduralist/institutional representative models of democracy (what they refer to as "liberal hegemonic" democracy)[71] from participatory democracy amongst other things on the basis of the attitude of such models of democracy to the state bureaucracy. The liberal hegemonic model of democracy tends to insulate the state bureaucracy from democratic

---

[67] Williams "Social Roots of Poverty" in *The Politics of Law* 569; Ross (1991) *Georgetown LJ* 1501-1502; N Fraser & L Gordon "A Genealogy of Dependency: Tracing a Keyword of the US Welfare State" (1994) 19 *Signs: Journal of Women in Culture and Society* 309 323-324. Examples of this kind of "depoliticizing rhetoric" abound in South Africa – think of the tendency of state agencies to speak of a "culture of non-payment" as the reason for the high rate of default in payment for municipal services, implying in the process a lack of social responsibility and trustworthiness on the side of the impoverished (without the political justification of resistance to the apartheid regime that operated in campaigns of non-payment in the 1980s). Instead, as Desai points out, there is an "economics of non-payment" – impoverished people are simply too poor to pay because of the operation of a certain politically determined economic system and related politically determined state policies (A Desai *We are the Poors: Community Struggles in Post-Apartheid South Africa* (2002) 17). See also further D Brand "The 'Politics of Need Interpretation' and the Adjudication of Socio-Economic Rights in South Africa" in AJ van der Walt (ed) *Theories of Social and Economic Justice* (2005) 17 18-25.

[68] Fraser (1989) *Ethics* 298; Ross (1991) *Georgetown LJ* 1509-1513. Cousins & Claassens, for example, point to the "mismatch between the needs and realities of the poor and anti-poverty policies ... in relation to housing policy and the erroneous assumptions that poor people will benefit from mortgage finance" that arises from the exclusion of the poor from policy formulation processes (Cousins & Claassens "Communal Land Rights and Democracy" in *Democratising Development* 247).

[69] Fraser (1989) *Ethics* 299.

[70] J Habermas "Law as Medium and Law as Institution" in G Teubner (ed) *Dilemmas of Law in the Welfare State* (1986) 204 210.

[71] De Sousa Santos & Avritzer "Introduction" in *Democratizing Democracy* xxxv.

control on the argument that in modern societies there is an increase in social and political problems that require technical solutions. Such technical problems, so the argument proceeds, require for their resolution technical expertise and skill that reside in the bureaucracy and not the democratic process. As such, decision of such technically complex issues must be removed from the democratic process and left to the state bureaucracy.[72] Participatory democracy by contrast recognises the "monocratic" nature of the bureaucracy – that it "advocate[s] a homogenizing solution for each problem confronted"[73] and so fails to account for the fact that social problems most often require plural solutions. It also recognises the inability of a centralised, insulated bureaucracy to acquire and process all the information that is required to implement complex social policies. This means that the "knowledge held by social actors" outside the bureaucracy – by the "common citizen", the democratic participant – becomes important for solutions to social problems, so that ways must be found to enable their participation in decision-making with respect to such problems.[74]

But what does this have to do with deference, apart from mirroring the conception of democracy that judicial deference is based on? The use by courts of judicial deference in socio-economic rights cases, so runs my claim, replicates this process of the technicisation of poverty and in the process works to limit the capacity for political action of impoverished people in a particularly powerful way. If one operates according to the broader, substantive view of democracy outlined above, it becomes clear that judicial deference operates to depoliticise the issues of poverty, need and social provisioning that arise in socio-economic rights cases in three closely related respects.[75] First, and most obviously, deference depoliticises in that it describes the issues in question as difficult ones that the court and the claimant party before the court alone might not have the capacity to deal with. The first step in deference in this context is after all always to recognise the fact that the issue before the court is complex. This first depoliticising step is to some extent inevitable and indeed desirable. One cannot and should not wish away the complexity of the issues in question or, for that matter the incapacity of a court, relative or otherwise, to deal with them on its own.[76] However, second, deference depoliticises in that it then almost inevitably describes the problems

---

[72] xxxix-xl. The point is of course not that issues of a technical nature are apolitical in some way – it is in fact exactly the opposite, that the issues are described as technical and therefore devoid of political content by those with an interest in removing them from political contestation.

[73] xl-xli.

[74] xli.

[75] It is important to be clear here. Deference operates, of course, on the basis of an understanding of what is political and what is not – courts defer to the other branches of government in part precisely because what are seen as "political" issues are left to the "political branches", being the legislature and executive. However, my point is that this move – deferring to the supposedly "political" branches – is based on an impoverished, limited understanding of what the "political sphere" or the proper space for democratic politics is. Leaving certain decisions to these supposedly political branches – authoritatively stating that these are the only places where they may be decided – insulates them from real democratic/political control.

[76] In fact, recognising complex issues as such and as issues that neither the court, nor the other branches of the state, nor civil society can engage with alone is an important first step in the approach of judicial prudence that I propose below.

at issue as technical rather than political in nature. On the understanding that a technical approach to a problem such as impoverishment and the standard of efficiency that underlies it is politically a neutral approach, the problems of impoverishment at issue in socio-economic rights cases are in this way bluntly depicted as devoid of politics, problems that can be solved without the need to engage political questions of redistribution and social justice.[77] And third, and most problematically, deference depoliticises in that it explicitly cedes the authority to deal with these complex issues to the formally constituted "political" branches of government "whose responsibility [and exclusive right] it ... [becomes] to deal with such matters".[78] This third move sends a particularly strong, legally countenanced message to impoverished people, social movements, nongovernmental organisations and others who might want to engage in a democratic, political sense with homelessness, hunger, ill-health and other incidences of impoverishment. What a court employing deference to account for any one of the range of institutional problems confronting it on review tells them is not only that these are difficult issues in a technical sense, requiring of them sustained, informed engagement which they, like the Court, might not on their own have the capacity for. Deference also tells them that such issues are, as with the Court, simply not their business. In this way the rhetoric of deference casts them not as active participants in democratic life, capable of political action to address their particular socio-economic needs, but as the passive recipients of services – their needs, predefined by the political branches of government, are administered to them through a process of therapeutic assistance.[79]

One response might be that what I describe here as a powerful depoliticising move is simply rhetoric that has no discernible effect on democratic politics and political agency. Such a response would be inaccurate. When courts engage with issues of impoverishment in socio-economic rights cases they also in different ways engage with, participate in and influence the political discourse about impoverishment. First, courts' work in socio-economic rights cases is part of this political discourse, even a medium for it. Participants in the political discourse use socio-economic rights litigation as tools for democratic political action, with judgments becoming political currency in

---

[77] See JW Singer "Property and Coercion in Federal Indian Law: The Conflict Between Critical and Complacent Pragmatism" (1990) 63 *S Cal L Rev* 1821 1824, where he points out that a "complacent" pragmatist (a technocratic) approach to social problems with its exclusive focus on "what works" is adopted precisely to avoid the need to engage substantive political questions of redistribution and social justice.

[78] *Soobramoney v Minister of Health, KwaZulu-Natal* 1998 1 SA 765 (CC) para 29.

[79] Habermas "Law as Medium" in *Dilemmas of Law* 210; Fraser (1989) *Ethics* 307. As will become clear below, I do not propose instead of deference an activist court that decides complex technical and politically contested questions unilaterally. Quite the contrary: I propose a court that recognises its own limitations, but that, instead of then deferring only to the other branches of government, opens itself and the issues up to a broader arena of democratic politics in which it remains itself engaged. See also Brand "Politics" in *Theories of Social and Economic Justice* 31-33.

political struggles.[80] Second, courts also play a symbolic or exemplary role in political discourses about impoverishment. Because of its authority, their vocabulary and rhetorical strategies are used in and so influence political discourses about impoverishment, influencing in particular perceptions about the role and political agency of participants in that debate.[81]

In sum then, judicial deference not only reflects a limited understanding of democracy at odds with the Constitution's substantive participatory vision of democracy, it also replicates the depoliticisation of issues of poverty that routinely occurs in other spheres of society and so actively works against rather than promotes the political capacity of impoverished people and the "establish[ment of] a ... democratic society" in the constitutional sense. In this light – and this is the strongest claim of this chapter – judicial deference is an inappropriate (and in relation to its democratic justification, a counter-productive) strategy to account for the range of institutional problems courts face in the exercise of their review powers in socio-economic rights cases, at least there where it is used unreflectively and in isolation. Something must be found in its stead.

4 Proposal

Emilios Christodoulidis provides a critique of the idea of representation and the counter-majoritarian dilemma as a central preoccupation of constitutional theory that is suggestive for my purposes.[82] In short (and I apologise for the inevitable reduction and reformulation) he points out that to describe the democratic problem with constitutional review in only binary institutional terms, as a counter-majoritarian depiction of that problem does – that is, as simply a problem of the relationship between courts and a constitution on the one hand and a legislature and executive as repositories of the democratic will on the other – is a limited view of the problem. He reminds us that, although this binary relationship is an important aspect of the democratic problem, one should not forget about popular sovereignty – "the people" – something that resides outside of, obviously, courts and a constitution, but also outside of the representative branches of government. Instead of seeing the democratic

---

[80] See R Ballard "Social Movements in Post-Apartheid South Africa: An Introduction" in P Jones & K Stokke (eds) *Democratising Development. The Politics of Socio-Economic Rights in South Africa* (2005) 78 87-88; M Heywood "Preventing Mother-to-Child HIV Transmission in South Africa: Background, Strategies and Outcomes of the Treatment Action Campaign Case Against the Minister of Health" (2003) 19 *SAJHR* 278 314-315; Liebenberg (2003) *LDD* 159.

[81] Consider the manner in which the reasonableness test with which courts evaluate the state's social provisioning activities has shaped civil society monitoring of planning and delivery with respect to social services and the political advocacy informed by that monitoring on the one hand and state responses to such advocacy on the other. See, for example, J Streak & J Wehner "Children's Socio-Economic Rights in the South African Constitution: Towards a Framework for Monitoring Implementation" in E Coetzee & J Streak (eds) *Monitoring Child Socio-Economic Rights in South Africa: Achievements and Challenges* (2004) 50 79. The kind of disabling, depoliticising rhetoric about the political role of impoverished people that I identify here in judicial language is of course prevalent in official and elite discourses about impoverishment, in a particularly acute way. The impoverished are routinely described as lazy, devious and greedy, requiring instead of state assistance, motivation through the withholding of such assistance. As such current political discourse about impoverishment is fertile ground for courts' depoliticising rhetoric. See Brand "Politics" in *Theories of Social and Economic Justice* 20.

[82] Christodoulidis (2002) *TSAR* 108-124.

problem with constitutional review in binary terms, he concludes, we should recognise that it occurs within a more complex triangular relationship – between a constitution and courts, the representative branches of government and popular sovereignty/the people.[83]

This seems like a simple point, but it is important – important because it is precisely the failure to see the triangular nature of the democratic problem with judicial review in socio-economic rights cases and the insistence to depict that problem in binary institutional terms that leads to the problems with judicial deference outlined above. This analysis, simple as it might seem, therefore suggests possibilities for my critique of judicial deference as a response to institutional problems in socio-economic rights adjudication. In short, my proposal is that courts should move away from regarding the institutional problems they face in deciding socio-economic rights cases in binary, institutional relations terms and to seek to resolve these problems by deferring to the other branches of government. Instead they should recognise that, with respect certainly to the democratic problem with judicial review, they stand in relationship not only to the representative branches of government, but also to Christodoulidis' third point of the triangle, the sovereign people. This shift of perspective, should they be able to operationalise it in their doctrine, techniques and reasoning, would enable them to embrace instead of deference with its attendant problems, an approach of what can perhaps be called judicial prudence. Such an approach would, on the understanding that courts in the exercise of their review powers stand in a complex triangular relationship with the other branches of government and the rest of the world (civil society, ordinary people), indeed recognise the difficulty of the institutional problems of capacity, legitimacy, integrity and security. But such an approach would in fact seek both to engage with these problems in every case in which they arise, and to do so by looking for inventive solutions to them elsewhere than simply in a deferral to the other branches of government.[84]

How would an approach of judicial prudence differ from judicial deference? Prudence and deference are similar in that in both approaches courts are aware of their institutional limits and seek ways in which to overcome them.[85] But once this first step (recognition of which issues a court cannot resolve on its own and why it cannot do so) is over, judicial prudence departs from judicial

---

[83] 108 and 112. These are my terms – he uses "constitutional reason", "democratic will" and "the sovereign people".

[84] This point resonates with Lucy Williams' recent argument on the operation of separation of powers concerns in socio-economic rights cases (Williams (2010) *CCR* 141-199). She makes the argument there that institutional concepts such as "separation of powers", or "institutional capacity" have no self-evident meaning that provides "guidance to or restraint upon decision-making" (142) in socio-economic rights cases. Instead, so she proposes, courts should in each specific case engage with the issues before them to determine themselves, for example, the extent of their institutional capacity or incapacity for those particular issues, relative to the legislature or executive. My point is similar – that concepts such as "separation of powers" cannot become place-holders for judgment – but broader. Whereas Williams' criticises the *manner* in which the South African Constitutional Court has employed deference, I criticise deference as such.

[85] Acting wisely in the Socratic sense, that is ("[all I know is] that I know nothing at all". Socrates quoted in Plato *The Republic* (transl B Jowett) (1894) <http//:classics.mit.edu/Plato/republic.2.i.html> (accessed 01-11-2011) 354b (conclusion of book 1)).

deference in two important ways, both related to how a court then deals with its institutional limits. The first is that it seeks assistance in resolving the issues not only from the other branches of government – instead it seeks to engage, together with the other branches of government, the particular claimants in a case, groups more generally interested in the issues that arise in a case and perhaps organs of civil society that can make a contribution in a process aimed at resolving the complex issues at stake. The second difference is less clear-cut than the first, but amounts to the following: A court employing judicial prudence instead of judicial deference precisely does not defer, in the sense of leaving decision of an issue to another forum (the "political" branches). In the context of administrative law review, a theory of judicial deference has been described as a set of principles to "guide [judicial] intervention and non-intervention".[86] In the general architecture of an approach of deference, the choice is in other words between the court itself deciding an issue, or leaving it be, for the other branches of government to decide. Although the sterling efforts of a number of administrative-law scholars to develop a theory of deference has in part been aimed at "grading" involvement of a court in particular decisions – softening the edges of deference so to speak so that it doesn't amount to an either/or proposition[87] – the basic structure of deference remains that it is either the court that decides an issue or certain aspects of an issue (leaving others to the administration), or it is the administration. In addition, with notable exceptions our courts, in particular in the context of socio-economic rights claims, have primarily employed judicial deference as a "judicial can't",[88] indicating either unilateral judicial decision or complete deference to the other branches.[89] In an approach of judicial prudence by contrast, the emphasis would be on the court *retaining involvement* in the resolution of difficult or contested issues, to the extent of its capacity. Instead of leaving decision of certain matters to other forums, the court would engage those other forums in a process aimed at resolving the issues in question both by creating such a process in institutional terms[90] and by setting the normative parameters within which any resolution must occur.

An approach of judicial prudence so described would in the first place be a more coherent and defensible response to the institutional problem with review that has been the focus of this chapter – the problem of its democratic legitimacy. If courts could find ways in their work in socio-economic rights cases of involving not only the other branches of government, but also elements of "the people" (the claimants before court; social movements and

---

[86] Cockrell "Paradigm" in *Administrative Law Reform* 227.

[87] It is in particular the work of Cora Hoexter that has been prominent in this respect (proposing an approach of variability of stringency of review depending on a contextual determination by a court of the relative limits of its powers with respect to a particular issue). See Hoexter (2000) *SALJ* 499-503; Hoexter *Administrative Law* 142-147. See also, in general, Cockrell "Paradigm" in *Administrative Law Reform* 227-247 but in particular 247; Dyzenhaus "The Politics of Deference" in *Province of Administrative Law* 279-307.

[88] R Cover *Justice Accused: Anti-Slavery and the Judiciary Process* (1975) 119-120.

[89] With respect to socio-economic rights cases, see Williams (2010) *CCR* 141-199 and with respect to administrative law, see Quinot (2010) *CCR* 111-139.

[90] See below for indications of what this means in operational terms.

other pressure groups) in the resolution of politically and socially contentious issues this would both accord more clearly with and so confirm the broader constitutional vision of substantive participatory democracy outlined above and avoid the depoliticising, democracy-limiting effect that deference's privileging of the legislature and executive has.

An approach of judicial prudence could also provide more coherent and practically more viable answers to at least the institutional problem of competence, which I have only touched on in passing in this chapter. Deference as a response to institutional competence concerns, by leaving decision of technically complex issues of social transformation that arise in socio-economic rights cases to the legislature, executive or state administration, reflects a centralist, "top-down" approach to socio-economic transformation in terms of which a "benevolent and rational state" "sets the agenda for" socio-economic transformation "and other actors and stakeholders have to embrace and support the path chosen".[91] Such an understanding of the nature of and requirements for sustainable socio-economic transformation conflicts with the general consensus in the fields of development studies and economics that sustainable and viable socio-economic transformation is only possible with broad participation by a range of social actors other than the state in development processes – participation that can be enabled through fostering and strengthening the political agency of impoverished individuals and groups on the one hand,[92] and fashioning developmental institutions and processes that allow for effective political contestation around issues of poverty and need on the other.[93] An approach of judicial prudence instead of deference, that recognises and attempts to involve in decision-making the third leg of Christodoulidis' triangle – social actors other than the state – better accords with this updated account of socio-economic transformation and development and is simply a more realistic response to problems of complexity and the resultant incapacity of a court.[94]

What would an approach of judicial prudence so described be in institutional terms – how, in other words, to operationalise it? At the outset it seems that an approach of judicial prudence would require our courts to

---

[91] E Pieterse & M van Donk "The Politics of Socio-Economic Rights in South Africa. Ten Years after Apartheid" (2004) 5 *ESR Review* 12 14. See also E Pieterse & M van Donk "Incomplete Ruptures: The Political Economy of Realising Socio-Economic Rights in South Africa" (2002) 6 *LDD* 193 195-196; P Heller "Local Democracy and Development in Comparative Perspective" in E Pieterse, S Parnell, M Swilling & M van Donk (eds) *Consolidating Developmental Local Government* (2008) 152 152.

[92] See, for example, A du Toit *Chronic and Structural Poverty in South Africa: Challenges for Action and Research* PLAAS Chronic Poverty and Development Policy Series No 6, Chronic Poverty Research Centre Working Paper No 56 (2005) 16-17 <http://www.plaas.org.za/pubs2/downloads/CP6%20du%20Toit. pdf/?searchterm=None> (accessed 22-11-2011). See also Cousins & Claassens "Communal Land Rights and Democracy" in *Democratising Development* 247 and particularly S Mnisi Weeks & A Claassens "Tensions between Vernacular Values that Prioritise Basic Needs and State Versions of Customary Law that Contradict Them: 'We Love these Fields that Feed Us but Not at the Expense of a Person'" in S Liebenberg & G Quinot (eds) *Law and Poverty* (2012) 381, 387-88, 392-95 for a thorough conceptual account and a graphic practical illustration of the dangers of unilateral, top-down developmental approaches, within the context of rural land rights.

[93] E Pieterse, S Parnell, M Swilling & M van Donk "Consolidating" in E Pieterse, S Parnell, M Swilling & M van Donk (eds) *Consolidating Developmental Local Government* (2008) 18-20.

[94] See Brand *Transformative Politics* 26-31. See also Liebenberg *Socio-Economic Rights* 437 for a brief account of this point.

develop fundamentally new approaches to access to court. The concern that courts in terms of an approach of judicial prudence would have to show for participation in litigation by actors other than the state would require that it be much easier than currently is the case for such non-state social actors to approach courts with socio-economic rights claims. This is not only so with respect to the rules of standing, other justiciability issues and the processes of approaching courts, but also with respect to the nature of the litigation process itself and the doctrine and forms of reasoning employed in it. Also, an approach of judicial prudence rather than deference, given the premium that it would place on a court's actual engagement with both politically contested and technically complex issues that come before it, would require adaptation of the currently still fundamentally adversarial approach to constitutional adjudication in South Africa toward a more inquisitorial model, with the more directly involved role for courts that such a model entails.

But quite apart from these two fundamental structural adaptations, a number of other obvious, more concrete ways in which our courts can operationalise an approach of judicial prudence present themselves, some of which have already taken root in our courts' socio-economic rights jurisprudence. First, courts, when confronted with technically complex or socially contested questions that they feel incapable of deciding on their own can instead of falling back on deference, employ different techniques of involving persons or institutions in litigation that are not directly party to that litigation but who possess the expertise or political representivity required to assist the court to resolve those issues. One thinks here in the first place of the possibility of joinder – our courts have recently, most notably in *Blue Moonlight Properties 39 (Pty) Ltd v Occupiers of Saratoga Avenue*,[95] joined local authorities to eviction proceedings between private property owners and squatters on the argument that such local authorities, although they have no direct interest in the litigation, have a constitutional duty to provide adequate housing that is implicated in the dispute.[96] This technique might be extended to allow courts to join also parties that don't have a direct interest in the litigation, or whose constitutional duties are not implicated by the litigation, but who possess particular expertise that might be helpful to the court, or represent particular interests that are implicated by the case. More obviously applicable perhaps, courts can expand existing practices of inviting friends of the court to make submissions in litigation, or more directly, appoint a *curator ad litem* to investigate and report to the court on complex matters that the court feels incapable of deciding, as our Constitutional Court has done in

---

[95]   2009 1 SA 470 (W).

[96]   Other cases in which the same technique was employed are: *ABSA Bank Ltd v Murray* 2004 2 SA 15 (C); *Cashbuild (South Africa) (Pty) Ltd v Scott* 2007 1 SA 332 (T); *Lingwood v The Unlawful Occupiers of R/E of Erf 9 Highlands* 2008 3 BCLR 325 (W); *Sailing Queen Investments v The Occupants La Colleen Court* 2008 6 BCLR 666 (W); *Chieftain Real Estate Incorporated in Ireland v Tshwane Metropolitan Municipality* 2008 5 SA 387 (T). For a discussion and evaluation of these joinder developments in eviction law, see G Muller *The Impact of Section 26 of the Constitution on the Eviction of Squatters in South African Law* LLD thesis Stellenbosch (2011) 231-255.

the past, most notably in the case of *S v M*.[97] A more radical development in this respect would have our courts following the example of apex courts in other jurisdictions deciding cases that raise complex and contested question of a technical nature. In jurisdictions such as Colombia, Argentina and India, courts have employed techniques of engagement in the course of deciding a case, to assist them in gathering information or resolving difficult technical or contentious political issues – courts have ordered, that is, the creation of discussion or negotiation forums both to advise them on complex technical issues that arise in the course of litigation and to reach agreement on contested questions that stand in the way of final judicial decision.[98]

In a slightly different vein, another obvious way in which our courts can introduce mechanisms of participation in their processes to assist them in resolving technically complex or politically contested questions presents itself; one that has of late been quite prominently used by our courts in socio-economic rights cases. South African courts have over the last several years displayed a growing inclination to resolve politically contentious or technically difficult issues that arise in the course of socio-economic rights litigation by requiring the parties before the court – the claimants and the state – to, as it has come to be called, "engage" with each other.

This has happened in a variety of ways. In cases such as *Modderfontein Squatters v Modderklip Boerdery (Pty) Ltd*,[99] *Port Elizabeth Municipality v Various Occupiers*[100] and *Occupiers of 51 Olivia Road Berea Township and 197 Main Street Johannesburg v City of Johannesburg*[101] our courts established that there is a constitutional duty on state agencies seeking to remove people from land to attempt to resolve the problem through "engagement" (read negotiation intended to reach agreement) with the occupiers of the land in

---

[97] 2008 3 SA 232 (CC). In this case, which concerned the constitutionality of the imposition of a term of imprisonment for fraud on a primary caregiver of minor children, the Court issued an invitation to interested parties to address it as *amici curiae* on a number of specified issues (para 5). The Centre for Child Law at the University of Pretoria joined as *amicus* and "made wide-ranging written and oral submissions on the constitutional, statutory and *social context* in which the matter fell to be decided" (para 6) (own emphasis). The Court also appointed a *curator ad litem* who, with the aid of a social worker, compiled a report that was considered by the Court. Finally, counsel for the Department of Social Development and the Department of Justice and Constitutional Development also submitted an extensive report on the position of children whose primary caregivers were sentenced to terms of imprisonment, compiled by a group of social workers.

[98] See, for example, the Colombian Constitutional Court decision T-760/2008 (decision requiring dramatic restructuring of the health care system, which has to be effected in part through a participatory process involving a range of stakeholders) (for a discussion and evaluation of this decision see A Ely Yamin & O Parra-Vera "How Do Courts Set Health Policy? The Case of the Colombian Constitutional Court" (2009) 6 *PLoS Medicine* 1); and the decision of the Argentinian Supreme Court in *Mendoza, Beatriz Silvia y otros c/ Estado Nacional y otros s/dānos y perjuicios (danā derivados de la contaminatión ambiental del Río Matanza-Riachuelo)* (decision attributing responsibility for the degradation of a river, reached on the basis of a participatory process managed by the Court during which interested parties participated in determining the decision of the Court) (summary in English available at <http//www.farn.org.ar/participacion/riachuelo/resumen_ingles.html> (accessed 03-08-2011)); and the Indian Supreme Court case of *People's Union for Civil Liberties v Union of India* (Writ Petition [Civil] 196 of 2001) *Right to Food Campaign* http://www.righttofoodindia.org/mdm/mdm_scorders.html> (accessed 03-08-2011) (a range of interim orders issued with judgment pending, including orders that a commission be appointed to investigate aspects of the case).

[99] 2004 6 SA 40 (SCA).

[100] 2005 1 SA 217 (CC).

[101] 2008 3 SA 208 (CC).

question before seeking an eviction order from a court, such that courts may deny an application for an eviction order in the absence of a showing that a reasonable such effort had been made.[102] Indeed, in *Olivia Road* Yacoob J went so far as to remark in passing that a duty to engage is also an aspect of the reasonableness test used to determine the constitutional cogency of measures intended to give effect to socio-economic rights in general,[103] a possibility that seems to have been applied by the Court subsequently in *Residents of Joe Slovo Community, Western Cape v Thubelisha Homes*.[104]

In *Port Elizabeth Municipality* the possibility was mooted to make the granting of an eviction order subject to the resolution through mediation or negotiation between the parties of technically complex or politically intractable aspects of the dispute – in that case, the question in particular of what would be suitable alternative accommodation for the potential evictees.[105] This technique was applied subsequently in *Joe Slovo* where the implementation of the eviction order granted in that case was made dependent on the parties reaching agreement on, among other things, the timing and manner of removal of the occupiers.[106]

Finally, in *Joseph v City of Johannesburg*[107] the scope of application of administrative-law procedural fairness guarantees was broadened through an inventive interpretation of a variety of sections of the Constitution and legislation to apply to any decisions related to the "public law duty" of the state to provide basic services effectively, efficiently and fairly and the concomitant "public law right" of people to receive those services in that manner.[108]

In South Africa these developments are still in their infancy, and it is unclear what their purpose and implications are and whether or not there is

---

[102] See with respect to *Modderfontein Squatters v Modderklip Boerdery (Pty) Ltd* 2004 6 SA 40 (SCA) paras 27 and 33-38 (see also *President of the Republic of South Africa v Modderklip Boerdery (Pty) Ltd (Agri SA, amici curiae)* 2005 5 SA 3 (CC) paras 27-38); with respect to *Port Elizabeth Municipality v Various Occupiers* 2005 1 SA 217 (CC) paras 45, 55-57 and 59; and with respect to *Occupiers of 51 Olivia Road Berea Township and 197 Main Street Johannesburg v City of Johannesburg* 2008 3 SA 208 (CC) paras 13-21.

[103] *Occupiers of 51 Olivia Road Berea Township and 197 Main Street Johannesburg v City of Johannesburg* 2008 3 SA 208 (CC) paras 17-21.

[104] 2010 3 SA 454 (CC) para 117.

[105] *Port Elizabeth Municipality v Various Occupiers* 2005 1 SA 217 (CC) paras 39-46.

[106] *Joe Slovo Community, Western Cape v Thubelisha Homes* 2010 3 SA 454 (CC) para 7, ss 5, 6, 7 and 11 of the order.

[107] 2010 4 SA 55 (CC).

[108] Paras 34-47. In *Occupiers of 51 Olivia Road Berea Township and 197 Main Street Johannesburg v City of Johannesburg* 2008 3 SA 208 (CC) the Constitutional Court also signalled its willingness to leave the resolution of a case wholly to the parties by ordering them to resolve their dispute through "engagement" prior to handing down judgment – effectively to order the parties to settle the case on the basis of engagement (paras 5-6). This particular instance of the use of engagement in adjudication is clearly problematic from my perspective. In fact, as one of the anonymous reviewers of this chapter pointed out, it amounts to an extreme form of deference in which the Court wholly abdicated its decision-making powers to the parties (the Court gave no indication either beforehand or after the fact when approving the agreement that was reached of the normative parameters within which agreement must be sought). As such it is not an example of a technique that gives expression to an approach of prudence.

scope for their further development.[109] But in a variety of other jurisdictions the engagement techniques employed by our courts have been developed far beyond the manner in which they have played a role thus far in South Africa.

So, for example, in a jurisdiction such as Colombia the Constitutional Court has issued what we would in South Africa call structural or supervisory interdicts that, apart from retaining for the Court jurisdiction over the implementation of its orders require all manner of broader societal involvement in the resolution of difficult technical or contentious political issues that remain after the court has decided a case.[110] The scope and ambition of the "engagement" aspects of these orders far exceed the role it has thus far played in South Africa.

These engagement techniques are themselves by no means unproblematic. Apart from the significant practical or logistical problems that attend their use – how to decide who to involve in different processes of engagement; where the numbers of involved parties are large, how to set in place manageable structures and processes for the negotiation; and how to ensure equality in power in ensuing negotiations or discussions – the utility of rights as particular kinds of tools in political struggles might be argued to suffer if their content is to be determined through negotiation between interested parties rather than through authoritative interpretation and pronouncement by a court.

Nevertheless, such techniques of engagement, if carefully developed by courts, achieve exactly the kind of shift in perspective from a binary to a triangular view of institutional problems in constitutional review that I advocate above – they enable courts, when confronted with contested political questions or technically complex issues in socio-economic rights litigation, to turn not only to the other branches of government, but also to the "sovereign people" for their resolution.

SUMMARY

In this chapter I present a problematisation of deference as a judicial strategy to account for institutional problems with judicial review in socio-economic rights cases. On the assumption that deference operates as an obstacle to effective judicial enforcement of socio-economic rights, I describe certain internal inconsistencies in its conception and use. In particular I point out that the democratic justification often offered for deference – that courts as unaccountable institutions defer to the democratically accountable branches out of concern for democracy – both reflects an

---

[109] For recent commentary on these developments see in this issue G Muller "Conceptualising 'Meaningful Engagement' as a Deliberative Democratic Partnership" in S Liebenberg & G Quinot (eds) *Law and Poverty* (2012) 300-316; L Chenwi "A New Approach to Remedies in Socio-Economic Rights Adjudication: *Occupiers of 51 Olivia Road v City of Johannesburg*" (2009) 2 *CCR* 371 and "'Meaningful Engagement' in the Realisation of Socio-Economic Rights: The South African Experience" (2011) 26 *SAPL* 128; WA Holness "Equality of the Graveyard: Participatory Democracy in the Context of Housing Delivery" (2011) 26 *SAPL* 1; K McLean "Meaningful Engagement: One Step Forward or Two Back? Some Thoughts on *Joe Slovo*" (2010) 3 *CCR* 223; Liebenberg *Socio-Economic Rights* 418-423. See also, for a well-developed and established engagement with the use of these techniques in the context of remedies in socio-economic rights adjudication C Mbazira *Litigating Socio-Economic Rights in South Africa: A Choice Between Corrective and Distributive Justice* (2009) 165-223 and in particular 215-217; and Liebenberg *Socio-Economic Rights* 434-438.

[110] See T025/04, a judgment of the Colombian Constitutional Court with respect to the rights of internally displaced persons (the "IDP case"). For a discussion, see MJ Cepeda-Espinosa "How Far May the Colombian Constitutional Court Go to Protect IDP Rights?" (Dec 2006) *Forced Migration Review* 21 <http://www.fmreview.org/FMRpdfs/BrookingsSpecial/13.pdf> (accessed 09-11-2011).

impoverished conception of democracy and actively counteracts a more substantive conception of democracy, by confirming and legitimising political discourse that seeks to exclude broad participation in development-related decision-making. I describe an alternative approach to take account of institutional problems in socio-economic rights-related judicial review that better accords with and affirms a broader vision of democracy. This approach would have courts both retain rather than relinquish judicial involvement in the resolution of issues that present them with institutional difficulties and actively involve in the resolution of such issues also social actors other than the state. I conclude by presenting a variety of possible judicial techniques through which this approach can be operationalised.

CHAPTER 11

NARROWING THE BAND: REASONABLENESS REVIEW IN ADMINISTRATIVE JUSTICE AND SOCIO-ECONOMIC RIGHTS JURISPRUDENCE IN SOUTH AFRICA

Geo Quinot

Sandra Liebenberg[*]

1   Introduction

The evolution of reasonableness as a standard of review has been one of the most significant developments in both socio-economic rights and administrative justice jurisprudence in South Africa under the Constitution of the Republic of South Africa, 1996 ("the Constitution"). However, the relationship between the development of reasonableness in these two areas of law has not received much attention and they remain seemingly distinct developments. At the same time, our courts' reasonableness model of judicial review for socio-economic rights has been variously criticised and praised as one premised on an administrative-law conception of review.[1] That is meant to convey a model that is relatively process orientated and pays little regard to developing the substance of the normative content and obligations imposed by socio-economic rights. Critics thus argue that such an administrative-law reasonableness model of review is ill-suited for socio-economic rights adjudication.[2]

But reasonableness is also argued to hold distinct advantages as a standard of constitutional review over more "absolutist" methods of interpreting rights.

---

[*]   Our thanks to the participants at the *Law and Poverty Colloquium* for responses to the chapter and in particular to Katie Young and Petrus Maree for valuable comments on an earlier draft.

[1]   See, generally, CR Sunstein "Social and Economic Rights? Lessons from South Africa" (2000-2001) 11 *Constitutional Forum* 123; D Brand "The Proceduralisation of South African Socio-Economic Rights Jurisprudence, or 'What are Socio-Economic Rights for?'" in H Botha, AJ van der Walt & J van der Walt (eds) *Rights and Democracy in a Transformative Constitution* (2004) 33; DM Davis "Adjudicating the Socio-Economic Rights in the South African Constitution: Towards 'Deference Lite'?" (2006) 23 *SAJHR* 301. See also S Liebenberg *Socio-Economic Rights: Adjudication under a Transformative Constitution* (2010) 173.

[2]   See Brand "Proceduralisation" in *Rights and Democracy* 51-56; Liebenberg *Socio-Economic Rights* 173.

Sadurski[3] identifies two such advantages. First, reasonableness review promotes greater transparency in legal reasoning[4] in that the competing value and policy considerations at stake, and the method and choices made in weighing them are openly acknowledged and set out in the reasoning. Second, reasonableness as a standard in judicial review is "consensus-orientated" in that it acknowledges that valid constitutional considerations and arguments are frequently made by both parties, and judicial review in the context of constitutional rights seeks to attain as far as possible to reconcile and accommodate competing values and interests.[5] Della Cananea points out that a reasonableness standard differs from a more rigid rule-based standard "in the sense that it escapes any all-or-nothing logic":

> "It instead makes it necessary to carefully weigh and balance all the circumstances in a case and all matters of fact and law. Which means that the kind of judicial review the principle involves goes well beyond the traditional review by which to determine legality."[6]

This conception of reasonableness review avoids normative closure and is capable of stimulating deliberative democracy both in court and in the broader public sphere.[7] It supports a dynamic concept of law, where law is responsive to changing circumstances and socio-political contexts. Sadurski observes that reasonableness involves a continuum or band between weak reasonableness aimed at the exclusion of manifestly unfair or irrational consequences,[8] and reasonableness in the strong sense of a proportionality analysis.[9]

---

[3]   W Sadurski "Reasonableness and Value Pluralism in Law and Politics" in G Bongiovanni, G Sartor & C Valentini (eds) *Reasonableness and Law* (2009) 129 145-146. He describes reasonableness review as follows:
> "By showing all the 'ingredients' of his/her reasoning, a judge conducting the proportionality analysis indicates that the final conclusion is not a result of a mechanical calculus: a syllogism in which the conclusion necessarily follows from the premises, but rather the outcome results from a complex, *practical* reasoning, in which significant but often mutually competing values have to be considered in their actual social context ... [P]roportionality analysis is more conducive to critical analysis and dissection of its elements than the 'absolutist' analysis which focuses on one constitutional right and on a thorough examination of its meaning." (139).

[4]   On the significance of promoting transparency of legal processes and legal reasoning for the project of transformative constitutionalism and deepening democratic culture, see K Klare "Legal Culture and Transformative Constitutionalism" (1998) 14 *SAJHR* 146 170-171.

[5]   This concept of reasonableness facilitates the relational, dialogic and fluid notion of constitutional rights and judicial review developed by scholars such as Jennifer Nedelsky "Reconceiving Rights as Relationship" (1993) 1 *Rev of Constitutional Studies* 1; and Henk Botha "Metaphoric Reasoning and Transformative Constitutionalism" (2003) *TSAR* 20.

[6]   G della Cananea "Reasonableness in Administrative Law" in G Bongiovanni, G Sartor & C Valentini (eds) *Reasonableness and Law* (2009) 299 307.

[7]   See Liebenberg *Socio-Economic Rights* 163-186.

[8]   Sadurski describes this standard of review as "safety valve" reasonableness and points out its connection with the standard laid down for the review of administrative decisions in *Associated Provincial Picture Houses v Wednesbury Corporation* [1948] 1 KB 223. See Sadurski "Reasonableness" in *Reasonableness and Law* 131-132.

[9]   Reasonableness in the strong sense involves two primary stages of inquiry:
Stage 1: The identification of the aim or purpose of a given measure, and an assessment of its nature and importance.
Stage 2: A three-tiered proportionality test, posing the following questions:
a)   Are the means adopted "suitable" or "reasonably and demonstrably justified"?
b)   Do the means adopted limit the constitutional rights in the least restrictive way (the "least restrictive means test")?
c)   Do the advantages of accomplishing the purpose outweigh the disadvantages and costs of restricting the specific constitutional right – "costs and benefits" analysis (proportionality *sensu stricto*)?
Sadurski "Reasonableness" in *Reasonableness and Law* 133-134. See the similar, but not identical formulation under s 36 of the Constitution.

In this chapter we argue that an approach to reasonableness review that builds on the development of reasonableness as a standard in *both* administrative justice and socio-economic rights jurisprudence offers us a strong and coherent model of judicial review. In our view an analysis of these developments in the two areas shows how reasonableness can be understood as a single model of review that captures the structural advantages of this standard, but at the same time is capable of facilitating the development of the substantive content of socio-economic rights.

We begin our analysis by noting the significant development of reasonableness as a standard of review in administrative law and the consequent shift towards a more substantive conception of review. In the first part of the chapter we thus consider the implications of that shift for cases involving review of administrative action impacting on socio-economic rights, what we call "overlap cases". One important purpose of this discussion is to show the extent to which substantive considerations may enter administrative-law review under this ground. This analysis also illustrates the significant development of a truly post-constitutional conception of administrative-law review. This is a notion of review that breaks with the narrow confines of common-law review and embraces an understanding of administrative-law review as part of administrative justice within a justiciable bill of rights. We then proceed to consider the application of the new reasonableness review model in administrative law in overlap cases. These cases raise the issue of overlapping standards of review under the banner of reasonableness and consequently the relationship between the different provisions regarding this standard.

The second part of the chapter examines reasonableness review in socio-economic rights cases where the cause of action is not formulated in terms of administrative law; what we call "non-overlap cases". This typically concerns cases where it is alleged that the legislature or executive branches of government have failed to fulfil the obligations imposed by socio-economic rights. In this section we examine the problems as well as potential of reasonableness review to do justice to the substantive commitments of the socio-economic rights provisions in the Constitution.

We conclude by showing that there can be a single model of reasonableness review across socio-economic rights and administrative justice cases. While the reasonableness standards under the different sections overlap, we argue that they do not simply result in duplication, but fulfil different functions in the review. Taken together, we conclude that reasonableness offers a model of review of socio-economic rights that promotes a number of key constitutional objectives. These include transparency and justification of all forms of public action, proper consideration of the factual and normative context, and the development of the substantive dimensions of the socio-economic rights in the Constitution. These we take to be strategic imperatives in realising "transformative constitutionalism"[10] and a "culture of justification"[11] in South Africa.

---

[10] Klare (1998) *SAJHR* 146.

[11] E Mureinik "A Bridge to Where? Introducing the Interim Bill of Rights" (1994) 10 *SAJHR* 31.

2   The reasonableness review standard in administrative law

2 1   Development of reasonableness as a standard in South African administrative law

Reasonableness enjoyed extremely limited status as a ground of review of administrative action in South African common law, as was the case in most common-law jurisdictions. As Stratford JA famously stated in *Union Government*:

> "There is no authority that I know of ... for the proposition that a court of law will interfere with the exercise of a discretion on the mere ground of its unreasonableness." [12]

The court went on to endorse the standard of gross unreasonableness as the level at which a court may take notice of unreasonableness upon review. As the court subsequently confirmed, proving unreasonableness as a ground of review involved "a formidable onus" requiring proof that the "decision was grossly unreasonable to so striking a degree as to warrant the inference of a failure to apply its mind".[13] Although common-law courts were prepared to adopt slightly higher standards of reasonableness review for the narrow categories of legislative administrative action (rule-making)[14] and judicial administrative action (tribunal decisions),[15] the vast bulk of administrative action remained subject only to the excessive standard of gross unreasonableness pointing to some other irregularity, aptly labelled "symptomatic unreasonableness".[16] This approach was closely aligned to the traditional approach to reasonableness in English administrative law that came to be known as *Wednesbury* unreasonableness.[17]

The Constitution of the Republic of South Africa Act 200 of 1993 ("the Interim Constitution") brought a decisive break with the common-law position by introducing the right to administrative action that is justifiable in relation to the reasons given for it in section 24(d). Despite the (ostensibly deliberate) avoidance of the term reasonableness in section 24,[18] early responses to this right raised the hope that reasonableness had at long last come to South African administrative law and with it a substantive dimension to review. A number of academic commentators labelled the standard to be adopted under section 24(d) as a reasonableness one.[19] Early case law expressly recognised the substantive dimension of this standard. One of the most significant of these early judgments was that of Froneman DJP in *Carephone (Pty) Ltd v Marcus*

---

[12]   *Union Government (Minister of Mines and Industries) v Union Steel Corporation (South Africa) Ltd* 1928 AD 220 236-237.

[13]   *National Transport Commission v Chetty's Motor Transport (Pty) Ltd* 1972 3 SA 726 (A) 735G.

[14]   *Kruse v Johnson* [1898] 2 QB 91; *R v Abdurahman* 1950 3 SA 136 (A).

[15]   *Theron v Ring van Wellington van die NG Sendingkerk in Suid-Afrika* 1976 2 SA 1 (A).

[16]   J Taitz "But 'Twas a Famous Victory" (1978) *Acta Juridica* 109 111.

[17]   HWR Wade & CF Forsyth *Administrative Law* 10 ed (2009) 293, 304; *Associated Provincial Picture Houses v Wednesbury Corporation* [1948] 1 KB 223.

[18]   Mureinik (1994) *SAJHR* 40 n 34.

[19]   J Klaaren "Administrative Justice" in M Chaskalson, J Kentridge, J Klaaren, G Marcus, D Spitz & S Woolman (eds) *CLoSA* (RS 5 1999) 25-20; J de Waal, I Currie & G Erasmus *The Bill of Rights Handbook* 3 ed (2000) 473.

NO[20] where he described section 24(d) as introducing "a requirement of rationality in the merit or outcome of the administrative decision" which "goes beyond mere procedural impropriety as a ground for review, or irrationality only as evidence of procedural impropriety".[21] Despite his reference to rationality, Froneman DJP had a substantive standard in mind. This is made clear by his important subsequent formulation of what the judicial enquiry under this standard entails:

> "In determining whether administrative action is justifiable in terms of the reasons given for it, value judgments will have to be made which will, almost inevitably, involve the consideration of the 'merits' of the matter in some way or another. As long as the Judge determining this issue is aware that he or she enters the merits not in order to substitute his or her own opinion on the correctness thereof, but to determine whether the outcome is rationally justifiable, the process will be in order."[22]

Froneman DJP concluded that the question to ask is whether there is "a rational objective basis justifying the connection made by the administrative decision-maker between the material properly available to him and the conclusion he or she eventually arrived at".[23]

Two important points regarding the standard of justifiability flow from these remarks. Firstly, the standard applied is not simply a process-orientated one, but involves a consideration of the substance or merits of the case, what Froneman DJP referred to as "substantive rationality".[24] Under this approach the review court does not only consider the way in which the decision was reached, that is the reasoning process leading to the decision, but indeed the decision itself. The substantive merits of the decision are measured against the material put forward, both facts and law, to justify the particular outcome.[25] Secondly, there are strong hints of the variability of the standard to be applied ranging from rationality to proportionality in particular cases.

The judgment in *Roman v Williams NO*[26] probably extended the section 24(d) standard most in this early jurisprudence by noting that it included the requirements of "suitability, necessity and proportionality" and that it therefore involved "the requirement of proportionality between the means and the end".

The hopes of a truly substantive standard of review were, however, dashed by the majority judgment in *Bel Porto School Governing Body v Premier, Western Cape*.[27] In that case the majority held that section 24[28] had not changed the common-law position regarding substantive review and had not "introduced substantive fairness into our law as a criterion for judging whether

---

[20]   1999 3 SA 304 (LAC).

[21]   Para 31.

[22]   Para 36.

[23]   Para 37.

[24]   Para 37.

[25]   As was stated in *Kotzé v Minister of Health* 1996 3 BCLR 417 (T) 425 the standard requires that "it must appear from the reasons that the action is based on accurate findings of fact and a correct application of the law".

[26]   1998 1 SA 270 (C) 284H-285A.

[27]   2002 3 SA 265 (CC).

[28]   The case was decided under the transitional reading of s 33 of the Constitution in terms of item 23(2)(b) of Sch 6 of the Constitution, which retained s 24 of the Interim Constitution pending the enactment of the Promotion of Administrative Justice Act 3 of 2000 ("PAJA").

administrative action is valid or not".[29] The Court noted that such a standard would drag judges into policy matters that should, in terms of the separation of powers, be left to the political and administrative decision-makers.[30] The Court also held that *Carephone* should not be read as suggesting otherwise and that the appropriate standard was simply whether there was "a rational decision taken lawfully and directed to a proper purpose".[31] The minority in stark contrast adopted a highly substantive test, which provided the groundwork for the later development of a substantive contextual conception of reasonableness under the Constitution and PAJA in *Bato Star Fishing (Pty) Ltd v Minister of Environmental Affairs*.[32]

In their minority judgment Mokgoro and Sachs JJ made a number of important remarks regarding the substantive test to be applied under section 24(d). They expressly endorsed proportionality as a dimension of the standard and noted that that includes "an element of substantive review".[33] They held that the test to be applied in a given case involves a sliding scale between a standard of correctness (whether the *correct* decision was taken on the merits) and a "mere rational connection" standard. In locating the relevant action between these extremes the context needs to be taken into account, including factors such as "the nature of the right or interest involved; the importance of the purpose sought to be achieved by the decision; the nature of the power being exercised; the circumstances of its use; the intensity of its impact on the liberty, property, livelihood or other rights of the persons affected; the broad public interest involved ... [and] whether or not there are manifestly less restrictive means to achieve the purpose".[34] In addition, the minority located their substantive review standard within the normative framework of the Constitution, which "prohibits administrative action which, however meritorious in its general thrust, is based on exclusionary processes, applies unacceptable criteria and results in sacrifice being borne in a disproportionate and unjustifiable manner, the more so if those who are most adversely affected are themselves from a disadvantaged sector of the community".[35] However, the minority acknowledged the need to respect the constitutional mandate of executive government and the challenges and constraints under which it operates and, in particular, the need for courts not to usurp the policy functions of the political branches.[36] In this regard the minority stated that respect for policymaking functions of other state organs must be balanced against the need to protect persons seriously affected by administrative decisions.[37] In a

---

[29]   *Bel Porto School Governing Body v Premier, Western Cape* 2002 3 SA 265 (CC) para 88.
[30]   Para 88.
[31]   Para 89.
[32]   2004 4 SA 490 (CC).
[33]   *Bel Porto School Governing Body v Premier, Western Cape* 2002 3 SA 265 (CC) para 162.
[34]   Para 165.
[35]   Para 155.
[36]   Paras 154-156.
[37]   Para 156.

striking expression the minority stated that "[t]here are circumstances where fairness in implementation must outtop policy".[38]

The minority in the final analysis concluded that all these factors led to the question whether "the decision can be defended as falling within a wide permissible range of discretionary options".[39] In the minority's view the standard of justifiability therefore involved not only a process enquiry into the appropriate reasoning method followed to reach the conclusion, but also a substantive enquiry in which, taking the substantive context into account, the decision falls within the band of outcomes that would be considered reasonable by the court.

Against this difference of opinion on what exact standard of review justifiability in section 24(d) incorporates, section 33(1) of the Constitution adopted the term reasonableness as a standard of administrative justice. Noting the clear difference in terminology between the two sections, Chaskalson CJ stated in *Minister of Health and Another NO v New Clicks South Africa (Pty) Ltd*[40] that the reasonableness standard under section 33(1) "is a variable but higher standard, which in many cases will call for a more intensive scrutiny of administrative decisions than would have been competent under the interim Constitution".

In giving effect to section 33 of the Constitution, PAJA contains two clear reasonableness grounds of review, namely section 6(2)(f)(ii), the rationality standard, and section 6(2)(h), the wording of which is strongly reminiscent of the *Wednesbury* test.[41] On its face, section 6(2)(h) involves a very narrow standard of reasonableness, something close to the gross unreasonableness test of the common law. However, building on the minority judgment in *Bel Porto,* the court in *Bato Star* rejected gross unreasonableness as an appropriate interpretation of section 6(2)(h) under section 33(1) of the Constitution and adopted a contextual reasonableness standard under PAJA. It is this standard that offers the most potential of a truly substantive test for reasonableness in South African administrative law.

2 2   Contextual reasonableness

In *Bato Star* O'Regan J held that section 6(2)(h) of PAJA should be understood as a simple reasonableness test, which asks whether the decision is one that a reasonable decision-maker could reach.[42] This formulation endorses the notion of a band of options and the standard of reasonableness simply requiring the relevant decision to fall within that band. O'Regan J confirmed the variability of reasonableness, particularly in relation to the context of the

---

[38]   Para 156 with reference to Sedley J in *R v Ministry of Agriculture Fisheries and Food, ex parte Hamble (Offshore) Fisheries Ltd* [1995] 2 All ER 714 (QB) 731.

[39]   *Bel Porto School Governing Body v Premier, Western Cape* 2002 3 SA 265 (CC) para 166.

[40]   2006 2 SA 311 (CC) para 108.

[41]   S 6(2)(h) of PAJA states that administrative action will be reviewable if "the exercise of the power or the performance of the function authorised by the empowering provision, in pursuance of which the administrative action was purportedly taken, is so unreasonable that no reasonable person could have so exercised the power or performed the function".

[42]   *Bato Star Fishing (Pty) Ltd v Minister of Environmental Affairs* 2004 4 SA 490 (CC) para 44.

decision and that reasonableness now contains both procedural and substantive dimensions.[43] She most helpfully provided a list of factors that may be taken into account in applying this approach, which includes "the nature of the decision, the identity and expertise of the decision-maker, the range of factors relevant to the decision, the reasons given for the decision, the nature of the competing interests involved and the impact of the decision on the lives and well-being of those affected".[44] Most of these factors can tell us very little about the actual reasonableness of a particular action. The factors rather serve to establish the level of scrutiny to be applied in a given case, which brings us back to the notion of a sliding scale or continuum of reasonableness advanced in the minority judgment in *Bel Porto*.

The *Bato Star* approach thus involves a two-stage enquiry, firstly establishing what the appropriate level of reasonableness scrutiny must be in a given case,[45] and secondly, assessing the decision at that level of scrutiny. Another way of looking at this approach is that the first step involves setting the markers of what would be the band of options available to the reasonable decision-maker under the particular circumstances. That involves developing some understanding as to what the minimum option would be, but also (at least notionally) what the maximum option would be in the given case, that is the maximum that a court can insist upon under a review. Once these markers have been set, the second step is to determine whether the administrator's choice falls within that band. The key consideration in all of this is the context of the particular decision, which includes both the normative context and the factual context.

Some of the factors listed by O'Regan J, such as "the nature of the decision" (especially where policy is at stake) and "the identity and expertise of the decision-maker", may point towards a lighter rationality type of reasonableness analysis. However, other factors such as "the nature of the competing interests involved and the impact of the decision on the lives and well-being of those affected" point to a standard beyond rationality and closer to proportionality, involving the consideration of the substantive impact of the decision. The very nature of this approach invites a proportionality analysis in which competing considerations are balanced.

This approach is a highly substantive one. O'Regan J pointed out that key questions are whether the decision taken "will reasonably result in the achievement of the goal", whether the decision is "reasonably supported on the facts" and that it is "reasonable in the light of the reasons given for it".[46]

The upshot of the contextual reasonableness approach in its most substantive dimension (in looking at the merits of the decision) is to define the band of decisions that an administrator may take and to check that the decision

---

[43]   Para 45.

[44]   Para 45.

[45]   This is not equivalent to the Canadian model of a certain and fixed number of predetermined levels of scrutiny, but a more fluid approach. See M Kidd *Following Bato Star: A Guide to Pinpointing Reasonableness* (2005) unpublished paper presented at the *Society of Law Teachers of South Africa* conference in Bloemfontein, 01-2005 (on file with authors).

[46]   *Bato Star Fishing (Pty) Ltd v Minister of Environmental Affairs* 2004 4 SA 490 (CC) para 48.

made is within those bounds. In "pure" administrative-law cases (cases not involving other fundamental rights) that involves a fairly broad band of well-reasoned decisions. However, the variability of the standard allows for the band to be narrowed where the context demands. Thus, in a particular context, typically involving a decision with a high policy dimension and insignificant impact, the appropriate standard may be rationality, which denotes a very wide band of options only requiring some substantive basis supporting the outcome. In other cases, primarily where a decision has a severe impact and/ or an impact on fundamental rights, a much stricter proportionality inquiry will be appropriate, which significantly narrows that band of options. The information must show that the decision arrived at was narrowly tailored to reach the desired outcome with minimal adverse impact and that there is evidence of a weighing of the negative and positive of the decision with an eventual balancing in the final outcome. In this approach the context will expand or narrow the band of options open to an administrator that will be considered reasonable.

2 3   Normative context

An important dimension of the context that informs the contextual reasonableness approach is the normative context. This refers to the relevance of the Constitution in general, in particular other fundamental rights, to the administrative decision at hand. The constitutional normative context plays a pivotal role in applying the contextual reasonableness approach in specific cases. In particular, it may result in a significant narrowing down of the band of options.

Bato Star itself provides one of the best examples of this role of the constitutional normative context. In the second majority judgment, Ngcobo J approached the review of the action at stake from a completely different angle to that of O'Regan J. His focus in determining whether the administrator's decision was reviewable under the circumstances was to assess the substantive goals to be achieved by the decision, in this case transformation of the fishing industry, and the administrator's substantive choice within the constitutional framework, particularly "the place of transformation in our constitutional democracy".[47] This approach led Ngcobo J to conclude that where the empowering provision required the administrator to "have regard to" a number of policy objectives, one of which was transformation of the industry, the band of options open to the administrator was significantly narrowed by the constitutional imperative of transformation. Given the importance of transformation in the normative context, options which simply "bear in mind" or do not overlook transformation were not open to the administrator. Instead, the administrator had to pick an option that actively promoted transformation. While Ngcobo J based his reasoning on a basic lawfulness premise, focusing on compliance with the empowering provision, rather than a reasonable basis,

---

[47]   Para 71.

his approach is a good example of the role that the normative context can play in narrowing the band of substantive choices open to an administrator.

The role of the normative context will be particularly important where other fundamental rights are at stake, such as socio-economic rights. In such cases, the substantive dimension of those rights impact directly on adjudicating the substance of the administrative action in terms of the contextual reasonableness approach. It is to these cases that we now turn.

2 4 The reasonableness of administrative action impacting on socio-economic rights

Applying the contextual reasonableness approach outlined above to cases where administrative action impacts on socio-economic rights requires the relevant socio-economic right to inform the normative context of the analysis. Put differently, when taking administrative action that affects socio-economic rights the band of substantive choices open to the reasonable administrator is narrowed to those options that conform to the substantive commitments of the relevant right. The implication is that a court should determine the substantive content of the relevant socio-economic right when testing for reasonableness under section 33 of the Constitution.

Two distinctive features of review in overlap cases can accordingly be identified. Firstly, the purpose of the measures required in terms of sections 26(2) and 27(2) of the Constitution should be provided by the normative goals underpinning the rights enshrined in sections 26(1) and 27(1). The explicit formulation of these provisions is that everyone should have access to the "adequate", "sufficient" or "appropriate" level of housing, health care, food, water and social security.[48] As human rights, socio-economic rights seek to promote and advance the fundamental values of this tradition, namely human dignity, equality and freedom.[49] They should also be interpreted according to the courts' core interpretive mandate in section 39(1)(a) of the Constitution to interpret the Bill of Rights so as to "promote the values that underlie an open and democratic society based on human dignity, equality and freedom". This provision requires the Court to develop a substantive and transparent account of the normative purposes and goals which the relevant rights should seek to advance. Developing the substantive content of socio-economic rights will require close attention to the relevant historical, social, economic and cultural meanings and experiential dimensions of the rights in the South African context as well as dialogic engagement with relevant international and comparative law standards and jurisprudence. This openness to considering developments in international law and other jurisdictions is expressly mandated in section 39(1)(b) and (c) of the Constitution.

---

[48] It is noteworthy that there is no adjective qualifying health care or social security, but arguably a qualitative dimension is intrinsic to nature of rights. This would certainly accord with international law standards (see, for example, United Nations Committee on Economic, Social and Cultural Rights (the "UN CESCR") *General Comment No 14: The Right to the Highest Attainable Standard of Health (art.12)* (2000) UN Doc E/C.12/2000/4 and UN CESCR *General Comment No 19: The Right to Social Security (art. 9)* (2007) UN Doc E/C.12/GC/19.

[49] See Liebenberg *Socio-Economic Rights* 97-101.

The substantive goals provided by the rights in sections 26(1) and 27(1) of the Constitution narrow the band of permissible policy choices. It is not enough that the objectives which the state sets itself fall within the broad range of what are regarded as "legitimate" state objectives. These objectives must be consistent with the normative purposes of the rights. This implies a rights-conscious social policy, planning and budgeting process. It is noteworthy in this context that one of the core obligations identified by the United Nations Committee on Economic, Social and Cultural Rights (the "CESCR") in relation to the rights protected in the International Covenant on Economic, Social and Cultural Rights (1966) (the "ICESCR")[50] is the adoption of a national strategy and plan of action aimed at the realisation of the relevant rights. Such a national plan must be participatory and transparent and set clear goals as well as indicators and benchmarks by which progress can be monitored. Particular attention must be given in the plan to vulnerable or marginalised groups.[51]

The second feature which should distinguish overlap cases from non-overlap cases concerns the relationship between the measures adopted and the constitutionally mandated goal. The state is obliged to take positive measures towards the realisation and protection of the relevant rights.[52] It may not remain purely passive when there are people within its jurisdiction lacking access to the relevant rights. In comparison, in non-overlap cases passivity would be an option as the state is not obliged to adopt positive measures. Passivity regarding a particular non-socio-economic rights substantive matter, say building roads, may pass the reasonableness test if the state can justify its choice to do nothing, for example with reference to competing substantive priorities, say improving rail connections. In the context of socio-economic rights, however, a positive duty to "realise" or "fulfil" the relevant rights implies scrutiny of whether the measures adopted are reasonably capable of fulfilling this objective. As O'Regan J pointed out in *Bato Star*, reasonableness means asking *inter alia* whether the decision taken "will reasonably result in the achievement of the goal".[53] In the absence of this linkage, the measures adopted are abstracted from the normative goal set in terms of sections 26(1) and 27(1) of ensuring that everyone has access to the relevant rights to the requisite standard of sufficiency.[54] In many circumstances, the state will have a range of options to choose from, but subject always to the need to justify through the presentation of evidence and argument that the measures chosen are capable of advancing the constitutionally mandated goals. In other circumstances, the context may indicate that the "choice of means" available to the state to give

---

[50] International Covenant on Economic, Social and Cultural Rights (1966) UN Doc A/6316.

[51] See, for example, UN CESCR *General Comment No 14* (2000) para 43 (f); UN CESCR *General Comment No 15: The Right to Water (arts. 11 & 12)* (2002) UN Doc E/C.12/2002/11 para 37(f) and paras 46-54.

[52] This is clear from the formulation of ss 26(2) and 27(2) of the Constitution, read with the overarching duty of the state to "respect, protect, promote and fulfil" the rights in the Bill of Rights in terms of s 7(2). For an application of the latter set of duties to the right to basic education, see *Governing Body of the Juma Musjid Primary School v Essay NO* 2011 8 BCLR 761 (CC).

[53] *Bato Star Fishing (Pty) Ltd v Minister of Environmental Affairs* 2004 4 SA 490 (CC) para 48.

[54] See, for example, M Pieterse "Coming to Terms with Judicial Enforcement of Socio-Economic Rights" (2004) 20 *SAJHR* 383 410-411; D Bilchitz *Poverty and Fundamental Rights: The Justification and Enforcement of Socio-Economic Rights* (2007) 159-162.

effect to the relevant rights is much narrower.[55] The narrowing of the band, and in particular the extent of the narrowing, thus depends on the substantive implications of the relevant right. In terms of the *Bato Star* approach to reasonableness the determination of this narrowing, by understanding what the substantive implications of the relevant right are under the circumstances, is a first step to assess the reasonableness of the administrator's substantive choice. In overlap cases the reasonableness analysis therefore requires more than simply indicating that the eventual choice was a properly reasoned one.

A rights-based analysis would furthermore imply a proportionality inquiry in assessing whether the means adopted are reasonably capable of advancing the normative goals and purposes of the relevant socio-economic rights. As noted above, this would entail inquiries into the extent of the impact on the relevant right, whether there are measures less restrictive or invasive of the rights which could be taken, and whether the state's justifications for not providing the service in question outweigh the impact of the deprivation on the claimant. This approach largely resembles the inquiry followed in respect of the general limitations clause and incorporates many of the factors identified by O'Regan J in *Bato Star* as relevant in determining the reasonableness of administrative decisions.[56]

How does this approach gel with the drafting of sections 26 and 27, specifically the qualifying phrases of "reasonableness", "within available resources" and "progressive realisation" found in their second subsections? Sections 26(1) and 27(1) consists of an initial assertion of the rights to which everyone is entitled, followed by a second subsection which describes the nature of the duty resting on the state in relation to the realisation of the rights specified in the first subsection. The first two subsections are separated into two distinct, but interrelated provisions. This formulation clearly implies that the right cannot simply be reduced to an obligation of the state to behave reasonably in the broad sphere of social policy. Such a reading would amount, in Danie Brand's words, to no more than an injunction for the state to observe "structural principles of good governance" in relation to socio-economic rights.[57] Rather, the obligation on the state to take reasonable measures refers to a very specific objective, namely, "the realisation" of the rights specified in sections 26(1) and 27(1). The reasonableness of the state's acts and omissions must thus be assessed in relation to the achievement of this constitutionally specified goal. In *Khosa v Minister of Social Development*,[58] the Court explicitly distinguished the "relatively low" test for rationality review from the standard of reasonableness review in the context of socio-economic rights.

---

[55] An example of such a situation would be the facts and circumstances of *Minister of Health v Treatment Action Campaign (No 2)* 2002 5 SA 721 (CC). But even then, the Court explicitly granted government the latitude to adapt its policy "if equally better methods become available to it for the prevention of mother-to-child transmission of HIV" (para 135, Order para 4).

[56] *Bato Star Fishing (Pty) Ltd v Minister of Environmental Affairs* 2004 4 SA 490 (CC) para 45.

[57] Brand "Proceduralisation" in *Rights and Democracy* 53.

[58] 2004 6 SA 505 (CC).

Certainly, the concept of reasonableness in itself implies a measure of the flexibility regarding the precise means to be adopted to achieve the goals, but this flexibility does not absolve a court from interrogating whether the means chosen are reasonably likely to advance the achievement of the goal, ie fall within the band of reasonable options.[59] Given the fact that the inquiry centres on the protection of rights in the Bill of Rights, "strong-form" reasonableness is appropriate, which incorporates a proportionality inquiry. The narrowing of the band of options resulting from such "strong form" reasonableness review does not, however, exclude innovative approaches to the realisation of rights. By the narrowing of the band we do not propose that the court will exhaustively formulate the actual measures that a reasonable administrator may take. Within the defined markers that set the band in a given case there should be ample scope for experimentation with different measures to realise the right. The concepts of "available resources" and "progressive realisation" in sections 26(2) and 27(2) represent specific considerations within the overall reasonableness inquiry which a court must give weight to in assessing the state's justificatory arguments in opting for a particular measure. However, while resource constraints and "progressive realisation" may constitute a basis for justifying the state's lack of progress in advancing access to socio-economic rights, these factors also set standards of accountability within the reasonableness inquiry. Thus the CESCR has held that the concept of "progressive realisation" in article 2 of the Covenant is, on the one hand, a "necessary flexibility device, reflecting the realities of the real world and the difficulties involved for any country in ensuring full realisation of economic, social and cultural rights". On the other hand, the UN CESCR states:

"[T]he phrase must be read in the light of the overall objective, indeed the *raison d'être*, of the Covenant which is to establish clear obligations for States parties in respect of the full realization of the rights in question. It thus imposes an obligation to move as expeditiously and effectively as possible towards that goal."[60]

Similarly, a failure to use available resources optimally (such as under-expenditure of allocated budgets) or efficiently (such as wasteful expenditure)

---

[59] The ICESCR uses the phrase "by all appropriate means, including particularly the adoption of legislative measures" in art 2. This is the equivalent of the concept of "reasonable legislative and other measures" used in ss 26(2) and 27(2) of the South African Constitution. In relation to the obligation "to adopt all appropriate means" in the Covenant, the CESCR has commented as follows in relation to the supervision of States' obligations in the periodic reporting process:

"While each State party must decide for itself which means are the most appropriate under the circumstances with respect to each of the rights, the 'appropriateness' of the means chosen will not always be self-evident. It is therefore desirable that State parties' reports should indicate not only the measures that have been taken but also the basis on which they are considered to be the most 'appropriate' under the circumstances. However, the ultimate determination as to whether all appropriate measures have been taken remains one for the Committee to make." (UN CESCR *General Comment No 3: The Nature of States Parties Obligations (art 2(1))* (1990) UN Doc E/1991/23 para 4).

It is noteworthy that in the Optional Protocol to the International Covenant on Economic, Social and Cultural Rights (2008) UN Doc A/RES/63/117 establishing an individual communications procedure, the examination (or "review" standard set in art 8(4)) is "the reasonableness of the steps taken by the State Party".

[60] UN CESCR *General Comment No 3* para 9 (cited with approval in *Government of the Republic of South Africa v Grootboom* 2001 1 SA 46 (CC) para 45).

should be strong indicators of unreasonableness in the context of socio-economic rights adjudication.

Reasonableness review described above is both a normative and context-sensitive standard. It is normative in the sense that the purposes and proportionality of the state's measures are assessed in relation to the overall objective to ensure the realisation of the relevant socio-economic rights. It is context-sensitive in the sense that this inquiry requires close attention to the factual context of relevant cases, how the deprivation in question impacts on the particular claimant group and the factual basis of the state's justifications for its conduct. Where the impact of the state's acts or omissions on socio-economic rights is severe, the review standard is correspondingly tightened (or narrowed). Much weightier justifications are required from the state to justify its actions or inaction, as the case may be. This was acknowledged by the Court in the context of reviewing the state's compliance with its positive duties to ensure the safety and security of persons using commuter trains. It held that the assessment of reasonableness should include, among other factors, "the extent of any threat to fundamental rights should the duty not be met as well as the intensity of any harm that may result".[61] O'Regan J went on to hold, "[t]he more grave is the threat to fundamental rights, the greater is the responsibility on the duty bearer".[62]

The potential of the contextual reasonableness approach of *Bato Star* has, however, not been fully exploited. The actual application of the approach in both judgments in *Bato Star* was fairly weak. Both applied little more than thin rationality, mostly by accepting the say-so of the administrator and being satisfied that attention had been given to the transformative objectives at issue in taking the decision.[63] There is very little interrogation of the actual substantive outcome of the decision, that is, to assess how the administrator's choice will in substance advance transformation. In this sense both judgments seem much closer to the test advocated in *Bel Porto* where any link between objective and decision will do, regardless of how tenuous that link may be in substance.

3   The reasonableness standard in socio-economic rights jurisprudence

In this part, we consider the model of review applied to socio-economic rights cases where the primary breach is identified as arising from executive or legislative acts or omissions. In other words, the impugned conduct does not constitute administrative action falling within the scope of section 33 of the Constitution and PAJA. Here we focus primarily on cases in which it is argued that the presence or absence of legislation, social programmes or policies infringe the obligations imposed by sections 26, 27, 28(1)(c) and 29 of the Constitution.

---

[61]   *Rail Commuters Action Group v Transnet Ltd t/a Metrorail* 2005 2 SA 359 (CC) para 88.
[62]   Para 88.
[63]   See Davis (2006) *Acta Juridica* 23.

We commence by tracing the developments in the socio-economic rights jurisprudence concerning cases where it is alleged that the state has failed to comply with an aspect of the positive duties imposed by sections 26(1) and 27(1) read with their second subsections. To place the discussion of this category of cases in context we provide a brief overview of the structure of the review model applied respectively to the negative and positive duties imposed by the socio-economic rights, and thereafter to the rights formulated as qualified and unqualified entitlements. Our overall objectives in this part are twofold. First, we seek to examine to what extent the courts have developed a model of review in socio-economic rights jurisprudence which is distinct from a more formalistic model of administrative-law review. Second, we examine how the more substantive reasonableness review criteria formulated in the context of South African administrative law (discussed in the previous part) can contribute to the development of principled, transparent criteria for reviewing socio-economic rights claims.

3 1   The model of review applied to different types of socio-economic rights claims

Before proceeding to assess the model of review applied to positive socio-economic rights claims in the light of this understanding of the appropriate method of review, it is useful to situate this analysis within a broad overview of the structure of review applied to different types of socio-economic rights claims. The first noteworthy feature of the jurisprudence is that the Court has drawn a categorical distinction between the model of review applied to negative and positive duties, respectively. Thus where state action is held to deprive people of the existing access that they enjoy to socio-economic rights, this is held to constitute a *prima facie* breach of the negative duty "to respect" the relevant rights which the Court has located in sections 26(1) and 27(1).[64] The state's justifications for the infringement are assessed according to the stringent purpose and proportionality requirements of the general limitations clause.[65] This is consonant with the traditional two-stage approach to constitutional review applied in respect of most other rights in the Bill of Rights.

In contrast, when the alleged infringement is classified as a breach of the positive duties in respect of socio-economic rights (which the Court locates in sections 26(2) and 27(2)), a different model of review is applied. The Court has expressly held that the positive duties to achieve the realisation of socio-economic rights for those who lack access to socio-economic rights, or whose current access is inadequate, *is both defined and limited* by the criteria of

---

[64] See *Government of the Republic of South Africa v Grootboom* 2001 1 SA 46 (CC) para 34; *Minister of Health v Treatment Action Campaign (No 2)* 2002 5 SA 721 (CC) para 46, *Jaftha v Schoeman; Van Rooyen v Stoltz* 2005 2 SA 140 (CC) paras 33-34; *Governing Body of the Juma Musjid Primary School v Essay NO* 2011 8 BCLR 761 (CC).
[65] S 36 of the Constitution.

reasonableness, progressive realisation and the state's available resources.[66]
In adopting the reasonableness standard of constitutional review, the Court
has eschewed a relatively more absolutist model based on a minimum core
approach.

3 2   The development of reasonableness review in the jurisprudence

In the first socio-economic rights case to come before the Constitutional
Court, *Soobramoney v Minister of Health, KwaZulu-Natal*,[67] the Court focused
its inquiry on whether the justifications provided by the state for rejecting
the applicant for kidney dialysis treatment at a state hospital were fair and
reasonable. Applying a costs-benefits analysis the Court held that the rationing
criteria for kidney dialysis were designed to allow more people to benefit from
scarce kidney dialysis facilities than would be the case in the absence of such
criteria.[68] Devoting further resources to the kidney dialysis programme would
prejudice both other health-related expenditure (including on primary health
care), and the other legitimate needs which the state is required to meet.[69]
In *Soobramoney* minimal attention was paid to the distinctive feature of the
normative goals and purposes of the right of access to "health care services"
in section 27(1)(a) read with 27(2). In contrast, greater attention was paid
to the scope of section 27(3) (the right to emergency medical treatment),
including at least some comparative references to Indian jurisprudence.[70] The
justificatory analysis is thus conducted without reference to the critical first
step of reasonableness review described by Sadurski – determining the nature
of the decision to be taken, and assessing its normative importance.

Government of the Republic of South Africa v Grootboom[71] signalled the
evolution of a more clearly articulated model of review in respect of positive
socio-economic rights claims. The Court indicated that it would adopt, as
described by Danie Brand, the "means-end" justificatory model characteristic
of reasonableness review.[72] Thus it held in the context of the right of access to
adequate housing that measures must be adopted that

> "establish a coherent public housing programme *directed* towards the progressive realisation of the
> right of access to adequate housing within the State's available means. *The programme must be
> capable of facilitating the realisation of the right.* The precise contours and content of the measures

---

[66]   See *Soobramoney v Minister of Health, KwaZulu-Natal* 1998 1 SA 765 (CC) para 11; *Minister of Health
v Treatment Action Campaign (No 2)* 2002 5 SA 721 (CC) paras 30-39. For a critique of the different
models of review applied in respect of negative and positive duties, see S Liebenberg "*Grootboom* and the
Seduction of the Negative/Positive Duties Dichotomy" (2011) 26 *SAPL* 38-59.

[67]   1998 1 SA 765 (CC).

[68]   Paras 25-26.

[69]   Para 28.

[70]   Paras 12-21. For criticisms of the restrictive, and purely "negative duties" meaning given to s 27(3), see
Liebenberg *Socio-Economic Rights* 137-139; C Scott & P Alston "Adjudicating Constitutional Priorities
in a Transnational Context: A Comment on *Soobramoney's* Legacy and *Grootboom's* Promise" (2000) 16
SAJHR 206 245-248.

[71]   2001 1 SA 46 (CC).

[72]   Brand "Proceduralisation" in *Rights and Democracy* 40.

to be adopted are primarily a matter for the legislature and the executive. They must, however, ensure that the measures they adopt are reasonable."[73]

This is strongly suggestive of a proportionality approach. Government is allowed a margin of discretion relating to the specific policy choices – or band of options – it is free to choose from in giving effect to socio-economic rights.[74] However, the Court is required to inquire whether such measures constitute a reasonable response to the socio-economic deprivation in question, taking into account the constitutionally mandated goal in section 26(1) and 26(2) of ensuring that everyone has access to an adequate level of the relevant social services and resources.[75] Reasonableness must be assessed in the light of the normative goals that the relevant socio-economic rights seek to advance.[76]

The Court devoted attention to developing some of the substantive features of housing as a human right and how it contributes to the promotion of foundational constitutional values as well as other rights in the Bill of Rights. Thus Yacoob J held that housing "entails more than bricks and mortar".[77] He goes on to refer in this context to land, various services (such as water and sewage removal) as well as the physical structure. Moreover, the Court highlights some of the broader constitutional objectives that housing as human right is designed to foster such as enabling people to enjoy the other rights in the Bill of Rights, the advancement of racial and gender equality and "the evolution of a society in which men and women are equally able to achieve their full potential".[78] Human dignity is the value-based underpinning of the Court's key finding in *Grootboom* that reasonableness requires as a minimum or basic step short-term measures of relief for those whose needs are urgent and "who are living in intolerable conditions or crisis situations".[79] Thus a statistical improvement in housing delivery will not pass the reasonableness test if it is not appropriately attuned and responsive to the circumstances of those in desperate need.[80]

The Court also explicitly engages with international law in its judgment, specifically the ICESCR. While not endorsing the direct application of a minimum core approach[81] (outside the framework of reasonableness

---

[73] *Government of the Republic of South Africa v Grootboom* 2001 1 SA 46 (CC) para 41 (emphasis added). The overarching requirement that a reasonable programme in the context of socio-economic rights must be geared towards the realisation of the relevant right is also implicit in the further criteria for assessing the reasonableness of the programme referred to in *Grootboom*: the programme must be comprehensive, coherent, coordinated (paras 39-40, 95); appropriate financial and human resources must be allocated to it (paras 39, 68); and the programme must be balanced and flexible, making appropriate provision for short-, medium- and long-term needs (para 43).

[74] *Government of the Republic of South Africa v Grootboom* 2001 1 SA 46 (CC) para 41. See also *Rail Commuters Action Group v Transnet Ltd t/a Metrorail* 2005 2 SA 359 (CC) para 87.

[75] Frank Michelman describes the objectives of socio-economic rights to be the creation of "legal obligations on lawmakers to make their best effort to devise, adopt and execute policies and measures that will result in the desired social-outcome targets". F Michelman "Socioeconomic Rights in Constitutional Law: Explaining America Away" (2008) 6 *I CON* 663 667-668.

[76] See in this regard, *Government of the Republic of South Africa v Grootboom* 2001 1 SA 46 (CC) para 44.

[77] Para 35.

[78] Para 23.

[79] Paras 63-64, 99.

[80] Para 44 ("[T]he Constitution requires that everyone must be treated with care and concern").

[81] Paras 26-33.

review),[82] it did, as noted above, endorse the CESCR's interpretation of the concept of "progressive realisation" in General Comment No 3.[83]

Reasonableness will be assessed in the light of the relevant social, economic and historical context, and the capacity of institutions responsible for implementing the programme,[84] and allowance must be made for the availability of resources and the latitude of progressive realisation. Nevertheless, the overall inquiry remains whether the impugned measures are sufficiently effective and expeditious in achieving the goal of the full realisation of the relevant socio-economic rights. The more serious the socio-economic deprivation and its consequences, the proportionately greater the response expected from relevant organs of state.

In *Grootboom, Khosa, Minister of Health v Treatment Action Campaign (No 2)*[85] and the recent eviction-related jurisprudence,[86] a number of open-ended, non-exhaustive indicators[87] of the reasonableness of the measures adopted by the state have been developed. These include: reasonable formulation and implementation of programmes;[88] transparency;[89] non-discrimination against groups in their access to relevant programmes;[90] the impact of the deprivation on other rights such as life, dignity and equality[91]; and "meaningful engagement" with affected groups.[92] Most of these indicators express aspects of the central constitutional values of human dignity, non-discrimination, transparency, and participatory democracy.[93]

---

[82] Note specifically the possibility left open by the Court that "[t]here may be cases where it may be possible and appropriate to have regard to the content of a minimum core obligation to determine whether the measures taken by the State are reasonable" (*Government of the Republic of South Africa v Grootboom* 2001 1 SA 46 (CC) para 33). See also *Minister of Health v Treatment Action Campaign (No 2)* 2002 5 SA 721 (CC) para 34.

[83] *Government of the Republic of South Africa v Grootboom* 2001 1 SA 46 (CC) para 45. See also UN CESCR *General Comment No 3* (2000) para 9 on the CESCR's interpretation of the concept of progressive realisation.

[84] Para 43.

[85] 2002 5 SA 721 (CC).

[86] *Port Elizabeth Municipality v Various Occupiers* 2005 1 SA 217 (CC); *Occupiers of 51 Olivia Road, Berea Township and 197 Main Street, Johannesburg v City of Johannesburg* 2008 3 SA 208 (CC); *Residents of Joe Slovo Community, Western Cape v Thubelisha Homes* 2010 3 SA 454 (CC); *Abahlali baseMjondolo Movement SA v Premier, KwaZulu-Natal* 2010 2 BCLR 99 (CC); *City of Johannesburg Metropolitan Municipality v Blue Moonlight Properties 39 (Pty) Ltd* 2011 4 SA 337 (SCA).

[87] The Court noted in *Khosa v Minister of Social Development; Mahlaule v Minister of Social Development* 2004 6 SA 505 (CC) that the factors identified in the assessment of reasonableness were not a closed list and that "all relevant factors have to be taken into account". The Court went on to observe that "[w]hat is relevant may vary from case to case depending on the particular facts and circumstances" (para 44).

[88] *Government of the Republic of South Africa v Grootboom* 2001 1 SA 46 (CC) paras 40-43.

[89] *Minister of Health v Treatment Action Campaign (No 2)* 2002 5 SA 721 (CC) para 123.

[90] *Khosa v Minister of Social Development; Mahlaule v Minister of Social Development* 2004 6 SA 505 (CC).

[91] Para 44.

[92] See the eviction cases listed in n 83 above and *Governing Body of the Juma Musjid Primary School v Essay NO* 2011 8 BCLR 761 (CC).

[93] Carol Steinberg argues that it is the heavier weighting of the values of human dignity and equality and the closer scrutiny of whether government programmes have been sufficiently attentive to these values that distinguishes reasonableness review in the context of socio-economic rights jurisprudence from an administrative-law model of review where constitutional rights are not implicated. C Steinberg "Can Reasonableness Protect the Poor? A Review of South Africa's Socio-Economic Rights Jurisprudence" (2006) 123 *SALJ* 264 277, 281.

While in *Khosa* there is some attempt to articulate the goals and values of social security as a human right,[94] very little explicit attempt is made by the Court in *Minister of Health v Treatment Action Campaign* to articulate the normative content of the right of access to health care services in section 27(1). The case is resolved in favour of the claimants primarily on the basis of reviewing the rationality of the arguments put forward by government in favour of its restrictive and inflexible approach to the provision of Nevirapine throughout the public health sector to reduce mother-to-child transmission of HIV in childbirth.[95] This is not far removed from the ground of review in administrative law that the decision is not rationally connected to the reasons given for it.[96]

3 3   Reasonableness review in *Mazibuko*

The leading recent case on the review of positive duties in the context of socio-economic rights claims is *Mazibuko v City of Johannesburg*.[97] We focus here on the first leg of the claim which concerned the sufficiency of the City of Johannesburg's policy relating to the quantum of a free basic water supply, although both legs of the claim are closely related.[98] In particular, the Court was requested to consider whether the decision by the City to limit its supply of free basic water to six kilolitres of free water per month to every accountholder in the city was in conflict with the right of access to "sufficient" water in section 27(1)(b) of the Constitution read with subsection (2), or with section 11 of the Water Services Act 108 of 1997.

In its judgment, the Court gave a narrow construction of the "reasonableness review" standard for assessing the positive duties imposed by socio-economic rights as developed in the *Grootboom, TAC* and *Khosa* cases.[99] The Court justified its deferential stance by reference to institutional concerns regarding the "proper role" of courts *vis-á-vis* the other branches of government. Thus O'Regan J stated:

"[O]rdinarily it is institutionally inappropriate for a court to determine precisely what the achievement of any particular social and economic right entails and what steps government should take to ensure progressive realisation of the right. This is a matter, in the first place, for the legislature and executive, the institutions of government best placed to investigate social conditions in the light of available

---

[94] See, for example, *Khosa v Minister of Social Development; Mahlaule v Minister of Social Development* 2004 6 SA 505 (CC) paras 74, 76-77, 79-81.

[95] See also Brand "Proceduralisation" in *Rights and Democracy* 50-51; Bilchitz *Poverty and Fundamental Rights* 152-162.

[96] See s 6(2)(f)(ii)(dd) of PAJA. In rebutting the rationality of the state's justifications, the Court accorded significant weight to the excellent medical evidence marshaled by the Treatment Action Campaign as well as the opinions of international and local expert bodies in the field such as the World Health Organisation and the Medicines Control Council. This arguably infuses a more substantive dimension in the degree of scrutiny applied in *Minister of Health v Treatment Action Campaign (No 2)* 2002 5 SA 721 (CC) than a mere *Wednesbury* review standard.

[97] 2010 4 SA 1 (CC).

[98] For a critique of the reasoning adopted by the Court in relation to the second leg of the claim relating to the installation of prepaid water meters, see G Quinot "Substantive Reasoning in Administrative-Law Adjudication" (2010) 3 *CCR* 111 124-136.

[99] For criticisms of the narrow construction and application of the reasonableness review standard adopted in *Mazibuko v City of Johannesburg* 2010 4 SA 1 (CC), see Liebenberg *Socio-Economic Rights* 468-472; L Williams "The Role of the Courts in the Quantitative Implementation of Social and Economic Rights: A Comparative Study" (2010) 3 *CCR* 141.

budgets and to determine what targets are achievable in relation to social and economic rights. Indeed, it is desirable as a matter of democratic accountability that they should do so for it is their programmes and promises that are subjected to democratic popular choice."[100]

She went on to hold that the Court's role in enforcing the positive duties imposed by socio-economic rights is restricted to two primary scenarios. First, if government does not take steps to realise socio-economic rights, "the courts will require the government to take steps".[101] Second, the courts will intervene if the measures adopted by government "fail to meet the constitutional standard of reasonableness".[102] Three basic situations would be indicative of unreasonableness: a) where no provision is made for those most desperately in need;[103] b) socio-economic policies contain unjustifiable exclusions or restrictions;[104] and c) a failure by government "continually to review its policies to ensure that the achievement of the right is progressively realised".[105]

Applying these criteria the Court found that it had not been shown that the refusal of the City of Johannesburg to provide more than the basic minimum water supply of 25 litres per person per day (or six kilolitres per household per month) prescribed in Regulation 3(b) of the National Water Standards Regulations[106] to the Water Services Act to the households in Phiri was unreasonable. Persuasive facts for the Court appear to have been that at least some basic water was being provided, that there were others who were "worse off" than the Phiri community,[107] there was provision for flexibility in the programme through the additional water available through the City of Johannesburg's indigency policy,[108] and it would be "administratively extremely burdensome and costly, if possible at all"[109] to provide water to households in Phiri on a per person universal basis instead of the set allowance of six kilolitres per month per household basis (based on the assumption of 25 litres per person per day in a household of eight persons).[110] It was argued that this resulted in an insufficient supply of water to larger households, particularly in the light of the fact that with the acute housing shortage in the townships stands were frequently occupied by more than one household, resulting in some stands, such as Ms Mazibuko's, accommodating as many as

---

[100]   *Mazibuko v City of Johannesburg* 2010 4 SA 1 (CC) para 61.
[101]   Para 67.
[102]   Para 67.
[103]   *Government of the Republic of South Africa v Grootboom* 2001 1 SA 46 (CC).
[104]   The Court cites its judgment in *Minister of Health v Treatment Action Campaign (No 2)* 2002 5 SA 721 (CC) as an example of a programme in which the Court simply ordered government to remove an "unreasonable limitation or exclusion". For criticism of this reading of the basis for the *Minister of Health v Treatment Action Campaign (No 2)* 2002 5 SA 721 (CC) decision, see Liebenberg *Socio-Economic Rights* 469.
[105]   *Mazibuko v City of Johannesburg* 2010 4 SA 1 (CC) para 67.
[106]   Regulations relating to compulsory national standards and measures to conserve water, GN R 509 in *GG* 22355 of 08-06-2001.
[107]   The Court referred to the fact that, according to Statistics South Africa *Census 2001* (2001), approximately a tenth of all households within the jurisdiction of the City of Johannesburg have no access to a tap providing clean water within 200 metres of their home. *Mazibuko v City of Johannesburg* 2010 4 SA 1 (CC) para 7.
[108]   Paras 90-102.
[109]   Para 89.
[110]   Paras 84, 86-89.

three families (20 people). In the end the Court refrained from engaging with the arguments regarding the sufficiency of the 25 litres per person per day basic water supply, despite acknowledging at the outset of its judgment that, "[w]ater is life" and that

> "[h]uman beings need water to drink, to cook, to wash and to grow our food. Without it, we will die."[111]

The considerations referred to above, which carried weight in the Court's judgment, should undoubtedly form part of the proportionality analysis in a case such as *Mazibuko*. However, these justifications are weighed without a prior rigorous analysis of the nature of the right at issue and the impact of the basic water allowance on households in the circumstances of Ms Mazibuko.[112] The result is that there is no narrowing of the bands of purpose and proportionality which should occur in judicial review where fundamental rights are at stake. Judicial review in *Mazibuko* accordingly has more in common with "weak form" rationality review than "strong form" reasonableness review.

Paradoxically, if one were to assume that the action at stake in *Mazibuko* qualified as administrative action,[113] the *Bato Star* test for reasonableness may have resulted in much closer scrutiny of the context than was actually done in that judgment, solely in terms of section 27. Especially the last two factors listed by O'Regan J in *Bato Star*, namely "the nature of the competing interests involved and the impact of the decision on the lives and well-being of those affected",[114] may have invited a closer look at both the decisions regarding the quantum of a free basic water supply and the installation of pre-payment meters against the substantive entitlements of section 27 and the real impact on the people of Phiri. Since the well-reasoned and rational decision-making dimension of the analysis would have been done in terms of section 33(1), the focus on section 27 could have remained entirely substantive. This indicates how the interaction of reasonableness under administrative justice and socio-economic rights in overlap cases can force a review court into truly substantive engagement with both socio-economic rights and administrative action. It also illustrates how the combination of the different provisions in a single model of reasonableness review can avoid a proceduralisation of socio-economic rights by locating that dimension of the review in section 33.

3 4 The relationship between the "internal" reasonableness test in sections 26 and 27 and the general limitations clause

The proportionality inquiry that we have put forward in reviewing socio-economic rights claims is identical to the justification inquiry normally taking place in terms of section 36. The potential overlap between the internal "reasonableness" inquiry in sections 26(2) and 27(2) and the reasonableness

---

[111] Para 1.
[112] See the more detailed engagement with these elements in the High Court and Supreme Court of Appeal judgments in *Mazibuko*: *Mazibuko v City of Johannesburg* 2008 4 All SA 471 (W); *City of Johannesburg v Mazibuko* 2009 3 SA 592 (SCA).
[113] This is not a particularly big assumption, see Quinot (2010) 3 *CCR* 135-136.
[114] *Bato Star Fishing (Pty) Ltd v Minister of Environmental Affairs* 2004 4 SA 490 (CC) para 45.

inquiry in the general limitations clause (section 36) was recognised by the Court in *Khosa*.[115] However, Mokgoro J did not decide whether a different threshold of reasonableness should be applied in section 36. She held that even if a different test should be applied, she was satisfied that the exclusion of permanent residents from the relevant social assistance scheme would not meet the criteria for reasonableness and justifiability in terms of section 36.[116]

As argued above, sections 26(2) and 27(2) both define the nature of the state's obligations in relation to the rights in sections 26(1) and 27(1), and permit the state to raise specific justificatory factors such as resource constraints and the latitude of "progressive realisation". "Reasonableness" in the second subsection can in fact incorporate the proportionality inquiry of section 36, making section 36 largely redundant in this context except for the threshold requirement that a limitation of rights must be in terms of a law of general application. However, the strategic danger of subsuming the limitations inquiry into the rights definitional stage of the inquiry is that the traditional two-stage methodology of constitutional analysis is blurred. This can lead to a lack of principled, focused attention on the scope and purposes of the relevant socio-economic right, before turning to consider the state's justificatory arguments.[117] As noted above, crucial to a proper application of the proportionality requirement is a clear understanding of the nature of the right affected,[118] and the impact of the challenged conduct or omissions on the normative purposes and values which the relevant right seeks to promote.[119]

The two-stage approach and an explicit consideration of the factors to be considered under the general limitations clause promotes transparency in identifying and weighing the relevant considerations underpinning the ultimate decision of the Court. If the trend is to continue whereby the internal reasonableness standard in sections 26(2) and 27(2) is to do the heavy lifting of definition and limitation, then the Court should at least separate out the different strands of the reasoning process and commence with an initial principled consideration of the relevant right asserted in sections 26(1) and 27(1), and the impact of the impugned conduct on the values and purposes promoted by the relevant right. The focus at this stage is on the right and rights-holder. Proper attention to this inquiry provides the normative and contextual framework for proceeding to apply a proportionality analysis to the state's arguments that its conduct meets the constitutional standard of reasonableness. This is the same approach that we have put forward for the

---

[115] *Khosa v Minister of Social Development; Mahlaule v Minister of Social Development* 2004 6 SA 505 (CC) para 83.

[116] Para 84. Compare the minority judgment of Ngcobo J (as he then was). See I Rautenbach "The Right to Access to Sufficient Water and the Two Stage Approach to the Application of the Bill of Rights" (2011) 74 *THRHR* 107 117-119 for an analysis of the different constructions of the relationship between ss 26 and 27 and the general limitations clause.

[117] See Liebenberg *Socio-Economic Rights* 201-202.

[118] This is the first factor to be considered in assessing the reasonableness and justifiability of limitations to rights in terms of s 36 (s 36(1)(a)).

[119] This corresponds with the third factor in the general limitation clause which requires consideration of the "nature and extent of the limitation" (s 36(1)(c)).

interaction between section 33 and socio-economic rights in overlap cases above. This will not only foster transparency in the judicial reasoning process in socio-economic rights claims, but will also ensure that reasonableness in the context of socio-economic rights adjudication is appropriately attuned to the normative considerations of human rights claims.

4 Conclusion

Our analysis above indicates that there can be a unified model of reasonableness review across cases involving administrative and non-administrative measures impacting on socio-economic rights. The various reasonableness standards found in distinct provisions of the Bill of Rights are capable of being interpreted in a way that promotes a coherent model of review. In terms of this model, reasonableness under the various provisions overlap, but do not duplicate the same function. There is rather an interaction between these standards that promote the core advantages of reasonableness as a model of review.

In administrative law, the best model for reasonableness review flows from the judgments in *Bato Star*. In terms of this model, reasonableness review is a contextual inquiry with the level of scrutiny being determined by a number of factors focusing on the context of the relevant case. This context involves both the normative context and the factual context. The former refers to the other constitutional provisions implicated in the case. The model allows the court to engage with the substance of the administrative decision at stake, but not in order to assess whether the correct decision was taken on the merits, but whether the decision falls within a band of reasonable decisions on the merits. The normative context plays a critical role in defining that band of options. In cases where administrative action impacts on socio-economic rights (what we call overlap cases) the substantive entitlements found in the relevant socio-economic right determines to a large extent the scope of the band of options available to the administrator. In effect, in overlap cases, the band is narrowed with reference to the substance of the relevant socio-economic right.

In cases involving measures impacting on socio-economic rights that are not administrative action, mostly executive or legislative measures (what we call non-overlap cases), the model of review is necessarily different from the one in overlap cases. In these cases, the Constitutional Court applies a different model of review depending on whether the case is classified as a breach of a negative duty imposed by the relevant socio-economic right, or a breach of a positive duty. In the former type of case the court assesses the justificatory analysis of the infringing measures within the strict proportionality analysis of the limitations clause. However, in the latter type of case the court subsumes all aspects of the reasonableness analysis within the relevant right. The effect, particularly in the context of cases involving the review of positive duties, is that very little attention is given to the substantive content of the relevant socio-economic right. All the work is done in the justificatory analysis.

Under the model we advocate here, a distinct role is given to reasonableness analysis in terms of the relevant socio-economic right as a first step of the model. This first step involves giving content to the relevant right in all types of cases before moving on to a justification analysis whether in terms of the internal reasonableness test of sections 26(2) or 27(2) or the general limitations clause analysis under section 36. Again, the band of options is narrowed down with reference to the substance of the right before the state's actions are analysed against those options.

This two-stage model of reasonableness analysis in both overlap and non-overlap cases facilitates many of the core advantages of reasonableness review. Firstly, it brings the context of the relevant case to the fore. Context, both normative and factual, plays a pivotal role in assessing the reasonableness of the measures at stake. Secondly, since the model is highly contextual, review can be appropriately individualised. There is thus less danger of setting substantive standards that may be inappropriate in another context or time. Thirdly, the model promotes greater transparency in legal reasoning in that the competing value and policy considerations at stake, and the method and choices made in weighing them are openly acknowledged and set out in the judgment, including judicial justification for the level of scrutiny applied. This promotes greater transparency in legal reasoning and enables a principled development of factors informing judicial intervention and non-intervention.[120] Since an assessment of the process and substance of the relevant measures are kept separate, there is less of a danger that these will be blurred with a resultant lack of transparency in the application of either one. Particular importance is accorded to the substantive dimensions of socio-economic rights in this model.

Despite the advantages noted above, our analysis indicates that the potential of a coherent reasonableness model of review has not been fully developed in the jurisprudence. The review standard in cases involving socio-economic rights has not been appropriately narrowed to reflect the particular purposes and values that these rights seek to advance. This leaves the judiciary ill-equipped to play a significant role in catalysing the public and private measures required to give effect to the substantive commitments of our transformative Constitution.[121]

SUMMARY

This contribution explores the standard of reasonableness review applied in both administrative justice and socio-economic rights jurisprudence in South Africa. The first part traces the development of reasonableness as a standard of review in administrative law, and the significant shift towards a more substantive conception of review. The implications of this shift for cases involving review of administrative action impacting on socio-economic rights (what we term, "overlap cases") are examined. The second part of the contribution examines reasonableness review in socio-economic rights cases where the cause of action is not formulated in terms of administrative law (what we term, "non-overlap cases"). This typically concerns cases where it is alleged that the legislature or executive branches of government have failed to fulfil the obligations imposed by socio-economic rights. In this section we highlight the failure of existing constitutional jurisprudence on socio-economic rights

---

[120] See A Pillay "Reviewing Reasonableness: An Appropriate Standard for Evaluating State Action and Inaction?" (2005) 122 *SALJ* 419 420; Davis (2006) *Acta Juridica* 33.

[121] On the catalytic function of judicial review see K Young "A Typology of Economic and Social Rights Adjudication: Exploring the Catalytic Function of Judicial Review" (2010) 8 *I CON* 385.

to develop a substantive account of the normative purposes and values promoted by these rights. We argue that it remains possible for such an account to be developed within the existing framework of reasonableness review applied to positive socio-economic rights claims. The chapter concludes with an argument in favour of the development of a single model of reasonableness review across socio-economic rights and administrative justice cases. While the reasonableness standards under the different sections overlap, they should not result in duplication, but fulfil different functions in the review. Taken together, reasonableness offers a model of review of socio-economic rights that promotes a number of key constitutional objectives. These include transparency, the justification of all forms of public action, proper consideration of the factual and normative context, and the development of the substantive dimensions of the socio-economic rights in the Constitution.

CHAPTER 12

TAKING POVERTY SERIOUSLY: THE SOUTH AFRICAN CONSTITUTIONAL COURT AND SOCIO-ECONOMIC RIGHTS

Stuart Wilson

Jackie Dugard

1 Introduction

The Constitutional Court ("the Court") has yet to develop a substantive account of the positive obligations socio-economic rights place on the state. It has suggested that it is precluded from doing so by the particular formulation of the separation of powers doctrine it has adopted in its later socio-economic rights jurisprudence. Accordingly, in *Mazibuko v City of Johannesburg*,[1] the Court held that

> "ordinarily it is institutionally inappropriate for a court to determine precisely what the achievement of any particular social and economic right entails and what steps government should take to ensure the progressive realisation of the right. This is a matter, in the first place, for the legislature and executive, the institutions of government best placed to investigate social conditions in the light of available budgets and to determine what targets are achievable in relation to social and economic rights. Indeed, it is desirable as a matter of democratic accountability that they should do so for it is their programmes and promises that are subjected to democratic popular choice."[2]

Consistent with the constraints identified above, the Court has adopted a framework which mediates the interpretation of the state's positive obligations through the prism of administrative law. This interpretive move has resulted in a test which requires policies giving effect to socio-economic rights to be "reasonable" and to be implemented in a procedurally fair manner.

In this chapter, we argue that this approach has not resulted in a jurisprudence which responds adequately to the interests of the poor. It is true that the Court regularly speaks, in general terms, of the need to adopt a transformative adjudicative paradigm.[3] Yet, in the area of socio-economic rights, the Court has chosen not to consider the full transformative potential of the role it might

---

[1] 2010 4 SA 1 (CC).

[2] Para 60.

[3] The Court has repeatedly recognised the transformative nature of the Constitution. See, for example, *Road Accident Fund v Mdeyide* 2011 2 SA 26 (CC) para 125; *Hassam v Jacobs NO* 2009 5 SA 572 (CC) para 28; *Biowatch v Registrar, Genetic Resources* 2009 6 SA 232 (CC) para 17; *Bato Star Fishing (Pty) Ltd v Minister of Environmental Affairs* 2004 4 SA 490 (CC) paras 73-74.

have in eliminating structural inequality and disadvantage. This is indicated
by the fact that it has instead turned away from what claimants say about their
lived experiences of poverty in favour of an abstract evaluation of the state's
justifications for its refusal to respond to them. Where lived experiences of
poverty and structural disadvantage are considered, they are afforded insufficient weight.

These interpretive moves construct poverty not as a *prima facie*
transgression of legal norms, but as a banal feature of the social order,
which judges are enjoined to "manage" rather than attempt to eliminate.
They have contributed to the depoliticisation and domestication of poverty
within fundamentally unjust pre-existing patterns of resource distribution,
social control and disempowerment.[4] The interests poor people seek to
vindicate through litigation have not been meaningfully addressed in the
Court's socio-economic rights jurisprudence. It seems that these interests
are, for the moment, to be defined and enforced through "democratic popular
choice" and not through adjudication. Yet it is precisely in the supposedly
"democratic" arena that poor peoples' claims for better access to social and
economic goods are marginalised and diminished. This is achieved in no
small measure by bureaucratic processes which systemically exclude them
and a dominant economic paradigm which tolerates high levels of structural
unemployment.[5]

We do not suggest that the Court can itself alter the balance of economic
forces that sustains structural disadvantage. We do, however, suggest that the
Court has underestimated the institutional role it can play in enabling poor
people to articulate and assert their entitlements to the basic social goods.[6] In
order for the Court's role in addressing poverty to move from the ameliorative
to the transformative, the Court must take much greater account, within its
interpretive and adjudicative paradigm, of the lived experience of poverty.
We agree with Sandra Liebenberg,[7] when she says that there is nothing in
the Constitution of the Republic of South Africa, 1996 ("the Constitution") or
the doctrine of the separation of powers that precludes the Court from taking
account of the needs, purposes and values which must be served by socio-
economic rights.[8] The Court can and must, we argue, develop a theory of
these needs and purposes, by listening more closely to what poor litigants say
in their papers about how the social context of poverty affects their access to
socio-economic goods. Legal practitioners, too, must be prepared to put time

---

[4]   See D Brand "The 'Politics of Need Interpretation' and the Adjudication of Socio-Economic Rights
      Claims in South Africa" in AJ van der Walt (ed) *Theories of Social and Economic Justice* (2005) 17 17-36;
      T Madlingozi "Good Victim, Bad Victim: Apartheid's Beneficiaries, Victims and the Struggle for Social
      Justice" in W le Roux & K van Marle (eds) *Law, Memory and the Legacy of Apartheid: Ten Years After
      AZAPO v President of South Africa* (2007) 107 107-126.
[5]   H Marais *South Africa: Pushed to the Limit: The Political Economy of Change* (2011) 126.
[6]   See S Gloppen "Courts and Social Transformation: An Analytical Framework" in R Gargarella, P
      Domingo & T Roux (eds) *Courts and Social Transformation in New Democracies: An Institutional Voice
      for the Poor?* (2006) 35 35-60.
[7]   S Liebenberg *Socio-Economic Rights: Adjudication under a Transformative Constitution* (2010).
[8]   180.

and effort into understanding these needs and experiences and to give voice to them in pleadings, affidavits and written argument.

We suggest that relatively small changes in the Court's interpretive paradigm can lead to big changes in outcomes. This may appear naïve to some. However, we choose to assume that the interpretive paradigm the Court has constructed for itself must shape how it responds to the claims poor people place before it. To assume otherwise would lead to the cynical conclusion that all the Court does when it decides socio-economic rights cases is pick an outcome acceptable to all or most of its members and reason back from it. We do not accept this. Instead, we propose changes to the paradigm which, in our view, would lead, over time, to a fairly substantial enhancement in the Court's role in addressing poverty and inequality. Yet, in what follows, we do not propose that the Court announces any fundamental departure from the doctrine of the separation of powers, or that it abandons completely the administrative law concepts it has deployed until now. The changes we advocate pre-suppose that the Court has over-constrained itself with these doctrines and concepts, which do not in fact limit opportunities for transformative adjudication in the way that the Court appears to assume that they do. In short, we seek to point out what we consider to be a blind spot in the Court's reasoning in socio-economic rights – one which is not apparent in other areas of its jurisprudence. Once this blind spot is addressed, we suggest that the Court's socio-economic rights jurisprudence will not only be better reasoned, but will also be more responsive to the needs of the most vulnerable of the claimants who turn to it for redress.

In the first part of this chapter, we sketch out the limitations of the Court's approach to the positive obligations imposed by socio-economic rights, including the justifications it offers for refusing to go further. We point out that, after rejecting the "minimum core" approach to the interpretation of socio-economic rights in *Government of the Republic of South Africa v Grootboom*,[9] the Court's later jurisprudence failed to engage with any contextual standards against which state action may be assessed. This is despite the Court having foregrounded such an approach in *Grootboom* itself.[10]

We then move on to consider how things could be different. We begin from the assumption that rights, at minimum, assign legal recognition to specific human interests. We set out a model of adjudication which pays appropriate regard to those interests, but still allows them to be weighed in the balance against the arguments based on general welfare, capacity and resource constraints which are generally advanced in order to justify the state's unwillingness to respond to them. We argue that the balancing exercise the Court performs in assessing the reasonableness of state policies is necessarily skewed against poor litigants unless weight is attached to the specific needs and interests they approach the Court to vindicate.

We go on to emphasise the role to be played, at every step of this analysis, by a contextual analysis of poverty and disadvantage in developing an account of the interests to be protected and advanced by socio-economic rights. We

---

9   2000 1 SA 46 (CC).
10   Paras 41, 43-45, 56.

do so with reference to three cases in which the Court, in our view, paid no or insufficient regard to the claimants' interests. In *Mazibuko*, we argue that uncontested contextual evidence of the urgent and intense distress caused by the claimants' lack of access to sufficient water was virtually ignored in preference to a generalised superficial examination of state policy. In *Residents of the Joe Slovo Community, Western Cape v Thubelisha Homes*,[11] the Court assigned insufficient weight to the hardship which would be caused by a forced eviction and long-range relocation from Langa Township to Delft in Cape Town. In *Nokotyana v Ekhurhuleni Municipality*,[12] the Court refused to consider whether a municipal policy of requiring ten families to share one toilet in an informal settlement was a reasonable measure to secure the dignity of those families. In each of these cases, we consider how a more contextual analysis of poverty and structural disadvantage could have led to an outcome that both granted appropriate relief to the claimants and at the same time allowed the Court to refrain from the kind of judicial policymaking, which would be inconsistent with its conception of the separation of powers.

2   The Court's general approach to positive socio-economic rights claims

Aspects of the Court's socio-economic rights jurisprudence have led some commentators to suggest that the Court has adopted an "administrative-law model" for the enforcement of socio-economic rights.[13] In its attempt to balance the need to hold the state accountable to the Constitution with deferring to its socio-economic policy choices, the Court has borrowed from administrative law to construct a framework within which to evaluate compliance with the state's positive obligations.

It would be a mistake to suggest that the Court's socio-economic rights jurisprudence as a whole can be reduced to an application of an adapted conception of administrative law. In protecting against negative infringements of socio-economic rights, the Court has given the right to housing substantive content. It has held that any measure that brings existing security of tenure to an end is *prima facie* a violation of the right of access to adequate housing.[14] *Grootboom* itself must also be understood as more than an exercise in

---

[11]   2010 3 SA 454 (CC).

[12]   2010 4 BCLR 312 (CC).

[13]   This part of the chapter relies to an extent on our exposition of the administrative-law model provided in our chapter "Constitutional Jurisprudence: The First and Second Waves" in M Langford, B Cousins, J Dugard & T Madlingozi (eds) *Symbols and Substance: The Role and Impact of Socio-Economic Rights Strategies in South Africa* (forthcoming Cambridge University Press, 2012). For a critique of the administrative-law model for socio-economic rights see D Bilchitz "Giving Socio-Economic Rights Teeth: The Minimum Core and its Importance" (2002) 118 *SALJ* 484 484-581; D Bilchitz "Towards a Reasonable Approach to the Minimum Core: Laying the Foundations for Future Socio-Economic Rights Jurisprudence" (2003) 19 *SAJHR* 1; D Brand "The Proceduralisation of South African Socio-Economic Rights Jurisprudence or 'What are Socio-Economic Rights For?'" in H Botha, A van der Walt & J van der Walt (eds) *Rights and Democracy in a Transformative Constitution* (2003) 33; S Liebenberg "The Interpretation of Socio-Economic Rights" in S Woolman, T Roux, J Klaaren, A Stein, M Chaskalson & M Bishop (eds) *CLoSA* 2 ed (OS 2004) 33-1; S Liebenberg "South Africa: Adjudicating Social Rights Under a Transformative Constitution" in M Langford (ed) *Social Rights Jurisprudence: Emerging Trends in International and Comparative Law* (2008) 75.

[14]   *Jaftha v Schoeman; Van Rooyen v Stoltz* 2005 2 SA 140 (CC) paras 25-34.

administrative-law reasoning, since it generated a substantive principle of broad application: that state policy must provide relief in the form of temporary shelter to desperately poor people facing housing crises.[15]

However, it is true that there are aspects of the Court's jurisprudence which indicate that it generally prefers to deploy the administrative-law concepts of rationality, reasonableness and procedural fairness in testing state policy. *Soobramoney v Minister of Health*,[16] *Minister of Health v Treatment Action Campaign ("TAC")*,[17] *Port Elizabeth Municipality v Various Occupiers*,[18] *Occupiers of 51 Olivia Road, Berea Township and 197 Main Street, Johannesburg v City of Johannesburg*[19] and *Khosa v Minister of Social Development*[20] are examples of this in that they all focus on the rationality of conscious decisions to exclude classes of persons from socio-economic programmes or on the procedural fairness of the implementation of those programmes. In *TAC*, the Court was asked to consider the reasonableness of government policy in facilitating access to antiretroviral treatment to prevent mother to child transmission of HIV. It found that the decision to limit access to antiretroviral treatment to a few test sites was irrational because there was no compelling reason not to provide treatment where it was medically indicated outside a limited number of research and testing sites. Likewise, *Khosa* characterised the exclusion of South African permanent residents from state social assistance programmes as irrational.[21] The Court in that case was guided by the impact of the exclusion on the applicants' right to equality. The right to social security, the Court held, vests in "everyone". To exclude permanent residents from its social security programme affected the applicant's rights to dignity and equality in material respects. Without sufficient reason being established to justify such an impairment of the applicants' equality rights, the exclusion was irrational and unconstitutional. *Soobramoney* was about the rationality of a health care rationing decision. *Port Elizabeth Municipality* and *Olivia Road* were chiefly concerned with the lack of adequate consultation with unlawful occupiers before an eviction order was made against them. Although it is true that both decisions hint at substantive entitlements for potential evictees, these merely echoed the entitlement to temporary shelter the Court had already developed in *Grootboom*.

The deployment of administrative-law concepts in this way has provided a device with which the Court can evaluate state policy without creating novel entitlements or designing new tests to which socio-economic policy may be subjected. It has also created an apparent overlap between the constitutional- and administrative-law concepts of reasonableness. Both the constitutional- and administrative-law concepts of reasonableness require more than a simple connection between means and ends, but admit of a range

---

[15] *Government of the Republic of South Africa v Grootboom* 2000 1 SA 46 (CC) para 99.
[16] 1998 1 SA 765 (CC).
[17] 2002 5 SA 721 (CC).
[18] 2005 1 SA 217 (CC).
[19] 2008 3 SA 208 (CC).
[20] 2004 6 SA 505 (CC).
[21] Paras 53 and 85.

of possibly reasonable decisions or policies within which a court will defer to the executive.[22] The question a court will ask in both cases is: on the facts placed before it, has the state adopted measures or taken a decision which can reasonably achieve the relevant legislative or constitutional purpose?[23]

Yet there is a crucial difference. In the case of the exercise of administrative power, the legislation in terms of which the decision is taken will normally define the purpose of the exercise of the power, and the interests to be taken into account, with some precision. This is almost never the case when considering the reasonableness of measures to give effect to socio-economic rights, because the purpose of the rights in question, or the interests they exist to satisfy, are not defined in the Constitution. The Court must identify them through interpretation.

In *TAC, Soobramoney, Khosa, Port Elizabeth Municipality* and *Olivia Road* the Court was able to come to a conclusion by weighing up the facts before it and making a value judgment as to whether or not the measures under scrutiny were rational, reasonable or procedurally fair. It did so without importing any particular conception of the interests to be served by the rights in question.

Grootboom alone is different, at least in the positive obligations jurisprudence. This is because that case saw the Court appeal to a second-order principle which gave some definition and purpose to the positive aspect of the right of access to adequate housing. This principle was that desperately poor people in situations of crisis should be provided with temporary shelter, pending the provision of permanent housing which will fully realise their rights of access to adequate housing. The *Grootboom* decision was a response to the urgent interests the claimants had in some form of shelter – as a temporary expedient – short of fully developed permanent housing.

What the Court has been reluctant to do since *Grootboom* is to exercise the power the Constitution assigns it explicitly to determine the interests socio-economic rights themselves exist to protect and advance. Reasonableness and procedural fairness are not sufficient to define these interests. They simply act as a prism through which the enforceability of these interests can be considered on the facts of a particular case. At best, they simply embroider the entitlements already guaranteed in section 33 of the Constitution.[24] What is required, as Danie Brand evocatively puts it, is an account of what socio-economic rights are for.[25] In relation to what needs and interests must the state's measures be reasonable?

The considerations that the Court has said count against such a substantive account are unconvincing. The first consideration, relied on in *Grootboom* and

---

[22] Compare, for example, *Government of the Republic of South Africa v Grootboom* 2000 1 SA 46 (CC) para 41 with *Bato Star Fishing (Pty) Ltd v Minister of Environmental Affairs* 2004 4 SA 490 (CC) para 49.

[23] Compare *Government of the Republic of South Africa v Grootboom* 2000 1 SA 46 (CC) para 41 with *Bato Star Fishing (Pty) Ltd v Minister of Environmental Affairs* 2004 4 SA 490 (CC) para 48.

[24] S 33(1) states that "[e]veryone has the right to administrative action that is lawful, reasonable and procedurally fair". S 33(2) states that "[e]veryone whose rights have been adversely affected by administrative action has the right to be given written reasons".

[25] Brand "The Proceduralisation of South African Socio-Economic Rights Jurisprudence" in *Rights and Democracy* 33.

TAC, albeit in the context of a minimum core argument, was that the Court lacks the institutional capacity necessary to embark upon a wide-ranging enquiry into what the realisation of socio-economic rights requires.[26] If this means that the Court cannot procure the information necessary to formulate a general policy, or calculate the resources necessary to fund it, or train the personnel necessary to implement it and so on, then that is undoubtedly correct. But, properly understood, that is not what the Court is required to do when it adjudicates socio-economic rights. The Court's role is to identify the purposes underlying the specific rights in the form of the interests they seek to protect and advance. As we shall argue below, that is exactly what litigants come to courts for – in the hope that the court will assign their interests a measure of legal recognition.

The second consideration is that it is not "institutionally appropriate"[27] for the Court to tell the executive and the legislature what the achievement of a particular right entails. The needs and interests to be responded to in the enforcement of a socio-economic right should be defined by the executive and legislature. This is more appropriate, so the argument goes, because the executive and the legislature are "more democratic" institutions than the courts, and more able to facilitate the participatory processes that are necessary to give popular content to socio-economic rights.

Accordingly, in *Mazibuko*, the Court defined its role in the definition and enforcement of socio-economic rights as a secondary one. It held:

> "The purpose of litigation concerning the positive obligations imposed by social and economic rights should be to hold the democratic arms of government to account through litigation. In so doing, litigation of this sort fosters a form of participative democracy that holds government accountable and requires it to account between elections over specific aspects of government policy.
>
> When challenged as to its policies relating to social and economic rights, the government agency must explain why the policy is reasonable. Government must disclose what it has done to formulate the policy: its investigation and research, the alternatives considered, and the reasons why the option underlying the policy was selected. The Constitution does not require government to be held to an impossible standard of perfection. Nor does it require courts to take over the tasks that in a democracy should properly be reserved for the democratic arms of government. Simply put, through the institution of the courts, government can be called upon to account to citizens for its decisions. This understanding of social and economic rights litigation accords with the founding values of our Constitution and, in particular, the principles that government should be responsive, accountable and open."[28]

This approach loses sight of the fact that litigants approach courts after the democratic process has failed. They do so on the basis that their interests are worthy of legal protection notwithstanding the fact that they are unpopular or have been overlooked in the democratic process. Having regard to the bourgeoning number of community-based protests concerning the failure of

---

[26] *Minister of Health v Treatment Action Campaign* 2002 5 SA 721 (CC) para 37.
[27] *Mazibuko v City of Johannesburg* 2010 4 SA 1 (CC) para 60.
[28] Paras 160-161.

the state to "deliver" socio-economic rights,[29] it may fairly be asked whether the executive and the legislature are routinely ensuring a truly democratic form of socio-economic development. Nonetheless, even if the process of policy formulation and implementation to give effect to socio-economic rights has not been perfectly democratic, the Court's job must be more than to foster further participation,[30] or even to consider whether the policy is, overall "reasonable". It must surely also be to decide whether vital interests and needs have been overlooked in the "democratic" process.

The Court should not, of course, prescribe in detail each of the administrative or legislative steps which must be taken to give effect to a particular socio-economic right. That is surely not what an interpretive exercise requires. Rather, all that is ultimately required of the Court is to identify the particular interests which fall within the boundaries of the right in question. The Court has had little difficulty with this in the adjudication of civil and political rights. The Court has prescribed in detail, for example, the ambit of interests protected by the positive obligations imposed by the right to vote, in the face of great administrative complexity.[31] In interpreting clauses of the Constitution beyond the Bill of Rights, the Court has assigned much interpretive meaning to the positive duties of Parliament and the provincial legislatures to facilitate public participation in the legislative process.[32] This has been done without prescribing the precise steps to be taken in doing so.[33] We do not see how the interpretation of socio-economic rights is any different. It should not raise any greater separation of powers concerns than the Court faced in *August v Electoral Commission* or *Doctors for Life International v Speaker of the National Assembly* in giving content to the right to vote and the concept of public participation. Yet the Court has refused to provide socio-economic rights with similar interpretive depth.

This suggests that much of the problem lies not in the doctrine of the separation of powers, but in the paucity of normative resources on which the Court can draw in the interpretation of socio-economic rights or a clear purposive understanding of a transformative role for the Court in relation to socio-economic inequality. Civil and political rights are buttressed by several centuries of history and a rich array of jurisprudence across a host of jurisdictions by reference to which they have been interpreted. Having rejected the notion that socio-economic rights entail a minimum core of goods and services which must be provided by the state,[34] the Court can only make limited use of the international law on the content of socio-economic rights.

---

[29] See J Hirsh "Community Protests in South Africa: Trends, Analysis and Explanations" in *Local Government Working Paper Series No 1* (2010) Community Law Centre, University of the Western Cape; J Dugard "Basic Services in Urban South Africa: Rights, Reality and Resistance" in M Langford, B Cousins, J Dugard & T Madlingozi (eds) *Symbols or Substance: The Role and Impact of Socio-Economic Rights Strategies in South Africa* (forthcoming).

[30] This was also the Court's approach in *Occupiers of 51 Olivia Road, Berea Township and 197 Main Street, Johannesburg v City of Johannesburg* 2008 3 SA 208 (CC), given effect to through an unprecedented "engagement order".

[31] *August v Electoral Commission* 1999 3 SA 1 (CC).

[32] *Doctors for Life International v Speaker of the National Assembly* 2006 6 SA 416 (CC).

[33] Paras 73-147.

[34] *Minister of Health v Treatment Action Campaign* 2002 5 SA 721 (CC) paras 26-39.

Foreign law is also of limited use, as few other common-law jurisdictions have socio-economic guarantees in a supreme law Bill of Rights. Those that do, appear to adopt a variation of the administrative-law model set out above,[35] are mostly advanced welfare states with relatively low levels of poverty, and do not contain the full range of socio-economic guarantees contained in South Africa's Constitution.[36] Other than the content of the South African government's own statutes and policies (which are usually at issue before it), the Court can draw on little other than its own interpretive resources in giving meaning to socio-economic rights.

This makes developing a substantive jurisprudence of socio-economic rights a daunting task. But if "reasonableness" is to add up to anything more than "the values, assumptions, and sensitivities" that the judges themselves bring "to the exercise of decision-making, whether consciously or not"[37] then the Court's approach needs to change. Such a change, we suggest, will require the Court to revisit some of its prior jurisprudence and reassess the manner in which it has conceptualised socio-economic rights litigation in its recent decisions.

In particular, two innovations are necessary. The first is to abandon the idea that socio-economic rights litigation is primarily a form of public participation in policymaking. The second is to develop an account of the particular interests socio-economic rights exist to protect and promote. This entails what Sandra Liebenberg has called "a context-sensitive assessment" of the impact the denial of a particular socio-economic good has on the claimants in question, including the "implications of the lack of access to the resource or service in question for intersecting rights and values such as the rights to life, freedom and security of the person, equality and dignity".[38] The raw material for such an examination is the situation of a particular claimant. More often than not, the claimant in question will be a person living in poverty, or at least a person who is very poor. It is accordingly with a claimant's lived experience of poverty and deprivation that a new theory of socio-economic rights must begin.

3   Towards a new theory

Claimants approach courts to vindicate their interests. When they receive a decision in their favour, it is because the law recognises that their interests are worthy of protection. We consider that this vindicatory purpose of litigation and the socio-economic interests litigants seek to advance are worthy of respect and attention. The first step in adjudicating positive socio-economic rights claims must be to identify the interest a litigant has come to court to advance or protect and to establish, as a matter of evidence, whether a particular socio-

---

[35] See L Williams' discussion of the German Constitutional Court's recent as yet unpublished decision in *Hartz IV* BVergG, judgment of 09/02/2009, 1 Bvl 1/09, 1 Bvl 3/09, 1 Bvl 4/09, in "The Role of Courts in the Quantitative-Implementation of Social and Economic Rights: A Comparative Study" (2010) 3 *CCR* 141 148-162.

[36] Germany and Canada are good examples.

[37] Williams (2010) *CCR* 142.

[38] Liebenberg *Socio-Economic Rights* 185.

economic interest is affected in the context of a given case. That is, after all, why claimants litigate – not primarily because they feel that the state's overall approach in an area of socio-economic policy is flawed, or unreasonable, but because they wish to make a difference in their own lives.

The second step is to consider whether that interest is one of the interests deserving of protection and fulfilment under the socio-economic right in question. The third step is to evaluate, with reference to the urgency and intensity of the interest in question, whether state policy and the manner of its implementation constitute an appropriate response to a person in the situation of the claimant, taking into account the range of other competing concerns the state must inevitably consider and prioritise. If the state's response, in the context of the particular case, is appropriate, then its policy is reasonable. If the state's response is inappropriate, then it is unreasonable and accordingly, on the Court's adopted test, a violation of the constitutional right at play. This broad conceptual schema grounds the right in question in a contextual account of the interests it must protect, while at the same time allowing the Court the necessary flexibility to assess whether or not the state has acted reasonably *in response to those interests*.

We now illustrate this argument by reference to the *Mazibuko, Joe Slovo* and *Nokotyana* decisions. In each case, we seek to expose the manner in which the Court's interpretive approach has prevented it from taking account of the real basis of the complaints before it. This has undercut the Court's ability to engage head on with the claimants' needs and lived experiences of poverty. Instead, the Court tends to prefer a facial examination of state policy, implicitly accepting the conceptions of reasonableness and possibility upon which those policies are drafted and implemented. This tends to reproduce the exclusion from policy formulation and implementation processes which have brought the claimants to court in the first place. Accordingly, we suggest that the Court's current approach falls at the first hurdle set up by the paradigm we propose: the interests driving the complaint – and the experiences of poverty and deprivation upon which they are based – are almost never properly defined and taken seriously.

3 1   An interest in sufficient water?

In *Mazibuko*, the Court had to consider whether the City of Johannesburg's Free Basic Water ("FBW") policy was reasonable in terms of section 27(1) and (2) of the Constitution, which guarantees everyone's right of access to sufficient water.[39] The thrust of the applicants' complaint was that the policy limited FBW provision to six kilolitres of water per household per month regardless of household size or need. The Court also had to consider whether both the

---

[39] The main respondents in the case were the City of Johannesburg and Johannesburg Water (Pty) Ltd, a wholly publicly owned municipal entity. For the sake of convenience, we make reference to "the City" to encompass the arguments of both parties, which were represented by the same legal counsel. There was a further respondent, the Department of Water Affairs and Forestry (now called Water and Environmental Affairs), but their arguments are not dealt with as they were largely irrelevant to the issues discussed here.

installation and operation of prepayment water meters, which automatically disconnected the water supply if additional water credit was not purchased following the exhaustion of the FBW allocation, were lawful.

It was common cause that the twin effects of the installation of prepayment water meters and limited FBW was that the applicants' water supply ran out around halfway through each month. This was in circumstances where they could not afford to pay for additional water to meet their basic washing, cooking, drinking, health and sanitation needs.

The applicants were five households from Phiri, Soweto. They were desperately poor, with household incomes of around R1 000 per month. Of the five applicants, four represented female-headed households and all the households were surviving mainly off government grants. It was not disputed that many Phiri households were fairly equally disadvantaged. It was common cause that Phiri is one of the most densely populated suburbs of Soweto, with numerous "backyard" shacks and many people on one stand. For example, Lindiwe Mazibuko, the first applicant, lived on a small stand with twenty people all sharing the same water supply:[40]

"Of the 20 people who are part of our household, one is a pensioner, 3 are small babies and six go to school. I suffer from arthritis and high blood pressure. My mother suffers from diabetes, high blood pressure and has a history of cardiac arrest. My sister, who recently moved into our house, suffers from a stroke. She moved in with us with her four children for us to take care of them. My mother is retired and receives a pension grant of R820 per month. The rest of us are unemployed. Other than her pension, my mother used to rely on R150.00 monthly rental she received from the three outside shacks. All of our boarders moved out in August 2005 however, following the change in our water situation. Between August and December 2005 we had to survive without this supplementary income. It was only in December 2005 that we finally found two new boarders … We charge them R70.00 and R50.00 each. I receive a child support grant of R180.00 per month in respect of two children in our household, namely Khosi and Zodwa Mazibuko. Our total monthly household income is accordingly R1 300. I am unsure of the exact figures of all my mother's expenses. However, she spends money on her own monthly doctor consultation fees in the amount of R140. She also spends another R140 for my doctor consultation fees. She then has to cater for all the transportation, food and clothing needs of the 14 Mazibukos, as well as schooling for the minor Mazibuko children, Thembi, Siphiwe, Zodwa, Nokuthula, Ntombikayise, Gift, Khosi, Zanele, Mabuntle and Mbali. Above that, she has to pay for the electricity and water expenses for the entire 20-person household … The people of Phiri are very poor. They are all black. There are many people who live in households with even more people than I do. Many of them are women who take care of children, elderly members of their family, or other members of the community who are ill. Many of the people in my community are HIV positive or have AIDS."[41]

Mazibuko's founding affidavit goes on to describe how the prepayment water meter system has compounded her adverse living conditions since it was installed on 11 October 2004:

"In October 2004, the first month that the meter was installed in our household, the 6 kilolitres ran out between 11 and 29 October 2004 [Mazibuko's prepayment meter was installed on 11 October and the free basic water supply was exhausted by 29 October]. The free 6 kilolitres of water per month has never lasted the entire month since it was installed on 11 October 2004. It usually finishes anytime between the 12th and 15th of each month. We can often not afford to buy further water. This means that our household is without any water for more than half of every month. When the free 6 kilolitres of water is finished, the water supply is discontinued without notice. There is no person to whom I can explain the reason why

---

[40] Lindiwe Mazibuko passed away just days after the High Court judgment was delivered, in May 2008. She was 36 years old and had suffered for many years from diabetes and high blood pressure.

[41] Founding Affidavit of Lindiwe Mazibuko (03-06-2006) *Mazibuko Record 1* 32-34 paras 69-77.

I cannot pay, or why I need the water to remain connected. The prepayment water meter automatically cuts off the water ... The amount of 6 kilolitres free water we are supplied with is simply not enough for our entire household's basic needs. This is despite the fact that we use water only for our basic needs. We cannot use less water in our household than what we are using at the moment. Our household uses water each day for drinking, cooking, sanitation, bathing, cleaning the house and laundry ..."

Mazibuko went on to point out that the effect of the City's FBW policy was that

"each person in our household of 20 would only be able to flush the toilet less than once every two days; each person could only have a 'body wash' every four days; 2 kettles of water, 1 sink full of dishes and half a clothes' wash per day would have to be used by 20 people. After all the free basic water budgeted for that day was used, no water would be left for anything else, such as drinking, cooking, cleaning the house and watering my food garden. We use very little water to bath with. We are now forced to do our laundry at my sister's house in Protea South, approximately 4 kilometres from our house. Sometimes, I do not drink sufficient water. This weakens my health ... We often do not flush our toilets. If we do, we use water that was used for bathing or washing dishes to flush our toilets. I used to have a small food garden but abandoned it when my water was cut off in March 2004. Now I have to buy the vegetables that I used to plant in my garden. The other applicants have suffered even more from prepayment water meters and the meagre rations of free basic water."[42]

In challenging the City's water supply measures, the applicants made several arguments.[43] We focus here on one of these arguments, which relied on an assessment of the context in which the policy was implemented. This was that the FBW policy was unreasonable because it was incapable of giving effect to the applicants' constitutional right of access to sufficient water.

The Court rejected this claim. It found that the City's FBW policy fell "within the bounds of reasonableness".[44] Yet its judgment attached no significance to the facts that the applicants were desperately poor, had inadequate access to water, and suffered greatly as a result. These undisputed facts relating to the applicants' circumstances received no real attention in the judgment. The Court did not ask whether the City had a reasonable programme that was "capable of facilitating the realisation of the right" in the context of its implementation.[45] Nor did it examine the evidence put up by the applicants that the City had the resources to provide additional FBW. It focused instead on a plethora of bureaucratic data concerning the difficulties the City said it faced in supplying water to Soweto.

In our view, the *Mazibuko* judgment fails to situate its analysis within a recognition of poverty and disadvantage. If it had done so, it would have been required to take a more critical, less deferential, approach to the City's claims. Without assigning any weight to the applicants' interests in having enough

---

[42] Founding Affidavit of Lindiwe Mazibuko *Mazibuko Record 1* 40-44 paras 100-118.

[43] We do not deal with all the arguments here. In the main, the other – more legally technical – arguments related to: the decision to install prepayment water meters in Phiri amounted to administrative action and, because it was taken without consultation, violated s 4(1) of the Promotion of Administrative Justice Act 3 of 2000 ("PAJA"); and that the automatic disconnection of prepayment water meters violated s 4(3) of the Water Services Act 108 of 1997, which requires reasonable notice and an opportunity to make representations prior to the limitation or discontinuation of water services. It could be argued that a more contextual appraisal of the right to water in this case might have rendered less deferential decisions on both the PAJA and Water Services Act rulings. This might result in a welcome move towards bringing a proportionality test into the Court's approach to deference, not dissimilar to the contextual test for reasonableness that we propose here.

[44] *Mazibuko v City of Johannesburg* 2010 4 SA 1 (CC) para 9.

[45] *Government of the Republic of South Africa v Grootboom* 2000 1 SA 46 (CC) para 41.

water to get through the month, and without reading that interest in the context of deep poverty, vulnerability and overpopulated residential stands, the Court deprived itself of the opportunity to subject the City's policies to much meaningful evaluation. The City's policies were, instead, evaluated in the abstract – meaning that the City's justifications for them had to be taken at face value. The sufficiency argument was accordingly disposed of by the Court in the following way:

"The fourth argument is that the 6 kilolitres per month per household is not sufficient in that it does not provide 50 litres per person per day across the board. There is a welter of evidence on the record indicating that household sizes in Johannesburg vary markedly. According to the 2001 Census there are one million households in the City. Of those households, 51% have a household income lower than R1 600 per month. What is clear is that in general the number of people per household is dropping, and the number of households is increasing sharply. The 2001 Census showed a decline in household density from 3,8 people per household in 1996 to 3,2 in 2001. The same period saw a 38,3% increase in the number of households. In addition, in 2001 only 20% of households had more than four people in them and only 2,5% of households more than nine.

The picture is further complicated, however, by the fact that there is often more than one household relying on one water connection. This is especially so in townships where there is still an acute housing shortage, a legacy of apartheid urbanisation policy. Stand-holders permit tenants to erect homes in their backyards, normally against payment of rental. So, for example, the 2001 Census data showed there to be 2,1 houses per stand in Phiri with an average 8,8 people per stand. In some cases, there are far more people per stand. As we have seen, Mrs Mazibuko's household at the time of the launch of the proceedings, for example, comprised three separate households with a total of 20 residents. Two of those households paid Mrs Mazibuko low monthly rentals. On the other hand, there were only three residents on the stand of Mrs Malekutu, the fourth applicant. What emerges from the record, thus, is that although the average household size is quite low, the variation in the number of occupants per water connection is significant. There are many water connections where there is only one resident, but there are some with as many as 20.

Where the household size is average, that is 3,2 people, the free basic water allowance will provide approximately 60 litres per person per day, considerably in excess of the amount the applicants urge us to establish as the sufficient amount of water as contemplated by section 27 of the Constitution. The difficulty is that many households are larger than the average, particularly where there is more than one family or house on a stand as is the case in Phiri and many other poor areas. Yet, to raise the free basic water allowance for all so that it would be sufficient to cover those stands with many residents would be expensive and inequitable, for it would disproportionately benefit stands with fewer residents.

Establishing a fixed amount per stand will inevitably result in unevenness because those stands with more inhabitants will have less water per person than those stands with fewer people. This is an unavoidable result of establishing a universal allocation. Yet it seems clear on the City's evidence that to establish a universal per person allowance would administratively be extremely burdensome and costly, if possible at all. The free basic water allowance established is generous in relation to the average household size in Johannesburg. Indeed, in relation to 80% of households (with four occupants or fewer), the allowance is adequate even on the applicants' case. In the light of this evidence, coupled with the fact that the amount provided by the City was based on the prescribed national standard for basic water supply, it cannot be said that the amount established by the City was unreasonable."[46]

The difficulty with this line of reasoning is that it deals with the applicants as a deviation from a convenient average and divorces the question of the sufficiency of the free basic supply from the hardship caused by the disconnection of water once the free component has been exhausted. Because the City's policy is assessed separately from the particularities of the applicants' needs

---

[46] *Mazibuko v City of Johannesburg* 2010 4 SA 1 (CC) paras 79-82.

(and the automatic disconnection is ignored altogether)[47] the policy appears reasonable because its contextual impact is ignored. The lived reality of having a water supply cut off in circumstances where one cannot afford to pay more is airbrushed out of the picture by a compartmentalised, abstracted approach to the impact of the City's policy in the context of manifold deprivation. The needs of the 20% of residents whom the court acknowledges will have insufficient water in the applicants' case, form no part of the analysis.

On our approach, the *Mazibuko* case would have been relatively easy. There was no dispute that *prima facie* many Phiri households had insufficient water to meet their basic needs. A person's interest in the provision of a sufficient amount of the good itself must be at the very heart of what the right of access to sufficient water is supposed to protect. Given this, the City would then have had to show that the frustration of the claimant's basic needs was justified by some other competing interest or concern. The Court should, therefore, have turned to examine the City's justifications for not providing more FBW. In the main, these related the fact that the City said it had more pressing policy priorities, chief among which was the provision of basic water supplies to informal settlements.

The approach taken by the Court did not require it to question whether it was reasonable to prioritise the needs of informal settlers over the needs of the applicants. It is, however, necessary for us to address it because the question would have arisen had the Court followed the approach we urge. Although it may appear reasonable to prioritise the needs of informal settlers over the residents of Phiri on the surface, once the appropriate contextual factors have been taken into account, the picture is not so clear. The only significant difference between the two groups was that the Phiri residents had access to formal housing and waterborne sanitation, whereas informal settlers tend to rely on pit latrines or chemical toilets. This meant that the Phiri residents would ordinarily need more water than residents of informal settlements. This was obviously not their fault. There was no difference in income or socio-economic status between the Phiri residents and people living in informal settlements. It would accordingly be absurd to suggest that the water needs of the residents of Phiri ought not to be met because, by historical accident, they live in formal housing and accordingly require more water to meet their waterborne sanitation needs. The City did not seriously contend that it did not have sufficient resources to meet the needs of both.[48] On this basis, the Court could and should have ruled that the City was able and required to do so.

Lucy Williams suggests that by comparing the South African Constitutional Court's approach in *Mazibuko* with the German Constitutional Court's approach in *Hartz IV*, it is possible and entirely appropriate for even relatively

---

[47] The lawfulness of prepayment meters is considered later in the judgment, but without reference to sufficiency.

[48] In the High Court leg of the case, *Mazibuko v City of Johannesburg* 2008 4 All SA 471 (W) para 51, Tskoa J noted that Mogale City, a poorer municipality than the City of Johannesburg, provided ten kilolitres of FBW per household per month, in comparison to the City's provision of six kilolitres. Indeed, the applicants placed on record an econometric analysis of water tariffs and FBW allocations in South Africa's main metropolitan areas that revealed that other metropolitan municipalities provided more FBW and had more pro-poor water tariffs than Johannesburg.

deferential courts to interrogate governmental reasons for not satisfying the interests at stake in any case.[49] However, we consider that those interests must be defined and taken seriously for the interrogation of the state's justificatory framework to have any real force. The Court's failure to define and evaluate the interests at stake in *Mazibuko* undercut its ability to hold the City to any meaningful standard of reasonableness. Because it had little to no regard for the needs and interests articulated by the applicants, it was able to conclude that it was "reasonable" to deprive them of sufficient water.

3 2 An interest in location: "convenience" or survival?

In *Joe Slovo*, 20 000 people (the residents) from Joe Slovo informal settlement in Cape Town appealed to the Court to set aside an order for their eviction granted by the Cape High Court. The High Court ordered the eviction of the residents and their forced relocation to temporary housing in a new development near Delft, some fifteen kilometres away.

The residents claimed that the proposed relocation would cause considerable hardship and fundamentally compromise their access to hospitals, schools, employment and social, cultural and family life. They presented (substantially undisputed) evidence about the likely adverse impact of the move.[50] This included the facts that residents were not being offered security of tenure or guaranteed access to formal housing, and that the new location did not have public amenities such as a clinic, a school or any community hall. Moreover, the new location was far away from residents' existing jobs and livelihoods and in most cases the cost of commuting between existing jobs and the new settlement would have doubled (amounting to upwards of half or more of their monthly incomes). In addition, being further away from Cape Town's city centre and linked settlements, Delft did not provide the opportunities for piece jobs that kept many of the residents financially afloat.

In short, the relocation would have been an economic and social disaster, despite the fact that better constructed housing (as opposed to shacks) was being offered on the relocation site. The residents, together with two *amici curiae*, argued that the advantages their current location afforded them, in the context of their poverty, economic vulnerability and social disadvantage, ought to be protected by the right of access to adequate housing. Housing is, after all, more than mere bricks and mortar.[51]

Although Moseneke DCJ's judgment did acknowledge the need for "special concern where settled communities face the threat of being uprooted to other neighbourhoods distant from employment, schooling or other social

---

[49] Williams (2010) *CCR* 197-198.

[50] There were two other main legal grounds not dealt with here: namely, that the occupiers were not unlawful occupiers and could not therefore be lawfully evicted; and that the province's promises had given rise to a legitimate expectation that 70% of the formal houses in the upgraded Joe Slovo settlement would be allocated to them.

[51] As the Court itself held in *Government of the Republic of South Africa v Grootboom* 2000 1 SA 46 (CC) para 35.

amenities",[52] the Court trivialised the clearly devastating impact the relocation would have had. The residents' interest in their location was reduced to one of mere "convenience".[53] The Court stated that while being relocated would be "an inevitably stressful process",[54] "there are circumstances in which there is no choice but to undergo traumatic experiences so that we can be better off later".[55]

The Court did not apply the reasonableness test to weigh up the interests of the residents and the harm to be suffered against the justifications of the government for the relocation. The hardships were largely written off as unfortunate consequences of policy choices over which the Court was unable to exercise any scrutiny:

> "In essence these are largely operational matters in relation to which the state should ordinarily have a large discretion. Courts would not normally intervene to decide how well or badly programmes are being managed."[56]

In upholding the eviction but placing conditions on the relocation, the Court seemed to conceive of its role as requiring the government to implement the best possible version of the policy it had presented. It did not attempt to delve into the question of whether the policy was appropriate to the community's objectively established needs.

Had it done so, we think the Court would have found the policy wanting. When weighed against the residents' clear interests and the dire consequences of the relocation, the City's eviction policy was plainly unreasonable. On our approach, state action resulting in the destruction of a whole community's economic and social base: its access to jobs, livelihoods, education and health care would require compelling justification. It cannot seriously be suggested that the mere provision of admittedly better constructed housing – with no guaranteed tenure security – can itself provide that justification.

By downgrading the residents' interests to matters of mere "convenience", the Court was not able properly to weigh them against state's eviction policy. Given that the province has since reversed its opposition to an *in situ* upgrade and, as a consequence, the eviction order has been discharged,[57] a harder look at the justifications for the relocation as against the residents' urgent interests in their current location as a means for survival may have produced a different result at the time.

3 3   An interest in going to the toilet in dignity?

In *Nokotyana*, the applicants were desperately poor residents of the Harry Gwala informal settlement in Ekurhuleni, who had been living for many years without formal access to water, sanitation or electricity while the

---

[52] *Residents of the Joe Slovo Community, Western Cape v Thubelisha Homes* 2010 3 SA 454 (CC) judgment of Moseneke DCJ para 165.
[53] Judgment of O'Regan J para 321.
[54] Judgment of Sachs J para 399.
[55] Judgment of Yacoob J para 107.
[56] Judgment of Sachs J para 381.
[57] See *Residents of the Joe Slovo Community, Western Cape v Thubelisha Homes* 2011 7 BCLR 723 (CC).

municipality failed to take a decision on whether to upgrade the settlement *in situ*. The applicants sued the municipality for access to water, the provision of high mast street lighting and access to basic sanitation. The High Court had, by agreement between the parties, ordered the municipality to expand the number of communal water taps to the applicants, but had dismissed the residents' claims for the installation of toilets and street lighting. Before the matter reached the Court, and undoubtedly spurred by the ongoing litigation, the municipality adopted a new policy in terms of which every informal settlement in its jurisdiction, including Harry Gwala, would be provided with one chemical toilet per ten households.

The applicants criticised this policy as unreasonable on two main grounds. First, they claimed that expecting ten households to share one communal toilet compromised their dignity. Second, they argued that they should receive Ventilated Improved Pit latrines ("VIPs") rather than chemical toilets, for which residents usually have to purchase costly chemicals to maintain.

The Court declined to take into account any of the contextual information the applicants adduced regarding sanitation (which included details comparing various forms of sanitation), electricity, health care, dignity and privacy. In connection with sanitation the Court held that evidence related to the new sanitation policy was inadmissible because it fundamentally changed the issues between the parties, making the Court one of first and last instance to a new policy adopted after the hearing in the High Court.[58] The Court also refused to order the municipality to implement the policy it had produced.

The Court's failure to grapple with the contextual evidence placed before it by the applicants in the run-up to the Court hearing put paid to any chances of the reasonableness test delivering a ruling that would vindicate the applicants' articulated interests. In order to see how the Court might have developed the reasonableness test through a contextualised examination of the interests at stake, it is instructive to look at another recent judgment concerning sanitation – that of Judge Erasmus of the Cape High Court in *Beja v Premier of the Western Cape*.[59]

In this case, which concerned the provision by the state of toilets in Silvertown near Khayelitsha in Cape Town, the Western Cape High Court had to determine whether the provision of unenclosed toilets, in the ratio of one toilet per five families, violated the residents' rights. The decision addressed the applicants' sanitation-related needs and interests head-on. Residents were left with toilets without doors, that were "in a bad state", "generally filthy and underserviced" with no street lighting, and which did not satisfy their claims to dignity or privacy.[60] The conduct of the Mayor and City of Cape Town in providing unenclosed toilets was found to be in violation of the residents' constitutional rights – particularly sections 10 (dignity), 12 (freedom and security of the person), 14 (privacy), 24 (environment), 26 (housing), and 27

---

[58]   *Nokotyana v Ekhurhuleni Municipality* 2010 4 BCLR 312 (CC) para 19.
[59]   2011 3 All SA 401 (WCC).
[60]   Paras 29-30.

(health care) of the Constitution. The Mayor and City of Cape Town were ordered to enclose all the toilets.[61]

Implicit in the approach of the High Court in *Beja* is an interpretive paradigm in which the court steps into the shoes of an ordinary informal settler faced with the choice of going to the toilet in the bush or using an unenclosed latrine. The court then asks whether the state's failure or refusal to address this state of affairs was reasonable in all the circumstances. In the absence of compelling justification for putting an informal settler to such an unconscionable election, the state's policy is found wanting.

It is virtually impossible to consider whether a ratio of ten families to one toilet is a reasonable measure capable of giving effect to constitutional rights to dignity in informal settlements, without an approach which delves in to the lived experience of informal settlers themselves, and develops an account of their interests from those experiences. Taking into account the privations of informal settlement living (all of which were before the Court in *Nokotyana*), and assuming that more is possible (a question which was never explored), such a measure appears undignified and objectionable. This is so even if it is accepted that the residents had nothing before – a fact upon which the Court in *Nokotyana* appeared to place implicit reliance in refusing to categorise the residents' needs as emergent. In any event, absence of services in the past cannot justify the provision of inadequate services in future. Whatever the case, the Court's failure to reach into the social context in which the services were provided in order to assess their adequacy rendered its approach in *Nokotyana* unsatisfactory.

4 Conclusion

In this chapter, we have urged a more substantive, interest-based approach to socio-economic rights adjudication. We have suggested that the current modes of adjudication adopted by the Court pay insufficient regard to the vindicatory purpose of litigation as well as the reasons why, and conditions under which, claimants turn to it for redress. It is neither appropriate nor coherent, we have suggested, to leave a substantive account of socio-economic rights to supposedly "democratic" processes beyond the Court's purview. The Constitution itself requires the Court to assign meaning to socio-economic rights through purposive interpretation which takes account of the specific needs and interests for which socio-economic rights exist to promote.

The Court has an important institutional role to play in addressing poverty and inequality in South Africa. It has the means and the opportunity to develop a socio-economic rights jurisprudence which adequately accounts for the lived experience of poverty, and which requires state policy to face up to the realities of that experience. The analysis of the cases in part three of this chapter demonstrates that the Court has deprived itself of the conceptual tools necessary to forge a sufficiently rich account of the interests protected by socio-economic rights. It is only through a bold engagement with those

---

[61] Paras 1-3.

interests, and the lived reality of the claimants who articulate them, that the Court can fulfil its institutional potential. If it does so, the Court will not only contribute more effectively to social transformation, but will also enhance the legitimacy of the constitutional project in the eyes of the poor. If the popular protests which have recently engulfed townships and informal settlements across South Africa tell us anything, it is that the basic needs of people participating in them have not been well-served by the "democratic" process upon which the Court says they must rely.

SUMMARY

The Constitutional Court's socio-economic rights jurisprudence fails to meaningfully address the needs and interests that poor people approach the Court to vindicate. This has resulted in a body of jurisprudence which cannot realistically contribute to the elimination of poverty and inequality and the transformation of social relations. This need not be so. We argue here that the Court's existing approach to socio-economic rights claims can be adapted to contribute substantively to the progressive elimination of poverty and disadvantage. The starting point is to identify the specific needs and interests claimants come to Court to vindicate and weigh them against the state's justifications for its refusal to respond to them. The seeds of such an approach were sown in *Government of the Republic of South Africa v Grootboom* 2001 1 SA 46 (CC). However, since *Grootboom*, the Court has turned away from an evaluation of the intensity of the interests litigants approach it to vindicate, preferring instead to embark upon an abstracted and empty facial evaluation of state policy. In this chapter we sketch out an alternative, interests-based approach which, we argue, may be adopted within the confines of the version of separation of powers doctrine the Court appears to have adopted. We then apply the approach to three practical examples and seek to demonstrate that it is better suited to responding to the needs and interests of the poor.

CHAPTER 13

AN APPRAISAL OF INTERNATIONAL LAW MECHANISMS FOR LITIGATING SOCIO-ECONOMIC RIGHTS, WITH A PARTICULAR FOCUS ON THE OPTIONAL PROTOCOL TO THE INTERNATIONAL COVENANT ON ECONOMIC, SOCIAL AND CULTURAL RIGHTS AND THE AFRICAN COMMISSION AND COURT

Lilian Chenwi[*]

1 Introduction

The effective implementation of socio-economic rights ("SERs") is crucial in the fight against poverty and underdevelopment,[1] as they provide a framework through which accountability for poverty can be strengthened. These rights are aimed at addressing some of the underlying conditions of poverty such as lack of access to food, social security and assistance, health care and housing. They are therefore useful tools through which people can gain access to basic social services and resources, in order to improve their situations and live a dignified life.[2] This is particularly important for disadvantaged groups such as those living in poverty. However, the extent to which SERs have and can contribute towards improving the situations of people living in poverty has been limited, to some extent, by the fact that their justiciability was (and in some cases still is) unsettled.[3] Though the Universal Declaration of Human Rights, 1948 ("UDHR") recognised SERs as fundamental to a person's well-being and dignity,[4] their justiciability was subsequently questioned, resulting in the adoption, in 1966, of the International Covenant on Economic, Social and Cultural Rights ("ICESCR")[5] without a complaints[6] mechanism, as was the case with its sister covenant, the International Covenant on Civil and

---

[*] I would like to thank Professor Sandra Liebenberg for her useful comments on an earlier draft of this chapter; and the Community Law Centre for its institutional support during the preparation of the first draft of this chapter.

[1] See C Mbazira "Enforcing the Economic, Social and Cultural Rights in the African Charter on Human and Peoples' Rights: Twenty Years of Redundancy, Progression and Significant Strides" (2006) 6 *AHRLJ* 333 333, where a similar point is advanced.

[2] S Liebenberg "South Africa's Evolving Jurisprudence on Socio-Economic Rights: An Effective Tool in Challenging Poverty?" (2002) 6 *LDD* 159 159.

[3] For further reading on reasons advanced for non-justiciability of socio-economic rights, see M Brennan "To Adjudicate and Enforce Socio-Economic Rights: South Africa Proves that Domestic Courts are a Viable Option" (2009) 9 *QUTLJJ* 64 65.

[4] Art 22 of the Universal Declaration of Human Rights (1948) UN Doc A/810 at 71 ("UDHR").

[5] International Covenant on Economic, Social and Cultural Rights (1966) UN Doc A/6316 ("ICESCR").

[6] The term "complaints" as used in this chapter includes "communications" or "petitions".

Political Rights ("ICCPR").[7] In addition, while the ICCPR explicitly required states "to develop the possibilities of judicial remedy",[8] the ICESCR did not contain such an explicit provision. Consequently, until recent years, not much attention was paid to developing mechanisms for their enforcement, particularly at the United Nations ("UN") level. The lack of a dedicated mechanism for these rights was seen as "starving the law of oxygen needed to develop a more coherent understanding" of these rights.[9]

The situation changed in 2008 with the adoption of the Optional Protocol to the International Covenant on Economic, Social and Cultural Rights ("OP-ICESCR"),[10] which makes provision for a complaints mechanism for violations of SERs.[11] The Protocol is seen as "an important mechanism to expose abuses that are typically linked to poverty, discrimination, and neglect, and that victims frequently endure in silence and helplessness".[12] Once a state ratifies the OP-ICESCR, the effective enforcement of SERs and the provision of an effective remedy for their violation is the only way it can escape the adjudication of these rights under this new mechanism.[13]

Increasingly, litigation[14] is becoming an attractive tool for human rights movements worldwide and is fundamental to building international justice.[15] International law mechanisms for litigating rights are useful for marginalised groups and people living in poverty based on their important role of ensuring that states meet the obligations they have committed to through the ratification of treaties, including the provision of effective remedies in cases of violations. The existence of international litigation mechanisms therefore encourages governments to ensure the availability of more effective local remedies in respect of SERs. The ability to litigate SERs at the global and regional levels further "enables international jurisprudence on these rights to develop in the context of concrete cases", which would be a useful resource in developing national jurisprudence on SERs.[16] However, it should be noted that national jurisprudence can also influence the development of international law.

---

[7]   International Covenant on Civil and Political Rights (1966) UN Doc A/6316 ("ICCPR").

[8]   Art 2(3)(b).

[9]   M Scheinin & M Langford "Evolution or Revolution? – Extrapolating from the Experience of the Human Rights Committee" (2009) 27 *Nordic Journal of Human Rights* 97 100.

[10] The Optional Protocol to the International Covenant on Economic, Social and Cultural Rights (2008) UN General Assembly Resolution 63/117 ("OP-ICESCR") is not yet in force, as it requires ten ratifications. As of September 2011, it had been ratified by four States (Ecuador, El Salvador, Mongolia and Spain) and signed by 32 others.

[11] The path to the adoption of the OP-ICESCR can be traced to as far back as 1948 when the UDHR was adopted. See L Chenwi "Correcting the Historical Asymmetry between Rights: The Optional Protocol to the International Covenant on Economic, Social and Cultural Rights" (2009) 9 *AHRLJ* 23 26-29, where it is traced from 1990; M Langford "Closing the Gap? – An Introduction to the Optional Protocol to the International Covenant on Economic, Social and Cultural Rights" (2009) 27 *Nordic Journal of Human Rights* 1 3-9, where it is traced to as far back as 1948.

[12] L Arbour "Human Rights Made Whole" (2008) *Policy Innovations* <http://www.policyinnovations.org/ideas/commentary/data/000068> (accessed 17-06-2011).

[13] Brennan (2009) *QUTLJJ* 65.

[14] "Litigation" is used in this chapter broadly to refer to the process of taking a case through a judicial or quasi-judicial treaty-body.

[15] Carnegie Council on Ethics and International Affairs "Litigating Human Rights: Promise v. Perils – Introduction" (2000) 2 *Human Rights Dialogue* 1 1.

[16] S Liebenberg *Socio-Economic Rights: Adjudication under a Transformative Constitution* (2010) 117.

In this chapter I assess the mechanisms for litigating SERs at the international level. In particular, it focuses on four aspects (standing; admissibility criteria; standard of reviewing state compliance; and remedies and enforcement) of the complaints mechanisms under the OP-ICESCR and of the African Commission on Human and Peoples' Rights ("African Commission") and the African Court on Human and Peoples' Rights ("African Court"). With regard to the OP-ICESCR and the African Court, the fact that the former mechanism is not yet in force and the latter is relatively new yet undergoing structural changes, implies that the scope of this chapter is limited to an analysis of their potential. While reference is made to some case law, the scope of the chapter does not allow for a detailed analysis of these. Some broad principles are borne in mind in assessing the effectiveness of the complaints mechanisms. An effective complaints mechanism should be able to provide states with clear authoritative guidance on the meaning of treaty provisions and the obligations, as well as an understanding of SERs in general. It should also be able to augment the practical relevance and status of the particular treaty. It should further have a broad and flexible approach to standing so as to ensure that its use is maximised in a way that facilitates accessibility for the poor and marginalised groups. The kind of remedies issued should be concrete, targeted and clear so as to facilitate implementation and improve rights enjoyment on the ground. An effective mechanism must also be able to address complaints within reasonable time, and ensure prompt and effective action in cases where violations have occurred. Effectiveness can also be affected by the kind of language used in the treaty provisions (for example, the OP-ICESCR has been criticised for using weak language that would impact negatively on its effectiveness), and whether the mechanism takes into consideration current realities,[17] as seen in the case of the African Commission.

It should be noted that the structure and approach to litigation at the international level is different from that at the national level. For instance, at the international level, human rights litigation occurs in quasi-judicial and judicial mechanisms. The complaints mechanisms of treaty bodies fall under the former. Quasi-judicial complaints mechanisms differ from judicial or court proceedings in that they are seen as "a distinctive form of adjudication".[18] They involve a body of independent experts (not necessarily having a legal background) that decides a claim of violation by applying international human rights norms and then makes its decision with recommendations on appropriate remedies for a violation, which are then transmitted to the parties. Generally, there are no oral proceedings and individual complaints are considered in

---

[17] See A Vandenbogaerde & W Vandenhole "The Optional Protocol to the International Covenant on Economic, Social and Cultural Rights: An *Ex Ante* Assessment of its Effectiveness in Light of the Drafting Process" (2010) 10 *HRLR* 207 207-237, where it is stated that potential effectiveness is jeopardised by weak wording since a weak procedure is unlikely to be able to respond adequately to violations of rights. The authors also state that "[a] potentially effective mechanism is one that is attuned to the specificity of [socio-economic] rights and to current realities, rather than to the prejudices that have compromised [these] rights" (237).

[18] K Mechlem "Treaty Bodies and the Interpretation of Human Rights" (2009) 42 *Vand J Transnat'l L* 905 926.

closed sessions.[19] Another difference between international and national litigation processes relates to the question of access to the mechanisms. While national courts adopt a very broad approach to access (granting everyone access and state consent is not required), access to international mechanisms is restricted by a number of factors including whether a state is a party to the mechanism's constitutive treaty and/or has recognised the competence of the relevant body to receive complaints. The question of access is discussed further in this chapter when dealing with standing in relation to quasi-judicial bodies and also in the discussion on the African Court, which highlights other factors that impact on access.

2   Quasi-judicial mechanisms: The OP-ICESCR and the African Commission

2 1   Overview

Before considering the four aspects – standing; admissibility criteria; standard of reviewing state compliance; and remedies and enforcement – of the complaints mechanisms under the OP-ICESCR and the African Commission, a brief overview of quasi-judicial mechanisms at the UN and regional levels is relevant for two reasons. First, it would place the OP-ICESCR and the African Commission mechanisms in context. Second, it would provide further understanding of the structure and approach to international litigation processes under quasi-judicial mechanisms.

As regards the UN system, treaty-based quasi-judicial mechanisms for litigating rights have been established by:[20] the ICCPR; the Optional Protocol to the International Covenant on Civil and Political Rights, 1966 ("OP-ICCPR");[21] the International Convention on the Elimination of All Forms of Racial Discrimination, 1965 ("CERD");[22] the Convention against Torture and Other Cruel, Inhuman or Degrading Treatment or Punishment, 1984 ("CAT");[23] the International Convention on the Rights of All Migrant Workers and Members of Their Families, 1990 ("CRMW");[24] the Optional Protocol to the International Convention on the Elimination of All Forms

---

[19] Regional mechanisms, such as that of the African Commission, allow oral representation. See Rule 99 of the Rules of Procedure of the African Commission on Human and Peoples' Rights (2010) ("African Commission Rules of Procedure"). See also R Murray "Decisions by the African Commission on Individual Communications under the African Charter on Human and Peoples' Rights" (1997) 46 *Int'l & Comp LQ* 412 427. Also, in order to enhance the complaints procedure under the OP-ICCPR, the use of oral hearings has been encouraged. See H Steiner, P Alston & R Goodmand *International Human Rights in Context: Law, Politics, Morals* 3 ed (2007) 895.

[20] At the time of writing, an optional complaints mechanism for the Convention on the Rights of the Child (1989) UN Doc A/44/49 ("CRC") had been adopted by the Human Rights Council and transmitted to the UN General Assembly for adoption.

[21] Optional Protocol to the International Covenant on Civil and Political Rights (1966) UN Doc A/6316 ("OP-ICCPR"). See also art 41 of the ICCPR.

[22] Art 14 of the International Convention on the Elimination of All Forms of Racial Discrimination (1965) UN Doc A/6014 ("CERD").

[23] Art 22 of the Convention against Torture and Other Cruel, Inhuman or Degrading Treatment or Punishment (1984) UN Doc A/39/51 ("CAT").

[24] Arts 76 and 77 of the International Convention on the Rights of All Migrant Workers and Members of Their Families (1990) UN Doc A/45/49 ("CRMW"). This mechanism requires ten declarations from states accepting the mechanism in order for it to enter into force.

of Discrimination against Women, 1999 ("OP-CEDAW");[25] the Optional
Protocol to the Convention on the Rights of Persons with Disabilities, 2006
("OP-CRPD");[26] the International Convention for the Protection of All Persons
from Enforced Disappearance, 2006 ("CPED");[27] and the OP-ICESCR.

With the exception of the OP-ICESCR, whose scope extends to all economic,
social and cultural rights, the scope of the other mechanisms are limited to
some SERs or the rights of certain groups. The mechanisms further provide
for both individual[28] and inter-state[29] complaints mechanisms. However, some
of the mechanisms or procedures require states to either opt in or opt out.
That is, a state has to make a declaration upon ratification or subsequently,
recognising (opt-in) or not recognising (opt-out) the competence of the relevant
committee to receive and consider complaints under specific procedures. The
opt-in approach is adopted in the case of the complaints mechanism under
the CAT, the CRMW, and the CPED; the inter-state procedures under the
ICCPR and OP-ICESCR; and the individual complaints procedures under
CERD. The OP-CRDP adopts an opt-out approach for individual and inter-
State complaints.

The OP-ICESCR is consistent with existing UN complaints mechanisms as
it allows for the possibility of interim measures in exceptional circumstances
in order to prevent irreparable damage to victims.[30] This is one of the most
important functions of any judicial or quasi-judicial body adjudicating
complaints, as it ensures such body's effectiveness. The practical challenge
would be to get states to comply with a request to take interim measures, since
many states are yet to accept that interim measures specified by international
quasi-judicial bodies are binding on them.[31] The OP-ICESCR also allows for
the friendly settlement of disputes.[32] The UN Committee on Economic, Social
and Cultural Rights ("CESCR") is further empowered to conduct inquiries
into grave or systematic violations of SERs, based on reliable information
it receives, which is an opt-in procedure.[33] The initiation of the inquiry is
at the discretion of the Committee and not based on the receipt of a formal

---

[25] Optional Protocol to the International Convention on the Elimination of All Forms of Discrimination against Women (1999) UN Doc A/54/49 (Vol I) ("OP-CEDAW"). The main treaty being the International Convention on the Elimination of All Forms of Discrimination against Women (1979) UN Doc A/34/46 ("CEDAW").

[26] Optional Protocol to the Convention on the Rights of Persons with Disabilities, (2006) UN Doc A/61/49 ("OP-CRPD"). The main treaty being the International Convention on the Rights of Persons with Disabilities (2006) UN Doc A/61/49 ("CRPD").

[27] Arts 31 and 32 of the International Convention for the Protection of All Persons from Enforced Disappearance (2006) UN Doc A/RES/61/177 ("CPED").

[28] Complaints brought by individuals or groups of individuals or by others on their behalf.

[29] Complaints brought by a state against another state, relating to a failure to meet obligations under the applicable treaty. The OP-CRPD is silent on inter-state complaints.

[30] Art 5 of the OP-ICESCR.

[31] J Pasqualucci "Interim Measures in International Human Rights: Evolution and Harmonization" (2005) 38 *Vand J Transnat'l L* 1 2. See also F Viljoen *International Human Rights Law in Africa* (2007) 326-329, which illustrates states' uniform disregard for interim measures made by the African Commission.

[32] Art 7 of the OP-ICESCR.

[33] Arts 10-11 of the OP-ICESCR.

complaint.[34] This is therefore useful in instances where individuals are precluded or prevented by circumstances beyond their control from submitting a complaint.

Pending the entry into force of the OP-ICESCR, the Human Rights Committee established under the ICCPR is seen as "the most important forum for the further evolution of jurisprudence in respect of equality and non-discrimination in the enjoyment of economic, social and cultural rights".[35] The Committee has interpreted article 26 of the ICCPR – on equality and non-discrimination – not only as an independent right, but also as a right that is applicable to the rights in the ICESCR. It has found a violation of this provision regarding access to social security rights,[36] the right to work and right to property; and has also addressed issues relating to the rights to education, health, reproductive rights and the right to culture.[37] Similarly, the CERD Committee has found a breach of the right to equality in relation to the right to housing.[38] The CEDAW Committee has also found a state in breach of its obligation to provide information and obtain full consent for reproductive health procedures.[39] While these decisions are commendable, their scope is restrictive in that it addresses SERs through the equality lens only, or as it relates to women. Hence the need for a separate individual complaints mechanism specifically for SERs that deals with all its dimensions and assesses its implementation through various lenses.

At the African regional level, the African Commission's complaints mechanism has been used in the litigation of SERs contained in the African Charter on Human and Peoples' Rights, 1981 ("African Charter"),[40] and the Protocol to the African Charter on Human and Peoples' Rights on the Rights of Women in Africa, 2003 ("African Women's Protocol").[41] Children's SERs in the African Charter on the Rights and Welfare of the Child, 1990 ("African

---

[34] The inquiry and inter-state mechanisms can be used to draw attention to issues relating to extra-territorial violations of rights in the ICESCR. See C Courtis & M Sepúlveda "Are Extra-territorial Obligations Reviewable under the Optional Protocol to the ICESCR?" (2009) 27 *Nordic Journal of Human Rights* 54 61.

[35] M Scheinin "Human Rights Committee: Not only a Committee on Civil and Political Rights" in M Langford (ed) *Social Rights Jurisprudence: Emerging Trends in International and Comparative Law* (2008) 540 552. See also M Scheinin "Economic and Social Rights as Legal Rights" in A Eide, C Krause & A Rosas (eds) *Economic, Social and Cultural Rights: A Textbook* 2 ed (2001) 29 32-34, in relation to cases in which provisions of the ICCPR such as equality and non-discrimination have been used to protect socio-economic rights.

[36] See, for example, *Young v Australia* Communication 941/2000 UN Doc CCPR/C/78/D/941/2000; *Gueye et al v France* Communication 196/1985 UN Doc CCPR/C/35/D/196/1985; *Zwaan de Vries v the Netherlands* Communication 182/1984 UN Doc Supp No 40 (A/42/40) 160. See also *Broeks v The Netherlands* Communication 172/1984 UN Doc CCPR/C/OP/2 196.

[37] See Scheinin "Human Rights Committee" in *Social Rights Jurisprudence* 540-552; Scheinin "Economic and Social Rights" in *Economic, Social and Cultural Rights* 32-34; A Rosas & M Scheinin "Implementation Mechanisms and Remedies" in A Eide, C Krause & A Rosas (eds) *Economic, Social and Cultural Rights: A Textbook* 2 ed (2001) 425 440-441.

[38] *L.R. et al v Slovakia* Communication 31/2003 UN Doc CERD/C/66/D/31/2003.

[39] *A.S. v Hungary* Communication 4/2004 UN Doc CEDAW/C/36/D/4/2004.

[40] African Charter on Human and Peoples' Rights (1981) OAU Doc CAB/LEG/67/3 rev. 5 ("African Charter").

[41] Protocol to the African Charter on Human and Peoples' Rights on the Rights of Women in Africa (2003) OAU Doc CAB/LEG/66.6 ("African Women's Protocol").

Children's Charter")[42] can be litigated through the complaints mechanism of the African Committee of Experts on the Rights and Welfare of the Child ("African Committee on Children's Rights").[43]

In contrast with the OP-ICESCR, there is no provision in the African Charter requiring the African Commission to resort to the friendly settlement of disputes or to adopt provisional measures in the case of individual complaints. However, the power to make provisional measures is contained in its African Commission Rules of Procedure;[44] and in practice, the Commission has occasionally resorted to the amicable settlement of disputes.[45] The Rules of Procedure go a step further than article 5 of the OP-ICESCR by including a follow-up mechanism for provisional measures; and, where there is non-compliance, the Commission can refer the case to the African Court.[46] As mentioned earlier, the ability to prescribe provisional measures is one of the most important functions of a judicial or quasi-judicial body adjudicating rights claims. For such a body to be effective, it should be able to perform a pre-emptive function – that is, stop harm before it can occur, stop an ongoing harm from continuing, or at least mitigate the effects of that harm.[47] The inclusion of the friendly settlement of disputes mechanism is important because friendly settlement is a general principle of international law.

Since the African Court is still in its early years, and undergoing structural changes as noted earlier and explained further subsequently in this chapter, the African Commission remains the principal body through which SERs can be litigated.[48] The African Commission has dealt substantively with SERs in a few cases.[49] The decisions provide some guidance on the obligations and substantive content of the rights in the African Charter, including augmenting the explicit rights in it. The Commission also made extensive recommendations in the cases, which would have far reaching implications for the poor if implemented effectively.

The most notable case is *Social and Economic Rights Action Centre and the Centre for Economic and Social Rights v Nigeria*[50] ("*SERAC*"), in which the Commission found the Nigerian government to be in violation of the rights to health, food, housing and environmental rights, among others. It is the first case in which the Commission delineated the negative and positive obligations

---

[42] African Charter on the Rights and Welfare of the Child (1990) OAU Doc CAB/LEG/24.9/49 ("African Children's Charter").

[43] At the time of writing, the Committee was finalising its first decision in the case of *Nubian Children in Kenya v Kenya* Communication 002/2009.

[44] Rule 98 of the African Commission Rules of Procedure.

[45] Viljoen *International Human Rights Law* 329.

[46] Rule 118(2) of the African Commission Rules of Procedure.

[47] Chenwi (2009) *AHRLJ* 37.

[48] For the steps in the litigation process, see SM Weldehaimanor "Towards Speedy Trials: Reforming the Practice of Adjudicating Cases in the African Human Rights System" (2010) 1 *University for Peace LR* 14 19-21.

[49] In addition to the cases below, the Commission has found violations of specific socio-economic rights in *Malawi African Association and Others v Mauritania* Communications 54/91, 61/91, 98/93, 164/97-196/97 and 210/98 (2000) AHRLR 146; *Free Legal Assistance Group and Others v Zaire* Communications 25/89, 47/90, 56/91, 100/93 (2000) AHRLR 74.

[50] *Social and Economic Rights Action Centre and the Centre for Economic and Social Rights v Nigeria* Communication 155/96 (2001) AHRLR 60.

of states in relation to SERs in the African Charter. The Commission also read some missing rights – food and housing, including the prohibition against forced eviction – into the African Charter.

In *Purohit and Moore v The Gambia*[51] (*"Purohit"*), while finding a violation of the right to health, among others, the Commission fleshed out its substantive content. The Commission took into account African realities in defining the SERs obligation of states. In particular, the Commission considered the fact that "millions of people in Africa are not enjoying the right to health maximally because African countries are generally faced with the problem of poverty which renders them incapable to provide the necessary amenities, infrastructure and resources that facilitate the full enjoyment of this right".[52]

Based on this "depressing but real state of affairs", the Commission read into the relevant provision "the obligation on part of States party to the African Charter to take concrete and targeted steps, while taking full advantage of its available resources, to ensure that the right to health is fully realised in all its aspects without discrimination of any kind".[53]

The Commission, with reference to a previous decision, read the right to water into the African Charter in *Sudan Human Rights Organisation v The Sudan Communication 279/03 and Centre on Human Rights and Evictions v The Sudan*[54] (*"Sudan"*). This decision speaks to the indivisibility of human rights and advances SERs such as housing, food, water and health, as well as the need for effective domestic remedies. The Commission elaborated on the right to property,[55] the prohibition on forced eviction,[56] and the right of peoples to their economic, social and cultural development.[57] In its most recent case, *Centre for Minority Rights Development (Kenya) and Minority Rights Group International on behalf of Endorois Welfare Council v Kenya*[58] (*"Endorois"*), the Commission for the first time recognised the rights of indigenous peoples to own land and to development. This case is important in its elaboration of the right to development. It also places emphasis on empowerment, better processes, respecting the agency of all individuals and improving their capabilities and choices in the realisation of rights. The decision further emphasised the need for states to give an equivalent degree of constitutional protection to civil, political, economic, social and cultural rights.

---

[51] *Purohit and Moore v The Gambia* Communication 241/2001 (2003) AHRLR 96.
[52] Para 84.
[53] Para 84.
[54] *Sudan Human Rights Organisation v The Sudan* Communication 279/03 and *Centre on Human Rights and Evictions v The Sudan* Communication 296/05 (2009) AHRLR 153.
[55] See paras 191-205
[56] See, for example, paras 177, 186-189 and 216.
[57] See paras 217-224.
[58] *Centre for Minority Rights Development (Kenya) and Minority Rights Group International on behalf of Endorois Welfare Council v Kenya* Communication 276/2003 (2010).

2 2 Some key aspects

2 2 1 Standing

Standing is an unqualified pre-condition to all legal actions and is different from admissibility. Standing refers to the "'right to appear as a party' before a judicial tribunal or quasi-judicial body", while admissibility relates to the substantive basis of a claim.[59]

The mechanisms under the OP-ICESCR and the African Commission recognise standing for victims, the representatives of victims, and third parties acting on behalf of victims with or without their consent.[60] Where consent has not been obtained, the author has to justify why it is acting without such consent. With regard to others submitting on behalf of victims, the OP-ICESCR is not clear on whether or not an organisation or institution acting on behalf of victims must have consultative status with the UN Economic and Social Council. The position under the African Commission mechanism is clear. A non-governmental organisation ("NGO") for instance, need not have observer status with the Commission, the author need not be a national or be registered in the territory of the state concerned, and there is no requirement on the author to be African, be based in an African state, or to be composed of people of African origin. However, what is clear in relation to the OP-ICESCR is that NGOs cannot submit a complaint in the public interest, as they have to act on behalf of individuals or groups of individuals.[61]

The OP-ICESCR can be contrasted with the African Commission mechanism in this regard. The African Commission has adopted a generous approach to standing. In addition to allowing individuals, groups of individuals or NGOs, the African Commission has allowed the submission of a complaint in the public interest. The *SERAC* case is instructive in this regard. The Commission in this case thanked the two NGOs that had brought the case, stating that it "is a demonstration of the usefulness to the Commission and individuals of *actio popularis*, which is wisely allowed under the African Charter".[62]

2 2 2 Admissibility criteria

Complaints can only be received and considered if they meet certain admissibility criteria. Key among the criteria is that all available domestic remedies – judicial and administrative – must have been exhausted. This requirement is based on the principle that the full and effective implementation of international human rights obligations is intended to improve the enjoyment of rights at the national level.[63] When taking a case to UN bodies, the exhaustion of regional remedies is not part of this requirement. This ensures

---

[59] Viljoen *International Human Rights Law* 323.
[60] Art 2 of the OP-ICESCR. This is also the position of the African Commission. A victim is different from the author of a complaint, as the person submitting a compliant does not have to be the victim.
[61] The OP-ICESCR does not include "collective complaints" as used in the European System.
[62] *Social and Economic Rights Action Centre and the Centre for Economic and Social Rights v Nigeria* Communication 155/96 (2001) AHRLR 60 para 49.
[63] NJ Udombana "So Far, So Fair: The Local Remedies Rule in the Jurisprudence of the African Commission on Human and Peoples' Rights" (2003) 97 *Am J Int'l L* 1 9.

that a hierarchy is not established between the UN and regional mechanisms, especially because regional mechanisms ordinarily play a complementary role to UN mechanisms rather than provide a basis for denying complaints from regions where regional remedies are available. Moreover, regional mechanisms are better placed to take into account a state's level of development and regional specificities. This is not to say that the UN mechanisms would not consider regional specificities if they are aware of them or if placed before them.

Since a remedy should be available (that is, it can be used without impediment), effective (that is, it should offer a prospect of success) and sufficient (that is, it is capable of redressing the wrong complained about),[64] exceptions to the rule exist. The particular circumstance of a case is relevant in any determination of whether domestic remedies are in fact available. In the *Sudan* case, for example, it was impossible to bring issues of human rights violations before independent and impartial courts, since the state was under a military regime, resulting in intimidation, threats and harassment when a case was brought.[65] Displacements into remote regions also made it impossible for people to avail themselves of any remedies.[66] The African Commission, while finding the case to be admissible, stated that "the scale and nature of the alleged abuses, the number of persons involved *ipso facto* make local remedies unavailable, ineffective and insufficient".[67]

Since the *Sudan* case involved a large number of people – in fact tens of thousands who had been forcibly evicted and had their properties destroyed – the Commission found it impracticable and undesirable to expect them to exhaust local remedies that were in any case ineffective.[68] The African Commission has interpreted the requirement to exhaust domestic remedies substantively, identifying instances where local remedies would be non-existent.[69]

In addition, complaints must be submitted within a specific time frame following the exhaustion of domestic remedies. While the OP-ICESCR stipulates a one-year time frame (with room for justifiable exceptions),[70] the African Commission is more flexible in its approach, as complaints have to be submitted "within a reasonable period from the time local remedies are exhausted".[71] This implies that establishing what amounts to a reasonable time is done on a case-by-case basis, taking into consideration the facts and circumstances of the particular case. In this regard, the African system is acclaimed for its "responsiveness to the African landscape's fluidity rather than an adherence to inflexible time standards".[72] Other admissibility grounds

---

[64] Viljoen *International Human Rights Law* 336

[65] *Sudan Human Rights Organisation v The Sudan* Communication 279/03 and *Centre on Human Rights and Evictions v The Sudan* Communication 296/05 (2009) AHRLR 153 para 64.

[66] Para 67.

[67] Paras 96-102.

[68] Paras 101-102.

[69] See Udombana (2003) *Am J Int'l L* 1-37; F Viljoen "Admissibility under the African Charter" in M Evans & R Murray (eds) *The African Charter on Human and Peoples' Rights: The System in Practice, 1986-2000* (2002) 61 81-99; Viljoen *International Human Rights Law* 331-340.

[70] Art 3(2)(a) of the OP-ICESCR.

[71] See art 56(6) of the African Charter.

[72] Viljoen *International Human Rights Law* 339.

common to the OP-ICESCR and African Commission are contained in article 3(2)(b)-(g) of the OP-ICESCR and article 56 of the African Charter.

A novel requirement, absent in the African Commission mechanism but included in the OP-ICESCR, is the discretion given to the CESCR to "decline to consider a communication where it does not reveal that the author has suffered a clear disadvantage, unless the Committee considers that the communication raises a serious issue of general importance".[73] The provision adds a threshold that would allow the CESCR not to deal with complaints of minor importance and to prevent a flood of cases. However, caution would have to be used in applying this provision so as not to eliminate cases that do not on the face of it reflect serious violations, which would otherwise have been considered. Caution is important because, as noted by Vandenbogaerde and Vandenhole, it is only at the merits stage that the substantive issues of a case can be adequately investigated. They also state that adding admissibility requirements reduces potential effectiveness since this implies additional hurdles of a procedural nature before the substance of a complaint can be examined.[74]

2 2 3   Standard of review

The standard of reviewing a state's compliance with its obligations is clearer under the OP-ICESCR than under the African Commission mechanism. Consistent with both international and domestic standards of review in the field of SERs, the standard to be applied under the OP-ICESCR when considering complaints and in assessing state compliance is that of reasonableness.[75] The African Commission has also referred to reasonable steps but with very limited elaboration on what it means.

As rightly observed by Porter, the wording of the relevant provision in the OP-ICESCR is derived from the South African Constitutional Court's jurisprudence.[76] In fact, during the negotiations of the OP-ICESCR, the way in which courts in various systems, including South Africa, have approached the question of enforcement of SERs was considered. The interpretation and application of the reasonableness standard, as Porter has observed, is at the core of the effectiveness of the OP-ICESCR in providing relief to litigants.[77] He

---

[73]   Art 4 of the OP-ICESCR. See also Scheinin & Langford (2009) *Nordic Journal of Human Rights* 110, where the importance of the CESCR adopting such an approach is stated with reference to the Human Rights Committee's experience.

[74]   Vandenbogaerde & Vandenhole (2010) *HRLR* 235.

[75]   Art 8(4) of the OP-ICESCR. For the various instances in which the concept of reasonableness has been used, see UNHRC Working Group on an Optional Protocol to the International Covenant on Economic, Social and Cultural Rights *The Use of the 'Reasonableness' Test in Assessing Compliance with International Human Rights Obligations* (2008) UN Doc A/HRC/8/WG.4/CRP.1.

[76]   B Porter "The Reasonableness of Article 8(4): Adjudicating Claims from the Margins" (2009) 27 *Nordic Journal of Human Rights* 39 49-51, which also explains what the reasonableness standard in the OP-ICESCR means. The South African Constitutional Court first developed the reasonableness standard in *Government of the Republic of South Africa v Grootboom* 2000 11 BCLR 1169 (CC) para 41, which it now applies in assessing the state's compliance with its obligation to take steps towards realising socio-economic rights. See also L Chenwi "Putting Flesh on the Skeleton: South African Judicial Enforcement of the Right to Adequate Housing of Those Subject to Evictions" (2008) 8 *HRLR* 105 119, where the South African reasonableness standard is discussed.

[77]   Porter (2009) *Nordic Journal of Human Rights* 40.

goes further to describe it as a "double edged sword".[78] From one standpoint, it can be used to deny adequate adjudication of, or effective remedies for, substantive SERs claims based on the margin of discretion accorded to states. From another standpoint, it can be used to respond to challenges that go to the systemic causes of poverty and exclusion. Since the OP-ICESCR is not yet in force, there is no jurisprudence from the CESCR on this standard of review. However, the Committee has identified a number of factors (which are not exhaustive) that it would take into account in assessing states' compliance with their obligations under the ICESCR, as well as to determine whether the measures they have taken are adequate or reasonable. The factors identified by the Committee were the following: measures taken must be deliberate, concrete and targeted; the state must exercise its discretion in a non-discriminatory and non-arbitrary manner; whether decisions relating to resources accord with international human rights standards; whether the policy option adopted is the one that least restricts rights; the time frame within which the measures were taken; and whether the situation of the disadvantaged and marginalised has been taken into account and priority given to grave situations or situations of risk.[79] The reasonableness standard in the OP-ICESCR therefore acknowledges the institutional roles and limitations in giving effect to the right to effective remedies. Where states use resource constraints as an excuse for a retrogressive step taken, the Committee has indicated other factors that it would take into account in its assessment.[80] Furthermore, importance is placed on transparent and participative decision-making processes at the national level.[81]

It should be noted that the reasonableness standard (as is the case in the South African context) has not been without challenges, including placing a heavy burden on the claimants to prove the unreasonableness of measures.[82] Accordingly, a number of suggestions have been made in relation to strengthening the standard under the OP-ICESCR. These include the need, in applying the standard, to ensure that the voices of rights claimants are adequately heard; that appropriate and effective remedies are fashioned, taking into consideration the needs and context of claimants and the purpose of the OP-ICESCR; and that the standard be interpreted as a recognition of the multiplicity of entitlements and actors that are involved in allegations of SERs violations.[83]

The African Commission's jurisprudence does not provide much clarity as regards the standard it applies. In *SERAC*, the Commission referred to the state's obligation to "take *reasonable and other measures*" in relation to the

---

[78]   40.

[79]   UN Committee on Economic, Social and Cultural Rights *An Evaluation of the Obligation to Take Steps to the "Maximum of Available Resources" under an Optional Protocol to the Covenant* (2007) UN Doc E/C12/2007/1 para 8.

[80]   Para 10.

[81]   Para 11.

[82]   See S Liebenberg "South Africa: Adjudicating Social Rights under a Transformative Constitution" in M Langford (ed) *Social Rights Jurisprudence: Emerging Trends in International and Comparative Law* (2008) 75 89-91, where the challenges in the South African context are highlighted.

[83]   Porter (2009) *Nordic Journal of Human Rights* 52-53.

right to a satisfactory (or healthy) environment favourable to development,[84] but failed to elaborate on what constitutes reasonable steps. Subsequently, in *Purohit*, the Commission read into the right to health in the African Charter, an obligation on states to "take *concrete and targeted steps*, while taking full advantage of its available resources, to ensure that the right to health is fully realised in all its aspects without discrimination of any kind".[85]

Again, it failed to link this to the "reasonable measures" in *SERAC* or to national jurisprudence that applies the reasonableness concept. Questions such as whether "concrete and target steps" should be considered within South Africa's reasonableness concept or within the CESCR's interpretation, or whether state obligations should be discharged as a matter of priority where resources are lacking, have therefore been left unanswered in the Commission's decisions.[86]

In *Endorois*, the African Commission stated that the state bears the burden of proving that a measure it has adopted is reasonable.[87] This would be useful to poor litigants who lack the resources to prove unreasonableness. The Commission also acknowledged the need for measures adopted to be based on objective and reasonable grounds, and based on equality[88] But again, the Commission made these statements without linking them to its previous SERs jurisprudence. However, the case is illustrative of the importance attached by the Commission to the participation of beneficiaries in the planning and implementation of measures that affect them. This is in line with the standard that the CESCR intends to apply, which also speaks to participative decision-making.

Furthermore, the Commission in *Endorois* engaged in a proportionality analysis, with reference to its previous jurisprudence and that of the Human Rights Committee. The Commission acknowledged that it may be necessary in some instances to place some form of limited restrictions on a right protected by the African Charter.[89] However, such restrictions must be established by law, not be applied in a manner that would completely vitiate the right, be applied only for those purposes for which they were prescribed, be directly related and proportionate to the specific need on which they are predicated, be based on exceptionally good reasons, and not be negligible.[90] In the *Sudan* case as well, the Commission held that restrictions on the enjoyment of rights should be proportionate and necessary to respond to a specific public need or

---

[84] *Social and Economic Rights Action Centre and the Centre for Economic and Social Rights v Nigeria* Communication 155/96 (2001) AHRLR 60 para 52 (emphasis added).

[85] Para 84 (emphasis added).

[86] DM Chirwa "African Regional Level: The Promise of Recent Jurisprudence on Social Rights" in M Langford (ed) *Social Rights Jurisprudence: Emerging Trends in International and Comparative Law* (2008) 323 326-327.

[87] *Centre for Minority Rights Development (Kenya) and Minority Rights Group International on behalf of Endorois Welfare Council v Kenya* Communication 276/2003 (2010) para 172.

[88] Para 234. See also paras 227, 228, 296.

[89] Para 172.

[90] Para 172.

pursue a legitimate aim.[91] The burden is again on the state to prove that an interference with a right is proportionate.[92]

The Commission has further made statements that imply its acknowledgement of the minimum core approach. In *SERAC*, for example, the Commission stated that

> "the minimum core of the right to food requires that the Nigerian Government should not destroy or contaminate food sources. It should not allow private parties to destroy or contaminate food sources, and prevent peoples' efforts to feed themselves".[93]

It then found the government to be in breach of its minimum duties of the right to food.[94] However, Chirwa has criticised the statements in *SERAC* as not reflecting an understanding of the minimum core approach as developed by the CESCR. It is rather, as he states, a misunderstanding of the concept as the pronouncements speak to the duty to respect as opposed to the government taking positive measures to satisfy minimum essential levels of the right.[95] Notwithstanding, it is evident from its jurisprudence and standards on SERs that the Commission recognise the minimum core approach as applicable to these rights in the African Charter.[96]

2 2 4   Remedies and enforcement

The OP-ICESCR does not explicitly refer to remedies. It states that the CESCR shall transmit its views (decision) together with recommendations to the state party after the consideration of a complaint.[97] However, the CESCR has identified the following remedies that it could issue: compensation; requesting the state to remedy the violation; suggesting a range of measures to be adopted; or recommending a follow-up mechanism to ensure ongoing accountability of the state.[98]

Similarly, the African Charter does not explicitly recognise the African Commission's role in granting remedies. Notwithstanding this, the Commission has issued remedies, some of which are open-ended, such as requesting a state to bring its laws in line with the African Charter. This is problematic in that it does not spell out what the state is supposed to do or shed light on the entitlements of the claimant. In other instances, relatively clear and targeted or detailed remedies have been issued – for example, requesting a state: to rehabilitate economic and social infrastructure, such

---

[91]   *Sudan Human Rights Organisation v The Sudan* Communication 279/03 and *Centre on Human Rights and Evictions v The Sudan* Communication 296/05 (2009) AHRLR 153 para 188.

[92]   *Centre for Minority Rights Development (Kenya) and Minority Rights Group International on behalf of Endorois Welfare Council v Kenya* Communication 276/2003 (2010) para 172.

[93]   *Social and Economic Rights Action Centre and the Centre for Economic and Social Rights v Nigeria* Communication 155/96 (2001) AHRLR 60 para 65. See also para 61 on the right to housing.

[94]   Para 66.

[95]   Chirwa "African Regional Level" in *Social Rights Jurisprudence* 325-326.

[96]   See the African Commission on Human and Peoples' Rights *Principles and Guidelines on the Implementation of Economic, Social and Cultural Rights in the African Charter on Human and Peoples' Rights* (formally launched in October 2011).

[97]   Art 9 of the OP-ICESCR.

[98]   UN Committee on Economic, Social and Cultural Rights *An Evaluation of the Obligation to Take Steps* para 13.

as education, health, water, and agricultural services, and to resolve issues of water rights;[99] to repeal the challenged law and adopt a new legislative regime, create an expert body to review the cases of all persons detained under challenged legislation, and provide adequate medical and material care for persons suffering from mental health problems;[100] to investigate violations and provide adequate compensation, including relief and resettlement;[101] and to provide compensation for loss suffered and restitution of land.[102]

However, enforcement of the decisions of treaty bodies is a challenge, as their decisions are not binding. Their implementation is therefore largely dependent on political will. Accordingly, follow-up mechanisms are relevant in ensuring implementation of the decisions. Follow-up is also a means of assessing direct impact of decisions. With regard to follow-up mechanisms, the OP-ICESCR requires states to submit to the CESCR, within six months, a written response to its views and recommendations.[103] The state may also be invited to submit further information on any measures taken in response to the views or recommendations in its subsequent state report under the ICESCR.[104] This follow-up mechanism provides an opportunity for the CESCR to become aware of and address problems encountered by the state when implementing its views and recommendations, so as to ensure their effective implementation. This follow-up mechanism is similar to that of other treaty bodies. For instance, the Human Rights Committee requires states to reply within a period not exceeding 180 days; in practice, it usually indicates a period of 90 days.[105] The difference, however, is that the requirement under the OP-ICESCR is explicitly stated in the treaty.

Compliance with the CESCR's decisions can also be facilitated through article 14 of the OP-ICESCR. It requires the Committee to transmit, when appropriate and with the consent of the state party, to UN specialised agencies, funds and programmes and other competent bodies, its views and recommendations concerning communications and inquiries that indicate a need for technical advice or assistance.[106] The CESCR can also bring to the attention of these bodies "the advisability of international measures likely to contribute to assisting States Parties in achieving progress in implementation of the rights [recognised] in the Covenant".[107]

---

[99] *Sudan Human Rights Organisation v The Sudan* Communication 279/03 and *Centre on Human Rights and Evictions v The Sudan* Communication 296/05 (2009) AHRLR 153 para 229.

[100] See *Purohit and Moore v The Gambia* Communication 241/2001 (2003) AHRLR 96 110.

[101] See *Social and Economic Rights Action Centre and the Centre for Economic and Social Rights v Nigeria* Communication 155/96 (2001) AHRLR 60 para 71.

[102] See *Centre for Minority Rights Development (Kenya) and Minority Rights Group International on behalf of Endorois Welfare Council v Kenya* Communication 276/2003 (2010) Recommendation 1(a) and (c).

[103] See art 9(2) of the OP-ICESCR.

[104] See art 9(3) of the OP-ICESCR.

[105] E de Wet "Recent Developments Concerning the Draft Optional Protocol to the International Covenant on Economic, Social and Cultural Rights" (1997) 13 *SAJHR* 514 514.

[106] Art 14(1) of the OP-ICESCR. The OP-ICESCR also provides for the establishment of a fund in order to facilitate international assistance and cooperation, through which states can receive expert and technical, as opposed to financial, assistance (art 14(3)).

[107] Art 14(2) of the OP-ICESCR.

With regard to the African Commission, the impact of its decisions has been limited by the lack of a mechanism to monitor implementation. Therefore, follow-ups to its decisions have for the main part been very limited, with the state reporting procedure being the main avenue used. This has been exacerbated by the lack of political will of states to implement its decisions, which further erodes the Commission's credibility.

The Commission has explicitly, though mainly in very weak language, required states to report back on implementation but failed, in some instances, to give a time frame. In *SERAC*, for example, the Commission urged the Nigerian government to keep it informed;[108] and in *Purohit*, it went a step further to require the Gambian government to include in its next periodic report, measures taken to comply with its recommendations and directions.[109] The Commission adopted a more stringent stance in line with its 2006 resolution in the *Endorois* case, requiring the Kenyan government to engage in dialogue with the complainants for the effective implementation of its recommendations and to report within three months on their implementation.[110] The Commission further avail its good offices to assist the parties in the implementation of the recommendations.[111]

In 2006, in order to strengthen the implementation of its recommendations, the Commission adopted a resolution requiring states to "respect without delay the recommendation of the Commission"; "submit at every session of the Executive Council a report on the situation of the compliance with its recommendations"; and to indicate within 90 days of being notified of the recommendations, "the measures taken and/or the obstacles in implementing the recommendations".[112] The African Commission has incorporated this follow-up mechanism in its Rules of Procedure, but extended the number of days within which a state should respond after being notified of the recommendation to 180 days.[113] Also, the Commission may request further information on measures taken in response to its decision, within 90 days of receipt of the state's written response.[114] In situations of non-compliance, the Commission can bring the case to the attention of the Sub-Committee of the Permanent Representatives Committee and the Executive Council on the Implementation of the Decisions of the African Union;[115] or submit it to the African Court.[116] Despite the adoption of the follow-up mechanism in 2006, implementation of decisions is still to be improved.

---

[108] *Social and Economic Rights Action Centre and the Centre for Economic and Social Rights v Nigeria* Communication 155/96 (2001) AHRLR 60 para 72.

[109] *Purohit and Moore v The Gambia* Communication 241/2001 (2003) AHRLR 96 110

[110] *Centre for Minority Rights Development (Kenya) and Minority Rights Group International on behalf of Endorois Welfare Council v Kenya* Communication 276/2003 (2010) Recommendation 1(g).

[111] Recommendation 2.

[112] African Commission on Human and Peoples' Rights *Resolution on the Importance of the Implementation of the Recommendations of the African Commission on Human and Peoples' Rights by States Parties* (2006) *ACHPR/Res.97(XXXX)06* <http://www.achpr.org/english/resolutions/resolution102_en.html> (accessed 17-06-2011).

[113] Rule 112(2) of the African Commission Rules of Procedure.

[114] Rule 112(3).

[115] Rule 112(8).

[116] Rule 118(1).

3   Judicial mechanisms: The African Court

This section focuses on the judicial mechanisms at the African regional level. A consideration of the judicial mechanisms in the European and Inter-American regional systems is beyond the scope of this chapter.

In 1998, a Protocol to the African Charter on Human and Peoples' Rights on the Establishment of an African Court on Human and Peoples' Rights ("African Court Protocol")[117] was adopted – establishing and empowering the African Court to, among other things, consider violations of human rights. The judicial mechanisms were initially constituted as two separate courts – the African Court to deal with allegations of human rights violations, and the African Court of Justice[118] to deal with issues of a political and economic nature. However, due to the possibility of overlap and concerns around institutional redundancy, as well as a desire to alleviate financial resources constraints,[119] a decision was taken in 2004 to integrate both courts into a single court. The overlap in competence and jurisdiction can be seen from the following: The African Court of Justice has jurisdiction over disputes and applications that relate to, among other things, the interpretation and application of treaties and subsidiary instruments of the African Union (AU), and public-international law.[120] The African Court also deals with disputes regarding interpretation and application of AU treaties, among others.[121] Therefore, the conflict of jurisdiction has been seen as one of the overlaps that the merger would address.[122] Consequently, in 2008, a Protocol on the Statute of the African Court of Justice and Human Rights was adopted ("2008 Protocol"), invalidating the 1998 and 2003 Protocols.[123] However, the African Court Protocol remains valid until the 2008 Protocol comes into force, and following that, for a transitional period not exceeding one year or any other period determined by the Assembly of Heads of States and Governments of the AU.[124] The joint court consists of a General Affairs Section and a Human and Peoples' Rights Section;[125] and once the joint court is in operation, it would take over cases that were pending before the African Court.[126]

---

[117]   Protocol to the African Charter on Human and Peoples' Rights on the Establishment of an African Court on Human and Peoples' Rights (1998) OAU Doc OAU/LEG/EXP/AFCHPR/PROT (III) ("African Court Protocol").

[118]   See Protocol of the Court of Justice of the African Union (2003) AU Doc Assembly/AU/Dec 45 (111) ("2003 Protocol").

[119]   A Zimmermann & J Bäumler "Current Challenges facing the African Court on Human and Peoples' Rights" (2010) 7 *KAS International Reports* 38 48-49. See also GM Wachira (Minority Rights Group International) *African Court on Human and Peoples' Rights: Ten Years On and Still No Justice* (2008) 14.

[120]   Art 19 of the 2003 Protocol.

[121]   Art 3 of the African Court Protocol.

[122]   African Legal Aid *Introducing the New African Court of Human and Peoples' Rights: Narrative Report* (2006) 13.

[123]   See art 1 of the Protocol on the Statute of the African Court of Justice and Human Rights (2008) AU Doc Assembly/AU/Dec.196 (XI) ("2008 Protocol").

[124]   Art 7 of the 2008 Protocol.

[125]   Art 16 of the 2008 Protocol. At the time of writing, discussions on amendments to the 2008 Protocol were underway in order to create a third section to the joint court – the International Criminal Law Section.

[126]   Art 5 of the 2008 Protocol.

The African Court can consider both individual and inter-state complaints; and is also empowered to give advisory opinions on any legal matter relating to the African Charter or other relevant human rights instruments, provided that the subject matter of the opinion is not related to a matter being examined by the Commission.[127] However, direct access to the Court is limited to the African Commission, the applicant and respondent states, the state of the victim of the human rights violation, and African Intergovernmental Organisations.[128] While NGOs with observer status before the African Commission and individuals can also have access, this is subject to the relevant state making a declaration upon ratification or thereafter recognising the competence of the Court to receive complaints from these groups.[129] Though access for individuals and NGOs is subject to a state making the necessary declaration, the Court still has the discretion to decide whether or not to consider the case, for example, if it does not meet other jurisdictional grounds.

Though there is the possibility of individual complainants accessing the Court through the African Commission,[130] restricting standing for NGOs and individuals is in fact a setback. The African Charter, as seen above, does not contain such restrictions and the African Commission has adopted a generous approach to standing. Therefore, the use of litigation, in the context of the African Court, by marginalised groups and peoples living in poverty to access their rights will be further restricted. There is already a restriction in the sense that states have to first become a party to the Court's constitutive treaty. In addition to that, the state party must enter a declaration allowing individuals to bring a case before the Court. As a result, the first case that came before the Court was dismissed on the basis that the Court had no jurisdiction because Senegal had not made the necessary declaration granting standing to individuals.[131]

Concerning the African Court's procedure in considering complaints, the African Court Protocol does not provide much. However, the Interim Rules of Procedure of the Court indicate that the Court would first conduct a

---

[127] Art 4(1) of the African Court Protocol. Arts 5-6, 8 and 33 of the Protocol, as well as part 4 of the African Commission Rules of Procedure, set out this complementarity relationship.

[128] Art 5(1) of the African Court Protocol.

[129] Arts 5(3) and 34(6) of the African Court Protocol. This restrictive standing is also contained in art 30(f), read with art 8, of the 2008 Protocol. Of the 26 states that have ratified the African Court Protocol, only five – Burkina Faso, Ghana, Malawi, Mali and Tanzania – have made such a declaration (see African Union "List of Countries which have Signed, Ratified/Acceded to the Protocol to the African Charter on Human and Peoples' Rights on the Establishment of an African Court on Human and Peoples' Rights" (11-03-2011) *African Union* <http://www.au.int/en/sites/default/files/992achpr.pdf> (accessed 17-06-2011)).

[130] By virtue of art 5(1)(a) of the African Court Protocol, the African Commission can refer cases it receives to the Court; or file cases (as a complainant) based on its own findings, even where the state concerned has not made the declaration giving individuals standing before the Court (see also Rule 118(3) and (4) of the African Commission Rules of Procedure). However, the Commission is yet to identify clear criteria for referring cases to the African Court (see African Commission on Human and Peoples' Rights "Communique Final de la 49ème Session Ordinaire de la Commission Africaine des Droits de l'Homme et des Peuples qui s'est tenue a Banjul, Gambie du 28 Avril au 12 Mai 2011" (12-05-2011) *African Commission on Human and Peoples' Rights* para 37 <http://www.achpr.org/english/communiques/Final%20Communique_49.pdf> (accessed 17-06-2011), where the Commission requested its Secretariat to conduct further research and propose criteria for referral of cases to the African Court, for the Commission to consider at its next extraordinary session).

[131] See *Yogogombaye v Senegal* Application 001/2008 (2009) AHRLR 315.

preliminary examination of its jurisdiction and admissibility before going on to consider substantive issues .[132]

With regard to admissibility, the criteria under the African Charter are applicable; and when considering the admissibility of complaints from NGOs or individuals, the Court may seek the opinion of the African Commission. The African Court may also refer cases to the Commission.[133] These provisions show the complementarity between the Commission and the Court, which is recognised in the Court's constitutive treaty.[134]

Conversely, due to the lack of clarity on when one could use the Commission or the Court, Steiner, Alston and Goodman have seen the bodies as being in competition with each other, without any clear hierarchy, which could result in duplication of efforts.[135] Looking at other regional systems, the Inter-American system for example sets a hierarchy between the Inter-American Court of Human Rights and Inter-American Commission on Human Rights, where cases must first go through the latter before they can be brought before the former.[136]

Furthermore, similar to UN and other regional bodies, the Court can try to settle a case amicably.[137] Similar to the OP-ICESCR, the protection of witnesses or persons that appear before the Court is guaranteed.[138]

A distinguishing point between the Court and UN treaty bodies and the African Commission is that the hearings are held in public, and therefore presumably include oral hearings, except where it is necessary to consider a complaint *in camera*.[139] This provision is a relief for many who have been concerned about the African Commission's closed hearings. As Udombana has pointed out, it ensures that "justice is not only done but manifestly seen to be done".[140] Also, free legal representation during hearings is available, where the interest of justice so requires.[141] However, the provision does not say if this extends to the filing of complaints. This would be crucial since one of the constraints of the African Commission's complaints mechanism has been the submission of poorly written and unclear cases that may likely allege serious violations but are difficult to process due to their format.[142]

---

[132] Rule 39 of the Interim Rules of Court of the African Commission on Human and Peoples' Rights, adopted and entered into force on 20-06-2008 <http://www.chr.up.ac.za/images/files/documents/ahrdd/theme03/african_court_rules.pdf> (accessed 17-06-2011).

[133] Art 6 of the African Court Protocol.

[134] See Rules 114-123 of the African Commission Rules of Procedure.

[135] Steiner et al *International Human Rights in Context* 1082.

[136] See TJ Melish "The Inter-American Court of Human Rights: Beyond Progressivity" in M Langford (ed) *Social Rights Jurisprudence: Emerging Trends in International and Comparative Law* (2008) 371 378.

[137] Art 7 of the African Court Protocol.

[138] Art 10(3).

[139] Art 10(1) and (2).

[140] NJ Udombana *The African Regional Human Rights Court: Modelling its Rules of Procedure* (2002) Danish Centre for Human Rights Research Partnership 5/2002 110 <http://www.humanrights.dk/files/Importerede%20filer/hr/pdf/udombana_-_african_human_rights_court.pdf> (accessed 17-06-2011).

[141] Art 10(2) of the African Court Protocol.

[142] J Harrington "The African Court on Human and Peoples' Rights" in M Evans & R Murray (eds) *The African Charter on Human and Peoples' Rights: The System in Practice, 1986-2000* (2002) 305 324.

The African Court is required to pass its judgment within 90 days after hearing a case.[143] This addresses a deficiency in the African Commission's mechanism, where there is a huge time lapse between the hearing and the issuance of a decision in some instances.[144] Upon finding a violation, the Court can grant remedies, including the payment of fair compensation and reparation.[145] It can also take provisional (interim) measures *proprio motu* in cases of extreme gravity and urgency in order to avoid irreparable harm.[146] However, the African Court Protocol fails to say if these measures are binding as is the case with the Court's judgments. The Court recently, in its second ruling, issued an order for provisional measures in the case of *African Commission on Human and Peoples' Rights v Great Socialist People's Libyan Arab Jamahiriya*[147] ("*Libya*"). This is the first case brought before it by the African Commission. It relates to alleged serious and massive violations, by Libyan authorities, of human rights guaranteed under the Charter, including the state's obligation to adopt legislative and other measures to give effect to the rights and ensure non-discrimination in the enjoyment of rights. Though the Commission did not request in its application that the Court should grant provisional measures, the Court found it necessary to do so due to an imminent risk of loss of life and the difficulties in serving the application on Libya due to the ongoing conflict.[148] The Libyan authorities were ordered to "immediately refrain from any action that would result in loss of life or violation of physical integrity of persons, which could be a breach of the provisions of the Charter or of other international human rights instruments to which it is a party".[149]

The case does not specifically deal with SERs but deals with rights such as non-discrimination and the obligations of states, both of which are relevant to SERs. The case also illustrates the potential use of provisional measures to protect the rights of those who cannot access the Court; of course, subject to the measures being implemented. This is particularly important for individuals in Libya because Libya has not made the necessary declaration recognising the competence of the Court to receive complaints from individuals. Also, though implementation of the order is uncertain because of the ongoing conflict in Libya, it is significant as it is the first judicial response to the situation in Libya and would influence how other bodies and institutions respond to the situation.

The implementation of the decisions of the African Court is monitored by the Council of Ministers.[150] This is reinforced by the undertaking by state parties to guarantee the execution of the Court's decisions and to implement

---

[143] Art 28 of the African Court Protocol.
[144] Harrington "African Court on Human and Peoples' Rights" in *African Charter on Human and Peoples' Rights* 325.
[145] Art 27(1) of the African Court Protocol.
[146] Art 27(2).
[147] *African Commission on Human and Peoples' Rights v Great Socialist People's Libyan Arab Jamahiriya* Application 004/2011 (2011).
[148] Paras 9-13.
[149] The authorities were also required to report to the Court within fifteen days on the measures taken to implement the order (see para 25).
[150] Art 29(2) of the African Court Protocol.

them within the time frames stated by the Court.[151] This addresses some of the deficiencies in the African Charter relating to remedies and follow-up, mentioned earlier, which have impacted on the effectiveness of the complaints mechanism of the African Commission. The remedial and enforcement powers granted to the Court present better prospects for the protection of SERs, as some judgments would require supervision in order to ensure their effective implementation.[152]

4 Concluding remarks

International complaints mechanisms are important in complementing domestic mechanisms. The UN High Commission for Human Rights, for example, has noted the contribution of UN treaty bodies to the development of jurisprudence that is frequently referred to by national and regional tribunals and in the provision of individual relief for victims.[153] International law complaints mechanisms have gone beyond providing justice to individuals or groups before it. For example, through the consideration of complaints, the African Commission has provided individual relief such as ordering compensation, as well as recommended proactive measures to prevent similar violations from occurring, such as requiring a state to review the relevant domestic legislation and monitor institutions providing services.

The OP-ICESCR is not yet in force, so an assessment of its efficacy is limited to its potential. Through the consideration of complaints, the CESCR would gain more insight into the challenges and limitations in the realisation of SERs, enabling it to develop jurisprudence that is sensitive to global realities. This would provide a useful framework through which subsequent complaints can be analysed and understood.[154] However, for it to be effective, a number of practical points need to be taken into consideration. Scheinin and Malcolm have pointed to the need for the CESCR to make its decisions expansive and in-depth in their legal reasoning; and to consider experiences and jurisprudence from other jurisdictions or regions so as to refrain from further promoting the fragmentation of public-international law.[155] Langa has, among other things, cautioned against the CESCR using too formalistic and technical approaches in analysing complaints; and emphasised the importance of the Committee using the tools of dignity and equality in addition to reasonableness in upholding and enforcing SERs.[156] In addition, effective implementation of the decisions of the Committee is crucial to ensuring that rights claimants have access to remedies and that the decisions have an impact on the ground.

The individual complaints mechanism of the African Commission has been instrumental in enforcing and expanding the SERs in the African

---

[151] Art 30.
[152] Chirwa "African Regional Level" in *Social Rights Jurisprudence* 337.
[153] UN Human Rights Instruments *Concept Paper on the High Commissioner's Proposal for a Unified Standing Treaty Body* (2006) UN Doc HRI/MC/2006/2 para 13.
[154] P Langa "Taking Dignity Seriously – Judicial Reflections on the Optional Protocol to the ICESCR" (2009) 27 *Nordic Journal of Human Rights* 29 31.
[155] Scheinin & Langford (2009) *Nordic Journal of Human Rights* 111-112.
[156] Langa (2009) *Nordic Journal of Human Rights* 37.

Charter, as seen in *SERAC*, *Purohit*, *Sudan* and *Endorois*, for example, where the Commission further developed the substantive content of these rights, clarified to some extent the obligations of states, and adopted a progressive interpretation of the African Charter and the doctrine of implied rights. However, the complaints mechanism of the Commission is not without drawbacks, many of them, procedural. While the Commission has been commended for developing the individual complaints mechanism into a "higher level human rights mechanism", the need to reform its practice of adjudicating cases has also been stressed.[157]

In addition to the limitation in terms of remedies, the binding nature of its decisions and their enforcement, the Commission – as is the case with UN treaty bodies – is inaccessible to the poor because of where it is located. Complaints also take a long time to be finalised – a problem common to quasi-judicial treaty bodies. It takes two-and-a-half to three years for a case to be disposed of; which is clearly at odds with the notion of a speedy trial.[158] This has frustrated many, particularly rights claimants. The complaint mechanism has therefore been criticised for doing very little to protect an individual complainant, "as it 'starts too late, takes too much time, does not lead to a binding results and lacks any effective enforcement'".[159] There is an urgent need for an effective complaint procedure that is accessible and relatively speedy, and for the rapporteurs of the Commission to be diligent in gathering information relating to the facts stated in complaints before it.[160]

The effectiveness of the African Court becomes relevant in complementing the African Commission's mechanism. In fact, its recent ruling on Libya has been seen as a practical example of how "the Commission and the Court may cooperate in responding to human rights situations in the region".[161] Despite the limitations in the African Court Protocol, such as taking a step back in terms of standing, generally, the Court's procedure and enforcement goes further than that of the Commission. It would therefore be instrumental in giving meaning to the SERs in the African Charter and other treaties. The initial omission of the Court was in fact seen as undermining public confidence in the African human rights system, since its absence made it impossible to compel violating states to conform to international norms and to provide remedies to victims.[162] Whether in practice the Court would be a more powerful and structured body than the Commission remains to be seen; this would depend on the aptitude, boldness and creativity of the judges. It would seem the Court is moving in this direction if one considers its recent order of provisional measures that indicate that the Court is taking its mandate seriously. It is

---

[157] Weldehaimanor (2010) *University for Peace LR* 19.

[158] 18.

[159] Udombana *African Regional Human Rights Court* 19.

[160] Udombana (2003) *Am J Int'l L* 36-37. Weldehaimanor (2010) *University for Peace LR* 27-19 also makes a number of useful suggestions relating to reforming the adjudication mechanism.

[161] AA Mulugeta "A Landmark Provisional Ruling of the African Court on Human and Peoples' Rights on Libya" (02-04-2011) *International Law Observer* <http://internationallawobserver.eu/2011/04/02/acthpr_provisional_ruling_on_libya/> (accessed 31-08-2011).

[162] NJ Udombana "An African Human Rights Court and an African Union Court: A Needful Duality or a Needless Duplication?" (2003) 28 *Brook J Int'l L* 811 826.

premature to make a decisive assessment on the Court's aptitude based on this single landmark ruling; but it is illustrative of the fact that Court's potential cannot be overruled.

SUMMARY

Litigation of socio-economic rights at international level is a viable option where access to justice at the national level is unattainable. International law mechanisms for litigating these rights are therefore useful for marginalised groups and people living in poverty. This is also based on the important role of these mechanisms in ensuring that states meet the obligations they have committed to in human rights treaties, and provide effective remedies in cases of violations. In this chapter I assess, taking into consideration some broad principles, the international law mechanisms for litigating socio-economic rights at the UN and African regional levels, particularly the Optional Protocol to the International Covenant on Economic, Social and Cultural Rights ("OP-ICESCR") and the African Court on Human and Peoples' Rights and the African Commission on Human and Peoples' Rights complaints mechanisms. The chapter illustrates that while these mechanisms have the potential to advance the rights of the poor and marginalised, and in some case have been successful in doing so, they are not without drawbacks that impact on their effectiveness.

CHAPTER 14

LIBERAL CONSTITUTIONALISM, PROPERTY RIGHTS, AND THE ASSAULT ON POVERTY

Frank I Michelman[*]

1 Introduction

Suppose we have three factors in play: a national project of post-colonial recovery from distributive injustice, prominently including land reform; express constitutional protection for property rights; and a Constitution whose other main features bring it recognisably within the broad historical tradition of liberal constitutionalism. Have we got a practical contradiction on our hands?

To what extent, if any, does or must the constitutional property clause (as distinct from its companion-liberal constitutional guarantees) particularly impede the social-transformation project? Crucially, the answer is not preordained but rather rests on how the clause is construed and applied by whoever is to decide which actions of the state the clause does and does not interdict.[1] Suppose that is a body of courts. The next question, then, might be about the extent, if any, to which we must expect that the Constitution's overall liberal affiliation will incline the courts toward deployments of that clause that are especially troublesome from the standpoint of reform.

The narrower claim of this essay is that the attractions of liberal constitutionalism do not come necessarily laden with a counter-reformative property clause. In what I would call a proper liberal view, the office of a constitutional property clause is to signal recognition of the connection between a decent respect for property and a decent respect for human dignity and freedom; it is *not*, however, to provide defenses for property rights beyond what constitutional protections for freedom, security, dignity, equality, and legality would anyway provide.

It may, even so, be true that the conditions of distributive justice within a national society will not always be achievable by means meeting the demands of an up-and-running liberal constitutional order. The essay's broader claim is that the fault in such cases does not, however, lie in a liberal conception of justice.

---

[*] My thanks go to STIAS. A fellowship there provided time and wonderfully supportive surroundings for the preparation of this chapter.

[1] This point receives apt emphasis from GS Alexander *The Global Debate Over Constitutional Property Rights* (2006) 6, 9, 29, 57-59. Throughout this essay, my necessarily summary observations in regard to the current state of the debate share much with Alexander's richly extended explorations.

1 1   A puzzle of transformative constitutionalism

Plain, deep, and insuperable are the South African Constitution's[2] liberal genes. So insists Sanele Sibanda in his highly compelling contribution to this colloquium,[3] even as he both grants and applauds the Constitution's "post"-liberal, transformation-minded reworkings of its liberal birthright.[4] With Sibanda's uncompromising placement of the Constitution in liberal territory, I could not more wholeheartedly agree. Indeed, I may go further down that road than Sibanda does; for I mean to resist as far as possible any suggestion of a divide or contradiction between the Constitution's social-transformative pretensions and its indwelling liberal identity. To resist the suggestion, I say, but not entirely to crush it. In the end, something beyond the trivial will remain of that concern. Whatever that is, though, it will not be an out-and-out indictment of a liberal constitutionalist transplant to African post-colonial soil.

Sibanda's own powerful work stops somewhere short of that, at least for now. But Sibanda does deeply doubt the receptiveness – much less the positive conduciveness – of any possible practice of liberal constitutionalism, let it be of the most left-leaning conceivable variety, to a truly redemptive project of social transformation in South Africa now or elsewhere on this continent. And yet, as I read Sibanda, it is not the liberal-constitutionalist *ideal* that he rejects, but rather the notion that a liberal-constitutionalist establishment *here* and *now* will permit – let alone can inspire and provoke – a consolidation of the political will and the political means required to move the country from its here and now to its envisioned, socially transformed future condition. However humanely conceived and intended, a liberal-constitutionalist transformative project in the South African here and now is bound, Sibanda believes, to meet with fatal blockage by a dominant drive in liberal constitutionalism to limit the state as opposed to empowering and obligating it. "Transformative constitutionalism" becomes, to that extent, a contradiction in terms, an oxymoron; perhaps not necessarily so on an abstract theoretical plane (where limitation might give more ground to obligation), but still surely so within the currently prevailing and reasonably foreseeable political-cultural context here, coddled as that context is by a more classical-liberal understanding.

Sibanda's reservations start out from what we may all agree are fixed points of substance and procedure in liberal constitutionalism. Procedurally, constitutionalism means the channelling of raw political desire through institutional filters for deliberation, accountability, and control: representative government, divided powers, institutional checks and balances – "procedural democracy in the form of free and fair elections and the balancing of institutional power dynamics between the branches of government".[5] Substantively, constitutionalism no doubt involves distinct limits on the lawful powers of the

---

[2]   Constitution of the Republic of South Africa, 1996 ("the Constitution").
[3]   S Sibanda "Not Purpose-Made! Transformative Constitutionalism, Post-Independence Constitutionalism and the Struggle to Eradicate Poverty" in S Liebenberg & G Quinot (eds) *Law and Poverty* (2012) 40.
[4]   See generally KE Klare "Legal Culture and Transformative Constitutionalism" (1998) 14 *SAJHR* 146.
[5]   Sibanda "Transformative Constitutionalism" in *Law and Poverty* 52.

state, although I would be cautious about how far to go in positing a liberal commitment to political and legal sequestration of a "private sphere that [is] the preserve of private citizens".[6]

As I read Sibanda, the problem he perceives is not that these liberal-constitutionalist ideas must necessarily, in the abstract or in all circumstances, act as obstacles to poverty-prevention by organised political means. There might, he allows, well be room to construe and apply them so that they need not. But liberalism's characteristic instinct to fall back on procedural responses to otherwise seemingly intractable social conflicts suggests to Sibanda an overwhelming likelihood, in the current South African *milieu*, of a slide to moderation and complacency and even to callous indifference in the halls of power to the indefinite persistence here of what few would deny are morally intolerable conditions of poverty, indignity, and dispossession.

That crude summary misses the power, refinement, and pathos of Sibanda's argument. Even as thus wanly restated, the argument is not one that I would know how to reject or rebut. Rebuttal, however, is not my aim, but rather a kind of interpretative next step. What I want to suggest is that the heart of the difficulty lies neither in the broadly speaking liberal nor in the specifically constitutionalist elements in the current South African regime. That is partly because the location of the heart of the difficulty is not within South Africa but in the world at large. Drain South African politics and law, if you could, of liberal normative ideas and ideals, to be replaced by something more radically solidaristic, communalistic, or perhaps (but now I stray beyond my competence) indigenous and African. Free South African politics and law, if you could, from constitutionalistic procedural and institutional fetters, to be replaced by some "constitution without constitutionalism" on the African model unforgettably and brilliantly described, explained, and analysed by Okoth-Ogendo.[7] The obstacle, as I see it, would remain. It would, to be sure, be a fellow-traveller with liberalism; I think a corruption of it, but that may be controversial. The obstacle would not, in my view, be liberalism pure and simple; it would not be the liberal normative essence or ideal. I do not take such a claim to contradict Sibanda. I want to partner, in a way, with his argument: to leave it standing, only shorn of some possible misunderstandings.

In fact my claim here will be cast in somewhat narrower terms. Its specific focus will be on the guarantees respecting property and property rights that inevitably are somewhere found, implicit if not explicit in any practice of liberal constitutionalism.

---

[6]   Sibanda "Transformative Constitutionalism" in *Law and Poverty* 51 n 64. Compare J Rawls *Justice as Fairness: A Restatement* (2001) 166:

"The principles defining the equal basic liberties and fair opportunities of citizens hold in and through all so-called [spheres or] domains ... [T]he spheres of the political and the public, and of the not-public and the private, take their shape from the content and application of the conception of justice and its principles. If the so-called private sphere is a space alleged to be exempt from justice, then there is no such thing."

[7]   HWO Okoth-Ogendo *Constitutions Without Constitutionalism: Reflections on an African Paradox* (1988).

1 2   Plan of the reflection

I offer, in what follows, a reflection on connections among three factors: constitutional property clauses, liberal constitutional culture, and national projects of recovery from post-colonial distributive injustice. I want to sort out, if I can, a tangle of ideas about the effects – for the better or for the worse – of constitutional protections for property rights on a society's vigour in addressing the causes and cures of poverty; and I want to consider how the effects might be conditioned by the presumably liberal – or at any rate "postliberal"[8] – mindset of constitutions containing such protections.

The reflection proceeds through a series of questions running from quite narrow to quite broad, as follows:

i) What special, concrete legal work (if any) is done by the inclusion of a property clause in an otherwise complete constitutional bill of rights?

ii) Aside from any such work it is expected to do, what other sorts of aims or concerns might prompt or explain the inclusion of a property clause in an otherwise complete constitutional bill of rights?

iii) Which among the results from our preceding queries best explain the inclusion of a property clause in a so-called "transformative" constitution that also contains evident, strong commitments to the eradication of poverty, the achievement of equality, and the fulfilment of human dignity for all from a starting position of wide-scale, unjust dispossession?

iv) What (if anything) follows regarding the normatively preferred judicial deployment of a property clause when found within such a constitution?

v) What (if anything) follows regarding the sustainability, in concept and in practice, of an idea of "transformative constitutionalism", occurrent within the broad current of the traditions, discourses, practices, and cultures of liberal constitutionalism?

The earlier questions in my series may seem aimless or ungrounded when first taken up. My hope is that by the end they will not seem so, but rather will stand justified as parts of an agenda of questions for further study and debate, by and among those currently committed to the pursuit of socially transformative aims (including the eradication of poverty), by what I will broadly call constitutional-legal means, in what I will broadly call post-colonial settings. I emphasise "for further study and debate" because the reflection here can only, on the whole, be rudimentary – to the point, indeed, of being merely cursory in some places. But let us begin.

---

[8]   Klare (1998) *SAJHR* 151-156.

2   Special, concrete legal work from a constitutional property clause?

What special, concrete legal work (if any) is done by the inclusion of a property clause in an otherwise complete constitutional bill of rights?

Several terms require definition: "property clause", "otherwise complete", and "special, concrete legal work" – in that order.

As I use the term here, a *constitutional property clause* is a guarantee – as represented, say, by the first three sub-paragraphs of section 25 of the Constitution of South Africa[9] – of (i) supreme-law support for (ii) defensive claims against (iii) disturbances of proprietary positions duly established under (iv) an extant legal regime that supports private ownership. Thus, my concern here is with constitutional guarantees respecting control and retention of assets currently recognised as yours, not with guarantees respecting what you will not be suffered at any time, or for long, to go without. (A constitution also may contain commitments of the latter sort – as does South Africa's[10] – but those are not what I mean here by property clauses.)

A constitutional property clause typically appears as one substantive guarantee in a list of several – a "bill" or "charter" of "rights". That list may or may not be what I here call *otherwise complete*. Picture, if you will, a constitution that already includes (as, for example, South Africa's does) robust substantive guarantees respecting personal freedom, security, dignity, and privacy; respecting non-discrimination and equality under the law; respecting legality and due process – but that contains nothing that refers specifically to property. By "guarantees respecting" these matters, I do not mean absolute and unconditional assurances. I rather mean what our constitutions typically are taken to mean: assurances against non-trivial infringements for which (or for the law's allowance of which by others) the state does not provide a sufficient justification, in terms of some appropriately weighty or urgent moral or social purpose that is served by the infringement or by the law that authorises or allows it.

My question, at this first stage of the reflection, is about what (if any) *special, concrete legal work* is expected to be done by addition of a property clause to such an otherwise complete bill of rights. Now, by "special, concrete legal work" I mean making a directly traceable difference in the disposition of some identifiable subset of cases at law from what the disposition otherwise would have been. What (if any) difference of that sort have we reason to

---

[9]   See s 25 of the Constitution:

"(1)   No one may be deprived of property except in terms of law of general application, and no law may permit arbitrary deprivation of property.

(2)   Property may be expropriated only in terms of law of general application –

(a)   for a public purpose or in the public interest; and

(b)   subject to compensation, the amount of which and the time and manner of payment of which have either been agreed to by those affected or decided or approved by a court.

(3)   The amount of the compensation and the time and manner of payment must be just and equitable, reflecting an equitable balance between the public interest and the interests of those affected ..."

[10]   See ss 25(5), 25(7), 26-28 of the Constitution.

expect from the introduction of a property clause into an otherwise complete constitutional bill of rights?

Especially if you are a lawyer, you will find it hard to free yourself from the thought that inclusion of the property clause must have been aimed at raising the litigation-success rate for some subset of constitutional claims above where it otherwise ought to lie. Given our definition of "property clause", the subset tagged for advantage would have to consist of claims stemming from disturbances of extant ownership positions, either perpetrated by the state or permitted by its laws. But now consider the fact (and is it not a fact?) that every conceivable instance of such a disturbance can support at least a bare claim of a *prima facie* infringement of one or more of a person's constitutional claims to freedom, security, dignity, privacy, equality (non-discrimination), legality, or due process, thus putting the state to its burden of justification. Appreciation of that point allows us to enrich somewhat our account of the concrete legal work (if any) that addition of the property clause to an otherwise complete bill of rights must be expected to do. It seems that some but not all cases of alleged infringement on those other rights – freedom, dignity, *et cetera* – will involve an ownership disturbance as occasioning the alleged infringement. Addition of the property clause must be expected to give claimants *in that particular subset of cases* some sort of extra litigation benefit or advantage they would not otherwise enjoy. I shall soon try to be a bit more precise about the sort of extra advantage the property clause might be expected to provide for ownership-disturbance claims. But to aid us in seeing what could be going on here, we can make use of a hypothetical case.

Let it be a case of a law on eviction control.[11] Say it is a law that bars an owner from evicting anyone from quarters occupied by that person as his home, unless and until a court has determined that replacement housing is available to that person, within his means and also within practicable reach of that person's established place of work, if he has one, or of locations where work will be available for him if he is capable of working. This statutory barrier to eviction is plainly written to apply to any and all cases of attempted evictions of people from their current homes, regardless of any conceded entitlement of the applicant to immediate possession under basic and simple property and contract law (because, for example, the applicant is the owner and the lease has expired, or perhaps the occupation is nakedly illegal).

Under a constitution containing an otherwise complete bill of rights but lacking a property clause, sundry applicants for eviction, when first met by blockage from this law, could be expected to invoke against it their constitutional rights to freedom, security, dignity, privacy, equality, and legality. At least at the beginning, before courts had been able to develop any

---

[11] I must ask South African lawyers to set aside the obvious special bearing on this instance of ss 25(6) and 26(3) of the Constitution. Those familiar with the South African mineral-resources legislation recently held unconstitutional in *Agri South Africa v Minister of Minerals and Energy* 2011 3 All SA 296 (GNP), or with the burial-rights provision, s 6(2)(DA) of the Extension of Security of Tenure Act 62 of 1997 as amended, held constitutional in *Nhlabati v Fick* 2003 7 BCLR 806 (LCC), might want also to have those laws in mind.

substantial body of qualifying doctrine,[12] a great many such claims should easily suffice to establish a *prima facie* limitation of one or another of those rights, thus putting the state to its burden of justification. Now, while the state could easily lose some fraction of the cases, it doubtless would prevail in others. (Perhaps, say, the violation of the lease-condition was accidental and endurable, the owner has no different use in mind for the space, the tenant is poor and lacks alternatives, and (for good measure) the eviction is prompted by spite.)

Add a property clause to the mix. Might cases now arise under our anti-eviction law in which a court would find an unconstitutional infringement *of the property clause*, even though, in context, the court would have detected no unjustified infringement of anything else in the otherwise complete bill of rights? If the answer is no, then addition of the property clause is not doing any special, concrete legal work. But how can the answer possibly be yes?

Here is how. We suppose that the presence of the property clause, and only the presence of the property clause, allows the owner to argue approximately as follows:

> My owner's title to this land is an asset, an item of property. The law in question, as applied to this case, has created in the current occupant a new asset, consisting of his legally protected, indefinitely continuing privilege to occupy the space in question. The law's bestowal of that asset on him perpetrates a redistribution from me to him – thus, a withdrawal from my asset portfolio, a contraction of its boundaries. The property clause flatly prohibits withdrawals of assets from owners by the state without just and equitable compensation, and no compensation has been provided.

Suppose that argument is allowed to go through just as stated. Then we can easily see a special, concrete legal consequence from the addition of the property clause to the otherwise complete bill of rights. When – and only when – what is up for decision is a claim to supreme-law protection against disturbances of existing positions of asset-holding or asset-definition, the property clause gives the claimant a special entitlement to a strongly rule-formalist style of adjudication, as opposed to the more insistently contextualised, proportionality approach that is used in regard to all the rest of the bill. Where owners cry out only in terms of "liberty", or "dignity", or "privacy", or "equality", or "legality", the gravity of the claimed infringements is tested – "weighed" – against the state's countervailing moral purposes. Where owners cry "property" and can show a non-compensated asset-redefinition or redistribution wrought by or pursuant to the state action in question, there is no such further weighing that the claim is required to undergo.

---

[12] As, for example, the Constitutional Court of South Africa has done for the property clause in the lines of cases beginning with *First National Bank of SA Limited t/a Wesbank v Commissioner for the South African Revenue Services; First National Bank of SA Limited t/a Wesbank v Minister of Finance* 2002 4 SA 768 (CC). See generally AJ van der Walt *Constitutional Property Law* 3 ed (2011); T Roux "The 'Arbitrary Deprivation' Vortex: Constitutional Property Law after FNB" in S Woolman & M Bishop (eds) *Constitutional Conversations* (2008) 265.

Granted, the property clause need not necessarily work that way.[13] The owner cries "property" and shows an infringement of his property right by non-compensated destruction, re-assignment, or impairment of an asset or of its value to him. The case could then proceed as usual to the justification stage, where the court tests the gravity of the property-right infringement against the state's moral or other social purposes. But then it seems that the property clause may be doing no special, concrete legal work, because – as we have seen – any instance of a property loss or impairment can always be re-described in terms of an infringement on freedom, security, privacy, dignity, equality, or legality. If or insofar as we lawyers really think that addition of the property clause *must* be meant to extend a "property" claimant's level of protection beyond what the other clauses would anyway provide, it seems that can only occur by somehow specially easing the claimant's burden, or specially toughening the state's, in that subset of bill-of-rights cases in which a claimed *prima facie* infringement on freedom *et cetera* takes the special form of a disturbance of an ownership position.

From decades of immersion in US constitutional property law, my sense of the way the property clause is supposed to do that is by making courts more receptive to rule-formalist argumentation in ownership-disturbance cases than in most other cases of claimed infringements on freedom or the rest.[14] Perhaps that is wrong, or perhaps it does not hold more widely in the world. My point remains that where it does *not* hold, the presence of the property clause in the otherwise complete bill of rights does no clear-cut, concrete legal work; and so lawyers (especially) may be tempted to think that the constitution containing the clause poses no more of an obstacle to social transformation than does the constitution lacking it. But such a restricted lawyer's-eye view would be incomplete.

3   Other grounds and explanations for inclusion

Aside from any special, concrete legal work it is expected to do, what other sorts of aims or concerns might prompt or explain the inclusion of a property clause in an otherwise complete constitutional bill of rights?

A number of possible answers come to mind. It will be convenient to give them labels, as follows: "signalling function", "property in the margins", "possessive individualism", "institutional guarantee", and "necessity".

Signalling function. Constitution-makers might be concerned about the legal culture's possible future insensitivity to the severity of the impairments of personal freedom and dignity that can result from disruptions of secure

---

[13]   As of course it does not in South Africa, but that may be in significant part because the South African property clause, in full context and with its nine sub-paragraphs, is specially and uniquely drafted to avoid such an effect, see Van der Walt *Constitutional Property Law* 16; *Phumalela Gaming and Leisure Limited v Gründlingh* 2006 8 BCLR 883 (CC) para 38:

"The constitutional property clause is not absolute and should not be employed in a manner that ignores other rights and values ... If the Court were to develop the common law test of wrongfulness to protect Phumalela's property rights to the detriment of the values on the other end of the scale, it would be discarding the nuanced test that has been developed through case law."

[14]   See generally FI Michelman "Takings, 1987" (1988) 88 *Colum L Rev* 1600. Critics from the right of US constitutional property law have objected that it moves insufficiently far in this direction. See RA Epstein "Property, Speech, and the Politics of Distrust" (1992) 59 *U Chi L Rev* 41.

control over things external to the self. The property clause then might be meant to serve as a firm and salient reminder of this political-moral truth (as the framers see it), so that policymakers and adjudicators will not overlook or disparage it.

The expected or desired signal might carry either or both of a left-leaning or a right-leaning inflection. To the left, we have "property in the margins"; to the right, we have "possessive individualism".

"Property in the margins".[15] In a transformative constitutional setting, and in alliance with the equality and other clauses, the property clause can serve as a call to recognise the dependency of a person's freedom and dignity no less (and oftentimes more!) on possessory positions traditionally classified as weak, subordinate, and vulnerable (labour tenancies, non-formalised occupations), than on positions of full, formal ownership. The clause works to demand full equality of consideration for these formally weaker claims when conflicts arise among contestants for the same space or other asset.

"Possessive individualism". (I take this term from Macpherson's widely known, adversarial exposition of an emphatically privatistic and self-centered form of liberal political thought.)[16] Our notion of "special, concrete legal work" was set up to look for some special advantage for constitutional claims involving proprietary disturbances as compared with claims that do not. But we must not overlook how inclusion of a property clause might work to signal a general "atomistic" tilt (as some might call it) in a country's overall political value-ordering – or, in other words, a wholesale stiffening, against socially compelled consideration for others, of individual defensive claims across the board, from free speech to free trade (or whatever), with consequent impediment to state efforts toward social transformation.[17]

Institutional guarantee. The normative prompt to include a property clause may not come at first from contemplation of the liberal individual entitled (by nature?) to strong supreme-law possessive-defensive rights. The aim may rather be toward the public or social good. It may be to provide to the world at large what is sometimes called an "institutional guarantee".[18] The clause, then, is put there to serve as a confirmation of the state's long-term commitment to an ownership-enabling (also efficiency-enabling) form of institutional order, in which persons, by voluntary action, can acquire, keep, exchange, and bestow positions of more-or-less secure and exclusive control over specified assets.

---

[15]   This neat term is drawn, of course, from AJ van der Walt *Property in the Margins* (2009).

[16]   See C Macpherson *The Political Theory of Possessive Individualism: From Hobbes to Locke* (1962).

[17]   Jennifer Nedelsky has written extensively on the property right's representation of the political-moral salience of the separateness of persons and boundaries around them, most recently in her *Law's Relations: A Relational Theory of Self, Autonomy, and Law* (2011) 91-96. See also J Nedelsky *Private Property and the Limits of American Constitutionalism: The Madisonian Framework and its Legacy* (1990) 1-9. For an account of spillover from property-as-boundary to controversies over free speech and democratic reform, see FI Michelman "Possession vs. Distribution in the Constitutional Idea of Property" (1987) 72 *Iowa LR* 1319 1340-1350.

[18]   *First National Bank of SA Limited t/a Wesbank v Commissioner for the South African Revenue Services; First National Bank of SA Limited t/a Wesbank v Minister of Finance* 2002 4 SA 768 (CC) para 85.

No doubt such a broadly programmatic guarantee can carry concrete legal consequences. A market order contemplates a characteristic assemblage of laws and facilities: background laws of delict (trespass) and contract, deeds registries and probate offices, and so on. Read as a programmatic guarantee, a constitutional property clause commits the state to the maintenance of the requisite public facilities and bodies of private law – so that, for example, a failure to uphold the laws of trespass or of contract,[19] or a move to socialise some economic sector,[20] becomes challengeable as an alleged deviation calling for specific justification.[21]

Necessity. Constitution-makers who see no other, normative reason of their own to include a property clause in an otherwise complete bill of rights might feel compelled to do so by explicit or implicit pressure from a global investment community. Without a specific (and perhaps hyper-formalised) constitutional guarantee against deprivation and appropriation of property, the drafters might conclude, the country will be unable to attract and hold the investment required to rebuild or sustain its economy.

4 Why, then, all things considered, a property clause?

Which among the results from our preceding queries best explain the inclusion of a property clause in a so-called "transformative" constitution that also contains evident, strong commitments to the eradication of poverty, the achievement of equality, and the fulfilment of human dignity for all from a starting position of wide-scale, unjust dispossession?

4 1 Normative reasons for constitutional property clauses

We have assembled a number of possible, normative reasons for adding a property clause to an otherwise compete bill of rights (in addition to "necessity", to which we will return later). The clause may be meant to accomplish any or all of the following:

a) to do some special, concrete legal work by providing a distinct litigation advantage to claims of unconstitutional infringement on freedom, dignity *et cetera* when the alleged infringement takes the form of a detraction from an ownership position;

---

[19] See, for example, *Truax v Corrigan* 257 US 312 (1921).

[20] See, for example, *Act of Nationalization* Decision No 81-132 DC of 16 January 1982 (*Conseil Constitutionnel*); BVerfGE 50, 361 [1985] ("Co-determination case"); *South African Post Office Ltd v Van Rensburg* 1997 4 All SA 523 (E). In *South African Post Office Ltd v Van Rensburg* 1997 4 All SA 523 (E), the (unsuccessful) challenge to the state's extensive monopolisation of the postal service was based on a clausal guarantee of freedom of economic activity, but a property clause construed as an institutional guarantee might also be cited in support of such a claim.

[21] The institutional-guarantee idea goes a long way to explain the attribution of constitutional property rights to juristic persons or corporations. If constitutional complaints about property confiscation all had to be pleaded in terms of *prima facie* infringements on human dignity and freedom, it seems that corporation property would lack full and firm protection by constitutional law, even allowing that confiscations of corporate property would still have to clear constitutional guarantees of equality and legality. "But then why worry?" you might ask, as long as no real person's freedom or dignity is affected. A felt need for an institutional guarantee to serve the public good provides an answer.

b)   without intending any such special *advantage* for property claims,
      merely to help ensure that policymakers and adjudicators do not overlook
      or downgrade the dependence of freedom, dignity *et cetera* on (some
      greater of lesser degree of) security of ownership;
c)   to signal an overall possessive-individualist tilt in the assessment of
      claims to bill-of-rights protection;
d)   to lay down a marker of national commitment to the maintenance, in
      general, of a more-or-less marketised system of economic organisation,
      activity, and relationships – thus, an institutional guarantee.

4 2   "Social liberalism"

In order to test the relative, normative cogency and weight of these reasons in
a given constitutional setting, we would need to have in hand some conception
of a political value-ordering – or call it a conception of political justice – with
which that constitution is understood to correspond. Here, we have specifically
in mind a detectably liberal but also a dedicatedly transformative constitution
– containing a property clause within its otherwise fulsome bill of individual
rights but also marked by evident, strong commitments to the eradication of
poverty and the achievement of equality from a starting position of wide-
scale, unjust dispossession. As a plausibly corresponding, normative political
conception, I here introduce an outlook that I will call "social liberal". Its
tenets include the following:

i)   Property – in some class or classes of objects, perhaps excluding some of
      society's means of production, but not excluding all of them – subserves
      basic human interests in freedom, dignity, autonomy (self-development,
      self-expression), privacy, and self-respect – all of which interests and
      values together, in what follows, we shall compendiously call "basic
      liberties".
ii)   A morally justified social order aims at assurance to all of enjoyment at
      all times of a full and adequate scheme of basic liberties.
iii) A morally justified social order further aims at maintaining at all times
      secure provision for the basic material needs of each person, regardless
      of ability to contribute, in a manner conducive to each person's dignity
      and self-respect.
iv)   A morally justified social order further aims at maintaining at all times a
      political-economic structure and practice that are consonant with "pure
      background procedural justice" – or, in different but equivalent terms,
      "fair equality of opportunity" to realise on one's exertions of choice,
      effort, talent, contribution, risk, and so on.[22]
v)   Without property, there are no markets. Markets (and very possibly
      only markets) enable levels of production permitting assurance to all
      of minimally acceptable levels of enjoyment of basic liberties (or the

---

[22] Rawls *Justice as Fairness* 42-43, 50.

achievement of basic human capacities defined in some other way).[23] Markets, furthermore, serve human dignity directly by maintaining connections, for those who seek them, between individual choice, effort, talent, contribution, risk, and so on, and the course of a person's life.[24]

Exactly how to specify these tenets further, and how to knit them together into a unified web of doctrine, are matters of debate among social liberals. John Rawls,[25] Ronald Dworkin,[26] and Martha Nussbaum[27] (say) would be leading exemplars of such differences.[28] But leaving such differences open, we can still see at least roughly how a broadly social-liberal outlook will respond to the various sorts of conceivable, normative reasons for a constitutional property clause we listed above (in part 4 1).

The first thing we can say is that reason (c) in our list ("possessive individualism"), would not occur to social liberals as a persuasive ground for inclusion of a property clause in an otherwise complete constitutional bill of rights. That is simply because social liberals will all be anxious to deny and reject any leaning in their creed toward possessive individualism (as conceived by Macpherson).

We can also easily see how social liberals might quite conceivably accept either or both of our reasons (b) (reminder of the property:liberty:dignity *nexus*) or (d) (institutional guarantee) as grounds for inclusion. But then the next point to notice will be that neither of those grounds will result in the clause's presence in the bill of rights doing any well-defined, special legal work – recalling that by "special legal work" we mean somehow specially easing the claimant's burden, or specially toughening the state's, in that subset of bill-of-rights cases in which a claimed *prima facie* infringement on freedom *et cetera* takes the specific form of a disturbance of an ownership position. For while reasons (b) and (d) do certainly demand that infringements on freedom or dignity, equality or legality, must not be ignored or discounted

---

[23] Compare *Minister of Health v New Clicks South Africa (Pty) Ltd* 2006 2 SA 311 (CC) para 520. Ngcobo J wrote that a regulatory reduction in medicines prices would not be "appropriate" in terms of s 226 of the Medicines and Related Substances Control Act 101 of 1965 (construed in the light of the Constitution) if it

> "will result in the closure of the pharmaceutical industry. For the need for the continued existence of pharmacies is implicit, if not explicit, from the [constitutionally mandated] objective to enhance the accessibility and affordability of medicines."

See also *Phumalela Gaming and Leisure Limited v Gründlingh* 2006 8 BCLR 883 (CC) para 36:

> "The Bill of Rights does not expressly promote competition principles, but the right to freedom of trade, enshrined in section 22 of the Constitution is, in my view, consistent with a competitive regime in matters of trade and the recognition of the protection of competition as being in the public welfare."

[24] Compare *Affordable Medicines Trust v Minister of Health* 2006 3 SA 247 (CC) para 59:

> "Freedom to choose a vocation is intrinsic to the nature of a society based on human dignity as contemplated by the Constitution. One's work is part of one's identity and is constitutive of one's dignity."

[25] See, for example, J Rawls *Political Liberalism* (1993) 289-371.

[26] See, for example, R Dworkin *Sovereign Virtue: The Theory and Practice of Equality* (2000) 120-303.

[27] See, for example, M Nussbaum *Frontiers of Justice* (2006) 1-95.

[28] My statement of the tenets will easily be recognised as loosely Rawlsian, although by-passing certain distinctively Rawlsian specifications of priority-rankings amongst them. In general, I believe that John Rawls' unpacking of the leading aims of liberal constitutionalism is amply spacious to take in not only the case, which I treat as central, of a liberal social democracy, but also societies leaning – as plotted from that "center" – either rightward toward a straight market-liberal conception or leftward toward (with thanks and a nod to Karl Klare) a "post-liberal" conception. See Klare (1998) *SAJHR* 146.

just because they do take the form of an ownership disturbance, neither of them self-evidently demands any special tenderness towards infringements taking that form, as compared with infringements taking other forms.

4 3   Special treatment for "property" claims: Is defense of property a basic human right?

What about reason (a), then? Do we include a property clause in a social-liberal constitution just in order to provide a special litigation advantage for claims of unconstitutional infringement on freedom, dignity (*et cetera*) when the alleged infringement takes the form of an infringement of an ownership position? The obvious question is about what reason (apart from possible "necessity") the authors of a social-liberal constitution could possibly have for wanting to do *that*. And the answer is that they would have no such reason.

Any positive answer would have to start by attributing to our authors a conviction that among the guaranteed basic rights that everyone should have in a just constitutional order is a firm shield against state-engineered and state authorised disturbances of asset-holdings lawfully established. But note, now – the point is crucial – that the reason for adding the property clause could not be merely a recognition that ownership-disturbances do sometimes amount to, or lead to, unacceptable infringements of other basic rights to freedom, privacy, dignity, quality, legality, or [you name it]. In the sight of social liberalism they surely sometimes do, *and when they do the clauses in an otherwise complete constitutional bill of rights should cover them.* The "basic right" reason for including a property clause would have to be that defense against ownership disturbances is a basic right *just in itself, regardless of any further ramification to freedom, dignity, equality and so on.*

Is it? We have among us those who emphatically answer yes. These are not confined to the neo-liberal or neo-con fringes, but include as well the so-called "classical" or "Lockean" liberals who regard strict constitutional barriers against ownership disturbances as an indispensable safeguard against encroachment by the state into matters morally reserved for resolution by the free acts and choices of individuals.[29] But here is where social liberals and classical ("possessive individualist"?) liberals part company. Social liberals deny that strict defense against asset-disturbances, severed from ramification to the other values informing an otherwise complete bill of rights, is either a basic human need or a demand of human dignity or of any other ascription to humankind that might plausibly motivate a universal human moral entitlement to political respect and regard.

Establishment beyond all dispute of this position's proper location within liberalism is beyond the scope of this essay. But by way of providing a bit of evidence, I offer here a brief summary of John Rawls' account of how, and to what extent, a guarantee respecting property belongs among what Rawls calls

---

[29]   See, for example, R Epstein "Beyond the Rule of Law: Civic Virtue and Constitutional Structure" (1987) 56 *George Washington LR* 149.

the liberal "constitutional essentials". Rawls' credentials as a liberal political philosopher will not, I take it, be widely doubted.

Rawls does include among the constitutional essentials a right "to hold and have the exclusive use of personal property".[30] But this Rawlsian liberal constitutional right to property does not stand on its own as a basic right; rather, it has a secondary, supportive role in the full Rawlsian scheme of basic rights.

In order to explain, I must next say a word about a certain idea of "moral powers" and that idea's place in Rawls' liberal political philosophy. In that philosophy, an ultimate aim or value, in whose overall pursuit the list or scheme of liberal basic rights or constitutional essentials is to be worked out, is service to an ascribed "highest-order interest" of every person in

> "the adequate development and the full and informed exercise of [certain so-called] moral powers … [A basic right] is more or less significant depending on whether it is more or less essentially involved in, or it is a more or less necessary institutional means to protect, the full and informed and effective exercise of the moral powers …"[31]

But then what are these moral powers? Familiarly to Rawlsians, they are a brace of capacities "connected," as Rawls says, "with … the idea of social cooperation":

> "[A] capacity for a sense of justice and a capacity for a conception of the good. A sense of justice is the capacity to understand, to apply, and to act from the public conception of justice which characterizes the fair terms of social cooperation … The capacity for a conception of the good is the capacity to form, to revise, and rationally to pursue a conception of one's [own] rational advantage or good."[32]

The secondary, supportive role of the Rawlsian constitutional property right can now be more precisely stated. That role is "to allow a sufficient material basis for a sense of personal independence and self-respect, both of which are essential for the development and exercise of the moral powers".[33] But of course the right then will extend no further than that purpose requires. Rawls therefore quite decidedly rejects the strong libertarian or Lockean idea (if it is, indeed, Locke's idea) of a fundamental or "natural" human right to guaranteed, undiminished, everlasting control over assets lawfully acquired.

Since, for example, powers of bequest and inheritance are (in Rawls' view) extraneous to providing a person with a sufficient basis of support for a sense of independence and self-respect, the constitutionally "essential" liberal property right does not encompass such powers. Nor does it necessarily, for all societies, encompass private ownership over "means of production and natural resources". It might do the latter, or it might not: Exactly what modes, forms, and extensions of private ownership should be "accounted for as necessary" to "a sense of independence and self-respect [and the] development and exercise of the moral powers," or to "the social bases of self-respect", will depend

---

[30] Rawls *Liberalism* 298 n 14.
[31] 333, 335.
[32] 13-14, 18-19.
[33] 298.

on other features of the society's historical traditions and political-economic structures.[34]

Rawls thus tailors the liberal constitutional property right to a certain specification of the core or ground of every person's equal and full entitlement to respect and regard in the operations of society and the state – or, in other words, to a certain conception of human dignity. As it happens, Rawls' particular specification of the "dignity" core in terms of the moral powers results from a special, philosophically grounded aim of his to develop what he calls a "political" conception of justice.[35] By no means do all (or perhaps most) philosophically inclined "social" or anti-poverty liberals share that aim or its closely linked moral powers-based conception of human personal dignity and entitlement to political respect. What it seems all anti-poverty liberals must, however, share with Rawls is (i) the notion of basic rights as components in a scheme aimed at overall service to *some* conception of human dignity to which all equally lay claim; and, following from that, (ii) a refusal to distend any liberal basic or constitutional right – including the property right – beyond what is called for by such service.

5   Constitutional interpretation

What (if anything) follows regarding the best judicial deployment of a property clause when found within [a social-liberal] constitution?

The property clause undoubtedly dictates some kind and measure of supreme-law support for defensive claims against disturbances of proprietary positions duly established under an extant legal regime that supports private ownership. In a social-liberal constitutional setting, the clause is understood to do so *not* in response to any recognition of a free-standing basic human right against ownership-impairments just as such, but rather as a part of the defence of valued human freedom and dignity against the kinds of impairments that ownership impairments can sometimes carry with them. But by valued freedom, then, we cannot mean – and social liberals never do mean – an unfettered right to dispose as you please of whatever you own, free of all social restraint. We must rather mean freedom relative to – freedom conceived and qualified in terms of – some conception of human dignity to which all equally lay claim. In a way, we might say, the only truly, ultimately basic right that is possible in a social-liberal constitution is everyone's equal right along with others to have one's dignity as a person duly recognised, respected, and protected. From that source spring further rights – to be defined accordingly – to freedom, security, privacy, equality, and legality.

It would follow, I think, that a property clause in a social-liberal constitution – verbiage permitting – should ideally be construed as if it carries the word "unfair" where the word "arbitrary" now appears in section 25(1) of the South African Constitution, thus:

---

[34]   Rawls *Justice as Fairness* 114.
[35]   See, for example, FI Michelman "The Subject of Liberalism" (1994) 46 *Stan L Rev* 1807 1816-1826.

"No one may be deprived of property except in terms of law, and no law shall permit the [unfair] deprivation of property."

I have in mind that the meaning of "unfair" in this context would be developed much as the South African Constitutional Court has developed it in the context of section 9(3)'s guarantee against (not "discrimination" unmodified, but only) "unfair discrimination". "Unfair," there, as many reading this will easily recall, has been construed to mean that the discrimination (or, as I would have it, the detraction from an ownership position) works "to impair the fundamental human dignity of persons as human beings or to affect them adversely in a comparably serious manner".[36] And then what might further be in order would be the sort of gloss on "dignity" advanced by Sachs J in the case of *City Council of Pretoria v Walker*.[37] As I have elsewhere summarised that view, it holds that in deciding whether a South African suffers damage to his dignity as a consequence of public actions that are differentially burdensome to a racial or other "suspect" group to which he belongs, we must pay him the respect of supposing that he shares the grand project of his country's Constitution, which "envisage[s]" equality as "something to be achieved through the dismantling of structures and practices which unfairly obstruct or unduly attenuate its enjoyment".[38] And so, it seems, it would have to be with defensive property rights under an avowedly transformative constitution.

Of course that may not be possible. Not pure normativity but rather necessity may dictate otherwise. In the world as we find it, an aim of bringing to an acceptable level the prospects of the economically least advantaged for exercise and enjoyment of basic liberties and capacities may not be achievable without a kind of institutional securitisation of investment that (as we might find) only a strongly rule-formalising form of defensive property guarantee can provide. And with that observation, we move toward the close of the reflection.

6 Conclusion

Where does all of this leave us? I will take up some thoughts that come to mind, in ascending order of probable anguish for those who place their stock in a social-liberal constitutionalist destiny for South Africa.

We start with necessity. In the social-liberal view as I have presented it, the property clause provides only (as we may say) soft but not hard legal protection for defensive property claims. That, indeed, is the turn in the story that social liberals hope and expect will allow the clause to recede from excessive legal blockage of the state's anti-poverty activities. But what if the

---

[36] *Harksen v Lane NO* 1998 1 SA 300 (CC) para 53.

[37] 1998 2 SA 363 (CC).

[38] See FI Michelman "Reasonable Umbrage: Race and Constitutional Antidiscrimination Law in the United States and South Africa" (2004) 117 *Harv L Rev* 1378 1413 (quoting from *City Council of Pretoria v Walker* 1998 2 SA 363 (CC) para 109). Compare *Bato Star Fishing (Pty) Ltd v Minister of Environmental Affairs* 2004 4 SA 490 (CC) para 76 (Ngcobo J):

"The measures that bring about transformation will inevitably affect some members of the society adversely, particularly those coming from the previously advantaged communities. It may well be that other considerations may have to yield in favour of achieving the goal we fashioned for ourselves in the Constitution. What is required, though, is that the process of transformation must be carried out in accordance with the Constitution."

world investment community simply insists on hard protection and on taking its play elsewhere if it does not get it? Well, social liberals can say, if it does so insist then it does. The country, then, will have to choose between providing hard defensive property protection and trying to conquer poverty by some internal distribution of the product available from a national economy cut off from private and outside capital investment. If the latter achievement is deemed impossible, and if poverty-eradication is not to be abandoned as a chief national commitment, then the necessitation of hard defensive property protection will supersede *any* choice of regime-form the country might make on (other) normative grounds. "Necessity," then, will pose no more of an argument against liberal/postliberal constitutionalism than it will against any regime-form that would reject neo-liberal doctrines of hard property protection.

Come, then, to *false* necessity. Maybe it is not true – we only rush to think it is – that soft-protection-only will deprive us of the requisite level of investment. Or maybe it is not true – we only rush to think it is – that a fully socialised national economy, severed from dependence on private and foreign capital investment (but not foreign trade; we can still aim to have diamonds, gold, crops *et cetera* to exchange with the outside), can possibly produce enough to lift and keep everyone here out of poverty. And maybe these false beliefs we hold spring from illusions inevitably bred in us by the same general cultural *milieu* that also sponsors our attraction to liberal/postliberal constitutionalism, so that ridding ourselves of that attraction, which we can only do by ridding ourselves of the practice, is a necessary part of the cure. To that, all that any dedicated social liberal can say is: "Believe it if you do, but I neither believe it nor have ever seen any good reason to believe it."

That was the easy part; now it gets harder. A judicial softening of protection against interference with property can only, within liberalism (however "post" you want to make it), take you so far. Unfair is still unfair, and "unfair", even in the version proposed by Sachs J, still carries its irreducible liberal (individualist) gloss. The freedom and the dignity *of the person*, and (in that light) legality and equality – perhaps especially equality when combined with dignity – still do set limits that it seems could be fatal, in practice if not in theory, to the transformative project laid down by the Constitution.

No doubt some headway is possible: The burial-rights law can surely be upheld as in *Nhlabati*. The *Agri-SA* judgment will be sharply contested before the Constitutional Court; if it is not overturned it may be substantially circumventable by a judicious re-write of the statute. The anti-eviction law can be given effect if many or most, if not in all, cases of its invocation, and ways can still be found to vindicate the claims of owners to fair treatment.[39] How much of a dent, though, does all of that really make on South Africa's post-apartheid legacy of poverty and dispossession? Dispossession, say, of the land and everything that means in regard not just to wealth but to power,

---

[39] See, for example, *Modder East Squatters v Modderklip Boerdery (Pty) Ltd, President of the Republic of South Africa v Modderklip Boerdery (Pty) Ltd* 2004 3 All SA 169 (SCA); *President of the Republic of South Africa v Modderklip Boerdery (Pty) Ltd* 2005 5 SA 3 (CC).

status, and dignity?[40] And not just of the land as land or natural resource but the land as capital input to housing? And how could it be judged remotely, liberally fair – or consonant with a decent care for liberal dignity – that the current owners of acreage should pay a hugely disproportionate share of society's (or even say of white society's) bill for repair? But how, otherwise, is it possible to make the repair within tolerable time, given the current and expected state of the economy and, relatedly, the public treasury?

To questions such as those, I think social liberals must choose between two lines of response. The first would be that we don't know until we really try, and we have not yet really tried. Maybe, with wisdom concertedly applied to issues of time, terms, trade, and taxation, there is a workable way to acquire land for redistribution that liberal equality and dignity can accept. That is a line that social liberals should not easily give up. The other response-line would be that, alas, we cannot get there from here by a liberal/postliberal constitutionalist path. That still does not sideline whatever (otherwise) normative preference for social-liberal/postliberal constitutionalism you may retain. Because on the morning after – after the blow-up of the current situation, after the start-over revolutionary redistribution of the land and natural resources – you will still want to start the country out again on the path you think is right, and so you will want to shape the intervening events in ways that do the least destruction possible to hopes for such a future. The words of Ngcobo J (as he then was) still ring in our ears. There can be, as he wrote, no "sacrifice" of transformation "at the altar of stability." But that does not give us free rein. The transformation still "must be carried out responsibly and its adverse impact must be minimised".[41]

SUMMARY

Suppose we have three factors in play: a national project of post-colonial recovery from distributive injustice, prominently including land reform; express constitutional protection for property rights; and a Constitution whose other main features bring it recognisably within the broad historical tradition of liberal constitutionalism. To what extent does or must that Constitution's overall liberal affiliation or its inclusion of a property clause impede the social-transformation project?

The narrower claim of this essay is that the attractions of liberal constitutionalism do not come necessarily laden with a counter-reformative property clause. In what I would call a proper liberal view, the office of a constitutional property clause is to signal recognition of the connection between a decent respect for property and a decent respect for human dignity and freedom; it is not, however, to provide defences for property rights beyond what constitutional protections for freedom, security, dignity, equality, and legality would anyway provide.

It may, even so, be true that the conditions of distributive justice within a national society will not always be achievable by means meeting the demands of an up-and-running liberal constitutional order. The essay's broader claim is that the fault in such cases does not, however, lie in a liberal conception of justice.

---

[40] See, for example, M Lipton *Land Reform in Developing Countries* (2009) 16-40.
[41] *Bato Star Fishing (Pty) Ltd v Minister of Environmental Affairs* 2004 4 SA 490 (CC) para 106.

CHAPTER 15

FARM LAND AND TENURE SECURITY: NEW POLICY AND LEGISLATIVE DEVELOPMENTS

Juanita Pienaar

Anna Kamkuemah

1 Introduction

On 24 December 2010 a new Draft Tenure Security Policy[1] and concomitant Draft Land Tenure Security Bill[2] were published for comment. These new measures focus on farm land in particular and have specific implications for two pieces of legislation, namely the Extension of Security of Tenure Act 62 of 1997 ("ESTA") and the Land Reform (Labour Tenant) Act 3 of 1996 (the "Labour Tenant Act"). Why was it necessary to introduce new tenure measures, seventeen years after an all-encompassing land reform programme was embarked on? What do these measures entail and what are the implications thereof? In order to answer these questions a brief historical background, with an emphasis on rural areas, we provide so that the reasons for tenure reform are clear. This will be followed by a brief evaluation of tenure reform to date. After the need for further progress has been established, an analysis of the new developments and proposals follows.

2 Brief historical background

Tenure refers to the manner in which land is held or in which control over land is exercised.[3] Therefore, in order for tenure to be secure, one needs to be protected against arbitrary eviction and against interference, abuse and violation of occupational rights. Secure tenure is thus the antithesis of vulnerability. Before an all-encompassing land reform programme was embarked on in 1994, of which tenure reform is one of the sub-components, tenure was directly linked to race.[4] The racial background of a person and the location of the land, determined the kind of tenure relevant.[5] In this

---

[1] RSA *Draft Tenure Security Policy* GN 1118 in *GG* 33894 of 24-12-2010.

[2] The Land Tenure Security Bill (draft) in GN 1118 *GG* 33894 of 24-12-2010.

[3] D Carey Miller & A Pope *Land Title in South Africa* (2000) 456.

[4] The other land reform sub-programmes are the redistribution programme under s 25(5) and the restitution programme under s 25(7) of the Constitution of the Republic of South Africa, 1996 ("the Constitution").

[5] See, generally, PJ Badenhorst, JM Pienaar & H Mostert *Silberberg and Schoeman's Law of Property* 5 ed (2006) 586, 607; Carey Miller & Pope *Land Title* 29-40; T Bennett "African Land – A History of Dispossession" in R Zimmermann & D Visser (eds) *Southern Cross: Civil and Common Law in South Africa* (1996) 65 65-94; C Walker *Landmarked: Land Claims and Land Restitution in South Africa* (2008) 11-31; CR Cross & RJ Haines *Towards Freehold? Options for Land and Development in South Africa's Black Rural Areas* (1988) 73-92.

regard, over many years, a complex, intricate web of tenure forms developed.[6] Essentially the approach in relation to rural areas was the following: the land in South Africa was divided into black areas and the rest of South Africa.[7] The areas allocated for the exclusive use of black persons were, over years, further divided into four independent national states,[8] six self-governing territories[9] and the South African Development Trust ("SADT") areas. Land tenure in the self-governing territories and the SADT-land was regulated by Proclamation R188 of 1969,[10] issued in terms of the Black Administration Act 38 of 1927,[11] and provided for quitrent and permission to occupy. Quitrent is the registered occupation of surveyed land in terms of which the holder received possession of the land while the state remained the owner. Accordingly, quitrent title could be suspended or cancelled by the Minister. Permission to occupy is the statutory form of communal land tenure in relation to unsurveyed land. It entitled the holder to occupy a residential and/or an arable site. Although both forms of tenure provided a permanent right of occupation to the holder and rights to use the commonage, these tenure forms were not identical to common-law ownership. Furthermore, different measures applied to towns within rural areas.[12] Land within the independent national states was also held under quitrent tenure and permission to occupy, although communal tenure was dominant in these areas.[13]

The complex system of racially based measures effectively led to the uprooting of a well-established, independent black farming community.[14] Apart from that, outside the self-governing territories and national states, where large commercial farms operated, tenure security of (usually) black occupiers and labour tenants diminished to those of mere wage-workers that left them extremely vulnerable to evictions.[15]

---

[6] CG van der Merwe & JM Pienaar "Land Reform in South Africa" in P Jackson & DC Wilde (eds) *The Reform of Property Law* (1997) 334 338; W du Plessis & JM Pienaar "The More Things Change, the More They Stay the Same: The Story of Communal Land Tenure in South Africa" (2010) 16 *Fundamina* 73 78-81; JM Pienaar "Customary Law of Property" in C Rautenbach, K Bekker & N Goolam (eds) *Introduction to Legal Pluralism* 3 ed (2010) 75 83-84.

[7] This was achieved through various racial statutes, for example, the Black Land Act 27 of 1913 which prohibited blacks from acquiring land outside the areas allocated to them, while also prohibiting whites from acquiring land in areas allocated for blacks. See in general Cross & Haines *Towards Freehold* 44; Bennet "African Land" in *Southern Cross* 79.

[8] Transkei, Bophuthatswana, Venda and Ciskei.

[9] KwaNdebele, QwaQwa, Gazankulu, Lebowa, KwaZulu-Natal and KaNgwane.

[10] Proc R188 in *GG* 2486 of 11-07-1969.

[11] Pienaar "Customary Law of Property" in *Legal Pluralism* 84.

[12] Van der Merwe & Pienaar "Land Reform" in *Reform of Property Law* 335-338; Pienaar "Customary Law of Property" in *Legal Pluralism* 83.

[13] Van der Merwe & Pienaar "Land Reform" in *Reform of Property Law* 334-338; Du Plessis & Pienaar (2010) *Fundamina* 73-81.

[14] See JM Pienaar "Farm Workers: Extending Security of Tenure in Terms of Recent Legislation" (1998) 13 *SAPL* 423 424-427 regarding the historical background of especially ESTA.

[15] See H Wolpe "Capitalism and Cheap Labour Power in South Africa: From Segregation to Apartheid" in W Beinart & S Dubow (eds) *Segregation and Apartheid in Twentieth-century South Africa* (1995) 60 60-91. See also, in general, C van Onselen *The Seed is Mine: The Life of Kas Maine, a South African Sharecropper 1894-1985* (1996); W Beinart, P Delius & S Trapido *Putting Plough to the Ground: Accumulation and Dispossession in Rural South Africa* (1986); and the publications of TJ Keegan, especially *Facing the Storm: Portraits of Black Lives in Rural South Africa* (1988) and *Colonial South Africa and the Origins of the Racial Order* (1996) 291-292.

Accordingly, prior to the new political dispensation, when the White Paper on Land Reform was published in 1991,[16] the tenure system in South Africa was diverse, fragmented, racially based and insecure. Following the new political dispensation, it is within this prevailing fragmented context that the White Paper on South African Land Policy was published in 1997, with a threefold point of departure relating to tenure reform:[17] to

- move away from the permit-based approach towards a rights-based approach;
- enable beneficiaries to choose the kind of tenure best suited for their needs; and
- focus on vulnerable sections of the population.

The aims of tenure reform were:[18] to

- rationalise and streamline the complex land tenure and land control system referred to above;
- improve security of tenure; and
- bring tenure in line with constitutional imperatives like equality and dignity.

In this regard the Constitution provides for the following:[19]

"A person or community whose tenure of land is legally insecure as a result of past racially discriminatory laws or practices is entitled, to the extent provided for by an Act of Parliament, either to tenure which is legally secure or to comparable redress" – section 25(6).

"Parliament must enact the legislation referred to in subsection (6)" – section 25(9).

Because insecure tenure can, to a large extent, be ascribed to past discriminatory laws and practices, both individuals and communities are entitled to secure tenure or equitable redress. From the above it is clear that the onus is on Parliament to draft and enact the necessary legislation to address insecurity. In fact, Parliament already promulgated tenure-related legislation *before* the new constitutional dispensation commenced, by way of the Upgrading of Land Rights Act 112 of 1991, the Less Formal Township Establishment Act 112 of 1991, and the Provision of Land and Assistance Act 126 of 1993.[20] Post 1994 two broad categories of tenure measures were issued: those aimed at regulating tenure on an interim basis, and those measures aimed at overhauling the tenure system as a whole.[21] The Interim Protection of Informal Land Rights Act 31 of 1996 ("Interim Protection Act") is an example of the first-mentioned category. The two legislative measures

---

[16]   RSA *White Paper on Land Reform* (1991).
[17]   Department of Agriculture and Land Affairs *White Paper on SA Land Policy* (1997) vi.
[18]   Badenhorst et al *Law of Property* 607; Carey Miller & Pope *Land Title* 456; AJ van der Walt *Constitutional Property Law* (2005) 308.
[19]   Constitution of the Republic of South Africa, 1996.
[20]   See for detailed discussions of these legislative measures JM Pienaar & J Brickhill "Land" in S Woolman, M Bishop & J Brickhill (eds) *CLoSA* 2 ed (RS 3 2011) 48–25-48–27; Badenhorst et al *Law of Property* 589, 604-605; Carey Miller & Pope *Land Title* 405-411.
[21]   See for more information Pienaar & Brickhill "Land" in *CLoSA* 48–25-48–27; H Mostert, JM Pienaar & J van Wyk "Land" in WA Joubert (ed) *LAWSA 14* (2010) paras 121, 125-140.

now in the spotlight, namely ESTA and the Labour Tenant Act, are examples of measures aimed at fundamentally altering the existing tenure disposition, especially in relation to white-owned commercial farms.[22]

3   Evaluating tenure reform performance in South Africa

If measured against the three main objectives of the tenure reform programme, namely (a) rationalisation; (b) increased security; and (c) the embodiment of constitutional imperatives, it becomes clear why Government deemed it necessary to introduce a new Policy and Bill at the end of 2010. Concerning the question of whether the complex system of permits and tenure rights was indeed rationalised and streamlined, it is important to underline that, although notorious racially based land measures were repealed by the Abolition of Racially Based Land Measures Act 108 of 1991, secondary or subordinate notices, proclamations and regulations issued under the main Acts, remained in force. Accordingly, quitrent and permission to occupy remained in force. Although some of these "old order" rights were automatically upgraded,[23] others remained insecure. With the commencement of the Interim Protection Act in 1996, the application of which is being extended on an annual basis,[24] informal, unregistered and undocumented rights were effectively elevated to real rights. The unconstitutionality finding of the Communal Land Rights Act 11 of 2004 ("CLARA") in the course of 2010,[25] has underlined that permit-based and other insecure rights are still a reality – seventeen years after the new political dispensation commenced. Apart from the fact that identical tenure forms prevalent in the former dispensation are still being used on a daily basis today, new land control forms have furthermore developed. One such an example is the use of a communal property association as a mechanism to acquire, hold and manage common property on behalf of communities.[26] The intricate tenure system has therefore not been dismantled and made more streamlined. Instead, to some degree, it has not only survived intact, but may even have become more complex.

Whether insecure tenure has indeed become more secure, is the second question to address. Mention has already been made of the upgrading of some of the insecure rights under the Upgrading of Land Rights Act.[27] However, many of the lesser rights, or "old order rights" are still prevalent today. Tenure forms in traditional areas, that were supposed to have been dealt with under

---

[22]   See for a detailed discussion of the tenure reform programme Pienaar & Brickhill "Land" in *CLoSA* 48-25-48-51.

[23]   For example, Schedule I – rights consisting of deeds of grant, leasehold and quitrent were upgraded to ownership – see Pienaar "Customary Law of Property" in *Legal Pluralism* 85.

[24]   Most recently by way of GN 745 in *GG* 33428 of 27-08-2010.

[25]   *Tongoane v The Minister of Agriculture and Land Affairs* 2010 6 SA 214 (CC). This case, though relevant in relation to communal areas only and not applicable to commercial farm land outside communal areas, has underlined the many complexities inherent to tenure reform. Whenever reform occurs in relation to communal areas, it will have to be consistent with reforms on commercial farms, thereby an all-encompassing approach is needed.

[26]   Badenhorst et al *Law of Property* 620-622.

[27]   588-589.

CLARA, are currently in limbo. Perhaps the clearest indication that insecure tenure is still as much a problem today as 20 years ago, is the number of evictions that occur in South Africa. Research done by Nkuzi Development has shown that evictions have in fact increased post 1994 and that the largest percentage by far relates to unlawful evictions.[28] It was especially in rural areas that ESTA, and to a lesser extent, the Labour Tenant Act, was supposed to have altered power relations and impacted on evictions. Unfortunately, these measures failed to achieve their respective aims.[29]

Lastly, the question of whether land tenure has been brought in line with constitutional imperatives, like equality and dignity, has to be answered in light of the prevailing backlog in the provision of housing and the living conditions in which some persons, especially rural and farm dwellers, often find themselves. After seventeen years it would seem real, effective tenure reform in especially rural areas, is still lacking.[30]

In light of the brief evaluation of the tenure reform programme above, it is clear that the overall tenure reform programme is in dire need of some kind of resuscitation. In order to determine whether the newly proposed measures would address the existing shortcomings in relation to farm land in particular, it is necessary to set out in detail what the proposals entail. The Draft Tenure Security Policy will be discussed first, followed by a discussion of the Draft Land Tenure Security Bill.

4   Draft Tenure Security Policy

4 1   Introduction

The importance of tenure reform is underlined in light of the point of departure that the Policy review "may not be unduly hamstrung by reluctance to depart from the traditional system of common law".[31] The aims of the current review are fourfold:[32] to

- protect relative rights;
- enhance security of tenure;
- effect peaceful and harmonious relationships; and
- sustain production discipline.

---

[28]   Nkuzi Development Association *Still Searching for Security: The Reality of Farm Dweller Evictions in South Africa* (2005) 40-48.

[29]   Various detailed analyses of the particular short-comings and failures of ESTA and labour tenancy legislation have been published to date and will accordingly not be repeated here. See *Draft Tenure Security Policy* 1-2. See also, for more detail, JM Pienaar & K Geyser "'Occupier' for Purposes of the Extension of Security of Tenure Act: The Plight of Female Spouses and Widows" (2010) 73 *THRHR* 248 248-260; JM Pienaar "Tenure Security: Overview and Challenges" (2011) 1 *Speculum Juris* 108 108-133 See also Lawyers for Human Rights "SFP challenges unlawful evictions" (2011) *Die Okkupeerder: Newsletter of the Security of Farmworkers Project* 2 2-3; Programme for Land and Agrarian Studies (PLAAS) *Umhlaba Wethu 5* (2008) 7; R Hall *Farm Tenure* PLAAS Occasional Paper No 3, University of the Western Cape (2003) 2-16; and R Hall *Land and Agrarian Reform in Integrated Development Plans* PLAAS Research Report No 23, University of the Western Cape (2006) 7-22.

[30]   B Cousins & R Hall *Rights Without Illusions: The Potential and Limits of Rights-Based Approaches to Securing Land Tenure in Rural South Africa* PLAAS Working Paper 18, University of the Western Cape (2011) para 2.2 <www.plaas.org.za/pubs/wp/WP18Cousins-Hall052011.pdf> (accessed 02-06-2011).

[31]   RSA *Draft Tenure Security Policy* 3.

[32]   4.

In the ensuing policy and legislative proposals the following critical issues need further attention:

- tightening up legislation by creating substantive rights in land for occupiers;
- information dissemination;
- effecting new settlements in farming areas; and
- monitoring evictions.

The following discussion is not a detailed discussion of the whole Policy. Instead, only the most important aspects, linked to the Bill below, will be highlighted.

4 2   Resettlement and agri-villages

Although the Policy specifically refers to agri-villages, this is no new development. In fact, agri-villages have been on the statute books since ESTA was promulgated in 1997. The underlying idea is that accommodation/ housing and employment on farms should be de-linked or separated. Not only would this enable workers to move freely from employer to employer, but tenure security would also be achieved, with all the benefits thereof, if land rights were vested in the workers and not the farm owners. In order for such an endeavour to succeed, a unique partnership between local authorities, land owners and farm workers is required. To date, these enterprises have hardly been successful. Revitalising agri-villages is therefore a priority for government.

The Policy refers to a "Farm Workers' Grouping", who could initially be title deed holder of the land that was acquired by way of donation, purchase or expropriation. State land may also be involved. Although the Workers' Grouping would be the initial title holder, the community would be in charge, in accordance with rules worked out by mutual consent of the "village community", the financier and the municipality. A permit system would form the basis of land holding and could include permits for pasture, residential and cultivation purposes.[33] The particular permit will set out the period involved as well as the necessary provisions and conditions. The Policy also states that the transfer of freehold land is possible "to persons who make better use of allotted land"[34] in accordance with particular rules. Persons who do not perform as required on the other hand, may lose their land. The challenge and difficulties in acquiring suitable land is underlined, thereby highlighting the future use of expropriation.[35]

---

[33]   6.
[34]   7.
[35]   7.

4 3   Arbitrary evictions

In order to monitor evictions in general, a Land Rights Management Board is proposed to deal proactively with evictions and their underlying causes.[36] Conditions for and limitations on evictions will be spelled out.

4 4   Development

Development of farm land is directly linked with the overall aims, objectives and strategies of the Comprehensive Rural Development Programme driven by government.[37]

4 5   Compliance and enforcement

In the past, numerous difficulties were experienced with compliance and enforcement of especially ESTA.[38] It is envisaged that the proposed Land Rights Management Board will play an integral role in improved compliance and enforcement of the new measures.[39] Further mechanisms identified in the Policy include alternative dispute resolution mechanisms and a Register of Interests on farms.[40]

5   Draft Land Tenure Security Bill

5 1   Introduction

Right from the outset, the Draft Land Tenure Security Bill proclaims a clear focus on farm land.[41] The objectives of the Bill and the Policy are identical, namely, to protect relative rights; to enhance security of tenure; to effect peaceful and harmonious relationships; and to sustain production discipline.[42]

The scope of the Bill is set out in clause 2 with an emphasis on agricultural land and land used for agricultural purposes, excluding land occupied by traditional communities.[43] The Bill essentially repeals the existing ESTA and Labour Tenant Act and combines them into one new legislative measure. However, Chapter III of the Labour Tenant Act still applies in relation to labour tenancy claims that have already been instituted.[44] The Prevention

---

[36] 8.
[37] 9. See also W du Plessis, NJJ Olivier & JM Pienaar "Land Matters and Rural Development: 2009 (2)" (2009) 24 *SAPL* 588 608-610 for an exposition of the approach followed in the restructured Department of Rural Development and Land Reform in which an emphasis is placed on rural development, coupled with increased commercialisation. See also R Hall *A Fresh Start for Rural Development and Agrarian Reform?* PLAAS Policy Brief 29 (July 2009) 1-6.
[38] RSA *Draft Tenure Security Policy* 10. See also Pienaar & Geyser (2010) *THRHR* 248; Pienaar (2011) *Speculum Juris* 108.
[39] RSA *Draft Tenure Security Policy* 10.
[40] 10.
[41] Long title and Preamble of the Draft Land Tenure Security Bill.
[42] Cl 2. However, there are no provisions in the Bill aimed at or focused on production discipline as such.
[43] These areas include land that would have been covered by CLARA had it not been found to be unconstitutional. It is questionable whether the overhaul of rural tenure can afford to exclude vast areas of rural land.
[44] These claims relate to land or rights in land under the current ss 16 and 17 of the Labour Tenant Act – see Badenhorst et al *Law of Property* 601-604 for more detail.

of Illegal Eviction from and Unlawful Occupation of Land Act 19 of 1998 ("PIE") and the Interim Protection Act are specifically excluded from the ambit of the Bill.[45]

Apart from the first introductory chapters, one and two, the Bill has eight further chapters dealing with the following: Chapter 3: categories of persons covered by the Bill; Chapter 4: relative rights and duties; Chapter 5: management of evictions; Chapter 6: agri-villages and land development measures; Chapter 7: management of resettlement units and agri-villages; Chapter 8: Land Rights Management Board; Chapter 9: Dispute Resolutions and Courts; and Chapter 10: Miscellaneous.

5 2   Persons covered by the Bill

The scope of the Bill, in relation to persons and categories of persons, is set out in Chapter 3. Five broad categories of persons are identified that fall within the ambit of the Bill, some of which overlap to some extent. These categories are: persons residing on farms;[46] persons working on farms;[47] persons associated with persons working or residing on farms;[48] farm owners and authorised agents;[49] and persons who have consent to reside.[50]

The first category, persons residing on farms, is the only group who face the risk of losing their homes when evicted. In order to qualify, a person must have consent to reside or must have another right in law to reside. This definition is similar to the definition in ESTA,[51] except that the Bill now includes this person's family members. This category also incorporates persons who meet the requirements of labour tenancy, as set out in the current Labour Tenant Act. In light of the difficulties experienced by spouses and partners to qualify as occupiers for purposes of ESTA,[52] the proposed definition provides slightly more protection in that family members are now specifically included in the definition.[53] This category of persons has an extensive list of rights, nineteen individual rights in total, set out in clause 15 and particular duties set out in clause 16. The rights provided for are formulated rather broadly and do not distinguish between persons who would formerly have fallen under ESTA and those that would have qualified as labour tenants. These rights listed include *inter alia* the right to own livestock that may not unreasonably be restricted,

---

[45]   Cl 4 of the Draft Land Tenure Security Bill. PIE has national application and applies to both rural and urban areas, whereas the Draft Land Tenure Security Bill will only apply to rural areas and land used for agricultural purposes. See for more information regarding the application of PIE Badenhorst et al *Law of Property* 247-250, 652-660.
[46]   Cl 7 of the Draft Land Tenure Security Bill.
[47]   Cl 8.
[48]   Cl 9.
[49]   Cl 10.
[50]   Cl 11.
[51]   S 1(1) of ESTA.
[52]   Pienaar & Geyser (2010) *THRHR* 248.
[53]   In terms of *Landbounavorsingsraad v Klaasen* 2005 3 SA 410 (LCC) a distinction is made between occupiers in the narrow sense and occupiers in the broad sense. Only persons who qualify as occupiers in the narrow sense may, for example, be served with eviction notices. This category includes only persons who have a legal *nexus* with the land owner. In reality, this usually excludes spouses and family members. Therefore, although spouses and family members presently fall within the scope of ESTA, they do not enjoy *full* protection.

cropping and grazing rights, the right to build homes and homesteads, the right to bury family members on the farm and access to burial grounds and ancestral land, the right not to be denied or deprived of educational and health services, the right to commercial farming and access to skills, the right to education for self and family, and the right to family life. All of these rights are subject to reasonable conditions.

The basic duties of this category include the duty to provide labour, as agreed. They must furthermore not intentionally and unlawfully harm persons; cause material damage and assist persons to occupy land unlawfully.

The second category of persons is those working on farms.[54] This category is especially broad as it includes *any* person who in *any* manner assists carrying on or conducting the business of farming. This includes a person employed in a home on the farm or engaged by the owner in farming activities and includes a domestic worker and security guard. Their rights relate to labour legislation, education for self and family, family life, and dignity.[55] Their duties are identical to persons residing on land.[56] This category may overlap with the first category and *vice versa*.

The third category relates to persons associated with persons working or residing on farms.[57] At first glance this category seems especially broad. However, most of the persons listed in this section have effectively already been incorporated into one of the other categories set out above, for example: spouse or partner; child (including niece and nephew under eighteen and over eighteen if still attending school); parents; and siblings. Many persons listed in this category would already have been included under clause 8 dealing with family members as part of the first category discussed above.

Farm owners and authorised agents constitute the fourth category.[58] A farm owner includes any person or institution that owns agricultural land or receives any pecuniary benefits therefrom. Persons who act as agents or managers of such land also fall within the ambit of the Bill. Under clause 13 this category has all of the rights set out in the Constitution, including the right to property and family life, employer's rights and a right to dignity. Any of these rights may be subject to reasonable conditions. Their duties are set out in clause 14 and include a prohibition to intentionally and unlawfully cause harm to any person or material damage to property. They must furthermore not prevent persons residing on farms or working on farms from accessing educational, health or any other public facilities. They are also prohibited from breaching labour-law provisions.

The last category identified in the Bill relates to persons who have consent to reside on the land. This is not a totally new category as it essentially relates to persons who already fall under clause 8 of the Bill, namely those residing on the land. Clause 11 is thus an elaboration of what consent entails, the consequences thereof, and the implications of withdrawal of consent.

---

[54] Cl 8 of the Draft Land Tenure Security Bill.
[55] Cl 17.
[56] Cl 18.
[57] Cl 9.
[58] Cl 10.

Persons who resided on or used land with the consent of the owner and such consent was lawfully withdrawn, shall be deemed to be a person still residing. However, this will only be the case if the person has resided continuously on the land for at least one year after consent was withdrawn.[59] For purposes of the Bill, consent will be effective, despite a defect or a failure to obtain the requisite authority. Persons who reside openly for six months are deemed to have consent. Consent contemplated in the Bill is binding on all successors in title.

In comparison to the existing legislative measures, it is notable that no distinction is drawn between persons who occupied land before and after February 1997, as is the case presently under ESTA.[60] There is also no specific distinction between long-term and other occupiers.[61] It is also interesting to note that, excluding persons residing on farms and land owners, the other two categories of beneficiaries have identical rights and duties. The long list of individual rights for persons residing on farms is general and unspecific. For example, a general right to burial is provided for, whereas the existing right in ESTA is more defined and delineated.[62] A general right to build homes and homesteads is also provided for in the Bill. Accordingly, no distinction is made between persons who would formerly have qualified as occupiers (ESTA) and persons who would have qualified as labour tenants.

The categories of beneficiaries and their corresponding rights overlap. Therefore, it is possible that one individual would enjoy protection under one or more provisions.

The duties of land owners are generally formulated negatively. This means there is a duty on them *not* to prevent access to housing, education *et cetera*, but there is no clear positive duty to provide housing or access to water and services.

Regarding persons associated with persons residing or working on farms (the third category), it is unclear how the land owner in practice would be able to realise rights of these persons to, for example, health and education.

5 3   Management of evictions

Chapter 5 of the Bill deals specifically with the management of evictions. Clause 19 sets out the scope of eviction. This entails an act or omission that results in temporary or permanent removal of persons against their will from their home or land that is being occupied. A new development consists of a long list of actions or omissions that would result in *constructive eviction*,[63] for example, the prevention of access to residence; interference with performance of cultural practices; refusal of allowing to bury someone on the land; denial of access to water or electricity; demolition of a home; forcing different families to live together; and forced relocation of a homestead.

---

[59]   There including persons who started off under cl 8.
[60]   See for more detail Badenhorst et al *Law of Property* 608-609.
[61]   As provided for under s 8(4) of ESTA – see Badenhorst et al *Law of Property* 610-611.
[62]   See especially Pienaar & Brickhill "Land" in *CLoSA* 48–32-48–36.
[63]   Cl 19(2) of the Draft Land Tenure Security Bill.

Clause 20 sets out the conditions or circumstances relating to lawful evictions. If residence and employment are linked,[64] then all labour legislation has to be complied with and formal eviction proceedings have to be lodged. In instances where the occupier has resided for a period longer than ten years and he or she is sixty years of age or is a former employee who cannot work due to ill health, injury or disability,[65] that person can generally not be evicted, except if that person is guilty of a section 16(2) breach.[66] When such a person dies, his or her family members can remain on the land for a further twelve months. If residence has indeed been terminated or family members remain on the land for a further twelve months, the parties can reach an agreement regarding the conditions of continued residence for the period following termination and preceding eviction. If no agreement can be reached, parties may also proceed to court for required conditions of continued residence.[67] Evictions may only proceed if all substantive and procedural requirements have been met. In this regard clause 20(10) provides a list of safeguards that have to be complied with, including that there must have been opportunity for genuine consultation; evictions cannot be carried out in bad weather or at night; that there must be legal representation; and that, where groups of people are evicted, government officials have to be present.

Clause 20(11) provides that no eviction may result in persons affected being rendered homeless or vulnerable to the violation of other human rights.[68] Effectively this means that persons cannot be evicted if there is no alternative accommodation available. For a provision like this to be employed sensibly, two qualifications immediately come to mind: (a) some kind of investigation or survey has to be done to determine the availability of accommodation; and (b) sufficient support and other mechanisms have to be in place to realise or provide accommodation if necessary. Caution is also required: the mere availability of alternative accommodation does not automatically guarantee an eviction. *All circumstances* still have to be considered. Clause 21 underlines that persons residing on farms may only be evicted in terms of an order of court issued under the Tenure Security Bill.[69]

The particular eviction proceedings are set out in clause 22. An owner has to give three months' notice of intention to lodge eviction proceedings to (a) the person to be evicted; (b) the municipal manager; and (c) the Land Rights Management Board (the "Board"). Urgent eviction proceedings are also provided for in identical terms to those currently provided for in ESTA.[70] In any application under clause 22 the owner furthermore has to give notice

---

[64]   This is mostly the case as farm workers are employed on the farm that they occupy.

[65]   This description incorporates the present definition of "long-term occupiers" in s 8(4) of ESTA.

[66]   Unlawfully injured another, caused damage, or unlawfully enabled or promoted occupation of land.

[67]   Cl 20(9) of the Draft Land Tenure Security Bill.

[68]   This is a *verbatim* reformulation of one of the procedural protections that was formulated under the UN Committee on Economic, Social and Cultural Rights *General Comment 7: The Right to Adequate Housing (Art 11.1): Forced Evictions* (1997) UN Doc E/1998/22 3.4 flowing from art 11(1) International Convention on Economic, Social and Cultural Rights (1966) UN Doc E/1998/22 that sets out the right to adequate housing.

[69]   This is also in line with s 26(3) of the Constitution that provides that no one may be evicted from their home without a court order and only after the court considered all relevant circumstances.

[70]   S 15 of ESTA.

to the municipal manager and the Board in advance. Although the reason for serving the various notices is clear, it is not clear why *different sets of bodies and institutions* receive the various notices in each instance.

Under clause 23 an eviction order may be granted if the person had not vacated the home after 30 days' notice and after the expiry of 30 days, the land owner had given at least three months' notice of intention to evict to the person affected, the municipal manager, the Board, and the Director-General. The particular provisions and the grounds for eviction have to be set out in the notice. Clause 23 provides for a probation report with certain required information to be requested within a reasonable time.[71]

Furthermore, an eviction order may be granted if the consent to reside was tied to a period in time and the time had lapsed.[72] In all other instances an eviction order may only be granted if it is just and equitable in the particular circumstances. In this regard the reason for the eviction and the fairness of particular terms and conditions are relevant.

If an eviction order is granted, it may only be executed after at least two months.[73] The court shall furthermore direct the municipal manager, the Board and the land owner to draft a plan to be submitted jointly with particulars relating to the person and the provision of suitable alternative accommodation. This plan has to be submitted within two months after the eviction order was granted.

5 4   Agri-villages and resettlement

The Draft Tenure Security Policy highlights the necessity of agri-villages and resettlement. As mentioned, clause 20(11) of the Bill provides that no eviction may render a person homeless. Accordingly, a clear synergy between the chapters dealing with eviction and resettlement is required. Of great importance is the role and function of the Board, with the assistance of the Minister, to establish sustainable human settlements.

Prior to the establishment of agri-villages, the owner may enter into agreements with persons residing on farms in terms of which these persons are to be relocated to suitable alternative land.[74] This agreement is subject to ministerial approval.[75] Furthermore, those likely to be affected by eviction are to be assisted to acquire suitable alternative accommodation, also in relation to productive land.[76] In the case of (lawful) evictions the Board also has to see to it that the rights of all groups are adhered to, including the right to safe, affordable, equitable alternative accommodation.[77] In the context of resettlement, the Board needs to ensure that various eviction criteria have been adhered to, including the rights of women, children and the vulnerable; that full and informed consent was given relating to the relocation; that

---

[71]   Cl 23(2) of the Draft Land Tenure Security Bill.
[72]   Cl 24(1).
[73]   Cl 25(1).
[74]   Cl 26(4).
[75]   Cl 26(5).
[76]   Cl 27(1).
[77]   Cl 27(2).

full consultation occurred; and that all plans, including those proposed by communities themselves, were taken into account.[78]

Relocation means to move a person from one piece of land to another piece of land.[79] Accordingly, relocation can be relevant *even before an eviction occurs* in that the land owner and the occupiers could agree to a relocation, which relocation is subject to ministerial consent.[80] It is unclear whether the Board is also a party in these kinds of agreements. However, because all eviction applications could render persons "likely to be evicted",[81] the Board is automatically involved in all eviction applications. It would seem that, although the Board is automatically involved in all evictions, it is not necessarily involved in agreements *prior* to eviction. If the Board is not involved in all relocations, how would it have an overall view of relocations and resettlements and be proactive? It is also unclear whether the removal of persons from one part of the farm to another part of the same farm constitutes a "resettlement" and whether the criteria listed above would then have to be adhered to as well.

Clause 28 provides that expropriation may be employed to further the objectives of the Bill. Where permanent expropriation is not desirable, clause 29 provides for a "temporary right" to use a piece of land for resettlement purposes. Would this settlement area be a settlement similar to a transit area? Can these temporary rights be upgraded or made permanent at a later stage? Do the criteria for resettlement areas have to be adhered to in these instances as well (interim settlement), or do those criteria only come into play where resettlement is permanent? What would be the case if the community is already present on the land and temporary use rights are acquired but no resettlement or relocation occurs? Would the criteria mentioned above also apply in these circumstances? These are but some of the questions remaining.

5 5   Management of resettlement units and agri-villages

Chapter 7 of the Bill deals with the management of resettlement areas and agri-villages. A committee of the resettled community or agri-village representatives is established under clause 33 to manage the affairs of the community. The committee is registered by the Board, reports to the Board and the total of the committee members is prescribed by the Board. The management rules, that have to be fair and reasonable, are made by the Board and relates to the administration, control, use and enjoyment of individual units and common areas. Although the community can amend the rules, the amendment has to be approved by the Board.[82] The other duties and functions of the committee are set out in clause 35 and include the duties to advise, aid, liaise and assist where necessary. From this exposition it is clear

---

[78]   Cl 27(5).
[79]   Cl 1.
[80]   Cl 26(4).
[81]   Cl 27(1).
[82]   Cl 34.

that, although the relevant committee runs the affairs of the community, the real power and authority are located in the Board.

5 6   Land Rights Management Board

The Board is established under clause 36 of the Bill, and the role and responsibilities thereof are set out in clause 37. These include *inter alia* the duty to enable and promote development, to manage land rights, to acquire land for resettlement; to provide guidelines for community committees and to provide and arrange for legal aid where necessary. The Board consists of between seven and nine members, and the required qualifications and experiences of members are set out in clause 39.

5 7   Dispute resolutions and courts

Chapter 9 of the Bill deals with dispute resolutions and courts. Although the Land Claims Court ("LCC") is the preferred court that has all the powers necessary to deal with all matters under the Bill, parties may also institute proceedings in the relevant magistrate's court.[83] In this regard, the magistrate's court has jurisdiction in relation to proceedings for the relocation or restoration of rights and criminal proceedings under the Act and can grant interdicts and issue declaratory orders.[84] Civil appeals from the magistrate's courts are to the LCC. Any orders made by the magistrate's court are subject to automatic review by the LCC, during which they can be confirmed, replaced, or substituted, or the case can be remitted to the magistrate's court. No review is available if an appeal has been lodged. Orders are suspended for the duration of the review. Proceedings lodged in the high courts are transferred to the LCC. Appeals from the LCC are to the Supreme Court of Appeal. Furthermore, parties are able to approach the Board to appoint persons to facilitate dispute resolution meetings.[85]

6   Discussion

Despite acting as overarching framework, the Draft Tenure Security Policy has various *lacunae* in relation to the Tenure Security Bill. Accordingly, a lack of synergy between the Policy and the Bill is the first aspect to be discussed here. Apart from this, the Bill itself is problematic in many respects.

6 1   Lack of synergy

Although the Policy focuses on farm land, the Bill refers to agricultural land only, with no clarification as to what "agricultural land" entails. The Constitutional Court judgment in *Wary Holdings (Pty) Ltd v Stalwo (Pty) Ltd*[86] has underscored how difficult it can be to establish whether land

---

[83] Cl 42.
[84] Cl 43.
[85] Cl 44.
[86] 2008 11 BCLR 1123 (CC); 2009 1 SA 337 (CC).

is "agricultural land", depending on where the land is located and which legislative measures apply.[87] Therefore, although the scope of the Bill is not as broad as that of the current ESTA, it is from the outset unclear what the *exact* scope of the Bill is.

Resettlement and agri-villages are highlighted as one of the main focus areas of government in the improvement of tenure security. Despite this emphasis and the long discussion thereof in the Policy, the whole of Chapter 7, which addresses resettlement and agri-villages, is rather vague and ambiguous. The exact stage at which time these provisions become relevant and how they function, remain uncertain. It is not clear from the Bill whether the provisions dealing with "resettlement" relate to occupiers or labour tenants. Although the Bill states that labour tenancy claims will continue to be dealt with under Chapter III of the Labour Tenant Act, the Policy and Bill provide for land for "productive purposes", thereby incorporating labour tenancy. Although the provisions are vague, it seems as if resettlement can be for shorter or longer periods of time. According to the Policy, settlement will be dealt with in accordance with permits, but it can also be in the form of freehold. It can furthermore be individual or in relation to communal areas and it can be residential or agricultural (for cultivation purposes). Mention is also made of the fact that rights can be taken away if the land is not used productively. Accordingly, it seems as if tenure can be (a) rather temporary as it is linked to a permit system; (b) conditional (as it may be lost if it is not used productively); and (c) can be of an "evolving" nature, as it can be "upgraded" to freehold if used productively. On all of these matters, the Bill is silent: there is no indication of the *kinds* of rights or interests available, who qualifies, when and what the content of the rights or interests would be. In this regard there is no translation of the constructs and ideals set out in the Draft Policy into the Bill itself.

Furthermore, in relation to resettlement and agri-villages, the Draft Policy states that the community rules will be "agreed on"[88] and thus drafted by the community themselves. That is not the case in the Bill. Instead, the drafting of community rules is the prerogative of the Board.

The Draft Policy also provides for an "efficient and accessible system to record and register rights"[89] whereas there is no mention thereof in the Bill itself. Therefore, neither the acquisition of rights, nor the recording thereof is dealt with.

The Draft Policy makes reference to new initiatives, including alternative dispute resolution mechanisms, legal aid and legal representation, and a register of interests on farms. The Bill provides that any person may approach the Board to appoint a person to facilitate dispute resolution meetings, without setting out the consequences of such meetings. Although the Labour Tenant Act presently provides that an arbitrator may be appointed[90] and that proceedings

---

[87]   See Mostert et al "Land" in *LAWSA 14* para 94.
[88]   RSA *Draft Tenure Security Policy* 6.
[89]   5.
[90]   S 18 of the Labour Tenant Act.

may be referred to arbitration,[91] it has hardly occurred in practice. Perhaps the reasons for the non-appointment need to be researched and the provision for alternative dispute resolution mechanisms in the Bill revisited.[92]

Despite the current provisions in ESTA and the Labour Tenant Act aimed at legal aid and representation, securing these services remains problematic. Hopefully the involvement of the Board in this regard will prove more successful. The reference to a Register of Interests in the Policy never resonated in the Bill itself. Surely such a Register would be necessary if a proactive approach is to be followed by the Board?

6 2   Inherent flaws and problems in the Bill

Although the exact scope of the Bill is unclear, persons occupying forestry areas, resorts and other land outside urban areas (including land within a township, but who used to be occupiers under ESTA immediately prior to the establishment, approval and proclamation of such townships) will not be protected under the Bill. These categories of persons currently enjoy protection under ESTA. Accordingly, the commencement of the Bill will decrease the number of persons who enjoy protection and will cause some confusion as to what "agricultural land" entails.

Some clauses in the Bill are drafted poorly. For example, the clauses and provisions dealing with eviction notices are confusing in relation to the different persons and entities that have to be notified and the time period involved. Throughout Chapters 6 and 7 various references are made to agreements. The exact time when these different agreements are to be entered into, as well as their implications, are unclear. Despite envisaging the proactive conduct of the Board, the Bill has yet to indicate *how exactly* the conduct of the Board is to be proactive. In order for it to play an overarching role, it would need clear guidelines, support and sufficient resources and information. Provisions dealing with resettlement and relocation are furthermore vague and ambiguous: would a relocation on the same farm constitute resettlement; does an *in situ* upgrading constitute resettlement; and would an interim resettlement require the same approach as a permanent resettlement area?

Although the submission of a plan to deal with persons facing eviction is supported, the time period (two months) for the plan to be submitted may be too short. Furthermore, additional guidelines are needed relating to the content of the plan and the possible responses of the court. For example, it has to be possible for the court to interdict the role players to address shortcomings in the plan or to provide more information when necessary and refer the plan back for re-submission. The most recent judgment in the case of *Residents of Joe Slovo Community, Western Cape v Thubelisa Homes*[93] has illustrated the crucial importance of precise instructions in this regard, as well as how complex and time-consuming these issues may be.

---

[91]   S 19.
[92]   See also T Roux "Pro-Poor Court, Anti-Poor Outcomes: Explaining the Performance of the SA Land Claims Court" (2004) 20 *SAJHR* 511 526.
[93]   2010 3 SA 454 (CC).

Section 14 of ESTA currently provides for the payment of compensation and/or damages in the event of eviction contrary to the provisions of the Act. The Bill does not have a similar provision.

The Bill formulates the duties of land owners negatively. This means that, although there is, for example, a duty not to cut off water supply, there is no positive duty to actually supply water. In instances where there is no existing water supply, there is thus no duty on the land owner to address the shortcoming. Furthermore, references to the right of "development" in clause 15 are vague and should be defined more precisely.

In short, although problems experienced in the implementation and effective application of especially ESTA necessitated a new, more holistic approach,[94] the Draft Policy and Draft Land Tenure Security Bill did not rise to the occasion. When the 1997 White Paper on South African Land Policy was published an emphasis was placed on, *inter alia*, the creation of *long-term security* for farm dwellers in particular.[95] Instead, the new Policy seems to move away from the secure rights paradigm towards a "settlement paradigm" in terms of which the particular rights; and the content, scope, acquisition and loss thereof are not defined and set out. It is questionable whether occupancy, essentially determined by the Management Board, would result in secure tenure within this context. In instances where occupiers are still resident on (commercial) farms, the proposed clause 20(11), which provides that eviction may not render a person homeless, will only be effective if (a) secure, effective support mechanisms are in place and if (b) institutions and departments involved have the necessary financial and other capacities to deal with these issues.

7 Conclusion

The farm land puzzle affects millions of South Africans: farm workers, labour tenants, rural dwellers, occupiers, communities, and land owners. The pieces of the puzzle consist of various policy documents, strategies, plans and legislative measures.[96] Recent developments propose that some pieces of the puzzle are to be reshuffled, new pieces added and other pieces removed. Unfortunately, the connections between the different pieces in the puzzle do not fit properly, resulting in important parts of the picture remaining incomplete. Tenure cannot be secure if the relevant rights have not been defined. Furthermore, rights cannot be acquired or transferred if the relevant enabling mechanisms are absent. Apart from the fact that the pieces are not sufficiently exact to make the perfect fit, the frame of the puzzle is incomplete: what exactly is the scope of the new Bill and what is "farm land"? Even though communal land had specifically been cut out of the picture, tenure reform relating to commercial farms on the one hand and communal areas on the other would have to correspond on some level. Can effective tenure reform

---

[94] Pienaar (2011) *Speculum Juris* 108; Cousins & Hall *Rights Without Illusions* para 2.2.
[95] Department of Agriculture and Land Affairs *White Paper on SA Land Policy* (1997) 3.25, 4.9.
[96] See Pienaar (2011) *Speculum Juris* 108.

relating to farm land and agriculture really occur when large portions of rural areas are excluded?

It seems that, seventeen years after work started on the puzzle, all the relevant pieces are as yet not on the table. It is imperative that the gaps be filled and the pieces refitted, but within a sound and well-constructed framework and in accordance with a clear vision. If re-evaluated again after seventeen years, will the piecemeal adjustment of the puzzle have stood the test of time?

SUMMARY

On 24 December 2010 a new Draft Tenure Security Policy and concomitant Draft Land Tenure Security Bill were published for comment. These new measures focus on farm land in particular and have specific implications for the Extension of Security of Tenure Act 62 of 1997 ("ESTA") and the Land Reform (Labour Tenant) Act 3 of 1996. In this contribution we briefly explore the reasons for the introduction of these new measures at this point in time; thereafter we analyse the Policy and Bill in detail. In light of our finding that the three main objectives of the tenure reform programme, namely (a) rationalisation; (b) increased security; and (c) the embodiment of constitutional imperatives, have not been achieved, some kind of intervention seventeen years after the tenure reform programme was embarked on, is to be expected. However, it is questionable whether the proposed Policy and Bill in their present formats will address the prevalent shortcomings sufficiently. In this regard we identify two main problem areas: (a) a glaring lack of synergy between the Policy and the Bill; and (b) inherent flaws in the Bill itself. Regarding the first problem, various concepts and constructs identified in the Policy remain unattended to in the Bill. Accordingly, new initiatives proposed in the Policy, for example, the introduction of a permit system, have not been given effect to in the Bill. In fact, neither the acquisition, nor the recording or transfer of rights, have been dealt with in the Bill. The Bill is furthermore drafted poorly, thereby resulting in confusing and ambiguous provisions, for example, relating to the service of notice in eviction proceedings and matters surrounding resettlement areas. In this regard numerous questions remain unanswered. We reach the conclusion that, although intervention in the tenure programme is necessary, the most recent proposals do not embody an all-encompassing approach, resulting in numerous *lacunae* leaving important issues unaddressed.

CHAPTER 16

CONCEPTUALISING "MEANINGFUL ENGAGEMENT" AS A DELIBERATIVE DEMOCRATIC PARTNERSHIP

Gustav Muller[*]

1 Introduction

Nearly four years ago the Constitutional Court introduced a new concept into the law of evictions. After hearing oral argument in *Occupiers of 51 Olivia Road, Berea Township, and 197 Main Street, Johannesburg v City of Johannesburg*[1] (*"Occupiers of 51 Olivia Road"*) the Constitutional Court issued an interim order[2] that directed the parties "to engage with each other meaningfully".[3] In this case the City of Johannesburg sought to evict approximately 400 people from six buildings in terms of the fire bylaws of the City, section 20 of the Health Act 63 of 1977 and section 12(4)(b) of the National Building Regulations and Building Standards Act 103 of 1977. The occupiers opposed the application because an eviction and relocation to an informal settlement on the outskirts of the city would destroy their livelihood strategies that depended on being able to conduct informal trading, domestic work and recycling in the inner city of Johannesburg.

The Court explained that the purpose of this engagement order was to determine whether the values of the Constitution of the Republic of South Africa, 1996 ("the Constitution"), the constitutional and statutory obligations of the City, and the rights of the applicants could direct the parties to resolve the dispute of the application amicably.[4] The engagement between the parties also had to determine whether the plight of the applicants would be alleviated if the dangerous and ailing buildings that they occupied could be

[*] I would like to thank the Overarching Strategic Research and Outreach Project on Combating Poverty, Homelessness and Socio-Economic Vulnerability under the Constitution for financial support. I would like to thank Prof Sandra Liebenberg (HF Oppenheimer Chair in Human Rights Law) and Prof AJ van der Walt (South African Research Chair in Property Law) for their comments on earlier drafts of this text which forms part of my LLD dissertation entitled "The Impact of Section 26 of the Constitution on the Eviction of Squatters in South African Law". I would also like to thank Prof Geo Quinot for actively engaging with me about meaningful engagement over the past four years and the anonymous peer reviewers for their helpful comments on the chapter.
[1] 2008 3 SA 208 (CC).
[2] The interim order was issued on 30-08-2007. *Occupiers of 51 Olivia Road, Berea Township, and 197 Main Street, Johannesburg v City of Johannesburg (Interim Order 30 August 2007)* (CCT 24/07) ZACC (30-08-2007) *Constitutional Court of South Africa* <www.constitutionalcourt.org.za/Archimages/10731.PDF> (accessed 17-11-2011) ("Interim Order").
[3] Order 1.
[4] Order 1.

upgraded.[5] Furthermore, the interim order directed the parties to report back to the Court on the results of the engagement between them.[6] This engagement process resulted in the parties reaching an agreement[7] on the interim measures that the City would take to improve the living conditions on the properties[8] and the status of the City's eviction application against the occupiers.[9] The Court subsequently endorsed this agreement.[10]

Five months later, the Court, in its judgment explained that a municipality would be acting in a manner that was generally at odds with the spirit and purpose of a range of constitutional obligations if it evicted people from their homes without first meaningfully engaging with them.[11] The Court explicitly linked meaningful engagement with the obligation to take reasonable legislative and other measures within its available resources to provide access to adequate housing.[12] The Court affirmed its interpretive approach to the right of access to adequate housing by also linking the obligation to engage with the right to human dignity[13] and the right to life.[14] Finally, the Court linked meaningful engagement with the obligations that municipalities have to strive towards the provision of services in a sustainable manner;[15] the promotion of social and economic development;[16] and the involvement of communities and community organisations in the affairs of local government.[17]

The Court makes it plain in these reasons for the engagement order that homelessness as a result of eviction is still a very real possibility for many people. Local authorities should therefore engage with these people before any decision is taken on the formulation and implementation of a housing policy or programme that will inevitably lead to their eviction and relocation.

The Court proceeded to define meaningful engagement as "a two-way process" in which a local authority and those that stand to be evicted would

---

[5]   Order 2.

[6]   Order 3.

[7]   The parties reached the agreement on 29-10-2007. *Occupiers of 51 Olivia Road, Berea Township, and 197 Main Street, Johannesburg v City of Johannesburg (Agreement 29 October 2007)* (CCT 24/07) ZACC (29-10-2007) ("Agreement").

[8]   Cl 1.1.1.

[9]   Cl 1.1.2.

[10] The order was issued on 05-11-2007. *Occupiers of 51 Olivia Road, Berea Township, and 197 Main Street, Johannesburg v City of Johannesburg (Order 5 November 2007)* (CCT 24/07) ZACC (05-11-2007) <www.constitutionalcourt.org.za/Archimages/11584.PDF> (accessed 17-11-2011).

[11] *Occupiers of 51 Olivia Road, Berea Township, and 197 Main Street, Johannesburg v City of Johannesburg* 2008 3 SA 208 (CC) para 16. See s 19 of the Local Government: Municipal Structures Act 117 of 1998; ss 16(1) and 17 of the Local Government: Municipal Systems Act 32 of 2000. See further the UN Committee on Economic, Social and Cultural Rights *General Comment No 4: The Right to Adequate Housing* (1991) UN Doc E/1992/23 paras 8, 12; UN Committee on Economic, Social and Cultural Rights *General Comment No 7: The Right to Adequate Housing: Forced Evictions* (1997) UN Doc E/1998/22 paras 13, 15.

[12] S 26(2) of the Constitution; s 9(1)(a)(i) of the Housing Act 107 of 1997.

[13] S 10 of the Constitution provides that "[e]veryone has inherent dignity and the right to have their dignity respected and protected". See *Government of the Republic of South Africa v Grootboom* 2001 1 SA 46 (CC) para 83; S Liebenberg "The Value of Human Dignity in Interpreting Socio-Economic Rights" (2005) 21 *SAJHR* 1 1-31.

[14] S 11 of the Constitution provides that "[e]veryone has the right to life".

[15] S 152(1)(b) of the Constitution.

[16] S 152(1)(c).

[17] S 152(1)(e).

talk to each other meaningfully in order to achieve certain objectives.[18] The Court held further that meaningful engagement had the potential to contribute towards the resolution of disputes and "to increased understanding and sympathetic care"[19] if both the local authority and those that stand to be evicted grappled with the issues that pertain to the achievement of housing development objectives.[20]

The Court found that the constitutional obligations of local authorities dictate that they should initiate the engagement process and continue to make reasonable efforts to engage unlawful occupiers when their initial efforts are resisted or rebuffed.[21] The Court foresaw that the unlawful occupiers will acquiesce in this process if it is managed by "careful and sensitive people"[22] with experience in housing matters. This process would enable a municipality to explore the vast range of possibilities that are available on the continuum spanning from eviction without more to the provision of permanent housing.[23] The Court found that the nature and extent of the engagement process would be determined by the underlying purpose of the eviction and the number of people that stand to be affected by the eviction.[24] Yacoob J noted that the City of Johannesburg should have been conscious of the fact that their Inner City Regeneration Strategy would have drastic consequences for its rapidly increasing poor population and that it would require "structured, consistent and careful engagement" with all the affected parties.[25]

The Court further underscored that the engagement process must be conducted in good faith and any attempt by the unlawful occupiers to derail the engagement process through unreasonable demands or by adopting an intractable attitude should not be tolerated.[26] The Court emphasised this point by clearly stating that

"[p]eople in need of housing are not, and must not be regarded as a disempowered mass".[27]

In conclusion, the Court noted that the constitutional value of openness should guide the engagement process so as to avoid the destructive allure of secrecy by ensuring that "a complete and accurate account of the process

---

[18] *Occupiers of 51 Olivia Road, Berea Township, and 197 Main Street, Johannesburg v City of Johannesburg* 2008 3 SA 208 (CC) para 14. L Chenwi & K Tissington *Engaging Meaningfully with Government on Socio-Economic Rights – A Focus on the Right to Housing* (2010) 9 observe that the objectives will depend on the specific situation. They add that the government should not be the only party to determine what these objectives should be or how such objectives could be achieved.

[19] *Occupiers of 51 Olivia Road, Berea Township, and 197 Main Street, Johannesburg v City of Johannesburg* 2008 3 SA 208 (CC) para 15.

[20] See also Centre for Applied Legal Studies *Workshop Report: Meaningful Engagement* (2009) 30-32 <http://web.wits.ac.za/NR/rdonlyres/D1176AF9-340B-413B-AF79-2F1152BE0CDA/0/Meaningful engagementreport_Dec09.pdf> (accessed 07-03-2010).

[21] *Occupiers of 51 Olivia Road, Berea Township, and 197 Main Street, Johannesburg v City of Johannesburg* 2008 3 SA 208 (CC) para 15.

[22] Para 15.

[23] Para 18.

[24] Para 19.

[25] Para 19.

[26] Para 20.

[27] Para 20. See also T Ross "The Rhetoric of Poverty: Their Immorality, Our Helplessness" (1991) 79 *Geo LJ* 1499 1499-1547.

of engagement, including at least the reasonable efforts of the municipality within that process" is considered the norm.[28]

In this chapter I wish to engage with Yacoob J's contention that the need for meaningful engagement could be inferred from the applicant's contention that the decision to evict constituted administrative action which required the occupiers to be heard before the decision was taken.[29] I am intrigued by this point because later in the judgment Yacoob J seems to contradict himself when he states that the obligation to engage meaningfully with occupiers who would be rendered homeless after an eviction was "squarely grounded" in section 26(2) of the Constitution. To my mind the question is whether, and to what extent, there is an intersection or duplication between the concept of meaningful engagement, in terms of section 26(2) of the Constitution; and procedurally fair administrative action, in terms of section 33(1) of the Constitution.[30] My aim is to show that firstly, procedural fairness is not the same as meaningful engagement from a conceptual and doctrinal point of view; and secondly, meaningful engagement should be construed as a deliberative democratic partnership between local authorities and unlawful occupiers.

2 Procedural fairness

2 1 Administrative action affecting the public

The Promotion of Administrative Justice Act 3 of 2000 ("PAJA"), like meaningful engagement, provides adequately for public participation with both individuals or a specific household of unlawful occupiers, in terms of

---

[28] *Occupiers of 51 Olivia Road, Berea Township, and 197 Main Street, Johannesburg v City of Johannesburg* 2008 3 SA 208 (CC) para 21.

[29] Para 9. In *Residents of Joe Slovo Community, Western Cape v Thubelisha Homes (Centre on Housing Rights and Evictions, Amici Curiae)* 2010 3 SA 454 (CC) O'Regan J added that "the obligation to engage meaningfully imposed by s 26(2) of the Constitution should be understood together with the obligation to act fairly imposed by s 33 of the Constitution, as spelt out in PAJA" (para 297).

[30] In *Minister of the Interior v Bechler* 1948 3 SA 409 (A) 451 the former Appellate Division of the High Court defined the theory of natural justice as "the stereotyped expression which is used to describe those fundamental principles of [procedural] fairness which underlie every civilised system of law". These principles have been reduced over time to the maxims *nemo iudex in sua causa* and *audi alteram partem* which constitute the core of fair administrative action. The *audi* principle affords people the opportunity to participate in decisions that will affect them by apprising the administrative functionary of additional facts and possible alternatives that might influence the outcome of those decisions. This ensures the legitimacy of the decision because the quality and rationality of the decision is enhanced through respect for the dignity and worth of the people that stand to be affected. The application of the *audi* principle to administrative action was limited during the era of parliamentary sovereignty by the illogically rigid classification of administrative functions and the focus on decisions that prejudicially affected the property or liberty of an individual. However, towards the end of apartheid the Appellate Division changed this position dramatically by introducing the doctrine of legitimate expectation in South African law. See *Administrator, Transvaal v Traub* 1989 4 SA 731 (A). Since then the courts have retreated from the narrow and formalistic approach to natural justice to embrace a broader and more flexible duty to act fairly in all cases. This change of direction gained constitutional legitimacy with the inclusion of a right to just administrative action in s 24 of the Constitution of the Republic of South Africa Act 200 of 1993 and s 33(1) of the Constitution. S 33(1) of the Constitution states that "[e]veryone has the right to administrative action that is lawful, reasonable and procedurally fair." The Promotion of Administrative Justice Act 3 of 2000 was enacted to give effect to s 33(1) of the Constitution.

section 3,[31] and with a community of unlawful occupiers, in terms of section 4,[32] who stand to have their right of access to adequate housing adversely affected by the administrative decision to evict. Section 4 of PAJA concerns administrative action that "materially and adversely affects the rights of the public".[33] This is an innovative provision that incorporates new procedures for public participation into the general administrative law that has nearly no equivalent in the common law.[34] However, this provision is "somewhat enigmatic"[35] because it is uncertain what the precise relationship is with administrative action "which materially and adversely affects the rights or legitimate expectations of any person" in terms of section 3 of PAJA.

Mass[36] argues that sections 3 and 4 are linked because there is no longer a need to limit the application of the *audi* principle if the aim is to "create a culture of accountability, openness and transparency in public administration".[37] Mass accordingly insists that there is a very close link between section 4 and the more general requirements for procedural fairness in section 3(2)(b). She finds support for this argument in the fact that section 4 does not contain all the requirements stipulated in section 3(2)(b). She therefore submits that

---

[31] S 3(2) of PAJA reads:
  "(a)   A fair administrative procedure depends on the circumstances of each case.
  (b)   In order to give effect to the right to procedurally fair administrative action, an administrator, subject to subsection (4), must give a person referred to in subsection (1) –
    (i)   adequate notice of the nature and purpose of the proposed administrative action;
    (ii) a reasonable opportunity to make representations;
    (iii) a clear statement of the administrative action;
    (iv) adequate notice of any right of review or internal appeal, where applicable; and
    (v)   adequate notice of the right to request reasons in terms of section 5."

[32] S 4(1) of PAJA reads:
  "In cases where an administrative action materially and adversely affects the rights of the public, an administrator, in order to give effect to the right to procedurally fair administrative action, must decide whether –
  (a)   to hold a public inquiry in terms of subsection (2);
  (b)   to follow a notice and comment procedure in terms of subsection (3);
  (c)   to follow the procedures in both subsections (2) and (3);
  (d)   where the administrator is empowered by any empowering provision to follow a procedure which is fair but different, to follow that procedure; or
  (e)   to follow another appropriate procedure which gives effect to section 3."

[33] S 1 of PAJA defines "public" as "any group or class of the public".

[34] Decisions that affected large numbers of people were usually classified as "legislative" administrative action during the pre-democratic era and therefore the *audi* principle did not apply to them. In *South African Roads Board v Johannesburg City Council* 1991 4 SA 1 (A) Milne JA rejected the classification of administrative functions as either "quasi-judicial", "purely administrative" or "legislative". Milne JA proposed:
  "[T]hat a distinction should be drawn between *(a)* statutory powers which, when exercised, affect equally members of the community at large and *(b)* those which, while possibly also having a general impact, are calculated to cause particular prejudice to an individual or particular group of individuals. Here I use the word 'individual' to include a legal *persona* such as a corporation or a local authority, clothed with corporate personality; and the word 'calculated' to mean not 'intended' but 'likely in the ordinary course of things' to have this result." (12E-G) (original emphasis).
  The effect was that cases which fell into the first category (the equivalent of s 4 of the PAJA) would not attract procedural fairness while cases which fell into the second category (the equivalent of s 3 of the PAJA) would attract procedural fairness unless a statutory provision specifically provided otherwise.

[35] C Hoexter *Administrative Law in South Africa* (2007) 364.

[36] C Mass "Section 4 of the AJA and Procedural Fairness in Administrative Action Affecting the Public: A Comparative Perspective" in C Lange & J Wessels (eds) *The Right to Know – South Africa's Promotion of Administrative Justice and Access to Information Acts* (2004) 63.

[37] Preamble of PAJA.

section 4 cannot be freestanding because it is an incomplete provision that must be interpreted with recourse to the more general provisions for procedural fairness contained in section 3. The effect is that the relationship between sections 3 and 4 is "one of *lex generalis* and (incomplete) *lex specialis*".[38] Mass argues further that this approach to the relationship between sections 3 and 4 promotes the spirit, purport and objective of the right to just administrative action much better than one founded on the semantic distinctions drawn between administrative action affecting "any person" and administrative action affecting "the public".[39]

Currie and Klaaren point to the drafting history of section 4 in support of their argument that this provision is completely freestanding.[40] Currie and Klaaren argue that the Justice and Constitutional Development Portfolio Committee severed the link between clauses 4 and 5 of the South African Law Reform Commission's Draft Bill[41] (currently sections 3 and 4 of PAJA) by changing the heading of clause 4 from "procedurally fair administrative action" to "procedurally fair administrative action affecting any person". This, according to Currie and Klaaren, "created two separate and unrelated procedural fairness regimes".[42] Administrative action with a particular effect would then fall under the purview of section 3, while administrative action with a general effect would fall under the purview of section 4.[43]

This approach to the relationship between section 3 and 4 is problematic because there is no statutory right to procedural fairness for administrative action affecting the public parallel to that of section 3(1). Currie and Klaaren argue that the most helpful interpretation is to read "the right to procedurally fair administrative action" in section 3(1) as indirectly creating a general right to procedural fairness. This general right to procedural fairness would then also shape the minimum requirements administrators must adhere to in instances of administrative action affecting the public, since the requirements of section 3(2)(b) would simply not apply.[44]

Hoexter also points to the drafting history of section 4 in support of her argument that this provision is not linked to section 3. Hoexter notes that the Justice and Constitutional Development Portfolio Committee mistakenly left a reference to section 3 in section 4(1)(e) during its amendment process. Hoexter attributes this to poor drafting and recommends that the reference should simply be expunged through the amendment of section 4.[45] Hoexter also notes that there are minimum requirements for procedurally fair administrative action in section 4 similar to those contained in section 3(2)(b).[46] Finally, Hoexter argues

---

[38] Mass "Section 4 of the AJA" in *The Right to Know* 66-67.
[39] 67.
[40] I Currie & J Klaaren *The Promotion of Administrative Justice Act Benchbook* (2001) 110-113.
[41] South African Law Reform Commission *Administrative Justice Project 115 Report* (1999) <www.justice.gov.za/salrc/reports/r_prj115_aja_1999aug.pdf> (accessed 30-01- 2010).
[42] Currie & Klaaren *Benchbook* 113.
[43] This is in accordance with the distinction that Milne JA made in *South African Roads Board v Johannesburg City Council* 1991 4 SA 1 (A) 12E-G.
[44] Currie & Klaaren *Benchbook* 113.
[45] Hoexter *Administrative Law* 369.
[46] 375.

that the attempted uncoupling of the two provisions and the narrower focus of section 3 is indicative of the "gulf" that exists between sections 3 and 4.[47]

The fact remains that section 4(1)(e) contains a reference to section 3 that cannot be ignored. Mass provides a workable approach that links sections 3 and 4 through this "hangover" of the South African Law Reform Commission's Draft Bill.[48] According to this approach an administrator will not be required to superficially classify an administrative action affecting "any person" in terms of section 3 or administrative action affecting "the public" in terms of section 4 when it is clear that the administrative action affects both "any person" and "the public".[49] Currie and Klaaren conceded this point when the administrative action presents itself along the factual lines of *South African Roads Board v Johannesburg City Council*.[50] In this case the South African Roads Board declared an existing road a toll road. Currie and Klaaren explain that this decision would have a particular impact (section 3 of PAJA) on the Johannesburg City Council because it would have to upgrade its current roads infrastructure and increase maintenance to support the additional traffic congestion caused by motorists choosing alternative routes. The decision would also have a general effect (section 4 of PAJA) on all the motorists' freedom of movement.

The result will be exactly the same where a local authority evicted a community of unlawful occupiers. The decision will have a particular impact on the surrounding local authorities because they would have to expand their housing programmes while also having a general impact on the community's right of access to adequate housing. Hoexter confirms that "decisions with a general impact often have a special impact on particular people".[51]

Furthermore, Mass does not focus disproportionately on the supposed intention of the legislature or its poor drafting abilities. Instead, her approach constitutes a purposive interpretation of the right to just administrative action that gives effect to the constitutional value of openness by making simpler and more efficient ways of public participation possible to the poor population of South Africa. While it is clear that PAJA provides simple and efficient forms of public participation it remains unclear whether these forms of participation follow the contours of meaningful engagement.

2 2   Participation procedures in section 4 of PAJA

It is clear from the structure of section 4 that a notice and comment procedure or a public inquiry or both are the default options available to an administrator.[52] However, section 4 does not provide specific instructions for an administrator to guide her in deciding which procedure to follow. Currie and Klaaren recommend that the following criteria should be used to decide

---

[47]   375.
[48]   Currie & Klaaren *Benchbook* 130.
[49]   116.
[50]   1991 4 SA 1 (A).
[51]   Hoexter *Administrative Law* 368.
[52]   Mass "Section 4 of the AJA" in *The Right to Know* 73.

the appropriate procedure:[53] the geographic impact; and the subject matter of the proposed administrative action. A notice and comment procedure is based on the consideration of written submissions, which makes it more suited to administrative action on general issues with national or regional impact. A public inquiry is driven by hearing testimony at a particular place on a given time, which makes it more suited to administrative action on specific issues with a local impact. Mass adds that the following criteria could also be helpful:[54] the cost and efficiency of the procedure; and the size and duration of the process. A notice and comment procedure is often simple and cheap because the administrator may not delegate her powers and consequently the procedure does not require many logistical arrangements. Public inquiries have the potential to be very complex and expensive because the administrator may delegate her powers to "a suitably qualified person or panel of persons"[55] who will conduct the public hearing.

A proposed decision to evict a community of unlawful occupiers will have a very specific impact on that particular community and could possibly extend to the surrounding local authorities as the unlawful occupiers move into other jurisdictions to find a place to stay. According to the abovementioned guidelines, circumstances of this nature will require conducting a public inquiry.

Regulation 5 of the Promotion of Administrative Justice Act, 2000: Regulations on Fair Administrative Procedures[56] adds a new dimension to a public inquiry that may be invaluable to unlawful occupiers that stand to be evicted. The aim of Regulation 5 is to provide assistance to communities "consisting of a considerable proportion of people who cannot read or write or who otherwise need special assistance".[57] Hoexter explains that

> "[t]his regulation sets out special steps to be taken to solicit the views of such people where they are likely to be affected by administrative action that may be taken as a consequence of a public inquiry. These steps may include the holding of public or group meetings where the issues are explained and views recorded, a survey of public opinion and the provision of secretarial assistance."[58]

This goes beyond the common-law understanding of the *audi* principle and embraces the constitutional value of openness in a way that ensures broader public participation.[59]

The public hearing will still be the core institutional feature of the public inquiry. While a public hearing is an effective way of obtaining the views and proposals of a community, it may be too adversarial[60] in the housing context to ascertain anything of significance regarding the rights and needs of the community given that the impact of an eviction on the lives of the poor may preclude any meaningful interchanges. It is similarly problematic to expect

---

[53]   Currie & Klaaren *Benchbook* 120.
[54]   Mass "Section 4 of the AJA" in *The Right to Know* 73-74.
[55]   S 4(2)(a) of PAJA.
[56]   Published in GN R 1022 in *GG* 23674 of 31-07-2002.
[57]   5.
[58]   Hoexter *Administrative Law* 372.
[59]   Mass "Section 4 of the AJA" in *The Right to Know* 74.
[60]   78.

impoverished communities to make effective use of a notice and comment procedure.

In these instances an administrator may follow "another appropriate procedure which gives effect to section 3".[61] Mass suggests that this provision allows an administrator to interact with "the public" on an individual basis by affording them a distinct opportunity to make representations or to follow other innovative procedures like "consultations, mediation, and negotiated rule-making".[62] These procedures require participation on a much smaller scale and their inquisitorial nature makes them cheaper and more efficient.[63]

This section shows that the public inquiry procedure provided for in terms of section 4 of PAJA could satisfy the need for two-way interaction between the local government and the unlawful occupiers, good faith interaction between the parties, and a transparent account of the interaction process. However, what section 4 fails to ensure is that the public inquiry will achieve certain objectives, lead to the resolution of disputes by increasing mutual understanding and respect, or ensure that the process is initiated and driven by skilled local government officials.

2 3   Procedural fairness does not equal meaningful engagement

In *Occupiers of 51 Olivia Road* and *Residents of Joe Slovo Community, Western Cape v Thubelisha Homes*[64] ("*Residents of Joe Slovo*") the *amici curiae*[65] argued that procedural fairness relates to the notion of participatory democracy because it ensured that individuals had an active role in state administration.[66] In *Doctors for Life International v The Speaker of the National Assembly*[67] the Constitutional Court explained that participation represents a powerful response to the legacy of apartheid by ensuring that excluded voices are empowered in wider participatory processes.[68] This conception of participatory democracy creates a unique link between the obligation of

---

[61] S 4(1)(e) of PAJA.

[62] Mass "Section 4 of the AJA" in *The Right to Know* 78.

[63] C Hoexter, R Lyster & A Currie *The New Constitutional and Administrative Law II: Administrative Law* (2002) 49.

[64] 2010 3 SA 454 (CC).

[65] In both cases the *amici curiae* were the Community Law Centre from the University of the Western Cape and the Centre on Housing Rights and Evictions (COHRE) from Geneva, Switzerland. *Occupiers of 51 Olivia Road, Berea Township, and 197 Main Street, Johannesburg v City of Johannesburg (Submissions of the Amici Curiae: Community Law Centre (UWC) and Centre on Housing Rights and Evictions (COHRE))* (CCT 24/07) ZACC (17-08-2007) *Constitutional Court of South Africa* <www.constitutional court.org.za/Archimages/10661.PDF> (accessed 07-03-2010) ("*Occupiers of Olivia Road amici* submissions"). *Residents of Joe Slovo Community, Western Cape v Thubelisha Homes (Submissions of the Amici Curiae: Community Law Centre (UWC) and Centre on Housing Rights and Evictions (COHRE))* (CCT 22/08) ZACC (30-07-2008) *Constitutional Court of South Africa* <www.constitutionalcourt.org.za/Archimages/12720.PDF> (accessed 07-03-2010) ("*Residents of Joe Slovo amici* submissions").

[66] *Occupiers of Olivia Road amici* submissions para 136; *Residents of Joe Slovo amici* submissions para 167.

[67] 2006 6 SA 416 (CC).

[68] I understand deliberative democracy to be a form of participatory democracy. The central tenet of participatory democracy is that participation in public debate and dialogue has transformative potential provided the participants in the process remain open-minded, are held accountable for their views, and do not evade the reality of deep structural inequalities. See S Liebenberg *Socio-Economic Rights: Adjudication under a Transformative Constitution* (2010) 28-34.

government to respect, protect and promote the fundamental rights in the Constitution and the right of excluded voices to access adequate housing. Section 4 of PAJA enables local government to fulfil this duty because "the public are likely to participate most robustly when their rights are materially and adversely affected".[69] Nedelsky explains that procedural fairness "offers the potential for providing subjects of bureaucratic power with some effective control as well as a sense of dignity, competence, and power".[70]

This must be understood against the background that administrative decisions are often taken in stages[71] and that procedural fairness must only be observed during the stage where a final decision is made.[72] Hoexter notes that it would be impossible to have an efficient administration if it had to "provide full-scale hearings at every stage".[73] This is supported by the fact that "administrative action"[74] must have a "direct" effect. The likelihood that preliminary decisions do not require the observance of procedural fairness is amplified by "pre-democratic reasoning",[75] which dictates the interpretation of the requirement that a right must be "adversely" affected by the administrative action.[76]

This conceptualisation of the *audi* principle is especially problematic in the housing context given that any investigation into the living conditions of unlawful occupiers or the upgrading of their informal settlement could result in the lodging of an eviction application and relocation to another site that is far away from *inter alia* employment opportunities. Put differently, any investigation without procedural fairness not only has the potential to aggravate the already insecure existence of the unlawful occupiers, but could also erode the fundamental values of accountability, responsiveness and openness[77] upon which our democracy is founded.[78] This is demonstrated unmistakably by the events leading up to the *Occupiers of 51 Olivia Road, Residents of Joe Slovo* and *Abahlali baseMjondolo Movement SA v Premier,*

---

[69] K Govender "An Assessment of Section 4 of the Promotion of Administrative Justice Act 2000 as a Means of Advancing Participatory Democracy in South Africa" (2003) 18 *SAPL* 404 409.

[70] J Nedelsky "Reconceiving Autonomy: Sources, Thoughts and Possibilities" (1989) 1 *YJLF* 7 27.

[71] Hoexter *Administrative Law* 392.

[72] See *Chairman, Board on Tariffs and Trade v Brenco Inc* 2001 4 SA 511 (SCA) paras 71-72.

[73] Hoexter *Administrative Law* 393.

[74] S 1 of PAJA defines "administrative action" as

"any decision taken, or any failure to take a decision, by – (a) an organ of state, when – (i) exercising a power in terms of the Constitution or a provincial constitution; or (ii) exercising a public power of performing a public function in terms of any legislation; or (b) a natural or juristic person, other than an organ of state, when exercising a public power or performing a public function in terms of an empowering provision, which adversely affects the rights of any person and which has a direct, external legal effect ...".

[75] Hoexter *Administrative Law* 396.

[76] In *R v Ngwevula* 1954 1 SA 123 (A) 127F Centlivres CJ explained that preliminary inquiries, according to pre-democratic reasoning, did not "prejudicially affect ... the property or liberty of an individual" because they were "purely administrative" in nature and, as such, did not require the observance of procedural fairness unless it was explicitly required by legislation. See Hoexter *Administrative Law* 351-353; *Law Society, Northern Provinces v Maseka* 2005 6 SA 372 (B) 382D-E.

[77] S 1(d) of the Constitution.

[78] See E Mureinik "Reconsidering Review: Participation and Accountability" (1993) *Acta Juridica* 35; G Quinot "Snapshot or Participatory Democracy? Political Engagement as Fundamental Human Right" (2009) 25 *SAJHR* 392.

Kwazulu-Natal[79] ("*Abahlali baseMjondol*") cases, where the applicants alleged that the conduct of municipal officials towards them had been characterised by tactics aimed at persuading them to accept the plans that the government had for their future, threats of violence when they did not succumb to these tactics, attacks on their person when they denounced the government plans which were made without addressing their concerns or incorporating their proposals, and announcements that decisions had been taken about their future. These examples of abuse of power and blatant disregard for the inputs of the unlawful occupiers at the beginning of multi-stage decision-making processes may fail to pass constitutional muster in the sense that they fall short of the lawful, reasonable and procedurally fair administrative action that the drafters of the Constitution had in mind or could even be excluded because it is executive action. The fact remains that these actions are common and reflect the lived reality of what the right to just administrative action amounts to for many poor people. *Occupiers of 51 Olivia Road, Residents of Joe Slovo* and *Abahali baseMjondolo* demonstrate that disastrous results can flow from preliminary inquiries into the housing conditions of unlawful occupiers where procedural fairness is not observed.

It is furthermore important to note that procedural fairness only applies to "administrative action". The definition of "administrative action" explicitly excludes "the executive powers or function of the Provincial Executive" – which includes the powers referred to in sections 126 and 139 of the Constitution[80] – and the executive powers or functions of a municipal council.[81] These exclusions are significant in the housing context because section 126 of the Constitution enables a MEC responsible for housing in a specific province to assign any power or function in terms of section 7 of the Housing Act to a municipality. Section 139 of the Constitution, on the other hand, obliges a MEC responsible for housing in a specific province to intervene where a municipality is unable or unwilling to fulfil its obligations in terms of section 9 of the Housing Act. Section 156 of the Constitution provides that municipalities have executive authority in respect of, and the right to administer all matters listed in, Schedule 4B and 5B of the Constitution which, significantly, includes the provision of electricity and gas reticulation; water and sanitation; local amenities; refuse removal, refuse dumps and solid waste disposal; and street lighting. The result is that many housing-related decisions are excluded from the operation of PAJA because they are considered to be of an executive nature. Meaningful engagement would therefore play an important role in adjudicating this category of decisions that do not require the observation of procedural fairness in terms of PAJA. This is where meaningful engagement transcends procedural fairness.

---

[79] 2010 2 BCLR 99 (CC).
[80] Subs (bb) of the definition of "administrative action" in s 1 of PAJA.
[81] Subs (cc) of the definition of "administrative action" in s 1 of PAJA.

3 Meaningful engagement as deliberative democratic partnership

Both the Housing Act and meaningful engagement flow from section 26(2) of the Constitution. Section 2(1)(b) and (1)(l) of the Housing Act lay the foundation for the establishment of a dialogic relationship between the executive and other role players in housing development which could be a useful reference for the interpretation of meaningful engagement. The general principles contained in these provisions concretise into obligations that require municipalities to ensure that they promote the resolution of conflicts that arise in the housing development process,[82] and facilitate and support the participation of other role players in the housing development process.[83] However, these general principles and obligations stop short of ensuring that the dialogue is managed by careful and sensitive people who will continue to make good faith efforts to engage so as to ensure that an increased understanding of the interests involved and sympathetic care for the unlawful occupiers are developed. Meaningful engagement therefore clearly foresees a change in the approach to and practice of participation – specifically its duration and nature – in housing development.

In *Occupiers of 51 Olivia Road* the Constitutional Court stated that meaningful engagement should ordinarily be initiated before litigation commences[84] because the outcome of the engagement process will be important for any court in determining whether it would be just and equitable to grant an eviction order.[85] In *Residents of Joe Slovo* the Court ordered the parties to engage on certain issues as part of the final order.[86] Meaningful engagement therefore requires the fostering of participation over a long period of time that commences with the conceptualisation of a plan, policy or piece of legislation, and culminates with the implementation and preservation of such plan, policy or legislation.[87]

Participation during this process cannot be characterised by manipulation, threats of violence, and similar announcements which the applicants in *Occupiers of 51 Olivia Road*, *Residents of Joe Slovo* and *Abahlali baseMjondolo* attested to because it would be at odds with the dialogic, transparent, "structured, consistent and careful"[88] engagement that the Constitutional Court described. The nature of the participation during the engagement process should rather be determined with reference to the ladder of citizen participation that Arnstein developed in the housing context from

---

[82] S 9(1)(e) of the Housing Act.
[83] S 9(2)(a)(vi).
[84] *Occupiers of 51 Olivia Road, Berea Township and 197 Main Street, Johannesburg v City of Johannesburg* 2008 3 SA 208 (CC) para 30.
[85] *Occupiers of 51 Olivia Road, Berea Township and 197 Main Street, Johannesburg v City of Johannesburg* 2008 3 SA 208 (CC) para 18. See also *Residents of Joe Slovo Community, Western Cape v Thubelisha Homes* 2010 3 SA 454 (CC) para 338.
[86] See *Residents of Joe Slovo Community, Western Cape v Thubelisha Homes* 2010 3 SA 454 (CC) para 7 order 5.
[87] See Chenwi & Tissington *Engaging Meaningfully with Government* 21.
[88] *Occupiers of 51 Olivia Road, Berea Township and 197 Main Street, Johannesburg v City of Johannesburg* 2008 3 SA 208 (CC) para 19.

the terminology used in US federal programmes that are directed at *inter alia* urban renewal.[89]

The ladder consists of eight rungs, with each rung representing a form of participation. The bottom two rungs – manipulation[90] and therapy[91] – describe levels where no participation takes place. These rungs are used as a substitute for genuine participation because the objectives of these forms of participation are to educate and cure citizens.[92] The following three rungs – informing,[93] consultation[94] and placation[95] – describe levels of tokenism where citizens are informed of government plans and may voice their concerns regarding these plans. Arnstein notes that these rungs do not ensure citizens that their concerns will be heeded and as such do not confer any real power to effect a change in the *status quo*.[96] The final three rungs – partnership,[97] delegated powers[98] and citizen control[99] – describe levels of citizen power, where citizens are afforded increasing degrees of decision-making power "by which they can induce significant social reform" and which "[enable] them to share in the benefits of the affluent society".[100]

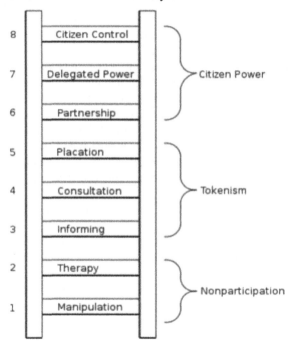

---

[89]   SR Arnstein "A Ladder of Citizen Participation" (1969) 35 *Journal of the American Institute for Planners* 216.
[90]   218.
[91]   218.
[92]   217.
[93]   219.
[94]   219.
[95]   220.
[96]   217.
[97]   221.
[98]   222.
[99]   223.
[100] 217.

The terminology used in the Housing Act and the experiences of the unlawful occupiers in *Occupiers of 51 Olivia Road, Residents of Joe Slovo* and *Abahlali baseMjondolo* indicates that participation in housing development currently occurs on the first five rungs of the participation ladder.[101] Conversely, the description of meaningful engagement indicates that it could not extend to the final two rungs of the participation ladder because that would have the effect of delegating or abdicating the constitutional duties of the executive to the unlawful occupiers. It is therefore clear that partnership, as a form of participation, most closely resembles the contours of meaningful engagement.

Arnstein explains that partnership, as a form of participation, would only work for as long as all the possible parties to the partnership find it useful to maintain the partnership.[102] The possible parties to an engagement process – the community that stands to be affected by the eviction and the government – will find it useful to maintain this partnership if their concerns and limitations are appreciated as legitimate and real. However, this will only occur if the parties, their legal representatives and other possible parties re-evaluate their respective roles.

A community cannot be allowed to persist with unreasonable demands and must rather focus its energy and resources on electing a community leader or committee that is empowered with a clear mandate to organise and mobilise the community. The community leader or committee must ensure that communication with the community is done in clear language and in a culturally appropriate manner. The community leader or committee must be able to engage openly with other parties and ensure that all outcomes of any engagement are referred back to the community for approval before finalisation.[103]

The legal representatives of the community must be prevented from approaching the case with so much vigour that they prejudice the rights of their clients. Instead, the legal representatives must ensure that they obtain a clear mandate from the community so as to position themselves as the secondary voice to the community leaders during the engagement process. This will not only ensure the fostering of a trust relationship between the community leaders and the legal representatives, but will also allow the legal representatives to facilitate the mobilisation and organisation of the community.[104]

---

[101] In *Residents of Joe Slovo Community, Western Cape v Thubelisha Homes* 2010 3 SA 454 (CC), Sachs J observed that

"[t]he evidence suggests the frequent employment of a top-down approach where the purpose of reporting back to the community was seen as being to pass on information about decisions already taken rather than to involve the residents as partners in the process of decision-making itself." (Para 378, footnote omitted).

[102] Arnstein (1969) *Journal of the American Institute for Planners* 221. The ladder of citizen participation provides a systematic characterisation of the types of participation that I found useful when evaluating the opposing accounts of the nature and duration of the public participation that took place in *Occupiers of 51 Olivia Road, Berea Township and 197 Main Street, Johannesburg v City of Johannesburg* 2008 3 SA 208 (CC), *Residents of Joe Slovo Community, Western Cape v Thubelisha Homes* 2010 3 SA 454 (CC) and *Abahlali baseMjondolo Movement of South Africa v Premier of KwaZulu-Natal* 2010 2 BCLR 99 (CC).

[103] Centre for Applied Legal Studies *Workshop Report: Meaningful Engagement* 37.

[104] 38.

Non-governmental organisations will also have to ply their advocacy[105] and research skills to support the engagement process. They can do so by facilitating the organisation and mobilisation of the community; ensuring that the legal representatives of the community are properly informed of existing international norms and examples from comparative jurisdictions that can be relied on to develop the law; and, finally, providing a court with a range of statistical data and budgetary information that may not appear in the papers of the parties.[106]

The government cannot be allowed to persist with its intractable institutional and bureaucratic attitude which dictates that all people living in intolerable conditions must be viewed as criminals or "at least to some degree as morally degenerate".[107] The government must rather ensure that it trains careful and sensitive officials to engage with communities in a manner that is characterised by access to information, flexibility, reasonableness, and transparency so that it can fulfil its constitutional and statutory obligations to provide access to adequate housing.

Conceived in this way, meaningful engagement is a type of public participation that transcends procedural fairness in terms of section 33 of the Constitution and sections 3 and 4 of PAJA in two ways. First, the process of meaningful engagement occurs over a long period of time, as opposed to the moment of decision-making in multi-staged administrative decision-making. Second, the nature of the participation required by meaningful engagement for it to be meaningful mandates the forging of a partnership between the government and the occupiers. It is only through the fostering of this long-term relationship that unlawful occupiers will be able to rise above the often misconceived perceptions of being helpless, passive and weak recipients of government largesse.[108]

4   Conclusion

Meaningful engagement creates a space for public participation that transcends procedural fairness in terms of PAJA. In this space the unlawful occupiers are required to appreciate the budgetary and policy challenges of providing for a range of interests, while the government must listen and respond with compassion to the plight of the urban poor.[109] Meaningful engagement must be viewed as an innovative mechanism for enforcing socio-economic rights.[110] In the long term individual engagement processes will create an incentive to develop the "multi-faceted and robust housing policies that section 26 arguably requires"[111] by incorporating the range of housing

---

[105]   See B Ray "Occupiers of 51 Olivia Road: Enforcing the Right to Adequate Housing Through 'Engagement'" (2008) 8 *HRLR* 703 711 for an explanation of why it is significant that the Constitutional Court envisaged an active role for civil society in the engagement process.
[106]   Centre for Applied Legal Studies *Workshop Report: Meaningful Engagement* 39.
[107]   42.
[108]   See Nedelsky (1989) *YJLF* 27.
[109]   See Chenwi & Tissington *Engaging Meaningfully with Government* 9.
[110]   Ray (2008) *HRLR* 708.
[111]   709.

needs of unlawful occupiers. Meaningful engagement requires government to take certain positive steps without mandating it to implement a specific court-directed housing development programme. The immediate remedial effect is that the unlawful occupiers may be able to retain their existing access to housing – with some improvements to render it safer and more suitable for human habitation – or to gain access to alternative accommodation that is of a relatively better standard.[112]

Furthermore, meaningful engagement ensures that a dialogic relationship is established between the local government and the unlawful occupiers.[113] This is preferable to a relationship which requires judicial intervention and control. The effect is that meaningful engagement will ensure that government appreciates the nature and scope of its constitutional and statutory obligations to provide access to adequate housing. Meaningful engagement will transform the way in which government approaches housing development projects in the sense that it will have to appraise itself of, *inter alia*: firstly, the full range of consequences that could flow from the proposed housing development; secondly, what will be required to alleviate the plight of those living in deplorable conditions and, finally, the cost and extent of interim measures it may need to take.

The only way in which this will happen is if both government and the unlawful occupiers approach the engagement process in good faith and with a renewed appreciation of their respective roles. This will ensure that the engagement process that creates the space for public participation and dialogue is open, honest and transparent. Proceeding from this foundation will make it easier for the parties to find common ground and thereby foster an increased understanding and appreciation by unlawful occupiers of the limitations of government, while simultaneously enabling government to respond to the plight of the unlawful occupiers with sympathetic care and concern.

In *Residents of Joe Slovo* the Constitutional Court made it clear that meaningful engagement could even have a role to play at the remedial stage of litigation in relation to controlling the effects of an eviction order. While engagement at this stage should by no means be viewed as a substitute for the engagement that precedes litigation, engagement at this stage could focus on the upgrading of the properties where the unlawful occupiers currently reside in order to make them safer or more suitable for human habitation.[114] However, engagement at this stage[115] will invariably pertain to the details

---

[112] See *Occupiers of 51 Olivia Road, Berea Township, and 197 Main Street, Johannesburg v City of Johannesburg (Agreement 29 October 2007)* (CCT 24/07) ZACC (29-10-2007) cls 5-13; *Residents of Joe Slovo Community, Western Cape v Thubelisha Homes* 2010 3 SA 454 (CC) para 7 order 10.

[113] In *Residents of Joe Slovo Community, Western Cape v Thubelisha Homes* 2010 3 SA 454 (CC), Sachs J observed that "[w]hen all is said and done, and the process [meaningful engagement] has run its course, the authorities and the families will still be connected in ongoing constitutional relationships" (para 408).

[114] See *Occupiers of 51 Olivia Road, Berea Township, and 197 Main Street, Johannesburg v City of Johannesburg (Interim Order 30 August 2007)* (CCT 24/07) ZACC (30-08-2007) orders 1 and 2.

[115] The recent judgment of the Constitutional Court in *Residents of Joe Slovo Community, Western Cape v Thubelisha Homes (Centre on Housing Rights and Evictions as Amici Curiae)* 2011 7 BCLR 723 (CC) illustrates that meaningful engagement at this late stage may not bear any fruits.

of the eviction,[116] possible relocation to temporary accommodation,[117] and ultimately the provision of permanent alternative accommodation.[118]

SUMMARY

Nearly four years ago the Constitutional Court created the concept of "meaningful engagement" in *Occupiers of Olivia Road, Berea Township, and 197 Main Street, Johannesburg v City of Johannesburg* 2008 3 SA 208 (CC). The Constitutional Court described meaningful engagement as a "two-way process" in which a local authority and those that stand to be evicted would talk to each other meaningfully in order to achieve certain objectives. In this chapter I question whether, and to what extent, there is an intersection or duplication between meaningful engagement, in terms of section 26(2) of the Constitution of the Republic of South Africa, 1996, and procedural fairness, in terms of section 33(1) of the Constitution and sections 3 and 4 of the Promotion of Administrative Justice Act 3 of 2000 ("PAJA"). I argue that meaningful engagement cannot be synonymous with procedural fairness because the definition of "administrative action" in section 1 of PAJA would limit the application of meaningful engagement by excluding executive action from its ambit. Furthermore, both the envisaged nature and duration of engagement ensures that meaningful engagement transcends procedural fairness. I therefore argue that meaningful engagement should rather be construed as a deliberative democratic partnership between local government and unlawful occupiers. This partnership demands that all the parties, including legal representatives and NGOs, involved in evictions should re-appreciate their respective roles. Finally, I posit that meaningful engagement is a welcome addition to South African law because it has the potential of fostering increased understanding and appreciation by unlawful occupiers of the limitations of government while simultaneously enabling government to respond to the plight of the unlawful occupiers with sympathetic care and concern.

---

[116] See *Residents of Joe Slovo Community, Western Cape v Thubelisha Homes* 2010 3 SA 454 (CC) para 7 orders 4-7, 11-15.

[117] Orders 8-10.

[118] Orders 17-20.

CHAPTER 17

RENTAL HOUSING AS ADEQUATE HOUSING

Sue-Mari Maass

1 Introduction

Despite the government's policies and housing legislation that aim to give effect to the housing provision (section 26 of the Constitution of the Republic of South Africa, 1996 ("the Constitution")), vulnerable households,[1] including previously disadvantaged households in urban areas, continue to occupy land and buildings with insecure tenure. This is evident from the evictions jurisprudence discussed in this contribution. Homeownership does provide tenure security to the marginalised, but the case law shows that these households should also be enabled to access other forms of formal tenure with strong tenure security. Recently the government has emphasised the importance of rental housing as a form of housing accessible to the urban poor. The current landlord-tenant laws are contract-based and premised on equal bargaining power. Generally, these laws provide sufficient tenure security for higher income groups who can easily access and exit the private rental market as they wish. However, it is questionable whether the free-market approach of the current rental housing laws provides satisfactory tenure security for the urban poor, because these households require increased tenure protection in order to establish themselves in their communities and actively participate in society.

The role of the state as public landlord is considered in light of the Constitution, while taking into account new policy developments in the area of public rental housing. This form of housing is also explored in the current socio-economic context of housing options for the urban poor. Finally, it is suggested that landlord-tenant law should develop in line with the Constitution and differentiate between different rental housing sectors in order to accommodate the desperately poor. It is also argued that such households should be enabled to access affordable public (and social) rental housing with strong tenure protection, which should be enacted in appropriate legislation.

2 The role of the state in the provision of housing

Section 26(1) and (2) of the Constitution ensures the right to have access to adequate housing, while it places an obligation on the state to take legislative

---

[1] The terms "vulnerable households", "desperately poor" and "urban poor" all refer to the same category of persons, namely the type of households who continuously struggle to find affordable formal accommodation, because of their financial weakness. These households often occupy informal housing because they are financially unable to afford formal housing.

and other measures to give effect to this right.[2] Furthermore, section 25(6) ensures that households who occupy land with insecure tenure as a result of past racially discriminatory laws are entitled to legally secure tenure and section 25(9) places an obligation on the legislature to enact laws that would give effect to this right. This provision forms part of the land reform programme as it initiates tenure reform, although one should consider its meaning within the broader context of transformation and specifically the transformation of the housing system.

The meaning of these provisions and specifically the role of the state in the provision of housing has developed in evictions jurisprudence. In *Government of the Republic of South Africa v Grootboom*[3] the Constitutional Court held that section 26(1) and 26(2) must be read together. It also decided that section 26(1) at least places a negative obligation on the state to desist from action that would impair the right of access to adequate housing.[4] In terms of section 26, the government must create a public housing programme aimed at realising the right of access to adequate housing.[5] In *Jaftha v Schoeman; Van Rooyen v Stoltz*[6] the Constitutional Court confirmed its decision in *Grootboom* and held that the right of access to adequate housing does contain a negative element, which means that a provision that permits a person to be deprived of existing housing restricts that person's constitutional housing right.[7]

Shortly after *Jaftha*, in *President of the Republic of South Africa v Modderklip Boerdery (Pty) Ltd*,[8] the Constitutional Court postponed

---

[2]   AJ van der Walt *Constitutional Property Law* (2005) 356 states that the constitutional obligation to give effect to the right of access to adequate housing often exists within policy frameworks, legislation and executive action.

[3]   2001 1 SA 46 (CC) para 34 per Yacoob J.

[4]   In *Government of the Republic of South Africa v Grootboom* 2001 1 SA 46 (CC) para 33 the Court rejected the contention that s 26(1) imposes a minimum core obligation on the state. The Court found that individuals' needs are too diverse to determine a minimum core threshold for all homeless members of society and that the court is unable to create such a threshold without the necessary information. See also S Liebenberg *Socio-Economic Rights: Adjudication under a Transformative Constitution* (2010) 163-173; S Russell "Introduction – Minimum State Obligations: International Dimensions" in D Brand & S Russell (eds) *Exploring the Core Content of Socio-Economic Rights: South Africa and International Perspectives* (2002) 11; P de Vos "The Essential Components of the Human Right to Adequate Housing – A South African Perspective" in D Brand & S Russell (eds) *Exploring the Core Content of Socio-Economic Rights: South Africa and International Perspectives* (2002) 23.

[5]   *Government of the Republic of South Africa v Grootboom* 2001 1 SA 46 (CC) para 41 per Yacoob J. This contention was confirmed in *Residents of Joe Slovo Community, Western Cape v Thubelisha Homes* 2010 3 SA 454 (CC) para 226 per Ngcobo J.

[6]   2005 2 SA 140 (CC).

[7]   *Jaftha v Schoeman; Van Rooyen v Stoltz* 2005 2 SA 140 (CC) para 34 per Mokgoro J. At paras 25-26 the Court emphasised that the aim of s 26 in relation to security of tenure had to be interpreted against the historical background of apartheid-type evictions and forced removals. The focus of s 26 is twofold, namely to reject the previous approach followed by the apartheid government with regard to evictions and to create a new dispensation in which the state must desist from interfering with individuals who occupy property. The state should only be allowed to interfere with an individual's access to housing when it is justifiable to do so: paras 26, 28. See also S Liebenberg "The Application of Socio-Economic Rights to Private Law" (2008) *TSAR* 464 467 on the negative obligation as developed in the case law. Liebenberg argues that in light of s 8(2) of the Constitution one should rather refrain from relying on a rigid distinction between positive and negative duties. A contextual approach should rather be followed in every case to determine whether a positive or negative duty should be imposed on (specifically) a private actor (Liebenberg (2008) *TSAR* 468-469).

[8]   2005 5 SA 3 (CC). See Liebenberg *Socio-Economic Rights* 281-286 for a discussion of the case.

the eviction of unlawful occupiers from private land until alternative accommodation could be provided by the state.[9] The state was also held liable to compensate the landowner because it failed to help execute the eviction order and therefore failed to protect the private landowner's property rights.[10] In *Residents of Joe Slovo Community, Western Cape v Thubelisha Homes*[11] Ngcobo J stated that the government does have a constitutional duty to make possible the realisation of the right to housing.[12]

The court has also held that the state should be joined in proceedings where private landowners claim eviction of unlawful occupiers (including previous tenants) and where the eviction order would result in the occupiers being homeless.[13] The court held that the interests of the occupiers, private landowner and state (municipality) would be protected if the state was joined, because the state has a duty to provide the evicted occupiers with adequate housing.[14]

In *Modderklip, Blue Moonlight Properties 39 (Pty) Ltd v Occupiers of Saratoga Avenue*,[15] and *The Occupiers, Shulana Court, 11 Hendon Road, Yeoville, Johannesburg v Steele*[16] the courts have recently interpreted the Prevention of Illegal Eviction from and Unlawful Occupation of Land Act 19 of 1998 ("PIE") to postpone eviction orders in the case where such an order would render the occupiers, including urban tenants, homeless. The courts allow the continued occupation of unlawful occupiers on private land until the state can make alternative accommodation available.

One could argue that the state does not have a positive duty to provide all homeless persons with access to adequate housing, even though the government is responsible for ensuring that the required laws (generally taking the form of legislation), policies and incentives are developed and sufficient to give effect to the duty enshrined in section 26 of the Constitution.[17] However, from the recent eviction cases it appears that the courts will force the state to be involved in some eviction proceedings with the aim to facilitate vulnerable occupiers who face homelessness. In *City of Johannesburg Metropolitan Municipality v Blue Moonlight*[18] the Supreme Court of Appeal decided that the local authority had a positive duty to provide temporary accommodation to marginalised evictees

---

[9] *President of the Republic of South Africa v Modderklip Boerdery (Pty) Ltd* 2005 5 SA 3 (CC) para 68. The same logic was followed in *Blue Moonlight Properties 39 (Pty) Ltd v Occupiers of Saratoga Avenue* 2010 JOL 25031 (GSJ); *The Occupiers, Shulana Court, 11 Hendon Road, Yeoville, Johannesburg v Steele* 2010 9 BCLR 911 (SCA).

[10] *President of the Republic of South Africa v Modderklip Boerdery (Pty) Ltd* 2005 5 SA 3 (CC) para 68. Van der Walt *Constitutional Property* 367-368. See also *City of Johannesburg Metropolitan Municipality v Blue Moonlight* 2011 4 SA 337 (SCA) paras 70-71.

[11] 2010 3 SA 454 (CC).

[12] Para 224.

[13] *Sailing Queen Investments v The Occupants La Colleen Court* 2008 6 BCLR 666 (W).

[14] Para 18.

[15] 2010 JOL 25031 (GSJ). At para 68 the Court stated that the state is directly involved in eviction cases where occupiers face homelessness, because the state has control over the housing policy and the available housing stock.

[16] 2010 9 BCLR 911 (SCA).

[17] *Government of the Republic of South Africa v Grootboom* 2001 1 SA 46 (CC) para 40 per Yacoob J.

[18] 2011 4 SA 337 (SCA).

who faced homelessness.[19] In light of the case law it seems that the courts are forcing the state to prevent an increase in homelessness by accommodating at least occupying persons who would be rendered homeless as a result of an eviction order. According to *Blue Moonlight*:

> "It is clear from the Constitutional Court and SCA judgments ... that the City has a positive constitutional duty to the desperately poor not to render them homeless should they be evicted."[20]

From the case law it is evident that the duty to make affordable housing available is a state duty. The state must be actively involved in the provision of housing and the state must be able to assist the most vulnerable who face homelessness. The case law shows that the state has not introduced a form of housing that is easily accessible to the desperately poor. Vulnerable evictees are unable to access formal housing other than homeownership, which might take years to establish.[21] The provision of homeownership for the urban poor is a time-consuming process[22] that might eventually be beneficial to some households, but in light of the case law it is clear that other forms of tenure must be introduced by the state to accommodate the marginalised who are in desperate need.

3   The rental housing option

3 1   The state's initial emphasis on homeownership

Since 1994, when the newly elected ANC government came into power, a number of policies have been introduced with the aim to provide adequate housing for vulnerable households. Part of the initial housing policy was to introduce and develop a variety of tenure forms that would provide access to housing and grant secure tenure, but individual ownership has been the main form of tenure delivered in urban areas.[23]

Providing tenure security in South African urban areas could be defined as "formalizing land rights through full formal private tenure".[24] The most

---

[19]   Paras 70-72.

[20]   *Blue Moonlight Properties 39 (Pty) Ltd v Occupiers of Saratoga Avenue* 2010 JOL 25031 (GSJ) para 128.

[21]   A concerning fact is that roughly 50% of state-subsidised housing, including RDP and BNG (the Department of Housing launched the Breaking New Ground (BNG) policy in September 2004, which strives to eradicate informal settlements; the aim is to upgrade informal settlements or relocate occupiers of informal settlements where development is impossible: Republic of South Africa, Department of Housing *Breaking New Ground Policy* (2004)) houses, have not been registered with the deeds office: K Tissington *A Resource Guide to Housing in South Africa 1994-2010: Legislation, Policy, Programmes and Practice* (2011) 31.

[22]   More than 12% of the population currently live in RDP houses, while almost 2 million households have at least one member on the waiting list for RDP housing. In Gauteng Province and the Western Cape more than 50% of the households have been on the waiting list for more than five years: Statistics South Africa *GHS Series II, Housing, 2002-2009* (2010) 19, 30. Since 1994, the housing backlog has grown from roughly 1.5 million to more than 2 million: Tissington *Resource Guide to Housing* 33.

[23]   L Royston "Security of Urban Tenure in South Africa: Overview of Policy and Practice" in A Durand-Lasserve & L Royston (eds) *Holding their Ground, Secure Land Tenure for the Urban Poor in Developing Countries* (2002) 165 176.

[24]   C Cross "Why the Urban Poor Cannot Secure Tenure: South African Tenure Policy under Pressure" in A Durand-Lasserve & A Royston (eds) *Holding their Ground, Secure Land Tenure for the Urban Poor in Developing Countries* (2002) 195 196. Conversely, the 1994 White Paper on housing stated that "[o]ne of the most significant and short-term interventions required of the Government will be to provide the widest range of options for the rapid attainment of secure tenure" (Republic of South Africa, Department of Housing *White Paper: A New Housing Policy and Strategy for South Africa* (1994) 3 2 2).

complete form of such tenure is private ownership, which is why this is the main form of tenure delivered until now.[25] By December 2008, government had built 2.8 million houses and provided such households (consisting of 13.5 million people in total) with private ownership.[26] The perception that ownership is the most important and valuable property right (as a right and a question of redress) has prevented a variety of tenure options from being developed and delivered in urban areas.[27]

It might seem that homeownership is the principal form of tenure for marginalised households, but ownership does not necessarily suit the needs of poor urban occupiers.[28] There is a preference among at least some of the urban poor to rent accommodation instead of acquiring ownership.[29] Marginalised occupiers who hold land under private tenure could easily be surprised by hidden costs which could lead to distress sales.[30]

Despite the preference of urban occupiers to rent housing, one could also argue that public rental housing is a better form of tenure (in comparison to owner-occupation) for poor occupiers because the state can regulate, assess and control the market to the extent that it is involved in the provision thereof. If the state is directly involved in the provision of rental housing, as a social landlord, the state would be able to provide marginalised occupiers with secure (adequate) housing, without having to place any unwanted financial burdens on these tenants. The success of such a form of housing depends on the enactment of effective legislation that affords tenure security while also being context-sensitive to the personal needs of the individual households.

In 2009, the government's prime target was to eradicate or upgrade all informal settlements by 2014/2015 through housing delivery, including the development of low-cost housing, medium-density accommodation and rental housing.[31] Currently, the government is again emphasising the need to develop different forms of tenure, especially in the area of rental housing through the development of differentiated public and social housing sectors.[32]

3 2   Landlord-tenant laws

Currently, rental housing legislation is limited to the private sector and the social sector. Private rental housing is regulated in terms of the Rental

[25] Cross "Why the Urban Poor Cannot Secure Tenure" in *Holding their Ground* 196.
[26] Republic of South Africa "Housing" (03-08-2009) *South African Government Information* <http://www.info.gov.za/aboutsa/housing.htm> (accessed 03-08-2009).
[27] Royston "Security of Urban Tenure in SA" in *Holding their Ground* 176-177. See also S Maass *Tenure Security in Urban Rental Housing* LLD dissertation Stellenbosch (2010) 119-120.
[28] V Watson & M McCarthy "Rental Housing Policy and the Role of the Household Rental Sector: Evidence from South Africa" (1997) 22 *Habitat International* 49 51-52. The authors state that globally, homeownership is not necessarily the best tenure option amongst poor urban dwellers.
[29] JM Pienaar "The Housing Crisis in South Africa: Will the Plethora of Policies and Legislation have a Positive Impact?" (2002) 17 *SAPL* 336 361. See also Watson & McCarthy (1997) *Habitat International* 53 for percentages of the population preferring rental housing, established during a survey in Cape Town.
[30] Cross "Why the Urban Poor Cannot Secure Tenure" in *Holding their Ground* 207.
[31] Republic of South Africa "Housing" (05-08-2009) *South African Government Information*.
[32] Republic of South Africa "Housing" (28-09-2011) *South African Government Information*. See also Tissington *Resource Guide to Housing* 8-9 for more detail on the government's revised target, namely *in situ* upgrading.

Housing Act 50 of 1999, while the Social Housing Act 16 of 2008 regulates social rental housing.

The Rental Housing Act is the primary statute that regulates private landlord-tenant relationships in urban areas. Generally, the Act supports a free-market approach to rental housing. It protects the rights of the parties in light of their contractual rights and duties. The legislature therefore assumes that the parties have equal bargaining power when entering into the lease and that this would remain their position throughout the term of the lease. The extent of tenure security granted to the tenant depends on the contract and therefore the will of both parties. The Rental Housing Act provides limited tenure protection because it does not override the landlord's common-law right to evict the tenant upon termination of the lease.[33] It follows that the Act entrenched the common-law rules governing termination of the lease and the consequential right of repossession, even though immediate repossession by the landlord might, in certain circumstances, be suspended. The landlord is entitled to reclaim his property upon termination of the lease by means of a court order.[34] Where the tenant fails to redeliver the property upon termination of the lease the landlord has his usual remedies for breach of contract, because the tenant is holding over.[35]

The Social Housing Act is a direct result of the government's social housing policy.[36] The Act makes provision for the creation of social housing institutions,[37] responsible for the provision and management of social housing stock,[38] while a "lease agreement" is defined as "a standard lease agreement utilised by a social housing institution".[39] The aim of the Act is to introduce a social housing sector that can provide affordable rental housing through the creation of social housing institutions (social landlords). The social housing model is suitable for persons earning more than R2 500 per

---

[33] AJ van der Walt "Exclusivity of Ownership, Security of Tenure, and Eviction Orders: A Model to Evaluate South African Land-Reform Legislation" (2002) *TSAR* 254 266; A Mukheibir "The Effect of the Rental Housing Act 50 of 1999 on the Common Law of Landlord and Tenant" (2000) 21 *Obiter* 325 329 agrees that the common-law rights will remain in force if they are not explicitly amended by the Act.

[34] S 4(5)(d) of the Rental Housing Act. See also T Legwaila "An Introduction to the Rental Housing Act 50 of 1999" (2001) 12 *Stell LR* 277 281; PJ Badenhorst, JM Pienaar & H Mostert *Silberberg & Schoeman's The Law of Property* 5 ed (2006) 429.

[35] Mukheibir (2000) *Obiter* 337-338. SI Mohamed *Tenant and Landlord in South Africa* (2003) 28 mentions that where the tenant refuses to vacate the premises upon termination of the lease, the landlord can lodge a complaint with the Rental Housing Tribunal because the act of the tenant amounts to an unfair practice. The tenant is obliged to pay the rent while the landlord can only recover arrears after a ruling was obtained from the tribunal. This position was amended by s 7(b) of the Rental Housing Amendment Act 43 of 2007.

[36] Republic of South Africa *A Social Housing Policy for South Africa* (2003). See also Tissington *Resource Guide to Housing* 98 for more detail on the Act and its underlying policy.

[37] S 2(1)(i)(xv) of the Social Housing Act. See s 13(1) and (5) for the definition of a social housing institution.

[38] Where there is a demand for social housing stock within a municipality's area, the municipality must take measures to facilitate the delivery of social housing within that area and encourage development of social housing through the conversion of existing non-residential stock and upgrading of existing stock: s 5(a) and (b) of the Social Housing Act.

[39] S 1 of the Social Housing Act.

month.[40] A number of social housing projects have been approved and funded by the government, but social housing is generally perceived as private and not a public housing initiative.[41]

Section 2(1)(h) states that government and social housing institutions must ensure secure tenure for residents in social housing stock. The extent of tenure security must be based on the general principles as stated in the Rental Housing Act. The Rental Housing Act does not provide strong tenure protection. Consequently, the Social Housing Act does not provide strong security of tenure either.

In light of the current housing laws one can conclude that the most vulnerable occupiers in urban areas are denied access to the social rental housing sector and to the extent that they can access the private rental sector, their tenure rights would be contract-based and therefore insecure. The government is currently emphasising the need for public rental housing that could accommodate poor households.[42]

3 3 Public rental housing

The Community Residential Units Programme[43] aims to provide public rental housing to very low-income households who currently access informal rental housing opportunities.[44] The purpose of this programme is to upgrade and make available existing hostels, residential units and dilapidated buildings that are owned by local government, to provide inexpensive rental housing to the very poor.[45] Apparently it would be more cost effective for local government to retain and upgrade buildings than to make them available for private ownership.[46] Overall, the programme would establish a formal public rental sector. The programme targets current public sector tenants; evictees and households from informal settlements; households who are on the housing backlog; and indigent groups who are able to afford some rent.[47] The programme is provincially funded,[48] but it is locally administered. The local municipality, acting as public sector landlord, must collect the rental payments, which should collectively cover the operating costs.[49] The local

---

[40] Development Action Group "Urban Land Matters: Tenure Options for Low Income Groups" (22-02-2011) *Resources* <http://www.dag.org.za/index.php?option=com_content&view=article&id=89:resources&cat id=9:research-reports&Itemid=8> (accessed 22-02-2011).

[41] Tissington *Resource Guide to Housing* 102.

[42] Republic of South Africa, Government Communication and Information System *Pocket Guide to South Africa Human Settlements* (2009/2010) 144-145 <http://www.gcis.gov.za/resource_centre/sa_info/ pocketguide/2009/019_human_settlemets.pdf> (accessed 22-02-2011).

[43] The details of the programme are explained in the Department of Human Settlements *National Housing Code: Community Residential Units Part 3 Vol 6* (2009) 11-87.

[44] Department of Human Settlements *National Housing Code* 11. Tissington *Resource Guide to Housing* 103.

[45] Department of Human Settlements *National Housing Code* 12 makes it clear that occupying tenants would not be enabled to purchase the public rental housing stock.

[46] 9.

[47] Department of Human Settlements *National Housing Code* 12. Tissington *Resource Guide to Housing* 103.

[48] Department of Human Settlements *National Housing Code* 15.

[49] 19.

municipality is responsible for the efficient management of the stock.[50] The rent is determined by using a standard square meter rate. In terms of the Housing Code the "[square meter] rate will be calculated by taking the total operating budget for the housing stock and dividing it by the total [square meter] of housing stock that the municipality or provincial department owns".[51]

The tenants are therefore charged the same amount of rent and annual rent increases are directly linked with the increase in operation costs.[52]

The municipality, who owns the rental stock, must ensure that the tenants sign leases in compliance with the Rental Housing Act.[53] The policy is a well-structured and valuable innovation that one can applaud for a number of reasons, including the introduction of a form of tenure that is regulated and administered by the state and that would accommodate the poorest of the poor. The incentive to restore dilapidated buildings in urban areas for residential purposes is also a welcome development, because the desperately poor often require housing options close to where they work, which is usually in the city centre. However, similar to the Social Housing Act, reference to the Rental Housing Act regarding tenure security is troublesome, because security of tenure in terms of the Rental Housing Act is contract-based and does therefore not provide the tenant with strong tenure protection.

The Community Residential Units Programme is still in an introductory phase and legislation has not been promulgated to give effect thereto. Nevertheless, the introduction of a formal public rental sector is a housing development that requires circumspection, as it was used during apartheid to provide weak tenure rights for black people to help orchestrate racial segregation. Public rental housing was the dominant form of tenure for black persons in urban areas during apartheid, specifically in the informal settlements. One of the many apartheid land laws, the Regulations Concerning the Administration and Control of Land in Black Urban Areas of 14 June 1968[54] serves as an example of how the laws ensured that the black majority occupied land with insecure tenure. The regulations provided that black individuals could occupy urban land under three different forms of tenure, namely "(i) a permit to erect a private dwelling; (ii) a resident's permit to rent a house from the Local Government; and (iii) a certificate of occupation of a house".[55] The rights allocated to black individuals were personal rights and derived from the contractual relationship between the local authority and

---

[50] 13.
[51] 19-20 includes the possibility of rent relief assistance, although the parties should agree to this arrangement when the lease is drafted.
[52] 20.
[53] 30.
[54] GN R 1036 in *GG* 2096 of 14-06-1968. See also s 14(1) of the Group Areas Act 41 of 1950, s 18(1) of the Group Areas Act 77 of 1957 and s 21(1) of the Group Areas Act 36 of 1966 for provisions that provided similarly weak tenure rights.
[55] N Olivier "Urbanisation: Policy/Strategy with Particular Reference to Urbanisation and the Law" (1988) 53 *Koers* 580 582.

the individual. The occupier could only enforce his personal right against the local authority, because he did not obtain a real right.[56]

The housing system in Khayelitsha (Cape Town) could be used as an example to illustrate some of the newly introduced tenure options generally used in informal settlements[57] shortly after apartheid was abolished.[58] In 1985 Khayelitsha was used to house thousands of black households as state tenants.[59] Households could either rent state property or rent a site in the informal settlement and build their own homes. As apartheid was abolished, the government introduced the option to purchase a site, but the purchaser had to pay an additional monthly service charge.[60] The Khayelitsha informal settlement, similar to a number of other informal settlements, was initially used by the apartheid government to accommodate black persons on a temporary basis, but when apartheid was abolished these households could acquire land as homeowners. Alternatively, they could lease public property (either a site or state property) and make rental payments to the state or they could lease land from a private homeowner.

4   Tenure options for the urban poor

To establish what forms of tenure the urban poor currently utilise, one can consider the tenure options accessible in informal settlements, because the majority of households who occupy land in informal settlements are poor.[61] More than 95% of the persons who occupy land in informal settlements are black and therefore presumably previously disadvantaged.[62] In 2009 it was established that more than 60% of persons living in informal settlements partially or fully "owned" their homes.[63] However, since 2002 owner occupation has generally decreased, while there has been a shift from owner occupation to renting.[64] More than 20% of the South African population rent their homes, while more than 19% of the entire group of renters (the 20%) live

---

[56]   N Olivier "Property Rights in Urban Areas" (1988) 3 *SAPL* 23 26; Olivier (1988) *Koers* 582. See also Olivier (1988) *SAPL* 26-29 for more detail regarding the various personal rights provided for in the Regulation.

[57]   The informal settlement in Khayelitsha refers to those areas not used as transit areas or site and service areas. The term "informal settlement" in the rest of this chapter refers to the general definition of an informal settlement, which excludes transit areas and site and service areas.

[58]   The most important laws that initiated the transformation of landholding and the abolishment of apartheid land laws were the Black Local Authorities Act 102 of 1982, the Black Communities Development Act 4 of 1984, the Black Communities Development Amendment Act 74 of 1986 and the Conversion of Certain Rights into Leasehold or Ownership Act 81 of 1988.

[59]   GP Cook "Khayelitsha: New Settlement Forms in the Cape Peninsula" in DM Smith (ed) *The Apartheid City and Beyond* (1992) 125. The literature clearly indicates that these occupiers made rental payments to the state and in exchange they could occupy state land. It is highly unlikely that the apartheid government would enter formal leases with these households, but the nature of the occupiers' tenure was still leasehold.

[60]   128-129. State tenants could therefore become homeowners with the help of state subsidies.

[61]   Statistics South Africa *Housing* 15. It is obvious that poor persons also occupy other forms of housing in areas different from informal settlements. These include a rented room in a township or a RDP house in a specific project: Tissington *Resource Guide to Housing* 26.

[62]   Statistics South Africa *Housing* 5.

[63]   12. One should note that some of these "owners" might occupy land in an unauthorised informal settlement, which indicates that they are formally not recognised as owners in the Deeds Registry. This is usually the case when they constructed their own structures or bought it from another.

[64]   9, 31.

in informal settlements. Unsurprisingly, the majority of households that rent dwellings in informal settlements are low-income occupiers.[65] A number of persons in informal settlements continue to rent public property from the state and are therefore public sector tenants.[66]

The relationship between public landlord and tenant is unclear, because these tenancies are not regulated formally in accordance with legislative authority. The Community Residential Units Programme is a new development and some public sector tenancies might be established as a result of this programme, but the programme merely refers to the Rental Housing Act regarding the relationship between state landlord and tenant. In terms of the Rental Housing Act the parties can agree on the period of the lease and once the lease has expired, the landlord can claim an eviction order.[67]

Currently, more than 14% of the population occupy their homes rent-free, while more than 30% of this group live in informal settlements.[68] In *Residents of Joe Slovo Community, Western Cape v Thubelisha Homes*[69] the Constitutional Court had to decide whether the occupiers of an informal settlement were unlawful occupiers in terms of PIE. The occupiers occupied state land since the early 1990s and in due course the settlement grew to roughly 20 000 people. The state provided various facilities to the occupiers, including tap water, toilets, electricity and roads. However, the state never negotiated the rights of the occupiers.[70] According to Yacoob J:

> "While it is understandable that the applicants would do everything possible to stay rent-free on municipal property, the circumstance points away from any concession of a right to occupation. The right to occupy, if it existed, would have been one free of charge. It is highly improbable that a concession of this kind would have been made."[71]

Yacoob J concluded that the occupiers never had consent to occupy the land and that they were therefore unlawful occupiers in terms of PIE[72] According to Moseneke DCJ, the occupiers' right to occupy the land was not evidenced by an express agreement but rather by the tacit acceptance by the state.[73] The City's consent was therefore tacit and the occupiers' lawful occupation was consequently also terminated tacitly by the City.[74] O'Regan J agreed with Moseneke DCJ that the City consented tacitly to the occupiers' occupation, at least until the permission was withdrawn.[75]

Sachs J agreed that the Council consented to the occupiers' occupation, but described their right to occupy differently. According to Sachs J, a special legal

---

[65] Tissington *Resource Guide to Housing* 38. Roughly 55% of tenants earn less than R3 500 per month.
[66] Watson & McCarthy (1997) *Habitat International* 50 state that the aim of public rental housing was tied to the apartheid government's objective of political control over the African labour force.
[67] S 4(5)(d) of the Rental Housing Act. See also Legwaila (2001) *Stell LR* 281.
[68] Statistics South Africa *Housing* 11.
[69] 2010 3 SA 454 (CC). See also *Residents of Joe Slovo Community, Western Cape v Thebelisha Homes* 2011 7 BCLR 723 (CC).
[70] *Residents of Joe Slovo Community, Western Cape v Thubelisha Homes* 2010 3 SA 454 (CC) para 22 per Yacoob J.
[71] Para 82.
[72] Para 85.
[73] Paras 147, 154.
[74] Para 160.
[75] Para 280.

relationship existed between the Council and the occupiers. This relationship was unique in the sense that it could not be located in the usual framework of common-law rights, but rather developed from a tension that existed between the public responsibility of the Council, namely to accommodate vulnerable households, and the social rights of the occupiers.[76] The Council's consent was of a temporary nature and the occupiers' right could be defined as a public-law right to temporarily occupy state land.[77] The fact that the occupiers failed to make any rental payments in return for the right to occupy the land was consistent with the special legal regime that existed between the occupiers and the Council.[78]

Ngcobo J was unwilling to "brand" the occupiers as unlawful occupiers and argued that the question whether the occupiers were unlawful occupiers in terms of PIE was not at the core of the dispute to determine whether the occupiers should be relocated to give effect to a policy that would provide vulnerable households with adequate housing and tenure security. Despite the occupiers' legal tenure status, the government would not have been able to evict the occupiers and render them homeless, because this would have been in conflict with section 26 of the Constitution.[79]

The decision illustrates the extent of the current uncertainty regarding the rights of some persons who occupy land in informal settlements. It seems that the majority agreed that the occupiers did have consent at some point, but it was either withdrawn (Moseneke DCJ, O'Regan J) or it was inherently of a temporary nature (Sachs J).

In light of these observations one can conclude that vulnerable urban occupiers are currently occupying land, specifically in urban informal settlements, by means of a variety of tenure options. Nevertheless, it is doubtful whether any of these forms of tenure is sufficient in light of sections 25(6) and 26 of the Constitution. The majority are owner occupiers; others rent land or property from either private persons or the state, while the remaining group occupy land rent-free. *Joe Slovo* illustrates that persons who occupy land in informal settlements who are neither homeowners nor renters are in all probability uncertain of their rights. One can conclude that marginalised occupiers in urban areas occupy land as homeowners, tenants (private or public), unlawful occupiers or lawful occupiers with some form of tacit consent that can easily be withdrawn. Apart from the formal homeowners, the remaining households occupy land with insecure tenure.

5   Adequate housing

In light of the previous sections one can reach certain conclusions regarding the potential development of landlord-tenant law, specifically related to its development for the purpose of providing housing for the most vulnerable. In addition to the constitutional right of access to housing and the government's

---

[76]   Para 343.
[77]   Para 359.
[78]   Para 361.
[79]   Para 216.

constitutional duty to introduce measures that would give effect to this right, section 25(6) of the Constitution provides that previously disadvantaged households are entitled to legally secure tenure. Unfortunately, previously disadvantaged persons continue to occupy urban land with legally insecure tenure. To a certain extent, recent policies indicate that the government is aware of this problem, because the government has suggested the development of differentiated rental housing sectors that would accommodate the most vulnerable. Unfortunately, the government has failed to emphasise the importance of security of tenure. The case law suggests that the state is primarily responsible to ensure that individuals can access adequate housing and if the government were to introduce a public rental housing sector, it would have to regulate, manage and administer such a sector as public rental landlord. The state would therefore have to be directly involved in the provision of housing on a daily basis. The duty of the state to accommodate the poor and provide access to adequate housing in the landlord-tenant framework is currently to a certain extent shared with social housing institutions as a result of the Social Housing Act.

If the aim of the government is to provide housing in the form of rental housing to give effect to section 26 of the Constitution, the question is how such housing would constitute *adequate* housing as defined in section 26(1). The Constitution does not define adequate housing, nor have the courts construed a fixed meaning for this term, except that government must refrain from depriving occupiers of existing housing and that government must enact legislation to give effect to this right. To construe some definition for adequate housing, reference to international law is justifiable since section 39(1) of the Constitution states that a court, tribunal or forum must consider international law when interpreting the Bill of Rights.

The International Covenant on Economic, Social and Cultural Rights ("ICESCR")[80] was signed by South Africa on 4 October 1994, although it has not been ratified yet.[81] Article 11(1) of the ICESCR recognises a right to an adequate standard of living, including housing, which is defined in General Comment No 4.[82] In General Comment No 4, the Committee on Economic, Social and Cultural Rights ("CESCR") states that the right to adequate housing should not be interpreted narrowly as merely a "roof over one's head",[83] but

---

[80] International Covenant on Economic, Social and Cultural Rights (1966) UN Doc A/6316 <http://www2. ohchr.org/english/law/cescr.htm> (accessed 20-06-2011). In *S v Makwanyane* 1995 3 SA 391 (CC), and later confirmed in *Government of the Republic of South Africa v Grootboom* 2001 1 SA 46 (CC), the Constitutional Court found that the court must consider international law that has been ratified by the government, although the court can also consider international law that has not been ratified.

[81] See Liebenberg *Socio-Economic Rights* 106.

[82] UN Committee on Economic, Social and Cultural Rights *General Comment 4: The Right to Adequate Housing* (1991) UN Doc E/1992/23 <http://www.unhchr.ch/tbs/doc.nsf/(symbol)/ CESCR+General+comment+4.En?OpenDocument> (accessed 20-06-2011).

[83] UN Committee on Economic, Social and Cultural Rights General *Comment No 4* para 7. This phrase is similar to the opinion of Yacoob J in *Government of the Republic of South Africa v Grootboom* 2001 1 SA 46 (CC) para 35.

that it should rather be seen as the right to occupy property with security.[84] The CESCR also states that the "adequacy" of a housing condition depends on various factors, although there are "certain aspects of the right that must be taken into account ... in any particular context".[85] One of these aspects is legal security of tenure, stipulated in paragraph 8(a) of General Comment No 4. This paragraph states that any type of tenure, including public and private rental accommodation, should ensure a degree of security of tenure.[86]

According to General Comment No 4 of the CESCR, security of tenure is a key component of the right to adequate housing. The question is whether the South African rental housing legislation (and programmes) give effect to the constitutional obligation as stated in section 26(2). The fact that the legislation does not make provision for tenure security is problematic considering its importance in international law and the repercussions that insecure tenure had for vulnerable occupiers during the apartheid era.[87] The effect of insecure tenure rights, or legal uncertainty, for vulnerable urban tenants is important to take into account, considering the growth in urbanisation and the increasing demand for urban rental housing. It is doubtful whether the provision of urban rental housing, either in the public or social sector, would comply with section 26 if the tenure rights of tenants are insecure.

There is also a link between urban poverty and tenure status, because tenure status is one of the core elements in the poverty cycle. Weak tenure security exacerbates poverty.[88] Weak tenure rights create problems such as unstable communities and discourage investment, which has an effect on socio-economic factors such as poverty, social exclusion and limited access to urban services.[89] Secure occupation rights have been described as the "main component of the right to housing".[90] The government realised the importance of secure tenure when it proclaimed that security of tenure is a cornerstone in its approach to provide housing for homeless persons.[91] However, the importance of urbanisation and the connection thereof with better tenure security has been neglected by the South African development policy.[92]

---

[84] UN Committee on Economic, Social and Cultural Rights *General Comment No 4* para 7. See also UN Commission on Human Settlements *Global Strategy for Shelter to the Year 2000* (1988) UN Doc A/43/8/Add 1 <http://ww2.unhabitat.org/programmes/housingpolicy/documents/A.43.8.Add.1.pdf> (accessed 20-06-2011).

[85] UN Committee on Economic, Social and Cultural Rights *General Comment No 4* para 8.

[86] Para 8(a).

[87] See L Chenwi "Recommendations of the United Nations Special Rapporteur on Adequate Housing Following his Mission to South Africa" (2008) 9 *ESR Review* 24 25. See also Tissington *Resource Guide to Housing* 25 where the author mentions a number of socio-economic factors that should be taken into consideration when determining the meaning of "adequate housing". These include, access to socio-economic goods such as water, sanitation, electricity and schools.

[88] A Durand-Lasserve & L Royston "International Trends and Country Contexts – From Tenure Regularization to Tenure Security" in A Durand-Lasserve & A Royston (eds) *Holding their Ground, Secure Land Tenure for the Urban Poor in Developing Countries* (2002) 1 7.

[89] Durand-Lasserve & Royston "International Trends" in *Holding their Ground* 9.

[90] 9.

[91] Royston "Security of Urban Tenure in SA" in *Holding their Ground* 172.

[92] A Bernstein *Land Reform in South Africa: A 21st Century Perspective* (2005) 44.

One of the challenges in urban land reform is to create statutory forms of tenure that would include substantive tenure security, although such protection should not be limited to existing tenure forms but should be extended and applied to a diverse variety of tenure options.[93]

6   Concluding remarks and recommendations

Tenure security is a fundamental component of the right to adequate housing. The urban rental market in South Africa is diverse. Black urban tenants are entitled to legally secure tenure (section 25(6) of the Constitution) and the courts have interpreted PIE and section 26(3) of the Constitution to ensure better tenure security for marginalised unlawful tenants based on their socio-economic weakness.[94] The landlord-tenant regime in South Africa should aim to accommodate all urban tenants and provide every household with the necessary level of tenure security.[95] The landlord-tenant laws in South Africa should therefore be context-sensitive and should preferably be divided in terms of different sectors. Landlord-tenant law is an ideal legal institution in terms of which the government can make affordable housing available to the lowest income group in dire need of housing, because the government can maintain control over the housing stock and be actively involved as landlord.[96]

The proposed public rental sector, as defined in the Community Residential Units Programme, would fail to give effect to the right to have access to adequate housing if it does not afford tenure security. The aim of the government should be to provide the lowest income households with the most secure form of tenure. The essence of this form of housing should be to allow marginalised households to establish themselves in their community in order to participate in society and achieve human development. With the aim to ensure tenure security, the public rental sector could, for example, provide state tenants with periodic tenancies combined with secure tenure. The point of departure should be that the parties may agree on the terms of the periodic tenancy. The basis for this proposition is that a periodic tenancy would allow the tenant to easily serve notice to the local authority and terminate the lease. Low-income households often require the necessary mobility to move to a different city or metropolitan area in search of new job opportunities.

---

93   Royston "Security of Urban Tenure in SA" in *Holding their Ground* 179.
94   See specifically *City of Johannesburg Metropolitan Municipality v Blue Moonlight* 2011 4 SA 337 (SCA) para 59; *The Occupiers, Shulana Court, 11 Hendon Road, Yeoville, Johannesburg v Steele* 2010 9 BCLR 911 (SCA) paras 9-13, 16-17.
95   In light of the mentioned case law and legislation, the exact scope and ambit of the constitutional right to secure tenure is unclear, especially in the landlord-tenant framework. As mentioned, the landlord-tenant laws entrench the common-law right of the landowner to claim eviction upon termination of the lease, which reflects a weak tenure right for the tenant in the sense that she cannot obstruct or prevent eviction by relying on the legislation. To determine the precise strength of a secure tenure right, as envisioned in the Constitution, requires greater reflection in a more dedicated piece since the answer to this question must be found in foreign law, which is a study beyond the scope of this chapter. In the following pages I briefly introduce some legal constructions that might be able to provide stronger tenure rights for tenants.
96   This does not mean that rental housing should be the only form of housing that the state should use to accommodate low-income groups.

Importantly, the essence of such a public sector periodic tenancy should be that the lease is in principle perpetual as far as the tenant is concerned. If the tenant should wish to continue occupying the premises, the local authority landlord would only be able to terminate the lease if there is a serious and legitimate ground for termination of the tenancy as provided for in the lease and appropriate legislation. Grounds for eviction should at least include the following: where the public sector tenant damaged the property or where the tenant caused a serious nuisance to neighbouring occupiers; where the tenant used the property for purposes other than housing; where the dwellings are unsafe or where the building requires reconstruction.

If there is a ground for termination of the lease, the local authority should be able to initiate eviction proceedings in court and firstly prove the ground for termination as stipulated in appropriate legislation. The grounds for possession function as a form of tenure protection, because the local authority landlord would not be able to end the periodic tenancy without successfully proving a ground for possession in court. This suggestion is very different from the current common-law position in terms of which the landlord does not have to show any reason for termination of a periodic tenancy.

The current social housing sector is also inadequate to the extent that it makes available rental housing for low-income households, but fails to provide tenure security. Currently, social housing institutions are able to let the residential premises to low- and medium-income households on either fixed-term or periodic tenancies. This is not necessarily problematic, because the parties can freely negotiate a lease that would suit their needs. Social sector tenancies should be concluded and enforced in terms of the common law, although statutory forms of protection should become applicable and provide the tenant with tenure security if she prefers to continue occupying the premises.

To give effect to the housing provisions and provide legally secure tenure for social sector tenants, a statutory tenancy should materialise upon termination of the contractual lease. A statutory tenancy entails that where the tenant continues to pay the agreed rent and fulfils the other terms of the lease upon termination of the contractual lease, the contractual lease would automatically convert into a statutory tenancy. The essence of this statutory tenancy would be to provide security of tenure, as the tenant's right to continue occupation would not come to an end and the social landlord would not be able to claim eviction upon termination of the contractual lease. The core of the social sector should be to allow the tenant to choose when she would like to end the tenancy.

The statutory tenancy would continue on a periodic basis until the tenant serves a notice to terminate the lease or until the landlord can prove one of the grounds for possession (listed in the legislation) in court. The grounds for eviction should generally be similar to those applicable in the public sector. The effect of these grounds should be to provide the tenant with tenure protection, as cancellation should be impossible in the absence of one of the listed grounds. If the landlord can prove a ground for possession in court, then the statutory tenancy would come to an end and the social landlord would be able to claim eviction.

The current public rental housing (as explained in the Community Residential Units Programme) and social housing (based on the Social Housing Act) sectors aim to provide affordable rental options for the most vulnerable households. Both these sectors also aim to increase rental housing stock in urban areas. Vulnerable households, such as evictees, would therefore be able to access formal housing, other than homeownership, and the state would be actively involved in the administration and maintenance of at least the public rental sector. In their current form, neither of these sectors provides secure tenure rights for vulnerable tenants, which is problematic in light of the Constitution. The public and social rental sectors are defective to the extent that they fail to provide vulnerable households with tenure security. Secure occupation rights are defined by the occupier's ability to continue occupying the property on a consecutive basis. The occupation right should in principle be perpetual and the period of occupation should mainly depend on the occupier's will. The tenant should be allowed to occupy the property legally until she wishes to terminate the lease and vacate the premises. Prior to her decision to terminate the lease, she should be enabled to establish herself in the rented property to such an extent that it constitutes her home. Security of tenure implies uninterrupted legal occupation devoid of uncertainty regarding termination of such legal occupation. A contract-based tenancy does not ensure tenure security, because termination of the tenant's occupation right is either fixed (fixed-term tenancy) or dependant on the will of the landowner (periodic tenancy). Security of tenure in landlord-tenant law should be made provision for in legislation and it should empower marginalised households to establish themselves in their community without fear of insecurity, uncertainty and eviction.

SUMMARY

Recently the government has emphasised the importance of rental housing as a form of housing accessible to the urban poor. The current landlord-tenant regime promotes equal bargaining power and contract-based tenure (occupation) rights for tenants. It is questionable whether this free-market approach would provide satisfactory tenure security for the urban poor. In terms of section 26 of the Constitution, the state must be actively involved in the provision of housing and the state must assist the most vulnerable who face homelessness. Public rental housing might be a suitable housing option for vulnerable occupiers because the state can regulate, assess and control the market to the extent that it is involved in the provision thereof. The success of such a form of housing depends on the enactment of effective legislation that affords tenure security while also being context-sensitive to the personal needs of the individual households. The purpose of the Community Residential Units Programme is to introduce a formal public rental sector. However, the tenure rights of these public sector tenants would be similar to those of private and social sector tenants, which is problematic since these tenancies are based on contract. Legislation has not been promulgated to give effect to this programme. If the aim of the government is to provide housing in the form of rental housing, the question is how such housing would constitute *adequate* housing. Security of tenure is a key component of the right to adequate housing. One of the challenges in urban land reform is to create statutory forms of tenure that would include substantive tenure security, although such protection should be extended and applied to a diverse variety of tenure options. Security of tenure implies uninterrupted legal occupation devoid of uncertainty regarding termination of such legal occupation.

CHAPTER 18

CONSTITUTIONAL PERSPECTIVES ON UNEMPLOYMENT SECURITY AND A RIGHT TO WORK IN SOUTH AFRICA

Avinash Govindjee

Ockert Dupper[*]

1   Introduction

South Africa's unemployment rate is one of the highest in the world, and significantly higher than those of other middle income economies.[1] When using the narrow International Labour Organisation ("ILO") definition[2] (which is the official definition in South Africa), South Africa's unemployment rate currently stands at 25%.[3] If the broad definition of unemployment is used (which includes discouraged work seekers), the unemployment rate swells to 36.6%.[4] While urban unemployment rates are already very high, particularly striking and unusual are the higher rural unemployment rates (particularly in the so-called former "homelands"), which are far higher than anywhere in the developing world.[5] Also noteworthy is that these unemployment rates differ greatly by race, age and gender.[6] In 2011 Africans had much higher (official or narrow) unemployment rates (28.9%), compared to Coloureds (23.6%), Indians (10.8%) and whites (5.6%).[7] Age is also a major determinant of unemployment. Unemployment disproportionately impacts on the youth,

---

[*]   The authors wish to acknowledge the technical assistance of Ms Zikhona Maroqa, an undergraduate student and research assistant at the Nelson Mandela Metropolitan University, and Mr Marius Roetz, a postgraduate student and research assistant at Stellenbosch University.

[1]   H Bhorat "Unemployment in South Africa: Descriptors and Determinants" (2007) *Developmental Policy Research Unit, University of Cape Town* 2 <http://www.commerce.uct.ac.za/Research_Units/DPRU/OtherPDFs/Unemployment_in_South_Africa4.pdf> (accessed 05-08-2011).

[2]   Art 20 of the ILO Social Security (Minimum Standards) Convention 102 (1952) ("ILO Convention 102") states:

> "The contingency covered shall include suspension of earnings, as defined by national laws or regulations, due to inability to obtain suitable employment in the case of a person protected who is capable of, and available for, work."

[3]   Statistics South Africa "Quarterly Labour Force Survey, Quarter 3, 2011" (2011) *StatsOnline* xii <http://www.statssa.gov.za/Publications/P0211/P02113rdQuarter2011.pdf> (accessed 01-11-2011).

[4]   Statistics South Africa "Quarterly Labour Force Survey, Quarter 4, 2010" (2011) *StatsOnline* 12 <http://www.statssa.gov.za/publications/P0211/P02114thQuarter2010.pdf> (accessed 01-11-2011).

[5]   S Klasen & ID Woolard "Surviving Unemployment without State Support: Unemployment and Household Formation in South Africa" (2008) 18 *J African Economies* 1 2.

[6]   On women and unemployment in general, see C Cooper "Women and the Right to Work" in B Goldblatt & K McLean (eds) *Women's Social and Economic Rights* (2011) 247 248.

[7]   Statistics South Africa "Quarterly Labour Force Survey, Quarter 3, 2011" (2011) *StatsOnline* xii <http://www.statssa.gov.za/Publications/P0211/P02113rdQuarter2011.pdf> (accessed 01-11-2011).

affecting about 35% of those below the age of 25.[8] Of particular concern is
the unemployment rate of African youth, which stood at 53.4% at the end of
2009.[9] There is also a noticeable gender differential, with females suffering
from higher unemployment rates among each age and race group.[10]

Protection against unemployment takes various forms in South Africa.
In the first place, partial and temporary income support is provided in the
form of social insurance *via* the Unemployment Insurance Fund ("UIF").
However, a proper unemployment policy framework requires more than just
partial and temporary income replacement. In this respect, South Africa
has made some modest attempts to develop what the ILO[11] refers to as both
"employment-enhancing measures" (primarily in the form of public works) and
"employment services" (which includes the most recent Employment Services
Bill[12] aimed at providing assistance to the unemployed in searching for new
employment). Nevertheless, the most glaring gap in the assistance provided
to the unemployed in South Africa is the exclusion of the structurally or the
long-term unemployed from any income replacement measures. For example,
there is no social assistance grant that particularly targets persons who have
either exhausted their limited unemployment insurance benefits, or those who
have never been formally employed and therefore never contributed to the
social insurance system.[13] Structurally unemployed youths and adults receive
limited or no support from the existing social assistance framework.[14]

In this chapter, we argue that the constitutional right to have access to
social security, as read with other existing rights, is an inadequate "umbrella
right" for purposes of covering the most recent policy developments which
attempt to address poverty by way of a combination of social security and
unemployment protection strategies. We also suggest that the disparity
between current policy developments and the existing statutory scheme of
laws requires address, given that current policymaking in this area operates
in the absence of a proper legal framework and that a real possibility exists for
a constitutional challenge in this regard.

In developing our argument, we introduce the concept of "unemployment
security" – one that is not common in the literature. The primary purpose for

---

[8] Department of Social Development *Creating Our Future: Strategic Considerations for a Comprehensive
     System of Social Security* (Discussion Paper) (2008) 7.
[9] See SAPA "Youth Unemployment is a 'Ticking Time Bomb': Mdladlana" (27-08-2010) *The Times*
     <http://www.timeslive.co.za/local/article625827.ece/Youth-unemployment-is-a-ticking-time-bomb--
     Mdladlana> (accessed 23-03-2011).
[10] Statistics South Africa "Quarterly Labour Force Survey, Quarter 3, 2011" (2011) *StatsOnline* 2-5 <http://
     www.statssa.gov.za/Publications/P0211/P02113rdQuarter2011.pdf> (accessed 01-11-2011)
[11] See ILO *World Social Security Report 2010-2011: Providing Coverage in Times of Crisis and Beyond*
     (2010) 57.
[12] Employment Services Bill (draft) in GN 1112 in *GG* 33873 of 17-10-2010.
[13] Although social grants cover those under the age of 18 and those over the age of 60 who are unable to
     support themselves, as well as all disabled persons, adults between the age of 19 and 59 who are not
     disabled are effectively not entitled to any social assistance – even when they are unable to support
     themselves.
[14] Department of Social Development *Creating Our Future* 8. Also see Government of the RSA *Decent
     Work Country Programme 2010-2014* (2010) *International Labour Organization* 9 <http://www.ilo.org/
     wcmsp5/groups/public/---dgreports/---integration/documents/genericdocument/wcms_145432.pdf>
     (accessed 24-03-2011).

using the term is to acknowledge the state prioritisation on matters relating to unemployment, while simultaneously linking the discussion to the well-known theme of social security. Used in this fashion, the term is defined to include both unemployment insurance and unemployment assistance. It is also intended to include both preventative and re-integrative components of unemployment protection – a concept which may be viewed as being one component of the broad notion of social protection. Unemployment protection would, for example, include state strategies to prevent employment loss as well as attempts to integrate people into employment, such as public works programmes. Unemployment security is accordingly defined to be practically synonymous with what is understood to be the unemployment protection-specific aspects of social protection, including social security strategies focusing on the problem of unemployment (unemployment insurance and unemployment assistance), as well as prevention and integration strategies directed at minimising unemployment. Skills development and training activities are clearly linked to such strategies and could be combined with any of the suggested sub-components of unemployment security.[15] The proposed definition also brings to the fore the possibility of a "right to work", which must be coupled with the developing notion of "decent work".[16]

The term may be diagrammatically represented as follows:

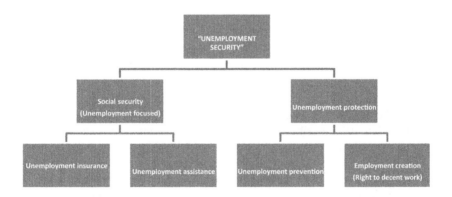

---

[15] This aspect is dealt with in greater detail in A Govindjee, M Olivier & O Dupper "Activation in the Context of the Unemployment Insurance System in South Africa" (2011) 22 *Stell LR* 205 205-227.

[16] In this chapter, the term "work" is used in the same way that the ILO has defined the concept, as an individual responsibility and a social activity, frequently involving collaboration in a team and occupying a central and defining place in people's lives, determining the stability and well-being of families and communities and being a key to social integration. The concept of "work" does not only refer to a paid job, self-employment and running a business, but any form of economic activity that increases the ability of an individual and their family not just to survive but to develop. As a result, it includes unpaid tasks related, for example, to helping in the home, the range of activities in the informal economy and the care economy: ILO *Changing Patterns in the World of Work: Report of the Director-General* (2006) v-vi as referred to in ILO *Skills Development through Community Based Rehabilitation (CBR): A Good Practice Guide* (2008) 7. Also see ILO Report of the Director-General: *Reducing the Decent Work Deficit – A Global Challenge* (2001) 5. The term "decent work" is considered, below.

This chapter is structured in two main parts. The first part provides a brief overview of each of the components represented in the diagram above. In part 2, we discuss the two related terms of social security and social protection, and then turn to a brief discussion of the current unemployment insurance and unemployment assistance systems in South Africa (parts 3 and 4). In parts 5 and 6 respectively, we examine the two sub-components of unemployment protection, namely unemployment prevention initiatives (including the training layoff scheme) and employment creation interventions (such as the expanded public works programme and the wage subsidy for incentivising the employment of the youth). This is followed by a brief explanation of the concept of "decent work" in part 7. In the second part of the chapter we turn to the crux of the chapter, namely a consideration of some constitutional perspectives related to unemployment security matters. The absence of direct statutory or constitutional provisions regarding the notion of unemployment security or a right to work is highlighted. Three potential options for constitutional and/ or legislative reform are considered, including an actual amendment to the Constitution of the Republic of South Africa, 1996 ("the Constitution") itself. It is argued that such redress is in accordance with the notion of transformative constitutionalism and could serve as a principled basis for the introduction of legislative and (further) policy developments aimed at achieving poverty alleviation.

2 Comprehensive social security

Although there is no universally acceptable definition of "social security", the concept has traditionally been split into social assistance (non-contributory) and social insurance (contributory) components.[17] These components are expected to combine so as to provide income protection and access to services upon the occurrence of certain defined events.[18] As indicated above, ILO Convention 102 describes social security as guaranteeing a stable income through medical care, sickness benefits, unemployment benefits, old-age benefits, employment injury benefits, family benefits, maternity benefits, and invalid benefits.[19] Social security has been trumpeted as representing one of the conditions for sustainable social and economic development, operating as an economic, social and political stabiliser, providing mechanisms to alleviate and prevent poverty, reducing income disparity to acceptable levels,

---

[17] Social insurance denotes contributory- and risk-based schemes giving rise to fixed-benefit payments aimed at income maintenance. Social assistance refers to tax-based benefit payments on a universal or targeted basis, aimed at minimum income-support (E Strydom "Introduction to Social Security Law" in EML Strydom (ed) *Essential Social Security Law* (2006) 1 6).
[18] Department of Social Development *Creating Our Future* 4.
[19] ILO Convention 102.

and enhancing human capital and productivity.[20] The development of comprehensive social security systems in countries where only rudimentary systems exist has been identified as being a key task to prepare global society for future economic downturns, as well as to achieve other objectives such as the Millennium Development Goals, sustainable economic development and fair globalisation.[21]

Social security must also be distinguished from the broader concept of "social protection".[22] This term has been used to describe a general system of basic social support which "is no longer linked to the regular employment relationship, and which is founded on the conviction that society as a whole is responsible for its weaker members".[23] The United Nations Social Protection Floor Initiative, for example, is based on the principle of progressive universalism and seeks to ensure a base level of benefits (or the so-called "social protection floor") for everyone.[24] In South Africa, it has been argued that the term also encapsulates elements and rights related and ancillary to social security itself.[25] As the Committee of Inquiry into a Comprehensive System of Social Security for South Africa (the "Taylor Committee") noted:

> "Comprehensive social protection for South Africa seeks to provide the basic means for all people living in the country to effectively participate and advance in social and economic life, and in turn to contribute to social and economic development. Comprehensive social protection is broader than the traditional concept of social security, and incorporates developmental strategies and programmes designed to ensure, collectively, at least a minimum acceptable living standard for all citizens. It embraces the traditional measures of social insurance, social assistance and social services, but goes beyond that to focus on causality through an integrated policy-approach including many of the developmental initiatives undertaken by the State."[26]

The South African social security system itself (that is, even ignoring broader social protection initiatives) is remarkably comprehensive by a middle-income developing country standard. While the system is largely

---

[20] See B Caracciolo "Social Protection: An Instrument for Poverty Reduction and Social Cohesion" in S Stocker (ed) *European Social Watch Report 2010* (2010) <http://www.socialwatch.eu/wcm/instrument_for_poverty_reduction_and_social_cohesion.html> (accessed 01-11-2011). The recent global economic crisis has, for some commentators, highlighted that investment in social security systems is an economic need (Caracciolo "Social Security" in *European Social Watch Report 2010*). The ILO found that the employment effect of automatic stabilisers, including social transfers, were as important as some of the stimulus packages introduced by countries as a response to the crisis. Governments with social protection systems in place were found to be in a better position to cope, as the impact on households was softened. ILO *Protecting People, Promoting Jobs: A Survey of Employment and Social Protection Policy Responses to the Global Economic Crisis* Report to the G20 Leaders' Summit, Pittsburgh, 24-09-2009 – 25-09-2009 (2009) 15 <www.ilo.org/public/libdoc/jobcrisis/download/protecting_people_promoting_jobs.pdf> (accessed 22-10-2010).

[21] Caracciolo "Social Security" in *European Social Watch Report 2010*.

[22] MP Olivier "The Concept of Social Security" in MP Olivier, E Kalula & N Smit (eds) *Social Security: A Legal Analysis* (2003) 23 26.

[23] 26.

[24] Caracciolo "Social Security" in *European Social Watch Report 2010*. On the relationship between this initiative and the International Social Security Agency (ISSA) strategy to extend social security coverage, see ISSA *Social Policy Highlight 18* (2011) 3.

[25] Olivier "The Concept of Social Security" in *Social Security: A Legal Analysis* 26.

[26] Committee of Inquiry into a Comprehensive System of Social Security for South Africa *Consolidated Report of the Committee of Inquiry into a Comprehensive System of Social Security in South Africa: Transforming the Present – Protecting the Future* (2002) 120 <http://www.sarpn.org/CountryPovertyPapers/SouthAfrica/taylor/report4.php> (accessed 01-11-2011).

formal employment-oriented (in particular as far as social insurance schemes and retirement provision are concerned), excludes many from participation, and adopts a categorical and means-tested approach as far as social assistance is concerned, numerous studies indicate that the system of social grants has contributed significantly to reducing overall poverty and (income)[27] inequality. As a recent report noted:

> "Not only do the grants have a significant impact on poverty [at the lower poverty line] but they also make a significant impact on inequality ... [T]he Gini coefficient on 'pre-grant' income is 0.03 higher than when calculated on either reported income or simulated income."[28]

The positive attributes of social transfers have been confirmed by evidence which suggests that social transfers are an effective tool to prevent and fight poverty.[29] The evidence suggests, in particular, that social security transfers increase domestic demand and encourage growth by expanding domestic markets. While the assimilation of more people into the labour market is at the heart of South Africa's poverty reduction strategy, there remains a need for programmes that provide income support to the unemployed and people that are unable to work. Social assistance cash grants provide income support to people whose livelihoods are most at risk.[30] The number of grant recipients has increased significantly during the past fifteen years, partly because social welfare was previously targeted mainly at white recipients.[31] Grants are generally well targeted and mostly reach the poorest of the poor.[32] For example, 62% of social grants go to the poorest 40% of households and 82% to the poorest 60%.[33] Almost fourteen million South Africans (nearly a quarter of the population) benefit from one grant or another (see table below).[34]

The post-apartheid government has been very active in reforming and expanding the system of social grants. A key aspect of the post-apartheid fiscal expenditure patterns has therefore been a widening and deepening of South Africa's social security system.[35] While spending on most big-item budget items such as education and health has remained fairly constant in real terms, consolidated expenditure on social assistance has increased from R30.1 billion (3.2% of GDP) in 2000/01 to R101.4 billion (4.4% of GDP) in

---

[27] See part 4 below for a discussion of the difference between income and non-income inequality.

[28] M Leibbrandt, I Woolard, A Finn & J Argent *OECD Social, Employment and Migration Working Papers No 101: Trends in South African Income Distribution and Poverty since the Fall of Apartheid* (2010) 66. For confirmation of these findings see H Bhorat, C van der Westhuizen & T Jacobs *Income and Non-Income Inequality in Post-Apartheid South Africa: What are the Drivers and Possible Policy Interventions?* Development Policy Research Unit (DPRU) Working Paper 09/138 (2009) 44-56.

[29] Caracciolo "Social Security" in *European Social Watch Report 2010*.

[30] On the positive impact of social grants on work-seeking behaviour and employment, see Department of Social Development *Creating Our Future* 11; M Samson "Social Cash Transfers and Employment: A Note on Empirical Linkages in Developing Countries" in OECD *Promoting Pro-Poor Growth: Employment* (2009) 179 179-186.

[31] K Pauw & L Mncube *Expanding the Social Security Net in South Africa: Opportunities, Challenges and Constraints* DPRU Working Paper 07/127 (2007) 2 <http://www.commerce.uct.ac.za/research_units/dpru/workingpapers/pdf_files/wp_07-127.pdf> (accessed 06-10-2011).

[32] Bhorat et al *Income and Non-Income Inequality in Post-Apartheid SA* 44.

[33] The Presidency *Towards a Fifteen Year Review* (2008) 19 <http://www.info.gov.za/view/DownloadFileAction?id=89475> (accessed 06-10-2011).

[34] National Treasury *Budget Review 2010* (2010) 103.

[35] Bhorat et al *Income and Non-Income Inequality in Post-Apartheid SA* 44.

2008/09.[36] In 2010, just over 2.5 million people received the old age grant, almost 9.5 million children benefited from the child support grant, and 1.3 million people were in receipt of the disability grant.[37] As Seekings notes:

"In no other country in the South does social assistance cover such a wide range of circumstances, reach so many of its citizens or cost so much in relation to GDP."[38][39]

SOCIAL GRANTS BENEFICIARY NUMBERS BY TYPE: 2005/06 – 2009/10[39]						
Type of grant	2005/06	2006/07	2007/08	2008/09	2009/10	% growth (average annual)
Old age	2 144 117	2 195 018	2 218 993	2 343 995	2 534 082	4.3%
War veterans	2 832	2 340	1 963	1 599	1 248	-18,5%
Disability	1 319 536	1 422 808	1 413 263	1 371 712	1 310 761	-0.2%
Foster care	312 614	400 503	443 191	476 394	569 215	16.2%
Care dependency	94 263	98 631	101 836	107 065	119 307	6.1%
Child support	7 044 901	7 863 841	8 195 524	8 765 354	9 424 281	7.5%
Total	10 918 263	11 983 141	12 374 770	13 066 118	13 958 894	6.3%

However, as a poverty-reduction strategy, this method is nearing the boundaries of its effective use, given fiscal constraints.[40] Various proposals to extend social assistance coverage in South Africa have failed to find favour within government circles, especially within the National Treasury.[41] Acknowledgement of the reality of resource constraint has resulted in increasing policy-focus being placed upon contributory social security arrangements, since these arrangements seek to draw from a reasonable proportion of individual or family income and do not place a direct strain on the availability of state resources.[42]

---

[36] Leibbrandt et al *Expanding the Social Security Net in SA* 52.

[37] See National Treasury *Budget Review 2010* 105.

[38] J Seekings "Employment Guarantee or Minimum Income? Workfare and Welfare in Developing Countries" (2006) 2 *International Journal of Environment, Workplace and Employment* 44.

[39] National Treasury *Budget Review 2010* 105.

[40] S van der Berg, R Burger, R Burger, M Louw & D Yu *Trends in Poverty and Inequality Since the Political Transition* DPRU Working Paper 06/104 (2006) 28 <http;//www.tips.org.za/files/forum/2006/papers/VanderbergTrends_in_Poverty.pdf> (accessed 06-10-2011). This is one of the general characteristics of non-contributory social security arrangements, namely that their effect is limited by a scarcity of resources (Department of Social Development *Creating Our Future* 4). In countries such as Costa Rica, the evidence has shown that even universal social security systems can only help reduce inequality and poverty if production regimes provide the required funding, the formal jobs and the demand for skills (JM Franzoni & D Sanchez-Ancochea "The Productive Bottlenecks of Progressive Social Policies: Lessons from Costa Rica and Beyond" (2011) Feb *Crop Poverty Brief* 1 2).

[41] For example, the Department of Social Development considered the introduction of a *conditional social assistance grant* for the long-term unemployed. The proposed value of the grant would have been low, and would have been conditional upon participation in labour activation programmes such as skills development programmes and special employment projects (see O Dupper "Actualités Juridiques Internationales: Afrique du Sud" (2009) *Bulletin de Droit Comparé du Travail et de la Sécurité Sociale* 335 337. The Taylor Committee suggested a similar intervention, arguing that a flat-rate social assistance grant (the so-called "Basic Income Grant") could be introduced, coupled with active labour policies (see Committee of Inquiry into a Comprehensive System of Social Security for SA *Transforming the Present – Protecting the Future* 71).

[42] Department of Social Development *Creating Our Future* 4. The proposed national retirement and national health insurance systems are examples of this mindset.

The realisation of the financial limitations of a society reliant upon social grants has left a glaring gap in South Africa's social security system: the exclusion of the structurally or the long-term unemployed from social security coverage. There is no social assistance grant that particularly targets persons who have either exhausted their limited unemployment insurance benefits, or have never been formally employed and thus never contributed to the social insurance system.[43] Structurally unemployed youths and adults receive limited or no support from the existing social assistance framework.[44] In addition, as will be illustrated, the existing unemployment insurance framework is woefully insufficient for purposes of dealing with this group of people.

3   Unemployment insurance in South Africa[45]

The Unemployment Insurance Act 63 of 2001 ("UIA")[46] and Unemployment Insurance Contributions Act 4 of 2002 ("UICA")[47] are applicable to all employers and employees except for those specifically excluded. Unless specifically excluded, participation in the unemployment insurance scheme is compulsory.[48]

The UIF recently announced that it had recommended certain legislative changes to the Minister of Labour. Three of those changes relate to the inclusion of some excluded categories, while the other two relate to the benefit replacement rate[49] and the benefit period[50] respectively. As far as the inclusion of currently excluded categories are concerned, the Fund recommended that public servants, legal migrants and those in learnerships

---

[43] Although social grants cover those under the age of 18 and those over the age of 60 who are unable to support themselves, as well as all disabled persons, adults between the age of 19 and 59 who are not disabled are effectively not entitled to any social assistance – even when they are unable to support themselves.

[44] Department of Social Development *Creating Our Future* 8. Also see Government of the RSA *Decent Work Country Programme* 9. The main source of income for this group of people is indirect, meaning that they rely on the labour incomes of other household members, or through a process known as "benefit dilution", rely on social grants received by other household members (in particular the old-age pension and the child support grant). It has been pointed out that reliance on such private safety nets can generate disincentive effects that can prolong unemployment, including low labour-market mobility and the reduction of job-search activities (Klasen & Woolard (2008) *J African Economies* 17).

[45] The following paragraphs are in the main based on O Dupper, MP Olivier & A Govindjee "Extending Coverage of the Unemployment Insurance-System in South Africa" (2010) 21 *Stell LR* 438 438-462.

[46] The Act provides for unemployment, sickness, adoption, maternity and survivor benefits in respect of workers and their dependants.

[47] This Act establishes the Unemployment Insurance Fund ("UIF"). Employers and employees contribute equally to the UIF.

[48] ET van Kerken & MP Olivier "Unemployment Insurance" in MP Olivier, E Kalula & N Smit (eds) *Social Security: A Legal Analysis* (2003) 415 435.

[49] The current graduated rate of 38-60% of previous income, although a rare example of the important principle of solidarity in the South African social security system, is nevertheless not in compliance with ILO Convention 102, which prescribes a minimum income replacement rate of 45%. The recommendation by the UIF, reportedly accepted by the Minister of Labour, that the minimum income replacement rate be increased from 38% of final monthly salary to 45% would align South African with international precedent. L Ensor "Strong Finances may Widen UIF Beneficiary Net" *Business Day* (13-09-2010).

[50] The Minister of Labour has apparently also accepted the recommendation from the UIF that the benefit period be extended from the current maximum benefit period of 238 days (about eight months) to 365 days (twelve months) (Ensor *Business Day* (13-09-2010)).

be included under its umbrella.[51] It has been reported that the Minister has agreed to the inclusion of public servants, which would cost the state about R3 billion annually.[52]

While the UIA has extended its scope of coverage over time, much more could be done to reduce exclusion and marginalisation in the unemployment insurance system. The reality is that the UIF currently only covers about 10% of South Africa's unemployed.[53] This is due to three main reasons. In the first place, the current maximum benefit period under the UIA is 238 days.[54] Studies indicate that almost half (44%) of the unemployed with previous work experience have been unemployed for more than a year, which means that they would have exhausted their benefits had they ever been eligible for them.[55] Second, slightly more than half (55%) of those unemployed report that they have never worked and have therefore not contributed to the UIF.[56] Finally, the UIF continues to exclude certain categories of workers from coverage, most notably the atypically employed, particularly independent contractors, so-called "dependent contractors", and those who are self-employed or informally employed; public servants in the national and provincial spheres of government; learners; and certain categories of migrant workers.[57] Therefore, while the UIF clearly has an important role to play in providing replacement income to the short-term unemployed with work experience, the vast majority of the unemployed fall outside of this system. This *lacuna* has resulted in attention being thrust upon the need for some form of non-contributory unemployment assistance in South Africa.

4   Unemployment assistance in South Africa?

Social assistance to low-income households is the primary way in which government tries to eliminate income poverty. The *Creating Our Future* government discussion paper launched by the Department of Social Development highlights the gaps in the social assistance framework in South Africa with respect to structurally unemployed "youth" (which it defines as people aged 19 to 25 years of age) and structurally unemployed "adults" (aged

---

[51] Ensor *Business Day* (13-09-2010).

[52] Ensor *Business Day* (13-09-2010). The exclusion of public servants has always been based on the assumption that the risk of unemployment for public servants is either low or non-existent. This assumption may be challenged, both legally and factually. The job security afforded to South African public servants is not as adequate as it is assumed to be. The risk of unemployment for private sector workers is often not greater than that of public servants in South Africa. In addition, it is doubtful whether the exclusion of public servants from the UIF is constitutionally tenable: see, for example, Olivier & Van Kerken "Unemployment Insurance" in *Social Security: A Legal Analysis* 438-440.

[53] M Leibbrandt, I Woolard, H McEwen & C Koep *Employment and Inequality Outcomes in South Africa* Southern Africa Labour and Development Research Unit & School of Economics, University of Cape Town (2010) 36 <http://www.oecd.org/dataoecd/17/14/45282868.pdf> (accessed 23-03-2010).

[54] S 13(3) of the UIA provides that unemployment insurance benefits accrue at a rate of one day's benefit for every completed six days of employment as a contributor subject to a maximum accrual of 238 days benefit.

[55] Leibbrandt et al *Employment and Inequality Outcomes in South Africa* 36.

[56] 36.

[57] Dupper et al (2010) *Stell LR* 448-459.

26 to 59).[58] The document acknowledges the short-term, inadequate benefits currently provided by the UIF and proposes a "continuation benefit" (at a value of 50% of a minimum wage still to be determined) for a maximum three-year period for people who exhaust their unemployment insurance entitlements without having been able to find suitable employment.[59] Importantly, it is proposed that recipients of the continuation benefit would need to participate in labour activation programmes where these have been implemented, possibly including skills development programmes, special employment projects with or without a skills development component and participation in surveys to evaluate the causes of continued unemployment.

A conditional social assistance grant, at a value equivalent to one-fifth of the proposed continuation benefit, is proposed for unemployed "adults" who have never been in formal employment and, consequently, have never qualified for unemployment insurance.[60] These proposals appear to be based, in part, on the proven positive correlation between receipt of a social grant and a person's attempts to find employment.[61] As such, the Department of Social Development suggests that reforming the social assistance system in this matter would prevent households with unemployed breadwinners from falling into extreme poverty, while simultaneously assisting their re-entry into formal employment (both because of the conditionalities attached to the proposed benefits, and because of the apparent relationship between receipt of social assistance and the search for employment).

The *Creating Our Future* document also promotes the idea of a conditional social assistance grant to unemployed youth, at a value of 30% of the unemployment insurance continuation benefit. Conditions for such a grant would include assessments by a labour and skills adviser, successful participation in skills-acquisition programmes, participation in employment structured to enhance skills development, and participation in surveys to evaluate the continuation of unemployment.[62] Failure to participate meaningfully in the programme, or to achieve set skills-acquisition goals, would be met with punishment in the form of a reduced grant payment for set periods.

It has been argued that the low value of such continuation benefits or grants will act as a deterrent against the problem of grant dependency and that implementing such proposals between now and 2015 would eradicate poverty experienced by over one-third of the population of the country.[63] It must be noted, however, that the feasibility of introducing such a costly form of social

---

[58] Department of Social Development *Creating Our Future* 21. The document specifically indicates that the proposals contained therein do not represent government's final position on any matter.

[59] Department of Social Development *Creating Our Future* 19-20. The proposals make two suggestions in this regard: either a conditional continuation benefit of up to three years to be funded from the existing UIF surplus; or, alternatively, an unlimited, reduced-value conditional continuation benefit to be funded out of general revenue.

[60] Department of Social Development *Creating Our Future* 18.

[61] Department of Social Development *Creating Our Future* 12; Samson "Social Cash Transfers and Employment" in *Promoting Pro-Poor Growth* 179, 180-185.

[62] Department of Social Development *Creating Our Future* 20.

[63] 17-18.

assistance at this stage of South Africa's development is questionable and does not appear to have found significant support at National Treasury level. There is also no available information to indicate that the UIF plans to implement such proposals (using the current surplus of the Fund, for example) in the foreseeable future.

5   Unemployment prevention strategies

Despite numerous amendments, the current UIA still reflects its origins as an Act designed to deal with cyclical unemployment in the 1940s.[64] In essence, the UIA retains the Fund as one designed to cater for the limited requirements of a historically privileged workforce not seriously threatened by unemployment.[65] Although it is questionable whether a fund based upon employer and employee contributions should be expected (or, indeed, was ever intended) to address large-scale problems related to unemployment, the UIA has rightly been criticised for its failure to appropriately contribute to preventing and combating unemployment as well as for its inability to reintegrate those who have become unemployed in the labour market.[66] The coupling of reintegration measures with compensation (as compared to compensation in isolation) would enhance the prospect of lasting change for the presently unemployed. However, there is little innovative attempt in the UIA to link entitlement to unemployment benefits with reintegration into the labour market. For example, in contrast with the previous legislation,[67] benefits are no longer available in the event of partial unemployment[68] and temporary suspension of work. Although it is required[69] of an applicant for benefits to register as a work-seeker with a labour centre,[70] and despite the fact that the refusal, without just reason on the part of an employee, to undergo training and vocational counselling for employment under any approved scheme is visited with disentitlement to unemployment benefits,[71] there is no further evidence of support for labour market integration in the UIA. These limitations are compounded by institutional challenges, human rights difficulties, and general problems of implementation. The cumulative effect of these factors complicates the ability of the UIF to act as a catalyst for employment activation. Most significantly, the UIA contains little in terms

---

[64]   P Benjamin *Labour Market Regulation: International and South African Perspectives* (2005) 39.

[65]   Committee of Inquiry into a Comprehensive System of Social Security for SA *Transforming the Present – Protecting the Future* ch v.

[66]   See, for example, Olivier & Van Kerken "Unemployment Insurance" in *Social Security: A Legal Analysis* 458.

[67]   Unemployment Insurance Act 30 of 1966.

[68]   For example, unlike the previous Act and except for the position of domestic workers, the UIA does not contain a provision that a contributor employed by two employers simultaneously, who lost one employment and continues in the other, does not lose his or her entitlement in respect of the lost employment simply because he or she retained the other employment (s 35(11) of the Unemployment Insurance Act 30 of 1966).

[69]   S 16(1)(c) of the UIA.

[70]   Established under the Skills Development Act 97 of 1998.

[71]   S 16(2)(b) of the UIA.

of a statutory framework for comprehensive unemployment policymaking, in particular in the area of preventing and combating unemployment.[72]

However, despite the fact that South Africa does not have a single, national employment policy, a number of initiatives have been undertaken to prevent unemployment and generate employment opportunities, the latter primarily by means of public works programmes. Both of these broad policy directions will now receive brief attention.

While the idea of bringing people who have become unemployed back to work through active measures (so-called "labour activation measures") is far from new (at least in developed economies), their application in developing middle-income or low-income countries may be problematic for a number of reasons, including institutional and capacity constraints, as well as the lack of job opportunities into which the unemployed may be "activated".[73] Nevertheless, there is significant support within government for making participation in active labour market policies a precondition for the receipt or the continuation of benefits – whether social insurance or social assistance benefits.[74]

For example, the recent Employment Services Bill contains a number of ambitious and varied goals all aimed at promoting active labour market policies. These include reducing unemployment, improving access to the labour market for all work-seekers, providing opportunities for work experience, improving the employment prospects of people with disabilities, assisting the unemployed, facilitating access by workers to training, improving workplace productivity, and promoting job security.[75] These objectives are to be achieved by providing "comprehensive and integrated public employment services", coordinating the activities of public sector agencies engaged in the provision of employment services, encouraging partnerships between the public and private sectors of the economy to provide employment services, providing a regulatory framework for the operation of private employment agencies, and promoting a constructive relationship between these agencies and the public employment service.[76] The draft provisions relating to private employment agencies reflects an evident attempt to align South Africa's international obligations in terms of the ILO Unemployment Convention[77] to endeavours to coordinate at a national scale the operations of public and private employment agencies where they exist.

---

[72] Olivier & Van Kerken "Unemployment Insurance" in *Social Security: A Legal Analysis* 418.

[73] For a more detailed discussion, see Govindjee et al (2011) *Stell LR* 205-227.

[74] See Department of Social Development *Creating Our Future* 19:

"Conditional social transfers can link grant recipients to a range of related government programmes and initiatives which form part of the common developmental package. These can include: 1. Participation in primary and secondary education; 2. Skills development targeted at the youth; 3. Skills development targeted at the long-term unemployed; 4. Preventive healthcare programmes; 5. Job placement programmes; and 6. Special employment programmes."

For a more detailed discussion, see Govindjee et al (2011) *Stell LR* 205-227.

[75] Cl 2(1) of the Employment Services Bill.

[76] Cl 2(2).

[77] ILO Unemployment Convention 2 (1919) ("ILO Unemployment Convention"). Ratification took place on 20-02-1924.

There are also a variety of measures in place that are aimed at preventing people from becoming unemployed in the first place, including strong protection against dismissal. One of the most innovative policies has been the so-called "Training Layoff Scheme", introduced during the aftermath of the 2008 international economic crisis. The scheme aims at avoiding the retrenchment of workers whose employers would ordinarily have retrenched them and instead allows workers to temporarily suspend their normal work to take part in training programmes. During the period of training, the worker agrees to forego his or her normal wage in return for a training allowance. The training allowance is set at 50% of the worker's salary subject to an overall cap of the UIF threshold. The amount is guaranteed for a three-month period with the possibility of an additional three-month extension. A National Jobs Fund was established in 2009 with an initial allocation of R2.4 billion to help finance the Training Layoff Scheme.[78]

6 Policies aimed specifically at creating work

In recent years, various macro-economic policies of the government have been developed to foster job-rich growth and to address persistent high levels of unemployment, poverty and unequal growth. For example, the Accelerated Shared Growth Initiative for South Africa ("AsgiSA") seeks to create an environment of, and opportunities for, an inclusive economy through the promotion of more labour-absorbing economic activities. In addition, the government's Industrial Policy Framework and the second Industrial Policy Action Plan ("IPAP2") are aimed at facilitating economic diversification beyond the current reliance on traditional commodities and non-tradable services towards a more labour-absorbing industrialisation path.[79]

An evaluation of these long-term employment-generating strategic policies falls beyond the scope of this chapter. However, it is clear that there is an urgent need for interventions that alleviate the current unemployment situation. According to the ILO, these interventions should include income support to the unemployed and underemployed (working poor) in the form of cash transfers, as well as certain forms of basic employment guarantees in the form of public works or similar programmes.[80] While the possibility of cash transfers will receive separate and more detailed analysis later in this chapter, two programmes aimed at ensuring basic employment guarantees merit attention here. These are the labour-intensive public works programme (also known as the "Expanded Public Works Programme" or "EPWP") as well as an employment-guarantee programme along the lines of India's much

---

[78] See, in general, L Ramutloa "A Guide to the Training Layoff Scheme" (2009) *Department: Labour* 1 1-11 <http://www.labour.gov.za/documents/useful-documents/skills-development/guide-to-training-lay-off-scheme> (accessed 08-09-2011).

[79] See RSA *Decent Work Country Programme* 12. The Programme was launched by the Government of the Republic of South Africa, the International Labour Organization, Representative Employers' and Workers' Organisations and the Community Constituency on 29-09-2010.

[80] The ILO considers both income support and employment guarantees to be among the foundations of the social protection floor. ILO *World Social Security Report 2010/2011* 63.

touted National Rural Employment Guarantee Scheme ("NREGS") (called the "Community Work Programme" or "CWP").

The EPWP was launched in 2004 and aims to create productive employment opportunities by increasing the labour intensity of all government programmes. The design of the EPWP seems to have been informed by proposals set out in the World Bank's 2001 *World Development Report*.[81] However, it has been pointed out that the World Bank proposals were meant to address problems of cyclical unemployment, not problems of structural and chronic unemployment as is the case in South Africa.[82]

In terms of the programme, all government bodies and state corporations are required to endeavour to increase the use of unskilled labour. Through the use of public expenditure, temporary, (generally) unskilled employment is created for the jobless. This temporary employment is coupled with on-the-job skills development and training. The intention is that this will provide the participants leaving the programme with a better chance of finding regular employment.[83] The size of the EPWP has grown considerably since its inception, and the intention is to increase the scale of the project to provide the full-time equivalent of more than 400 000 jobs a year over the medium term.[84] While the ability of the EPWP to have a positive impact on the unemployment figures has been questioned,[85] there is general agreement that the EPWP has the potential to make a significant contribution to poverty alleviation through the provision of short-term income support.[86]

The CWP was initiated in 2007 by the Second Economy Strategy Project – an initiative of the Presidency. The design phase of the CWP was initially implemented without direct control of government, namely with donor funding and strategic oversight from a Steering Committee comprising representatives of the Presidency and the Department for Social Development, and later also from National Treasury, the Department of Cooperative Governance and the Department of Public Works.[87] The CWP offers two days of work per week,

---

[81] World Bank *World Development Report* (2000/2001). See also Seekings *Employment Guarantee or Minimum Income?* 15.

[82] Seekings *Employment Guarantee or Minimum Income?* 15.

[83] Leibbrandt et al *Employment and Inequality Outcomes in South Africa* 36.

[84] 37.

[85] For example, Seekings points to the fact that most of the job opportunities are typically of short duration, and the training component suffers from general delivery problems typical of all government training programmes (Seekings *Employment Guarantee or Minimum Income?* 15). In addition, while the EPWP provided 1.4 million "work opportunities" between 2004/05 and 2008/09, it has been pointed out that the number of full-time person years of work created is about one quarter of the number of "work opportunities" reported as a result of the short-terms nature of these opportunities. See Leibbrandt et al *Employment and Inequality Outcomes in South Africa* 36.

[86] Leibbrandt et al *Employment and Inequality Outcomes in South Africa* 37. According to the latest available figures, the EPWP created 643 116 work opportunities in the 2010-2011 financial year (Government Communication and Information System "EPWP a Catalyst for Decent Work Opportunities" (23-06-2011) *BuaNews* <http://www.buanews.gov.za/news/11/11062311351001> (accessed 06-10-2011)). For a more detailed evaluation of the benefits and drawbacks of the EPWP, see Cooper "Women and the Right to Work" in *Women's Social and Economic Rights* 257-262.

[87] K Philip *Employment Guarantees: Innovation at the Interface between Social and Economic Policy* (2010) 7 paper prepared for the conference *The Global Economic Crisis and South Africa: Lessons in Long-Run Economic Growth and Development*, Johannesburg, October 2010 <http://www.commerce.uct. ac.za/research_units/dpru/DPRU_Conference_2010/Conference_Papers/Philip%20Employment%20 Guarantees%20DPRU%20TIPS.pdf> (accessed 25-03-2011).

and provides 100 days of work per person spread throughout the year. The programme targets unemployed and underemployed people and is area-based, meaning that it is implemented in a defined local area or site. A site operating at full capacity offers work opportunities to 1 000 people.[88] While the CWP is still small in comparison to the Indian NREGS that it is meant to replicate, it has nevertheless grown in less than two years from 1 500 participants in April 2009 to almost 83 000 participants by March 2011, which demonstrates its potential to grow to significant scale, and to mobilise the local partnerships and capacities required to do so.[89] In addition, with a labour-intensity of 65% at site level, it is highly cost effective. The aim is to establish a presence for CWP in every municipality by 2014, which could provide as many as 237 000 work opportunities.[90]

7 Decent work creation

Given the fiscal constraints which hamper the possibility of expanding social assistance coverage in South Africa, coupled with other concerns pertaining to the creation of a welfare-dependent society, it has been argued that the state should place renewed emphasis on the implementation of complementary policy measures such as the strengthening of labour market policies and improving the education system. This would make it easier for labour market entrants to secure employment which in turn "would make it easier to wean the South African society off the social security system that we so desperately depend on". [91] On a political level too, the government has recognised that addressing all the challenges facing the country, including growing the economy and reducing the high rates of poverty, inequality and unemployment, as well as improving the livelihoods of all South Africans, requires a "developmental state" with the capacity to actively intervene to achieve these goals.[92]

The creation of decent work opportunities serves the dual objective of acting as a complementary policy measure to the well-established social security system, as well as being a driving force behind the attempt to actually create a true developmental state in South Africa.[93] The concept of "decent work" is based on the understanding that work is

> "not only a source of income but more importantly a source of dignity, family stability, peace in community, and economic growth that expands opportunities for productive jobs and employment. The goal is not just the creation of jobs, but the creation of jobs of acceptable quality."[94]

---

[88] K Motlanthe *Address by Deputy President Motlanthe* (22-03-2011), a public address in the National Council of Provinces, 22-03-2011 <http:www.info.gov.za/speech/DynamicAction?pageid=461&sid=171 84&tid=30466> (accessed 06-10-2011).

[89] Philip *Employment Guarantees* 8.

[90] Motlanthe *Address by Deputy President Motlanthe*.

[91] Bhorat et al *Income and Non-Income Inequality in Post-Apartheid SA* 56.

[92] O Edigheji "Constructing a Democratic Developmental State in South Africa: Potentials and Challenges" in O Edigheji (ed) *Constructing a Democratic Developmental State in South Africa* (2010) 1 1.

[93] On the decent work deficit, see ILO *Reducing the Decent Work Deficit* 7-12.

[94] RSA *Decent Work Country Programme* 5; ILO *Skills-Development through CBR* 7. For further information in this regard, see ILO *Decent Work Agenda* <http:www.ilo.org/global/about-the-ilo/decent-work-agenda/lang--en/index.htm> (accessed 06-10-2011).

The decent work ideal has been encapsulated in the objectives of promoting fundamental principles and rights at work, promoting employment and income opportunities, expanding and improving social protection coverage and promoting social dialogue and tripartism. Decent work offers a way of combining employment, rights, social protection and social dialogue in developmental strategies.[95] The South Africa Decent Work Country Programme represents the culmination of a consultative process between the ILO, the South African government, business and labour (through the mechanism of the National Economic Development and Labour Council) in order to internalise and operationalise key international principles which facilitate decent work enhancement in this country.[96] The priorities and strategic focus of the South Africa Decent Work Country Programme intersect with the ILO strategic objectives and key outcome areas as outlined in the ILO Strategic Policy Framework (2010-2015)[97] and the ILO Programme and Budget for the 2010-2011 Biennium.[98]

In 2005, the United Nations Millennium Development Goals Summit agreed on the inclusion of a specific target for decent work, namely to "achieve full and productive employment and decent work for all".[99] One of the key elements of the development agenda of the government in South Africa is to eradicate poverty and unemployment through the promotion of decent work and employment.[100]

Despite the South African economy enjoying relatively strong economic growth during the first decade of the 21st century, the economy has seemingly been unable to create sufficient employment opportunities.[101] In order to attempt to address this anomaly, the past few years have seen a heightened

---

[95] ILO *Reducing the Decent Work Deficit* 11.

[96] RSA *Decent Work Country Programme* 4.

[97] ILO *Strategic Policy Framework 2010-2015* (Three Hundred and Fourth Sess of the Governing Body, March 2009) 5-25.

[98] ILO *Programme and Budget for the Biennium 2010-2011* (2009). The priorities of the Decent Work Country Programme also respond to other global and regional commitments to which South Africa is a part, notably: the ILO *Decent Work Agenda for Africa: 2007-2015* (Eleventh African Regional Meeting, Addis Ababa, April 2007) <http:www.ilo.org/public/English/standards/relm/rgmeet/11afrm/dg-tthematic.pdf> (accessed 06-10-2011); African Union *Ouagadougou Declaration and Plan of Action on Employment and Poverty Alleviation* (African Union Extraordinary Summit on Unemployment and Poverty Alleviation in Africa, Ouagadougou, Burkina Faso, 08-09-2004-09-09-2004) <http://www.africa-union.org/EMPLOYMENT/declaration%20on%20employment%20and%20poverty%20allevaition.pdf> (accessed 06-10-2011), and the SADC Regional Indicative Strategic Development Plan (2008) <http:www.sadc.int/index/browse/page/104> (accessed 06-10-2011).

[99] Para 47 of UN GA *2005 World Summit Outcome* Res 60/1 UN GAOR (2005) UN Doc A/60/L.1. This commitment was with direct reference to the first Millennium Development Goal of eradicating extreme poverty and hunger. Reconfirmed in para 70 of UN GA *Keeping the Promise: United to Achieve the Millennium Development Goals* Res 65/1 UN GAOR (2010) UN Doc A/60/PV.9. <http://www.un.org/en/mdg/summit2010/pdf/outcome_documentN1051260.pdf> (accessed 19-10-2010).
      The *ILO Declaration on Social Justice for a Fair Globalisation* included a framework for the implementation of the four pillars of decent work at international, regional and national levels (ILO *ILO Declaration on Social Justice for a Fair Globalisation* (2008) 5-7 <www.ilo.org/public/english/bureau/dgo/download/dg_announce_en.pdf> (accessed 22-10-2010)).

[100] RSA *Decent Work Country Programme* 5.

[101] Government of the Republic of South Africa *The New Growth Path: The Framework* (2010) 3. The ILO's implementation of its "decent work for all" programme has been criticised for its overwhelming focus on "decency", as opposed to a focus on "work for all" (see Cooper "Women and the Right to Work" in *Women's Social and Economic Rights* 251).

policy focus on the creation of decent work through a new growth path in South Africa.[102] It is now clear that the creation of decent work is practically at the centre of current economic and social policy ambition.[103] The number and quality of jobs created is presently entrenched as the first indicator of success of the so-called "New Growth Path", which seeks to direct limited state resources and capacity at activities that maximise the creation of decent work opportunities.[104] This advancement in the number of quality job opportunities is a key component of the present conceptualisation of South Africa as a developmental state.[105]

In support of this, the 2011 Budget Speech reflected an expansion of social protection initiatives as well as a strong enhancement of employment creation strategies.[106] In particular, a R9 billion jobs fund was set aside over the next three years to co-finance innovative public- and private-sector employment projects, with R73 billion earmarked over the same period for continued support of the expanded public works programme.[107] Manufacturing investment opportunities with a focus on job-creation potential received tax breaks of R20 billion and a targeted commitment to youth employment was backed by a R5 billion wage subsidy allocation.[108]

The recent proposed amendments to South Africa's existing labour legislation, as well as the proposed introduction of new employment-centred law and the reconsideration of broad-based black economic empowerment provisions is a consequence of this renewed focus, across all spheres of government, on job creation.[109]

Such developments raise a number of difficult issues. For example, there is arguably a trade-off required in order to balance attempts to create work for everyone who seeks it against the concept of "decent work" provision.[110] The capacity of the UIF to adequately address the malaise of the structurally or long-term unemployed is a serious concern, as is the sustainability of increased social grants provision, despite their positive attributes. The efficacy of unemployment prevention strategies and policies aimed specifically at creating work raise further questions. The next part of this contribution attempts to

---

[102] See, for example, RSA *New Growth Path* 1; JG Zuma *State of the Nation Address by His Excellency JG Zuma, President of the Republic of South Africa,* 03-06-2009 1, a public address at the Joint Sitting of Parliament at Parliament, Cape Town.

[103] RSA *New Growth Path* 1; P Gordhan *2011 Budget Speech* (2011) 41.

[104] RSA *New Growth Path* 6. At an international level, for example, the United Nations Chief Executive Board launched the "Global Jobs Pact" in 2009, aimed at focusing decision-makers' attention on employment measures and decent work as the foundation for long-term economic recovery. The key component of the Global Jobs Pact is employment promotion coupled with social protection (see United Nations Department of Economic and Social Affairs *The Global Social Crisis: Report on the World Social Situation 2011* (2011) UN Doc ST/ESA/334 7-9).

[105] RSA *New Growth Path* 28.

[106] Gordhan *2011 Budget Speech* 3.

[107] 16-17.

[108] 17. In total, an amount of R146.9 billion was reserved for social protection-related matters.

[109] E Patel *Comments in the State of the Nation Address Debate, National Assembly, by Minister of Economic Development Ebrahim Patel* (15-02-2011), a public address to the National Assembly in Parliament, Cape Town, 15-02-2011 <http://www.info.gov.za/speech/DynamicAction?pageid=461&sid=16545&tid=2890 6> (accessed 08-09-2011).

[110] Cooper "Women and the Right to Work" in *Women's Social and Economic Rights* 256-257.

contextualise these matters against the backdrop of the Constitution, in order to lay the foundation for the concluding arguments advanced.

8   The absence of a constitutional or legislative provision regarding unemployment security or a right to work

The Constitution was adopted so as to establish a society based on democratic values, social justice and fundamental human rights.[111] The Preamble specifically refers to the rationale of improving the quality of life of all citizens and the liberation of the potential of each person. In addition to important constitutional values such as human dignity, the achievement of equality, non-racialism and non-sexism, the founding provisions of the Constitution include the advancement of human rights and freedoms as a constitutional value.[112] The Constitution is characterised by a broad-ranging Bill of Rights, which includes socio-economic and environmental rights. The state must respect, protect, promote and fulfil the rights in the Bill of Rights.[113]

It is somewhat surprising, given the large-scale problem of unemployment and the state prioritisation of employment-creation activities, that the Constitution does not contain a provision pertaining to "non-social security" aspects of unemployment security (as defined above).[114] There is also no designated right to work contained in the Bill of Rights.[115]

The right of access to social security and appropriate social assistance contained in section 27 of the Constitution may not, strictly speaking, be read in such a manner so as to automatically incorporate all components of the broader notion of social protection.[116] The term "social security" is normally understood in a relatively narrow sense. The social insurance and social assistance components of social security are, similarly, limited by the manner in which they are generally conceptualised and understood in practice. Employment-creation initiatives would, for example, be excluded from the ambit of section 27. Employment-protection interventions such as the Training Layoff Scheme would also not be covered. The limited social insurance benefits available in cases of unemployment would be included, as

---

[111] Preamble to the Constitution.

[112] S 1.

[113] S 7(2).

[114] For an example of intensive investment by the Department of Labour (involving R35 billion from the UIF and R27 billion from the Compensation Fund), *via* the Public Investment Corporation, in the creation and sustainability of jobs, see Government Communication and Information System "Labour Dept Ploughs Billions into Job Creation" (08-07-2011) *BuaNews* <http://www.buanews.gov.za/news/11/11070809351001> (accessed 06-10-2011).

[115] A Govindjee "Assisting the Unemployed in the Absence of a Legal Framework: The Next Frontier for the Eastern Cape Bench?" (2011) 25 *Speculum Juris* 86 105. Also see Cooper "Women and the Right to Work" in *Women's Social and Economic Rights* 246.

[116] On the need for social security systems to move towards integrated forms of social protection, see ILO "Social Security and the Rule of Law" in *General Survey Concerning Social Security Instruments in Light of the 2008 Declaration on Social Justice for a Fair Globalization* Report III (Part 1B) (2011) 11 22. The idea that social security should serve as a means, among others, for promoting employment and must be coordinated with *other means* of employment and social policies serving the goal of employment protection (but is not synonymous with unemployment security) is also clear from a consideration of the ILO Employment Promotion and Protection against Unemployment Convention 168 (1988).

would any "continuation benefit" or other form of unemployment assistance introduced in future for groups of unemployed people.[117]

Similarly, the constitutional provisions pertaining to freedom of choice and practice of trade, occupation and profession, and the right to fair labour practices have neither been interpreted in a manner to suggest that unemployment protection activities are encompassed, nor in order to claim that there exists a constitutional right to work.

There is also no legislation which deals directly with employment-creation initiatives.[118] Furthermore, there are very few cases[119] which have considered the right to work in a South African context or the legalities of work in terms of public works programmes. Leaving aside the possibility of a constitutional amendment giving effect to a right to work, the speediest method of gaining more formal recognition for its attempts to create jobs would be for government to introduce legislation regulating its own employment creation activities. Section 39(3) of the Constitution states that the Bill of Rights does not deny the existence of a right or freedom that is recognised or conferred by common law, customary law or legislation, to the extent that it is consistent with the Bill. This would arguably serve as constitutional support for such law.

Passing legislation that formally regulates the state's efforts to create employment (in particular through its public works programmes) and prevents unemployment would arguably have contributed to greater accountability on the part of those involved in such initiatives. Furthermore, the passing of legislation would involve the judiciary by making it notionally easier for unreasonable state conduct pertaining to employment-creation initiatives to be challenged in court on a basis similar to the manner in which unreasonable policies pertaining to other socio-economic rights have been exposed and reformulated.[120] Policymaking in the area of job creation exists and operates largely in the absence of direct constitutional, legislative and case law guidance.[121]

There would appear to be little reason in principle for refraining from constitutionalising, or at the very least passing legislation relating to, unemployment security, including a progressively realisable right to work,

---

[117] S 27(1)(c) of the Constitution states that "[e]veryone has the right to have access to social security including, if they are unable to support themselves and their dependants, appropriate social assistance". Furthermore, s 27(2) provides that "[t]he state must take reasonable legislative and other measures, within its available resources, to achieve the progressive realisation of the right to have access to social security".

[118] On the absence of a formally legislated right to work, in general, see Cooper "Women and the Right to Work" in *Women's Social and Economic Rights* 245. It is arguable that various pieces of legislation and proposed legislation, such as the Skills Development Act and the Employment Services Bill, strive to encourage employment creation indirectly.

[119] See *City of Johannesburg v Rand Properties (Pty) Ltd* 2006 JOL 16852 (W) para 64; *Swartbooi v ACV Civils* CCMA 01-04-2004 case no ECPE 3157/03 <http://www.caselaw.co.za/search.php?court=0&stype=caselaw&query=ACV+Civils&sfunc=0> (accessed 12-06-2007); *Lewis v GATA/Coast Care* CCMA 29-04-2003 case no WE9080/02 <http://www.caselaw.co.za/search.php?court=0&stype=caselaw&query=gata&sfunc=0 > (accessed 12-06-2007).

[120] See Cooper "Women and the Right to Work" in *Women's Social and Economic Rights* 272.

[121] Govindjee *Assisting the Unemployed in the Absence of a Legal Framework* 3.

in South Africa.[122] One concern could be that a constitutional focus on unemployment security and work would permit individuals to utilise their freedom to contract in order to choose work at a standard below legislated basic conditions of employment or somehow otherwise undermine legislation prescribing such basic working conditions.[123] To the extent that it is necessary to do so, careful constitutional and legislative crafting should easily be able to circumvent this concern.[124] Another perceived concern may be that the advancements made with respect to realisation of the right to have access to social security will be lost by virtue of a constitutional focus on work. This argument may be rebutted by considering established principles of interpretation of socio-economic rights. For example, it is by now well known that the removal of existing access to rights, or the adoption of a retrogressive measure regarding a particular right, would not easily be justified.[125]

The right to work is, in addition, established in international and regional instruments such as the Universal Declaration of Human Rights (1948),[126] the International Covenant on Economic, Social and Cultural Rights (1966),[127] the European Social Charter (1961) and Revised Social Charter (1996),[128] the

---

[122] Regarding the fear that a right to work in the Constitution would promote untoward interference by the judiciary in the realm of the executive and legislature, or could result in rigidities in the labour market, see Cooper "Women and the Right to Work" in *Women's Social and Economic Rights* 274-275.

[123] See S Liebenberg *Toward a Right to Work in SA?* (2006), unpublished paper presented at the *AIDC Conference on the Right to Work*, 12-06-2006 (copy on file with the authors).

[124] S 36 of the Constitution, which provides that all rights may be limited by a law of general application to the extent that this is reasonable and justifiable in an open and democratic society, should, in any event, serve to "limit" a right to work in such a way that only the idea of "decent work" would be promoted. It is also important to note that there appears to be no justification for suggesting that international law sanctions a reduction in labour standards protection as a mechanism for advancing the right to work (Liebenberg *Toward a Right to Work* 3).

[125] See, generally, *Jaftha v Schoeman, Van Rooyen v Stoltz* 2005 2 SA 140 (CC); *Government of the Republic of South Africa v Grootboom* 2001 1 SA 46 (CC); *Minister of Health v Treatment Action Campaign (No 1)* 2002 5 SA 703 (CC). See also Liebenberg *Toward a Right to Work* 3-4. However, it might be true that the introduction of a new right relating to the fight against unemployment will be read together with s 27 in such a manner so as to more easily justify the limitation of the s 27 right or the failure to progressively continue to realise that right.

[126] Art 23(1) of the Universal Declaration of Human Right (1948) UN Doc A/810 provides that "[e]veryone has the right to work, to free choice of employment, to just and favourable conditions of work and to protection from unemployment".

[127] Art 6 of the International Covenant of Economic, Social and Cultural Rights (1966) UN Doc 14531 provides that
"(1)   The States Parties to the present Covenant recognise the right to work, which includes the right of everyone to the opportunity to gain his living by work which he freely chooses or accepts, and will take appropriate steps to safeguard this right.
(2)   The steps to be taken by a State Party to the present Covenant to achieve the full realisation of this right shall include technical and vocational guidance and training programmes, policies and techniques to achieve steady economic, social and cultural development and full and productive employment under conditions safeguarding fundamental political and economic freedoms to the individual."

[128] See Council of Europe, European Social Charter (1961) art 1 and Council of Europe, Revised Social Charter (1996) art 1 which states:
"With a view to ensuring the effective exercise of the right to work, the Contracting Parties undertake:
(1)   To accept as one of their primary aims and responsibilities the achievement and maintenance of as high and stable a level of employment as possible with a view to the attainment of full employment;
(2)   To protect effectively the right of the worker to earn his living in an occupation freely entered upon;
(3)   To establish and maintain free employment services for all workers;

Additional Protocol to the American Convention on Human and Peoples' Rights in the Area of Economic, Social and Cultural Rights (1988),[129] the African Charter on Human and Peoples' Rights (1981),[130] as well as in various ILO standards. There is also foreign precedent for the constitutional inclusion of some form of this right, as is evident from consideration of the law in Spain, Finland and France.[131]

In sum, there should be little disagreement about the merits of including a right to work, in one form or another, in the Constitution. Recognising a right to work would have the positive consequence of placing the values associated with work on an equal footing with other human rights contained in the Constitution, thereby elevating this aspect of life above other social interests.[132] Interestingly, there also appears to be a positive empirical relationship between government effort and the actual constitutionalisation of economic rights which a policymaker strives to achieve.[133] There exists at least some evidence to demonstrate that constitutionalisation is associated with increased government effort and higher economic rights fulfilment.[134] Put differently, countries that display high effort in fulfilling the human needs associated with economic rights also on average have the strongest economic rights provisions in their constitutions.[135]

At least two further options may be considered in order to achieve this end. Firstly, there would appear to be some opportunity for the courts to utilise the existing constitutional text and framework of constitutional values in order to identify "unenumerated" rights in appropriate and limited circumstances.[136] The judges of the Constitutional Court in *Ferreira v Levin NO*[137] all seemed

---

      (4)   To provide or promote appropriate vocational guidance, training and rehabilitation."

[129] See art 6 of the Additional Protocol to the American Convention on Human and Peoples' Rights in the Area of Economic, Social and Cultural Rights (1988), which states:

    "The States Parties also undertake to implement and strengthen programs that help to ensure suitable family care, so that women may enjoy a real opportunity to exercise the right to work."

[130] See art 15 of the African Charter on Human and Peoples' Rights (1981) OAU Doc CAB/LEG/67/3 rev 5,21 I.L.M 58, which states:

    "Every individual shall have the right to work under equitable and satisfactory conditions, and shall receive equal pay for equal work."

[131] Cooper "Women and the Right to Work" in *Women's Social and Economic Rights* 272-273.

[132] G Mundlak "The Right to Work: Linking Human Rights and Employment Policy" (2007) 146 *International Labour Review* 189 208; I Ahmed "Decent Work and Human Development" (2003) 142 *International Labour Review* 263 265. On the philosophical underpinnings of the right to work, in particular the relationship between this right and the attainment of social justice, see Cooper "Women and the Right to Work" in *Women's Social and Economic Rights* 249.

[133] L Minkler "Economic Rights and the Policymaker's Decision Problem" (2007) 5 *Economic Rights Working Paper Series* Human Rights Institute, University of Connecticut 1 3.

[134] 3. This is apparently because the constitutionalisation of economic rights results in the reduction of a policymaker's likelihood of making a "decision error".

[135] 26. It must be noted that there are a number of *caveats* to the conclusions reached by Minkler.

[136] R Kruger & A Govindjee "The Recognition of Unenumerated Rights in South Africa" forthcoming in (2011) 20 *SAPL*. On the recent, negative, view of the South African government of interventions of this sort, see the Keynote Address by President JG Zuma (3rd Access to Justice Conference, Pretoria, 8 July 2011) 5 <http://www.justice.gov.za/access-to-justice conference-2011/20110708_ajc_zuma-speech.pdf> (accessed 06-10-2011). It is interesting to note that British courts of appeal have on occasion in the past recognised a person's right to work based on an interpretation of English common law and with emphasis on the relationship between work and livelihood: see, for example, the judgments of Lord Denning in *Nagle v Feilden* [1966] 1 All ER 689; *Edwards v Society of Graphical and Allied Trades* [1970] 3 All ER 689.

[137] *Ferreira v Levin NO* 1996 1 SA 984 (CC).

to agree, for example, that the Constitution of the Republic of South Africa Act 200 of 1993 ("the Interim Constitution") protected both enumerated and unenumerated freedom rights.[138] There is nothing to suggest that the position has changed when it comes to the final Constitution.

Secondly, it is also open for judges (perhaps reluctant to take the seemingly drastic step of recognising an unenumerated right) to utilise an expanded interpretation of existing, enumerated constitutional rights in order to address a challenge relating to a right not expressly included in the Bill of Rights.[139] The right of everyone to have their dignity respected and protected[140] is probably most conducive to such an exercise.[141] In *Minister of Home Affairs v Watchenuka*[142] the Supreme Court of Appeal accepted that

> "[t]he freedom to engage in productive work – even where that is not required in order to survive – is indeed an important component of human dignity ... for mankind is pre-eminently a social species with an instinct for meaningful association. Self-esteem and the sense of self-worth – the fulfilment of what it is to be human – is most often bound by with being accepted as socially useful."

There is also a small body of jurisprudence that argues that the right to life in the South African Constitution may have to be construed in such a way that it includes socio-economic entitlements not contained in the Constitution or, at least, enhances those socio-economic rights guaranteed by the Constitution. As Pieterse argues:[143]

> "To be deprived of clothing, sanitation, *employment* or means to secure a livelihood can seriously encroach upon the quality of human life and may even threaten survival. The constitutional right to life must at least ensure access to these basic survival requirements if it is to have any significance for a large percentage of the population."[144]

In *S v Makwanyane*[145] it was suggested that the right to life, coupled with the right to dignity, may impose a positive duty on the state to create conditions which enable people to enjoy these rights as something more than a guarantee of mere physical existence.[146] In *City of Johannesburg*,[147] the court linked the absence of adequate housing for the respondents, as well as their potential

---

[138] Paras 184, 212.

[139] Kruger & Govindjee (2011) *SAPL*.

[140] S 10 of the Constitution.

[141] For example, the Constitutional Court's purposive interpretation of the right to dignity in *Dawood v Minister of Home Affairs* 2000 3 SA 936 (CC) paras 36-38 enabled it to give recognition to the importance of family life.

[142] *Minister of Home Affairs v Watchenuka* 2004 4 SA 326 (SCA) para 27. See also *Affordable Medicines Trust v Minister of Health* 2006 3 SA 247 (CC) para 59; *Reference Re Public Service Employee Relations Act (Alta.)* [1987] 1 SCR 313 (SCC); *Malik and Mahmud v Bank of Credit and Commerce International SA (in liquidation)* [1998] AC 20 para 37; *Johnson v Unisys Ltd* [2001] UKHL 13 [2001] IRLR 279 (HL) para 35.

[143] M Pieterse "A Different Shade of Red: Socio-Economic Dimensions of the Right to Life in South Africa" (1999) 15 *SAJHR* 373 384.

[144] Pieterse (1999) *SAJHR* 384 (emphasis added). See also, in general, *City of Johannesburg v Rand Properties (Pty) Ltd* 2006 JOL 16852 (W).

[145] 1995 3 SA 391 (CC).

[146] Para 25. Also note the minority judgment of Arbour J in *Gosselin v Quebec (Attorney General)* [2002] 4 SCR 429 holding that a minimum level of welfare is so closely connected to issues relating to a person's basic health and security, and possibly even survival, that such a right to minimum welfare must encompass these issues.

[147] 2006 JOL 16852 (W).

eviction, to the effect that this deprivation would have on their employment prospects, their livelihood, their dignity and their life:

> "An individual has as much right to work as the individual has to live, to be free and to own property. To work means to eat and consequently to live. This constitutes an encompassing view of humanity."[148]

International law and foreign law in the form of section 21 of the Constitution of India 1949 provides support for reading the right to work into either the right to dignity or the right to life, although at least one court in southern Africa has already rejected this notion expressly.[149]

9 The right to unemployment security and transformative constitutionalism

The impetus behind arguing for constitutional or statutory recognition of unemployment security and the right to work is enhanced by the inherent limitations of the South African social assistance system. A vast number of unemployed people are completely uncovered by the UIF, for reasons discussed above, and are not entitled, in terms of the provisions of the Social Assistance Act 13 of 2004, to any form of social assistance. There is a potential constitutional challenge to the current situation, details of which are summarised below.

The Constitution provides that everyone who is unable to support themselves and their dependants has the right to have access to social assistance, the state having the duty to take progressive steps, within its available resources, to achieve progressive realisation of the right. The definition of "social assistance" contained in the Social Assistance Act is currently restricted to social grants, including the social relief of distress grant.[150] This suggests that all other "state assistance" geared towards the unemployed in South Africa, barring the provision of unemployment insurance (which would count as part of the "social insurance" component of social security), cannot, by definition, amount to "social assistance" or "social security". Public works programmes which appear to be enjoying some success in terms of creating work opportunities would, for example, not be considered to be "social assistance".[151] Unemployment prevention initiatives, such as the Training Layoff Scheme, would similarly be excluded by definition. However, should the proposals mooted for the youth and adult unemployed in the *Creating Our Future* document[152] be implemented, the position might be different. The

---

[148] Para 64.

[149] *Baitsokoli v Maseru City Council* 2005 3 All SA 79 (LesCA) paras 17, 20, 23-24. See A Govindjee "Lessons for South African Social Assistance Law from India: Part 2 – Is There More to the Right to Life in South Africa?" (2006) 27 *Obiter* 33; *Olga Tellis v Bombay Municipal Corporation* [1987] LRC (Const) 351 368.

[150] The main social grants provided for are the Child Support Grant, the Older Persons Grant and the Disability Grant.

[151] Social assistance, as presently defined in South Africa, exists as a safety-net *in the event of unemployment.* To argue that there is a greater attempt to create employment or provide additional work opportunities cannot, therefore, absolve the state from its current duty in terms of s 27.

[152] Department of Social Development *Creating Our Future.*

difficulty with the current situation is that the obligation on the state to take progressive measures to provide social security, including social assistance, to unemployed adults who are unable to support themselves and their dependants, is largely being ignored.[153] The consequence of this is that the state may be challenged for failing to take steps, within its available resources, to respect, protect, promote and fulfil a right contained in the Bill of Rights, despite clearly prioritising employment creation at a policy level. The difficulty with implementing the Department of Social Development's proposals to deal with this *lacuna* relates primarily to concern regarding the financial viability of the suggested options.

Put differently, it is feasible that a group of unemployed youths, having attempted to unsuccessfully obtain sustained work *via* a public works programme and being unable to support themselves and their dependants (currently not being entitled to any UIF "continuation benefit" or social grant), could approach the court in order to challenge the constitutionality of the state social assistance system. Such a challenge could be based, for example, on the obligation of the state to take reasonable measures, within its available resources, to achieve the progressive realisation of the right to social assistance for "everyone" – not just for children, older persons and disabled persons. A defence to the effect that the state is taking progressive *policy* steps to create employment for the affected group would seemingly be ineffective, given the present wording of section 27 of the Constitution.

It may well be the case that such a matter has only not come before the courts to date due to the state's ability to progressively increase the scope of the Child Support Grant over the past few years, as well as the recent age equalisation of the Older Persons Grant. Should the state fail to expand the scope of social assistance further (for example, by refusing to pay social assistance progressively to able-bodied person between the ages of 19 and 59 years of age due to inadequate resources), the situation may be different.

Inserting a limited right to unemployment security, including work, into the Constitution will allow the state the possibility of justifiably limiting an unemployed person's right to social assistance on the basis that the state is striving, within its available resources, to progressively take reasonable legislative and other measures in order to create employment opportunities for that person. Such a right could be crafted, and limited, as follows:

> "Everyone has the right to have access to unemployment security, including the right to work. The state must take reasonable legislative and other measures, within its available resources, to achieve the progressive realisation of this right."

It may be argued that it should be left to the judiciary to chart the course of transformation and to secure a greater level of social justice for the people of South Africa.[154] For the unemployed person currently ineligible for any form of social security, this could involve the recognition of an unenumerated right or an expanded reading of an existing constitutional right, as discussed above.

---

[153] The mooted extension of coverage of the UIF system may provide a temporary reprieve in this regard.
[154] See D Moseneke "Transformative Adjudication" (2002) 18 *SAJHR* 314 318-319; F Michelman "A Constitutional Conversation with Professor Frank Michelman" (1995) 11 *SAJHR* 477 479.

There would appear, however, to be an even better argument in favour of *direct constitutional transformation* in order to address the current anomaly of policy focus on unemployment in the absence of a coherent legal framework.

In fact, the Constitution does not provide a specific method to achieve its transformative goals and the envisaged transformation could be achieved in various ways. While a process of transparent judicial decision-making may play a great role in transforming society, the courts should not be the sole bearers of the duty to transform society.[155]

As Moseneke has noted, the Constitution promised a new beginning and represented a collective quest for renewal, committing itself to improving the quality of life of all citizens, and to freeing the potential of each person.[156] Moseneke sees embedded in the "inner recesses of our transformative project" the meticulous observance of fundamental human rights as well as "the quest to ameliorate material deprivation and, so to speak, to bring the goal of a better life for all within reach".[157] Albertyn and Goldblatt have suggested as follows:

> "We understand transformation to require a complete reconstruction of the state and society, including redistribution of power and resources along egalitarian lines. The challenge of achieving equality within this transformation project involves the eradication of systemic forms of domination and material disadvantages based on race, gender, class and other grounds of inequality. It also entails the development of opportunities which allow people to realise their full human potential within positive social relationships."[158]

This clearly cannot be a challenge to be met only by the judiciary and, in fact, there is some opposition to the idea of *transformative adjudication* because of its perceived invitation to judges to accomplish political objectives.[159] The state is intimately involved in the protection of socio-economic rights and the advancement of the goal of a transformed, socially just society. In fact, it is generally acknowledged that the state carries the primary duty to protect socio-economic rights by regulating such rights through legislation and administrative conduct.[160] It is suggested that there may not always be a justifiable basis for limiting this primary duty to matters short of constitutional amendment.

The Constitution (incorporating the Bill of Rights) was drafted only a few years ago and its provisions are, in comparison to those of older constitutions, comprehensive. But this comprehensiveness does not imply that the provisions of the Constitution expressly cater for every eventuality.[161] Constitutions and Bills of Rights are necessarily products of their time and context. In order for these documents to continue to address important societal issues, it has been

---

[155] See, in general, S Liebenberg *Socio-Economic Rights: Adjudication under a Transformative Constitution* (2010).

[156] D Moseneke "Transformative Adjudication in SA – Taking Stock" in G Glover & PC Osode (eds) *Law and Transformative Justice in Post-Apartheid South Africa* (2010) 21 23.

[157] 24.

[158] C Albertyn & B Goldblatt "Facing the Challenge of Transformation: Difficulties in the Development of an Indigenous Jurisprudence of Equality" (1998) 14 *SAJHR* 248 248-249.

[159] Moseneke (2002) *SAJHR* 315.

[160] Moseneke "Transformative Adjudication" in *Law and Transformative Justice* 31.

[161] Kruger & Govindjee (2011) *SAPL*.

argued that constitutions need to reserve room for their own development through the addition of new rights and through new interpretations being given to "old" rights.[162] According to De Villiers, there are various reasons which explain why this is necessary.[163] Firstly, societal circumstances change and the interpretation given to bills of rights must keep track of the needs and requirements of society. Secondly, the legal obligation of the state to take certain active steps to realise and respect fundamental individual rights is facilitated by a "living Constitution" which evolves so as to keep pace with changes in society. Thirdly, human rights philosophy acknowledges that fundamental rights have to adapt as more insight into human nature and the organisation of government is gained.[164]

The wording of section 74 of the Constitution implies that the drafters understood the need for careful amendment to any part of the constitutional text.[165] Section 74 specifically provides the criteria and requirements for constitutional amendment.[166] It is arguable that constitutional amendment is sometimes desirable in order to accommodate the developing needs and requirements of a society. It is submitted that the constitutional goal to "heal the divisions of the past and guide us to a better future", which according to Langa is the core idea of transformative constitutionalism, can also be achieved through refinement of the Constitution.[167]

That the Constitution has already been amended several times supports this submission, although some of the amendments have related merely to technical matters. The Constitution prescribes the attainment of strict majorities prior to amendment of sections 1 and 74 (75% of the National Assembly and the supporting vote of at least six provinces) as well as for the amendment of chapter 2, including the Bill of Rights (two thirds of the members of the National Assembly and the supporting vote of at least six provinces).[168] Given that employment-related matters have become a primary policy focus, introducing a new constitutional right giving recognition to this reality may be the best method of ensuring that current unemployment security initiatives are continued and improved in a sustainable fashion.

10 Concluding remarks

The problems still experienced by the majority of people living in South Africa are well known and undeniable. These problems include gross inequality and abject poverty, coupled with an unacceptably high rate of unemployment and issues regarding basic service delivery. A complex and interrelated range of factors have contributed to creating this harsh reality

---

[162] B de Villiers *The Protection of Social and Economic Rights: International Perspectives* Occasional Paper 9 Centre for Human Rights, University of Pretoria (1996) 3.

[163] 4.

[164] 4.

[165] On the unlikely existence of the basic structure doctrine existing in South Africa, see A Govindjee & R Kruger "A Question of Interpretation: A Comparative Study of 'Unenumerated' Rights Recognition in India and South Africa" forthcoming in (2011) *Journal of the ILS Law College.*

[166] Govindjee & Kruger (2011) *Journal of the ILS Law College.*

[167] P Langa "Transformative Constitutionalism" (2006) 17 *Stell LR* 351 352.

[168] Subs 74(1) and 74(2) of the Constitution.

and the country remains on the back foot regarding the constitutional promise of a society underpinned by the values of human dignity, the achievement of equality, and the advancement of human rights and freedoms.

There is general consensus that the constitutional promise of upliftment will remain unfulfilled as long as the living conditions which currently torment millions of residents in the country prevail.[169] It has repeatedly been mentioned that a life which is perpetually stuck in circumstances of squalor is an affront to human dignity.[170] On an international level, agencies such as the ILO and the World Health Organisation have also realised that unemployment and poverty are global crises, and have increasingly focused on the creation of a basic "social floor", comprising both social transfers and the provision of essential services, as a possible solution.

This approach resonates with the emerging South African experience. South Africa has, during the course of the last two decades or so, endeavoured to utilise its available resources in a manner which progressively establishes a comprehensive system of social security. This system is, to some extent, targeted towards those inhabitants who are the most vulnerable, and, importantly, is underpinned by a constitutional right which grants everyone the right to have access to social security, including appropriate social assistance for those people unable to support themselves and their dependants. As Justice Mokgoro noted in *Khosa v Minister of Social Development; Mahlaule v Minister of Social Development*:[171]

> "The right of access to social security, including social assistance for those unable to support themselves and their dependants is entrenched because as a society we value human beings and want to ensure that people are afforded their basic needs. A society must seek to ensure that the basic necessities of life are accessible to all if it is to be a society in which human dignity, freedom and equality are foundational."[172]

The Constitutional Court has yet to engage substantively with the scope and content of the right to social security and assistance entrenched in section 27(1)(c).[173] While the positive attributes of social transfers have been confirmed by evidence which suggests that social transfers are an effective tool to prevent and fight poverty, it has been argued that as a poverty-reduction strategy, this method is nearing the limits of its effectiveness, given fiscal constraints. This realisation of the financial limitations of a society reliant upon social grants has left a glaring gap in South Africa's social security system: the exclusion of the structurally or the long-term unemployed from social security coverage.

---

[169] See *Soobramoney v Minister of Health, KZN* 1998 1 SA 765 (CC) paras 8-9; M Pieterse "Coming to Terms with Judicial Enforcement of Socio-Economic Rights" (2004) 20 *SAJHR* 383 385.

[170] See, for example, K Kallmann "Towards a BIG Paradigm Shift: A Rights Based Approach to Poverty Alleviation" (undated) *Economic Policy Research Institute* 1 <http://www.epri.org.za/KarenKallmannFullPaper.pdf> (accessed 20-06-2010). See also *Soobramoney v Minister of Health, KZN* 1998 1 SA 765 (CC) para 8.

[171] 2004 6 SA 505 (CC).

[172] Para 52.

[173] S Liebenberg "The Judicial Enforcement of Social Security Rights in South Africa: Enhancing Accountability for the Basic Rights of the Poor" in EH Riedel (ed) *Social Security as a Human Right* (2006) 69 74.

In this contribution we address this particular gap from a constitutional perspective. Given the terminological distinction between "social security" and the broader notion of "social protection", the idea of "unemployment security" has been conceptualised in order for inadequacies in the current system to be better identified and addressed. For example, the UIF has proven to be an insufficient tool to address the plight of people who find themselves in a situation of long-term, structural unemployment. Proposals regarding the introduction of some form of unemployment continuation grant or unemployment assistance scheme may stall due to the large costs associated with the idea. It is also clear that not all of the components of unemployment security are directly covered by the section 27 constitutional right to have access to social security (or any other constitutional right), despite government having unambiguously promoted unemployment protection interventions (such as unemployment prevention and employment creation schemes) in terms of recent policy pronouncements. There is also no legislation in place which regulates matters such as employment creation or protection interventions, or the notion of decent work, directly. This results in policy innovations on such matters failing to be grounded in a proper legal framework. This, in turn, contributes to a range of resulting difficulties due to the disparity between current policy developments and the statutory scheme of laws. There is also the real potential for a successful constitutional challenge (on the part of a group of unemployed people in South Africa) against the current situation.

We argue that there are a number of potential advantages to legislating such matters, not least because this will result in unemployment security interventions enjoying the same legal status (and level of accountability) as other existing attempts to progressively realise matters of a socio-economic nature. This will, for example, also limit the potential of government (or a new government) being able to back-track from the progress made to date in this regard. Going even further, it is suggested that there are few grounds for failing to constitutionalise a new right relating specifically and directly to unemployment security and work. The Committee for Economic Social and Cultural Rights has emphasised both the social and economic dimensions of the right to work. Work is viewed as a "good' activity in itself – and not merely as something which might just as well be substituted by income support in the form of a social grant.[174] In fact, it is precisely because of the inability of the social security system to provide for any form of "unemployment assistance" that the claim for a right to have access to work deserves heightened consideration. Such a right could be read into the Constitution as an example of a self-standing unenumerated right; alternatively some form of the right could be read into the Constitution *via* an expanded interpretation of, for example, the rights to dignity, life, fair labour practices, equality, or access to social security. It is suggested that directly constitutionalising such a right would be the ultimate expression of the notion of transformative constitutionalism and should result in a principled basis for the introduction of legislative and policy

---

[174] Mundlak (2007) *ILR* 364.

developments aimed at achieving poverty alleviation through minimising unemployment insecurity.

SUMMARY

The endemic problem of unemployment poses a serious challenge to the realisation of South Africa's constitutional goals and values. One of the most glaring gaps in the assistance provided to the unemployed in South Africa is the exclusion of the long-term unemployed from any income-replacement measures. While the state's focus, when it comes to people of working age, is on job creation (rather than extending the range of social grant recipients), policy interventions to reduce unemployment tend to operate largely in the absence of a proper legal framework. For example, there is no designated right to work in the Bill of Rights. No legislation deals specifically with employment creation initiatives and few court cases have considered this issue. In the absence of a right to work, there is a real possibility of a successful constitutional challenge to the current situation. Although we acknowledge indirect ways to give constitutional recognition to such a right, we favour a more direct approach in the form of the insertion in the Constitution of a limited, qualified right to unemployment security, including the right of access to employment opportunities and work. This would allow the state to limit an unemployed person's right to social assistance – the root of a potential constitutional challenge – on the basis that the state is striving, within its available resources, to progressively take reasonable legislative and other measures to create employment opportunities. In the absence of such an explicit right, the state may find it very difficult to use its attempts to create more jobs as a justification for its failure to pay social grants to the entire uncovered adult population. Significantly, constitutionalising such a right would embody transformative constitutionalism. We argue that the Constitution should be the starting point in the quest for meaningful social change. A new constitutional right would result in a principled basis for the introduction of legislative and policy measures aimed at defusing the time bomb of long-term unemployment and endemic poverty.

CHAPTER 19

PRIVATISATION OF THE COMMONS: WATER AS A RIGHT; WATER AS A COMMODITY

Khulekani Moyo[*]

1 Introduction

Access to safe water is necessary to sustain human life and indispensable to ensure a healthy and dignified life.[1] Furthermore, lack of access to water has been considered as one of the greatest obstacles to development. The linkage between poverty and water shortage is well established. Those who do not have access to sufficient water are geographically located in the poorer areas of the developing world.[2]

A 2010 joint World Health Organisation ("WHO") and United Nations Children's Fund's Joint Monitoring Programme report indicate that more than one in six people worldwide or 894 million people do not currently have access to safe water for domestic use.[3] The report further estimates that globally 88% of diarrhoeal deaths are due to inadequate availability of water for hygienic purposes.[4] The United Nations ("UN") Human Rights Council, in a key resolution, expressed its alarm that "approximately 1.5 million children under 5 years of age die and 443 million school days are lost every year as a result of water-related diseases".[5] The 2009 UN World Water Report points out that in sub-Saharan Africa, the percentage of the population living in absolute poverty is essentially the same as it was 25 years ago. The report further states that a staggering 340 million Africans lack access to safe drinking water.[6] A watershed resolution of the UN General Assembly adopted in 2010 on the right to water and sanitation, graphically illustrates the dire magnitude of the global water crisis.[7] This dire situation prompted the then Vice President of the World Bank, Ismail Serageldin to warn in 1995 that "if the wars of

---

[*] I would like to thank my LLD supervisor, Professor Sandra Liebenberg for commenting on earlier drafts of this chapter which forms part of my LLD thesis entitled "Water as a Human Right under International Human Rights Law: Implications for the Privatisation of Water Services". I would also like to express my appreciation to the two anonymous reviewers for their valuable comments.

[1] T Kiefer & V Roaf "The Human Right to Water and Sanitation-Benefits and Limitations" in M Mancisidor (ed) *The Human Right to Water: Current Situation and Future Challenges* (2005) 1 4.

[2] SMA Salman & S McInerny-Lankford *The Human Right to Water: Legal and Policy Dimensions* (2004) vii.

[3] See World Health Organisation *Progress on Sanitation and Drinking Water* (2010) 7 <http://www.who.int/water_sanitation_health/publications/9789241563956en/index.html> (accessed 06-03-2010).

[4] 7.

[5] See preamble to the UN Human Rights Council *Human Rights and Access to Safe Drinking Water and Sanitation* (2010) UN Doc A/HRC/15/L.14 para 6.

[6] World Water Assessment Programme *The United Nations World Water Development Report 3: Water in a Changing World* (2009) xii <http://www.unesco.org/water/wwap/wwdr/wwdr3/> (accessed 23-09-2010).

[7] See preamble to the UN General Assembly *The Human Right to Water and Sanitation* (2010) UN Doc A/64/L.63/Rev.1 and Add.1 para 4.

[the 20th] century were fought over oil, the wars of the [21st] century will be fought over water – unless we change our approach to managing this precious and vital resource".[8]

The global water crisis has become so urgent an issue that it has been put on top of the UN agenda, and is "generating debate that has been both extensive and complex".[9] The international community also expressed its determination to combat the water crisis at the global level by including it in the eight Millennium Development Goals ("MDGs").[10]

2 Global response to the water crisis

The global water crisis resulted in calls for the treatment of water as an economic good. This is predicated on the argument that water is increasingly a scarce resource which must be priced at full economic cost to facilitate access to water to those who currently lack access.[11] This saw the World Bank, the International Monetary Fund and regional development banks vigorously pushing for privatisation of water supply services. These institutions promoted the involvement of multinational water corporations as the panacea for the global water crisis.

The conception of water as an economic good also stimulated the lobby for the explicit recognition of water as a human right. Human rights practitioners argued that water is a basic need, a human right, and a public good; and its commodification[12] would lead to lack of access, especially by poor and vulnerable members of society.[13]

In the first part of this chapter we discuss the legal basis for a right to water under international human rights law. We proceed to analyse the various international human rights instruments in which the right to water has been recognised. We also analyse and evaluate the scope and content of the right to water under international human rights law. In the second part we explore the rise of privatisation as a political-economic concept and increased private sector participation in the water supply sector. We focus particularly on increased participation by non-state actors in the water services sector. This will be followed by an analysis of the nature of the obligations that the right to water imposes on states in the event of privatisation of water services. In the final section we focus on a human rights analysis of privatisation, paying particular attention to the importance of adopting independent regulatory and monitoring mechanisms.

---

[8] See V Shiva *Privatisation, Pollution and Profit* (2002) ix.

[9] Salman & McInerny-Lankford *The Human Right to Water: Legal and Policy Dimensions* vii.

[10] See United Nations *United Nations Millennium Declaration* (2000) UN Doc A/55/L.2 para 19.

[11] World Bank *The State in a Changing World: World Development Report* (1997) 64.

[12] Commodification is the process of converting a good or service formerly subject to many non-market social rules into one that is primarily subject to market rules.

[13] Shiva *Privatisation* ix.

3   Legal basis and scope of the right to water under international law

The Universal Declaration of Human Rights ("UDHR") does not expressly mention a human right to water.[14] Neither do the two major international human rights treaties – the International Covenant on Civil and Political Rights ("ICCPR")[15] and the International Covenant on Economic, Social and Cultural Rights ("ICESCR")[16] – explicitly refer to a right to water. The only explicit references to a right to water are contained in the Convention on the Elimination of All forms of Discrimination Against Women ("CEDAW"),[17] the Convention on the Rights of the Child ("CRC"),[18] and the International Convention on the Protection and Promotion of the Dignity and Rights of Persons with Disabilities (the "Disability Convention").[19] The following section discusses and analyses the legal basis for the right to water under international law.

3 1   International human rights treaties

Some authors had long argued that a human right to water is implicit in the provisions of the International Bill of Rights[20] as a derivative right.[21] These include the rights to an adequate standard of living, food, health and life. The argument is that the fulfilment of these rights is impossible without water.[22] The right to water has therefore been derived from the explicit rights to health and an adequate standard of living contained in the ICESCR. This is because the provision of safe and adequate water is necessary for the full realisation of such rights.[23] This section will examine whether a universal human right to water can be derived from international human rights law. The analysis will focus on the provisions of the ICESCR, CEDAW, CRC and the Disability Convention.

3 2   International Covenant on Economic, Social and Cultural Rights

Article 11(1) of the ICESCR, provides:

"The States Parties to the present Covenant recognise the right of everyone to an adequate standard of living for himself and his family, including adequate food, clothing and housing and to the continuous improvement of living conditions."

---

[14]   Universal Declaration of Human Rights (1948) UN Doc A/810.

[15]   International Covenant on Civil and Political Rights (1966) UN Doc A/6316.

[16]   International Covenant on Economic, Social and Cultural Rights (1966) UN Doc A/6316.

[17]   Convention on the Elimination of All Forms of Discrimination Against Women (1979) UN Doc A/34/46.

[18]   Convention on the Rights of the Child (1989) UN Doc A/44/49.

[19]   International Convention on the Protection and Promotion of the Rights of Persons with Disabilities (2006) UN Doc A/61/49.

[20]   The International Bill of Human Rights is the collective term for the UDHR, the ICESCR and its Optional Protocol, and the ICCPR and its two Optional Protocols.

[21]   See S McCaffrey "A Human Right to Water: Domestic and International Implications" (1992) 5 *Geo Int'l Envtl L Rev* 1 8-10.

[22]   M McFarland Sanchez-Moreno & S Higgins "No Recourse: Transnational Corporations and the Protection of Economic, Social and Cultural Rights in Bolivia" (2003) 27 *Fordham Int'l LJ* 1663 1726-1728.

[23]   P Gleick "Human Right to Water" (1998) 1 *Water Policy* 487 492.

The Committee on Economic, Social and Cultural Rights ("CESCR") sets forth in General Comment 15 its criteria for deriving the right to water from other related rights by stating that

"[a]rticle 11, paragraph 1, of the Covenant specifies a number of rights emanating from, and indispensable for, the realisation of the right to an adequate standard of living, including adequate food, clothing and housing ... The right to water clearly falls within the category of guarantees essential for securing an adequate standard of living, particularly since it is one of the most fundamental conditions for survival."[24]

It may be questioned why the drafters of the ICESCR did not explicitly mention access to water in article 11(1) while arguably less fundamental elements of an adequate standard of living such as adequate clothing and housing are explicitly referred to. The inference of the right to water from article 11(1) has provoked criticism from some scholars.[25] Stephen Tully, for instance, has argued that article 11(1) offered no interpretive space for the reading of new rights given the seemingly endless list of other rights that could be added.[26]

The overwhelming literature is supportive of such a stance of deriving the right to water from article 11 of the ICESCR.[27] The main explanation for the omission seems to be that fresh water was not the scarce and competed-for resource it is today at the time the ICESCR was drafted.[28] This position is supported by Langford in his ensuing debate with Tully.[29] The use of the word "including" makes clear that the enumeration of adequate food, clothing and housing was not intended to be exhaustive, but rather serves as an indication of constituent elements of an adequate standard of living.

There is no doubt that access to a basic supply of safe and adequate water is a *conditio sine qua non* for the sustenance of human life itself. Keifer & Brölmann, for instance, argue that water must be "considered as a fundamental precondition for the realisation of an adequate standard of living".[30] The two authors put the issue succinctly, arguing that the recognition of the right to an adequate standard of living necessarily encompasses the right to access essential freshwater supplies.[31]

The right to water has also been inferred from the right to health. Article 12(1) of the ICESCR recognises the right of everyone to the enjoyment of

---

[24] See UN Committee on Economic, Social and Cultural Rights *General Comment No 15: Right to Water* (2002) UN Doc E/C.12/2002/11 para 3.

[25] See S Tully "A Human Right to Access Water? A Critique of General Comment No 15" (2008) 26 *NQHR* 35 63. Two American lawyers have also criticised the derivation of the right to water from the provisions of the ICESCR, see M Dennis & D Stewart "Justiciability of Economic, Social and Cultural Rights: Should There be an International Claims Mechanism to Adjudicate the Rights to Food, Water and Health?" (2004) 98 *Am J Int'l L* 462 477-489.

[26] See Tully (2008) *NQHR* 35.

[27] See generally McCaffrey (1992) *Geo Int'l Envtl L Rev* 1; Gleick (1999) *Water Policy* 478. See also T Keifer & C Brölmann "Beyond State Sovereignty: The Human Right to Water" (2005) 5 *NSAIL* 183 208.

[28] See Keifer & Brölmann (2005) *NSAIL* 195.

[29] Tully (2008) *NQHR* 35-36; M Langford "Ambition that Overleaps Itself? A Response to Stephen Tully's Critique of the General Comment on the Right to Water" (2006) 24 *NQHR* 434 459; S Tully "Flighty Purposes and Deeds: A Rejoinder to Malcolm Langford" (2006) 24 *NQHR* 461 472; M Langford "Expectation of Plenty: Response to Stephen Tully" (2006) 24 *NQHR* 473 479.

[30] Keifer & Brölmann (2005) *NSAIL* 195.

[31] 195.

the highest attainable standard of physical and mental health. The CESCR also derived a right to water from the above provision, stating that "[t]he right to water is also inextricably related to the right to the highest attainable standard of health".[32] The CESCR further stated in General Comment 14, in its interpretation of the right to health in article 12(1) of the ICESCR, that the latter is not limited to a right to health-care services only. Rather, the right to health embraces such socio-economic factors that facilitate conditions in which people can lead a healthy life, such as access to safe and potable water.[33] This interpretation by the CESCR is persuasive in light of the strong causal link between inadequate freshwater supplies and ill-health or even death, highlighted in the opening section of this chapter. A purposive and teleological interpretation of article 12(1) of the ICESCR as done by the CESCR strongly endorses the argument that the right to health extends to the right of access to water. This is because safe water is perhaps the most fundamental underlying determinant of health.

The right to water has also been derived from the right to housing. The CESCR in General Comment 15 articulated the right to water as inextricably related to the right to adequate housing contained in article 11(1) of the ICESCR. Earlier on the CESCR had adopted the same interpretative stance in its General Comment 4.[34] The CESCR has interpreted the right to adequate housing in article 11(1) of the ICESCR to encompass access to safe drinking water.[35] The ICESCR provides in article 11(1) and (2) for the right of everyone to adequate food.[36] The CESCR has interpreted this provision by implying a right to water as a component of the right to food. It stated that "[t]he right to water is also inextricably related to the right ... to adequate food".[37]

The only explicit references to the right to water under the contemporary universal human rights instruments are in the CEDAW, CRC, and the Disability Convention. However, it must be conceded that none of these international instruments are meant to guarantee universal human rights. This is because these instruments are limited *ratione personae* since they target specific groups in society, namely, women, children and the disabled persons respectively.[38] The significance of these instruments lies in the fact that they explicitly provide for a right to water. The CEDAW explicitly refers to the right to water for rural women. It obliges state parties to cater for the specific

---

[32]   UN Committee on Economic, Social and Cultural Rights *General Comment No 15* para 3.
[33]   See UN Committee on Economic, Social and Cultural Rights *General Comment No 14: The Highest Attainable Standard of Health* (2000) UN Doc HRI/GEN/1/Rev.6 para 43(c).
[34]   See UN Committee on Economic, Social and Cultural Rights *General Comment No 4: Right to Adequate Housing* (1991) UN Doc HRI/GEN/1/Rev.6 para 8(b).
[35]   Para 8(b).
[36]   Art 11(1) and (2) of the ICESCR provides:
       "The States Parties to the present Covenant recognise the right of everyone to an adequate standard of living for himself and his family, including adequate food ... [and] recognising the fundamental right of everyone to be free from hunger."
[37]   UN Committee on Economic, Social and Cultural Rights *General Comment No 4* para 8(b).
[38]   See W Schreiber "Realising the Right to Water in International Investment Law: An Interdisciplinary Approach to BIT Obligations" (2008) 48 *Nat Resources J* 431 440.

needs of rural women and to ensure them the "the right to enjoy adequate living conditions, particularly in relation to ... water supply".[39]

The CRC is the most widely ratified universal human rights treaty.[40] Article 24(2)(c) of the CRC provides for the right of every child to clean drinking water.[41] Furthermore, article 27(1) recognises the right of every child to an adequate standard of living. The latter provision has been consistently interpreted by the Committee on the Rights of the Child to include access to clean drinking water.[42] Additionally, article 28 of the Disability Convention enjoins states to ensure disabled people and their families an adequate standard of living, similar to article 25 of the UDHR and article 11(1) of the ICESCR. As discussed above, the right to water has been derived from these provisions. Additionally, the Disability Convention explicitly provides for the right of equal access by persons with disabilities to clean water.[43] Article 28(2)(a) obliges states to "ensure equal access by persons with disabilities to clean water services, and to ensure access to appropriate and affordable services". The following section discusses the obligations that the right imposes on states.

3 3 Obligations imposed by the right to water

States have general, specific and core obligations in relation to the right to water.[44] The CESCR classifies the obligations imposed on states by the right to water into a threefold typology. These are the obligations to respect, protect and fulfil the right to water.[45] The obligation to promote is subsumed under the duty to fulfil in the General Comments of the CESCR.[46] The duty to respect enjoins the state to ensure that the activities of its institutions do not interfere with people's access to water.[47] The duty to protect imposes on states an obligation to take measures to prevent third parties from interfering with enjoyment of the right to water. Furthermore, the duty to protect arguably requires states to prevent third parties, when they control or operate water services, from compromising equal, affordable and physical access to sufficient, safe and acceptable water.[48] This duty is of cardinal significance in the light of privatisation of water services, as will be discussed below. This is because international human rights law has not sufficiently developed to address the accountability of private providers for impinging the right to water and the availability of adequate remedies against such entities. The

---

[39] See art 14(2)(h) of CEDAW.
[40] The US and Somalia are the only countries that have not ratified the CRC.
[41] See art 24(1), and (2)(c) and (e), of the CRC.
[42] See, for example, UN Committee on the Rights of the Child *Concluding Observations of the Committee on the Rights of the Child on Ethiopia* (2006) UN Doc CRC/C/ETH/CO/3 para 61.
[43] Art 28 of the Disability Convention guarantees the rights to an adequate standard of living and social protection for persons with disabilities.
[44] See R Pejan "The Right to Water: The Road to Justiciability" (2004) 36 *Geo Wash Int'l L Rev* 1181 1186. See also M Williams "Privatisation and the Human Right to Water: Challenges for the New Century" (2007) 28 *Mich J Int'l L* 467 486-488.
[45] UN Committee on Economic, Social and Cultural Rights *General Comment No 15* paras 20-29.
[46] Para 25.
[47] Williams (2007) *Mich J Int'l L* 486-488.
[48] Salman & McInerney-Lankford *The Human Right to Water: Legal and Policy Dimensions* 68.

duty to fulfil requires states to facilitate people's enjoyment of the right to water.[49] The question arises also in respect of this obligation in light of water privatisation, as a right-holder is invariably entitled to the realisation of her right to water notwithstanding public or private provision. This inevitably raises the question of enforcing the positive obligations against private entities involved in the provision of water services. There is an imperative need for conceptual development in this area. This would entail imposing direct obligations on private water operators to provide minimum amounts of water for personal and domestic uses in respect of those sections of the community who cannot afford it. This issue will be fully canvassed in the final section of this chapter where I discuss a privatisation model that is responsive to water as an internationally recognised human right.

General Comment 15 defines the right to water as requiring water to be accessible, affordable, safe, adequate for a life of dignity, and to be provided without discrimination.[50] Furthermore, General Comment 15 also establishes a strong presumption against retrogressive measures taken in connection with the right to water. However, this prohibition is qualified by stating that any party that deliberately resorts to retrogressive measures has a burden of justifying such measures "by the totality of the rights in the Covenant in the context of the full use of the State party's maximum available resources".[51]

States have, however, immediate obligations in relation to the right to water. These include the guarantee of non-discrimination in respect of the right to water, and the guarantee to take steps towards the full realisation of the right.[52] Such steps must be "deliberate, concrete and targeted towards full realisation of the right".[53]

The right to water imposes an overarching obligation on the state to ensure that access to adequate water is realised on a progressive basis if resource constraints are such that the right cannot be realised immediately.[54] This, according to the CESCR, is a flexibility device in light of the difficulties in ensuring full realisation of economic, social and cultural rights.[55] Progressive realisation of the right to water, however, does not alter the obligations of the state to marshal its resources in an expeditious manner towards the full realisation of the right.[56]

---

[49] UN Committee on Economic, Social and Cultural Rights *General Comment No 15* paras 25-29.

[50] Paras 11-12.

[51] Para 19.

[52] Para 17.

[53] Para 17. States also have core obligations in respect of the right to water. These include ensuring access to the minimum essential amount of water that is sufficient and safe for personal and domestic uses to prevent disease; ensuring the right of access to water and water facilities and services on a non-discriminatory basis, especially for disadvantaged and marginalised groups, ensuring physical access to water facilities within a reasonable distance from the household and with very little waiting period, ensuring equitable distribution of all available water facilities and services and most significantly, monitoring the extent of the realisation or non-realisation of the right. See UN Committee on Economic, Social and Cultural Rights *General Comment No 15* para 37.

[54] See UN Committee on Economic, Social and Cultural Rights *General Comment No 3: The Nature of State Parties' Obligations* (1991) UN Doc E/1991/23 para 9.

[55] Para 9.

[56] Para 9.

The above approach of deriving the right to water from related rights is in harmony with the purposes and values underlying human rights. Human rights constitute a mechanism to protect and advance certain values.[57] The above approach is also an endorsement that economic, social and cultural rights, such as the right to water, are a significant normative component of the International Bill of Rights.[58] Such a development is timely in light of the schism that had been created by the adoption of two distinct human rights instruments, the ICCPR and the ICECSR. This resulted in civil and political rights attracting much attention and recognition in theory and practice, whereas economic, social and cultural rights were often relegated to the periphery.[59] The recognition of the right to water under international human rights law should therefore be seen in light of the importance that is being attached to socio-economic rights. Most recently, in 2008 the UN General Assembly adopted the Optional Protocol to the ICESCR[60] which establishes an individual complaints mechanism for violations of economic, social and cultural rights.[61] At the domestic level, the Constitution of the Republic of South African, 1996 (the "South African Constitution"), as well as the 2010 Kenyan Constitution ("the Kenyan Constitution")[62] enshrines an assortment of justiciable socio-economic rights in their bills of rights, including the right to water.[63]

The full realisation of all human rights, including the right to water, therefore requires an understanding of the symbiotic relationship between all human rights. This is because human rights are deeply interconnected and cannot be realised in an isolated manner. Conceiving of human rights in this way works as a bulwark against an atomised and fragmented conception of human rights. Such an approach is in accordance with the interdependence and indivisibility of all human rights. The following section will discuss the rise of water privatisation as an alternative response to the global water crisis, as well as the ensuing debates.

---

[57] J Donelly *Human Rights and Dignity* (2009) 13, paper presented in June 2009 at the Geneva Academy of International Humanitarian Law and Human Rights in the framework of the Swiss Initiative to commemorate the 60th Anniversary of the Universal Declaration of Human Rights <www.udhr60.ch/report/donnelly-HumanDignity_0609.pdf> (accessed 09-02-2011).

[58] See M Scheinin "Economic and Social Rights as Legal Rights" in A Eide, C Krause & A Rosas (eds) *Economic, Social and Cultural Rights: A Textbook* (2001) 1 3.

[59] 3.

[60] Optional Protocol to the International Covenant on Economic, Social and Cultural Rights (2008) UN Doc A/RES/63/117.

[61] See generally L Chenwi "An Appraisal of International Law Mechanisms for Litigating Socio-Economic Rights, with a Particular Focus on the Optional Protocol to the International Covenant on Economic, Social and Cultural Rights and the African Commission and Court" in S Liebenberg & G Quinot (eds) *Law and Poverty* (2012) 241, where she discusses the Optional Protocol among other mechanisms for litigating economic, social and cultural rights at the international level.

[62] Constitution of the Republic of Kenya, 2010.

[63] The South African Constitution provides in s 27(1)(b) that "[e]veryone has the right to have access to sufficient ... water". The Kenyan Constitution provides in art 43(1)(d) for the right of every person to clean and safe water in adequate quantities.

4   Privatisation of water services

Privatisation has seen a move away from service provision by the state in key sectors, such as water provision, towards a fragmented model of provision and contracting out the responsibility to non-state actors. The privatisation, liberalisation and deregulation engendered by neoliberalism[64] are principally aimed at reducing the role of the state in economic and social systems. This has resulted in a shift from public management of water services to private management. The state is increasingly arrogated only the responsibility for setting down the framework within which non-state actors operate. Such a framework departs radically from what before was a focus on significant state control in the production, management and supply of water services.

Privatisation as a concept is mired in definitional uncertainty.[65] This is because private sector participation has taken a variety of forms. In some instances, privatisation represents state withdrawal from a field of activity or from responsibility for providing services, as for example when a public entity sells off a state-owned entity to a private entity.[66] The other, more common model of privatisation is when the state engages private entities to provide services to the public on the state's behalf. This form of privatisation is normally characterised by government agencies giving private entities significant control over and responsibility for the provision of basic services ordinarily provided by the state.[67]

Martin, for instance, suggested privatisation as entailing "a change in the role, responsibilities, priorities and authority of the state", rather than simply a change of ownership.[68] Such a definition will not only encompass divestiture (a complete transfer of hitherto publicly owned assets from state ownership to private ownership), but would also encompass an understanding of privatisation in which the state remains the primary service provider and producer. It also incorporates a more entrepreneurial approach, including market-stimulating decision-making techniques.[69] This may be through the adoption of market principles such as full-cost recovery.[70] This broad understanding is consistent with viewing concepts such as public-private partnerships as forms of privatisation. This chapter will adopt the latter expansive understanding of privatisation.

---

[64]   This chapter will adopt David Harvey's definition of neoliberalism as entailing a theory of political economic practices that proposes that human well-being can best be advanced by liberating individual entrepreneurial freedoms and skills within an institutional framework characterised by strong private property rights, free markets and free trade. The role of the state is to create and preserve an institutional framework appropriate to such practices. See D Harvey *A Brief History of Neoliberalism* (2005) 2.

[65]   See L Lundqvist "Privatisation: Towards a Concept for Comparative Policy Analysis" (1988) 8 *J Publ Pol* 1 1.

[66]   With this form of privatisation, which is to be found in England and Wales, publicly operated monopolies are transferred as a whole to a private enterprise-oriented provider. In England and Wales ten water service companies were created in this manner and their shares were sold on the stock exchange.

[67]   E Metzger "Privatisation as Delegation" (2003) 103 *Columbia LR* 1367 1370-1371.

[68]   DA Heald "Privatisation: Analysing its Appeal and Limitations" (1984) 5 *Fiscal Studies* 36 46.

[69]   K Bakker "From State to Market? Water Mercantilism in Spain" (2002) 34 *Environment & Planning A* 767 770.

[70]   770.

Although non-state actor involvement in the provision of water services has a long history, the defining point for the most recent privatisation wave in developed countries can be traced to the 1980s. This was embraced by many developing countries during the 1990s.[71] Privatisation of water services in developing countries should be understood in the context of policies of international financial institutions ("IFIs") and donor agencies. IFIs have particularly promoted a neo-liberal paradigm advocating for states to reduce public spending, including in the provision of water services. Some of the reforms leading to widespread privatisation have been imposed through loan or aid conditions conditionalities, debt reprogramming or loan forgiveness.[72]

The 1992 International Conference on Water and the Environment adopted what became known as the "Dublin Statement".[73] The Dublin Statement argued that water needed to be construed as an economic good in order to realise its optimal value. Although not legally binding, it became an extremely important tool in the conceptualisation of water as an economic good. Principle 4 in particular provides:

"Water has an economic value in all its competing uses and should be recognised as an economic good ... Managing water as an economic good is an important way of achieving efficient and equitable use."[74]

The World Bank adopted the economic good model of the Dublin Statement as its guiding principle.[75] It introduced the principle of full cost recovery – a corollary of applying the economic good model – as preconditions conditionality for loans in the water sector, especially in the developing world.[76] For instance, in 1997, the IMF, the World Bank and the Inter-American Development Bank demanded the privatisation of Bolivia's water utility, the Municipal Drinking Water and Sewage Service of Cochabamba ("SEMAPA") as a condition for debt renegotiation and forgiveness.[77] Bolivia complied with these structural adjustment conditions conditionalities by forging ahead with

---

[71] See C de Albuquerque *Report of the UN Independent Expert on the Issue of Human Rights Obligations Related to Access to Safe Drinking Water and Sanitation* (2010) UN Doc A/HRC/15/31 para 6 <http://daccess-dds-ny.un.org/doc/UNDOC/GE.pdf> (accessed 04-04-2010).

[72] Para 9.

[73] In 1992, the World Meteorological Organisation held an International Conference on Water and Environment in Dublin and the result was the Dublin Statement articulating various principles on water resources management which was commended to the world leaders participating at the UN Conference on Environment and Development in Rio de Janeiro. See Conference Participants of the International Conference of Water and the Environment *The Dublin Statement on Water and Sustainable Development* (1992) <http://www.gdrc.org/uem/water/dublin-statement.html> (accessed 03-04-2010).

[74] Principle 4.

[75] S Grusky & M Fiil-Flynn *Will the World Bank Back Down? Water Privatisation in a Climate of Global Protest* (2004) 7.

[76] See P Bond "Water Commodification and Decommodification Narratives: Pricing and Policy Debates from Johannesburg to Kyoto to Cancun and Back" (2004) 15 *Capitalism Nature Socialism* 7 8.

[77] T Kruse & C Ramos "Water and Privatisation: Doubtful Benefits, Concrete Threats" *Social Watch Report: The Poor and the Market* (2003) 98 <http://www.socialwatch.org/node/10835> (accessed 17-06-2011).

the privatisation of SEMAPA.[78] In Tanzania, the country obtained funding for US$140 million from the World Bank, African Development Bank and European Investment Bank for a comprehensive programme to repair and extend Dar es Salaam's water and sewerage infrastructure. The funding was conditional on having a private operator replacing the public water provider.[79]

The principle of full cost recovery meant that the state or non-state supplier of water services should be able to recover the full costs of supplying water to all users.[80] The proposal to treat water as an economic good was predicated on the belief that treating it as such would, firstly, ensure access to water resources for all. Secondly, it would minimise inefficiencies through pricing techniques.[81] This entailed introducing the cost recovery principle within the tariff system and opening up the water sector for private sector involvement and foreign investment.[82]

The privatisation movement in the water sector has generated immense debate, linked to the status of water as a human right on one hand, and the characterisation of water as an economic good on the other.[83] Opponents of privatisation argue that water is a human right, a public good and not a commodity that can be bought and sold for profit[84] and incompatible with guaranteeing the right to water.[85] They also point out that privatisation's focus on full cost recovery ignores the need to protect the poor and enhance universality of access to water.[86] On the other hand, proponents of water privatisation argue that water is an economic good and a price should be charged for treating and supplying it.[87] They argue that the private sector

---

[78] E Peredo Beltrán *Water, Privatisation and Conflict: Women from the Cochabamba Valley* (2004) iv
<www.funsolon.org/publicaciones/peredowaterwomenboliviaeng.pdf> (accessed 16-06-2011). In 1997,
the World Bank provided Bolivia with US$ 20 million in technical assistance for regulatory reform and
privatisation, including preparation of laws and regulations for the financial, infrastructure and business
sectors. Some of this funding was earmarked for the Major Cities Water and Sewerage Rehabilitation
Project which aimed to provide full coverage to Santa Cruz, Cochabamba and La Paz in the most efficient
and sustainable manner. One of the bank's conditions for the extension of the loan was the privatisation
of the La Paz and Cochabamba water and sewerage utilities.

[79] See a discussion paper by J Perez, M Gistelinck & D Karbala *Sleeping Lions: International Investment
Treaties, State-Investor Disputes and Access to Food, Land and Water* Oxfam Discussion Paper (2011)
19-20 < http://www.oxfam.org/sites/www.oxfam.org/files/dp-sleeping-lions-260511-en.pdf > (accessed
08-06-2011).

[80] EB Bluemel "Implications of Formulating Human Right to Water" (2004) 31 *Ecology Law Quarterly* 957
964.

[81] 962.

[82] See Bond (2004) *Capitalism Nature Socialism* 8. For further discussion on the principle of cost recovery
within the water delivery and management sector, see also V Petrova "At the Frontiers of the Rush for
Blue Gold: Water Privatisation and the Human Right to Water" (2006) 31 *Brook J Int'l L* 557 578-580;
K Bakker "The 'Commons' Versus the 'Commodity': Alter-Globalization, Anti-Privatisation and the
Human Right to Water in the Global South" (2007) 39 *Antipode* 430 431.

[83] JW de Visser "Comparing Water Delivery in South Africa and the Netherlands" in JW de Visser & C
Mbazira (eds) *Water Delivery: Public or Private?* (2006) 29 29.

[84] Grusky & Fiil-Flynn *Will the World Bank Back Down?* 3.

[85] For an overview of the water anti-privatisation debate see Petrova (2006) *Brook J Int'l L* 578-580.

[86] Grusky & Fiil-Flynn *Will the World Bank Back Down?* 3.

[87] WL Megginson *The Financial Economics of Privatisation* (2005) 6 notes that the water industry is one
industry where privatisation, as well as increasing welfare, has been very ambiguous.

constitutes an obvious alternative for the delivery of services in the face of state failure to ensure universal access to safe water.[88]

Another position in the contestation argues for the recognition of water's economic good status as well as recognising its status as a basic human right. It advocates for the guarantee of universal access to safe water despite the involvement of non-state actors.[89] This group envisages private sector participation, with the state having regulatory oversight in order to protect the water's public nature.[90]

This group further points out that human rights do not envisage the state as the sole provider of basic services.[91] Rather, it is permissible within the human rights framework for private actors to be involved in the provision of human rights sensitive services such as water.[92] Reference is made to the pronouncements by treaty bodies on this issue. In General Comment 3, the CESCR has asserted that human rights law does not require a particular political or economic system within which human rights can best be realised.[93] Consequently, it is argued that private sector involvement in the provision of basic goods and services is not in conflict with human rights.[94]

The thrust of the argument is that privatisation of human rights sensitive services does not absolve the state of its human rights obligations in respect of the privatised services. This implies that, by privatising the provision of basic services and goods, the state remains responsible for ensuring the enjoyment by all people of the rights relevant to the privatised service.[95] Agreements with private service providers must therefore be structured by the relevant human rights norms.[96] The state has a duty to regulate and monitor the activities of private actors. Williams has pointed out that the state has a duty to monitor and regulate the activities of the private actor during the duration of the privatisation arrangement so that human rights are not imperilled.[97] The state's duty to protect is of utmost significance in the context of privatisation.[98] The CESCR, for instance, has elaborated this obligation to include the duty to prevent violations of these rights by private actors as well as to control and regulate them. In respect of the right to water, for example, the CESCR has stated that the state has an obligation to prevent third parties from "compromising equal, affordable, and physical access to sufficient, safe and acceptable water".[99] It appears that both proponents and opponents of water privatisation agree on the importance of monitoring and regulation in

---

[88] PD Lopes *Water Privatisation and the Human Right to Water* (2006) 6.
[89] 21.
[90] 22.
[91] DM Chirwa "Privatisation of Water in Southern Africa: A Human Rights Perspective" (2004) 4 *AHRLJ* 218 230.
[92] 230.
[93] UN Committee on Economic, Social and Cultural Rights *General Comment No 3* para 8.
[94] Chirwa (2004) *AHRLJ* 231.
[95] 231.
[96] 233.
[97] Williams (2007) *Mich J Int'l L* 501
[98] Chirwa (2004) *AHRLJ* 235.
[99] UN Committee on Economic, Social and Cultural Rights *General Comment No 15* para 24.

the event of privatisation.[100] It is argued that the state's obligation to protect and fulfil the right to water survives the privatisation arrangement. Consequently, a duty is imposed on the state to monitor and regulate the activities of private enterprises involved in the management and distribution of water services.[101] The following section discusses some of the regulatory challenges engendered by water privatisation.

5   Regulatory challenges

Water provision normally enjoys monopoly status because of the high costs involved in transporting bulky water products.[102] In other utilities such as telecommunications and electricity, monopoly power is gradually being eroded by technological innovation and the development of competitive substitutes.[103] Such a development is unlikely to occur to any significant extent in the water sector in the foreseeable future. Naturally, monopoly in the water services sector is likely to remain a long-term feature.[104] It is pertinent to note that the difficulties involved in protecting the public from private monopoly power abuses was one of the significant historical factors which led to the development of public water utilities in many countries.[105] This clearly calls for regulation of these private enterprises involved in the provision and management of water services. Opponents of privatisation have also pointed out the often weak regulatory institutions associated with privatisation. This is because private corporations often prefer regulatory discretion to be minimised and for the contract to be the major regulatory mechanism.[106]

Privatisation by states of their traditional domestic functions such as water provision has in some cases weakened regulation at national level, because of investor pressure and new international free trade rules and bilateral investment treaties.[107] This is further compounded by the sheer size and scale of some non-state actors involved in the human rights sensitive services such as the provision of water. Globalisation has led to the emergence of powerful non-state actors who have resources greater than those of many states.[108] Consequently, most of the private entities have outgrown the ability of individual states to regulate them effectively.[109] The sheer size and influence of some corporations is such that they are capable of determining

---

[100] Williams (2007) *Mich J Int'l L* 501. See also UN Committee on Economic, Social and Cultural Rights *General Comment No 15* para 24, which envisages an effective regulatory system to be established, providing for independent monitoring, genuine public participation and imposition of penalties for non-compliance with set rules where water services have been privatised.

[101] Williams (2007) *Mich J Int'l L* 501-502.

[102] JA Rees "Regulation and Private Participation in the Water and Sanitation Sector" (1998) 22 *Nat Resource Forum* 96 96.

[103] 96.

[104] 96-97.

[105] 97.

[106] 104.

[107] International Council on Human Rights Policy *Beyond Voluntarism: Human Rights and the Developing International Legal Obligations of Companies* (2002) 10.

[108] D Shelton "Protecting Human Rights in a Globalised World" (2002) 2 *BC Int'l & Comp LR* 273 273.

[109] International Council on Human Rights Policy *Beyond Voluntarism* 11.

national policies and priorities.[110] In some cases, weak states, especially in the developing world, are unable or unwilling to control their activities. Opponents of water privatisation particularly emphasise that the nature of multinational corporations in today's global economy also makes it more difficult for individual governments, especially those from developing countries, to regulate them and hold them to account. For instance, a recent study revealed that the largest private multinational corporations in the water sector are Suez (111 479 116 customers), Veolia Environment (130 924 000 customers), RWE AG (38 235 000 customers), Aguas de Barcelona (29 511 718 customers), Saur (12 999 000 customers), Acea (14 305 000 customers), Biwater PLC/Cascal (8 834 000 customers) and United Utilities (24 028 000 customers).[111] Such a development poses challenges to the international human rights movement, because for the most part, that law was designed to foreclose violations by states and state actors, and has not adequately developed to regulate the conduct of non-state actors.[112]

Of particular note is the lack of independence and expertise of regulatory bodies. This was buttressed by Nils Roseman's study of the Manila water privatisation in the Philippines. Roseman's study concluded that it was mainly the erroneous design of the privatisation process and the lack of political will to create a powerful regulatory agency that led to the partial failure of that privatisation scheme.[113] In South Africa, the local authority in Nelspruit did not have the capacity to effectively regulate the water concession contract, hence its failure.[114] Mcdonald and Ruiters further pointed out that in the Lukhanji, Amahlati and Nkokobe municipalities in the Eastern Cape, most of the councillors mandated to monitor and regulate the privatisation contracts lacked the requisite expertise to do so.[115] In the following section, I carry out a human rights analysis of water privatisation.

6   International human rights law and privatisation

International human rights instruments are neutral as regards the economic models of service provision. Consequently, it is permissible within the human rights framework for private entities to be involved in the provision of human rights sensitive services such as water, health and education. The CESCR clearly stated that the realisation of human rights obligations enshrined in the ICESCR prescribes no particular form of government or economic system "provided that it is democratic and all human rights are thereby respected".[116]

---

[110]   Shelton (2002) *BC Int'l & Comp LR* 273.
[111]   See Pinsent Masons "Pinsent Masons Water Yearbook 2009-2010" (2009) *Pinsent Masons* 222-223 <http://www.pinsentmasons.com/PDF/PMWaterYearbook2008-09.pdf> (accessed 20-08-2011).
[112]   Shelton (2002) *BC Int'l & Comp LR* 279.
[113]   N Rosemann (Friedrich Ebert Foundation) *The Human Right to Water under the Conditions of Trade Liberalisation and Privatisation: A Study on the Privatisation of Water Supply and Wastewater Disposal in Manila* (2003) 6 <http://library.fes.de/pdf-files/iez/01949.pdf> (accessed 27-06-2011).
[114]   DA McDonald & G Ruiters "Theorising Water Privatisation in Southern Africa" in DA McDonald & G Ruiters (eds) *The Age of Commodity: Water Privatisation in Southern Africa* (2005) 13 28.
[115]   160.
[116]   UN Committee on Economic, Social and Cultural Rights *General Comment No 3* para 8.

Privatisation *per se* does not relieve the state of its legal responsibility under international human rights law.[117] states are the primary duty bearers under the international human rights system. It necessarily follows that states do not relinquish their international human rights obligations by privatising the delivery of water services. A state should ensure that it continues to exercise adequate oversight in order to meet its obligation to realise the right to water when it engages non-state actors to manage and supply water services. The state's duty towards beneficiaries of the right from the breach of their right by such private entities becomes crucial. Should a water privatisation scheme leads to the violation of any of the constituent elements of a right to water discussed above, the state may be liable for failing to discharge its duty to protect.[118] For a state to effectively discharge its protective mandate particularly where water services have been privatised, it is important for it to put in place a regulatory and monitoring mechanism to monitor the performance of water services providers.[119]

Privatisation of water services necessarily raises the issue of accountability of both policymakers and private entities involved in the management or provision of water services. It is of utmost importance that privatisation policies entrench legal and administrative measures to guarantee democratic accountability, particularly by those affected by the privatisation of a particular service. Of great significance also, is the principle of participation.[120] International human rights law emphasises the need for policies to be conceived and implemented in a manner that enables popular participation.[121] All those affected by a privatisation policy, particularly the poor and the marginalised sections of the community, must be given the opportunity to participate and give input in key decisions directly or indirectly affecting their socio-economic rights. This consequently entails a right of access to sufficient, adequate and timely information pertaining to any proposed water privatisation process.[122] The following section discusses the importance of effective monitoring and evaluation in the context of water privatisation.

6 1   Towards effective monitoring and regulation of water services providers

One of the key issues raised in the cases of water privatisation in Tanzania, Bolivia and South Africa highlighted above was the paucity of effective monitoring and regulatory mechanisms to exercise oversight over the private providers. Chirwa has pointed out that the duty to regulate and monitor enjoins the state to take appropriate positive action to protect its citizens from

---

[117] W Vandenhole & T Wilders "Water as a Human Right – Water as an Essential Service: Does it Matter?" (2008) *NQHR* 391 409-410.

[118] See A Kok "Privatisation and the Right to Access to Water" in K Feyter & FG Isa (eds) *Privatisation and Human Rights in the Age of Globalisation* (2005) 259 268.

[119] 268.

[120] DM Chirwa "Water Privatisation and Socio-Economic Rights in South Africa" (2004) 8 *LDD* 185 185-186. See also, generally, S Tsemo "Privatisation of Basic Services, Democracy and Human Rights" (2003) 4 *ESR Review* 2.

[121] Chirwa (2004) *LDD* 185-186.

[122] 185-186.

potentially deleterious acts of private actors.[123] The CESCR has stated in General Comment 15 that the state has an obligation to prevent third parties from threatening access to equal, affordable, sufficient, safe and acceptable water.[124] The Maastricht Guidelines on Violations of Economic, Social and Cultural Rights (Maastricht Guidelines) enshrine a similar approach, providing that in the interpretation of economic, social and cultural rights, the state has a duty to ensure that private providers over which they exercise jurisdiction do not deprive individuals of their economic, social and cultural rights.[125] The Maastricht Guidelines further provide for the responsibility of states for any violations of economic, social and cultural rights that result from their neglect to exercise the necessary control on the behaviour of such non-state actors.[126] The state will only fulfil this duty to protect through the establishment of an effective regulatory system which provides for independent monitoring, genuine public participation and provision of appropriate relief to those negatively impacted by the acts of such non-state actors.[127] This means that states should establish regulation and control mechanisms, which include independent monitoring, genuine public participation and the provision of remedies for non-compliance.[128]

General Comment 15 makes it clear that in the event of privatisation, states must prevent such entities from "compromising equal, affordable, and physical access to sufficient, safe and acceptable water".[129] Furthermore, "arbitrary or unjustified disconnection from water services or facilities" and "discriminatory or unaffordable increases in the price of water" constitute *prima facie* violations of the states' obligation in respect of the realisation of the right to water.[130] Such safeguards are very significant for the protection of the human right to water in the event of involvement of non-state actors in the provision of water services. These independent monitoring mechanisms should ensure that the minimum international standards with regard to the right to water are maintained. The monitoring mechanism should also have the mandate to scrutinise privatisation contracts to ensure that their provisions and implementation do not encroach on the right to water by specifying that the private or public operator of water services will meet the minimum quantitative or qualitative levels of water provision.[131] Significantly, the monitoring mechanism should have in place a strict water tariff control to prevent the private entity from charging exorbitant water tariffs thereby impeding the economic accessibility of water.[132] It is also important that water services should be immune from disconnections where a water user is unable

[123]   Chirwa (2004) *AHRLJ* 235.
[124]   UN Committee on Economic, Social and Cultural Rights *General Comment No 15* para 24.
[125]   TC van Boven, C Flinterman & I Westendorp *The Maastricht Guidelines on Violations of Economic, Social and Cultural Rights* (1998) UN Doc E/C.12/2000/13 para 18.
[126]   Para 16.
[127]   UN Committee on Economic, Social and Cultural Rights *General Comment No 15* para 24.
[128]   Paras 23-24.
[129]   Para 24.
[130]   Para 44(a).
[131]   Kok "Privatisation" in *Privatisation and Human Rights* 271.
[132]   286.

to pay for the service. Kok has suggested that rather, the supplier should only be allowed to adopt measures necessary to limit an indigent beneficiary's supply to the minimum levels provided for under international law – or national law, if the national minimum standards are higher than the international minimum standards.[133] Another additional tier towards ensuring the realisation of the right to water in the event of privatisation is to explore the possibility of extending direct negative and positive human rights obligations on non-state actors involved in the provision of water services. This is discussed in the next section.

6 2   Direct human rights obligations on corporations?

Privatisation of hitherto publicly provided services also puts into question the public/private dichotomy. Liebenberg has critiqued the public/private dichotomy in the context of adjudicating socio-economic rights, noting that "both methodological and ideological considerations constrain the potentially transformative effect of socio-economic rights on private law rules and doctrines".[134] The weakening of the public/private partition is particularly necessary in the context of privatisation of water services, which has led to the involvement of non-state entities in the functions usually exercised by state organs.[135] Despite the fact that the development of other branches of international law such as international criminal law have focused attention on individual criminal responsibilities of non-state actors, the question of direct human rights obligations for non-state actors, particularly corporations, is still a nascent area – especially at the international level. The orthodox position is to omit private actors from the purview of international human rights law and holding states as constituting the proper addressees of international law. Private actors are deemed to fall within the rubric of domestic law. There is a growing concern that the enforcement of human rights imperatives set out in international human rights law is hindered by the lack of direct human rights obligations placed on non-state actors. This is more so when public functions are delegated to them by the state.[136]

John Ruggie, the Special Representative of the Secretary-General on the issue of human rights and transnational corporations and other business enterprises, recently proposed a new framework for dealing with non-state actors such as businesses, namely the Guiding Principles on Business and Human Rights: Implementing the United Nations "Protect, Respect and Remedy" Framework ("UN Guiding Principles").[137] The UN Guiding Principles are based on three

---

[133] 286-287.

[134] S Liebenberg *Socio-Economic Rights: Adjudication under a Transformative Constitution* (2010) 375.

[135] See G van Harten "The Public-Private Distinction in the International Arbitration of Individual Claims against the State" (2007) 56 *Int'l & Comp LQ* 371 394.

[136] A Mahinney *Harmonising Good Governance* (2002) 3.

[137] See J Ruggie *Report of the UN Special Representative of the Secretary-General on the Issue of Human Rights and Transnational Corporations and Other Business Enterprises – Guiding Principles on Business and Human Rights: Implementing the United Nations "Protect, Respect and Remedy" Framework* (2011) UN Doc A/HRC/17/31 <http://www.ohchr.org/Documents/Issues/Business/A-HRC-17-31_AEV> (accessed 05-04-2011). The UN Guiding Principles were officially endorsed by the UN Human Rights Council on 21-06-2011.

main principles, namely the state's duty to protect against human rights abuses by third parties, the corporate responsibility to respect human rights and the need for more effective access to remedies.[138] Although the UN Guiding Principles provide that international law firmly establishes that states have the duty to protect against human rights abuses by non-state actors within their jurisdiction, they seem to suggest that international law does not impose any direct duties on such entities to observe human rights norms. Instead corporations need only engage in "due diligence" to consider whether their business activities might contribute to the abuse of human rights.[139] The UN Guiding Principles thus use the term "responsibility" instead of "duty" or "obligation" in respect of non-state actors.

The above marks a significant departure from the Norms on the Responsibilities of Transnational Corporations and Other Business Enterprises with Regard to Human Rights ("Norms"), adopted by the UN Sub-Commission on the Promotion and Protection of Human Rights in 2003.[140] The Norms assert that, even though states have the primary responsibility to promote, protect, ensure the respect of, and ultimately fulfil human rights, transnational corporations and other business enterprises, as organs of society "within their respective spheres of activity and influence ... have the obligation to promote, secure the fulfilment of, respect, ensure respect of, and protect human rights recognised in international as well as national law".[141]

The distinction between state and non-state bodies for the purposes of determining the reach, or applicability, of human rights law becomes questionable and, it is suggested, requires adjustment in light of changing modes of governance.[142] The impact non-state actors have on the realisation of human rights through their business activities makes many of the underlying assumptions of the arguments against imposing human rights obligations on them hard to sustain. This is because arguments against extending human rights obligations to non-state actors are based on a "remarkably resilient model of a liberal market society characterised by a clear distinction between the public and private spheres".[143] In the case of water privatisation, this will provide another layer of protection in ensuring that water privatisation does not impede the realisation of the right to water.

7 Conclusion

Water is far too important to the well-being of humans to be treated solely as an economic good. Privatisation of water services to non-state actors has the potential to assist in the realisation of the right to water. The experience from the 1990s saw the acceleration in the privatisation of water services,

---

[138] Paras 11-14.

[139] Para 12.

[140] UN Sub-Commission on the Promotion and Protection of Human Rights *Norms on the Responsibilities of Transnational Corporations and Other Business Enterprises with Regard to Human Rights* (2003) UN Doc E/CN.4/Sub.2/2003/12/Rev.2.

[141] Para 1.

[142] Mahinney *Harmonising Good Governance* 3.

[143] PT Muchlinski "Human Rights and Multinationals: Is There a Problem?" (2001) 77 *Int'l Affairs* 31 36.

with both successful and dramatic failures. Less effort has been made to understand the risks and limitations of water privatisation, and to put in place safeguards to protect the marginalised from violation of their right to access water. Water is a human right and cannot be equitably protected by purely treating it as an economic good through the utilisation of markets for its distribution. Ownership of the water delivery systems, be it through public or private entities, should not compromise accessibility, availability, quality and acceptability of basic services.[144] Privatisation of water services should also not result in denial of access to vulnerable and poor people to socio-economic rights, hence independent monitoring and regulatory mechanisms must be put in place. There is also an urgent need for further research and development of an international process with the necessary normative force to directly impose binding human rights obligations on non-state actors, especially those involved in the provision of human rights sensitive services such as water. This is particularly relevant where states are unable or unwilling to protect human rights.

SUMMARY

In this contribution I seek to propose an accountability framework for states and non-state actors involved in the provision and management of water services. I contend that states have a legal obligation under international human rights law to fulfill, respect, protect and promote the human right to safe and sufficient water for personal and domestic uses. While acknowledging both the potentially deleterious and beneficial implications of privatisation of water services, I suggest two mutually reinforcing approaches to foreclose any breaches of the right. The first approach advocates for the strengthening of the state's duty to protect, in particular the putting in place of independent monitoring and regulatory mechanisms to ensure that the minimum conditions imposed by the right to water are not abridged. The difficulty of enforcing positive human rights obligations against non-state actors is now extant in literature. The second approach argues for a doctrinal progression towards the imposition of direct obligations on non-state actors engaged in the provision of water services, not only to not impede the realisation of the right to water but also a positive obligation to provide minimum amounts of water for personal and domestic uses, particularly in respect of poor and marginalised members of society.

---

[144] United Nations Office of the High Commissioner for Human Rights *Liberalisation and Human Rights* (2003) 197.

CHAPTER 20

TENSIONS BETWEEN VERNACULAR VALUES THAT PRIORITISE BASIC NEEDS AND STATE VERSIONS OF CUSTOMARY LAW THAT CONTRADICT THEM

"WE LOVE THESE FIELDS THAT FEED US, BUT NOT AT THE EXPENSE OF A PERSON"

Sindiso Mnisi Weeks

Aninka Claassens

1   Introduction

"A field is yours when it is yours ... no-one will come and take it from you. [But] when [residential] stands must be cut [from the fields], they are cut ... *These fields are very important to us; we love the food we get from them. But then we won't love them to the extent that we would jeopardise another human being.* We don't do that. As I'm saying that we are rural and indigenous (sisintfu) ... As rural, indigenous people, we agree with that [giving up our fields so that someone else can have a site on which to build a home]. We agree that a person is welcome, except a person who comes and does things that are not right."

These were the words of an elderly widow who sat on the Mbuzini Traditional Council, in Mpumalanga.[1] We were discussing the possible reallocation of fields (one of which was her own) in order to create additional residential sites for members of the community. She explained the principle that a field belongs to an individual and is secure in that sense, but that rights to fields are also subject to the more pressing needs of those who do not have land on which to establish a home. She described this as an intrinsic indigenous value, and one with which she agrees. As she saw it, the basis for the value was that "we want each person to live and we also want our lifestyle to continue". She felt that providing for people's basic needs is important enough that those with greater material security – that is, those who have homes and fields – would forgo a key source of their own livelihoods (fields) in order to help meet the basic needs of others to establish a home.

As we demonstrate below, she is not alone in her subscription to a relative concept of rights in land – this is a key aspect of vernacular land rights systems. This chapter therefore argues that legal "reforms" that fail to recognise and support the processes of social cohesion and mutual support

---

[1]   Interview conducted by Sindiso Mnisi Weeks on 12-09-2007 (on file with authors) (emphasis added).

that characterise vernacular systems are likely to have serious unintended consequences especially insofar as they distort power relations. Interventions that prop up unaccountable power fundamentally undermine the reciprocal relationships that are intrinsic to the proper functioning and expression of indigenous entitlements.

In this chapter we discuss recently passed laws such as the Traditional Leadership and Governance Framework Act 41 of 2003 that frustrate the realisation of the value of prioritising need. This is to the detriment of the socio-economic rights of people whose welfare the government is purporting to ensure by these laws. We argue that "rural development", "community empowerment" and socio-economic rights security are undermined by prioritising the powers of senior traditional leaders over those of ordinary rural people. Socio-economic rights security cannot be realised by top-down authority given to traditional leaders but by processes that operate democratically on the ground and give expression to the values that people hold to.

Based on literature that broadens the discourse on rights to reflect that in practice rights do not function primarily as boundaries of exclusion, it is possible to see how vernacular values that prioritise need could be instruments for realising socio-economic rights in rural areas. These theories speak to how the content of rights is defined by the contexts[2] in which they evolve and operate to facilitate people's autonomy by mediating the relationships on which people depend.[3] In other words, if rights are to have the same usefulness for people in vastly different situations,[4] they must be relevant to the contextual needs and relationships of those people.[5] The capacity and opportunities of rights users to participate in the processes in which rights are defined and distributed hereby also emerge as fundamental.[6]

While the arguments we make relate closely to the jurisprudence of "living customary law" emanating from the Constitutional Court, we choose to use the term "vernacular" rather than "indigenous" and "customary" law.[7] "Indigenous" suggests pre-colonial existence and seems to emphasise continuity through history, which we do not suggest is a necessary attribute

---

[2] See generally J Nedelsky "Reconceiving Rights as Relationship" (1993) 1 *Review of Constitutional Studies* 1; C Nyamu Musembi "Towards an Actor-Oriented Perspective on Human Rights" in N Kabeer (ed) *Inclusive Citizenship: Meanings and Expressions* (2005) 31; M Mamdani "The Social Basis of Constitutionalism in Africa" (1990) 28 *J Mod Afr Stud* 359.

[3] Nedelsky (1993) *Review of Constitutional Studies* 7-8.

[4] N Lacey *Feminist Legal Theory and the Rights of Women* (2003) 31, paper presented at a conference on *Citizenship, Borders and Gender: Mobility and Immobility* hosted by the Crossing Borders Initiative, Woodward Lecture Fund, Women Faculty Forum, Yale Centre for International and Area Studies and Yale Law School at Yale University, 05 2003 <http://www.yale.edu/wff/cbg/pdf/LaceyPaperFeministLegalTheory.pdf> (accessed 18-03-2010).

[5] Lacey *Feminist Legal Theory* 31; S Mnisi Weeks "'Take Your Rights Then and Sleep Outside, on the Street': Rights, Fora and the Significance of Rural South African Women's Choices" forthcoming in (2010) *Wis Int'l LJ*.

[6] Nedelsky (1993) *Review of Constitutional Studies* 4; A Claassens & S Mnisi Weeks "Rural Women Redefining Land Rights in the Context of Living Customary Law" (2009) 25 *SAJHR* 491 514.

[7] We adopt an inclusive approach to the concept of law that includes the interaction of "rules" and "processes" in non-state normative orders. For a comprehensive description of the relationship between rules and processes in vernacular legal systems, see J Comaroff & S Roberts *Rules and Processes: The Cultural Logic of Dispute in an African Context* (1981) ch 3.

of the norms of which we speak. Our preferred word "vernacular", when used in relation to law and its underlying values, carries a similar meaning to that which the term has in relation to language: namely, that it is emic, locally evolved and not imposed from the outside nor judged in terms of an external logic or scheme. This is unlike the word "customary", which has been tainted – especially as it is often associated with official forms of the law, rather than what is commonly coming to be known as "living customary law". The use of the term "living customary law" by the courts introduces further complexity, however, in that one can no longer be sure whether the reference is to that form of the living law that is articulated by the courts or that which continues to develop within the groupings that use vernacular law.

2 Relative property rights in vernacular settings

Studies of Mbuzini and other rural areas yield evidence of underlying similarities in the rules that govern the possession and reallocation of "communal" land.[8] These rules relate to weighing different entitlements and needs against each other, and prioritising accordingly.[9] Therefore, occupation (especially of residential land) would typically have first preference over use (such as farming an allocated field), which would, in turn, be preferred over mere access (such as for grazing or collecting grass and firewood).[10] Moreover, there are principles of consultation and/or consent that govern the process of reallocation so as to prevent unfair dispossession.[11] These latter principles implicitly recognise that multiple rights and interests in land often overlap.

Similar norms pertain to succession, in which many of the same issues arise in the context of distribution within the family, as opposed to between the family and the wider society. The rules governing inheritance of family property (usually land or a home) are guided by the same basic value as those applicable to land (re)allocation: the prioritisation of need. Likhapha Mbatha describes studies of two rural communities in the North West Province conducted by the Centre for Applied Legal Studies in the mid to late 1990s.[12] The research was completed before the rule of male primogeniture was declared unconstitutional in *Bhe v Magistrate, Khayelitsha; Shibi v Sithole*[13] in 2004. At the time, there were many accounts of how "customary heirs" (that is, male primogenitors) abused their legal rights and thus dispossessed other dependents – disadvantaging women and children, above all. Mbatha's report

---

[8] R Kingwill "Custom-Building Freehold Title: The Impact of Family Values on Historical Ownership in the Eastern Cape" in A Claassens & B Cousins (eds) *Land, Power and Custom: Controversies Generated by South Africa's Communal Land Rights Act* (2008) 184; B Cousins *Imithetho Yomhlaba YaseMsinga: The Living Law of Land in Msinga District, Kwa-Zulu Natal, PLAAS Research Report 43* (2011) <http://www.plaas.org.za/pubs/rr/RR%2043%20Msinga%20web%20FINAL.pdf> (accessed 20-10-2011); S Mnisi *The Interface Between Living Customary Law(s) of Succession and South African State Law* DPhil thesis Oxford (2010).

[9] C Cross "An Alternate Legality: The Property Rights Question in Relation to South African Land Reform" (1992) 8 *SAJHR* 305 315-318; Cousins *Imithetho Yomhlaba YaseMsinga* 33-35, 42.

[10] Cross (1992) *SAJHR* 305 315-318; Mnisi *Interface Between Living Customary Law(s) of Succession and SA State Law* 292-294.

[11] Mnisi *Interface Between Living Customary Law(s) of Succession and SA State Law* 293-294.

[12] L Mbatha "Reforming the Customary Law of Succession" (2002) 18 *SAJHR* 259.

[13] 2005 1 SA 580 (CC).

of the study provided useful evidence of how families and wider vernacular groupings were developing vernacular law in response to the challenges that were presented by official customary law and the resultant corruption of underlying indigenous values. This information would later serve as evidence in the court challenge to male primogeniture as the default rule of vernacular succession.[14]

The findings of the study are summarised as follows:

> "The research confirmed that the primary value underlying customary succession is an egalitarian one aimed at ensuring the maintenance of the family ... Families have changed their practices to ensure that the family rather than an individual heir is cared for ... We came across several community practices designed to realise the responsibilities entrusted to the heir by customary succession rules. In all of these practices, the concern is with who will control the parents' property. Parents wanted to leave their properties as family properties to be accessed in accordance with need and in acknowledgement of children who contribute to the welfare of family members, especially parents ... The common practice is to bring children up in the belief that the residential home is family property, the use of which should be based on need rather than entitlement."[15]

As Mbatha recounts, parents clearly sought to protect the rights of all of their dependants and curb the abuses of the typically male "heirs" recognised by the codified customary law set out in section 23 of the Black Administration Act 38 of 1927.[16] The value underlying succession practices consequently gained pronounced articulation and prominence through this process: prioritisation on the basis of need. When applied, the principle meant that the people who would inherit occupation, use and administration of the family home were most likely to be widows,[17] orphans, unmarried, separated or divorced sisters, and disabled people.[18] Indeed, daughters were generally well positioned to be recognised because, for the most part, they were the ones who had also most contributed to the family's well-being and cared for their parents.

Rosalie Kingwill describes how in both Fingo Village in Grahamstown and Rabula, a rural area near Keiskammahoek, both in the Eastern Cape, Africans acquired freehold title to their land over 150 years ago. This ownership has passed down over generations and is highly valued. However, there is a very low incidence of subsequent generations registering transfer of title; therefore the vast majority of title deeds reflect the registered owner as someone who has long since died. This is not an isolated phenomenon in African freehold areas. Kingwill states that "[i]n black freehold areas the concretised property relationships between various associated members of families and lineages are more relevant in defining ownership than currency of title deeds".[19]

The scale of "non-compliance" by African owners in respect of updating individual title deeds has been so extensive as to necessitate a state-subsidised system of updating titles in terms initially of a special provision of the Black

---

[14]   *Bhe v Magistrate, Khayelitsha; Shibi v Sithole* 2005 1 SA 580 (CC).
[15]   Mbatha (2002) *SAJHR* 268-269.
[16]   269.
[17]   B Cousins "Characterising 'Communal' Tenure: Nested Systems and Flexible Boundaries" in A Claassens & B Cousins (eds) *Land, Power and Custom: Controversies Generated by South Africa's Communal Land Rights Act* (2008) 109 120; Claassens & Mnisi (2009) *SAJHR* 501.
[18]   Mbatha (2002) *SAJHR* 269 n 41.
[19]   Kingwill "Custom-Building Freehold Title" in *Land, Power and Custom* 185.

Administration Act of 1927 and subsequently the Land Titles Adjustment Act 111 of 1993.[20]

The scale of "non-compliance" reflects the strength and resilience of vernacular understandings of land ownership as "essentially 'family property' subject to a range of family obligations" [21] – as opposed to individualised exclusive ownership. Kingwill quotes Letitia Siziwe Mnyamana of Fingo Village:

> "We call it family property because sometimes someone is disabled or unemployed. They can come back to that home. If a son or daughter [falls on hard times] you will take them in, even my grandchildren ..."[22]

Kingwill describes family membership as "a process of active engagement rather than a uniform set of rules. Rights are kept active through ongoing participation in family affairs and by contributing to the physical maintenance of the home and caring for the young and aged".[23]

Kingwill identifies the following norms:

> "[A]ll family members have rights; the rights of those who live at home and maintain contact are strongest; land is not ordinarily alienable; succession relates to management of property rather than to partible inheritance; the responsibility for maintaining family property is undertaken by a caretaker or custodian identified by the family; property is important in holding together extended families; and registration in the name of particular persons poses risks to the property."[24]

Like Mbatha, Kingwill reports that women are increasingly identified as the most suitable caretakers for family property, as they are seen as more likely to care for the property and destitute family members, and less likely to attempt to sell it or evict family members. As Kingwill points out, the high incidence of females appointed by their families as custodians in Fingo Village stands in strong contrast with previously entrenched legal and institutional models of customary law that restricted succession and control to men.[25]

The above examples in land distribution and succession illustrate the point that in vernacular groupings rights in property are often shared and exist in overlapping ways.[26] When competing claims are made, a process of mediation and prioritisation takes place, in which all stakeholders are involved. Of overriding value is that the outcome should protect the survival and security of the group and its members.[27] What this means is that those with the greatest need are prioritised, and those who occupy and use the asset, as well as those who have made the largest human contribution by giving the

---

[20] 189.
[21] 191.
[22] 192.
[23] 198.
[24] 198.
[25] 195.
[26] Cousins "Characterising 'Communal' Tenure" in *Land, Power and Custom* 109, 123-126; HMO Okoth-Ogendo "The Nature of Land Rights under Indigenous Law in Africa" in A Claassens & B Cousins (eds) *Land, Power and Custom: Controversies Generated by South Africa's Communal Land Rights Act* (2008) 95 101.
[27] TR Nhlapo "The African Customary Law of Marriage and the Rights Conundrum" in M Mamdani (ed) *Beyond Rights-Talk and Culture-Talk: Comparative Essays on the Politics of Rights and Culture* (2000) 136 142; Mnisi *Interface Between Living Customary Law(s) of Succession and SA State Law* 135-136, 157, 302; Mbatha (2002) *SAJHR* 269.

most care to others.[28] At least, that is the underlying principle in vernacular law.

The picture can be far less idyllic in practice. As socio-economic, political and legal conditions change, relationships on the ground are subjected to some stress.[29] Therefore, conflicts and tensions arise over even these fundamental values and people's rights in terms of them.[30] State laws have the potential to either improve or exacerbate the distortions of vernacular norms and values that often result, as well as the extent of disadvantage to women and children that accompanies this. The example of the abuse of the principle of male primogeniture and how such abuse by male heirs was facilitated by rigid and illiberal codification in state laws illustrates this.[31] The contemporary examples of some traditional leaders selling off the land underneath the "traditional communities" over which they are given extensive authority by government constitute another instance of abuse elicited and aided by state laws.[32] In this context, it is crucial that state law and policy proceed from a nuanced understanding of underlying vernacular values and processes of change as they unfold in practice – here, we refer to the balancing of relative rights to land according to criteria that prioritise survival needs.

3 Theories on relative rights and processes

It has long been acknowledged that vernacular groupings observe what Catherine Cross calls "the indigenous social land ethic which structures the social values attaching to land".[33] Cross describes the fact that land is perceived by vernacular groupings as reflecting both a relationship between people and a means of production.[34] She discusses the misunderstanding that often emerges in land reform programmes aiming to deliver "tenure security";[35] specifically, that development "experts" assume that "security" is exclusively about "production". Instead, as Cross articulates, African groupings arrange land rights along strong relational lines and their relationships form the foundation for their strategies of survival.[36] In other words, the relationships between them provide the main basis upon which security is obtained.

Most critically, Cross observes that

> "[r]esearch suggests that the indigenous land right is built on a set of principles that balance off providing land to the landless against upholding possession by landholding families and limiting

---

[28] Mbatha (2002) *SAJHR* 268-269; Claassens & Mnisi (2009) *SAJHR* 501.
[29] Cousins "Characterising 'Communal' Tenure" in *Land, Power and Custom* 113.
[30] 113.
[31] Mbatha (2002) *SAJHR* 263-264; Mnisi *Interface Between Living Customary Law(s) of Succession and SA State Law* 108-146.
[32] Claassens "Power, Accountability and Apartheid Borders: The Impact of Recent Laws on Struggles over Land Rights" in A Claassens & B Cousins (eds) *Land, Power and Custom: Controversies Generated by South Africa's Communal Land Rights Act* (2008) 262 286; Cousins "Characterising 'Communal' Tenure" in *Land, Power and Custom* 118.
[33] Cross (1992) *SAJHR* 314.
[34] 314.
[35] 314.
[36] 314-315.

conditions of access and transfer. The land ethic recognises the prior right of settlers, and also the community's obligation to the poor."[37]

Cross discusses the elements that are common to most vernacular land systems,[38] which she recognises as contextually varying.[39] And, in the end, she summarises her findings thus:

"Without providing general co-ownership of land, these tenures offer a basis for either common property rights or different forms of individual property rights under community supervision."[40]

In this way, she contradicts the fallacy that "communal areas" are marked by the recognition of exclusively communal property rights with no recognition for individual rights in property.

Cross' account of land rights in vernacular groupings is consistent with the account given by the elderly member of the traditional council quoted at the beginning of this chapter. It offers support to our claim that the recognition and prioritisation of socio-economic rights is consistent with, and indeed foreshadowed by resilient values within vernacular law. Ben Cousins has written about the relative stability of land rights secured in terms of vernacular values. He observes that recent developments in relation to single women being allocated land rights (initially only women with children), are consistent with a fundamental value that is being given broader expression:

"The principle that families need land to establish an independent base for their livelihoods is still widely upheld."[41]

He further argues that land that has been allocated is then generally secure, and the rights of the landholders not to be dispossessed similarly so, except where they elect to leave the area permanently or commit a severe offence.[42]

It scarcely needs saying that there is limited scope for the accommodation of vernacular socio-legal values of this kind in classic state conceptions of law. The general incompatibility of a system based on bounded and centralised rules and authorities with a much less rigid one that depends on expansive and multivocal participation in law-making and decision-making processes accounts for this. Responding to this long-standing challenge, Wilmien Wicomb takes an atypical approach to the task of adapting the conventional, positivist notions of law and rights in state law to the contextual needs of law-users and rights-holders in vernacular groupings. She appeals to complexity theory as a means to an "ethical" relationship between state and vernacular

---

[37]   315.
[38]   315-318.
[39]   318.
[40]   Cross (1992) *SAJHR* 318. See also Okoth-Ogendo "The Nature of Land Rights" in *Land, Power and Custom* 102.
[41]   Cousins "Characterising 'Communal' Tenure" in *Land, Power and Custom* 116.
[42]   116-117.

groupings, and their respective systems of law. In her view, "[t]o be ethical, state law must be able to accommodate customary law *in its difference*".[43]

Wicomb draws on Jacques Derrida to illustrate the importance of seeing vernacular law as a complex system. As such, vernacular law has a system structure that is identifiable but is also flexible and constantly changing. This tension between the stability of the system's structure and its persistent change is resolved by means of "self-organisation": the interactions between the individuals who all participate in contributing to the meaning of the system, thus creating meaning "all over the system".[44]

Wicomb refers to the latter as "distributed meaning".[45] In keeping with the principle of "distributed meaning", the meaning of the system and the grouping to which it applies cannot be confined to fixed boundaries.[46] She illustrates this by the analogy of language as a complex system that reconciles structure and adaptability to changing circumstances and communication needs. Wicomb thereby emphasises the fact that "change cannot be the choice of an individual or the instruction of a centre of power ... it must be the result of interaction between many individuals using the language".[47] She concludes that vernacular law also cannot be defined by a single power or authority (whether within a vernacular grouping or external to it)[48] but must be the product of the broad range of users and decision-makers at different levels of the vernacular-law system. In this, decision-making at the local level emerges as most important.[49]

With regard to women's security in the system, Wicomb draws attention to how understanding vernacular law as a complex system of distributed meaning is consistent with the possibility that women can contribute to the determination of those meanings. Moreover, it recognises that new meanings can possibly emerge with regard to women's roles and rights within the system.[50] Consequently, it recognises the potential space for women to advance their rights by using vernacular values as a basis.[51] And it also explains the system's resilience as it internally adapts to changing social circumstances and needs.[52] In addition, it highlights the importance of women's ability to participate in law- and decision-making processes.

We have previously made the case that in practice when rural women argue for the advancement of their rights they often combine rights-based arguments

---

[43] W Wicomb *Law as a Complex System: Facilitating Meaningful Engagement Between State Law and Living Customary Law* (2011) 3, unpublished paper presented at conference on *Sustaining Commons: Sustaining our Future* hosted by the International Association for the Study of the Commons at Dr Marri Channa Reddy Human Resource Development Institute of Andhra Pradesh, 14-01-2011 (copy on file with authors) (original emphasis).

[44] 6-7.

[45] 5-6, 13, 22.

[46] 13, 19.

[47] 7.

[48] 13, 22.

[49] 13.

[50] 22.

[51] Wicomb *Law as a Complex System* 12, 14; Claassens & Mnisi (2009) *SAJHR* 499-502.

[52] Wicomb *Law as a Complex System* 14; Okoth-Ogendo "The Nature of Land Rights" in *Land, Power and Custom* 99.

with those based on vernacular values and entitlements.[53] More specifically, women rely on vernacular values as a basis upon which their rights can be extended.[54] A number of scholars make arguments that are in keeping with this notion of rights as being defined within the context in which they serve and in the terms that make the most sense to those that they will protect.[55]

Jennifer Nedelsky contends that the processes by which rights are defined are central to their defence. Furthermore, because rights (embodied in formal law) are the articulation of fundamental social values, the specific terms in which the underlying values are articulated as "rights" is always debatable, even when it seems as if the underlying values are fixed.[56] Therefore, broad and democratic participation in the process of defining the content of rights is essential to their protection.[57] This is particularly important to keep in mind when we consider the differences between the extent to which traditional leaders and ordinary rural people are able to contribute to the definition of rights under the new laws discussed in the following section.

Nedelsky's theory has another key element to it. She argues for a relational view of rights. She disputes the plausibility of the primary function of rights, in practice, being to provide people with an exclusive autonomy that separates them from one another. She therefore rejects the predominant view that

> "rights are barriers that protect the individual from intrusion by other individuals or by the state. Rights define boundaries others cannot cross and it is those boundaries, enforced by the law, that ensure individual freedom and autonomy."[58]

Instead, she develops the more compelling understanding that "[w]hat makes autonomy possible is not separation, but relationship",[59] whereby she seeks to move the existing notion of autonomy away from individual independence to relationships that facilitate autonomy. She explains this on the basis that dependence is a necessary element "in the relationships ... which provide the security, education, nurturing, and support that make the development of autonomy possible".[60]

Applied to land rights as discussed above, it is easy to see how the Western legal construct of ownership as providing people with exclusive rights over a thing and absolute protections against others with respect to that thing is flawed and ahistorical. This is true even in the European context;[61] but

---

[53] Claassens & Mnisi (2009) *SAJHR* 500.

[54] 501.

[55] Nedelsky (1993) *Review of Constitutional Studies* 4; Lacey *Feminist Legal Theory* 7; Nyamu Musembi "Towards an Actor-Oriented Perspective" in *Inclusive Citizenship* 37.

[56] Nedelsky (1993) *Review of Constitutional Studies* 4.

[57] Claassens & Mnisi (2009) *SAJHR* 512, 514.

[58] Nedelsky (1993) *Review of Constitutional Studies* 7.

[59] 8.

[60] 8.

[61] CM Hann *Property Relations: Renewing the Anthropological Tradition* (1998) 4 stresses that property relations can only exist between people with regards to things and not between people and things. He quotes EA Hoebel's writing in 1966:
> "The essential nature of property is to be found in social relations rather than in inherent attributes of the thing or object that we call *property*. Property, in other words is not a thing, but a network of social relations that governs the conduct of people with respect to the use and disposition of things." (EA Hoebel *Anthropology: The Study of Man* (1966) 424) (original emphasis).

the model and concept of exclusive property rights is particularly distorting in the vernacular context. However, Nedelsky's theory opens up room for contextualising the system of relative rights – marked by often shared and overlapping rights in property – that is comprised by the vernacular relations and values concerning property.

The perennial question regarding the extent to which women's rights can be fully expressed and secured through the individual rights paradigm rather than the protection of group rights is raised directly by Nicola Lacey. Along with that question, she asks how the rights framework that exists can be better sensitised to "the contextual factors which shape the capacities of differently situated subjects to take up and realise their rights".[62] Along similar lines as Nedelsky, Lacey and Celestine Nyamu Musembi argue for the contextual definition and functioning of rights to give effect to the needs of people in that precise *milieu* in which they live and develop their needs.[63] Nyamu Musembi adopts the concept of "vernacularisation" that was developed by Sally Engle Merry to describe the process by which rights are given meaning in localised struggles.

Likewise, Lacey invites us to "think of rights not just in formal but equally in substantial terms: if the underlying value of rights lies in human equality, we have to think about the content and enforcement of rights in terms of their equal value to differently situated subjects".[64]

She speaks to the strong tie between rights and values – namely, the fact that certain articulations of rights prevail and along with them particular values and conceptualisations of personhood and freedom.[65]

As Nedelsky's theory was earlier used to demonstrate, a conception of autonomy based on boundaries of exclusion has undergirded Western rights discourse and therefore provides no room for the accommodation of vernacular conceptions of rights as relational. This serves to exclude the more positive articulation of freedom that is provided for in vernacular rights protections that seek to strengthen fair and accountable relationships as the primary means by which people obtain security and ensure survival.

With the help of these theories we come to recognise that, to the extent that in vernacular groupings claims of entitlement to share are legitimate and socially recognised, they constitute rights against the wider society. Furthermore, their social recognition and the mediatory role they serve between people supports systems of mutual security and the enhanced autonomy of individuals within those systems. In recognising the nature of vernacular rights – and implicitly, the values that that they give expression to – it is fundamentally important to recognise and protect the processes by which the rights are articulated. Unless we understand that vernacular systems of distributed meaning require

[62] Lacey *Feminist Legal Theory* 7.

[63] Mamdani (1990) *J Mod Afr Stud* 1; Lacey *Feminist Legal Theory* 7; Nyamu Musembi "Towards an Actor-Oriented Perspective" in *Inclusive Citizenship* 37; C Nyamu Musembi "Are Local Norms and Practices Fences or Pathways? The Example of Women's Property Rights" in AA An-Na'im (ed) *Cultural Transformation and Human Rights in Africa* (2002) 126 133-134.

[64] Lacey *Feminist Legal Theory* 31.

[65] 19.

and are dependent on the involvement of the vernacular grouping at large in the ongoing definition and redefinition of rights and meaning, we fail to grasp their inherent nature. The involvement of ordinary members of the vernacular grouping in law- and decision-making is therefore foundational and indispensible to vernacular law.

4   Contradictory state versions of customary law

Recent laws pertaining to "customary law" fundamentally undermine the vernacular values and the conditions for effective rights protection set out above in three primary ways. First, these laws entrench the fixed and arbitrarily established "tribal" boundaries delineated during apartheid on vernacular groupings as the jurisdictional boundaries of the future. They thereby subsume and distort the identity of vernacular groupings within "traditional communities", the imposed and often controversial boundaries of which coincide with those of apartheid tribes. Second, by prioritising the top-down powers of traditional leaders within these imposed boundaries, the laws effectively exclude the voices of ordinary rural people from participation in law- and decision-making. Vernacular systems are internally nested with land rights and decision-making authority coexisting at layered levels of social organisation including the family, the clan, user-groups and village councils. The fixed tribal boundaries and forms of unilateral chiefly power imposed by the new laws trump both countervailing vernacular identities and layered and decentralised decision-making processes that mediate centralised power. And third, this privileging in legislation of traditional leaders and their undemocratically assigned powers undercuts the relational interdependence between them and ordinary people, and therefore their accountability to them.

The Traditional Leadership and Governance Framework Act 41 of 2003 ("TLGFA") is misleading in that the opening sections imply a process of recognition for "traditional communities" based on self-definition. Yet hidden near the end are provisions that re-establish apartheid authorities over bounded "traditional communities" (formerly known as "tribes") in the manner of apartheid. This is done explicitly. Section 28(1) deems "[a]ny traditional leader who was appointed as such in terms of applicable provincial legislation and was still recognised as a traditional leader immediately before the commencement of this Act ... to have been recognised as such in terms of section 9 or 11, subject to a decision of the Commission in terms of section 26".[66] Likewise, in section 28(3), "[a]ny 'tribe' that, immediately before the commencement of this Act, had been established and was still recognised as such, is deemed to be a traditional community contemplated in section 2 ..."

---

[66]   The Commission on Traditional Leadership Disputes and Claims has only just completed investigations of paramountcies and has issued a controversial decision on these. It is an extremely long way from determining the legitimacy of the existences of senior traditional leaders (that is, chiefs), and headmen thereafter. See Commission on Traditional Leadership Disputes and Claims *Determinations on the Position of the Paramount Chiefs* (2010) <http://www.info.gov.za/view/DownloadFileAction?id=129114> (accessed 15-07-2011).

Therefore, boundaries and structures established by the Bantu Authorities Act 68 of 1951 are reinforced by this legislation.

Put differently, the TLGFA entrenches the existence of apartheid structures and boundaries under the guise of legislation by a democratic government. It does so under the heading, "transitional arrangement", yet seven years after the Act was enacted, there is no sign of the arrangement's transience and every sign of its permanence. To begin with, the TLGFA allows national and provincial government to provide a role for traditional councils or traditional leaders in a range of areas including land administration; agriculture; health; welfare; administration of justice; safety and security; registration of births, deaths and customary marriages; economic development; environment; tourism; disaster management; the management of natural resources; and dissemination of information relating to government policies and programmes.[67] This is a list with wide scope indeed, and these roles are to be exercised by what is at present an essentially untransformed institution.

The TLGFA's successor, the Communal Land Rights Act 11 of 2004 ("CLARA"), that the Constitutional Court declared unconstitutional in May 2010, did likewise. In the Constitutional Court's words, under this Act, "traditional leaders, through traditional councils, [would] now have wide-ranging powers in relation to the administration of communal land".[68]

Disputes concerning the definition and boundaries of "community" were at the heart of the CLARA litigation. Previous land reform laws[69] had defined the term "community" to include "part of a community". This was in recognition of the reality of the layered and internally segmented nature of vernacular social organisation and governance structures. It opened up space for conversations about self-definition and enabled groupings within layered systems to constitute themselves as separate units and decisions about land rights to be taken at different levels by those most directly affected. CLARA dropped the phrase "part of a community". At the same time it provided for the recognition of traditional councils of the said "communities" as land administration committees and gave them power over communal land. By centralising decision-making authority to the traditional council, CLARA trumped these other levels of decision-making authority and so undermined the land rights and tenure security of families and sub-groupings at lower levels. Recognising one "community" as the official structure, as CLARA did, violates the ongoing terms of interaction between coexisting larger and smaller units. It also privileges particular types of groupings as "community", while ignoring others.

The Traditional Courts Bill B15-2008, which aims to empower "senior traditional leaders" as "presiding officers" – and thus effective law- and decision-makers – in traditional courts would grant the widest powers of all. The Bill allows no legal representation in the courts, even to those criminally

---

[67] S 20 of the TLGFA.
[68] *Tongoane v National Minister for Agriculture and Land Affairs* 2010 6 SA 214 (CC) para 80.
[69] Restitution of Land Rights Act 22 of 1994; Interim Protection of Informal Land Rights Act 31 of 1996.

accused.[70] Significant powers of summons are given to the traditional leader, denying people the right to opt out of the territorial jurisdiction of the local chief's court regardless of whether they deem the chief legitimate or not.[71] Severe sanctions (such as forced labour)[72] and limited grounds of appeal or review are permitted.[73] Most crucially, the Bill only outlaws banishment in criminal cases and not in civil disputes.[74] Yet the Bill permits the presiding officer to deprive parties to disputes of "community benefits".[75] Since, as we have demonstrated, land rights are secured in the context of relationships and the balancing of relative claims, disputants' vernacular land rights and membership of their vernacular grouping would not be secure under the Bill. Basically, in terms of the Bill, traditional leaders would be able to singlehandedly determine the content and decide the application of vernacular law.

There is no provision in the Bill for women's ability to form part of the constitution of the traditional courts, and no assurance given to them that they would be able to represent themselves as litigants in disputes, as opposed to being represented by male family members as is commonly the case.[76] In vernacular groupings where women are not permitted to appear at all in traditional courts that are deemed to be sacred (and thus male) spaces,[77] there would be no assurance that this practice would be discontinued.

The fact that, under the Traditional Courts Bill, only one level of courts – namely, chiefs' courts – would be recognised[78] is contrary to the multilayered nature of vernacular social organisation and multi-levelled authority.[79] Moreover, traditional leaders' statutory entitlement to hold judge-like positions and thereby exclude the essential contributions of ordinary members of their vernacular groupings stands in stark contrast to the nature of vernacular systems as earlier described. The Bill would therefore effectively close down the avenues currently available for women to participate in the definition of law and rights in their communities which are, in fact, increasingly employed by women in practice. The fact that in practice the availability of these potential pathways for women's involvement would depend on the decision of the traditional leader alone, is contradictory to both vernacular law and democracy.

---

[70]   S 9(3)(a) of the Traditional Courts Bill.

[71]   S 20(c).

[72]   S 10(2), especially s 10(2)(g)-(h).

[73]   Ss 14(1)(a)-(d), 16(3)(a)-(b).

[74]   S 10(1)(b).

[75]   S 10(2)(i).

[76]   See s 9(3)(b) of the Traditional Courts Bill. Also see A Claassens & S Ngubane "Women, Land and Power: The Impact of the Communal Land Rights Act" in A Claassens & B Cousins (eds) *Land, Power and Custom: Controversies Generated by South Africa's Communal Land Rights Act* (2008) 154 173; Claassens & Mnisi (2009) *SAJHR* 512, 514. Compare this with s 9(2)(a)(i) of the Traditional Courts Bill, which, even though it says that women should participate as men do, is undercut by s 9(3)(b) and the exclusion of ordinary voices by the Traditional Courts Bill in general.

[77]   E Curren & E Bonthuys "Customary Law and Domestic Violence in Rural South African Communities" (2005) 21 *SAJHR* 607 633.

[78]   S Mnisi Weeks "The Traditional Courts Bill: Controversy around Process, Substance and Implications" (2011) 35 *SACQ* 3 6.

[79]   Okoth-Ogendo "The Nature of Land Rights" in *Land, Power and Custom* 101.

We have argued elsewhere that women are able to make their claims more successfully in lower level decision-making forums which are often more sympathetic.[80] Wicomb's notion of lower level decision-making being significant to the distributed meanings of complex systems supports this.[81] Under the Traditional Courts Bill, women would have only one sphere in which to fight the struggle for greater rights protection – the highest and most socially removed level, that is the chief's court. Not being able to participate in substantial ways in that forum, they would therefore have great difficulty in their attempts to advance their rights locally. By the same token, even if community practices were changing in progressive ways – as in the succession example provided by Mbatha – under the Bill these changes in vernacular law would be dependent on the goodwill of the senior traditional leader and their wider manifestation would depend upon his disposition. Ultimately, the vernacular law of any grouping would be contingent upon the chief being progressive in his views and changing the law from the top down. This fundamentally contradicts the reciprocal and consensual nature of the vernacular systems of distributed meaning under discussion.

These laws render it virtually impossible for a "traditional community" subject to a "senior traditional leader" recognised by government to hold the leader accountable. As previously mentioned, vernacular systems are inherently flexible – in relation to their boundaries as well as the changing content of the law. There is much evidence that a key mechanism for holding leaders accountable was the fact that leaders' powers, authority and legitimacy depended on their attention to the will of their people.[82] The leader's supporters could otherwise defect, and indeed they did. Accordingly, the rather porous boundaries of vernacular groupings expanded and contracted with the legitimacy of particular leaders.[83] And, the members of the vernacular grouping at large were essential to the law- and decision-making processes.[84] The colonial and apartheid imposition of fixed (and often controversial) boundaries and authorities, and distortions of vernacular law, damaged this relationship between leader and populace. These laws, by entrenching the old boundaries and reinforcing the unilateral power of chiefs within them, further erode indigenous accountability mechanisms.

As Govan Mbeki wrote, in 1964, about the chiefs and headmen who agreed to the Bantu Authorities that are the predecessors of today's Traditional Councils:

"Gone was the old give-and-take of tribal consultation, and in its place there was now the autocratic power bestowed on the more ambitious Chiefs, who had become arrogant in the knowledge that government power was now behind them."[85]

---

[80]   Claassens & Mnisi (2009) *SAJHR* 514.
[81]   Wicomb *Law as a Complex System* 13.
[82]   WD Hammond-Tooke *Command or Consensus: The Development of Transkeian Local Government* (1952) 67; A Claassens "Women, Customary Law and Discrimination: The Impact of the Communal Land Rights Act" (2005) *Acta Juridica* 42 75. See also Comaroff & Roberts *Rules and Processes* 80-83.
[83]   Claassens "Power, Accountability and Apartheid Borders" in *Land, Power and Custom* 286-287.
[84]   See discussion in Mnisi Weeks (2011) *SACQ* 31.
[85]   G Mbeki *South Africa: The Peasants' Revolt* (1964) 119-120.

Whereas a principle of most vernacular systems in South Africa is that only members are entitled to land allocations to meet their basic needs, these days traditional leaders give land to those who can pay for it.[86] This results in large sums commonly exchanging hands between traditional leaders and development, pharmaceutical and mining companies.

5 Selling land allocations

The powers of traditional leaders in respect of land allocation is one of the most disputed areas of "customary law",[87] particularly in relation to the increasing problem of traditional leaders "selling" land allocations and attempting to justify the sales as customary tribute or *khonza* fees. This gives rise to serious disputes in which members of vernacular groupings allege that, not only have traditional leaders failed to preserve the land base of the grouping, on which members depend, they have also changed the grouping's composition by bringing in large numbers of "outsiders" for profit. The scale and seriousness of the problem is reflected in a 2007 resolution adopted at the ANC national conference in Polokwane to

"[e]nsure that the allocation of customary land be democratised in a manner which empowers rural women and supports the building of democratic community structures at village level, capable of driving and coordinating local development processes. The ANC will further engage with traditional leaders, including Contralesa, to ensure that disposal of land without proper consultation with communities and local governments is discontinued."[88]

The disputed content of vernacular law in relation to traditional leaders "selling" land allocations arose in *Tongoane v National Minister for Agriculture and Land Affairs*[89] challenging CLARA. Applicants from Makgobistad, a Tswana area in North West, insisted that their chief and headman were acting contrary to custom and precedent in establishing a housing project on farming land without first consulting the long-term owners of the fields. They also argued that it was contrary to custom for traditional leaders to charge "outsiders" large amounts of money for land belonging to the vernacular grouping.

The case was defended by the National Department of Provincial and Local Government, which referred to the expert testimony of Dr Freddy Khunou. In his affidavit, Khunou stated:

"It was a long standing rule and common practice of the Barolong-boo-Ratlou-ba-ga-Mokgobi to allocate land to immigrants on certain conditions."[90]

---

[86] Claassens "Power, Accountability and Apartheid Borders" in *Land, Power and Custom* 286; Cousins "Characterising 'Communal' Tenure" in *Land, Power and Custom* 118.

[87] Cousins "Characterising 'Communal' Tenure" in *Land, Power and Custom* 113-115; Claassens & Ngubane "Women, Land and Power" in *Land, Power and Custom* 169-171; Claassens "Power, Accountability and Apartheid Borders" in *Land, Power and Custom* 282-286.

[88] ANC *52nd National Conference – Resolution 10* (2007) under the heading "Rural Development, Land Reform and Agrarian Change".

[89] 2010 6 SA 214 (CC).

[90] Affidavit of Samuel Freddy Khunou on the DVD Rom of Court Papers accompanying A Claassens & B Cousins (eds) *Land, Power and Custom: Controversies Generated by South Africa's Communal Land Rights Act* (2008) para 21.13.

In a footnote, he added that at the time he conducted his research, the allocation fee was R4 000, and might change according to the determination of the council.[91]

The Kalkfontein residents, the first applicants in the *Tongoane* case, are the descendants of a diverse group of farmers who clubbed together so that they could collectively pay the purchase price of farming land north of Pretoria, which they managed to buy by obtaining an exemption from the Natives' Land Act 27 of 1913. An elected community authority was established to represent the co-owners and manage their affairs. Life continued as such for 50 years, until the apartheid government imposed a "tribal authority" on the Kalkfontein farms in 1979 and elevated one of the co-owners to be chief of the newly created Ndzundza Traditional Community. This happened pursuant to its efforts to carve out and create a separate Ndebele "homeland". The newly elevated Chief Daniel Mahlangu instituted a reign of terror over the other co-owners[92] during which he sold off over 1 000 sites to people from outside the community. In reply to concerns that CLARA would bolster the power of the "traditional leader" and enable a return to past abuses of their property rights, the acting chief of the Ndzundza Traditional Community argued that the previous allocations had been consistent with customary law.[93]

The Kalkfontein applicants argued that the powers given to traditional leaders by CLARA would undermine their vernacular system of joint decision-making, land allocation and control over common property resources. Like the other applicants, they administer the land according to the vernacular precedent of each family having its own secure residential site and fields, together with shared rights of access to the *veld* for grazing and shared resources such as water, wood and grass. Also, as with the other applicants, a structure referred to as a *kgotla* oversees the process of land allocation to descendants of the co-owners when they come of age and establish families of their own.

The government's response, supported by an expert affidavit from the President of Contralesa, Inkosi Pathekhile Holomisa, was that customary law does not, and cannot exist in the absence of traditional leaders.[94] Holomisa states in his affidavit that "[i]t is inconceivable that a community whose affairs are administered through a 'Kgotla', as described by the Applicants, could not

---

[91] Affidavit of Samuel Freddy Khunou in *Land, Power and Custom* n 58.

[92] Kruger Commission of Enquiry *Report* (1990) National Archives of South Africa, NTS files, established by the Minister of Co-operation and Development to investigate the "unrest" in Kalkfontein. The Commission reported in 1990 and recommended that Mahlangu's recognition as chief be withdrawn and consideration be given to the disestablishment of the tribal authority. While Mahlangu was deposed, the tribal authority was never disestablished and has therefore been deemed to be a "traditional council" in terms of s 28(4) of the TLGFA.

[93] Answering affidavit of Christopher Salabantu Mahlangu on the DVD Rom of Court Papers accompanying A Claassens & B Cousins (eds) *Land, Power and Custom: Controversies Generated by South Africa's Communal Land Rights Act* (2008) para 20.2.

[94] Affidavit of Dr Sipho MD Sibanda on the DVD Rom of Court Papers accompanying A Claassens & B Cousins (eds) *Land, Power and Custom: Controversies Generated by South Africa's Communal Land Rights Act* (2008) paras 31.2, 47.1.

have someone who is the equivalent of a traditional leader, be it a headman or a Kgoshi".[95]

The basis of the new laws is that chiefly power, as opposed to actual practice, is the starting point and defining feature of "customary law". With this assumption, they support the ability of corrupt traditional leaders to undermine the access of members of vernacular groupings to resources upon which they depend for their survival.

6 Constitutional support for vernacular law

By contrast, instead of government bolstering the power of traditional leaders to unilaterally define the content of custom, government should partner with rural people as stakeholders in their own development. If ordinary people were supported in their efforts to debate and influence the content of locally recognised rights in line with fundamental values, we might see more broad-based social security. Put differently, were ordinary people enabled to make more broad-based distribution decisions by means of locally embedded democratic processes, there would be greater potential for the eradication of poverty in rural areas than exists under the centralised and unaccountable power relations entrenched by the traditional leadership laws. However, positive outcomes would be dependent on the ability of ordinary people to hold their leaders to account. Instead of facilitating this, the new laws make it virtually impossible.

There exists a robust constitutional basis for our argument that socially recognised claims within vernacular systems constitute rights recognised by the Constitution of the Republic of South Africa, 1996 ("the Constitution"), and that these rights are undermined by the new traditional leadership laws. In addition to its recognition of conventional rights in the Bill of Rights and living customary law under sections 30, 31 and 211(3), section 39(3) of the Constitution provides that "[t]he Bill of Rights does not deny the existence of any other rights or freedoms that are recognised or conferred by common law, customary law or legislation, to the extent that they are consistent with the Bill".

Our argument here is that vernacular values that prioritise need are justifiable and protected under our Constitution. These values are embodied in the ongoing mediation of systems of relative rights that seek to balance vernacular entitlements such as birth and inheritance rights on the one hand, with the prioritisation of basic survival needs on the other. Such mediation processes require the active participation and consent of those whose entitlements are at issue in order to arrive at accommodations that all can accept as legitimate. In such processes, values and rules are not simply applied, they are debated, interpreted and (re)made. Intrinsic to the nature of vernacular systems of relative rights, we argue, is the participation of those who hold them, in both

---

[95] Supporting affidavit of Sango Phathekile Holomisa (A! Dilizintaba) MP on the DVD Rom of Court Papers accompanying A Claassens & B Cousins (eds) *Land, Power and Custom: Controversies Generated by South Africa's Communal Land Rights Act* (2008) para 9.4.

their definition and their mediation. We therefore argue that laws which prioritise the powers of traditional leaders over the participatory nature of vernacular systems of relative rights are inconsistent with the Constitution.

In keeping with the latter point, the Constitutional Court stated in *Shilubana v Nwamitwa*:[96]

> "As has been repeatedly emphasised by this and other courts, customary law is by its nature a constantly evolving system. Under pre-democratic colonial and apartheid regimes, this development was frustrated and customary law stagnated. This stagnation should not continue, and the free development *by communities of their own laws* to meet the needs of a rapidly changing society *must be respected and facilitated.*"[97]

Likewise, in *Alexkor Ltd v the Richtersveld Community*,[98] the Constitutional Court interprets customary law to be "the living law" which "evolves as the people who live by its norms change their patterns of life".[99] Consequently, in light of Constitutional Court precedent, there is a compelling basis upon which to suggest that the widespread participation of ordinary people in the adaptation of vernacular law to the ever-changing demands of their circumstances is required by the Constitution. By necessity then, the inverse prioritisation of traditional leaders as sole law- and decision-makers in their "communities" is contrary to the Constitution. This reading also accords with the emphasis given by the Court to the fundamental nature of the constitutional requirement of public participation in *Tongoane*.[100] In fact, as we have shown, the centralisation to traditional leaders of law- and decision-making power is inconsistent with the very notion of democracy that the Court emphasises in that judgment as being essential to South Africa's constitutional order.[101]

Nedelsky's observations about the intricate connection between the content of rights and the process by which they are defined apply similarly to policy- and law-making more generally. The new traditional leadership laws exemplify that those privileged in the legislative process are those who benefit from the content of the new laws. This point is well understood by rural people. A 1991 discussion of interviews with rural women concerning their views about women's access to land and power after apartheid concluded by drawing attention to the fact that for rural women to benefit from future laws and policy it is essential that they be included in the process of policy formulation.[102] The same point is brought home by a rural man's response to the Traditional Courts Bill. He rejects

---

[96] 2009 2 SA 66 (CC).

[97] Para 45 (emphasis added). The Court cites: *Bhe v Magistrate, Khayelitsha; Shibi v Sithole* 2005 1 SA 580 (CC) paras 82-87, 90, 152-153; *Alexkor Ltd v the Richtersveld Community* 2004 5 SA 460 (CC) paras 52-53; *Du Plessis v De Klerk* 1996 3 SA 850 (CC) para 172; *Mabuza v Mbatha* 2003 4 SA 218 (C) paras 26, 28; *Mabena v Letsoalo* 1998 2 SA 1068 (T) 1075B-C.

[98] 2004 5 SA 460 (CC).

[99] Para 52.

[100] Para 66.

[101] See ss 1 and 7 of the Constitution. See also *Doctors for Life International v Speaker of the National Assembly* 2006 6 SA 416 (CC) para 211; *Tongoane v National Minister for Agriculture and Land Affairs* 2010 6 SA 214 (CC) paras 106-107.

[102] J Small & L Kompe *Demanding a Place Under the Kgotla Tree: Rural Women's Access to Land and Power* TRAC Publication 13 (1991) (copy on file with authors).

it on the basis that the people who drafted it never consulted rural people and reiterates that

> "we as South Africans, in the rural or communal lands, we want the big or small laws that refer to us to start with us. Only after our inputs should such proposals become law."[103]

The new laws that we have discussed must therefore be unconstitutional on both grounds: they violate legitimately defensible vernacular socio-economic values and rights; and they undermine vernacular democratic processes of participation. In the next section, we point to the danger that the new traditional leadership laws would also undermine progressive democratic and socio-economic rights practices that are developing within vernacular systems on the ground.

7 Socio-economic rights as negotiated in practice

Rural people are negotiating changes in "customary" precedents to accommodate the needs of families headed by single women. The previous "rule" in most vernacular systems was that residential land should be allocated only to men, and only when men marry and establish families. The underlying rationale was that only families, and not individuals, are entitled to establish themselves as separate units within the vernacular grouping. However, a recent survey undertaken by the Community Agency for Social Enquiry ("CASE") confirmed anecdotal evidence from large rural consultative meetings held between 2002 and 2009 that significant processes of change are underway in relation to single women accessing residential sites.[104] The changes are borne out by research in various former homeland areas.[105] They are also consistent with trends in other parts of sub-Saharan Africa.[106]

In our experience, single women use a range of arguments to advance their claims to residential sites. Many are couched in terms of vernacular values. One such value is that all members of the community are entitled (by birthright) to land to fulfil their basic needs and support their children. In their claims, women point to the fact that men are entitled to land only when they marry and establish families. Now that the structure of the family is changing

---

[103] A Claassens (ed) (translation and transcription by T Charles with S Mnisi) *Traditional Courts Bill Workshop* (2009) 177, a workshop organised by the Law, Race and Gender Research Unit, Legal Resources Centre and TRAC Mpumalanga, held in Mpumalanga, 03-06-2009–04-06-2009 <http://www.lrg.uct.ac.za/publications/other/> (accessed 20-03-2011).

[104] See D Budlender, S Mgweba, K Motsepe & L Williams *Women, Land and Customary Law* (2011) 91-95; A Claassens *Community Views on the Communal Land Rights Bill* PLAAS Research Report No 15, University of the Western Cape (2003) 1 11, 15-16, 21, 28; Claassens & Mnisi (2009) *SAJHR* 499-502.

[105] C Cross & M Friedman "Women and Tenure: Marginality and Left Hand Power" in S Meer (ed) *Women, Land and Authority* (1997) 1 13; S Mpilo *Communal Land Tenure Versus Individual Housing Tenure? Working Together in Housing Provision* (2004), unpublished paper presented to the National Rural Housing Symposium in Johannesburg, 13-05-2004 (copy on file with author); R Alcock & D Hornby *Traditional Land Matters: A Look into Land Administration in Tribal Areas in KwaZulu-Natal* Legal Entity Assessment Project Occasional Paper (2004) 1 14; S Turner *Land Rights and Land Administration in the Herschel and Maluti Districts, Eastern Cape* PLAAS Occasional Paper No 10, University of the Western Cape (1999) 1 1-17.

[106] R Odgaard & AW Bentzon "Rural Women's Access to Landed Property: Unearthing the Realities Within an East African Setting" in A Hellum, J Stewart, SS Ali & A Tsanga (eds) *Human Rights, Plural Legalities and Gendered Realities: Paths are Made by Walking* (2008) 202 213-222.

and women are fulfilling the role of providing for the family, often without men, they argue that they are entitled to be allocated land on the same basis as men with families to support.

Often the principle of equality is asserted, and women refer to "democracy" and the Constitution. They say that the times and the laws have changed, and that discrimination is no longer legal. In many instances, arguments about the values underlying vernacular systems (in particular, the primacy of claims of need) and entitlements of birthright and belonging are woven together with the right to equality and democracy in the claims made.

Some of the dynamics at play in relation to land allocation to women were illuminated at a lively meeting in Kalkfontein[107] in Mpumalanga in 2004. Young women challenged the community trust as to why women were not represented on the land allocation sub-committee. Single mothers in Kalkfontein have been allocated residential sites since the transition in 1994 on the basis that as "daughters and granddaughters", they were just as much "descendants" of the original purchasers of Kalkfontein as sons were, and that they also needed to be able to house their children.

Both the men and women at the meeting agreed that these days any adult "heir" could apply for a stand – son or daughter, married or unmarried. There was some concern expressed by the committee and women alike about "outside" men marrying Kalkfontein women and then causing trouble by refusing to acknowledge the authority of the committee. But, they ultimately agreed that single women were in desperate need of residential sites and that no one could say for sure that a single woman would subsequently marry or that her husband would be "troublesome". The tenor of the debate was passionate and engaged, but also good-humoured and pragmatic. Women engaged forcefully but respectfully. The trustees present, who were all men, articulated their concerns but conceded the merits of the women's arguments. Women have subsequently been co-opted onto the allocation committee.

Another form of agency is that of women living on family land who resist being evicted by male relatives and assert that they must be accommodated within the family land. Often they, too, rely on arguments that combine both custom and equality. Claassens and Ngubane tell the story of a woman who successfully challenged her brother's attempts to evict her on the basis that as a family member she had a "birthright" to belong.[108] They refer to widows and divorcees who managed to hold on to their married homes despite attempts to evict them.[109] As previously noted, there are increasing numbers of women whose parents have bequeathed them (not their brothers) control of the family home and land in recognition of the role they have long played in supporting their parents and in balancing the interests and needs of other family members.

A striking feature of anecdotal stories about how changes come about – particularly in relation to women being allocated residential sites – is how

---

[107] Attended by Aninka Claassens and Moses Modise from the Legal Resources Centre, 04-11-2004.
[108] Claassens & Ngubane "Women, Land and Power" in *Land, Power and Custom* 158.
[109] 160.

often they are described as starting with a particular woman's brave attempts to challenge the *status quo*. Time and again "1994" is given as the date when change began. Another striking feature of stories of change is the supportive actions of key men in the community. Many women and men saw 1994 as a key turning point that heralded the victory of the values which had informed the struggle against apartheid: democracy, equality and human rights. In many instances people saw no inherent contradiction between these values and those that underlay vernacular systems before they were distorted by apartheid. Both women and men simply got on with the task of hammering out local solutions that reconciled vernacular values with human rights.

In the *Shilubana* case, for example, a woman was appointed chief when her uncle died in 2001. Her father, who had been the previous chief, had only daughters and so his brother was appointed chief when he died in 1986. But on the death of the uncle the royal family called a general meeting at which all present resolved that the original chief's daughter should now be made *hosi*. The resolution noted:

> "[T]hough in the past it was not permissible by the Valoyis that a female child be heir, in terms of democracy and the new [Constitution of the Republic of South African] it is now permissible that a female child be heir since she is also equal to a male child."[110]

New law and policy should depart from an awareness of these changes that people are making through local, participatory processes on the ground, and encourage them rather than reinforce the patriarchal power relations of the apartheid era as the new laws do. When it comes to enacting laws that impact on vernacular systems of relative land rights and mediated power, Lacey's caution is apt:

> "Interventions within one set of practices often have unseen and sometimes adverse implications for others ... The challenge is to try to understand how social institutions interact with each other, which are the most open to change, and which means of changing them are likely, in particular contexts, to be least dangerous or most successful."[111]

8   Conclusion

We have argued in this chapter that vernacular values that attempt to prevent and address poverty are remarkably resilient at local level despite the slew of laws and policies that ignored them in the past. Property rights in "communal areas" remain shared and overlapping, and vernacular precedents are regularly used in people's attempts to resolve competing claims by balancing the relative rights and interests of those who possess land and those who are poor.

With Nedelsky, we contended that the protection of rights is integrally connected with the processes by which the content of rights is determined. Moreover, given that essential to vernacular law are its ability to change and the contributions of diverse people to the structure and meaning of the system, the exclusion of ordinary voices from law- and decision-making by the TLGA and the TCB offends vernacular law's very essence. We argued that the

---

[110]   Quoted in *Shilubana v Nwamitwa* 2009 2 SA 66 (CC) para 4.
[111]   Lacey *Feminist Legal Theory* 29.

TLGFA and the laws built on its foundation privilege the powers of traditional leaders at the expense of the intrinsic nature of vernacular systems.

In our view, vernacular systems of relative rights that prioritise basic needs constitute a valuable resource that government could build on in engaging rural people in poverty reduction initiatives and strategies. We argue for an approach that builds on and supports the processes of positive change that rural people in many areas are already engaged in – with regard to women's rights, especially. The transition from apartheid to democracy inspired many people to engage in finding synchronicities between inclusive indigenous precedents and the principles of equality and democracy. Instead of supporting such initiatives government has chosen to enact laws that take us back to apartheid power relations and outdated notions of absolute and exclusive property rights.

SUMMARY

This chapter starts with a statement made by an elderly female traditional councillor in a Swati-speaking area when consideration was being given to reallocating some farming fields as residential stands for others. She communicated that she loved her field but that she would not choose to retain it if that meant that someone else would have no place to live. She expressed this as a fundamental value in her society.

Other studies have found similar values embraced by different vernacular groupings in South Africa. In these "communal" areas, rights in property are often overlapping and shared. Competing claims over shared property are prioritised on the basis of need, use, contribution made, and care given to others. This is so especially in land distribution and succession wherein security and survival are key motivating factors.

We reflect on these vernacular rural value systems in light of scholarship that challenges conceptions of rights as boundaries functioning exclusively – to protect autonomy by keeping others out. This literature rather conceives of rights in more inclusive terms, focusing on how they work in practice to structure the relationships on which people depend for basic survival. Moreover, this literature perceives the content of rights as contextually defined, through inclusive participatory processes. This body of theory is particularly useful when applied to the realm of socio-economic rights wherein a primary ethic in living customary law is that the basic needs of each member should be prioritised in balancing relative rights.

We go on to show how official versions of customary law apply top-down conceptions of authority that privilege the powers of senior traditional leaders in ways that compromise the rights of ordinary people. Accordingly, we argue that the often more democratic and egalitarian rights existing in terms of living customary law provide a better departure point in attempts to give effect to socio-economic rights and alleviate poverty in rural areas.

CHAPTER 21

DEVELOPING THE COMMON LAW OF CONTRACT IN THE LIGHT OF POVERTY AND ILLITERACY: THE CHALLENGE OF THE CONSTITUTION

Dennis M Davis[*]

"What he [Hale] has to teach us is that the legal ground rules of economic struggle constitute the economic bargaining power of the combatants ... The process of circular causation works between the private economic system and the public law making system as well as within the economy."[1]

1 Introduction

South Africa is one of the most unequal countries in the world, a condition which is a product of more than three hundred years of colonial and racist rule. The constitutional settlement that ushered in democracy did not summarily erase apartheid from the social, economic landscape. To an extent, the drafters of the Constitution of the Republic of South Africa, 1996 ("the Constitution") understood that erasure would not be achieved by way of one silver bullet. It could only occur by way of a journey towards the egalitarian vision prefigured in the constitutional text. At the same time the drafters understood that legal rules which reinforced patterns of power required reconfiguration if the journey was to be undertaken.

For this reason the Constitution, after a long and anxious debate, prompted in significant part by the decision of the Constitutional Court in *Du Plessis v De Klerk*,[2] in which the application of the substantive provisions of the Bill of Rights as contained in the Constitution Act 200 of 1993 ("the Interim Constitution") was narrowed almost exclusively to a vertical application, boldly insisted that disputes between private parties should be subjected to constitutional scrutiny.

Section 8 reflected the determination of the constitutional drafters to ensure that private parties should also be bound by constitutionally entrenched rights. A threefold process was envisaged in terms of this section:

(i) A court must determine whether a private person is bound by the constitutional right as alleged.

(ii) If the private person is so bound, the court must apply legislation giving effect to the right.

---

[*] This chapter owes a great intellectual debt to Karl Klare and Duncan Kennedy for educating me about the importance of Robert Hale and thus opening up a new intellectual vista. Thanks are also due to Sandra Liebenberg and Geo Quinot for encouraging me to write this chapter.

[1] D Kennedy "The Stakes of Law or Hale and Foucault" (1991) 15 *Legal Studies Forum* 327 336.

[2] 1996 3 SA 850 (CC).

(iii) If there is no legislation giving effect to the applicable right, the court must develop a rule of common law. In so doing, a court is empowered to develop the rule of common law, both to give content to the constitutional right as well as to limit the right, provided the limitation accords with section 36(1) (the general limitations clause) of the Constitution.[3]

In addition, the text provided for a further mechanism to infuse all law with constitutional values, namely section 39(2),[4] which was designed to engage both law and conduct not specifically covered by any of the provisions set out in the Bill of Rights.

Whatever the disputes about the scope of these provisions and their impact upon existing common law,[5] the idea was that the Constitution, whether through a specific right or the influence of its normative framework – itself based upon the foundational principles of dignity, freedom and equality – would be central to a reconfiguration of the background rules in terms of which all economic activity took place.

The need for a post-apartheid legal order to interrogate existing rules of law on the basis that private-law rules empower some actors, while subordinating others, was well articulated by Madala J in the *Du Plessis* case where he wrote:

"Ours is a multi-racial, multi-cultural, multi-lingual society in which the ravages of apartheid, disadvantage and inequality are just immeasurable. The extent of the oppressive measures in South Africa was not confined to government/individual relations but equally to individual/individual relations. In its effort to create a new order, our Constitution must have been intended to address these oppressive and undemocratic practices at all levels. In my view, our Constitution starts at the lowest level and attempts to reach the furthest in its endeavours to restructure the dynamics in a previously racist society."[6]

Viewed within the matrix of this compelling observation, it was to be hoped that the distributive importance of the ground rules of contract would have been the subject of careful interrogation by the courts, now mandated to adjudicate all law in terms of a constitutional text, which, the Constitutional Court has *asserted,* contained a particular normative framework of justice.[7]

In this chapter I seek to engage with key cases in which South African courts, in effect, ignored these challenges when deciding disputes based upon the law of contract. The record reveals that the courts either eschewed the significance of the Constitution or simply nodded in the direction of the Constitution, before proceeding in the opposite direction. I employ the realist work of Robert Hale

---

[3] MH Cheadle "Application" in MH Cheadle, DM Davis & NRL Haysom (eds) *South African Constitutional Law: The Bill of Rights* 2 ed (RS 3 2005) 3-1 3-4.

[4] S 39(2) states that "[w]hen interpreting any legislation, and when developing the common law or customary law, every court, tribunal or forum must promote the spirit, purport and objects of the Bill of Rights".

[5] The most restrictive approach is that adopted by A Fagan "The Secondary Role of the Spirit, Purport and Objects of the Bill of Rights in the Common Law's Development" (2010) 127 *SALJ* 611.

[6] *Du Plessis v De Klerk* 1996 3 SA 850 (CC) para 163.

[7] *Carmichele v Minister of Safety and Security* 2001 4 SA 938 (CC) para 54. The problem is that when the Constitutional Court asserted the existence of an objective normative framework sourced in the Constitution, it failed to provide a clear explication or application in this judgment or any other subsequent judgment of the content and hence the implications of this framework for further jurisprudential development.

to illustrate that rules which assign property rights and which impact upon the nature and enforcement of contractual claims profoundly shape economic relationships. In short, if the ground rules are changed, an alteration of social and economic relationship may well take place.

2   The contested nature of contract law

In a conventional analysis of the general principles of the law of contract, Dale Hutchison notes that, apart from issues of consensus and reliance, the cornerstone of the law of contract remains the concept of freedom of contract which, in his view, means a general liberty to choose whether to contract, with whom to contract and on what terms to so contract.[8] Accordingly:

"The sanctity of contract entails holding the parties bound to their agreement, once it has been properly reached; for it is a fundamental principle, based on the need for certainty in commercial dealings as much as on considerations of morality, that agreements should be honoured, *pacta sunt servanda.*"[9]

Admittedly, Hutchison concedes that freedom of contract is limited by the dictates of public policy and the closely related concept of good faith. For him the latter is

"an ethical value or controlling principle founded upon community standards of fairness and decency. Good faith underlies and informs the entire law of contract, shaping its content and finding concrete expression in its technical rules and doctrines."[10]

This is as promising an engagement with the Constitution as the standard approach to contract appears to admit. There is one further concession that agreements can be contrary to public policy when they conflict with the appropriate norms of the objective value system embodied in the Constitution,[11] but the reader will search in vain for guidance as to how this claim is to find any practical application. The invocation of public policy thus becomes no more than a basis by which to employ a ritual incantation of the existence of the Constitution before moving on to deal with the "real" law of contract.

So much for the standard approach to the law contract, which asserts the centrality of *pacta sunt servanda*, makes some undefined concessions to public policy, and affords little guidance to courts, in particular, in the legal community, in general, as to the manner in which public policy may shape the law of contract.[12]

There are exceptions to this approach even in South Africa. Contrast Hutchinson to the following:

"[C]ontract law is the mechanism meant to regulate market relations. In doing so, its foundations in 18th and 19th century classical liberal theory buttress contemporary neo-liberal policies for macro-

---

[8]   D Hutchison & F du Bois "Contracts in General" in F du Bois (ed) *Wille's Principles of South African Law* 9 ed (2007) 733 737.

[9]   737. There are many examples of what I have termed the standard approach to contract law. However, I have simply chosen a relatively short but lucid version for illustrative purposes.

[10]   737-738.

[11]   763.

[12]   Not all the South African literature thus eschewed a critical engagement with underlying legal norms.

economic growth where there is a continued emphasis on, and respect for, the voluntary choices (liberty) of participants in the market."[13]

In this passage, the individualistic approach to contract law, which promotes self-interest and self-reliance, is contested. The "neutral" idea that contract law promotes a particular conception of autonomy and that this can be equated with a generalised view of the "good life" is brought sharply into question. It will be argued in the light of recent case law that this alternative vision has attracted little serious attention from the highest courts over the past decade, notwithstanding its resonance with the framework for legal development as envisaged in sections 8 and 39(2) of the Constitution.

3   Robert Hale: Who is he?

An alternative view to the law of contract, albeit hardly examined in South Africa,[14] finds a rich resonance beyond these shores. In particular, the work of Robert Hale is directed towards the importance of legal rules in shaping the determination of the distribution of income. As he writes:

> "The market value of a property or a service is merely a measure of the strength of the bargaining power of the person who owns the one or renders the other, under the particular legal rights with which the law endows him, and the legal restrictions which it places on others."[15]

In order to substantiate this claim, Hale categorises legal rules into two specific groups, rules governing the conduct of parties during the process of bargaining and rules that structure the alternatives to remaining in a specific bargaining situation.[16]

The first category includes rules that provide how a contract will be enforced, the provision of remedies for a breach of contract as well as terms and conditions which may be implied by law. The second category concerns those laws that impose rights and obligations upon parties, such as their rights to property, which rules, in turn, inform the very nature of the strength that each side brings to the bargaining table.[17]

This second category of legal rules is often overlooked in the analysis of the law of contract, notwithstanding their clear influence on a contractual outcome. The following passage from Hale is illustrative of the critical importance of this category of legal rules:

> "If the non-owner works for anyone, it is for the purpose of warding off the threat of at least one owner of money to withhold that money from him (with the help of the law). Suppose, now, the worker were to refuse to yield to the coercion of any employer, but were to choose instead to remain under the

---

[13]   D Bhana "The Role of Judicial Method in the Relinquishing of Constitutional Rights through Contracts" (2008) 24 *SAJHR* 300 303.

[14]   I have been unable to find any reference to Hale in the standard literature such as RH Christie *The Law of Contract in South Africa* 5 ed (2006) or AJ Kerr *The Principles of the Law of Contract* 6 ed (2002).

[15]   In preparing this chapter, an academic colleague was bemused by the idea that contract law could, in any way, have an effect on poverty, assuming that the common law of contract was a value-neutral system which had no distributional consequences of note. For most South African academic lawyers who write about private law, Hale is an unknown figure. Sadly, his work appears never to have found its way to Oxbridge! See for a riposte to my colleague, R Hale "Bargaining, Duress and Economic Liberty" (1943) 43 *Columbia LR* 603 625.

[16]   Kennedy (1991) *Legal Studies Forum* 330.

[17]   330.

legal duty to abstain from the use of any of the money which anyone owns. He must eat. While there is no law against eating in the abstract, there is a law which forbids him to eat any of the food which actually exists in the community – and that law is the law of property. It can be lifted as to any specific food at the discretion of its owner, but if the owners unanimously refuse to lift the prohibition, the non-owner will starve unless he can himself produce food. And there is every likelihood that the owners will be unanimous in refusing, if he has no money. There is no law to compel them to part with their food for nothing. Unless, then, the non-owner can produce his own food, the law compels him to starve if he has no wages, and compels him to go without wages unless he obeys the behests of some employer. It is the law that coerces him into wage-work under penalty of starvation – unless he can produce food. Can he? Here again there is no law to prevent the production of food in the abstract; but in every settled country there is a law which forbids him to cultivate any particular piece of ground unless he happens to be an owner. This again is the law of property."[18]

I have cited extensively from Hale, as the passage highlights the critical impact of background legal rules on the distribution of income and wealth, which in turn is continuously fashioned by legal rules. A party who enjoys the protection afforded by a property right can exert considerable pressure in order to induce another party to enter into a bargain. In addition, the law endows the property owner with power to have recourse to governmental authority, if necessary, to enforce his or her property rights. It follows that:

"It is with these unequal rights that men bargain and exert pressure on one another. These rights give birth to the unequal fruits of bargaining. There may be sound reasons of economic policy to justify all the economic inequalities that flow from unequal rights. If so, these reasons must be more specific than a broad policy of private property and freedom of contract. With different rules as to the assignment of property rights, particularly by way of inheritance or government grant, we could have just as strict a protection of each person's property rights, and just as little governmental interference with freedom of contract, but a very different pattern of economic relationships."[19]

It is important to emphasise that Hale did not adopt a Marxist or a liberal analysis of law. In neither of the conventional Marxist nor liberal accounts of law, is a major role given to the causal role of law in patterns of distribution. Unlike the Marxist position, distribution is analysed in terms of the impact of legal rules and not on the basis of relations of production. Contrary to the liberal scheme, legal rules are not seen to emerge as a matter of inexorable logic from basic principles like unfettered individualism, private poverty or from the will of the people.[20] In the work of Hale, all legal systems, no matter their ideological pedigree, give rise to rules that effect distribution. Hence the need to read Hale beyond Marxism or liberalism.

The true significance of Hale lies in the emphasis placed upon the idea that the defining of powers, liabilities, immunities and privileges produces particular results, empowering some and disempowering others. In the process of definition, the judge is involved in a choice. In developing the implications of this choice, Friedrich Kessler contended that the role played by a dominant form of contract, as fashioned by the courts, promotes a concept of individualism "of which freedom of contract is the most powerful symbol",[21]

---

[18]   R Hale "Coercion and Distribution in a Supposedly Non Coercive State" (1923) 38 *Political Science Quarterly* 470 472-473.

[19]   Hale (1943) *Columbia LR* 628.

[20]   Kennedy (1991) *Legal Studies Forum* 332-333.

[21]   F Kessler "Contract of Adhesion – Some Thoughts about Freedom of Contract" (1943) 43 *Columbia LR* 629 640.

the principles of which are linked to a form of free market capitalism, based in turn, on the idea that an individual who serves his or her own interests also serves the interests of the community.[22]

In summary, Kessler and Hale developed an examination of the law of contract which seeks to interrogate its foundations and the normative framework upon which the idea of freedom of contract, so central to prevailing rules of contract law, was predicated. This literature, which is generally ignored by South African private lawyers and hardly, if ever, taught in any course on South African contract law, provides important guidance for the implementation of the task mandated by the Constitution – that is, to interrogate the prevailing foundations of all law so as to test whether all rules of law are congruent with the normative commitments of the Constitution.

Hale and Kessler thus point the way towards a deconstruction of existing norms of contract law. Absent this process, it is difficult to envisage how the constitutional interrogation of the law of contract can take place, as was intended, either by means of section 8 or the application of section 39(2) of the Constitution. Simply put, the analysis developed in this literature provides a mechanism to interrogate whether the body of contract law received from the pre-constitutional period can promote the foundational values of the Constitution, which were intended to infuse all law. To engage in this process is to commence with a deconstruction of all values immanent in prevailing legal concepts. Without this step, it becomes extremely difficult to see how a coherent application of the framework envisaged in section 8 and section 39(2) can take place. In particular, section 39(2) can only be applied after a consideration as to whether the values and principles that infuse specific rights are in alignment with the normative framework set out in the Constitution. If a positive answer is forthcoming, then a court has development work to do in order to change, extend or restrict an existing rule.

Within this theoretical context, it is possible to examine the approach that the highest South African courts have adopted to the law of contract during the constitutional era.

4   The response of the Constitutional Court and the Supreme Court of Appeal to contract and the Constitution

The decision in *Afrox Health Care Bpk v Strydom*[23] is an appropriate judgment with which to commence, in that it illustrates the consequences of ignoring realist insights as can be gleaned from the expositions of Hale and Kessler. A patient was admitted to a private hospital for an operation. On admission, he signed a standardised form. The form contained an exemption clause, in terms of which he absolved the hospital from liability for damages caused by personal injury or death resulting from any default, excluding only wilful default, on the part of the hospital staff. Certain complications arose which, it appears, were caused by the negligence of a nurse. The plaintiff sued

---

[22]   641.
[23]   2002 6 SA 21 (SCA).

the hospital for damages that he had suffered as a result of these complications. The hospital relied on the indemnity provided for in the agreement.

The plaintiff contended that this clause was contrary to public policy, alternatively, that it was in conflict with considerations of good faith, equity and fairness sourced in section 27(1)(a) of the Constitution, which provides that everyone has the right to access to health care.[24]

While the Court went through the motions of noting that these clauses are to be strictly interpreted against the *proferens*, it eschewed all consideration of the principle of good faith, but devoted great energy in emphasising the critical role of the doctrine of *pacta sunt servanda*. The constitutional imperative to examine the substance of legal norms and their congruence with the normative framework of the Constitution was given short shrift. Without more, the freedom of contract, in its most literal and interrogated form, had become a core constitutional value. Ironically, the Court found support for this proposition in a *dictum* of that quintessential apartheid judge, Chief Justice LC Steyn,[25] in *SA Sentrale Ko-op Graansmaatskappy BPK v Shifren*;[26] truly a double irony in the light of the jurisprudence of the erstwhile Chief Justice and the restrictive approach to anti-variation clauses adopted in the *Shifren* judgment.

Brand JA, on behalf of the Court, found that there was no evidence that the plaintiff had occupied a weaker bargaining position than the hospital.[27] In itself, this is a breathtaking proposition, namely that evidence is required to determine whether a person, in serious need of an operation, enjoys equality of bargaining power with the very hospital which can provide this essential medical service.

The Court found further that gross negligence had not been pleaded. Only negligence was claimed. Hence, the pleadings did not require an interrogation of the exemption clause beyond the question of negligence. On its own, the Court found that this was an inadequate foundation to argue that public policy should override the contract.[28]

This finding notwithstanding, the approach of the Court to the role of good faith in contract law is illuminating:

---

[24] Paras 11-14.

[25] I am aware that by adopting a form of social amnesia, it may be possible to level an accusation of "tar brushing" about this description of Steyn CJ. However, the description employed is but shorthand for the magisterial contribution of E Cameron "Legal Chauvinism, Executive-mindedness and Justice – LC Steyn's Impact on South African Law" (1982) 99 *SALJ* 38.

[26] 1964 4 SA 760 (A) 767A.

[27] *Afrox Health Care Bpk v Strydom* 2002 6 SA 21 (SCA) para 12.

[28] Para 13. That gross negligence had not been pleaded may well have represented an obstacle for the plaintiff. However, it is of interest that the Supreme Court of Appeal seeks to adopt a particularly rigid approach to pleadings. By contrast, in *Robinson v Randfontein Estates Gold Mining Co Ltd* 1925 AD 173 198 Innes CJ adopted a far less rigid approach:

"The object of pleading is to define the issues; and parties will be kept strictly to their pleas where any departure would cause prejudice or would prevent full enquiry. But within those limits the Court has a wide discretion. For pleadings are made for the Court, not the Court for pleadings. And where a party has had every facility to place all the facts before the trial Court and the investigation into all the circumstances has been as thorough and as patient as in this instance, there is no justification for interference by an appellant tribunal, merely because the pleading of the opponent has not been as explicit as it might have been."

"As to the role and function of abstract notions such as good faith, reasonableness and fairness, it was decided by the majority in *Brisley v Drotsky* that, although these considerations constitute the substructure of our law of contract, they do not provide an independent or 'free floating' basis for setting aside or limiting the operation of contractual provisions. Otherwise stated, although these abstract notions represent justification for and inform the rules of 'hard law', they do not constitute rules of 'hard law' themselves. When it comes to the setting aside or the enforcement of contractual provisions, a court has no general discretion to act on abstract notions such as good faith and fairness. It is bound to apply the rules of hard law."[29]

The judgment in *Afrox* illustrates the extent of the conceptual myopia which has so limited the vision of law in South Africa for more than one hundred years. Compare the judgment in *Afrox* with a passage from a thoughtful article co-written by Douglas Brodie and the author of the *Afrox* judgment, Brand JA, who ironically, commenting on the *Afrox* judgment, write:

"In the course of its judgment, the Court referred to s 39(2) of the Constitution which enjoins South African courts 'when developing the common law [to] promote the spirit, purport and objects of the Constitutions.' In the light of these provisions, so the Court held, a decision as to whether a particular provision in a contract is contrary to public policy cannot be taken without reference to the provisions of the Constitution. It can therefore be predicted that constitutional values such as equality (s. 9), dignity (s. 10), freedom of trade, occupation or profession (s. 22), and others are bound to play an ever-increasing role in the law of contract."[30]

It is submitted that it is almost impossible to reconcile this comment with the *Afrox* judgment, in that no attempt was made in the latter to investigate the potential role of constitutional values; in particular whether the constitutional right to health could have any impact on applicable contractual principles. Indeed the application of the law as developed in *Afrox* had an effect of gutting the guarantee to the right to health care for persons in the position of plaintiff. In summary, if the values of the Constitution "are bound to play an increasing role in the law of contract", as Brodie and Brand have argued, then on what possible basis is the reasoning set out in the *Afrox* judgment to be justified?

In the light of the sustained academic criticism of *Afrox*,[31] the next instalment of litigation in this area prompted the hope that the Constitutional Court would rise to the challenge posed by sections 8 and 39(2) of the Constitution, interrogate the values underlying the law of contract, examine their compatibility with the normative constitutional framework and, if necessary, engage in legal development.

In *Barkhuizen v Napier*,[32] the essential dispute turned on a 90-day time bar clause in a short-term insurance contract. Appellant contended that this clause amounted to an unreasonable and unjustified limitation of a constitutional

---

[29] *Afrox Health Care Bpk v Strydom* 2002 6 SA 21 (SCA) para 32 (translation) (footnotes omitted).

[30] D Brodie & F Brand "Good Faith in Contract Law" in R Zimmerman, D Visser & K Reid (eds) *Mixed Legal Systems in Comparative Perspective* (2004) 94 108-109.

[31] See for example L Hawthorne "Closing of the Open Norms in the Law of Contract" (2004) 67 *THRHR* 294; G Lubbe "Taking Fundamental Rights Seriously: The Bill of Rights and its Implication for the Development of Contractual Law" (2004) 121 *SALJ* 395; D Bhana & M Pieterse "Towards Reconciliation of Contract Law and Constitutional Values: *Brisley* and *Afrox* Revisited" (2005) 122 *SALJ* 865; S Liebenberg *Socio-Economic Rights: Adjudication under a Transformative Constitution* (2010) 361-365.

[32] 2007 7 BCLR 691 (CC).

right of access to courts as enshrined in section 34 of the Constitution and, accordingly, that it was contrary to public policy and unenforceable.

When the case came before the Constitutional Court,[33] Ngcobo J (as he then was), on behalf of the majority of the Constitutional Court, noted that the appellant had raised two different arguments, namely a reliance on section 34, from which it was sought to derive the content of public policy, and an invitation to the Court to apply section 34 directly to the applicable time bar clause.[34]

Ngcobo J rejected the section 34 argument, namely that the time bar clause had breached section 34. He held that the particular clause was not a law of general application and therefore could not be subjected to a limitation analysis in terms of section 36(1). It was not sufficient to find that the rule under examination was a common-law principle of contract, expressed in the maxim *pacta sunt servanda,* namely that legal agreements are binding.[35] Further, in terms of section 172(1)(a) of the Constitution, a court is required to declare "any law or conduct" that is inconsistent with the Constitution, to be invalid. The applicable clause was not "conduct" within the meaning of the provision and hence could not be construed to be a law of general application.[36]

Following these observations, the majority found that

> "[t]he proper approach to the constitutional challenges to contractual terms is to determine whether the term challenged is contrary to public policy as evidenced by constitutional values, in particular those found in the Bill of Rights. This approach leaves space for the doctrine of *pacta sunt servanda* to operate, but at the same time, allows courts to decline to enforce contractual terms that are in conflict with applicable constitutional values, even though the parties may have consented to them."[37]

Ngcobo J proceeded to enquire whether the time bar clause under scrutiny was so manifestly unreasonable that it offended public policy.[38] He found that there was nothing in the evidence to suggest that the contract of insurance had not been freely concluded between the appellant and respondent or that the appellant had not been aware of the clause.

The judgment then laid out a test which might apply to cases of this nature:

> "Thus where a claimant seeks to avoid the enforcement of a time-limitation clause on the basis that non-compliance with it was caused by factors beyond his or her control, it is inconceivable that a court would hold the claimant to such a clause."[39]

However, on the available evidence, the Court found that it was not possible to conclude whether the enforcement of the clause against the appellant would be unfair and thus contrary to public policy, in that the appellant had furnished no reason for non-compliance with the clause.[40] Accordingly, the

---

[33] An earlier appeal had failed before the Supreme Court of Appeal. See *Napier v Barkhuizen* 2006 4 SA 1 (SCA).

[34] *Barkhuizen v Napier* 2007 7 BCLR 691 (CC) para 13.

[35] Paras 23-24.

[36] Para 25.

[37] Para 30.

[38] Para 62.

[39] Para 73.

[40] Para 84.

stated facts, which represented the total factual matrix, in terms of which the Court was required to adjudicate the dispute, disclosed no reason for non-compliance with the time bar clause and there was therefore no basis to strike down the clause in the circumstances of this case.

Much has been written about this case and, in particular, the majority judgment delivered in the Constitutional Court.[41] For the purposes of this chapter, the key criticisms can be set out thus: although the majority judgment recognises that public policy imports notions of fairness, justice and reasonableness and that the doctrine of *pacta sunt servanda* cannot be upheld if it results in unfairness or an unreasonable consequence, the judgment fails to examine critically the doctrine of freedom of contract. As a consequence, contractual autonomy continues to feature as the dominant conceptual construct which underpins the mandated inquiry. There is a striking absence of any interrogation of the basis upon which contractual autonomy is predicated. In turn, the constitutional impact of *pacta sunt servanda* is hardly canvassed.

This minimalist approach is best exemplified in the manner in which the majority judgment deals with the context of the conclusion of contracts in a society where it concedes that "poverty and illiteracy abound and differences of culture and language are pronounced".[42] Consequently, the majority judgment recognises that contracts are concluded in South Africa by persons who have little bargaining power and without much understanding of the content of the contract. But that is as far as the majority is prepared to go, for Ncgobo J insist that there should be clear evidence presented to the court in order to determine whether the principle of *pacta sunt servanda* should give way to other policy considerations.

By contrast, in his minority judgment, Moseneke DCJ points out that

> "[p]ublic policy cannot be determined at the behest of the idiosyncrasies of individual contracting parties. If it were so, the determination of public policy can be held ransom by the infinite variation as to be found in any set of contracting parties."[43]

The approach of the majority appears to accept that the principle of autonomy remains the decisive consideration in any of these enquiries, save where individualised evidence is brought to discharge the relevant onus. This conclusion finds support in the manner in which Moseneke DCJ dissents with regard to the insistence of the majority that contractual terms can only be tested for their congruence with public norms by an examination of the particular situation of the contracting parties. The Deputy Chief Justice was blunt in his dissent:

---

[41] See PJ Sutherland "Ensuring Contractual Fairness and Consumer Contracts after *Barkhuizen v Napier* 2007 5 SA 323 (CC)" (2008) 19 *Stell LR* 390; PJ Sutherland "Ensuring Contractual Fairness and Consumer Contracts after *Barkhuizen v Napier* 2007 5 SA 323 (CC) – Part 2" (2009) 20 *Stell LR* 50; Bhana (2008) *SAJHR* 300.

[42] *Barkhuizen v Napier* 2007 7 BCLR 691 (CC) para 64 quoting from *Mohlomi v Minister of Defence* 1997 1 SA 124 (CC) para 14.

[43] *Barkhuizen v Napier* 2007 7 BCLR 691 (CC) para 98.

"To defeat a complaint that a contractual term offends public policy by holding that the complainant has not shown individual unfairness is, in effect, to extol the *laissez faire* notions of freedom of contract at the expense of public notions of reasonableness and fairness."[44]

A further problem with the majority judgment is the rather surprising conclusion that the question of horizontality, that is the direct application of the Bill of Rights to private persons as set out in section 8 of the Constitution, has not been considered by the Court.[45] This is a problematic finding, in that the judgment of O'Regan J in *Khumalo v Holomisa*,[46] clearly found that the Constitution did have horizontal reach.

Not only did the majority judgment appear to ignore the *Khumalo* judgment, but it went on to eschew any engagement with the direct application of the Bill of Rights to private persons, on the basis that there was no law to be analysed but rather a contract between private parties. That simply cannot be correct. The principles upon which contractual disputes are predicated, are part of our law of contract. If the principles of the law of contract are in contravention of section 34 of the Constitution, the court must determine whether section 34 is applicable to such disputes between private persons. Manifestly, this was such a case. The enquiry should have shifted to whether the principles of contract upon which the time bar clause is predicated were congruent with section 34 of the Constitution, that is, once this provision of the Constitution had been determined to apply to private disputes. But the challenge posed by section 8 is ignored and that contained in section 39(2) overlooked. Small wonder therefore that Stuart Woolman has written:

"*Barkhuizen* is so badly reasoned, and so at odds with the court's existing jurisprudence, that it is hard to know where to start."[47]

The majority judgment in *Barkhuizen*, as could have been predicted, has played an extremely important role in the further development of the law of contract. The failure of the majority to engage with the ramifications of good faith and this concept's relationship to the Constitution or to public policy, infused as it must be by the foundational values of the Constitution, represented a lost opportunity.

These consequences are best shown in a more recent decision in *Bredenkamp v Standard Bank of SA Ltd*.[48] Briefly, *Bredenkamp* concerned the right of a bank to terminate the account of a client. The bank had become aware that the United States Department of Treasury had listed the appellant as being a "specially designated national". Once a person is listed, US banks are prohibited from conducting any business, directly or indirectly, with such a person or entity. By virtue of its relationship with Master Card, Standard Bank was placed in a similar position. It appeared that appellant had been listed because he was said to be "a crony" of President Mugabe and had provided financial and logistical

---

[44] Para 104.
[45] Para 23.
[46] 2002 5 SA 401 (CC) paras 31-32.
[47] S Woolman "The Amazing, Vanishing Bill of Rights" (2007) 124 *SALJ* 762 772.
[48] 2010 4 SA 468 (SCA). My insight into this judgment has been greatly enriched by a contribution of Jaco Barnard-Naudé "Deconstruction is What Happens" (2011) 22 *Stell LR* 160.

support to the "regime" that had enabled Mugabe "to pursue policies that seriously undermined democratic processes and institutions in Zimbabwe".[49]

In terms of its contract with appellant, the bank was entitled to terminate the account, upon reasonable notice having been so given. In addition, it was not contractually obliged to provide reasons for termination. The appellant approached the High Court for an interim interdict to restrain the bank from terminating his facilities. He first contended that there was no express term which entitled the bank to act as it has done and, to the extent that there was an implied term, this was *contra bonos mores* and thus unconstitutional.[50]

After the interim interdict was granted, it was discovered that the appellant "had an unenviable and dubious reputation locally and internationally"[51] which included allegations of sanctions busting in relation to the US and the UK, as well as a range of acts of tax evasion and fraud.

On the return day, appellant contended that the bank's decision to terminate offended constitutional values and, accordingly, it had no right to so act. This argument was rejected by the court *a quo* and the matter proceeded to the Supreme Court of Appeal, which upheld the right of the bank to terminate appellant's bank account.

To the argument that the enforcement of the termination clause was unfair, the Court said:

> "The argument proceeded on the basis that *Barkhuizen* stands as authority for the proposition that fairness is a core value of the Bill of Rights and that it is therefore a broad requirement of our law generally. This would mean that any conduct (including legislation), which is unfair, would be in conflict with the Constitution and, accordingly void – a novel proposition, at least for me. In any event, according to the argument, fairness and reasonableness have infused the law of contract to such an extent that ordinary principles, such as those relating to mistake, misrepresentation, cancellation and all else have been subsumed by constitutional fairness."[52]

However, Harms DP was careful not to ignore entirely the link between the Constitution and the common law. He accepted that

> "every rule has to pass constitutional muster. Public policy and the boni mores are now deeply rooted in the Constitution and its underlying values".[53]

Then comes a significant passage:

> "This does not mean that public policy values cannot be found elsewhere. The constitutional principle that tends to be overlooked when generalised resort to constitutional values is made is the principle of legality. Making rules of law discretionary or subject to value judgments may be destructive of the rule of law."[54]

This comment is made in direct response to the argument that public policy now derives its content from the broad normative framework of the Constitution, which is intended to infuse our entire legal system with its spirit, purport and objects. What could Harms DP mean when he claims that making rules discretionary or subject to value judgments may be destructive of the

---

[49] *Bredenkamp v Standard Bank of SA Ltd* 2010 4 SA 468 (SCA) para 14.
[50] Paras 6-9.
[51] Para 19.
[52] Para 27.
[53] Para 39.
[54] Para 39.

rule of law? The learned judge of appeal can surely not have contended that value judgments play no role in the process of adjudication or that the judicial operation is no more than a jurisprudential slot machine in which material is fed into the machine, which then spews out the only correct result.

What I take him to mean within the specific context of the law of contract is that, once the parties have so contracted, courts should not, save in the most exceptional of circumstances, reject the rules which flow from the contract by means of what Harms DP considers to be a value judgment – but which others would consider to be an engagement with the normative framework of the Constitution and its lack of congruence with the applicable rules of contract.

Barnard-Naudé[55] reveals a further contradiction in the judgment when he refers to Harms DP's comment that, once a contractual clause limits a constitutional right the limitation "is not *per se* contrary to public policy, but it would be if the limitation was 'unreasonable or unfair'".[56] Suddenly, fairness looms large as a principle and, arguably, even larger in this case, albeit by implication. A reading of the judgment as a whole supports the conclusion that it is based on the idea that the enforcement of a right to cancel a bank account in the circumstances of this case was not unfair. Further, it did not amount to an abuse of bargaining power, because it was the appellant and his entities who were guilty of bad faith, fraud, corruption and complicity in criminal activity.[57]

The judgment in *Bredenkamp* again illustrates a notional acceptance by the Court of the reach of the Constitution into the domain of private law while, at least by implication, reaffirming a commitment to the standard version of the ground rules of contract. No attempt is made to engage in a process of contractual deconstruction. To illustrate how Hale would be applied to those disputes, a recent decision of the Supreme Court of Appeal provides rich material.

5 *Maphango*: the conceptual chickens come home to roost

The cases examined so far in this chapter do not touch directly upon the questions of poverty save, arguably, for *Afrox*, which raises issues relating to health care. However, it is central to the argument of this chapter that the retention of the dominant paradigm may have a direct effect upon poverty. This is now luminously illustrated in the case of *Maphango v Angus Lifestyle Properties (Pty) Ltd*.[58] The appellants were lessees of flats located in a ten-storey building. The respondent, which was the owner of the building, brought an application for the eviction of the appellants and their families on the basis that the leases had been duly terminated by a notice on its behalf. The appellants opposed the application on two grounds, namely that the purported termination of leases was invalid and, secondly, even if the leases were validly

---

[55] Barnard-Naudé (2011) *Stell LR* 169-170.
[56] *Bredenkamp v Standard Bank of SA Ltd* 2010 4 SA 468 (SCA) para 44.
[57] Barnard-Naudé (2011) *Stell LR* 170.
[58] [2011] ZASCA 100 (01-06-2011) *SAFLII* <http://www.saflii.org/za/cases/ZASCA/2011/189.html> (accessed 07-10-2011).

terminated, this act to so terminate was not just and equitable in terms of the provisions of section 4(6) of the Prevention of the Illegal Eviction from and Unlawful Occupation of Land Act 19 of 1998.[59]

It was common cause that, from November 2008 to March 2009, written notices of termination of the leases were provided to each of the appellants. The appellant had generated these notices because its business model was to acquire buildings in the central business district of Johannesburg. Many of these buildings, which were derelict, were then renovated and rented out to tenants. It was also common cause that the notices informed the appellants that, if they wished to remain as tenants beyond the date for termination of the agreement, they would be required to enter into new lease agreements at rentals which were approximately 100% to 150% higher than what had been paid at the time.[60]

The appellants contended that each of the lease agreements contained a tacit term which forbade the use of the termination clause to increase the rental beyond the increment provided in the respective agreements. They further argued that to allow the respondent to terminate the agreements in this fashion was unreasonable and unfair, constituted an infringement of the right to access to adequate housing in terms of section 26(1) of the Constitution and was an unfair practice as contemplated in the Rental Housing Act 50 of 1999.[61]

For the limited purposes of this chapter, the second argument, namely that the termination of the leases was unreasonable and unfair and should not be enforced on grounds of public policy, is particularly relevant. The Court found that there was nothing unreasonable in the conduct of the respondent to terminate the leases. It justified its conclusion thus:

> "[S]ince the respondent is not a charitable organisation, it cannot be blamed for its unwillingness to pursue this commendable business venture at a loss as would be the result if the current leases were to be maintained at the agreed rentals. The respondent therefore decided to terminate the leases, as it was contractually entitled to do, to save its business from commercial demise. In doing so, it behaved transparently by disclosing its motive, which it was not obliged to do. Had it not done so, the present litigation would probably not have ensued. Objectively, I can find nothing in the respondent's conduct that can justifiably be described as unreasonable and unfair."[62]

Turning to the argument based on section 26(1) of the Constitution, namely that everyone has the right to adequate housing, the Court, without any explanation or justification, concluded that the provision does not bind private persons. In the next sentence, it conceded that "*in its negative aspect*" private persons are bound because, in the words of the Court, "it thus forbids private persons from interfering with the rights of any other persons in terms of the section".[63]

---

[59] Para 1.
[60] Para 8.
[61] Para 12.
[62] Para 25.
[63] Para 26 (emphasis added).

Appellants contended that, although the rights enshrined in section 26(1) did not prevent the termination of a lease, a party in the position of the respondent was bound to exercise a right to terminate in a reasonable and fair manner. In the present case, appellants argued that the termination was unreasonable and was therefore contrary to public policy.[64]

The Court rejected this argument. In concluding that a lessee of property enjoys no security of tenure in perpetuity, it held that the duration of a lease is governed by the terms thereof. Beyond the period of the lease, a lessee has no rights with regard to tenure.[65] Distinguishing this case from *Jaftha v Schoeman; Van Rooyen v Stoltz*[66] and *Standard Bank of South Africa Ltd v Saunderson*[67] on the basis that these latter cases dealt with interference with the rights to security of tenure of an owner to his or her home, the Court held that this case dealt with appellants who had no security of tenure beyond the duration of the lease and thus could not be afforded any relief by the courts.[68]

The factual matrix confronting the Court in cases such as *Saunderson* was, admittedly, different in form to that with which the Court was dealing in *Maphango*. But, in substance, there were considerable similarities. For example, in *Saunderson*, a bank sought judgment against a number of home-owners in respect of the amount of their debts and, in accordance with the ordinary procedures, for a further order declaring the mortgage property executable. While the Court, on the facts, found that the property that was the subject of the mortgage bond was executable, it noted:

> "[T]he defaulting debtor should be informed, in the process of initiating action, that s 26(1) may affect the bond-holder's claim to execution. Should it be held that the negative obligation of s 26(1) binds even the bond-holder, the debtor would have the right to invoke circumstances that may persuade a court to grant extenuation in the execution of the order (albeit that the bond-holder's summons need not attempt to justify in advance a possible constitutional infringement). Section 172 permits a court when deciding a constitutional matter to make an order that is 'just and equitable' and it is in our view desirable to lay down a rule of practice requiring a summons in which an order for execution against immovable property is sought to inform the defendant that his or her right of access to adequate housing might be implicated by such an order."[69]

This approach follows that of the Constitutional Court in *Jaftha*, where Mokgoro J, writing for the Court, noted that the right to have access to adequate housing is enshrined in section 26(1) of the Constitution. Thus, the Court could determine, on the facts, that there was unjustifiable interference with any person's existing access to adequate housing and that "at the very least, any measure which permits a person to be deprived of existing access limits the rights protected in section 26(1)".[70]

---

[64] Para 12.
[65] Paras 28-29.
[66] 2005 2 SA 140 (CC).
[67] 2006 2 SA 264 (SCA).
[68] *Maphango v Angus Lifestyle Properties (Pty) Ltd* [2011] ZASCA 100 (01-06-2011) *SAFLII* para 30.
[69] *Standard Bank of South Africa Ltd v Saunderson* 2006 2 SA 264 (SCA) para 25.
[70] *Jaftha v Schoeman; Van Rooyen v Stoltz* 2005 2 SA 140 (CC) para 34.

In *Maphango,* there is a marked absence of any examination as to how the conduct of land owners such as the respondent, which sought to buy up derelict buildings and evict those who were living precariously in order to make a significant profit, could not constitute a measure which unfairly limited rights protected in terms of section 26(1). At the very least, this enquiry would have compelled the Court to consider a further extenuation of the decision to so terminate the lease. Nowhere in this judgment is there an engagement with the substance of the constitutional implications of the law of contract or the effect on people living in a precarious situation, who were significantly affected by the approach to the contract of lease as articulated in the judgment.

The background rules, as applied by the Court, therefore reinforce one property claim and ignore another, or, at least, refuse to recognise that the latter has any legal significance. Brand JA holds that the lessee "has no security of tenure in perpetuity. The duration of the lessee's tenure is governed by the terms of the lease."[71] Thus, existing property rules, as argued by Hale, have the consequences that one party has no rights and the other party has the power to determine the fate of the former. Notwithstanding that the Constitution has been interpreted to soften the harshness of this conception of property law,[72] the Court eschews any consideration thereof. Hence the manner in which the law reproduces patterns of power and distribution that reproduce poverty and hence despair is of no forensic moment, even within the context of a Constitution that contains majestic claims about curbing abuses of power, even if sourced in private power.[73]

There is nothing natural or automatic about the outcome reached by Brand JA regarding the rights of a lessee. Rather, as Hale has shown, it is the uncritical acceptance in this case of a background rule of property law that shapes the outcome, against the poor and in the favour of the property owner. Hale JA would have examined the basis of the rules of law upon which the lessor's rights were predicated, set out their implications and then tested these against the Constitution. Brand JA treats existing background rules as universal, a natural product of the legal system, and hence axiomatic.

6   A legislative intervention

Subsequent to a number of these decisions, the Consumer Protection Act 68 of 2008 has now come into force. This legislation is designed to address many of the concerns that have been articulated in this chapter and to strengthen the protection that the law affords consumers.[74]

A superficial reading of the Consumer Protection Act may justify an argument that the concerns articulated in this chapter are now irrelevant. However, as Sutherland has noted:

---

[71]   *Maphango v Angus Lifestyle Properties (Pty) Ltd* [2011] ZASCA 100 (01-06-2011) *SAFLII* para 28.

[72]   See *Port Elizabeth Municipality v Various Occupiers* 2004 12 BCLR 1268 (CC).

[73]   Recall the important point of Hale in this connection: the exercise of private power takes place through law which provides remedy enforced by public authority. Hale (1943) *Columbia LR* 627. So much for the exercise of autonomy which is immune from public power.

[74]   Sutherland (2009) *Stell LR* 72.

"[T]hese legislative reforms should be accommodated within a general contract law ... that [is] in harmony with it."[75]

Take for example section 49 of the Consumer Protection Act, which has the potential to put an end to *Afrox*-type jurisprudence. Section 49 provides for the provision of a notice drawing attention of the consumer to certain types of risk. These are defined as any risk

"(a) of an unusual character or nature;
(b) the presence of which the consumer could not reasonably be expected to be aware or notice, or which an ordinary alert consumer could not reasonably be expected to notice or contemplate in the circumstances; or
(c) that could result in serious injury or death."[76]

In general, in dealing with these provisions, a court may have to consider the application of a concept of good faith and fair dealing in order to determine whether a particular term is unfair as well as to give content to the phrase "a significant imbalance" in the rights and obligations of the parties which is *"not reasonably necessary to protect the legitimate interest of the supplier"*.[77]

In terms of section 52 of the Consumer Protection Act,[78] a court may make an order to the effect that the transaction agreement is, in whole or in part, unconscionable, unjust, unreasonable or unfair and that it should be just and reasonable to order the restoration of money or property to the consumer or to compensate the consumer for losses or expenses. In making such an order, the court is obliged to consider the following:

"(a) the fair value of the goods or services in question;
(b) the nature of the parties to that transaction or agreement, their relationship to each other and their relative capacity, education, experience, sophistication and bargaining position;
(c) those circumstances of the transaction or agreement that existed or were reasonably foreseeable at the time that the conduct or transaction occurred or agreement was made, irrespective of whether this Act was in force at that time;
(d) the conduct of the supplier and the consumer, respectively;
(e) whether there was any negotiation between the supplier and the consumer, and if so, the extent of that negotiation;
(f) whether, as a result of conduct engaged in by the supplier, the consumer was required to do anything that was not reasonably necessary for the legitimate interests of the supplier ...
(i) the amount for which, and circumstances under which, the consumer could have acquired identical or equivalent goods or services from a different supplier ..."[79]

For the jurisprudence that emerges from the Consumer Protection Act to be coherent, the courts will no longer be able to eschew an interrogation of the ground rules upon which the contractual arrangement has been ultimately fashioned, and as has been analysed by Hale. Inequality of bargaining power and the consequences thereof lie at the heart of the considerations of which the court is required to take into account in terms of section 52(2). The ultimate

---

[75]   72.
[76]   See s 49(2)(a)-(c) of the Consumer Protection Act.
[77]   T Naude "The Consumer's 'Right to Fair, Reasonable and Just Terms' under the New Consumer Protection Act in Comparative Perspective" (2009) 126 *SALJ* 505 517-518 (emphasis added).
[78]   The provisions should be read together with s 48 of the Consumer Protection Act.
[79]   S 52(2) of the Consumer Protection Act.

problem with unfair contractual terms is not with the standard term *per se* but with the existence an exercise of market power.[80]

This new legislation introduces a number of value-laden concepts such as whether an agreement is "excessively one sided in favour of any person other than the consumer" or "the terms are so adverse to the consumers to be inequitable".[81] Thus the recent judicial record, in which the substance of the contractual outcome circumvents the implications of the Constitution and thus restricts the development of the general principles of the law of contract, would, to a large degree, work to subvert the very purpose of this legislation.

However, the courts may finally have to infuse a variable range of contracts with a more coherent concept of fairness and reasonableness. Regulation 44 of the Regulations to the Consumer Protection Act,[82] read together with section 120 of the Act, creates a presumption of unfairness. This will work to the advantage of the consumer where a term of a contract has the purpose or effect of creating a range of consequences, including, for example, the exclusion or restriction of a consumer's right to rely on the statutory defence of prescription or excluding or limiting the liability of a supplier for death or personal injury caused to the consumer through an act or omission of a supplier. In turn, the breadth of the new Act, even when read with the Regulations, will depend on a willingness of courts to interrogate principles of law which have, to date, assumed iconic status that implies uncritical acceptance and application.

7 Conclusion

The work of Robert Hale draws attention to the manner in which the rules of law produce and reproduce patterns of wealth, poverty, power and powerlessness. It emphasises that the law of contract cannot simply be viewed as an arena of private autonomy which is devoid of profound public implications. These implications include the production and reinforcement of patterns of access to resources and this occurs because the nature and scope of background rules condition the consequences of distributional conflict. It must follow therefore that a change to these legal rules may alter the bargaining outcome. That the outcome should matter to a judiciary, enjoined to examine the congruence of all law with the normative framework of the Constitution, follows from a reading of sections 8 and 39(2) of the Constitution.

Hale showed that law is responsible, at least in part, for patterns of distribution which, in turn, means that the invitation to adhere to the contractual shibboleths of the past should be declined if we are concerned with inequality and its clear companion in South Africa – poverty.

Viewed within broader theoretical terms, Hannah Arendt has argued that the constitution of freedom requires a constitution that does not merely

---

[80] I am indebted for these insights to Robert Petersen SC and his unpublished paper R Petersen *The Constitution and the Private Law: the Case Study of Unfair Contracts* (2009) (copy on file with author).
[81] S 48(2) of the Consumer Protection Act.
[82] GN R 95 in *GG 9515* of 01-05-2011.

entail government guaranteeing private rights but also the development of a constitutional scheme whereby everyone is admitted to the public realm.[83] That is not to suggest that Arendt was not concerned about the qualities that constitutional government can provide in terms of stability and endurance of the legal system. Rather, she was anxious that the empowerment of the citizenry within the society was equally important to ensure that all would be able to participate meaningfully in civic life. An uncritical acceptance of private autonomy, as is evidenced in the prevailing contractual jurisprudence, goes no further than the protection of existing private rights.

Admittedly, a concept of contract law, in particular, and private law, in general, which embraces this constitutional vision, is a value-laden exercise. But is it more value laden than the argument of Brand JA when, in criticising the minority judgment of Sachs J in *Barkhuizen*, he writes:

"One cannot help wondering, if his approach would have been endorsed by courts as a general principle, how many Lloyds' contracts would be concluded in South Africa."[84]

Hence the debate is not about the existence of a contest of values. Contest is inevitable in any process of adjudication, whether the dispute is grounded in the principles of the general law of contract or derived from the provisions of the Consumer Protection Act, even buttressed by the Regulations. In either case, the process of adjudication is involved in the application of open-ended legal standards that require an interrogation of values and policy considerations. The absence of the kind of analysis embarked upon by Hale endangers our constitutional ambition of ensuring that all law is congruent with the normative framework set out in the Constitution. In turn, this normative framework holds implications for continued patterns of poverty, particularly because of the latter's effect upon freedom and dignity.

The decisions discussed in this chapter have, in effect, circumvented the implications of this normative constitutional framework. An engagement with the foundational values has been prominent in its absence rather than in any process of coherent judicial work. Unfortunately, it appears as if the courts are more concerned, when dealing with implications of the law of contract, with the conclusion of Lloyd's policies in South Africa than with the effect of existing law upon the living conditions of the majority of South Africans.

SUMMARY

The constitutional settlement that ushered in democracy in South Africa did not summarily erase apartheid from the social and economic landscape. The drafters of the Constitution understood that erasure would not be achieved by way of one silver bullet. It could only occur by way of a journey towards the egalitarian vision prefigured in the constitutional text. At the same time the drafters understood that legal rules which reinforced patterns of power required reconfiguration if the journey was to be undertaken. The idea was that the Constitution, whether through a specific right or the influence of its normative framework, itself based upon the foundational principles of dignity,

---

[83] See in particular the arguments developed in H Arendt *On Revolution* (1963).
[84] FJ Brand "The Role of Good Faith, Equity and Fairness" (2009) 126 *SALJ* 71 87.

freedom and equality, would be central to a reconfiguration of the background rules in terms of which all economic activity took place. Viewed within the matrix of this compelling observation, it was to be hoped that the distributive importance of the ground rules of contract would have been the subject of careful interrogation by the courts. In this chapter I seek to engage with key cases in which South African courts, in effect, ignored these challenges when deciding disputes based upon the law of contract. The record reveals that the courts either eschewed the significance of the Constitution or simply nodded in the direction of the Constitution, before proceeding in the opposite direction. I employ the realist work of Robert Hale to illustrate that rules which assign property rights and which impact upon the nature and enforcement of contractual claims profoundly shape economic relationships. In short, if the ground rules are changed, an alteration of social and economic relationship may well take place.

CHAPTER 22

CONCLUDING REFLECTIONS: LEGAL ACTIVISM AFTER POVERTY HAS BEEN DECLARED UNCONSTITUTIONAL

Karl Klare[*]

1 Introduction

I had the honour – and daunting task – of offering concluding reflections at the Law and Poverty Colloquium with an eye toward drawing together some major threads of the discussion. I repeat here the gratitude I then expressed for the energy and imagination of the many people who made the colloquium a great success.[1] In the brief compass of these remarks, I cannot possibly survey the rich array of research and analysis we shared, and I have precious little insight to add. I particularly regret short-changing the challenging papers on policy questions.

Preliminarily, I want to highlight Professor Liebenberg's remark that the colloquium was blessed to have so many distinguished jurists in attendance, including some heroes of the liberation struggle. I doubt that South African academics appreciate just how extraordinary it is that judges of the Constitutional Court and other courts would attend a gathering like this, sit with us, take our enterprise seriously, engage with our arguments and concerns, and contribute to the dialogue. We were particularly fortunate to hear former Chief Justice Pius Langa's moving dinner address.[2] Nothing like this ever occurs in the United States. I suspect that there are very few, if any, other places in the world where it does. In this respect, South African lawyers and academics are indeed very privileged.

2 Poverty-eradication as a constitutional imperative

A tacit premise of the colloquium that merits explicit statement is that poverty-eradication is not only a desirable policy-direction for South Africa, it is a *constitutional imperative*. This observation may be trite in South Africa, but it is decidedly novel almost everywhere else in the world. In their scholarship

---

[*] This is a lightly edited and annotated version of informal remarks delivered at the conclusion of the Law and Poverty Colloquium, Stellenbosch Institute for Advanced Study (STIAS), University of Stellenbosch, 29-05-011–31-05-011.

[1] Special thanks in particular to Professor Sandra Liebenberg, Academic Director of the Colloquium; Project Manger Gustav Muller; Dean Gerhard Lubbe and the Faculty of Law, Stellenbosch University; the STIAS community; and the many students and others who facilitated the programme.

[2] Reprinted here as P Langa "The Role of the Constitution in the Struggle against Poverty" in S Liebenberg & G Quinot (eds) *Law and Poverty* (2012) 4.

and activism, colloquium participants fight to eradicate poverty both because poverty is wrong and because it is *prima facie* illegal. The continued existence of widespread poverty in South Africa is plainly inconsistent with the vision of freedom and democracy embraced by the Constitution.[3] As former Chief Justice Langa put it, complacency in the face of continuing poverty "contradicts the Constitution".[4] The Constitutional Court has held that "[t]he State is *obliged* to take positive action to meet the needs of those living in extreme conditions of poverty, homelessness or intolerable housing".[5]

The success of South Africa's constitutional project will be judged in large part by the effectiveness of the measures taken by government and civil society under the command of the Constitution to eradicate poverty. As former Chief Justice Langa argued, the elimination of poverty "is critical to democracy, development and the stability of our constitutional state".[6] No one is so naïve as to think that, by themselves, the stated aspirations of the Constitution can deliver clean water, food, medical care, education, social security or housing. Still, it is a remarkable development in legal history for a jurisdiction to affirm that its constitution requires the abolition of poverty.

3   The multidimensional nature of poverty

A salient theme of the colloquium was attention to the variegated and multidimensional nature of poverty. Sandra Fredman showed why merely defining "poverty" is a complicated and contested task.[7] Lucy Williams' chapter developed the important analytical observation that poverty cannot be defined or understood independent of the ways in which legal practices and discourses characterise or "construct" it.[8] The distinct dimensions of poverty are inextricably intertwined, yet each has unique aspects that cannot be reduced to or neatly mapped onto the others. Similar cross-cutting complexities arise in plotting the relationship between poverty and inequality or the inter-relationships between material deprivation, social and cultural life, and political life.[9] Nancy Fraser raised a further complication: intersecting with each of the multiple dimensions

---

[3]   The Constitution of the Republic of South Africa, 1996 ("the Constitution").

[4]   Langa "The Role of the Constitution" in *Law and Poverty* 4, referencing the Preamble of the Constitution.

[5]   Langa "The Role of the Constitution" in *Law and Poverty* 7, quoting *Government of the Republic of South Africa v Grootboom* 2001 1 SA 46 (CC) paras 23-24 (emphasis added).

[6]   Langa "The Role of the Constitution" in *Law and Poverty* 4. Langa further states that "[p]overty ... may bring with it complex and interrelated challenges that threaten to interfere with our society's commitment to the rule of law, which is a foundational concept and element of our constitutional existence".

[7]   S Fredman "The Potential and Limits of an Equal Rights Paradigm in Addressing Poverty" in S Liebenberg & G Quinot (eds) *Law and Poverty* (2012) 124, 125-132.

[8]   L Williams "The Legal Construction of Poverty: Gender, 'Work' and the 'Social Contract'" in S Liebenberg & G Quinot (eds) *Law and Poverty* (2012) 21.

[9]   In his discussion of the dichotomy Hannah Arendt draws between the social and the political, Emilios Christodoulidis rightly argued that human freedom is at stake both socially and politically and that "social questions" are necessarily sites of political contestation over the meaning of freedom. See E Christodoulidis "De-Politicising Poverty: Arendt in South Africa" in S Liebenberg & G Quinot (eds) *Law and Poverty* (2012) 59.

of poverty are three different scales or levels of the injustice of poverty, namely national, transnational, and global.[10]

The problem here is not simply to get the taxonomy right for academic purposes. Poverty-eradication strategies must be sensitive to the different ways in which poverty and deprivation are experienced. Well-intended anti-poverty measures designed to "raise all ships" simultaneously may differentially impact on particular social groups or on particular types of injury. "One-size-fits-all" thinking insensitive to the complexity and "thickness" of social context may wind up entrenching status-inequalities and relative economic deprivation.[11]

One axis along which presenters arrayed the social context and experience of poverty is the dimension of social and cultural status. Cathi Albertyn argued, for example, that "the need to address the distinctive forms of poverty and inequality experienced by women" is central to fulfilling the Constitution's commitment to equality, improved quality of life, and the freeing of human potential "although [this is] often not recognised as such".[12] Lucy Williams argued that as decision-makers in both the US and South Africa "translated the supposedly universal values of 'dignity', 'self-sufficiency' and 'independence' into policies, institutions, and legal rules, they consistently filled them with gendered content that ultimately reinforces the social and economic subordination of women".[13] Several speakers noted that even progressive anti-poverty advocates sometimes need to be reminded of the distinctly racial and gender dimensions of poverty.[14]

A distinct dimension of poverty is the range of harms it causes. Material deprivation is only one aspect (and there is dispute within the anti-poverty community about whether material deprivation should or can be defined in absolute or in relative terms). The poor are also denied agency and self-determination in daily life and in their life-course. Poverty is associated with stigma and shame. The poor, particularly poor women, are disproportionately vulnerable to violence. Some speakers invoked the notion of "social exclusion",[15] although in response, Lucy Williams argued the concept of social exclusion, now particularly salient in the European discussion, is problematical in that

---

[10] N Fraser "Social Exclusion, Global Poverty, and Scales of (In)Justice: Rethinking Law and Poverty in a Globalising World" in S Liebenberg & G Quinot (eds) *Law and Poverty* (2012) 10.

[11] See, for example, Fredman "An Equal Rights Paradigm" in *Law and Poverty* 132-4 stating that policy responses focused only on poverty without considering issues of inequality among the poor risk entrenching inequality. See also S Mnisi Weeks & A Claassens "Tensions Between Vernacular Values that Prioritise Basic Needs and State Versions of Customary Law that Contradict Them" in S Liebenberg & G Quinot (eds) *Law and Poverty* (2012) 381, asserting that law and policies that ignore dense local contexts may increase rather than eradicate poverty.

[12] See C Albertyn "Gendered Transformation in South Africa Jurisprudence: Poor Women and the Constitutional Court" in S Liebenberg & G Quinot (eds) *Law and Poverty* (2012) 149. Albertyn also states that the need to address gendered poverty and inequality is central to South Africa's constitutional project (149). Albertyn's approach is not a matter of "adding on" concerns about gender inequality to concerns about economic deprivation. Rather, the need is to address *intersectional* claims, for example, to appreciate the unique experience and needs of poor women (150-152).

[13] Williams "The Legal Construction of Poverty" in *Law and Poverty* 21.

[14] It was altogether fitting that a session of the Law and Poverty Colloquium celebrated the launch of B Goldblatt & K McLean (eds) *Women's Social & Economic Rights: Developments in South Africa* (2011).

[15] See, for example, Fraser "Social Exclusion" in *Law and Poverty* 10.

that it may valorise "inclusion" into or conformity with the going system.[16] Nancy Fraser's keynote address theorised the types of harms poverty causes or of which it consists, which in her formulation include material deprivation, denial of recognition, and denial of voice.[17] Sandra Fredman offered a four-dimensional analytic framework for understanding questions of poverty in relationship to substantive equality.[18]

Once again, sorting out these complexities is not a matter of simply academic concern. The point is that virtually all of the critical concepts upon which progressive, anti-poverty thinking is grounded – such as "deprivation," "equality," "dignity," and "poverty" itself – point us in a general direction but are indeterminate as to their concrete meaning(s). What these terms mean in people's lived experience is something about which the poor and their advocates can and from time to time should disagree. These concepts and values are not self-defining. Except as evocative rhetoric, they become useful to us only if we fill them with ever-more fine-grained, substantive content. The indeterminacy of our fundamental values does not mean we cannot make rational decisions about the way forward or that anyone's idea of "equality" or "dignity" is as good as anyone else's. What it does mean is that we cannot *derive* policy approaches from the foundational values without making intermediate and contestable ethical and political judgments that are not prescribed by the abstract values. Moreover, we need to bring a great deal of local knowledge to bear on the effort in order to do a satisfactory job of translating the values into effective policies, always bearing in mind that all knowledge about society is at least partially shaped by the preoccupations and world view of the actor or investigator. Conscious or unconscious moral and political sensibilities come into play whenever we address a question like "what is the scope and what are the characteristics of poverty among single-parent households in rural KwaZulu-Natal?" All of this is elementary to social scientists, policy analysts, and activists on the ground. As will be seen, however, special difficulties arise when *lawyers* attempt to give substantive content to abstract legal concepts like equality or dignity.

4   Poverty and democracy

Another thread of the conversation concerned the interpretive frame in which we should understand democracy. Henk Botha and Danie Brand argued that the Constitution embraces a new conception of democracy that assumes but is not exhausted by free elections and representative government.[19]

---

[16]   Fredman "An Equal Rights Paradigm" in *Law and Poverty* 125 deploys the concept of social exclusion, but also states that policy "should not exact conformity as a price of equality" (135).

[17]   Fraser "Social Exclusion" in *Law and Poverty* 10. This corresponds to her three-axis conception of justice, comprising distributive justice, equal recognition, and democratic representation (455).

[18]   Fredman "An Equal Rights Paradigm" in *Law and Poverty* 135 (redistribution, recognition, transformation, and participation as distinct dimensions of substantive equality in relationship to poverty).

[19]   H Botha "Representing the Poor: Law, Poverty, and Democracy" in S Liebenberg & G Quinot (eds) *Law and Poverty* (2012) 79, 80. D Brand "Judicial Deference and Democracy in Socio-Economic Rights Cases in South Africa" in S Liebenberg & G Quinot (eds) *Law and Poverty* (2012) 172, 179-82. For an excellent overview, see T Roux "Democracy" in S Woolman, T Roux & M Bishop (eds) *CLoSA* 2 ed (RS 1 2009) 10-1–10-77.

We thought aloud about the shape and contours of this new understanding of democracy and whether it might open political space for the poor to challenge their continued subordination and exclusion. Danie Brand argued that the constitutional vision of democracy embraces the idea that poverty-eradication is not a technical problem for solution by experts and elites but fundamentally a political problem. The implication is that the poor must be actively engaged in the design and implementation of measures to eliminate poverty. Frank Michelman spoke of a "social-liberal constitution" concerned to eliminate poverty,[20] but acknowledged that there is a "space of doubt" about whether the divide between liberal constitutionalism and socially progressive goals can be straddled.[21] Sanele Sibanda feared that an interpretation of South Africa's transformative constitution anchored within a liberal paradigm – even a modernised and "socially conscious" version – would narrow and stunt the transformative project and the promise of eradicating poverty.[22] This outcome might eventuate, he argues, because of the general conservatism of the local legal culture.

Colloquium participants used an array of emblems to evoke this richer conception of democracy toward which the Constitution points including "advanced democracy", "radical democracy", "social democracy", "social-liberal democracy",[23] "participatory democracy",[24] "thick democracy",[25] "substantive democracy",[26] and "post-liberal democracy".[27] The conversation did, however, make two things clear. First, that the eradication of poverty will go hand-in-hand with the invention of a richer vision of democracy. Second, specifying the content of this advanced conception of democracy is every bit as complicated and difficult as concretising the meanings of poverty, deprivation, inequality, and social recognition. It will be the work of a generation.

In general conception, democracy is a set of political, institutional, social, and material arrangements and conditions that enable and allow all people to be self-determining in their individual choices, in their life-course, and in their collective existence. The Constitutional Court has provided a few,

---

[20]   FI Michelman "Liberal Constitutionalism, Property Rights, and the Assault on Poverty" in S Liebenberg & G Quinot (eds) *Law and Poverty* (2012) 264, 274-275.

[21]   Cathi Albertyn insightfully addresses a parallel if also ambiguous debate within equality theory between a "liberal-egalitarian" and more "critical" or redistributive conceptions of substantive equality. See Albertyn "Gendered Transformation" in *Law and Poverty* 163-167.

[22]   S Sibanda "Not Purpose-Made! Transformative Constitutionalism, Post-Independence Constitutionalism, and the Struggle to Eradicate Poverty" in S Liebenberg & G Quinot (eds) *Law and Poverty* (2012) 40, 44. See also 50, where Sibanda expresses doubt that transformative constitutionalism "conceived within a liberal democratic paradigm" has the potential to empower the poor as true political agents or to provide the legal framework for eradicating poverty.

[23]   Michelman "Liberal Constitutionalism" in *Law and Poverty* 274-276.

[24]   Botha "Representing the Poor" in *Law and Poverty* 79.

[25]   Brand "Judicial Deference" in *Law and Poverty* 180.

[26]   181.

[27]   See K Klare "Legal Culture and Transformative Constitutionalism" (1998) 14 *SAJHR* 146 151-156.

encouraging glimmers of authority for this broader vision.[28] But at this stage we are for the most part still groping in the dark in our efforts to fill the abstract idea with more precise content. Various speakers in various ways suggested at least the following components of advanced democracy (in addition to free and fair elections and representative government):

- ongoing and robust popular engagement and political participation down to grass-roots level;[29]
- more complex conceptions of procedural fairness;[30]
- transformative conceptions of separation-of-powers;[31] and
- reorganisation of the background social and economic conditions so that all people live in circumstances affording them the capacity authentically to experience self-determination and the meaningful pursuit of personal and political choices.

The last point gives rise to a suggestion and a wholly tangential observation. The suggestion is that future colloquiums of this kind devote greater attention to questions of private law to complement our discussions of constitutional law and public policy. South Africans cannot create a just society by superimposing a transformative Constitution suffused with the spirit of *ubuntu*[32] onto a largely untransformed legal infrastructure.[33] As Lucy Williams reminded us, all of the hidden and obscure background rules that partially constitute social and economic life must be brought into the foreground, interrogated, and renovated with an eye toward transformation.[34] Not enough of this has occurred so far in the new South Africa,[35] with the notable exception of the field of residential property and evictions.

The tangent concerns an irony in our evolving understanding of the rule of law. Curiously, some of the most important and progressive stepping stones in poverty-eradication have involved disruption and transgression of law. One thinks of *Modderklip*[36] and *Olivia Road*, for example, as cases in which *illegal* occupation of land provoked noble advances in legal understanding and law enforcement. "Rights and remedies of illegal occupiers of land" is a bona fide field of legal scholarship in South Africa. I can assure you that this

---

[28] Among other cases, Botha "Representing the Poor" in *Law and Poverty* 81-87 refers us to *Doctors for Life International v Speaker of the National Assembly* 2006 6 SA 416 (CC); *Matatiele Municipality v President of the RSA* 2007 6 SA 477 (CC); *Merafong Demarcation Forum v President of the Republic of South Africa* 2008 5 SA 171 (CC); *Poverty Alleviation Network v President of the Republic of South Africa* 2010 6 BCLR 520 (CC); *Occupiers of 51 Olivia Road, Berea Township v City of Johannesburg* 2008 3 SA 208 (CC); *Port Elizabeth Municipality v Various Occupiers* 2005 1 SA 217 (CC).

[29] Botha "Representing the Poor" in *Law and Poverty* 80.

[30] Symbolised, for example, by the concept of meaningful engagement launched in *Occupiers of 51 Olivia Road, Berea Township and 197 Main Street, Johannesburg v City of Johannesburg* 2008 3 SA 208 (CC); and *Residents of Joe Slovo Community, Western Cape v Thubelisha Homes* 2009 9 BCLR 847 (CC).

[31] Brand "Judicial Deference" in *Law and Poverty* 179-195.

[32] See *Port Elizabeth Municipality v Various Occupiers* 2005 1 SA 217 (CC) para 37 (Sachs J).

[33] See, generally, DM Davis & K Klare "Transformative Constitutionalism and the Common and Customary Law" (2010) 26 *SAJHR* 403 403-509.

[34] Williams "The Legal Construction of Poverty" in *Law and Poverty* 26-28.

[35] See DM Davis "Developing the Common Law of Contract in the Light of Poverty and Illiteracy: The Challenge of the Constitution" in S Liebenberg & G Quinot (eds) *Law and Poverty* (2012) 403, 404-405, 408-415.

[36] *President of the Republic of South Africa v Modderklip Boerdery (Pty) Ltd* 2005 5 SA 3 (CC).

is not the case in the US. So primitive are the legal entitlements of occupiers in the US that it is an exaggeration to call them "rights". I am not sure where this point goes exactly, but I sense it warrants study, particularly in light of the current rash of service-delivery protests (to which the police response has sometimes been quite harsh).

5 Technologies of judicial review

The Colloquium grappled with a particular institutional aspect of "advanced democracy", namely, how we should conceive judicial review of legislative or executive action affecting or giving effect to social and economic rights. Manifestly, a significant challenge facing progressive South African lawyers and activists is the task of inventing new legal approaches to (or what I call "technologies of") judicial review that reflect a richer, more nuanced conception of separation of powers and relative institutional competence.

Numerous papers worked on aspects of this problem. Danie Brand argued that the Constitutional Court's conception of separation of powers and judicial deference is at odds with the theory of democracy embedded in the Constitution.[37] He called for a revised theory of judicial review that would replace the current binary and exclusively institutional conception of separation of powers (the judicial deference question seen as concerning relationship between (i) courts and (ii) legislatures and executives) with a triangular understanding inspired by the substantive aspirations of the Constitution (judicial deference now understood as involving (i) courts, (ii) legislatures and executives, and (iii) engaged, popular sovereignty outside the normal representative institutions). Jackie Dugard and Stuart Wilson proposed a substantively oriented (as distinct from purely procedural and institutional) framework for judicial review in which the test for reasonableness is whether the government's policy or omission in a socio-economic rights case adequately responds to the lived, situational context of the case with respect to the interests meant to be protected by the right.[38]

Geo Quinot and Sandra Liebenberg strove valiantly to bring some coherence to South Africa's existing jurisprudence of "reasonableness review".[39] Building on this effort, they offered a refined, hi-tech proposal as to what reasonableness review should become. The core of their idea is that legislative and executive decision-making (or omissions) affecting or giving effect to socio-economic rights must fall within a constitutionally permissible "band" of options, but that the range or "band-width" of legislative or executive discretion varies from case to case. They argued further that *prior* to any balancing or proportionality exercise, the band-width, and consequently the level of judicial scrutiny must be determined and justified based on a substantive analysis of the normative

---

[37] Brand "Judicial Deference" in *Law and Poverty* 182-188.

[38] S Wilson & J Dugard "Taking Poverty Seriously: The South African Constitutional Court and Socio-Economic Rights" in S Liebenberg & G Quinot (eds) *Law and Poverty* (2012) 222, 230-231.

[39] G Quinot & S Liebenberg "Narrowing the Band: Reasonableness Review in Administrative Justice and Socio-Economic Rights Jurisprudence in South Africa" in S Liebenberg & G Quinot (eds) *Law and Poverty* (2012) 197, 200-219.

content and goals of the right. By analogy to a zoom-lens camera, the first stage of inquiry is equivalent to composing the picture by moving the lens in or out to determine focal length; the balancing or proportionality phase of the inquiry, equivalent to rotating the lens to put the image in focus, is secondary.

Filling out the meaning of transformative conceptions of judicial review and separation of powers will be, too, the work of a generation. But the idea is not to come up with neat and tidy doctrinal solutions. Discussion at the colloquium generally reflected a "chastened" or "anti-formalistic" view of the constraining power of legal doctrine. No one suggested that if we can only come up with the correctly formulated test for judicial review in socio-economic rights cases we would have the "magic bullet" that will secure the right outcomes. Indeed, few participants exhibited a great deal of faith in the notion that legal rules and standards tightly confine and channel judicial action. At the end of the day, the words and concepts of the doctrinal formulation matter much less than how they are applied in practice, as Lucy Williams develops in a very helpful recent paper.[40]

On the other hand, no one argued that legal reasoning is content-less or infinitely plastic and therefore that it can be assimilated to political or ethical argument. Scepticism about the constraining power of legal rules leads not to an instrumental or nihilistic approach but to an appeal to decision-makers to be more self-conscious and transparent about their reasoning processes. Several speakers urged greater self-understanding by and candour from the courts about what they are doing when they make legal decisions.

6   The challenge of the 'law/politics' relationship in legal advo-
cacy

These threads of conversation brought the colloquium back to a familiar topic, the distinction between law and politics. But there was a new twist. Our project confronts a dilemma growing out of a critical understanding of the law/politics distinction.

As *advocates* we wish to invoke the cachet of legal necessity; we want to be able to say that our proposals for transformation and poverty-eradication are legally, indeed constitutionally required. This interpretative leaning is not simply a reflection of our personal political commitments. Our claim is that transformative, equality-seeking approaches are congruent with what is legally the best reading of the Constitution. In truth, the reason why we are so keen on transformative constitutionalism and social and economic rights is precisely because they make our fondest hopes and dreams appear to be legally necessary.

However, our work as *analysts and critics* demonstrates that the broad values and transformative aspirations embraced by the Constitution are indeterminate with respect to their legal and institutional implications. They can only be given concrete application on the basis of a myriad of intermediate judgments

---

[40]   See generally L Williams "The Role of Courts in the Quantitative-Implementation of Social and Economic Rights: A Comparative Study" (2009) 3 *CCR* 141 141-199.

and choices that reflect moral and political perspectives and sensibilities. Central themes of the colloquium were that the meaning of a constitution is not given or self-defined by its text,[41] and that the progressive values we champion in the name of transformation are indeterminate, evolving, contestable, and sometimes internally contradictory. The proper understanding of these values is contested within the anti-poverty community, let alone within the general political culture.

At least on the surface, what we say to each other in gatherings such as this colloquium seems different from what it is prudent to say in a courtroom. We urgently need to develop a language in which to address courts and other decision-makers that is faithful to our analytical insights, yet persuasive as advocacy. We need to develop the capacity to reassure adjudicators that recourse to ethical and political judgment is inevitable in the adjudication process, and can be legitimate provided it is done transparently, self-critically, and faithfully to the broad vision of the Constitution. At the same time, we must avoid falling into the trap of being heard to approve of "politicising" adjudication in the primitive and corrupt sense of that phrase, ie that responsible adjudicators may pursue the self-serving agendas of individuals and interest groups to whom they are beholden.

It was common cause among colloquium participants that legal reasoning based on a duty of interpretive fidelity to legal authorities is a distinct discourse from "purely" political or ethical argument. Some argument-types that are perfectly acceptable in a philosophical treatise are inappropriate or unpersuasive in legal argument as lawyers know it. The project of deepening transformative constitutionalism in which we are engaged is a *constitutional* project, never "simply" an ideological project or an expression of personal inclination. On the other hand, all agreed that the boundaries between law and politics and between legal argument and political or philosophical argument are indistinct, blurred, and porous. In making the intermediate judgments and choices essential to translating legal norms into concrete applications, adjudicators have resort – and, since there is no other way the requisite intellectual operations can be performed – *must* have resort, consciously or unconsciously, to ideological considerations.[42] Indeed, adjudicators' understanding of the very authorities to which they owe interpretive fidelity is partly constructed by their interpretive activity which, consciously or unconsciously, filters through their ethical and moral preoccupations and sensibilities.

Moving forward, we must continually debate among ourselves as well as with broader publics about what the transformative values are and what they should mean in concrete application. We must debate the real-world content that should be poured into social and economic rights. We must be aware that these debates will never and should never reach closure, and that any conclusions we reach are always provisional. We must also acknowledge

---

[41] Sibanda "Transformative Constitutionalism" in *Law and Poverty* 50-52.

[42] See H Botha "Rights, Limitations and the (Im)possibility of Self-Government" in H Botha, A van der Walt & JWG van der Walt (eds) *Rights and Democracy in a Transformative Constitution* (2003) 13 13 n 4:
   "[A] judge cannot simply invoke the authority of the Constitution, as if the Constitution speaks to us directly, unmediated by the interpretations of relevant social actors and legal decision-makers."

that transformation involves trade-offs that will rest in part on judgments of an ethical and political nature. An elderly, traditional councillor vividly illuminated this point. As reported by Sindiso Mnisi Weeks and Aninka Claassens, she spoke movingly about the love she and her community have for the fields that sustain them, but then said, without hesitation, that the community would provide a family in need with a parcel of land taken from others. This would be both for the benefit of the family in need and for the sustainability of the entire community.[43]

But therein lays a danger. Candidly engaging in these debates, as we must, risks de-legitimating our reading of the Constitution by revealing it to be in some way morally and politically grounded after all, not textually required (at least in any simple sense). Getting the law/politics relationship right is going to be hard work. It brings to mind Sisyphus rolling the rock up the hill. But that is what we do. It is a worthy task, and we should continue to work at it. I do not mean even slightly to suggest that resolving this jurisprudential conundrum is a priority on a par with delivering water, electricity, food, shelter, housing, medical care, and social security to the poor. My point is narrower. It is that these questions and paradoxes are pertinent and potentially significant to legal work to eradicate poverty. As Cathi Albertyn said, lawyers are partly responsible for the development of the law.[44] The substantive content of law is influenced by how we conceive and frame our cases, what theories we choose to advance, and what understanding of the legal process and the scope of judicial review we offer to courts.[45] Working on these questions is at best a modest contribution to establishing a just society. But it is *our* contribution, and if this work is exemplified by the learning, insight, imagination, and intellectual daring on display at this colloquium, we can feel good about it.

---

[43] Mnisi Weeks & Claassens "Tensions Between Vernacular Values and State Versions of Customary Law" in *Law and Poverty* 381.

[44] Dennis Davis, Cathi Albertyn, and other participants commented during the discussion that the way in which advocates and courts frame legal arguments, and therefore the conscious or unconscious political and ethical sensibilities advocates and judges bring to their work, plays a large role in determining what the rights mean.

[45] Albertyn "Gendered Transformation" in *Law and Poverty* 171.

INDEX

I

L

M

P

T

Lightning Source UK Ltd.
Milton Keynes UK
UKOW07f0959180915

258853UK00006B/64/P